Rome and Byzantium in the Visigothic Kingdom

Rome and Byzantium in the Visigothic Kingdom

Beyond Imitatio Imperii

Edited by
Damián Fernández,
Molly Lester, and
Jamie Wood

Routledge
Taylor & Francis Group
LONDON AND NEW YORK

First published in 2023 by Amsterdam University Press Ltd.

Published 2025 by Routledge
4 Park Square, Milton Park, Abingdon, Oxon OX14 4RN
605 Third Avenue, New York, NY 10158

Routledge is an imprint of the Taylor & Francis Group, an informa business

ISBN: 9789463726412 (hbk)
ISBN: 9781041185642 (pbk)
ISBN: 9781003703167 (ebk)
NUR 684

Cover illustration: Roman architectural spolia, reused in the Visigothic period in Mérida. Museo Nacional de Arte Romano, Colección Visigoda.

Cover design: Coördesign, Leiden

DOI: 10.5117/9789463726412

For Product Safety Concerns and Information please contact our EU representative:
GPSR@taylorandfrancis.com
Taylor & Francis Verlag GmbH, Kaufingerstraße 24, 80331 München, Germany

Table of Contents

List of Figures and Tables

Abbreviations

Aug. De civ. Dei	Augustine of Hippo, *De civitate Dei*, ed. and trans. by R. W. Dyson, *The City of God Against the Pagans* (Cambridge: Cambridge University Press, 1998)
Avit. Ep.	Avitus of Vienne, *Epistulae*, ed. by Rudolph Peiper, *Alcimi Ecdicii Aviti Viennensis episcopi opera quae supersunt*. MGH Auctores Antiquissimi, VI.2 (Berlin: Weidmann, 1883)
Braul. Ep.	Braulio of Zarazoga, *Epistulae*, ed. by Ruth Miguel Franco and José Carlos Martín-Iglesias, *Braulionis Caesaraugustani Epistulae et Isidori Hispalensis Epistulae ad Braulionem. Braulionis Caesaraugustani Confessio vel professio Iudaeorum civitatis Toletanae*. CCSL 114B (Turnhout: Brepols, 2018)
CCSL	Corpus Christianorum. Series Latina
Chron. Muz.	*Chronica Muzarabica*, ed. by Juan Gil, *Chronica Hispana saeculi VIII et IX*. Corpus Christianorum. Continuatio Mediaevalis 45 (Turnhout: Brepols, 2018)
CILAE	*Corpus Inscriptionum Latinarum Augustae Emeritae. Inscriptiones Hispaniae Latinae* (*CIL II*^{2}), ed. by Antonio Alvar Ezquerra, Jonathan Edmondson, José Luis Ramírez Sádaba, et al. (Alcalá de Henares: Universidad de Alcalá de Henares, 2019–), https://cil2digital.web.uah.es/
CIPTP	*Catálogo das inscrições palaeocristãs do território português*, ed. by Maria Manuela Alves Dias and Catarina Isabel Sousa Gaspar (Lisbon: CEC-UL, 2006)
CJ	*Codex Justinianus*, ed. by Paul Krüger, *Corpus iuris civilis*, vol. II, *Codex Iustinianus*. 9th stereotype edition (Berlin: Weidmann, 1914)
Coll. Hisp.	*Collectio Hispana*, ed. by Gonzalo Martínez Díez and Félix Rodríguez, *La colección canónica hispana*, 6 vols (Madrid: Consejo Superior de Investigaciones Científicas, 1966–2002)
Conc.	*Concilios visigóticos e hispano-romanos*, ed. and trans. by José Vives (Madrid: Consejo Superior de Investigaciones Científicas, 1963)
Cons. Caes.	*Consularia Caesaraugustana*, ed. by Carmen Cardelle de Hartmann, *Victoris Tunnunensis Chronicon cum reliquiis ex Consularibus Caesaraugustanis et Iohannis Biclarensis Chronicon*. CCSL 173A (Turnhout: Brepols, 2001)

CTh	*Codex Theodosianus*, ed. by Theodor Mommsen and Paul M. Meyer, *Theodosiani libri XVI: cum Constiutionibus Sirmondianis et Leges novellae ad Theodosianum pertinentes*, 2 vols (Berlin: Weidmann, 1905)
Fredegar	*Fredegarii Chronicon*, ed. by Bruno Krusch, *Fredegarii et aliorum chronica*. MGH Scriptorum rerum Merovingicarum, II (Hannover: Hahn, 1888)
FW	*Formulae Wisigothicae*, ed. by Juan Gil, *Miscellanea Wisigothicae* (Seville: Publicaciones de la Universidad de Sevilla, 1972)
Gai Inst.	*Gai Institutiones*, ed. by Emil Seckel and Gustav Kuebler (Leipzig: Teubner, 1935)
Greg. Mag. Dial.	Gregory the Great, *Dialogui*, ed. and trans. by Adalbert de Vogüé, *Grégoire le Grand. Dialogues*, 3 vols. Sources Chrétiennes, 251, 260, and 265 (Paris: Les Belles Lettres, 1978–1980)
Greg. Mag. Reg.	Gregory the Great, *Registrum epistularum*, ed. by Dag Norberg, *S. Gregorii Magni opera. Registrum epistularum*, 2 vols. CCSL 140 and 140A (Turnhout: Brepols, 1982)
Greg. Tur. Decem libri	Gregory of Tours, *Decem libri historiarum*, ed. by Bruno Krusch and Wilhelm Levison, *Gregorii Episcopi Turonensis libri historiarum X*. MGH Scriptores rerum Merovingicarum, I.1 (Hannover: Hahn, 1951)
Greg. Tur. In gloria confess.	Gregory of Tours, *Liber in gloria confessorum*, in *Gregorii Episcopi Turonensis Miracula et opera minora*, ed. by Bruno Krusch. MGH Scriptores rerum Merovingicarum, I.2 (Hannover: Hahn, 1969)
Greg. Tur. In gloria mart.	Gregory of Tours, *Liber in gloria martyrum*, in *Gregorii Episcopi Turonensis Miracula et opera minora*, ed. by Bruno Krusch. MGH Scriptores rerum Merovingicarum, I.2 (Hannover: Hahn, 1969)
HE	*Hispania Epigraphica*
Hist. Wamb. reg.	Julian of Toledo, *Historia Wambae regis*, ed. by Jocelyn N. Hillgarth, B. Bischoff, and Wilhelm Levison, *Iulianus Toletanus. Opera I. Prognosticon futuri saeculi libri tres. Apologeticum de tribus capitulis. De comprobatione sextae aetatis. Historia Wambae regis. Epistula ad Modoenum*. CCSL 115 (Turnhout: Brepols, 1976)

Hyd.	Hydatius, *Chronicon*, ed. and trans. by R. W. Burgess, *The Chronicle of Hydatius and the Consularia Constantinopolitana: Two Contemporary Accounts of the Final Years of the Roman Empire* (Oxford: Clarendon Press, 1993)
ICERV	*Inscripciones cristianas de la España romana y visigoda*, ed. by José Vives, 2nd ed. (Barcelona: Consejo Superior de Investigaciones Científicas, 1969)
Ildef. De viris	Ildefonsus of Toledo, *De viris illustribus*, ed. by Valeriano Yarza Urquiola and Carmen Codoñer, *Ildefonsi Toletani De virginitate Sanctae Mariae, De cognitione baptismi, De itinere deserti, De viris illustribus*. CCSL 114A (Turnhout: Brepols, 2007)
Ioh. Bicl.	John of Biclarum, *Chronicon*, ed. by Carmen Cardelle de Hartmann, *Victoris Tunnunensis Chronicon cum reliquiis ex Consularibus Caesaraugustanis et Iohannis Biclarensis Chronicon*. CCSL 173A (Turnhout: Brepols, 2001)
Isid. De eccl.	Isidore of Seville, *De ecclesiasticis officis*, ed. by Christopher M. Lawson, *Sancti Isidori episcopi Hispalensis De ecclesiasticis officiis*. CCSL 113 (Turnhout: Brepols, 1989)
Isid. De viris	Isidore of Seville, *De viris illustribus*, ed. by Carmen Codoñer Merino, *El 'De viris illustribus' de Isidoro de Sevilla* (Salamanca: Consejo Superior de Investigaciones Científicas, Instituto 'Antonio de Nebrija', Colegio Trilingüe de la Universidad, 1964)
Isid. Etym.	Isidore of Seville, *Etymologiae*, ed. by W. M. Lindsay, *Isidori Hispalensis episcopi Etymologiarum sive originum libri XX*, 2 vols. (Oxford: Oxford University Press, 1911)
Isid. Hist. Goth.	Isidore of Seville, *Historia Gothorum*, ed. by Cristóbal Rodríguez Alonso, *Las historias de los godos, vándalos y suevos de Isidoro de Sevilla. Estudio, edición crítica y traducción* (León: Centro de Estudios e Investigaciones 'San Isidoro', 1965)
Isid. Sent.	Isidore of Seville, *Sententiae*, ed. by Pierre Cazier, *Isidorus Hispalensis Sententiae*. CCSL 111 (Turnhout: Brepols, 1998)
LI	*Liber Iudiciorum* or *Lex Visigothorum*, ed. by Karl Zeumer, *Leges Visigothorum*. MGH Leges nationum Germanicarum, I (Hannover: Hahn, 1902)

Lib. Const.	*Liber Constitutionum*, ed. by Ludwig Rudolf von Salis, *Leges Burgundionum*. MGH Leges nationum Germanicarum, II.1 (Hannover: Hahn, 1892)
LRV	*Lex Romana Visigothorum*, ed. by Gustav Haenel (Leipzig: Teubner, 1849)
Mart. De trina	Martin of Braga, *De trina mersione*, ed. by Claude W. Barlow, *Martini episcopi Bracarensis opera omnia* (New Haven, CT: Yale University Press, 1950)
MGH	Monumenta Germaniae Historica
Nov. Just.	*Novellae Justiniani*, ed. by Rudolf Schöll and Wilhelm Kroll, *Corpus iuris civilis*, vol. 3, *Novellae*. 4th stereotype edition (Berlin: Weidmann, 1912)
Oros. Hist.	Orosius, *Historiae adversus paganos*, ed. and trans. by Marie-Pierre Arnaud-Lindet, *Orose. Histoires contre les Païens*, 3 vols. Collection des universités de France. Série latine, 291, 296, and 297 (Paris: Les Belles Lettres, 1990–1991)
PH	*Pasionario Hispánico: introducción, edición crítica y traducción*, ed. and trans. by Pilar Riesco Chueca (Seville: Universidad de Sevilla, Secretaría de Publicaciones, 1995)
PL	*Patrologiae cursus completus. Series latina*, ed. by J. P. Migne (Paris: Garnier, 1844–1865)
Proc. Bell.	Procopius, *Bella*, ed. by Jakob Haury, rev. by Gerhard Wirth, *Procopii Caesariensis opera omnia*, 2 vols (Leipzig: Teubner, 1962–1963)
Prud. Peri.	Prudentius, *Peristephanon*, ed. by Maurice P. Cunningham, *Aurelii Prudentii Clementis Carmina*. CCSL 126 (Turnhout: Brepols, 1966)
Sid. Apol. Carm.	Sidonius Apollinaris, *Carmina*, ed. by André Loyen, *Sidoine Apollinaire. Poèmes*. Collection des universités de France. Série latine, 161 (Paris: Les Belles Lettres, 1960)
Sid. Apol. Ep.	Sidonius Apollinaris, *Epistulae*, ed. by André Loyen, *Sidoine Apollinaire. Correspondence*, 2 vols. Collection des universités de France. Série latine, 198 and 199 (Paris: Les Belles Lettres, 1970)
VA	Braulio of Zaragoza, *Vita Aemiliani*, ed. by Ignazio Cazzaniga, 'La Vita di S. Emiliano scritta da Braulione vescovo di Saragozza: edizione critica', in *Bolletino del Comitato per la preparazione della Edizione Nazionale dei Classici Greci e Latini* 3 (1954), pp. 7–44

Val. Ord. quer.	Valerius of Bierzo, *Ordo querimonie prefati discriminis*, ed. by Manuel C. Díaz y Díaz, *Valerio del Bierzo. Su persona, su obra* (León: Centro de Estudios e Investigación 'San Isidoro', 2006)
VF	*Vita Fructuosi*, ed. by Manuel C. Díaz y Díaz, *La vida de San Fructuoso de Braga. Estudio y edición crítica* (Braga: Empresa do Diário do Minho, 1974)
VSPE	*Vitas sanctorum patrum Emeretensium*, ed. by Antonio Maya Sánchez, CCSL 116 (Turnhout: Brepols, 1992)

Acknowledgements

This book originated at a workshop held at Princeton University on 3–4 May 2019, 'Rome, Byzantium, and the Visigothic Kingdom of Toledo: Imitation, Reinvention, or Strategic Adoption?'. We would like to thank the Committee for the Study of Late Antiquity, the Center for Collaborative History, the Program in the Ancient World, and the Seeger Center for Hellenic Studies, all at Princeton University, for their generous support. In particular, we would like to give thanks to Helmut Reimitz for co-ordinating this workshop and to him and Stefan Esders for helping to bring the project to fruition. Northern Illinois University History Department also provided financial support for the production of this volume. Special gratitude must also go to Erin Dailey at Amsterdam University Press for his expert editorial oversight. Erik Goosman of MappaMundi Cartography made an excellent map of the Iberian peninsula, while Sarah Longair traced the map of Mérida in Graham Barrett's chapter from the original. Finally, the anonymous reviewers provided invaluable and constructive feedback.

OTHER SITES:

1. Ambérieux
2. Carouge
3. San Martín de Asán (?)
4. Haro
5. Vergegio
6. Peña Amaya
7. Castrum Petrense (?)
8. San Juan de Baños
9. San Juan de Hornija
10. Mogarraz
11. Alange
12. Puebla de Sancho Pérez
13. Vallclara

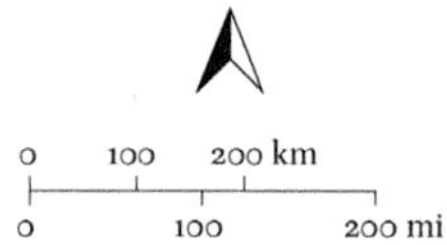

Figure 1: Map of Visigothic Gaul and Spain

Introduction

Damián Fernández, Molly Lester, and Jamie Wood

As western Roman society refashioned itself into multiple 'little Romes' in the fifth, sixth, and seventh centuries, the Visigothic kingdoms of Toulouse and Toledo actively preserved and transformed much of the Roman world that preceded them. They were not alone in this, as several other kingdoms, including the eastern Roman empire, explored the legacy of Rome while navigating the social, political, and economic shifts that accompanied the transition to the early medieval period. The 'Romanness' of such kingdoms, as well as what being Roman actually meant in the post-Roman west, frequently plays a pivotal role in debates about the 'transformation' of the Roman world, functioning for some scholars as a key marker of continuity and change across the period.[1]

In post-Roman Iberia and southern Gaul, scholarly debate over the legacy of Rome in the Visigothic kingdom has long grappled with the survival of Roman (or so-called Germanic) identities and practices and with the importation of Roman traditions from other polities. To a large extent, the modern origins of this debate trace back to discussions of the nature of Visigothic institutions, particularly the controversy over the putative Roman or Germanic origins of Visigothic law.[2] Those who stressed the Visigoths' *romanitas* were also particularly interested in Visigothic relations with the empire in the east. As Céline Martin explores in her contribution to this volume, art historians and archaeologists have long spoken of a 'Byzantine imprint' on Iberian evidence, a characterization which scholars eventually extended to political culture as well. In the twentieth century, the political and diplomatic policies of the Francoist regime strongly shaped Spanish scholarly insistence on Iberian uniqueness within the western

1 Some notable recent contributions to this debate from different perspectives are Conant 2012; Arnold 2014; Pohl, 2014; Pohl, Gantner, Grifoni, and Pollheimer-Mohaupt 2018; Kaldellis 2019; Fafinski 2021; Papadopoulos 2021.

2 Some fundamental works are Zeumer 1898a, 1898b, 1899a, 1899b, 1899c, and 1901; Torres López 1926; Sánchez Albornoz 1942; D'Ors 1960; King 1972; Alvarado Planas 1997.

Fernández, D., Lester, M. & Wood, J. (eds.), *Rome and Byzantium in the Visigothic Kingdom: Beyond* Imitatio Imperii. Taylor & Francis Group 2023
DOI: 10.5117/9789463726412_INTRO

Mediterranean and on the markedly 'imperial' influences on Visigothic art, culture, and institutions.[3] Outside of Spain, many Anglophone scholars argued for a strong imperial presence within the Iberian peninsula as well, such as P. D. King's statement that there are 'plenty of examples [...] of the constant Byzantine influence in practically every walk of Visigothic life'.[4] For those advocating for imperial models, however, the source of these models was far less clear, and scholars debated whether the Visigoths drew on the late Roman empire,[5] the Byzantine political centre of Constantinople,[6] the 'East' more generally,[7] or closer Byzantine societies such as Ravenna, southern Iberia, or northern Africa.[8]

In particular, the relationship between the Visigothic kingdom and the Byzantine empire has been the subject of much recent work.[9] The Byzantine empire was certainly a rival for the Visigothic kingdom of Toledo, and Byzantine presence in southern Iberia led to tension, and even conflict, between the two states. Yet the relationship between Toledo and Constantinople was one of exchange and dialogue as well as conflict. Numerous studies have suggested that, over the sixth and seventh centuries, eastern Roman imperial practices and ideas were adopted in the Visigothic kingdom, a process sometimes referred to in scholarly literature as *imitatio imperii*. Michael McCormick's influential *Eternal Victory*, for instance, argued that some rituals of military victory in Toledo were modelled after Byzantine political ceremonies.[10] Others have suggested that Visigothic kings' reforms of the Visigothic monarchy were in conversation with late Roman and Byzantine emperorship,[11] and several scholars have argued that Toledo became a smaller version of Constantinople in its topography and its conception as a capital city.[12] Studies of the intellectual, religious, and material culture of the Iberian peninsula have also emphasized the strong cultural and economic ties that bound Hispania to Byzantine territories, especially Africa, as well as the impact of Byzantine religious debates

3 Linehan 1993; Salvatierra Cuenca 2015, 250–52; Moreno 2019.

4 King 1972, 12, n. 6.

5 Claude 1971.

6 Stroheker 1963.

7 García Moreno 1972.

8 See Céline Martin's chapter in this volume.

9 Vallejo Girvés 1993; Arrese 2002; Pérez Martín and Bádenas de la Peña 2004; Vallejo Girvés 2012.

10 McCormick 1986, 297–327.

11 Hillgarth 1966; Díaz and Valverde 2000; Valverde Castro 2000, 181–95; García Moreno 2008, 81–95.

12 Velázquez and Ripoll 2000; Martin 2003, 205–68.

on Iberian ecclesiastics.[13] Finally, some have suggested that Visigothic anti-Judaism in the seventh century was related to a desire to imperialize the monarchy or even to emulate the anti-Jewish policies of Byzantine emperors such as Heraclius.[14]

As suggested by recent characterizations of Visigothic Iberia as imperial or 'Byzantinizing',[15] however, scholars must continue to question and refine their assumptions about the nature of Visigothic engagement with Rome more broadly and with Byzantium in particular. As a case in point, the popular characterization of Visigothic practices as *imitatio imperii* risks conceptually simplifying a dynamic process of exchange. The idea of 'imitation' can lead to misrepresenting people of post-imperial Iberia as passive recipients of Byzantine norms, and many features of Visigothic cultural and political life as derivative mirror images of Byzantine models. Such a conceptualization of the relationship could lead to applying outdated 'Romanization' models to the post-Roman kingdoms, with Constantinople replacing Rome as the imperial centre acting upon a range of provincial peripheries. Such a position is incompatible with the historical evidence, and recent scholarship has increasingly begun to demonstrate that while individual and collective actors certainly adopted Roman and Byzantine ideas and practices, they did so via a process of intelligent, creative, and strategic adaptation.[16] Iberian actors were not simply preserving or importing imperial traditions and legacies: they resignified these ideas and practices within contexts specific to Visigothic society. In other words, Visigothic customs were not an uncritical adoption and *imitatio* of contemporary Roman models (an 'acculturation' model), but unique interpretations of a common pool of symbols, practices, and institutions that formed the legacy of Rome.

We must also be wary of oversimplifying what was 'Roman' about the Roman models for Visigothic kingdoms. As mentioned above and explored more fully in Martin's contribution, scholars have historically considered multiple Romes when searching for origins and models of imperializing tendencies. Although 'Rome' could certainly relate to the contemporary eastern Roman empire or to the Roman empire of the past, it could also refer to various parts of the eastern empire outside of the Constantinopolitan centre.[17] Nor was Rome exclusively associated with empire in the early medieval world: the city of Rome and the

13 Herrin 1986, 229–33; Collins 2004, 147–61; Castillo Maldonado 2005; Vizcaíno Sánchez 2007; Reynolds 2010; García Vargas 2011; Fernández Fernández 2014; Ihnat 2019.

14 Gil 1977; Saitta 1995, 35–40; Esders 2018, 109–15.

15 Arce 2004; Koch 2008; Arce 2020.

16 Wood 2012; Walker 2016; Fernández 2017; Esders 2019.

17 García Moreno 2002, 2011.

Roman popes, both past and present, had their own unique relationships with the Iberian peninsula.[18] And ultimately, characterizing Visigothic practices as *imitatio imperii* leans towards presenting Rome as outside of or even oppositional to Visigothic culture. We must recall the deep history of Visigothic relations with Romans, and that a range of different 'Gothic' groups had been part of the Roman world for several centuries.[19] Exchange long predated the foundation of the kingdoms of Toulouse and Toledo. Although we should be wary of over-Romanizing the Visigoths and indirectly implying Roman cultural superiority, any discussion of *imitatio imperii* must acknowledge the rich web of traditions and customs that were already present in Gothic societies, including the long-established Roman provincial traditions of Gaul and Spain.

The essays in this volume seek to explore engagement with Rome and Byzantium in the Visigothic kingdoms without falling back onto *imitatio imperii* as a blanket explanatory model. Instead, the authors emphasize how Iberian and Gallic actors continually resignified and redefined Rome over the fifth, sixth, and seventh centuries and uncover the multiple meanings and uses of Rome that circulated in the Visigothic worlds. Authors have taken a variety of approaches and draw on a wide range of sources, from the legal and canonical sources that have long been the staple of Visigothic studies to under-appreciated texts such as the *passiones* and material artefacts that speak to everyday and elite interactions with the Byzantine world. We do not claim to be comprehensive in our coverage, but we have tried to be inclusive as part of an effort to capture the rich variety of Visigothic-era engagement with Rome and Byzantium.

Several authors explore how Visigothic rulers used and interpreted Roman customs and legacies. Beginning in the Visigothic kingdom of Toulouse, Ian Wood and Merle Eisenberg investigate how Visigothic kings engaged with the traditions and practices of the fifth-century western Roman empire. Long before the reign of Leovigild, whom traditional historiography considered as the 'imperializing' king par excellence, Ian Wood traces developments in court etiquette in Toulouse that were rooted in contemporary Roman practices, focusing in particular on resonances between Roman (imperial, provincial, military) and Visigothic royal banqueting. Moving to the early sixth century, Eisenberg problematizes scholarly categorizations of 'imitative' and 'pseudo-imperial' Visigothic coinage, arguing that despite formal similarities in numismatic imagery, Alaric II's minting and monetary reforms

18 Madoz 1951; García Moreno 2002; Deswarte 2010; Ferreiro 2020; Martín-Iglesias, Díaz, and Vallejo Girvés 2020.

19 Heather 1996; Berndt and Steinacher 2014; Kulikowski 2015; Delaplace 2015.

were due to internal transformations of the Visigothic state in southern Gaul rather than to a basic desire to mimic Roman practice.

Royally driven engagement with Roman and Byzantine traditions continued in the sixth- and seventh-century kingdom of Toledo. By comparing imperial and Visigothic laws prescribing the punishment of exile, Margarita Vallejo Girvés suggests that Visigothic reliance on Roman law in royal legislation did not preclude selective adaptation and even abandonment of Roman punitive practices to adapt law to a new economy of punishment. Such adaptability also characterizes elite consumption of Byzantine material culture, and in her exploration of the incorporation of a deluxe (perhaps even imperial) Byzantine cross into King Recceswinth's famous votive crown, Cecily Hilsdale demonstrates how the original meaning and usage of the cross was simultaneously activated and redefined in its new setting. Damián Fernández re-evaluates sixth- and seventh-century applications of Roman and Byzantine notions of capitalhood in the Visigothic kingdom of Toledo. He argues that terminological similarities in references to Rome, Constantinople, and Toledo as *urbes regiae* in Visigothic sources does not mean that Visigothic actors had the same understanding of capitalhood as their Roman predecessors and contemporaries. Instead, they relied on Roman terminology for specifically local purposes.

Iberian churchmen, of course, availed themselves of Roman legacies as well, and the contributions of Molly Lester, Erica Buchberger, and David Addison focus on ecclesiastical and clerical actors who plumbed the Roman past—and present—to articulate and address contemporary concerns. Turning to the Christian liturgy, Lester examines Iberian adoptions of eastern and Roman liturgical practices to unpack when and why bishops proudly identified Roman antecedents for their rites as well as when they obscured them. Erica Buchberger explores how Isidore of Seville maintained and massaged classical Roman ethnic terms and categories to apply the Roman past to his post-Roman reality. David Addison turns to the Visigothic-era *passiones* of Roman martyrs to demonstrate how early medieval hagiographers recreated an urban Roman and Christian past. By making this past come alive for Visigothic audiences, Addison reminds us that Roman-era martyrdoms remained a living memory long after they had ceased in practice, reshaping how that past was viewed by contemporaries.

Connections with the Roman past and the Byzantine present were not restricted to royal and episcopal elites—they also found expression in multiple local and regional contexts. Hagiography has long been recognized for its potential to unmask the workings of the small worlds of Late Antiquity, and Santiago Castellanos advises us to look beyond explicit Visigothic recognition of Roman heritage to understand how Roman institutions and social structures implicitly shaped Iberian saints' worlds. While Castellanos explores Romanness (or lack thereof) in the lives of sixth- and seventh-century saints, Jamie Wood and Graham Barrett encourage us to move beyond the centre, focusing on urban elites and humble consumers. Barrett reappraises evidence associated with the bishopric of Mérida and its interactions with the Visigothic kings in the late sixth century, concluding that conflicts that have long been viewed as confessional in origin may be better interpreted as the result of late Roman-style factional politics within the city. Jamie Wood deploys ceramics, inscriptions, and hagiography to explore connections between the southwestern cities of Mérida and Mértola and the Byzantine worlds of North Africa and the eastern Mediterranean, arguing that we must look to local and regional elites if we are to understand the mechanics of interactivity.

Finally, Iberian adaptation and resignification of Roman legacies did not end with the collapse of the Visigothic monarchy in the early eighth century. While later Arabic and Latin textual accounts respectively advocated for sharp breaks and strong continuities with the Roman and Visigothic past, Ann Christys uses early Andalusi Arabic coins and lead seals to explore how Arab and Berber actors selectively mobilized eastern Roman minting practices. Like the Visigoths before them, Andalusi elites navigated several Roman models, including the Byzantine East, the formerly Byzantine North Africa, and Visigothic Hispania itself.

Individually, the essays make significant interventions, but the volume as a whole makes three major contributions. First, it builds on recent scholarship to disaggregate further what 'Rome' could mean in a Visigothic context. Instead of concentrating on one particular model of Romanness, the essays present multiple temporally and spatially diverse visions of Romanness that Iberian actors used to understand, mould, and influence their social worlds. Some contributions explore Visigothic engagement with the Roman past, showing how classical and imperial memories and concepts were put to work in the fifth, sixth, and seventh centuries. Others consider Visigothic relationships with contemporary Roman polities, examining how practices, materials, and institutions from the fifth-century western empire and the sixth- and seventh-century eastern empire simultaneously evoked their original context and, when recontextualized in Hispania, generated new meanings. In particular, the volume reinforces the idea that Byzantium was not, nor was it regarded as, a homogenous entity identified exclusively with Constantinople. In North Africa, Iberia, and Italy there were western Mediterranean iterations of the Byzantine empire, the inhabitants of which interacted with the people of Visigothic Hispania across the period. And finally, the city of Rome exerted a strong conceptual and ecclesiastical presence in the early medieval world, and Visigothic Christians and rulers continually had to negotiate their relationship to the Apostolic See. Taken together, the chapters remind us that the Visigoths had before them a constellation of 'Romes' across the Mediterranean and that such imperial, provincial, and local reimaginings of Roman past and Byzantine present were not mutually exclusive of one another.

Second, the volume suggests that unpacking the concept of *imitatio imperii* requires not only a disaggregation of 'Rome' as a source for and a product of resignification, but also a disaggregation of 'Visigothic Hispania'. Studies of Visigothic Hispania frequently focus on royal and ecclesiastical centres and authorities. Of course, kings and bishops are the best documented actors in Visigothic history: they have certainly not been ignored in past scholarship, and several essays in this volume speak to ongoing royal and episcopal engagement with Roman traditions and legacies. But like the Byzantine empire, the Visigothic kingdom was not monolithic. The fifth-century kingdom of Toulouse differed in many ways from the sixth- and seventh-century kingdom in Iberia. Moreover, Visigothic scholarship is increasingly interested in individual bishops and local elites outside of Toledo, who had their own agendas and contexts that did not necessarily align with political and ecclesiastical centres. Outside of capital cities and powerful urban centres such as Toledo, Braga, and Mérida, actors in what are often considered peripheral areas interacted with the Roman and Byzantine worlds, their day-to-day contacts inscribed in saints' lives and material culture. By exploring areas that were not under direct Visigothic control and the experiences of local and regional elites, what begins to emerge are a multiplicity of centres and peripheries operating at a variety of levels across the peninsula.

Finally, the essays illustrate the wide variety of mediums through which Visigothic engagement with the Roman and Byzantine worlds took place. As indicated above, scholarship has traditionally prioritized examining *imitatio imperii* in political and material terms, and several authors in this collection of essays take up these threads from a variety of perspectives. From practices such as banqueting, lawgiving, the minting of coinage, and rhetorics of capitalhood, many essays look at royal reuse of the Roman-Byzantine legacy and its present instantiations. This focus on kings carries through in examinations of material culture, particularly the material production of votive crowns and coins. But material culture went beyond the royal centre, and noble production of seals in post-Visigothic Iberia and local trade can demonstrate how more lowly actors in provincial contexts interacted materially with the worlds of Rome and Byzantium. Finally, many essays move beyond political and material considerations. From religious ideologies and practices to conceptions of ethnicity and the underlying social structures of the Roman world, the chapters in this volume show that the engagement with 'Rome' was far more diverse and complex than models based on concepts of influence or imitation allow.

The mediums of engaging with Romanness, and the explicit uses as well as eloquent silences, reveal that Gallic and Iberian actors did not have a fixed—or necessarily a very clear—idea about what 'Rome' was in the past or the present, or about the uses to which it could be put. If anything, the contributions to this volume show that they may have had multiple, coexisting, and highly contingent notions of 'Rome'. It should be clear that this volume was not designed to find the 'true' Rome, or to discover a single Visigothic view, conceptualization, or experience of the late antique or Byzantine empire. The chapters reveal the plurality and flexibility of the concept of *romanitas*, and the production of new discourses in rapidly changing contexts in southern Gaul and Hispania across the course of three centuries.

Bibliography

Alvarado Planas, Javier, *El problema del germanismo en el derecho español* (Madrid: Marcial Pons, 1997)

Arce, Javier, 'Ceremonial visigodo/ceremonial "bizantino": un tópico historiográfico', in *Bizancio y la Península Ibérica: de la antigüedad tardía a la Edad Moderna*, ed. by Inmaculada Pérez Martín and Pedro Bádenas de la Peña (Madrid: Consejo Superior de Investigaciones Científicas, 2004), pp. 101–15

Arce, Javier, 'Las tumbas de los reyes visigodos: un problema histórico', in *Pyrenae*, 51.2 (2020), 131–40

Arnold, Jonathan, *Theoderic and the Roman Imperial Restoration* (Cambridge: Cambridge University Press, 2014)

Arrese, M. C. (ed.), *Toledo y Bizancio* (Cuenca: Ediciones de la Universidad de Castilla-La Mancha, 2002)

Berndt, Guido M., and Roland Steinacher (eds), *Arianism: Roman Heresy and Barbarian Creed* (Burlington, VT: Ashgate, 2014)

Castillo Maldonado, Pedro, 'Una aproximación a la presencia de Oriente en Occidente: rechazo y atracción hacia el mundo cristiano oriental en las iglesias hispanas de la Antigüedad Tardía', in *'Ilu Revista de Ciencias de las Religiones*, 10 (2005), 5–19

Claude, Dietrich, *Adel, Kirche und Königtum im Westgotenreich* (Sigmarigen: Thorbecke, 1971)

Collins, Roger, *Visigothic Spain, 409–711* (Oxford: Blackwell, 2004)

Conant, Jonathan, *Staying Roman: Conquest and Identity in Africa and the Mediterranean, 439–700* (Cambridge: Cambridge University Press, 2012)

D'Ors, Álvaro, *El Código de Eurico. Edición, palingenesia, índices* (Madrid: Consejo Superior de Investigaciones Científicas, 1960)

Delaplace, Christine, *La fin de l'Empire romain d'Occident: Rome et les Wisigoths de 382 à 551*. Histoire. Série Histoire ancienne (Rennes: Presses Universitaires de Rennes, 2015)

Deswarte, Thomas, *Une Chrétienté romaine sans pape. L'Espagne et Rome (586–1085)* (Paris: Classiques Garnier, 2010)

Díaz, Pablo C., and M. R. Valverde, 'The Theoretical Strength and Practical Weakness of the Visigothic Monarchy of Toledo', in *Rituals of Power from Late Antiquity to the Early Middle Ages*, ed. by Frans Theuws and Janet L. Nelson (Leiden: Brill, 2000), pp. 59–93

Esders, Stefan, 'Kingdoms of the Empire, AD 608–616. Mediterrane Konnektivität, Synchronität und Kausalität als analytisches und darstellerisches Problem der Frühmittelalterforschung', in *Neue Wege der Frühmittelalterforschung: Bilanz und Perspektiven*, ed. by Walter Pohl, Maximilian Diesenberger, and Bernhard Zeller (Vienna: Austrian Academy of Sciences Press, 2018), pp. 93–136

Esders, Stefan, '*Regem iura faciunt, non persona*. Der westgotische Treueid im kräftefeld personaler und transpersonaler Konzepte der Legitimität politischer Herrschaft', in *Die Macht des Herrschers. Personale und transpersonale Aspekte*, ed. by Mechthild Albert, Elke Brüggen, and Konrad Klaus (Göttingen: Vandenhoeck & Ruprecht, 2019), pp. 70–152

Fafinski, Mateusz, *Roman Infrastructure in Early Medieval Britain: The Adaptations of the Past in Text and Stone* (Amsterdam: Amstersam University Press, 2021).

Fernández, Damián, *Aristocrats and Statehood in Western Iberia, 300–600 C.E.* (Philadelphia, PA: University of Pennsylvania Press, 2017)

Fernández Fernández, Adolfo, *El comercio tardoantiguo (ss. IV–VII) en el noroeste peninsular a través del registro cerámico de la Ría de Vigo* (Oxford: Archaeopress, 2014)

Ferreiro, Alberto, *Epistolae Plenae: The Correspondence of the Bishops of Hispania with the Bishops of Rome (Third Through Seventh Centuries)* (Leiden: Brill 2020)

García Moreno, Luis A., 'Colonias de comerciantes orientales en la Península Ibérica. S. V–VII', in *Habis*, 3 (1972), 127–54

García Moreno, Luis A., '*Urbs cunctarum gentium victrix gothicis triumphis victa*. Roma y el Reino visigodo', in *Roma fra Oriente e Occidente* (Spoleto: CISEM, 2002), pp. 239–322

García Moreno, Luis A., *Leovigildo: Unidad y diversidad de un reinado* (Madrid: Real Academia de la Historia, 2008)

García Moreno, Luis A., 'Relaciones internacionales del reino godo de Toledo en el siglo VII: De la *faida* gótica a la obsesión bizantina', in *Le relazioni internazionali nell'alto medioevo* (Spoleto: CISEM, 2011), pp. 481–559

García Vargas, Enrique, 'Oriental Trade in the Iberian Peninsula During Late Antiquity (4th–7th centuries AD): An Archaeological Perspective', in *New Perspectives on Late Antiquity*, ed. by David Hernández de la Fuente (Newcastle: Cambridge Scholars Publishing, 2011), pp. 76–117

Gil, Juan, 'Judios y cristianos en la Hispania del siglo VII', in *Hispania sacra*, 30 (1977), 9–110

Heather, Peter, *The Goths* (Oxford: Blackwell, 1996)

Herrin, Judith, *The Formation of Christendom* (Princeton, NJ: Princeton University Press, 1986)

Hillgarth, J. N., 'Coins and Chronicles: Propaganda in Sixth-Century Spain, and the Byzantine Background', in *Historia*, 15 (1966), 483–508

Ihnat, Kati, 'Orígenes y Desarrollo de La Fiesta Litúrgica de La Virgen María En Iberia', in *Anuario de Estudios Medievales*, 49.2 (2019), 619–43

Kaldellis, Anthony, *Romanland: Ethnicity and Empire in Byzantium* (Cambridge, MA: Harvard University Press, 2019)

King, P. D., *Law and Society in the Visigothic Kingdom* (Cambridge: Cambridge University Press, 1972)

Koch, Manuel, 'La imperialización del Reino visigodo bajo Leovigildo. ¿Es la *imitatio imperii* de Leovigildo la manifestación de un momento de cambio en la pretensión de poder y la ideología visigodas?', in *Pyrenae*, 39.2 (2008), 101–17

Kulikowski, Michael, *Rome's Gothic Wars: From the Third Century to Alaric* (Cambridge: Cambridge University Press, 2015)

Linehan, Peter, *History and the Historians of Medieval Spain* (Oxford: Oxford University Press, 1993)

Madoz, José, 'Tajón de Zaragoza y su viaje a Roma', in *Mélanges Joseph de Ghellinck, SJ, II. Moyen Age* (Gembloux: Éditions J. Duculot, 1951), pp. 345–60

Martin, Céline, *La géographie du pouvoir dans l'Espagne visigothique* (Lille: Septentrion, 2003)

Martín-Iglesias, Pablo Díaz, and Margarita Vallejo Girvés, *La Hispania tardoantigua y visigoda en las fuentes peninsulares. Antología y comentario*. Nueva roma, 52 (Madrid: Consejo Superior de Investigaciones Científicas, 2020)

McCormick, Michael, *Eternal Victory: Triumphal Rulership in Late Antiquity, Byzantium and the Early Medieval West* (Cambridge: Cambridge University Press, 1986)

Moreno Martín, Francisco J., '*Gesta dei per hispanos*. Invención, visualización e imposición del mito de cruzada durante la Guerra Civil y el primer franquismo', in *La Reconquista. Ideología y justificación de la Guerra Santa Peninsular* (Madrid: La Ergástula, 2019), pp. 438–518

Papadopoulos, Ioannis, *The Idea of Rome in Late Antiquity: From Eternal City to Imagined Utopia* (Amsterdam: Amsterdam University Press, 2021)

Pérez Martín, Inmaculada, and Pedro Bádenas de la Peña (eds), *Bizancio y la Península Ibérica: de la antigüedad tardía a la edad moderna* (Madrid: Consejo Superior de Investigaciones Científicas, 2004)

Pohl, Walter, 'Romanness: A Multiple Identity and its Changes', in *Early Medieval Europe*, 22.4 (2014), 406–18

Pohl, Walter, Clemens Gantner, Cinzia Grifoni, and Marianne Pollheimer-Mohaupt (eds), *Transformations of Romanness: Early Medieval Regions and Identities* (Berlin: De Gruyter, 2018)

Reynolds, Paul, *Hispania and the Roman Mediterranean, AD 100–700: Ceramics and Trade* (London: Duckworth, 2010)

Saitta, Biagio, *L'antisemitismo nella Spagna visigotica* (Rome: 'L'Erma' di Bretschneider, 1995)

Salvatierra Cuenca, Vicente, 'El lugar de visigodos y omeyas en la historiografía de los siglos XIX y XX. Aportaciones a un debate sobre continuidad y ruptura', in *Archivo Español de Arqueología*, 88 (2015), 247–61

Sánchez Albornoz, Claudio, *En torno a los orígenes del feudalismo*, vol. 1 (Mendoza: Universidad Nacional de Cuyo, 1942)

Stroheker, Karl Friedrich, 'Das spanische Westgotenreich und Byzanz', in *Bonner Jahrbücher*, 163 (1963), 252–74

Torres López, Manuel, 'El Estado Visigótico', in *Anuario de historia del derecho español*, 3 (1926), 307–475

Vallejo Girvés, Margarita, *Bizancio y la España tardoantigua (SS. V–VIII): Un capítulo de historia mediterránea* (Alcalá de Henares: Universidad de Alcalá de Henares, 1993)

Vallejo Girvés, Margarita, *Hispania y Bizancio: una relación desconocida* (Madrid: Akal, 2012)

Valverde Castro, María R., *Ideología, simbolismo y ejercicio del poder real en la monarquía visigoda: un proceso de cambio* (Salamanca: Universidad de Salamanca, 2000)

Velázquez, Isabel, and Gisela Ripoll, 'Toletum: la construcción de una *vrbs regia*', in *Sedes Regiae, ann. 400–800*, ed. by Gisela Ripoll and Josep M. Gurt (Barcelona: Real Acadèmia de Bones Lletras, 2000), pp. 521–578

Vizcaíno Sánchez, Jaime, *La presencia bizantina en Hispania (siglos VI–VII): la documentación arqueológica*. Antigüedad y Cristianismo, 24 (Murcia: Universidad de Murcia, 2007)

Walker, Rose, *Art of Spain and Portugal from the Romans to the Early Middle Ages: Routes and Myths* (Amsterdam: Amsterdam University Press, 2016)

Wood, Jamie, *The Politics of Identity in Visigothic Spain: Religion and Power in the Histories of Isidore of Seville* (Leiden: Brill, 2012)

Zeumer, Karl, 'Geschichte der westgotischen Gesetzgegung. I', in *Neues Archiv der Gesellschaft für ältere deutsche Geschichtskunde*, 23 (1898a), 419–516

Zeumer, Karl, 'Über zwei neuentdeckte westgotische Gesetze: I. Das Processkostengesetz Königs Theudis; II. Der Titel: *De nuptiis incesitis* des *Codex Euricianus*', in *Neues Archiv der Gesellschaft für ältere deutsche Geschichtskunde*, 23 (1898b), 72–112

Zeumer, Karl, 'Geschichte der westgotischen Gesetzgebung. II', in *Neues Archiv der Gesellschaft für ältere deutsche Geschichtskunde*, 24 (1899a), 39–122

Zeumer, Karl, 'Geschichte der westgotischen Gesetzgegung. III', in *Neues Archiv der Gesellschaft für ältere deutsche Geschichtskunde*, 24 (1899b), 571–630

Zeumer, Karl, 'Zum westgothischen Urkundenwesen', in *Neues Archiv der Gesellschaft für ältere deutsche Geschichtskunde*, 24 (1899c), 13–38

Zeumer, Karl, 'Geschichte der westgotischen Gesetzgebung. IV', in *Neues Archiv der Gesellschaft für ältere deutsche Geschichtskunde*, 26 (1901), 90–149

About the Authors

Damián Fernández is Associate Professor of History at Northern Illinois University. He has published on the social, institutional, and economic history of the Iberian peninsula in Late Antiquity, including a monograph titled *Aristocrats and Statehood in Western Iberia, 300–600 CE*. He is currently co-authoring a translation and commentary of the *Liber Iudiciorum*.

Molly Lester is Assistant Professor of History at the United States Naval Academy. She is a historian of late antique and early medieval Christianity and has published on orthodoxy and heresy, liturgy, and canon law in Visigothic Iberia. Her current book project is *The Word as Lived: Orthodoxy and Liturgy in Early Medieval Iberia*.

Jamie Wood is Professor of History and Education at the University of Lincoln. He has published extensively on Isidore of Seville's historiography, bishops in Visigothic Hispania, and the social functions of violence. His current project explores political, economic, and religious connections between the Iberian peninsula and the Byzantine world in Late Antiquity.

1 Visigothic Spain and Byzantium

The Story of a Special (Historiographical) Relationship

Céline Martin

Abstract

Most late twentieth-century studies dealing with the Visigothic kingdom of Toledo mentioned its alleged imitation of Byzantium as its hallmark, singling it out from the rest of barbarian Europe. This was not a general *imitatio imperii*, but an imitation of the only Roman empire contemporary to the Gothic polity: eastern, Greek-speaking, exotic Byzantium. This chapter discusses the origins of Byzantinism in Visigothic historiography, its occasionally scant grounding in the evidence, and the ideological functions it fulfilled for historians. In the twentieth century, the Byzantinist paradigm produced well-arranged yet often contradictory narratives of one of the longest-lived post-Roman kingdoms in the West. Only lately has political and scientific globalization dispelled both the illusion of the uniqueness of Spanish features and the necessity for grounding it in Byzantinism.

Keywords: historiography; Byzantium; late antique archaeology, ritual; Mediterranean; Germanism; Romanism; National Catholicism; Marxism

In one of his last articles, the late Gilbert Dagron pointed out how Byzantium was purposely 'forgotten' in historiographical constructions of Europe stretching back to the First World War and continuing through the *Annales* school. The racist myth that Europe was produced by a merger between an exhausted Romanity and a young and vital Germanity was then replaced by the idea that Europe had emerged out of the mosaic of peoples in Charlemagne's empire. Significantly, in this new narrative, Charlemagne's Europe had moved to the north, away from the Mediterranean area, and Byzantium

Fernández, D., Lester, M. & Wood, J. (eds.), *Rome and Byzantium in the Visigothic Kingdom: Beyond* Imitatio Imperii. Taylor & Francis Group 2023
DOI: 10.5117/9789463726412_CH01

had no further role in European memory.[1] This historiographical perspective left aside not only Mediterranean Byzantium, but also the Iberian peninsula, which had entered the European community fairly late, just as, centuries before, it stood on the margins of the Carolingian sphere of influence. It should hardly be surprising that, whereas the rest of Europe built a collective memory by deliberately forgetting Byzantium and the Mediterranean, Spain used Byzantium to work out parts of its own memory.

Still, such diverging paths do not account enough for the fact that, for several decades, many historians of the Visigothic kingdom were seemingly so fascinated by the Byzantine empire that they strove to uncover similarities between both polities, or even the imitation of the latter by the former—an obsession we will call 'Byzantinism'.[2] This term evokes the 'neogothicism' displayed by early medieval authors of Christian Iberia who were eager to rely on their alleged Visigothic roots in order to legitimize new political constructions. The concept of 'Byzantinism' also stresses the label itself; when modern historians emphasize the similarities between Visigothic Spain and its contemporary, the eastern Roman empire, they almost always speak of 'Byzantium', however debatable that terminology is.[3] Even if scholars frequently use the term 'Byzantine' for the sixth and seventh centuries, it is more accurate to refer to the 'proto-Byzantine' period or the eastern Roman empire before Leo III's accession in 717.[4] This distinction avoids an otherwise deceptively stable representation of the eastern Roman empire.[5] Moreover, in the work of some historians, the comparison between the Visigothic kingdom and 'Byzantium' added overtones of exoticism, refinement, and independence from the papacy, in striking contrast with the northern, barbarian Frankish kingdom (which nonetheless outlived its Visigothic neighbour and ended up creating an empire of its own type, closely bound to the pope.) Given its problematic nature, where did this paradigm come from, and what was its enduring appeal? In the following pages, I will recover the origins of what we could call the historiographical vogue for Byzantinism, and what functions it

1 Dagron 2007, 150–54.

2 In López Pérez's words, in art history at least, Byzantinism can be seen as an explanatory model very close to 'historiographical legendarism' (López Pérez 2012, 213).

3 Arce 2004, 101.

4 Haldon 1990, 1; Ducellier 1988, 15.

5 See McCormick 1987, 217: 'In part, Byzantium's ideology of continuity combined with historians' love of their subject to foster the assumption of Byzantine civilization's unchanging superiority over the contemporary West at all times and in all respects, with the further implication that medieval westerners shared that appreciation.'

may have fulfilled among the historians of the second half of the twentieth century.

I will start with an overview of the most important reference works on the Visigothic kingdom available to scholars in the last three decades of the last century: Thompson's *The Goths in Spain*, Claude's *Adel, Kirche und Königtum*, Orlandis's *Historia de España. España visigótica*, Collins's *Early Medieval Spain*, and García Moreno's *Historia de España visigoda*.[6] As indicated in its title, Edward Thompson's book recounted the history of the Gothic dominance over the Iberian peninsula. Although a historian with a Marxist background, his scope was less social than ethnic: the bulk of his narrative rests on the relations between a small Gothic elite and the Roman population. In his view, a policy of 'separation of nationalities' prevailed under Leovigild which allowed for a 'joint administration' of the kingdom.[7] This separation had disappeared by the end of the sixth century, when the Goths experienced a gradual Romanization and were nearly absorbed by Romans.[8] The reforms of the mid-seventh century under Chindaswinth and Recceswinth, however, 'almost completely ousted' the Romans from the government of the realm, which finally stayed in Gothic hands.[9] Although almost devoid of bibliographical references and making the controversial choice to rely only on primary (largely legal) sources,[10] Thompson's book did rely on secondary literature especially for archaeology, culture, and religion—areas in which he had little interest.[11] Given the authority he was to have on Visigothic studies for the rest of the century, it is important to stress this point. Thompson dealt only indirectly with the 'involved question of Byzantine influence on the Gothic kingdom', as put by a seemingly sceptical Byzantinist colleague.[12] With regard to archaeology, Thompson relied mainly on the work of Hans Zeiss[13] and argued that Germanic elements had been replaced by 'peculiarly Spanish varieties of what had once been the tastes and styles of Byzantium' in the material culture of the seventh century.[14] In the field of art history, he

6 Thompson 1969; Claude 1971; Orlandis 1977; Collins 1983; García Moreno 1989.

7 Thompson 1969, 312.

8 Thompson 1969, 109.

9 Thompson 1969, 313.

10 As noted by reviewers at the time. See Hillgarth 1973; Orlandis 1969, whose furious review rested on Thompson's alleged disregard of Spanish scholarship; yet an overview of his footnotes mostly reveals Thompson's lack of interest for bibliography in general.

11 Markus 2001, 691.

12 Walter 1970.

13 Zeiss 1934.

14 Thompson 1969, 152.

followed Helmut Schlunk in pointing out that some rural Hispanic churches resembled the North African version of Byzantine architectural style.[15] In the field of numismatics, Thompson followed Díaz y Díaz and Hillgarth in noting the Byzantine nature of the legend *Regi a Deo vita* in a coin minted under Hermenegild.[16] Most strikingly, he described without any textual support Leovigild's reform of royal ceremonial as an 'introduction of Byzantine ceremonial'.[17] In this claim, Thompson was probably following Stroheker's work,[18] even if he did not refer to him explicitly, since the only evidence that might suggest such reform (a much discussed passage of Isidore of Seville) does not give any support to the idea of a Byzantine imitation.[19]

In 1971, two years after Thompson's monograph, the German historian Dietrich Claude published his *Adel, Kirche und Königtum im Westgotenreich*. Claude did not intend to uncover Byzantine connections in the political and social history of the Visigothic kingdom, despite his familiarity with Byzantine sources.[20] He advanced the idea of an imperialization of the Gothic monarchy, but only as an inward-looking phenomenon: in his view, the imperial ritualization of the monarchy was meant to be displayed *inside* the kingdom, not outwardly to Francia or the empire itself.[21] Even if Claude admitted that King Erwig, possibly the son of a Byzantine exile, could have exerted some limited eastern Roman influence towards the end of the seventh century,[22] he argued that the main model for the kingdom of Toledo was the late Roman empire, not the contemporary eastern Roman polity.[23] In his mind, the imperial imprint on Visigothic Spain was so strong that the kingdom 'appeared, after Byzantium, as the most centralised state formation in the early Middle Ages, a fact which should primarily be ascribed

15 Thompson 1969, 331. Cf. Schlunk 1945, 203.

16 Thompson 1969, 68. Cf. Díaz y Díaz 1958; Hillgarth 1966.

17 Thompson 1969, 109.

18 Stroheker 1965, 230. See below.

19 'Aerarium quoque ac fiscum primus iste auxit, primusque inter suos regali ueste opertus solio resedit, nam ante eum et consessus et habitus communi ut genti ita ac regis erat' (Isid. Hist. Goth. 51: 'He was the first to increase the treasury and the fisc, and the first to sit on a throne among his peers dressed in royal wear, for before him the seat as well as the garment were common to the people and the king'). On this topic, cf. Arce 2004, 106–7.

20 Claude 1969.

21 Claude 1971, 74–75.

22 Claude 1971, 76 and 125.

23 E.g., in coinage, where he held that the mentions of military victories or the epithets *pius* or *felix* referred to the fourth and fifth centuries, not to contemporary monetary practices (Claude 1971, 71–72).

to the monarchy'.[24] This key idea led Claude to situate the kingdom on a par with Byzantium and therefore to suggest a strong exceptionalism of late antique Hispania within the West. He did not conclude, however, that the Visigothic kingdom followed a Byzantine model.

Unlike Thompson's book, José Orlandis's *Historia de España. España visigótica* (1977) paid close attention to bibliography.[25] An Opus Dei priest and a professor of legal history, Orlandis was one of the major twentieth-century specialists in Visigothic studies. He argued for the existence of strong Byzantine influences in the arts and culture of the Visigothic kingdom as well as in Suevic Gallaecia.[26] He believed that King Leovigild had deliberately imitated a range of Byzantine aspects beyond the ceremonial,[27] and he concluded that the Iberian peninsula underwent a 'genuine orientalization' in the sixth and seventh centuries.[28] José Orlandis appeared far more convinced than Claude and Thompson that in Visigothic times, the Byzantine imprint on Spain had been decisive.

Such was not the view of Roger Collins, who published in 1983 a reference work on the Visigothic kingdom in English.[29] Contrary to the then popular idea of the 'isolationism' of Visigothic Spain, Collins emphasized the peninsula's deep integration into the Mediterranean world. Rather than a 'Byzantine influence', he detected a 'great continuity' with the late Roman world in chronological terms and with the wider Mediterranean environment in geographical ones.[30] I will come back later to the isolationist position, but for now, it is sufficient to note that it was often associated (paradoxically enough) with the idea of Byzantine influence over late antique Hispania. Conversely, asserting the integration of the Iberian peninsula within the Mediterranean world could undermine the paradigm of Byzantinism.

Finally, in 1989 Luis A. García Moreno published an overview of the sixth and seventh centuries that stands as a historiographical landmark of Visigothic Byzantinism.[31] He argued that during the two centuries of Gothic

24 'Das Westgotenreich erscheint – nächst Byzanz – als die am stärksten zentralisierte frühmittelalterliche Staatsbildung, was in erster Linie auf das Königstum zurückzuführen ist' (Claude 1971, 208).

25 Orlandis 1977.

26 Orlandis 1977, 102 and 207.

27 Orlandis 1977, 104 and 196.

28 Orlandis 1977, 198.

29 Collins 1983.

30 Collins 1983, 90 and 104. Collins had already challenged the 'unfounded belief in Spanish isolationism, especially in the seventh century' as well as the very idea of Byzantine influence in an anterior important publication (Collins 1980, 203–5).

31 García Moreno 1989.

dominance over the Iberian peninsula—that is, from the Ostrogothic period to the end of the seventh century—the monarchy underwent a process of 'imperialization' (a concept already put forward by Claude) which consisted mainly in imitating contemporary Byzantium.[32] García Moreno alleged that the reign of Leovigild, a king literally 'obsessed by the Justinianic model', had been a key milestone in this process.[33] He also traced Byzantine imitation throughout the reigns of Reccared, Sisebut, Chindaswinth, and Recceswinth in the military, administrative, religious, artistic, and architectural fields.

This brief survey of important historical synthesis works is illustrative of different approaches to the Byzantine paradigm in Visigothic studies, although these studies are only a glimpse into the topic. We can gain further insight into the question from the set of publications that led those historians, primarily Thompson, Orlandis, and García Moreno, to identify parallels between the Visigothic kingdom and the Byzantine empire, and, on some occasions, to affirm that the former had deliberately imitated the latter.

Dating back to the discovery of the treasure of Guarrazar in 1858, archaeologists and art historians were the first to draw parallels between both ends of the late antique Mediterranean world. Amador de los Ríos coined the category of 'Latin-Byzantine' in early medieval sculpture to describe the objects from the treasure, and most of these scholars followed him in identifying conspicuous Byzantine features in the Hispanic findings of the period.[34] In the twentieth century, Hans Zeiss, Helmut Schlunk, and Theodor Hauschild continued this trend.[35] These scholars were positive that they recognized a much more marked 'Byzantine' imprint in the peninsula than, for instance, in Merovingian Francia. Nevertheless, as early as 1945, Schlunk warned against simplifications, arguing that such an imprint was most probably connected not to the Justinianic occupation, but rather to a sixth-century influence from Ravenna.[36]

Initially restricted to cultural and art history, Byzantinism subsequently extended to political history. The German historian Karl Friedrich Stroheker provided a strong impetus in that direction in two important articles, both republished in a 1965 book.[37] The first piece, from 1939,[38] presented King

32 García Moreno 1989, 99, 112, 120, 136, 148, 322 and so forth.

33 García Moreno 1989, 322–23.

34 Amador de los Ríos 1861. On all this topic, see Martínez Jiménez, Sastre de Diego, and Tejerizo García 2018, 30–35.

35 Zeiss 1934; Schlunk and Hauschild 1978. See also Hilsdale in this volume.

36 Schlunk 1945.

37 Stroheker 1965.

38 Stroheker 1939, in Stroheker 1965, 134–91.

Leovigild as the genuine creator of a unitary Visigothic state, crediting him, and not his Catholic son Reccared, with having deeply reorganized the kingdom. In Stroheker's narrative, Leovigild entrenched his power by drawing freely on a Justinianic model, associating his sons with the throne, altering the royal ceremonial and monetary types, buying peace from the Byzantines in a proper Byzantine way, and founding a new city, Reccopolis, with the name of his son. In 1963, Stroheker reapproached the subject from a broader perspective and sought to demonstrate how contacts with the Byzantine empire had affected the inner functioning of the Visigothic kingdom.[39] According to this article, Justinian's intervention in Hispania made the direct relationship between both polities possible, with the result that Leovigild's Visigothic political construction relied far more on the Byzantine than on the western Roman model. Byzantine military aggression added another reason for Leovigild's state building, namely a political self-awareness that led him to pursue a political, ethnic, and religious unity similar to that which the eastern imperial efforts strove to achieve.[40]

Stroheker's significant impact on Visigothic studies epitomizes the powerful influence that German academics had in Spanish scholarship since the beginning of the twentieth century, not only in archaeology, but also in legal history and history in general.[41] References to Stroheker's writings are recurrent in all the general surveys mentioned above, as well as in the more specific studies of Barbero, King, or, somewhat later, Díaz, along with many others.[42] However, attributing the success of Byzantinism to one scholar would be an oversimplification. A crucial factor to this success was the condition of the Visigothic historiographical field in the central decades of the twentieth century.

As is well known, European scholarly interest in the early medieval period was often related to modern national claims over the historical heritage of preceding medieval polities.[43] Hence, in contrast with German scholarly interest in *all* of the so-called 'Germanic kingdoms', the Visigothic kingdom of Toledo was predominantly studied by Spanish historians, and the historiography of Visigothic Iberia is intrinsically connected to the

39 Stroheker 1963, in Stroheker 1965.

40 Stroheker 1965, 229–33.

41 In the Visigothic field, the two main figures were Felix Dahn (Dahn 1870 and 1885) and Karl Zeumer (Zeumer 1944, a collection of his articles translated into Spanish published in the review *Neues Archiv* from 1897 to 1900).

42 Barbero 1970, 249–50: Leovigild strove to imitate Justinian not only in political issues, but also in religious ones; King 1972, 11–14; Díaz 1998, 185.

43 The classic reference is Geary 2003. See also Wood 2013.

contemporary history of Spain. Although the history of Byzantinism has deeper roots, a crucial moment for its development within the Spanish national context happened in 1943, when the Francoist regime imposed National Catholicism on university teaching through the University Law.[44] Whether this was forced or not, adhesion to this ideology entailed the endorsing of a narrative which emphasized the construction of political and religious unity. Spain, as expressed by the fascist leader José Antonio Primo de Rivera, was 'a unity of destiny in the universal' ('unidad de destino en lo universal'). In an essentialist fashion typical of the period, Primo de Rivera claimed that the essence of Spain had transcended over the course of the centuries, connecting modern Spain directly with the Visigothic era. Moreover, post-war Spanish historians championed the already deep-rooted idea of Spain's historical uniqueness, a position particularly advanced in the 1940s and 1950s by Menéndez Pidal.[45] The well-known and heated debate between Américo Castro and Claudio Sánchez-Albornoz over the essence of Spain did nothing to modify these ideological premises, since they were essentially shared by both authors.[46] The idea of the specificity of Spanish history was then (and to a surprising point, still is) quite widespread, not only in Spain, but also among non-Spanish scholars. As I mentioned above, Dietrich Claude advanced a similar notion of distinctiveness for the Visigothic period.

In addition to Francoist ideology, Spain's international isolation after the Second World War and the defeat of other fascist states heavily conditioned Spanish medieval studies of the 1940s and 1950s. Not only had Menéndez Pidal projected the contemporary situation of Spain onto his vision of medieval Spanish culture,[47] but the nation's diplomatic isolation also engendered a moral need to build a peculiarly Spanish history outside of the general evolution of Europe. In this context, Spanish scholars wholeheartedly embraced the Byzantinist paradigm, which presented Spain as a unique case in the West, comparable only to Byzantium, a distant and prestigious polity totally foreign to Europe. But not only Francoist ideology and diplomatic isolationism worked in favour of Byzantinism. It also fitted well in the Romanist current the Spanish authorities favoured from the 1950s onwards.

44 National Catholicism, a combination of nationalism and Catholicism, is the name usually given to the ideology of the Francoist regime. Cf. De la Rasilla 2018, 271–72.

45 Cf. Bonch Reeves 2016, 26–30.

46 On this debate, which he correctly labelled 'ahistorical', see Díaz 2007.

47 Catalán 1982, 61–62. Cf. Bonch Reeves 2016, 56–57.

Given the strong German influence on Spanish historiography, the Romanism and Germanism dispute strongly shaped Spanish research for decades, especially in the fields of archaeology and legal history, where debates over the prevalence of Germanic or Roman heritage framed historiographical agendas. Whereas the Germanist approach had prevailed until the middle of the twentieth century, in the 1950s the tide began to favour Roman influence. In 1954, archaeologist Julio Martínez Santaolalla, who had been the main representative in Spain of the previously German orientation of research that had focused on 'national' or 'racial' origins, was dismissed from the position of *Comisario General de Excavaciones*. In line with the contemporary 'liberal-catholic' turn in the political sphere, the Francoist regime ceased to support an approach so close to Nazi ideas and promoted existing scholarly interest in the Christian ('paleocristianos') origins of Spain.[48] Pere de Palol, an expert on Christian archaeology and a self-proclaimed Romanist, dominated Spanish archaeology roughly from 1950 to the end of the 1980s. In his view, Spain's Christian substrate had brought about a synthesis of Latin and Germanic elements, which merged into a 'Hispano-Visigothic' profile with strong Byzantine influence.[49] Thus, Palol accepted the Byzantinist paradigm, but contrary to Stroheker and the Germanists, he attributed the main role in the alleged Byzantinization to the first Catholic (i.e., Nicene) king, Reccared, and not to his Arian father Leovigild.

The evolution of legal history or 'institutional history' during the same years followed a similar pattern. At the end of the 1950s, Germanist legal historians were either liberal (Sánchez-Albornoz, who was then living in exile in Argentina) or supporters of the fascist Falange (Torres López), who had become political opponents of the Francoist regime.[50] As mentioned earlier, the intellectual orientation of Franco's dictatorship had departed from Germanism and had begun to promote the (not so new) Romanist notion of a Visigothic kingdom deeply rooted in the Mediterranean world and unified through Catholicism. Prominent Romanists such as Martínez Díez and the above-mentioned Orlandis (who were also members of the clergy) dominated the field of legal history, and the academic tradition they

48 See the illuminating exposition by Tejerizo García (2016), drawing on prior categorization by Olmo (1991) of the Spanish archaeological approaches of the first half of the twentieth century.

49 Tejerizo García 2016, 152–55. See for instance Palol 1955, 125.

50 The opposition of some members of the (highly divided) fascist Falange to Franco's dictatorship began even before the end of the Spanish Civil War and became only broader in the following years, for a variety of reasons.

initiated continued into the twenty-first century.[51] In Martínez Díez's view, the political functioning of the kingdom of Toledo was purely Byzantine, a characterization that explained the seeming peculiarities of the relation between the civil authority and the church. In his interpretation, Chindaswinth's judicial reform of the mid-seventh century that gave bishops an intermediate judicial authority between the count of the city and the king followed Justinian's novel 86 issued nearly a century earlier.[52] Moreover, he argued that the 'subordination' of the general councils of Toledo to the Visigothic king was a distinctly Byzantine feature, possibly adopted through the mediation of Leander of Seville, who had lived in Constantinople for three years before playing a decisive role in Reccared's conversion and presiding over the Third Council of Toledo.[53]

Consciously or unconsciously, ecclesiastical historians of the early 1950s likely associated the situation of the Visigothic church with their own contemporary situation.[54] As pointed out by Díaz,[55] these historians of Visigothic Spain could not ignore the arduous negotiations between Spain and the Holy See to reach a new Concordat, which Franco finally signed in 1953.[56] Facing the post-war papacy's lack of enthusiasm for Franco's regime, Spanish historians may have found some comfort in the memory of the uncompromising attitude that Braulio of Zaragoza and Julian of Toledo had shown toward the popes of the seventh century.[57] The Visigothic church's obedience to Rome seemed tenuous, a fact that post-war Spanish scholars attributed to an essential, ahistorical feature of Spanish Christianity rather than to a characteristic of western Christianity before the Gregorian Reform. Moreover, the conflict between the papacy and the Byzantine empire, the best known early medieval case of a clash between Rome and a state, contributed to explaining that the relative independence of the Visigothic church was properly Byzantine.

José María Lacarra's classical exposition of this topic in 1959 is probably the best example of this approach.[58] Lacarra drew a close parallel between the Visigothic and the Byzantine churches, both of which were in his view equally centralized. In the seventh century, he argued, Byzantium and the

51 García Moreno 1990b.
52 Nov. Just. 86. Cf. Martínez Díez 1960.
53 Martínez Díez 1971.
54 In Linehan's view, such association was deliberate (Linehan 2011, 61).
55 Díaz 2007, 39, n. 168.
56 Payne 1987, 420–21.
57 Braul. Ep. 16; Hillgarth 1976, ix–xi.
58 Lacarra 1960.

Visigothic kingdom were the only polities to hold one single faith, canon and civil law, and liturgy. According to Lacarra, by the end of the Isidorian period, relations between Spanish bishops and the papacy became infrequent, probably because of the papacy's rapprochement to the eastern empire. In response, the Visigothic kingdom closed ranks with the king, even if his supervision was inconveniently closer than that of the pope. The rise of the metropolitan see of Toledo by the time of Julian mirrored the status of Constantinople in the East, the *Nea Roma*. It was not a coincidence that Erwig, the son of a Byzantine exile in Spain, granted the primacy of Toledo.[59] Lacarra adopted Stroheker's idea that Visigothic Byzantinism was to a large extent the result of a political self-awareness induced by Byzantine aggression, but he transposed it to the ecclesiastical field.[60]

A few years later, British scholar Jocelyn Hillgarth followed Lacarra's idea, albeit with important nuances. He detected a strong integration between Visigothic church and state since the conversion to Nicene Christianity in 589, an integration which led to Hispania's growing isolationism and which motivated papal suspicion: 'Toledo had become the Spanish Byzantium, almost the Spanish Rome.'[61] Yet in his view, such an imitation of Byzantium was 'artificial' and short-lived, as Toledo lacked Byzantium's sufficient 'armature' to fight the 'advance of feudalism'.[62] He developed this idea further only many years later, at the end of the lecture he delivered in 1989 at the very official symposium that commemorated the Third Council of Toledo of 589. On that occasion, he claimed that the strong Byzantine influence in Visigothic Hispania could not prevail because of the kingdom's lack of schools to integrate elites.[63]

To sum up, the political context in 1950s Spain as well as the country's diplomatic situation encouraged scholars to present the Visigothic kingdom as a self-contained polity strikingly distinct from its northern neighbours, and where the Roman, Christian substrate was much stronger than the Germanic contribution of the fifth and sixth centuries. From premises quite different from those defended by historians and archaeologists in previous decades, these scholars retained the Byzantinist paradigm that first appeared in a Germanist environment. However, Byzantinism was now in the service of the idea of Spanish

59 Lacarra 1960, 376–79.
60 See above n. 40.
61 Hillgarth 1966, 500.
62 Hillgarth 1966, 500–501.
63 Hillgarth 1991.

history's uniqueness. In contrast to the rest of Europe, which had been significantly influenced by Germanization, the Iberian peninsula had preserved the legacy of the Roman empire so well that its only peer could be another empire, the Byzantine empire, with which Spain shared even its conflictual relationship with the pope. As suggested in Hillgarth's remarks, comparing Spain with Byzantium seemed less audacious and more acceptable than drawing a direct comparison between a former Roman province and Rome itself.

While remaining external to the lingering politically charged Spanish debates over the supposed Germanic or Roman nature of the Visigothic kingdom, scholars outside of Spain usually accepted the paradigm of Visigothic Byzantinism. For example, P. D. King, whose 1972 study on Erwig's version of the Visigothic code stands as a landmark work in Visigothic legal history, agreed with the idea of an 'extreme Byzantine influence upon Visigothic Spain'.[64] Relying mostly on Stroheker and Thompson, King attributed this influence to Justinian's occupation of Spain, with the exception (following Schlunk) of the architectural field.[65] In matters of church and state, King followed Lacarra's views on the existence of a close parallel between the Visigothic kingdom and Byzantium.[66] Yet curiously enough, Byzantine influence was not a key idea of King's book even though he opened his work with a strong assertion of Byzantinism.[67] Instead, he identified different legal influences on Visigothic law of which the Byzantine element was only one among others.[68] One gets the impression that his adherence to Byzantinism was motivated more by respect for other scholars in fields outside of legal history than by genuine conviction.

King's approach mirrored that of many other non-Visigothicists, who frequently applied the Byzantinism paradigm to Iberia without overstressing Byzantine parallels or their uniqueness. In 1963, in a comprehensive study of western *sedes regiae* and capitals of Late Antiquity and the early Middle Ages, Eugen Ewig grouped Toledo into a general thesis on early medieval urban centres, claiming that '[o]n the threshold of the Middle Ages, cities-residences seem to have been more or less exact replicas of the "capitals" of the late Roman empire. The continuity was obvious at Ravenna, but the imperial model exerted an influence in the other germano-latin kingdoms

64 King 1972, 197.
65 King 1972, 197, n. 8.
66 King 1972, 123–24.
67 'There will be plenty of examples in the pages which follow of the constant Byzantine influence in practically every walk of Visigothic life' (King 1972, 12, n. 6).
68 E.g., King 1972, 121.

as well.'[69] In this vein, he asserted that Saints Peter and Paul, the titulature of Toledo's *ecclesia praetoriensis* (which he labelled a 'palatine chapel'), echoed the dedication of Constantinople's Holy Apostles. Ewig's assertion was probably shaped less by evidence and more so by prevailing ideas of Visigothic imitations of Byzantium, as Constantine's Holy Apostles were the Twelve, not Saints Peter and Paul, while the closest, western examples of Toledo's precise titulature were churches in Rome and the Paris basilica erected by Clovis.[70] Finally, Ewig claimed that the primacy that Toledo gained in 683 was 'borrowed from the rights of Constantinople's patriarchate' ('empruntée au droit patriarcal de Constantinople').[71] Despite these statements, Ewig did not accord Visigothic Spain any special kind of Byzantinism in comparison to the rest of the Mediterranean south, and situated Toledo at the same level as Ravenna or Pavia.

A similarly nuanced approach (admittedly with better attention to sources) can be observed twenty years later in Michael McCormick's comprehensive study of triumphal rulership. The chapter he dedicated to Visigothic Spain stressed imperial influence on celebrations of victory and liturgy.[72] More accurately, he identified Visigothic rituals as both a preservation and transformation of the Roman tradition and a conscious borrowing and adaptation of some elements of the contemporary Byzantine ceremony. He explained the latter by the analogous political conditions of 'insecurity' both polities experienced from the lack of a dynastic monarchy (unlike the Franks),[73] and argued that a similar political experience drove historical actors to adopt similar solutions. At the same time, McCormick rejected some insufficiently grounded assertions of Byzantine imitation, such as Leovigild's alleged Byzantinization of ritual.[74] His position can be summarized in his statement '[w]hen legitimacy was in question, Byzantium provided reassurance. This was nowhere truer than in Visigothic Spain.'[75] In the particular field of rituals of rulership, McCormick identified important parallels with Byzantium, sought to explain them, and set those parallels

69 'À l'aube du Moyen Âge, les villes-résidences semblent avoir été les répliques plus ou moins exactes des "capitales" du Bas-Empire. La continuité est évidente à Ravenne, mais le modèle imperial exerçait son influence aussi dans les autres royaumes germano-latins' (Ewig 1963, 70). See Fernández in this volume.

70 Greg. Tur. Decem libri 10.2.43.

71 Ewig 1963, 35.

72 McCormick 1986, 297–327.

73 McCormick 1986, 316.

74 McCormick 1986, 298–300. See above n. 19.

75 McCormick 1986, 393.

within a continuum, but he did not suggest any striking specificity of the Visigothic kingdom in that respect.

Turning back to specifically Visigothic historiography, the political evolution of Spain in the 1970s led to the field's gradual diversification. Not only did the field become more ideologically diverse, but it also included a growing number of scholars from non-peninsular countries.[76] Even before Franco's death in 1975, Marxist historiography surfaced in Spain. In Visigothic studies, Marcelo Vigil and Abilio Barbero led the way with works that offered a new perspective on the transition from Antiquity to the Middle Ages in the Iberian peninsula.[77] However, their firm support for the concept of feudalism in Spanish medieval history did not entail a shedding of old narratives. Barbero and Vigil stuck to Byzantinism for a variety of reasons, one of which was possibly their respect for Thompson's work. Furthermore, despite their direct opposition to Sánchez-Albornoz's institutional approach and despite rejecting his arguments for the lack of feudalism in medieval Spain, they did not totally dismiss the deeply rooted idea of Spain's historical singularity. In the field of military organization, they asserted that the Visigothic kingdom had set up a *limes* facing the Byzantine area and had maintained another one, originally Roman, in the north of the peninsula against the 'northern barbarians' (Astures, Cantabri, and Vascones).[78] The Visigoths supposedly improved these *limites* following a Byzantine model, 'not only because of the superiority of [Byzantine] state administration and their prestige of being the heir to Rome, but also due to the precise historical fact that they occupied part of the Iberian peninsula'.[79] Vigil and Barbero essentially relied on the current or past scholarship on Byzantine military organization, especially the works by Haussig,[80] and deemed central to their argument the appearance of *castra* in Visigothic sources, such as Isidore of Seville's *Historia Gothorum*,[81] or even more importantly Julian of Toledo's *Historia Wambae*.[82] At least in military affairs, they endorsed the

76 The growing number of scholars 'from outside Spain' in Visigothic studies was underlined in 1994 by García Moreno (1994, 117).

77 Mainly Barbero and Vigil 1978.

78 The idea of a *limes hispanus* against the 'northern barbarians' made up by Barbero and Vigil is now outdated. See, among others, Novo Güisán 1993; Menéndez Bueyes 2001, 198–206; Kulikowski 2004, 338, n. 56.

79 '[N]o solo por la superioridad de su administración estatal y su prestigio de ser el heredero de Roma, sino también por el hecho histórico concreto de que ocupó parte de la Península Ibérica' (Barbero and Vigil 1974, 71).

80 Haussig 1957.

81 Isid. Hist. Goth. 42 and 47.

82 Hist. Wamb. reg. 10 and 11.

idea that the prestige of Byzantium and the circumstantial border with the Byzantine province of Spania induced Visigothic authorities to imitate Byzantine organization in order to confront dangers that the Roman empire itself had previously faced in the peninsula.

Barbero and Vigil's works exerted a significant influence on Visigothic studies in the 1980s. The above-mentioned Luis García Moreno, a student of Vigil, not only authored several reference works, but he also wrote multiple studies on very diverse issues. In his academic production of the 1970s and 1980s, Visigothic Byzantinism was a key topic, as reflected in his *Historia de España visigoda*.[83] Although he soon refrained from taking sides in the thorny debate over the *limes* against the northern barbarians, García Moreno stated that the Visigoths had erected a peninsular *limes* against the Sueves, which he described as a 'real military border of late Roman type'.[84] The fullest articulation of his support for Byzantinism appeared in a major study on Visigothic administration released in 1974,[85] an influential article that promptly became the classic exposition of the subject. Two main ideas drove his thorough examination of Visigothic judicial, fiscal, and military organization: a very strong Late Roman and Byzantine imprint, and a high degree of feudalization affecting not only the economy and the society, but also the administration. The administration's growing militarization during the seventh century paralleled, and to a large extent imitated, the process experienced in the contemporary Byzantine empire, admittedly with a poorer result in strengthening the monarchy.[86] García Moreno, like other scholars at the time, maintained that Visigothic authorities had implemented eastern solutions in order to solve political and social problems similar to those faced by Byzantium. His deliberately exhaustive discussion of the sources led him to apply this idea to many aspects of Visigothic society, and the momentous influence he exerted on Visigothic studies ensured Byzantinism a privileged position until the end of the twentieth century.

In the 1970s and 1980s, the question of Byzantine influence was also at the centre of a controversy between two other specialists of Visigothic Spain, Jacques Fontaine and Jocelyn Hillgarth. Their debate is interesting because it includes a French philologist (Fontaine) and a British historian (Hillgarth), which shows that the Byzantinism question was not limited

83 See above.

84 '[U]na auténtica frontera militar de tipo tardorromano' (García Moreno 1990a, 463). See also García Moreno 1987.

85 García Moreno 1974.

86 García Moreno 1974, especially 152–55.

to the peninsular context. As mentioned earlier, Hillgarth defended the position that the Visigothic regime had imitated Byzantium in a number of aspects, although such imitation was short-lived and contrary to the social evolution of the kingdom. Fontaine, on the other hand, was very sceptical of the mere existence of such parallels, and he energetically supported the idea of nationalism among Hispano-Gothic authors (which, in turn, Hillgarth deemed an 'anachronism *par excellence*'). In 1969, during the seventeenth *Settimana di Studio* in Spoleto, Fontaine questioned Hillgarth's allegation of Byzantine influence in political theology. Instead, he argued in favour of a common late antique legacy, mediated especially, in the case of Hispania, through Orosius.[87] Their discussion shows that Visigothic Byzantinism, although closely related to the early twentieth-century essentialist views of Spanish identity, could also be maintained from a position that rejected such views. The controversy was still alive nearly two decades later when Suzanne Teillet, a disciple of Fontaine, published her dissertation in a book arguing for a distinctive nationalism among the writers of the Visigothic period (her book was in turn subject to a very harsh review by Hillgarth).[88] Hillgarth attacked Fontaine's views again at a multidisciplinary conference that took place in 1988 (*The Seventh Century: Change and Continuity*), a conference that was co-directed by Fontaine and Hillgarth.[89] On that occasion, Hillgarth also defended Visigothic Byzantinism following Averil Cameron's lecture,[90] but once again, Fontaine kept a prudent distance in his own conclusions to the conference.[91]

I will conclude this tour through the vicissitudes of Visigothic Byzantinism in twentieth-century historiography with a choice morsel that illustrates several of the points already made and provides a final variation of the topic. In 1990, the French Centre National de la Recherche Scientifique organized a conference on *Europe, Heir to Visigothic Spain* at the Casa Velázquez of Madrid.[92] Spain and Portugal had joined the European Union four years earlier, as pointed out by Jacques Fontaine in his introduction to the meeting: it was time for Europe to amend its selective memory and to acknowledge

87 Hillgarth 1970, 347–52.

88 Teillet 1984; Hillgarth 1988.

89 'To introduce the term "nation" into a discussion of Late Antiquity is to mislead the reader of today by inducing in him a false feeling of familiarity with a world very different from that of the late twentieth century' (Hillgarth 1992, 230).

90 Cameron 1992.

91 Fontaine and Hillgarth 1992, 282.

92 Fontaine and Pellistrandi 1992.

its debt to the historical legacy of Visigothic Spain.[93] Michel Rouche's lecture on that occasion partially adopted the form of a metaphor. He asserted that, in the seventh century, Visigothic Spain had been completely isolated diplomatically. The eastern empire, through its Spanish province, was its only link with the outside world, and the Visigothic kingdom kept its eyes fixed on the 'light from the east' because 'the light comes from the East, be it politically, religiously, or cosmically'.[94] Spain's 'splendid isolation' was related to Visigothic obsession for internal unity and finally led the kingdom to a 'crisis of civilization'. In the end, 'when instead of the light from the East came the devastating fire of Islam, the shock was such that it opened Spanish Christians' eyes on their [European] neighbours'.[95] In the face of catastrophe, Visigoths stopped staring at the eastern mirage and raised their eyes to the Pyrenees: Spain opened to Europe and started to reassume its European heritage, paid attention to Rome, and quietly submitted to the Carolingians. The year 711 marked the end of Visigothic Byzantinism. Rouche assumed that the 'genuine orientalization' of Spain alleged by Orlandis[96] had finally led to its destruction, an annihilation that was only prevented when the country accepted northern dominance.[97] For him, Visigothic imitation of Byzantium was not synonymous with prestige or national pride; it was a historical mistake, fortunately dispelled at the beginning of the Middle Ages.

To conclude, the most outstanding aspect of the Byzantine paradigm in Visigothic studies was probably its enduring character. It persisted through Germanism, Romanism, Marxism, deep religious convictions, Spanish nationalism, and opposition to Spanish nationalism, and responded until recently to the agendas of diverse historians. Aside from Collins's unobtrusive but clear criticism of 1980,[98] Byzantinism was first denounced overtly at the beginning of the twenty-first century by Javier Arce, who harshly deemed the Visigothic imitation of Byzantium as a 'historiographical myth'.[99] He was followed by Manuel Koch, who criticized not only Byzantinism, but

93 Fontaine and Pellistrandi 1992, 5–7.

94 'La lumière vient de l'Orient, que ce soit sur le plan politique, religieux ou cosmique' (Rouche 1992, 46).

95 'Lorsqu'au lieu de la lumière venue de l'Orient, cefut le feu dévastateur de l'Islam, le choc fut tel qu'il ouvrit les yeux des chrétiens espagnols sur leurs voisins' (Rouche 1992, 50).

96 See above, n. 25.

97 In Rouche's view, Einhard's assertions in *Vita Karoli* 16 on Alfonso II's vassalic submission to Charlemagne were real (Rouche 1992, 50).

98 See above n. 29.

99 Arce 2004, 115. See also Arce 2001.

even the mere idea that Leovigild undertook an 'imperialization' of the realm, an idea which endured in the literature of the 2000s.[100] This idea was still supported by Margarita Vallejo in 2012,[101] although her book, dedicated to relations between the Byzantines and the Visigoths, strove mainly to reposition Visigothic Hispania in a broader Mediterranean context rather than highlight its Byzantine influences. In art history, scepticism against the Byzantine paradigm now seems to be established.[102] In numismatics, the imitation of Byzantine iconography starting from Leovigild's coins is not questioned, but it has been noted that such an imitation declined throughout the seventh century.[103] A very recent general study of Visigothic coinage reasserted the idea, defended by Collins since the 1980s, that Hispania was deeply integrated into the Mediterranean.[104] This position accounts for a number of so-called Byzantine parallels and is likely to retain support from most scholars in the near future: the 'Spanish exception' has lost the intellectual appeal it used to have. Since the 1990s, political and scientific globalization have both decreased the isolation of Spanish scholars and undermined the notion of Visigothic solipsism, and the intellectual necessity of a separate Spanish history is less apparent to scholars. Increased contacts with specialists in other geographic areas, notably Frankish Gaul, have cleared up the false impression of the uniqueness of the Spanish features, thereby integrating the Visigoths into a global, post-Roman world to which Byzantium also belonged by its own right. Visigothic Byzantinism is probably out of fashion now, but it remains as a major historiographical milestone of twentieth-century historiography of the early Middle Ages.

Bibliography

Amador de los Ríos, José, *El arte latinobizantino en España y las coronas visigodas de Guarrazar: ensayo histórico-crítico* (Madrid: Imprenta Nacional, 1861)

Arce, Javier, '*Leovigildus rex* y el ceremonial de la corte visigótica', in *Visigoti e Longobardi*, ed. by Javier Arce and Paolo Delogu (Florence: All'Insegna del Giglio, 2001), pp. 79–92

100 Koch 2008. About 'imperialization' in Leovigild's times, García Moreno (2008, 81–92) still maintained the same line as in 1989, with some new arguments (celebration of the king's *decennalia*) but also with outdated mentions of 'cesaropapism' (at p. 92).

101 Vallejo Girvés 2012, 232–33.

102 López Pérez 2012.

103 Pliego 2009.

104 Kurt 2020.

Arce, Javier, 'Ceremonial visigodo / ceremonial "bizantino": un tópico historiográfico', in *Bizancio y la Península Ibérica: de la antigüedad tardía a la edad moderna*, ed. by I. Pérez Martín and P. Bádenas De la Peña (Madrid: Consejo Superior de Investigaciones Científicas, 2004), pp. 101–15

Barbero, Abilio, 'El pensamiento político visigodo y las primeras unciones regias en la Europa medieval', in *Hispania*, 30 (1970), 245–326

Barbero, Abilio, and Marcelo Vigil, *Sobre los orígenes sociales de la Reconquista* (Barcelona: Ariel, 1974)

Barbero, Abilio, and Marcelo Vigil, *La formación del feudalismo en la Península Ibérica* (Barcelona: Crítica, 1978)

Bonch Reeves, Ksenia, *Visions of Unity after the Visigoths: Early Iberian Latin Chronicles and the Mediterranean World* (Turnhout: Brepols, 2016)

Cameron, Averil, 'Byzantium and the Past in the Seventh Century: The Search for Redefinition', in *The Seventh Century: Change and Continuity. Proceedings of a Joint French and British Colloquium Held at the Warburg Institute 8–9 July 1988*, ed. by J. Fontaine and J. Hillgarth (London: University of London, 1992), pp. 250–76

Catalán, Diego, 'Ensayo introductorio: España en su historiografía: de objeto a sujeto de la historia', in *Los españoles en la historia*, ed. by Ramón Menéndez Pidal (Madrid: Espasa-Calpe, 1982), pp. 9–67

Claude, Dietrich, *Die byzantinische Stadt im 6. Jahrhundert*. Byzantinisches Archiv. H. 13 (Munich: C. H. Beck, 1969)

Claude, Dietrich, *Adel, Kirche und Königtum im Westgotenreich* (Sigmarigen: Thorbecke, 1971)

Collins, Roger, 'Mérida and Toledo: 550–585', in *Visigothic Spain: New Approaches*, ed. by E. James (Oxford: Clarendon Press, 1980), pp. 189–219

Collins, Roger, *Early Medieval Spain: Unity in Diversity, 400–1000* (London: Macmillan, 1983)

Dagron, Gilbert, 'Oublier Byzance. Éclipses et retours de Byzance dans la conscience européenne', in *Praktika tès Akadèmias Athènôn*, 82 (2007), 141–58

Dahn, Felix, *Die Könige der Germanen*, vol. 5 (Würzburg: Georg Olms, 1870)

Dahn, Felix, *Die Könige der Germanen*, vol. 6 (Leipzig: Georg Olms, 1885)

De la Rasilla, Ignacio, *In the Shadow of Vitoria: A History of International Law in Spain (1770–1953)* (Leiden: Brill, 2018)

Díaz, Pablo C., 'Rey y poder en la monarquía visigoda', in *Iberia*, 1 (1998), 175–95

Díaz, Pablo C., 'Los godos como epopeya y la construcción de identidades en la historiografía española', in *Anales de Historia Antigua, Medieval y Moderna*, 40 (2007), 25–73

Díaz y Díaz, Manuel C., 'La leyenda Regi a Deo Vita de una moneda de Ermenegildo', in *Analecta Sacra Tarraconensia*, 31 (1958), 261–69

Ducellier, Alain, *Les Byzantins. Histoire et culture* (Paris: Seuil, 1988)

Ewig, Eugen, 'Résidence et capitale pendant le haut Moyen Âge', in *Revue Historique*, 230.1 (1963), 25–72

Fontaine, Jacques, and Jocelyn N. Hillgarth (eds), *The Seventh Century: Change and Continuity. Proceedings of a Joint French and British Colloquium Held at the Warburg Institute 8–9 July 1988* (London: University of London, 1992)

Fontaine, Jacques, and Christine Pellistrandi (eds), *L'Europe héritière de l'Espagne wisigothique* (Madrid: Casa de Velázquez, 1992)

García Moreno, Luis A., 'Estudios sobre la organización administrativa del reino visigodo de Toledo', in *Anuario de Historia del Derecho Español*, 44 (1974), 5–155

García Moreno, Luis A., 'La arqueología y la historia militar visigoda en la península ibérica', in *Arqueología Medieval Española. II Congreso* (Madrid: Comunidad de Madrid, Consejería de Cultura y Deportes; Dirección General de Patrimonio Histórico, 1987), pp. 331–36

García Moreno, Luis A., *Historia de España visigoda* (Madrid: Cátedra, 1989)

García Moreno, Luis A., 'Zamora del dominio imperial romano al visigodo. Cuestiones de Historia militar y geopolítica', in *Actas del I Congreso de Historia de Zamora*, vol. 2 (Zamora: Diputación Provincial de Zamora; Instituto de Estudios Zamoranos Florián de Ocampo, 1990a), pp. 455–66

García Moreno, Luis A., 'La historia de la España visigoda. Líneas de investigación (1940–1989)', in *Hispania*, 50.175 (1990b), 619–36

García Moreno, Luis A., 'El hoy de la historia de la España visigoda', in *Medievalismo*, 4 (1994), 115–32

García Moreno, Luis A., *Leovigildo. Unidad y diversidad de un reinado* (Madrid: Real Academia de la Historia, 2008)

Geary, Patrick J., *The Myth of Nations: The Medieval Origins of Europe* (Princeton, NJ: Princeton University Press, 2003)

Haldon, John, *Byzantium in the Seventh Century: The Transformation of a Culture* (Cambridge: Cambridge University Press, 1990)

Haussig, H. W., 'Die Anfänge der Themenordnung', in *Finanzgeschichte der Spätantike*, ed. by F. Altheim and R. Stiehl (Frankfurt am Main: Klostermann, 1957), pp. 82–114

Hillgarth, Jocelyn N., 'Coins and Chronicles: Propaganda in Sixth-Century Spain and the Byzantine Background', in *Historia*, 15 (1966), 483–508

Hillgarth, Jocelyn N., 'Historiography in Visigothic Spain', in *La storiografia altomedievale. XVII Settimana di studio del Centro italiano di studi sull'alto medioevo* (Spoleto: Centro italiano di studi sull'alto Medioevo, 1970), pp. 261–352

Hillgarth, Jocelyn N., 'Review of *The Goths in Spain* by E. A. Thompson', in *Speculum*, 48 (1973), 591–93

Hillgarth, Jocelyn N., 'Introduction', in *Sancti Iuliani Toletanae sedis episcopi Opera*, ed. by Jocelyn N. Hillgarth, CCSL 115 (Turnhout: Brepols, 1976), pp. viii–lxiv

Hillgarth, Jocelyn N., 'Review of Suzanne Teillet, *Des Goths à la nation gothique*', in *Journal of Ecclesiastical History*, 39 (1988), 578–81

Hillgarth, Jocelyn N., 'El concilio III de Toledo y Bizancio', in *Concilio III de Toledo: XIV Centenario: 589–1989* (Toledo: Arzobispado de Toledo, 1991), pp. 297–306

Hillgarth, Jocelyn N., 'Eschatological and Political Concepts in the Seventh Century', in *The Seventh Century: Change and Continuity. Proceedings of a Joint French and British Colloquium Held at the Warburg Institute 8–9 July 1988*, ed. by J. Fontaine and J. Hillgarth (London: University of London, 1992), pp. 212–35

King, P. D., *Law and Society in the Visigothic Kingdom* (Cambridge: Cambridge University Press, 1972)

Koch, Manuel, 'La imperialización del Reino visigodo bajo Leovigildo. ¿Es la *imitatio imperii* de Leovigildo la manifestación de un momento de cambio en la pretensión de poder y la ideología visigodas?', in *Pyrenae*, 39.2 (2008), 101–17

Kulikowski, Michael, *Late Roman Spain and Its Cities* (Baltimore, MD: Johns Hopkins University Press, 2004)

Kurt, Andrew, *Minting, State, and Economy in the Visigothic Kingdom* (Amsterdam: Amsterdam University Press, 2020)

Lacarra, José María, 'La iglesia visigoda en el siglo VII y sus relaciones con Roma', in *Le Chiese nei regni dell'Europa occidentale e i loro rapporti con Roma sino all'800. VII Settimana di studio del Centro italiano di studi sull'alto Medioevo* (Spoleto: Centro italiano di studi sull'alto Medioevo, 1960), pp. 353–85

Linehan, Peter, *Historia e historiadores de la España medieval* (Salamanca: Universidad de Salamanca, 2011)

López Pérez, Iván Pablo, '¿Somos todos griegos ... incluso en el exilio? Algunas reflexiones acerca de las "influencias bizantinas" en la plástica hispánica de la tardoantigüedad y la Alta Edad Media', in *Anales de Historia del Arte*, 22 (2012), 213–19

Markus, Robert A., 'Edward Arthur Thompson 1914–1994', in *Proceedings of the British Academy*, 111 (2001), 679–93

Martínez Díez, Gonzalo, 'Función de inspección y vigilancia del episcopado sobre las autoridades seculares en el período visigodo-católico', in *Revista Española de Derecho Canónico*, 15 (1960), 579–89

Martínez Díez, Gonzalo, 'Los Concilios de Toledo', in *Anales toledanos*, 3 (1971), 119–38

Martínez Jiménez, Javier, Isaac Sastre de Diego, and Carlos Tejerizo García, *The Iberian Peninsula between 300 and 850: An Archaeological Perspective* (Amsterdam: Amsterdam University Press, 2018)

McCormick, Michael, *Eternal Victory: Triumphal Rulership in Late Antiquity, Byzantium and the Early Medieval West* (Cambridge: Cambridge University Press, 1986)

McCormick, Michael, 'Byzantium's Role in the Formation of Early Medieval Civilization: Approaches and Problems', in *Illinois Classical Studies*, 12.2 (1987), 207–20

Menéndez Bueyes, Luis Ramón, *Reflexiones críticas sobre el origen del reino de Asturias* (Salamanca: Universidad de Salamanca, 2001)

Novo Güisán, José Miguel, 'El *limes hispanus*, un concepto llamado a desaparecer de nuestros libros de historia', in *Galicia: da romanidad e á xermanización* (Santiago de Compostela: Universidad de Santiago de Compostela, 1993), pp. 61–90

Olmo Enciso, Lauro, 'Ideología y arqueología: los estudios sobre el período visigodo en la primera mitad del siglo XX', in *Historiografía de la arqueología y de la historia antigua en España (siglos XVIII–XX): Congreso Internacional, Madrid, 13–16 diciembre 1988*, ed. by R. Olmos and J. Arce (Madrid: Instituto de Conservación y Restauración de Bienes Culturales, 1991), pp. 157–60

Orlandis, José, 'Un libro inglés sobre los Godos en España', in *Cuadernos de Historia de España*, 49.50 (1969), 310–22

Orlandis, José, *Historia de España. España visigótica* (Madrid: Gredos, 1977)

Palol, Pere de, 'Esencia del arte hispánico de época visigoda: romanismo y germanismo', in *I goti in occidente. III Settimana di studio del centro italiano di studi sull'alto Medioevo* (Spoleto: Centro italiano di studi sull'alto Medioevo, 1955), pp. 65–126

Payne, Stanley G., *The Franco Regime, 1936–1975* (Madison, WI: University of Wisconsin Press, 1987)

Pliego Vázquez, Ruth, *La moneda visigoda. 1: Historia monetaria del reino visigodo de Toledo (c. 569–711). 2: Corpus* (Seville: Universidad de Sevilla, 2009)

Rouche, Michel, 'Du royaume de Tolède à la future Europe', in *L'Europe héritière de l'Espagne wisigothique*, ed. by J. Fontaine and C. Pellistrandi (Madrid: Casa de Velázquez, 1992), pp. 45–50

Schlunk, Helmut, 'Relaciones entre la península ibérica y Bizancio durante la época visigoda', in *Archivo Español de Arqueología*, 18 (1945), 177–204

Schlunk, Helmut, and Theodor Hauschild, *Hispania Antigua. Die Denkmäler der frühchristlichen und westgotischen Zeit* (Mainz: Von Zabern, 1978)

Stroheker, Karl Friedrich, 'Leowigild', in *Die Welt als Geschichte*, 5 (1939), 446–85

Stroheker, Karl Friedrich, 'Das spanische Westgotenreich und Byzanz', in *Bonner Jahrbücher*, 163 (1963), 252–74

Stroheker, Karl Friedrich, *Germanentum und Spätantike* (Zurich and Stuttgart: Antemis Verlag, 1965)

Teillet, Suzanne, *Des Goths à la nation gothique: les origines de l'idée de nation en Occident du Ve au VIIe siècle* (Paris: Belles-Lettres, 1984)

Tejerizo García, Carlos, 'Arqueología y nacionalismo en (el) movimiento: Apuntes sobre la arqueología de época visigoda durante el segundo Franquismo', in *Arqueoweb: Revista sobre Arqueología en Internet*, 17.1 (2016), 144–62

Thompson, E. A., *The Goths in Spain* (Oxford: Clarendon Press, 1969)
Vallejo Girvés, Margarita, *Hispania y Bizancio. Una relación desconocida* (Madrid: Akal, 2012)
Walter, Christopher, 'Review of Thompson (E. A), *The Goths in Spain*', in *Revue des Études Byzantines*, 28 (1970), 308
Wood, Ian, *The Modern Origins of the Early Middle Ages* (Oxford: Oxford University Press, 2013)
Zeiss, Hans, *Die Grabfunde aus dem spanischen Westgotenreich* (Berlin: W. de Gruyter, 1934)
Zeumer, Karl, *Historia de la legislación visigoda* (Barcelona: Universidad de Barcelona, 1944)

About the Author

Céline Martin is Maître de Conférences in Medieval History at the Université Bordeaux Montaigne. Her research deals with political theory and practice, particularly the normative corpus of Visigothic *leges* and *concilia*. Her international projects include 'Les élites dans le haut Moyen Âge occidental' (2003–2007) and 'Valère du Bierzo (VIIe s.)' (2006–2013).

2 The Development of the Visigothic Court in the Hagiography of the Fifth and Sixth Centuries

Ian Wood

Abstract

Discussions of the Visigothic court have tended to concentrate on the reforms brought in by Leovigild. For the previous century and a half, we do have some evidence in the letters of Sidonius Apollinaris, and in various hagiographic accounts, notably the Lives of Orientius of Auch, Bibianus of Saintes, and Epiphanius of Pavia. These highlight the importance of formal dining (the *convivium*), and they also imply that royal banquets followed the traditions of aristocratic dining, rather than any elaborate ceremonial. The archaeology of late Roman villas gives us some insight into the reality of the *convivium*.

Keywords: *convivium*; Sidonius Apollinaris; Euric; Theodoric II; *Vita Orientii*; *Vita Bibiani*

An obvious point of departure when considering Byzantium and the Visigothic kingdom of Toulouse is the reign of Leovigild (568–586). In Edward Thompson's words, Leovigild 'dressed himself "in royal raiment and seated himself upon a throne". Hitherto the kings had worn much the same dress as their subjects, and had been accessible to all, like the old Germanic chieftains. But Leovigild surrounded the throne with something of Byzantine pomp, though the details of what he did are not recorded.'[1] The reign of Leovigild, however, will be my end point. I am interested in what the Visigothic court was like before Leovigild's reforms. This will take us to

1 Thompson 1969, 57: citing Isid. Hist. Goth. 51.

Fernández, D., Lester, M. & Wood, J. (eds.), *Rome and Byzantium in the Visigothic Kingdom: Beyond* Imitatio Imperii. Taylor & Francis Group 2023
DOI: 10.5117/9789463726412_CH02

Toulouse rather than Toledo, and to the courts of western emperors rather than Byzantium. It will not take us to the dress of 'old Germanic chieftains'.

Our image of the Visigothic court in the fifth century is largely derived from Sidonius's accounts of the courts of Theodoric II and Euric.[2] Certainly this is the most vivid material. But there are several small anecdotes and snippets of information that add to his. For the reign of Athaulf there is Orosius's story of the Narbonnensian *familiarissimus* of the king, in which we learn that the king decided not to overthrow the empire, but rather to support it with Gothic arms.[3] The story is clearly symbolic, and we do not need to believe the detail, but there was a Roman coterie surrounding Athaulf, Galla Placidia, and Attalus, including the senator Paulinus of Pella, although his view of Athaulf's reign is very much less happy.[4] We can trace the continuing association of Romans and Visigothic leaders in the links between Theodoric II and Avitus,[5] Euric and Leo,[6] and Alaric II, Apollinaris, the son of Sidonius,[7] and the various Romans we can connect with the creation of the *Breviarium Alarici*.[8] Pablo Díaz has lucidly summarized a tradition of scholarship that looks back to the work of K. F. Stroheker in talking about the integration of the Gallo-Roman aristocracy into the *concilium regis* by the time of Euric, and arguing that the *Officium Palatinum* 'was made up of the aristocratic élite of the kingdom, especially the Gothic élite, but in time also the Roman élite, that it included those holding important military and civil offices, and that the presence of the high clergy was also to be taken into consideration'.[9]

Some colour is added to this reading in the hagiographical material relating to the Visigothic court, notably the *Lives* of Orientius of Auch,[10] Bibianus of Saintes,[11] and Epiphanius of Pavia.[12] These have all been dealt with for what light they shed on the practice of diplomacy,[13] but they have been used

2 Sid. Apol. Ep. 1.2; 8.9.5; also, ep. 4.8. For a critique of Sidonius's description of Theodoric see Díaz 1999, 332.

3 Oros. Hist. 7.43.6.

4 Paulinus of Pella, *Eucharisticos* 2.291–327 (ed. Moussy 1974).

5 Delaplace 2015, 215–20.

6 See below pp. xx–xx.

7 Avit. Ep. 51–52. See Shanzer 2012, 66.

8 Dumézil 2008, 73.

9 Díaz 1999, 330–35, esp. 334.

10 *Vita Prima Orientii* 3 (*Acta Sanctorum, Mai I*, 62–63). On the *Vita Orientii* see Griffe 1966, vol 2, 31–33, 276–77. See also the brief comments in Dumézil 2005, 82, 246, 549, n. 14, 728.

11 *Vita Bibiani* 4 (ed. Krusch 1896). Griffe 1966, vol 2, 70–71, 274–75; Dumézil 2005, 722.

12 Ennodius, *Vita Epifanii* (ed. Vogel 1885, 84–109).

13 Gillett 2003, 138–71; Becker 2014.

less often for what they tell us about early Visigothic rule. Another bishop who had dealings with Alaric II was Caesarius of Arles, but unfortunately the comments to be found in the *Vita Caesarii* lack any useful detail on the Visigothic court.[14]

There are good reasons why the *Lives* of Orientius and Bibianus have received little attention. The *Vita Bibiani* is one of the hagiographical works condemned as post-Merovingian by Bruno Krusch, although more recent scholarship has accepted that it was probably written between the battle of Vouillé in 507 and the early 530s.[15] The *Vita Orientii* is now regarded as a *réécriture*, based on a text written before 507.[16] Both works, moreover, have been shown to be dependent on the *Vita Epifani* of Ennodius,[17] a point of some importance not just for our reading of the Gallic hagiographical texts, but also for what it tells us about the early circulation of Ennodius's work, for which there is no manuscript earlier than the Carolingian period.[18] That works of the bishop of Pavia circulated in Gaul in the early sixth century should occasion no surprise: quite apart from the fact that Theodoric the Great intervened to protect what remained of the Visigothic kingdom after 507, Ennodius had close family ties with Provence,[19] and he also corresponded with Caesarius of Arles.[20] Another work linked to the *Vita Bibiani*,[21] which also has an anecdote relating to the court of Euric and which again survives only as a *réécriture*, is the *Vita Marcelli Deiensis*[22]—although, like the *Vita Caesarii*, this tells us little about the court other than that it was based in Toulouse, and it does so in words similar to those of the *Vita Bibiani*.[23] Modern awareness of the *réécriture* of hagiography, however, has transformed our appreciation of these texts.[24] It is now clear enough that these hagiographical narratives refer to the same world that one can see in the letters of Sidonius, in his descriptions of the courts of Theodoric II and Euric.

14 Cyprian of Toulon, Firminus of Uzès, Viventius, Messianus, and Stephanus, *Vita Caesarii* 1.20–24 (ed. Morin 1942).

15 *Vita Bibiani* (ed. Krusch 1896, 94–100). Dated to 520/30 by Dolbeau 1983, 108, nn. 63–64; Lot 1929, 467–77 (reprinted in Lot 1970, 101–11); Courcelle 1947; Heinzelmann 2010, 61; Godding 2001, xxxix. Also, Gillett 2003, 143–48.

16 Heinzelmann 2010, 61, n. 151; Dumézil 2005, 728.

17 Courcelle 1947.

18 Kennell 2000, 222.

19 See Stroheker 1948, 236.

20 Ennodius, *Epistula* CDLXI (= ep. IX, 33) (ed. Vogel 1885).

21 Dolbeau 1983, 107–9.

22 *Vita Marcelli Diensis episcopi et confessoris* 5 (ed. Dolbeau 1983, 119–21).

23 See *Vita Bibiani* 5 (ed. Krusch 1896). Dolbeau 1983, 119, n. 30.

24 Goullet, Heinzelmann, and Veyrard-Cosme 2010.

I begin with Sidonius's account of the court of Theodoric II.[25] The king's day started with religious ceremonies, which were followed, for the rest of the morning, by royal duties, including the reception of the representatives of foreign nations. Thereafter there was a visit to the treasury and the stables, followed sometimes by a hunting expedition. Next there was a meal, the *convivium*, where discussion was weightier than the food ('maximum tunc pondus verbis est, quippe cum illic aut narrentur aut seria').[26] Jeremy Rossiter has noted that Sidonius's words suggest that the king sat down to eat, as if in private (*simile privato*),[27] though one should note that this is explicitly the case on non-festive days (*diebus profestis*). The implication is surely that on feast days Theodoric dined in the normal manner of a Roman *convivium*—reclining with guests. The king then took a short rest, before indulging in table games, which in Sidonius's view was the time to ask for favours.[28] Further requests were made at the ninth hour. This was followed by dinner, which was sometimes accompanied by mimes—something that may suggest that it took place in a *triclinium*, a standard setting for entertainment provided in the course of a *convivium*.[29] After leaving the table the king set the guard over the treasury, before retiring for the night.

Other significant comments on the Visigothic court to be found in Sidonius come from the letter addressed to Lampridius containing what is a mini verse-panegyric describing the court of Euric, and the suitors from various nations.[30] The author states that, not being present when the verses are read, he will not be able to perform as *chori pantomimorum* are able to do. Here the reference to mimes suggests that Sidonius envisaged the recitation of verse in the course of a *convivium*—or perhaps, following the model of the timetable of Theodoric, after the evening meal. There are some slight differences to be noted between the courts of Theodoric and Euric—Sidonius seems to have assumed that singers regularly performed at the court of the latter, whereas the former did not encourage musical performance, although he occasionally admitted mimes (*sales mimici*).[31] A further hint at life in the Visigothic court comes in a letter of Sidonius to his friend Evodius,[32] which contains verses to be engraved on a vase for Euric's

25 Sid. Apol. Ep. 1.2.4–9.
26 Sid. Apol. Ep. 1.2.6.
27 Rossiter 1991, 206.
28 Sid. Apol. Ep. 1.2.8. On Toulouse in the time of Theodoric, see Guyon 2000.
29 See below, pages xx, for the discussion of the villa of Noheda.
30 Sid. Apol. Ep. 8.9.5.
31 Sid. Apol. Ep. 1.2.9.
32 Sid. Apol. Ep. 4.8.

queen Ragnahild. In addition Sidonius comments on several occasions on the role at court of another acquaintance, Leo,[33] adviser to at least two Visigothic kings, who not only acted as counsellor but also delivered panegyrics and verses in Euric's honour.[34] Sidonius's own panegyrical lines would seem to be the sole surviving example of what appears to have been a significant outpouring of political verse delivered at the Visigothic court.[35] Leo also appears in Ennodius's account of the mission of Epiphanius to Euric.[36] In Gregory of Tours's *Liber in gloria martyrum* he advises Alaric II to order the demolition of part of the church of St Felix at Narbonne because it obstructed the view from the palace (*palatium*).[37] As a result he was struck blind.

We can compare Sidonius's descriptions of the courts of Theodoric and Euric with what is to be found in the hagiography. According to the *Vita Prima Orientii*, despite the king's Arianism the saint was persuaded by Theodoric I to negotiate with Aetius and Litorius, to dissuade them from attacking the Visigoths.[38] On seeing Orientius, Aetius, in an action that has parallels in Constantius's *Vita Germani*[39] and in the *Vita Lupi*,[40] dismounted from his horse and agreed to the request, asking the saint to pray for him. Litorius, however, refused to desist from war, and was subsequently killed in the attack on Toulouse. It is an episode that caught the attention of Salvian, who remarked on Roman rejection of an episcopal legation sent by the Goths.[41] In a later chapter of the *Vita Orientii* we find the bishop interceding at court for a Spaniard who was subject to an unjust accusation. The bishop was invited to a dinner (*convivium*), where there was a huge banquet, which began with a table loaded with meat: 'at the start of the royal banquet, the table was laden, as is the custom of the barbarians, with huge platters of meat' ('et cum initio regalis prandii, more solito barbarorum, mensa magnis fuisset carnium ferculis onerata'). Theodoric, knowing of the saint's abstinence, asked him for once not to abstain, stating that in return he would grant any request. Orientius blessed the food, praised it, ate, and asked that the life of the accused Spaniard be spared.[42]

33 Sid. Apol. Ep. 4.22.3; 8.3.3; 9.13.2; 9.15.1. On Leo, see also Sid. Apol. Carm. 9,l.314; 23,l.446.
34 See the assessment of Helmut Reimitz in Reimitz 2014, 41.
35 Sid. Apol. Carm. 9,ll.312–17; Loyen 1943, 82, 90, and 103.
36 Ennodius, *Vita Epifanii* 85 (ed. Vogel 1885).
37 Greg. Tur. In gloria mart. 91.
38 *Vita Prima Orientii* 3 (*Acta Sanctorum, Mai I*).
39 Constantius, *Vita Germani* 6.28 (ed. Borius 1965).
40 *Vita Lupi* 5 (ed. Krusch 1896).
41 Salvian, *De Gubernatione Dei* 7.9.39 (ed. Lagarrigue 1975). Dumézil 2005, 549, n. 14.
42 *Vita Prima Orientii* 5 (*Acta Sanctorum, Mai I*). Griffe 1966, vol 2, 69 and 276.

Turning to the *Vita Bibiani* we hear of the saint's intervention on behalf of numerous *mediocres* and *nobiles* who had failed to respond to demands for tribute (*iniunctio*) and had subsequently had their goods sequestered and been taken in chains to court.[43] The bishop of Saintes travelled to Toulouse, where he visited the shrine of Saturninus. Theodoric I heard of his presence in the city and invited him, along with other bishops, to a *convivium*. Bibianus dined sparingly, but for doctrinal reasons refused a cup of wine that was offered to him by the king, who was furious at the bishop's refusal. The saint then returned to the shrine of Saturninus, where he kept vigil. The dead saint intervened to tame the king, who came to beg forgiveness, and freed the imprisoned men. The story has its parallel in the contemporary *Life* of Bishop Anianus of Orléans where the oppressor is not the Visigothic king, but the Roman *magister militum* Agripinus, who acceded to the request of the saint after being hit by a piece of falling masonry in the church where he had gone to pray.[44] As for the importance of the ruler offering the cup to an individual, it was already an issue in the *Vita Martini*—another likely influence on the *Lives* of Orientius, Bibianus,[45] and Marcellus—where Magnus Maximus offered a cup of wine to the saint. Martin, who was sitting, unlike the other diners, who were reclining, drank and then passed the cup on to his priest, in defiance of standard decorum.[46]

To the *Lives* of Orientius and Bibianus we can add Ennodius's account of Epiphanius's mission, on behalf of the Emperor Julius Nepos, to the court of Euric.[47] When the bishop arrived in Toulouse, where the king was, he spoke to the local episcopate ('sacerdotibus praecipue eiusdem regionis').[48] Leo, friend of Sidonius and counsellor of Euric at the time, was delighted by the bishop's arrival and informed the king, who summoned him to court. Having successfully concluded his diplomatic negotiations, the bishop refused to attend Euric's *polluta convivia*, and returned to Italy. Once again, a visit to the Visigothic court involves an invitation to a *convivium*: the pollution is clearly a reference to Euric's Arianism.

Although there are parallels that link the text of the *Vita Epifani* and the *Lives* of Orientius and Bibianus, as noted by Pierre Courcelle, the narrative

43 *Vita Bibiani* 4–6 (ed. Krusch 1896, 96–98).

44 *Vita Aniani* 3 (ed. Krusch 1896). For the date of the *Vita Aniani*, Godding 2001, xxiii–iv.

45 Griffe 1966, vol 2, 70–71

46 Sulpicius Severus, *Vita Martini* 20.6 (ed. Fontaine 1967, 296–98). See the comments of Dunbabin 2003, 193.

47 Ennodius, *Vita Epifanii* 85–94 (ed. Vogel 1885, 94–96).

48 Sid. Apol. Ep. 8.3.3; Harries 2001, 48–49.

similarities are not such as to suggest that the Gallic hagiographers were simply borrowing from Ennodius. We should, however, pause for a moment to consider the embassy of Epiphanius. This refers to a full-scale diplomatic mission sent by Julius Nepos in 475.[49] It was hugely important in that it resulted in the concession of a large amount of territory in southern Gaul to Euric, much to the fury of Sidonius, as is clear in his letter to Basilius of Aix.[50] It also enraged the Burgundian Gibichungs, who had been governing much of the territory ceded, and who had also opposed the appointment of Julius Nepos (which provoked the departure of Gundobad from Italy).[51] Epiphanius's mission, then, was of a very different order from the interventions of Orientius and Bibianus. But despite the difference between a public embassy and the personal intervention of a bishop, there are important points of similarity in these narratives.

In the *Vita Epifani* Ennodius refuses to partake of the *convivia polluta*. In the case of Orientius, Theodoric I persuades him not to abstain, and in return he grants the bishop's request. In the case of Bibianus, the bishop dines sparingly but refuses the proffered chalice, which enrages Theodoric. The king, however, does as the bishop asked after the latter kept vigil, and thus unleashed divine torment on the king.

Here there is an interesting conflict between the norm of the *convivium* and the problem of dining with heretics. It is an issue that is raised in the late fifth-century *Statuta ecclesiae antiqua*, which states: 'A cleric should avoid the banquets and gatherings [guilds?] of heretics and schismatics' ('Clericus haereticorum et schismaticorum tam convivia quam sodalitates aequaliter vitet').[52] It is also a problem that raises questions in some other literary and hagiographical texts. For instance in a letter of Sidonius to Patiens of Lyon we learn that the Gibichung *magister militum* Chilperic liked the feasts (*prandia*) of Patiens, while his wife liked the fasts (*ieiunia*).[53] Although Nicene bishops clearly did dine with Arian monarchs, as is apparent from the *Vitae* of Orientius and Bibianus and as may be implied by some of the letters of Avitus of Vienne,[54] the question of whether or not an orthodox bishop could dine with an Arian ruler was a serious issue in the mid-fifth century, which unquestionably occasioned some soul-searching. The fact

49 Harries 1994, 236–37; Gillett 2003, 148–71.

50 Sid. Apol. Ep. 7.6.4.

51 See Wood 2022.

52 *Statuta ecclesiae antiqua* 80 (LXX) (ed. Munier 1963).

53 Sid. Apol. Ep. 6.12.3.

54 Avit. Ep. 80, 85, and 86; see Shanzer and Wood 2002, 331–32, 334–36, and 279–84. In each of these, however, the king may be the orthodox Sigismund.

that, according to Sidonius, the Burgundian *magister militum* Chilperic enjoyed attendance at the feasts of Bishop Patiens of Lyon should perhaps be taken as an indication that the barbarian was a Nicene.[55] A similar conclusion can be drawn from the account of Chilperic's encounter with the holy man Lupicinus in the *Vita Patrum Iurensium*.[56]

It is worth pausing on the importance of the *convivium* as a political institution.[57] The phrase *convivium regis* occurs in Anglo-Saxon sources,[58] not least in Bede, where Aidan left the *convivium regis* of King Oswald.[59] Presumably the banquet was held in a great mead-hall of the sort envisaged by the Beowulf-poet.[60] In the sources for fifth-century Gaul we find the word *convivium*, but not the phrase *convivium regis*. In so far as the phrase *convivium regis* does appear in late antique sources it is in the Latin Bible, in the Old Testament.[61] The importance of the king's banquets in the Book of Esther has, not surprisingly, attracted attention.[62] The biblical use of the phrase, of course, may have been a factor in Bede's choice of words. However, the *Vita Orientii* refers to a *regale prandium*, and Avitus of Vienne talks of *pompam convivii principalis*.[63] It is, therefore, reasonable to understand the banquets of fifth- and sixth-century kings as occasions of political significance. Outside of Anglo-Saxon England and possibly northern Francia, they would not have taken place in a mead-hall. Rather, the evidence suggests that royal banquets took place in villas or official residences, few of which, in the fifth and sixth centuries, would have been newly built. The Ostrogoth Theodoric did feast in a recently erected *triclinium*,[64] but the rebel Vandal leader Gunthiarius dined in traditional style in the old proconsular residence in Carthage.[65] Visigothic rulers of the fifth and sixth centuries presumably made use of what had been the official residences of governors in Toulouse, Bordeaux, and Narbonne—where we hear that Alaric II had part of the church of St Felix pulled down to improve the view

55 Sid. Apol. Ep. 6.12.3.

56 *Vita Patrum Iurensium* 92–95 (ed. Martine 1968).

57 Courcelle 1947. See also the observations on feasts in Shanzer 2001, 217–39; also, Dierkens 2008, 9–21.

58 See Bullough 1993, 105–8.

59 Bede, *Historia Ecclesiastica* 3.5 (ed. Colgrave and Mynors 1969).

60 See, in general, Gautier 2006.

61 I Samuel, 25, 36; II Samuel, 13, 27; Esther, 14, 17. Bullough 1993, 105.

62 Kahana 2007, 17–32.

63 Avit. Ep. 86.

64 Agnellus, *Liber Pontificalis ecclesiae Ravennatis* 94 (ed. Deliyannis 2006); Ward-Perkins 1984, 160–63; Rossiter 1991, 206–7.

65 Proc. Bell. 4.28.1; Rossiter 1991, 206.

from the palace.[66] For Toulouse we have tantalizing evidence provided by Fredegar in his account of the breakdown of relations between Alaric and Clovis, where there is reference to an *aula palatiae*, before which the Frankish legate, Paternus, sat on horse-back while the Goths showered him with *solidi*, and also to a *solarium*.[67] Subsequently Alaric displayed his treasure to Paternus—which may call to mind Theodoric II's concern for his treasure in Sidonius's account.[68] From the *Consularia Caesaraugustana* we know that there was a palace in Barcelona, where Goeric was killed in 510. It was surely a residence of the imperial period, given that the Goths had only established themselves properly in the Iberian peninsula in 498, according to the chronicle,[69] although Jordanes dates the expansion into the peninsula to the reign of Euric (466–484).[70] Their Burgundian counterparts had official residences in Lyon, where they made use of the *principium*,[71] and Chalon, but also in villas at Carouge (which was fortified) and Ambérieux.[72]

Ancient historians have had a good deal to say about the history of dining.[73] In Late Antiquity dining still took place in what was an essentially classical manner: the diners reclined on couches (*stibadia*) arranged in *triclinia*. An ordinary *triclinium* might seat seven diners, though between five and nine are known.[74] Some grand houses boasted dining areas that were triple-apsed, which would have three clusters of couches, perhaps accommodating two-dozen diners.[75] Discussing the large *triclinium* of the late antique villa discovered at Noheda near Cuenca, Miguel Ángel Valero Tévar has stated:

> These large spaces with their rich ornamentation provided an ideal setting for banquets and associated ceremonies through their studied, hierarchical layout for participants in the *convivium*, something reserved for a select group of guests; at Noheda the central (E) apse would have been reserved for the *dominus* and his family and/or a special guest, and lesser

66 Greg. Tur. In gloria mart. 91. For further discussion, see pp. xx and xx–xx.

67 Fredegar 2.58.

68 Sid. Apol. Ep. 1.2, 4–9.

69 Cons. Caes., s.a. 498, 510.

70 Jordanes, *Getica* 47.244 (ed. Mommsen 1882).

71 Sid. Apol. Ep. 4.20; Bonnet and Reynaud 2000, 244. Unfortunately, the *regia* cited by Bonnet and Reynaud is only mentioned in the *Collatio Episcoporum* (ed. Peiper 1883, 163), a forgery of Jérôme Vignier.

72 Bonnet and Reynaud 2000, 243–44, 247, 256, 264.

73 E.g., Dunbabin 2003. See also Brown 2012, 198–99.

74 Rossiter 1991, 202–3.

75 Dunbabin 2003, 172.

> guests would occupy the other two apses, while the square open space in the centre of the room would provide a stage for musicians, dancers, actors, and perhaps even activities relating to *ludi* (gymnastics or boxing exercises), while also for use by servants and others coming and going.[76]

Jeremy Rossiter has noted that *triclinia* were often part of a bipartite scheme, in which the dining space was preceded by a reception area.[77] Such space provides an appropriate context for the banquets of Theodoric and Euric as described by Sidonius and fits well with his references to music and mimes. On occasion the initial reception took place in the library of the villa, as described by Macrobius, and also by Sidonius in his description of the villa of Tonantius Ferreolus.[78] If we are to envisage the banquets of kings as taking place in *triclinia*, we should note that we are dealing with relatively small-scale affairs, attended only by a few choice guests.

Despite the value of Priscus's account of Attila's banquets,[79] historians of Late Antiquity have rarely paused to discuss the political importance of the meals of barbarian kings. The *convivium* was, nevertheless, an important aspect of political life, both under the later empire[80] and in the so-called successor states, where protocol was as important as it had ever been.[81] Indeed, one can see this in the anecdotes contained in the *Lives* of Orientius and Bibianus. Although conviviality was supposed to mean that politics were avoided, as Konrad Vössing has noted in his discussion of imperial banquets the *convivium* could act as a type of *audientia*,[82] albeit one for a very restricted clientele. The continuing importance of the banquet is clear from Isidore, who insisted that there was a particular word for royal banquets, which in his vocabulary is actually *dapes*, and not *prandium*, *convivium*, or *cena*.[83] In his *Historia Gothorum*, however, when he records that King Theudegisel was killed in the course of a banquet he uses the phrase *inter epulas cenae*.[84] Royal meals are, indeed, attested as being important throughout the sixth century.[85] For an indication of what a festal meal might

76 Valero Tévar 2013, 312–22. I am indebted to Graham Barrett for drawing this article to my attention.

77 Rossiter 1991, 202.

78 Macrobius, *Saturnalia* 1.74 (ed. Kaster 2011); Sid. Apol. Ep. 2.9.5. See Rossiter 1991, 200–201.

79 Priscus, fr. 13, 14 (ed. Blockley 1983, 282–93); see also fr. 11, 2 (266–67).

80 See, however, Vössing 2007, 165–73. Also, Becker 2018, 204.

81 See Dierkens 2008, 18–19.

82 Vössing 2007, 165 and 169.

83 Isid. Etym. 20.2.5.

84 Isid. Hist. Goth. 44.

85 Shanzer 2012.

involve our best evidence is probably to be found in the letters of Avitus of Vienne,[86] not least in his extraordinary satire, penned under the name of Leonianus, of the food served on such an occasion.[87]

Gregory of Tours talks of several banquets held by Guntram: at one the king criticized Egidius of Rheims, and also restored lands to his nephew Childebert;[88] at another he discussed matters with his bishops;[89] at a third he commanded Gregory's deacon to sing;[90] at a fourth the king talked of his vision of Chilperic tormented in hell by Bishops Tetricus, Agricola, and Nicetius;[91] and Guntram also held a dinner after the baptism of Chlothar.[92] Nor was Guntram the only king with whom Gregory dined, for we hear of the bishop dining with Childebert II.[93] In addition Gregory was offered food and wine when he was interviewed by Chilperic during the trial of Praetextatus, which he only accepted after the king had promised to act in accordance with the canons.[94]

In the seventh century, Jonas of Bobbio relates a story that takes us closer to the behaviour of the fifth-century bishops, when Columbanus rejected an offer of food from Theuderic II and the king's grandmother Brunhild.[95] In Fredegar, the Breton leader Iudicael refused to eat with Dagobert following negotiations with the king at the *palatium* at Clichy, apparently because he had reservations about the king's godliness—instead 'he went to dine at the residence of the referendary Dado, whom he knew to lead a religious life'.[96] In the *Passio Praejecti* the Easter meal at court was an occasion of importance.[97]

The significance of food in the transaction of political business perhaps provides a context for the presentation to the Merovingian king Theuderic I (511–534) of a cookery book by the Ostrogothic ambassador Anthimus.[98]

86 Avit. Ep. 66, 74, 76–77, and 86 (trans. Shanzer and Wood 2002, 235–37 and 276–84). Also, Shanzer 2001.
87 Avit. Ep. 86.
88 Greg. Tur. Decem libri 7.33.
89 Greg. Tur. Decem libri 8.1.
90 Greg. Tur. Decem libri 8.3.
91 Greg. Tur. Decem libri 8.5.
92 Greg. Tur. Decem libri 10.28.
93 Greg. Tur. Decem libri 8.14.
94 Greg. Tur. Decem libri 5.18.
95 Jonas, *Vita Columbani* 1.19 (ed. Krusch 1905).
96 Fredegar 4.78 (trans. Wallace-Hadrill 1960, 66).
97 *Passio Praejecti* 19 (ed. Krusch 1910). See also *Passio Praejecti* 8.
98 Anthimus, *De observatione ciborum* (ed. Grant 1996). On the career of Anthimus, see Anthimus, *De observatione ciborum* 12–21. Also, Hen 2006, 99–110 and Dierkens 2008, 19–21.

Anthimus had an interesting career: a doctor in the eastern empire, he was caught up in negotiations between Theodoric the Amal and Theodoric Strabo, as a result of which he was sent into exile. He seems to have accompanied the former to Italy, and he subsequently acted as an ambassador for the Ostrogoths. Clearly he understood food to be an appropriate subject for a diplomatic gift.

Dining was, of course, also an important aspect in the formalities involving the emperor in the fourth, fifth, and sixth centuries. Although the imperial court was developing elaborate rituals of audience at this period—rituals of the sort that we see Leovigild adopting at the end of the sixth century—at least during the fourth and fifth centuries we also seem to see patterns of activity close to what we have noted for the fifth-century Visigothic court. Thus, according to Zosimus, it was at a dinner with Theodosius I that Fravitta and Eriulf fell out.[99] In the *Vita Martini* the saint, along with a host of notables, was invited to a meal (*convivium*) with Magnus Maximus as if on a *diem festum*.[100] Just as he describes the formal meals of Theodoric and Euric, so too Sidonius tells us of an *epulum* hosted by Majorian,[101] in a passage that Katherine Dunbabin has seen as a classic description of a *stibadium* banquet.[102] It is worth noting that in the anecdotes relating to Maximus and Majorian we are dealing with the feasts of military emperors who were not resident in a fixed capital, where court rituals might have been more advanced. Away from the great imperial residences of the capital cities, eating with the emperor may have been relatively informal, but could be politically loaded.

When Fredegar relates the time spent by Theodoric the Ostrogoth at the imperial court in Constantinople, however, he envisages a *convivium*, and indeed one that illustrates one aspect of the potentially political nature of the banquet. It is at a formal dinner that Tolomeus warned the barbarian that his life was in danger.[103] It was on such occasions that skilled politicians were noted as being expert storytellers, *iocundus in fabulis*.[104] In the parable related by Tolomeus a stag is killed at a banquet hosted by a lion. This story may well not reflect the realities of the court of the Emperor Leo. But the fable may be more enlightening than one might assume: there were indeed plenty of occasions when men were killed or arrested at dinner. Julian had

99 Zosimus, *Historia Nova* 4.56 (ed. Paschoud 1979). Esders 2009, 424.

100 Sulpicius Severus, *Vita Martini* 20.4–7 (ed. Fontaine 1967, 296–98)

101 Sid. Apol. Ep. 1.11, 10–16.

102 Dunbabin 2003, 193. See also Rossiter 1991, 205.

103 Fredegar 2.57.

104 Wood 2015, 327–38.

Vadomarius seized at a banquet held by the Rhine commander.[105] Lupicinus attempted to kill Fritigern and Alavivus at a formal dinner.[106] According to Procopius, Odoacer was killed at a banquet,[107] while, as we have noted, Isidore gave a similar context for the murder of Theudigisel.[108] Gregory of Tours included several such stories: Guntram Boso and Gripo were both attacked while dining,[109] while Fredegund organized the killing of a group of quarrellers at table.[110] In Fredegar Godinus was killed at mealtime.[111] This, of course, reflects the weak position in which a diner might find himself—unarmed and probably drunk. Murder in the course of a *convivium* was regular enough to warrant a clause in the *Pactus legis Salicae* ('De homicidio in contubernio facto').[112]

Some of these anecdotes take us away from formal dining, and as we have noted Isidore makes a distinction between *epulae* and *dapes*,[113] although others do not use this vocabulary. Before the days of Leovigild it is possible that we should see the formal dinners of the rulers of the successor states as being similar to the dinners of emperors away from their capitals, of senators, and of *patroni*, rather than anything more loaded with ceremony. In which case, we might compare Sidonius's account of the meals of Seronatus, who tended to preach to his guests praising the laws of Theodoric over those of Theodosius.[114] Here we are not that far from the *convivium* of Theodoric II. Indeed, when we compare Byzantine court ritual of the later fifth and sixth centuries with what we see at the courts of the western kings, in the latter instance we seem to be looking at a set of protocols which have more in common with the traditions of senatorial life than with that of the imperial court as it evolved in Constantinople.

But it is not just the rites of the imperial court that were evolving. We began with Leovigild's adoption of a new style of rulership. It may well be that Merovingian rulership was evolving at much the same period. Historians have long pointed to Theudebert I, Theudebald, and Chilperic I aping imperial style.[115] Josiane Barbier, in her study of the Merovingian

105 Ammianus Marcellinus, *Res Gestae* 21.4.3 (ed. Rolfe 1939–1950).
106 Ammianus Marcellinus, *Res Gestae* 30.5.4–7 (ed. Rolfe 1939–1950).
107 Proc. Bell. 5.1.24–25.
108 Isid. Hist. Goth. 44.
109 Greg. Tur. Decem libri 9.31 (Boso); 10.2 (Gripo).
110 Greg. Tur. Decem libri 10.27. See also 10.19, on Sichar and Chramnesind.
111 Fredegar 4.54.
112 *Pactus legis Salicae* 43 (ed. Eckhardt 1962, 165). See Dierkens and Périn 2008, 31.
113 Isid. Etym. 20.2.5.
114 Sid. Apol. Ep. 2.1.3.
115 Collins 1983, 7–12. Greg. Tur. Decem libri 4.17; Dierkens 2008, 17–18.

audientia, has emphasized the significance of the royal *aula* and the throne in the reigns of Guntram and his successors.[116] Whether in the late sixth and seventh centuries the banquets of Merovingian kings, or indeed those of other rulers of the successor states, took place in the traditional setting of a *triclinium* one might doubt. In so far as we have evidence for royal and aristocratic buildings in the sixth, seventh, and early eighth centuries it would seem that new *triclinia* were not being built in the West until there was a revival of the design in the eighth century.[117] In Italy, the last, sixth-century phase of the villa of San Giovanni di Ruoti adopted a new plan.[118] Increasingly in the literature we find references to the *aula*.[119]

When looking at court ritual historians have tended to concentrate on the borrowings of imperial titles and *regalia*: Leovigild, Authari, and Chilperic are all cited.[120] But the norms of western royal behaviour in the fifth and early sixth centuries were not those of the Byzantine court of the period, but those of earlier emperors, senators, and generals. In so far as the rulers of the successor states compare to emperors, it is to Magnus Maximus or Majorian, whose style was clearly that of a military man.[121] In the provinces, at least, these were men whose imperial style was not the aloof protocol of Diocletian, or that of sixth-century Byzantium. Rather, it was rooted in the behaviour of the aristocracy. In her discussion of Sidonius's description of the banquet of Majorian, Katherine Dunbabin has argued:

> The whole passage makes eminently clear the degree of ceremonial and formality that was still inseparable from such an occasion, and the way the *stibadium* banquet, once designed for more informal dining, had in turn become governed by hierarchy and precedence. Indeed we may suspect that, precisely as the presence of the barbarians became more inescapable, in what had been the western Roman empire, those who clung to the old ways believed it all the more necessary to maintain what for them was the hallmark of civilised behaviour, and to assert the privileges of their traditions.[122]

116 Barbier 2007, 241–63.
117 Rossiter 1991, 206–7; Dunbabin 2003, 193; Rizzardi 2007, 232.
118 Rossiter 1991, 207.
119 Barbier 2007, 249.
120 Wolfram 1967.
121 Sid. Apol. Ep. 1.11.7.
122 Dunbabin 2003, 192–93.

But at the same time new barbarian rulers and aristocrats themselves wished to adopt Roman tradition as a mark of their legitimacy within the old empire. It is, then, not to the style of 'old Germanic chieftains', as Edward Thompson had it, but to campaigning emperors, *magistri militum*, and *patroni* that we should look to understand the style of the Visigothic kings in the kingdom of Toulouse.

Bibliography

Agnellus of Ravenna, *Liber Pontificalis ecclesiae Ravennatis*, ed. by Deborah Mauskopf Deliyannis, *Agnelli Ravennatis Liber Pontificalis ecclesiae Ravennatis*, Corpus Christianorum Continuatio Medievalis 199 (Turnhout: Brepols, 2006)

Ammianus Marcellinus, *Res Gestae*, ed. by J. C. Rolfe, *Ammianus Marcellinus. History*, 3 vols (Cambridge, MA: Harvard University Press, 1939–1950)

Anthimus, *De observatione ciborum*, ed. by Mark Grant, *Anthimus, De observatione ciborum: On the Observance of Foods* (Totnes: Prospect, 1996)

Barbier, Josianne, 'Un rituel politique à la cour mérovingienne: l'audience royale', in *L'Audience. Rituels et cadres spatiaux dans l'Antiquité et le haut Moyen Âge*, ed. by Jean-Pierre Caillet and Michel Sot (Paris: Picard, 2007), pp. 241–63

Becker, Audrey, 'Les évêques et la diplomatie romano-barbare en Gaule au Ve siècle', in *L'empreinte chrétienne en Gaule du IVe au IXe siècle*, ed. by M. Gaillard (Turnhout: Brepols, 2014), pp. 45–59

Becker, Audrey, *Dieu, le souverain et la cour. Stratégies et rituels de légitimation du pouvoir impérial et royal dans l'Antiquité tardive et au haut Moyen Âge. Approche historique et anthropologique* (Thèse d'habilitation, Université de Lille, 2018)

Bede, *Historia Ecclesiastica*, ed. by Bertram Colgrave and R. A. B. Mynors, *Bede's Ecclesiastical History of the English People* (Oxford: Oxford University Press, 1969)

Bonnet, Charles, and Jean-François Reynaud, 'Genève et Lyon, capitales burgondes', in *Sedes regiae (ann. 400-800)*, ed. by Gisela Ripoll and Josep Gurt (Barcelona: Reial Acadèmia de Bones Lletres, 2000), pp. 241–66

Brown, Peter, *Through the Eye of a Needle: Wealth, the Fall of Rome, and the Making of Christianity in the West, 350–550 AD* (Princeton, NJ: Princeton University Press, 2012)

Bullough, D. A., 'What Does Ingeld Have to Do with Lindisfarne?', in *Anglo-Saxon England*, 22 (1993), 93–125

Collatio Episcoporum, ed. by R. Peiper, *Alcimi Ecdicii Aviti Viennensis episcopi opera quae supersunt*, MGH Auctores Antiquissimi, VI.2 (Berlin: Weidmann, 1883)

Collins, Roger, 'Theodebert I, "*Rex Magnus Francorum*"', in *Ideal and Reality in Frankish and Anglo-Saxon Society*, ed. by Patrick Womald (Oxford: Oxford University Press, 1983), pp. 7–33

Constantius of Lyon, *Vita Germani*, ed. by René Borius, *Constance de Lyon, Vie de saint Germain d'Auxerre*, Sources Chrétiennes 112 (Paris: Éditions du Cerf, 1965)

Courcelle, Pierre, 'Trois diners chez le roi wisigoth d'Aquitaine', in *Revue des Études anciennes*, 49 (1947), 169–77

Cyprian of Toulon, Firminus of Uzès, Viventius, Messianus, and Stephanus, *Vita Caesarii*, ed. by Germain Morin, *Sancti Caesarii episcopi Arelatensis opera omnia nunc primum in unum collecta*, vol. 2 (Maredsous: Maretioli, 1942)

Delaplace, Christine, *La fin de l'Empire romain d'Occident: Rome et les Wisigoths de 382 à 531* (Rennes: Presses Universitaires de Rennes, 2015)

Díaz, Pablo C., 'Visigothic Political Institutions', in *The Visigoths from the Migration Period to the Seventh Century*, ed. by Peter Heather (Woodbridge: Boydell, 1999), pp. 320–72

Dierkens, Alain, 'Grande cuisine romaine à la table des premiers rois mérovingiens: contexte historique et enjeux culturels', in *Festins mérovingiens*, ed. by Alain Dierkens and Liliane Plouvier (Brussels: Le Livre Timperman, 2008), pp. 9–21

Dierkens, Alain, and Patrick Périn, 'Les cinque sens aux temps mérovingiens', in *Festins mérovingiens*, ed. by Alain Dierkens and Liliane Plouvier (Brussels: Le Livre Timperman, 2008), pp. 17–39

Dolbeau, François, 'La vie en prose de saint Marcel, évêque de Die, Histoire du texte et édition critique', in *Francia*, 11 (1983), 97–130

Dumézil, Bruno, *Les racines chrétiennes de l'Europe: Conversion et liberté dans les royaume barbares Ve–VIIIe siècle* (Paris: Fayard, 2005)

Dumézil, Bruno, 'Le comte et l'administration de la cité dans le Bréviare d'Alaric', in *Le Bréviare d'Alaric: Aux origines du Code civil*, ed. by Michel Rouche and Bruno Dumézil (Paris: Presses de l'Université Paris Sorbonne, 2008), pp. 73–90

Dunbabin, Katherine, *The Roman Banquet: Images of Conviviality* (Cambridge: Cambridge University Press, 2003)

Ennodius of Pavia, *Epistulae*, ed. by Friedrich Vogel, *Magni Felicis Ennodi Opera*, MGH Auctores Antiquissimi, VII (Berlin: Weidmann, 1885)

Ennodius of Pavia, *Vita Epifanii*, ed. by Friedrich Vogel, *Magni Felicis Ennodi Opera*, MGH Auctores Antiquissimi, VII (Berlin: Weidmann, 1885)

Esders, Stefan, 'Rechtliche Grundlagen frühmittelalterlicher Staatlichkeit: das allgemeine Treueid', in *Der frühmittelalterliche Staat: europäische Perspektiven*, ed. by Walter Pohl and Veronika Wieser (Vienna: Österreichischen Akademie der Wissenschaften, 2009), pp. 423–34

Gautier, Alban, *Le festin dans l'Angleterre anglo-saxonne, Ve–XIe siècle* (Rennes: Presses Universitaires de Rennes, 2006)

Gillett, Andrew, *Envoys and Political Communication in the Late Antique West, 411–533* (Cambridge: Cambridge University Press, 2003)

Godding, Robert, *Prêtres en Gaule mérovingienne* (Brussels: Société des Bollandistes, 2001)

Goullet, Monique, Martin Heinzelmann, and Christiane Veyrard-Cosme (eds), *L'hagiographie mérovingienne à travers ses réécritures* (Ostfildern: Thorbecke, 2010)

Griffe, Élie, *La Gaule chrétienne à l'époque romaine*, 3 vols, 2nd ed. (Paris: Letouzey et Ané, 1966)

Guyon, Jean, 'Toulouse, la première capitale du royaume Wisigoth', in *Sedes regiae (ann. 400–800)*, ed. by Gisela Ripoll and Josep Gurt (Barcelona: Reial Acadèmia de Bones Lletres, 2000), pp. 219–40

Harries, Jill, *Sidonius Apollinaris and the Fall of Rome* (Oxford: Oxford University Press, 1994)

Harries, Jill, 'Not the Theodosian Code: Euric's Law and Late Fifth-Century Gaul', in *Society and Culture in Late Antique Gaul: Revisiting the Sources*, ed. by Ralph Mathisen and Danuta Shanzer (Aldershot: Ashgate, 2001), pp. 39–51

Heinzelmann, Martin, 'L'hagiographie mérovingienne. Panorama des documents potentiels', in *L'hagiographie mérovingienne à travers ses réécritures*, ed. by Monique Goullet, Martin Heinzelmann, and Christiane Veyrard-Cosme (Ostfildern: Thorbecke, 2010), pp. 27–82

Hen, Yitzhak, 'Food and Drink in Merovingian Gaul', in *Tätigkeitsfelder und Erfahrungshorizonte des ländliche Menschen in der frühmittelalterlichen Grundherrschaft (bis ca. 1000). Festschrift für Dieter Hägermann*, ed. by Brigitte Kasten (Stuttgart: Franz Steiner, 2006), pp. 99–110

Jonas of Bobbio, *Vita Columbani*, ed. by Bruno Krusch, *Ionae Vitae Sanctorum Columbani, Vedastis, Iohannis*, MGH Scriptores Rerum Germanicarum in usum scholarum separatim editi (Hannover: Hahn, 1905)

Jordanes, *Getica*, ed. by Theodor Mommsen, *Iordanis Romana et Getica*, MGH Auctores Antiquissimi, V.1 (Berlin: Weidmann, 1882)

Kahana, Hanna, 'Fêtes et audiences royales dans le livre d'Esther', in *L'Audience. Rituels et cadres spatiaux dans l'Antiquité et le haut Moyen Âge*, ed. by Jean-Pierre Caillet and Michel Sot (Paris: Picard, 2007), pp. 17–32

Kennell, S. A. H., *Magnus Felix Ennodius: A Gentleman of the Church* (Ann Arbor, MI: University of Michigan Press, 2000)

Lot, Ferdinand, 'La *Vita Viviani* et la domination visigothique en Aquitaine', in *Mélanges Paul Fournier* (Paris: Sirey, 1929), pp. 467–77, repr. in *Recueil des travaux historiques de Ferdinand Lot*, vol. 2 (Geneva: Droz, 1970), pp. 101–11

Lot, Ferdinand, *Recueil des travaux historiques*, vol. 2 (Geneva: Droz, 1970)

Loyen, André, *Sidoine Apollinaire et l'esprit précieux en Gaule aux derniers jours de l'empire* (Paris: Les Belles Lettres, 1943)

Macrobius, *Saturnalia*, ed. by Robert Kaster, *Macrobius. Saturnalia, Volume I. Books 1–2* (Cambridge, MA: Harvard University Press, 2011)

Pactus Legis Salicae, ed. by K. A. Eckhardt, *Pactus Legis Salicae*, MGH Leges, IV.1 (Hannover: Hahn, 1962)

Passio Praejecti, ed. by Bruno Krusch, *Passiones vitaeque sanctorum aevi Merovingici (III)*, MGH Scriptores Rerum Merovingicarum, V (Hannover: Hahn, 1910)

Paulinus of Pella, *Eucharisticos*, ed. by Claude Moussy, *Paulin de Pella, Poème d'action de graces et prière*, Sources Chrétiennes 209 (Paris: Éditions du Cerf, 1974)

Priscus, *Fragmenta*, ed. and trans. by Robin Blockley, *The Fragmentary Classicising Historians of the Later Roman Empire: Eunapius, Olympiodorus, Priscus and Malchus*, vol. 2 (Liverpool: Francis Cairns, 1983)

Reimitz, Helmut, 'The Historian as Cultural Broker in the Late and Post-Roman World', in *Western Perspectives on the Mediterranean: Cultural Transfer in Late Antiquity and the Early Middle Ages, 400–800 AD*, ed. by Andreas Fischer and Ian Wood (London: Bloomsbury, 2014), pp. 41–54

Rizzardi, Clementina, 'Le sale di rappresentanza dell'episcopio di Ravenna nell'ambito dell'edilizia religiosa occidentale ed orientale dal tardoantico all'alto medioevo', in *L'Audience. Rituels et cadres spatiaux dans l'Antiquité et le haut Moyen Âge*, ed. by Jean-Pierre Caillet and Michel Sot (Paris: Picard, 2007), pp. 221–39

Rossiter, Jeremy, '*Convivium* and Villa in Late Antiquity', in *Dining in a Classical Context*, ed. by W. J. Slater (Ann Arbor, MI: University of Michigan Press, 1991)

Salvian of Marseilles, *De Gubernatione Dei*, ed. by Georges Lagarrigue, *Salvien de Marseille, Œuvres*, vol. 2, *Du gouvernement de Dieu*, Sources Chrétiennes 220 (Paris: Éditions du Cerf, 1975)

Shanzer, Danuta, 'Bishops, Letters, Fast, Food and Feast in Later Roman Gaul', in *Society and Culture in Late Antique Gaul: Revisiting the Sources*, ed. by Ralph Mathisen and Danuta Shanzer (Aldershot: Ashgate, 2001), pp. 217–39

Shanzer, Danuta, 'Vouillé 507: Historiographical, Hagiographical, and Diplomatic Reconsiderations and Fortuna', in *The Battle of Vouillé, 507 CE: Where France Began*, ed. by R. W. Mathisen and D. Shanzer (Boston, MA: De Gruyter, 2012), pp. 63–78

Shanzer, Danuta, and Ian Wood, *Avitus of Vienne, Letters and Selected Prose* (Liverpool: Liverpool University Press, 2002)

Statuta ecclesiae antiqua, ed. by Charles Munier, *Concilia Galliae A.314–A.506*, CCSL 148 (Turnhout: Brepols, 1963)

Stroheker, K. F., *Der senatorische Adel im spätantiken Gallien* (Tübingen: Alma Mater, 1948)

Sulpicius Severus, *Vita Martini*, ed. by Jacques Fontaine, *Sulpice Sévère; Vie de Saint Martin*, Sources Chrétiennes 130 (Paris: Editions du Cerf, 1967)

Thompson, E. A., *The Goths in Spain* (Oxford: Clarendon, 1969)

Valero Tévar, Miguel Ángel, 'The Late-Antique Villa at Noheda (Villar de Domingo García) Near Cuenca and its Mosaics', in *Journal of Roman Archaeology*, 26 (2013), 307–30

Vita Aniani, ed. by Bruno Krusch, *Passiones vitaeque sanctorum aevi Merovingici et antiquiorum aliquot*, MGH Scriptores Rerum Merovingicarum, III (Hannover: Hahn, 1896)

Vita Bibiani, ed. by Bruno Krusch, *Passiones vitaeque sanctorum aevi Merovingici et antiquiorum aliquot*, MGH Scriptores Rerum Merovingicarum, III (Hannover: Hahn, 1896)

Vita Lupi, ed. by Bruno Krusch, *Passiones vitaeque sanctorum aevi Merovingici et antiquiorum aliquot*, MGH Scriptores Rerum Merovingicarum, III (Hannover: Hahn, 1896)

Vita Marcelli Diensis episcopi et confessoris, ed. by François Dolbeau, 'La vie en prose de saint Marcel, évêque de Die, Histoire du texte et édition critique', in *Francia*, 11 (1983), 97–130

Vita Patrum Iurensium, ed. by François Martine, *Vie des Pères du Jura*, Sources Chrétiennes 142 (Paris: Éditions du Cerf, 1968)

Vita Prima Orientii, Acta Sanctorum, Mai I (Paris: Société des Bollandistes, 1866)

Vössing, K., 'Empereurs et banquets à Rome', in *L'Audience. Rituels et cadres spatiaux dans l'Antiquité et le haut Moyen Âge*, ed. by Jean-Pierre Caillet and Michel Sot (Paris: Picard, 2007), pp. 165–73

Wallace-Hadrill, J. M., *The Fourth Book of the Chronicle of Fredegar* (London: T. Nelson, 1960)

Ward-Perkins, Bryan, *From Classical Antiquity to the Early Middle Ages: Urban Public Building in Northern and Central Italy AD 300–850* (Oxford: Oxford University Press, 1984)

Wolfram, Herwig, *Intitulatio*, vol. 1, *Lateinische Königs- und Fürstentitel bis zum Ende des 8. Jahrhunderts* (Graz: Böhlau, 1967)

Wood, Ian, '*Iocundus in fabulis*: The Value of Friendly Advice', in *Splendor Reginae. Passions, genre et famille*, ed. by L. Jégou, S. Joye, T. Lienhard, and J. Schneider (Turnhout: Brepols, 2015), pp. 327–38

Wood, Ian, 'The Return of Gundobad to his Homeland', in *Omnium Magistra Virtutum, Studies in Honour of Danuta R. Shanzer*, ed. by A. Cain and G. Hays (Turnhout: Brepols, 2022), pp. 307–17

Zosimus, *Historia Nova*, ed. by François Paschoud, *Zosime, Histoire Nouvelle*, vol. 2 (Paris: Les Belles Lettres, 1979)

About the Author

Ian Wood is Emeritus Professor of Early Medieval History at the University of Leeds, where he taught from 1976 to 2015. He is the author of books on the end of the western Roman empire, the Merovingians, the hagiography of mission, the early Anglo-Saxon church, and the historiography of the early Middle Ages.

3 Experiments in Visigothic Rulership

Minting and Monetary Reforms under Alaric II

Merle Eisenberg[1]

Abstract

Analyses of coinage from the post-Roman West tend to assume a steady decline from idealized late Roman appearance and use. This article explores the early Visigothic state to understand how coinage and monetary policy were transforming. It first investigates features of the first two types of post-Roman Visigothic coins—imitative (418–507 CE) and pseudo-imperial (507–570s CE)—to suggest that they should be understood as responses to local changes in governance alongside changes to broader Mediterranean trajectories. It then compares the 'interpretations' added to the *Breviary of Alaric* that modified laws on coins in the *Theodosian Code* to argue that these changes helped shape both the appearance and use of money in the Visigothic world and were thus a means of transforming governance in the post-Roman West.

Keywords: economy; monetary policy; coinage; Visigothic coins; *Theodosian Code*; *Breviary of Alaric*

Introduction

Around the year 508 CE, Bishop Avitus of Vienne wrote to his brother Bishop Apollinaris of Valence asking for a gold monogrammed ring, whose features he described in detail. He asked Apollinaris to ensure that the

1 Thanks to Lee Mordechai for his comments and to Paolo Tedesco for his help with economic questions. My thanks as well to David Yoon at the American Numismatics Society for the images and the editors of the volume for their feedback. Work on this chapter was begun at Princeton University and SESYNC (supported by funding received from the NSF DBI 1639145), and completed at Oklahoma State University. All images of coins are courtesy of the American Numismatic Society (ANS).

Fernández, D., Lester, M. & Wood, J. (eds.), *Rome and Byzantium in the Visigothic Kingdom: Beyond* Imitatio Imperii. Taylor & Francis Group 2023
DOI: 10.5117/9789463726412_CH03

ring was not made from a 'corrupted mixture of gold' that was of the same debased metal content that the 'King of the Visigoths had commanded to the public mint'.[2] Avitus's letter offers a tantalizing hint that this Visigothic ruler, Alaric II (r. 484–507 CE), was reducing the fineness of his gold, which people including Avitus had noticed. A clause in the Burgundian law code, the *Liber Constitutionum* issued around a decade after Avitus's letter, corroborates that Alaric had apparently minted adulterated coinage, since the clause banned coins that 'had been debased at the time of king Alaric'.[3] Several other stories about the last few years of Alaric's reign discuss Visigothic money as well. The *Chronicle of Fredegar*, for example, recounts that Alaric II owed tribute to the ruler of the Merovingians, Clovis (d. 511). Alaric was required to pay Clovis the amount of gold required to cover a mounted Merovingian envoy and his spear. When Alaric could not fulfil this impossible demand, conflict broke out between the two rulers, with Clovis eventually victorious.[4] Likewise, both Gregory of Tours and Procopius of Caesarea explicitly mention that Clovis carried off Alaric's treasure at the end of the conflict.[5] Added together, scholars have argued that this economic dispute was a—if not the—cause for this early medieval conflict that led to Merovingian hegemony over Gaul and the shift of Visigothic power to Iberia.[6]

These stories and discussions of them have an underlying assumption of post-Roman monetary decline. Each state vied for power in a world no longer able to mint 'proper' coins or meet state fiscal obligations, and had to resort to stealing each other's treasury, for example, to remain economically sustainable. Rather than examine these monetary questions from the perspective of divergence from some ideal Roman type, this chapter suggests that a more useful approach is to contextualize these

2 'Nec quidem talis electri, quale nuper, ut egomet hausi, in sancto ac sincerissimo impollutae manus nitore sordebat, cui corruptam potius quam confectam auri nondum fornace decocti crederes inesse mixturam: vel illam certe, quam nuperrime rex Getarum secuturae praesagam ruinae monetis publicis adulterium firmantem mandaverat' (Avit. Ep. 87).

3 Lib. Const. Constitutiones Extravagantes 21.7; on the laws in context, Wood 2016; and on the laws and the making of the Burgundian state, Eisenberg 2019.

4 For this story: Fredegar 2.58; for a discussion of this passage, Shanzer 2012, 75; and on Fredegar, Collins 2007. For the war, Gómez Aragonés 2016.

5 Greg. Tur. Decem libri 2.37; Proc. Bell. 1.12.69.

6 For a discussion of the letter and debasement leading to conflict: Shanzer and Wood 2002, 251–53; and Wood 1994, 47; also, Shanzer 2012, 73–77. These coins have never been identified. For a suggestion of one coin that could be Alaric's, but which is not debased: Grierson and Blackburn 1986, 46. It is possible that few were minted, or that they were all reminted.

economic and monetary questions within broader changes in Visigothic governance. As a case study, I investigate changes to Alaric's coinage, which I argue are linked to concurrent changes to monetary laws in the *Breviary of Alaric*, whose interpretations of the *Theodosian Code* began to transform monetary norms and ideas. Taken as a package, Visigothic monetary ideas reveal how the state tested new methods of governing as they consolidated control over new regions. These nascent experiments, whose language sought 'simply' to clarify existing laws, began to transform regions into new states. While this small series of changes to monetary norms cannot reveal everything about how post-Roman state structures transformed, or resolve the specific chronology of this process, they do offer a methodological approach that suggests that comparisons between post-Roman states and the mid-fifth-century Roman past should be the basis for further work.[7] As the introduction to this volume and Ian Wood's chapter about the Visigothic court both suggest, the question is what specific concepts of Rome were transformed in contingent moments in time when states experimented with new ideas.

The beginning of the sixth century did mark a break in western European governance following the emergence of post-Roman spheres of influence. Post-500 western rulers, such as Theodoric (ruler of Italy, 493–526 CE), Gundobad (in power, 472–516 CE), and Alaric II, are often compared with emperors of the Roman past, to whom contemporary rhetoric linked them, or to contemporary eastern Roman emperors, who ruled in ways now unconnected to western reality.[8] Yet these post-500 rulers imagined their (Roman) power as primarily based upon the military rulership of the previous century, and not as explicitly building new structures.[9] Alaric's reforms were connected to the need to clarify governance and territorial boundaries after the emergence of de facto post-imperially controlled states in northern Gaul under Clovis, in south-eastern Gaul under Gundobad, and in Italy under Theodoric.[10]

In the context of a break between the Roman and post-Roman worlds, numismatists investigate change by tracing how new coins spread from

7 For narrative histories of the Visigoths, Wolfram 1988, Heather 1996, and Delaplace 2015. Alaric's efforts do not, of course, stand alone, but were alongside similar efforts in Ostrogothic Italy and in the Burgundian *regio*. For the historical context, Halsall 2007.

8 For the comparison between emperors and post-Roman rulers see, for example, Arnold 2014.

9 On late Roman rulership, McEvoy 2013; on post-Roman Burgundy, Wood 2014.

10 On mid-fifth-century power structures, McEvoy 2017; for the Ostrogoths, Vitiello 2017; on the Vandals, Conant 2012; and coinage, Hendy 1988.

a centre to the periphery. Based on numismatic classification, the first post-Roman Visigothic coins were the so-called 'Victory with Palm Wreath' (VPW) *tremisses*, which appeared for the first time in the early sixth century. The first issuing of the VPW coins is generally connected to the rule of Theodoric, who, as the 'most Roman' of the successor rulers, began a coinage reform that spread throughout the West.[11] The basis of this claim is the style of the VPW coins along with the assumption that Theodoric issued them after his defeat of Clovis and Gundobad in 508–510 CE In this narrative, the VPW coins declare Ostrogothic victory at the end of this war (hence Victory on the coin).[12]

Aside from a few famous legal clauses such as the one in the *Liber Constitutionum*, numismatics rarely questions this centre-periphery model even when the origins of the VPW coins can never be resolved satisfactorily.[13] At the same time as these coinage changes, Alaric II initiated a legal codification project—the so-called *Breviary of Alaric*, or *Lex Romana Visigothorum*, issued in 506—and supported the first Gallic church council in over fifty years at Agde in that same year. Among its many titles, the *Breviary* changed monetary laws and revised the tax system. The changes to legal monetary arrangements can be traced in the *interpretationes* ('interpretations') attached to the *Breviary*, which modified existing provisions that were originally codified in the *Theodosian Code* about seventy years earlier, but which claimed to be clarifying complex legal situations. Whether monetary reforms changed practice (i.e., top down) or the monetary laws responded to practice on the ground (i.e., bottom up) cannot be clearly distinguished, but the laws did reform normative practice.

This chapter begins by first discussing the traditional classification system of Visigothic coins and argues that these categories are problematic, since they ensconce Visigothic coinage in a 'decline' classification rather than examining them in their immediate context. It also demonstrates the limited ability of the coin evidence alone to reveal anything about the post-Roman economy and money. In the second part of this article, I offer a new path forward by linking these physical coin changes to the *Breviary of Alaric*'s modifications to existing *Theodosian Code* laws on monetary aspects.

11 This is exemplified in Tomasini 1964, 32–44; and Grierson and Blackburn 1986, 75–77.

12 Burgundian VPW coins should be dated to around 502 CE during a crisis in that state's governance. See Eisenberg 2019.

13 My thinking is shaped by Mitchell 2014.

Visigothic Coinage and Monetary Law

Surveys of western coins have focused on sketching out a paradigm of slow degradation from late Roman standards. As the decades progressed from 476 (and earlier in some cases), western post-Roman coins are judged first against plentiful fourth-century Roman coins and then against higher quality contemporary eastern Roman coins. After the last Roman emperor in the West, with the exception of Ostrogothic rule in Italy, coins are discussed as worse, uglier, and of lower quality than coins minted in the East or during the fourth century.[14] At the same time, the numismatic decline narrative cannot resolve key chronological and geographical questions such as: Who minted various post-Roman coin types first? Where were the first new coins minted? Early Visigothic coinage evidence alone—at least on the basis of existing evidence—cannot answer these questions.

After the fragmentation of western Roman political power, the major break between eastern and western minting dates to the Anastasian coinage reform of *c.* 498 CE. Anastasius's reform placed denominations on coins and was used throughout the central and eastern Mediterranean. (See Figure 3.1.) While the reform is named after the Emperor Anastasius and denominated coins were minted in the Byzantine empire for centuries, it remains unclear if the Byzantine empire actually initiated the reform or if it began in Ostrogothic Italy or Vandal North Africa.[15] (See Figures 3.2 and 3.3.) Moreover, attempting to pinpoint the origin point reveals far less than its implementation and long-term effect on structures and users.[16] The post-Roman states in the West, though, ignored these changes and continued to mint 'older' coins. The weight and fineness of the western coins remained within acceptable limits and they were presumably still accepted as legal tender across the Mediterranean. The question should not be why the Visigoths (or others) failed to mint reformed coins, but rather what experiments were tried on their coins and how this is connected to other monetary reforms.

14 The best introduction remains: Grierson and Blackburn 1986, 39–49; also, Carson, Kent, and Burnett 1994, 220–28; one of the few examinations of money and law is Depeyrot 1991. On monograms as 'outdated' coins, Garipzanov 2017 and 2018.

15 The starting point for discussions of post-Roman coins is Hendy 1988; the connections between reforms, Stahl 2012.

16 Coinage reforms during the late eighth century can be linked to transformations in how money should function. See Garipzanov 2009 and Naismith 2012, 175–76. The Anastasian reform can be more usefully thought about as a movement away from smaller *nummi* and monogrammed coins to a new system of bronze denominations.

Figure 3.1: Bronze 40 *nummi* of Anastasius I, Eastern Roman, Constantinople, 498–518 CE. ANS 1997.31.1.obv.600 and ANS 1997.31.1.rev.600

Figure 3.2: Bronze 40 *nummi* of Theodoric and Athalaric, Ostrogothic, Rome, 522–534 CE. ANS 1944.100.61978.obv.490 and ANS 1944.100.61978.rev.490

Figure 3.3: Bronze 42 *nummi* of Hilderic, Vandal, Carthage, 523–530 CE. ANS 1944.100.73746.obv.490 and ANS 1944.100.73746.rev.490

Visigothic coinage is divided into three phases: imitative (418–507 CE), pseudo-imperial (507–570s CE), and regal (570s–700s CE). Wilhelm Reinhart popularized these categories and, although there have been modifications, they have remained largely the same ever since.[17] Lee Mordechai and Alan Stahl have proposed an alternative classification of late antique and early medieval imitations, which can be applied to Visigothic coinage. Yet their classification retains the problems of the existing Visigothic phase system, since it depends on an ideal type—a stylistically superior Roman coin—and derivatives produced as the financial system in the West simplified.[18] The earliest Visigothic coins, which are labelled as Visigothic due to their 'worse' Roman style (although their attribution is uncertain), were theoretically minted soon after the arrival and settlement of the Visigoths in Aquitaine. From the 420s through the 470s, Visigothic leaders imitated Roman coins with coin obverses corresponding to the analogous chronological emperor through to the reign of Zeno (r. 474–491 CE). In other words, upon learning of the accession of a new emperor, Visigothic coins changed their obverse to match the new image.[19] Even though Visigothic coins are considered stylistically worse, their metal content was not initially adulterated.[20]

The pseudo-imperial phase supposedly began when Theodoric ordered the minting of new coins to demonstrate his power following his conquest and hegemony over southern Gaul between 508 and 510 CE. These new coins are implicitly classified as pseudo-Roman, since they appear different from 'proper' (i.e., eastern) Roman coinage in style and type.[21] The evidence for the Ostrogothic overhaul in coinage style is the addition of Victory to these coins (hence their modern name, 'Victory with Palm Wreath'), which supposedly celebrated Ostrogothic victory over the Merovingians and Burgundians.[22] Victory, though, had long been a symbol on Roman coins, which continued even after Constantine's Christianization of the Roman empire, despite Victory's pagan connotations. While in the history of Roman coinage, Victory was sometimes linked with a favourable military outcome, it just as often appeared to portend a hoped-for future conquest or else functioned as a statement of authority. The Emperor Jovian (r. 363 CE), for example, placed

17 Laid out in Reinhart 1938, 1942, and 1945. Generally still followed, Steinbach 2017.

18 Mordechai and Stahl 2021.

19 The pre-regal Visigothic coins lack further articulation. For an overview, Grierson and Blackburn 1986, 39–49, Pliego Vázquez 2009, 64–79, and Kurt 2020, 25–80.

20 Grierson 1953, and Metcalf, Cabral, and Alves 1992.

21 On Theodoric as the political break, while using similar ideas to the past, see Arnold 2012.

22 For the attribution to Theodoric although there is criticism of Tomasini's numismatic work, see Tomasini 1964; for the circulation patterns, Barral i Altet 1976, 147–48.

Victory on his coins despite ruling for just a few short months and whose only military action was to conclude an unfavourable treaty with Persia that ceded strategically important territories. Jovian's 'military victory' and his placement of Victory on coins, among many examples, was hardly a statement of military conquest.[23] VPW coins should likewise be detached from this problematic reasoning.

From approximately 510 CE onward, Visigothic VPW coins were minted until a newly consolidated Visigothic state in Iberia issued new regal, sometimes termed 'national', coins under Leovigild (r. 568–586) and his successors. Regal coins were then minted until the end of the kingdom in the early eighth century.[24] (See Figure 3.4.) Some mid-sixth-century VPW coins are certainly Visigothic, since their circulation patterns were increasingly localized in regions under Visigothic control and they have direct stylistic links with the early regal coinage.[25] The standard narrative of three coinage phases imagines a reactive Visigothic state as a passive recipient that responded to larger Mediterranean-wide trends in minting and monetary policy. On this interpretation, structural changes in more monetarily sophisticated states which witnessed less 'decline' (eastern Romans or Ostrogoths) drove transformations in Visigothic coinage until the Visigothic state emerged as sufficiently centralized and sophisticated under Leovigild, and was then able to mint its own coins.

The known VPW coins look similar to each other and do not have any features that allow numismatists to disaggregate them chronologically. 'Burgundian', 'Ostrogothic', and 'Visigothic' VPW coins have only rough stylistic differences.[26] (See Figures 3.5 and 3.6.) Circulation patterns of the various early VPW coins do not offer sufficient information to detail a more specific chronological pattern either. Xavier Barral i Altet mapped the known finds of early VPW coins, which have been located in a disparate arc from England to the Low Countries, down the Rhine River to Provence, and Iberia. This pattern follows rivers and known trade routes, but its spread and the relative paucity of coins hampers any chronological interpretation that might facilitate identification of which state might have minted VPW coins first. While more recent finds have updated this picture, no general pattern has emerged. The physical coin evidence, including both stylistic

23 For a link between Victory and these coins, see Tomasini 1964, 32–41. For one example of Jovian's coinage, Kent 1981, 533.

24 An earlier catalogue is Miles 1952; and comprehensive now is Pliego Vázquez 2009.

25 See Barral i Altet 1976, 147–48; and for a mixed hoard 86–91.

26 For the stylistic analysis, see Tomasini 1964, 88–103.

Figure 3.4: Visigothic Regal Coinage, Gold *tremissis* of Leovigild, Toledo, 575–586 CE. ANS 2016.29.9.obv.1800 and ANS 2016.29.9.rev.1800

Figure 3.5: Gold *tremissis* of Gundobad, 'Burgundian', after 501–516 CE. ANS 2014.44.55.obv.2300 and ANS 2014.44.55.rev.2300

Figure 3.6: Gold *tremissis* of the Visigoths, after 501–518 CE. ANS 1944.74.1.obv.3950 and ANS 1944.74.1.rev.3950

analysis of individual coins and a circulation pattern examination, cannot date the Visigothic VPW coins more precisely.[27] It is notable though that all types of VPW coins were interchangeable, which reflects continued connections across the broader region.

This broad survey has shown how until the mid-sixth century coins remained similar and interchangeable. Experimentations persisted within existing coinage types that could claim to continue existing precedents, but small changes slowly led to new practices. The first Visigothic VPW coins—as with all the VPW coins—cannot be definitively dated, given the small chronological window in which they all appeared in the West. Even if these could be precisely chronologically dated, this reveals little about how money, as a contingent social relation, was undergoing change. As a way to overcome purely numismatic questions, then, Visigothic VPW coins should be disassociated from their connection to a Roman imitative classification system and placed back alongside similar monetary changes occurring across the post-Roman West. Moreover, the numismatic evidence alone cannot answer the monetary, let alone economic, questions about how new states were formed. Broader governance reforms, of which coins were one of many at the turn of the sixth century, provide a more useful context within which to examine the Visigothic coinage in this period.

The *Breviary of Alaric* and Legal Monetary Changes

The legal landscape of southern Gaul at the turn of the sixth century transformed through new secular laws and the meeting of supra-regional church councils. Alongside secular legal changes, Alaric sanctioned the convening of the Council of Agde in 506 CE and both initiatives had the same legal experts present.[28] Among other changes, the meetings highlighted adjustments to physical forms of acceptable coinage and to the use of money and carved out a role for churches in facilitating economic transactions. This section explores the monetary laws in the *Breviary* to offer a new source that, when combined with the coinage evidence, suggests that monetary ideas were vital in governing the Visigothic state. It reveals how Alaric

27 Barral i Altet 1976, 147–48; and with updates in 'FLAME – Framing the Late Antique and Early Medieval Economy'.

28 For the connection between ecclesiastical and secular legal training, Humfress 2007; for the connection between Agde and the *Breviary*, Mathisen 2008, and the volume has other relevant articles on the *Breviary*; on post-Roman legal culture, Liebs 2002. For the church and changes to money, Wood 2013.

sought to clarify existing monetary precedents, but in the process began to transform monetary realities.

The *Breviary*, completed in 506, was created through a carefully articulated process. As with other western legal compendia from the late fifth through the first half of the sixth century, the *Breviary* modified existing Roman laws, particularly the *Theodosian Code* (CTh) and the later issued *novellae*, rather than overturning existing legal structures.[29] It subtly changed the focus of some existing laws, excluded irrelevant laws, and clarified debated passages of laws through jurisprudential readings. The *Breviary*'s compilers added interpretations to the existing laws that were retained in order to expand, update, and comment upon the existing laws. The interpretations demonstrate an active effort to adapt existing laws to a new context and many were compiled in the decades before the law code was issued in 506. They have generally been overlooked in analyses of changes at the turn of the sixth century, but they offer a useful point of comparison.[30]

A comparison between the *Breviary*'s monetary, financial, and few crucial tax laws and their Theodosian originals highlights a Visigothic attempt to clarify the central aspects of coinage in the Visigothic realm, as well as removing non-applicable laws. A number of laws from the *Breviary* discussed coinage to update the *Theodosian Code*, particularly CTh 9.22. Constantine had originally issued 9.22 in two parts (9.22.1 and 9.22.2). CTh 9.22.1 was the title's central focus and confirmed that all coins were legal tender, regardless of the size of the obverse's imperial image. In the second part (9.22.2), Constantine had ordered capital punishment for people who clipped the outer edge of a coin or who minted a debased counterfeit coin. The emphasis in this title was on the first part—the size of the imperial image on the obverse—since at the time the law was issued, there were differences in the size of the emperor's image on the obverses.[31] (See Figure 3.7.) Notably, the *Breviary*'s *interpretatio* ignored the question of imperial image size, since all

29 For a proposed dating of 507, Saint-Sorny 2001.

30 One of the few monographs is Lambertini 1991; for an initial investigation, Matthews 2001; also, Liebs 2003 and 2013. There are a few case studies such as on judges, Roux 2019; on Jews and the law, Nemo-Pekelman 2013; on Book 9, Di Cintio 2013. For a similar process to the north, Wood 2008.

31 CTh 9.22: 'Omnes solidi, in quibus nostri vultus ac veneratio una est, uno pretio aestimandi sunt atque vendendi, quamquam diversa formae mensura sit. Nec enim qui maiore habitu faciei extenditur, maioris est pretii aut qui angustiore expressione concluditur, minoris valere credendus est, cum pondus idem existat. Quod si quis aliter fecerit, aut capite puniri debet aut flammis tradi vel alia poena mortifera. Quod ille etiam patietur, qui mensuram circuli exterioris adroserit, ut ponderis minuat quantitatem, vel figuratum solidum adultera imitatione in vendendo subiecerit.'

Figure 3.7: Gold *Solidus* of Constantine I, Nicomedia, 315–316 CE. ANS 1948.19.315.obv.600 and ANS 1948.19.315.rev.600

Figure 3.8: Gold *solidus* of Julius Nepos, Visigoths, 474–480 CE. ANS 2014.44.12.obv.2300 and ANS 2014.44.12.rev.2300

minted coins in the late fifth-century West had an imperial portrait of the same size. (See Figure 3.8.) Earlier coins undoubtedly continued to circulate, but after two centuries of seeing various types of obverses in circulation, people had become accustomed to differences.[32]

Two other titles in the *Theodosian Code* were also related to aspects of minting: 9.21 ('On Counterfeit Money') and 9.23 ('On Melting down Money for Transport'). CTh 9.23 contained two laws, which were from the second half of the fourth century, and which outlawed the melting down of money for transport to the imperial fisc as tax payments. The *Breviary* excluded this entire title, since melted-down money was no longer transported for tax

32 For a brief discussion of CTh 9.22, see Matthews 2001, 26, especially note 28; for hoard data, 'FLAME – Framing the Late Antique and Early Medieval Economy'.

payments within the Visigothic state.[33] CTh 9.21 contained eight individual laws from Constantine (319 CE) through to the reigns of Valentinian II, Theodosius I, and Arcadius (392 CE). These laws banned a wide range of illegal actions regarding counterfeit coins and detailed punishments depending upon an individual's social status. For example, CTh 9.21.1 and 9.21.2 punished offenders according to sex and legal status, while offering inducements to those who reported illegal actions, such as freedom for slaves if they reported a counterfeiting operation. Constantine's titles also ordered the property upon which the illegal actions had occurred confiscated, while providing loopholes in other titles that, for example, protected widows' property as long as they were ignorant of the illegal minting.[34] Further titles in CTh 9.21 included bans on casting coins and adulterating silver coins, the latter of which were debased as a way to siphon off small amounts of silver for personal profit.[35]

The *Breviary* simplified both monetary laws that it included (9.21 and 9.22) and broadened their applicability, suggesting that the Visigothic state aimed to consolidate control over its monetary administration. It expanded the original two categories of a clipped coin and a 'debased counterfeit' of 9.22.1 to three stating: 'if any person should clip around a *solidus* or substitute a debased coin or make counterfeit money, he shall be capitally punished.'[36] A counterfeit was no longer assumed to be debased, but rather two separate categories were listed with the possibility that both coins of lesser value existed as did illegally minted coins. These new definitions allowed the state greater flexibility to define a counterfeit coin, given that they could now include coins outside appropriate state channels (not just debased counterfeit coins) since more types of coins were now minted and in circulation (i.e., from non-Visigothic regions of Gaul).

33 CTh 9.23: 'Quicumque vel conflare pecunias vel ad diversa vendendi causa transferre detegitur, sacrilegii sententiam subeat et capite plectatur.' For a brief discussion of the interpretations on monetary questions, Di Cintio 2013, 153–56. On tax payments: Tedesco (forthcoming).

34 CTh 9.21.4 on widows: 'Viduas autem ac pupillos speciali dignos indulgentia credidimus, ut viduae nec in proximo constitutae domo sua vel possessione careant, si nulla aput ipsas tam gravis conscientiae noxa resideat.' On Constantine and the family, Evans Grubbs 1995.

35 CTh 9.21.3 on casting coins: 'Si quis nummum falsa fusione formaverit, universas eius facultates fisco addici praecipimus, atque ipsum severitate legitima coherceri, ut in monetis tantum nostris cudendae pecuniae studium frequentetur.' CTh 9.21.6 on casters purging out silver: 'Comperimus nonnullos flaturarios maiorinam pecuniam non minus criminose quam crebre separato argento ab aere purgare.'

36 LRV CTh 9.18.1 (=CTh 9.22): 'Interpretatio: Quicumque solidum circumciderit, adulterum subposuerit aut falsam monetam fecerit, capite punietur.'

In addition to outlining new categories of problematic coins, CTh 9.21's provisions flattened social hierarchies by simplifying punishments for illegal minting operations. The *Breviary* removed most of the individual laws and its interpretation now clarified that 'if anyone should give up a counterfeiter of money, that person shall receive a reward, and the one who has been given over, if that person is convicted, that person should be burned by fire'.[37] Late Roman class and status were erased as categories and any special treatment (e.g., for widows) was removed. Everyone received the same capital punishment for illegal minting—an equalization of legal categories that can be found in other post-Roman legal codes.[38] Added together these provisions suggest a simplification and flattening of monetary categories and the accompanying punishments for illegal activities, which offered the state greater room for manoeuvre by removing legal loopholes.

The *Breviary* also removed the only discussion of debased Gallic coins in the post-*Theodosian Code* period, which suggests a greater recognition of its sphere of influence. In addition to Sigismund's law about Gothic coins that had been 'debased at the time of king Alaric' (*c.* 516 CE), a section of a novel of Majorian (7.14) issued in 458 CE had noted that Gallic *solidi* (*solidi Gallici*) had been debased and, therefore, could not be used to pay taxes. What coins this law referred to remains a matter of speculation, but metrology conducted on some coins minted in Gaul in the mid-fifth century seems to have demonstrated that at least a few gold coins deviated from a pure standard.[39] Yet these particular types of fifth-century debased Gallic coins were apparently no longer a concern for the Visigothic state, since the *Breviary*'s *interpretatio* removed this section while keeping other parts of the novel. It simply stated that this section of the novel's provisions were 'not in use' and did not require any interpretation.[40]

The laws the *Breviary* retained further demonstrate responsiveness to broader fiscal policy. The *Breviary*, for example, removed all mentions of

37 LRV CTh 9.17.1 (=CTh 9.21.1): 'Interpretatio: Praemium accipiat, quicumque adulterum monetarium prodiderit et is qui proditus est, si de monetae adulteratione convictus fuerit, ignibus concremetur.'

38 On citizenship, Mathisen 2006; on Romanness and its changing aspects, Pohl 2018.

39 Lib. Const. Const. Extr. 21.7. The relevant part is: 'Praeterea nullus solidum integri ponderis calumniosae inprobationis obtentu recuset exactor, excepto eo Gallico, cuius aurum minore aestimatione taxatur; omnis concussionum removeatur occasio.' For the standard interpretation, Kurt 2020.

40 CTh Nov. Maj. 7.8: 'Interpretatio: Reliqua vero pars legis interpretata non est, quia haec, quae continet, usu carent, et certe ad intelligendum non habentur obscura.' Alternatively, one could read that all Visigothic coins were debased and could be used in tax collection. This would still mean that monetary concerns were central to state efforts.

silver coins (*siliquae*) that had been included in the *Theodosian Code*, since silver coins were no longer used frequently in the West.[41] The *Breviary* also eliminated any discussions of gold:silver:bronze ratios along with previous attempts to fix their exchange rate. In contrast, Vandal coinage continued to control the exchange rate, with their bronze coin denominations reflecting this reality.[42] Likewise, the *Breviary* removed payment schedules for groups no longer applicable to regions under Visigothic control, such as the imperial bodyguards, particular clerical tax payments, and the cost of certain types of Italian fish.[43] These monetary reforms remained within a fifth-century Roman framework, without the changes that occurred in the central and eastern Mediterranean around the year 500, while also removing references to economic situations that might have applied to a Mediterranean-wide empire, but which no longer existed in one region of Europe.

Non-monetary financial matters regarding taxes were also transformed in the *Breviary* as part of this package of governance reforms. As John Matthews has argued, the *Breviary* jettisoned large portions of Roman tax law, since it did not use most of the *Theodosian Code*'s Book 13, which contained the heart of tax law.[44] Yet, the *Breviary* retained many of the recent tax laws (the novels) that were updated and more applicable to the administrative apparatus of the early sixth century. A novel of Marcian, for example, remitted tax payments for a ten-year period (437–447 CE), which was repeated in the *Breviary*. Its focus shifted to clarify that all taxes individuals had already paid remained in force, while back taxes from that ten-year period were no longer to be collected. Similarly, costs were shifted in order to be more applicable for a southern Gallic setting. Particular sections of this novel, such as references to advocates in Rome and Constantinople, were removed since the *interpretatio* stated that 'these provinces do not use them', although the language continued to mark the Visigothic state as part of the *res publica*.[45] Likewise, Valentinian's Novel 33

41 See CTh 8.4.9, 10.1.4, and 11.1.32 among others. On later Visigothic silver coins, De Crusafont, Benages, and Noguera 2016.

42 See CTh 8.4.27, 13.2.1, and Nov. Val. 16. These ratios appear correct based on the financial records in the Albertini Tablets found in North Africa (Courtois, Leschim, Perrat, and Saumagne 1952); and for a discussion, Conant 2004; on Vandal coinage, Berndt and Steinacher 2008; on the Vandal economy, Tedesco 2018.

43 For these laws respectively: CTh 6.24.3, 13.1.11, and 14.20.1.

44 Matthews 2001, 20. Matthews is referring specifically to CTh 13.1.13, 13.10.1, and 13.10.5. On tax issues, Tedesco (forthcoming).

45 CTh Nov. Mar. 2 with the *interpretatio* reading: 'Lex ista hoc continet, ut per provincias relaxatae beneficio principis tributorum reliquiae non quaerantur, tamen quod exactum est, si apud exactores residisse constiterit, id praecipit, ut publicis debeat utilitatibus non perire, sed

concerning people who sold their children or themselves into slavery was amended from a discussion of being sold to barbarians (*barbari*) and now read 'to foreign peoples' (*ad extraneas gentes*). Only the Burgundians seemed to have used the term 'barbarian' to refer to their soldiers, and the change in the *Breviary* removed any potential link between Visigoths and barbarians. The Visigoths, in this law at least, were Romans, while other groups were classified as foreign peoples.[46] Finally, land taxes were similarly updated to ensure that private citizens might retain marginal land or former public landholdings, but the focus was, as with monetary questions, broadened. In the case of public land that had passed into private hands, the new legal interpretation shifted the emphasis from city lands to the more general state fiscal lands. Municipal property holdings were no longer the focus.[47]

Many legal changes in the novels were based on a thirty-year statute of limitations for civil and criminal claims in order to create a single legal structure for the state. This included transactions, wills, and murders among a long list of procedures. For laws that did not adhere to this timeline, the *interpretatio* to Valentinian's Novel 35 extended the same timeframe to them, although it never delineated every crime.[48] The thirty-year statute of limitations was a late Roman legal standard, but its expansion to all laws mirrored more recent *novellae* and was also followed in a Burgundian law issued around the same time that likewise set a statute of limitations for the new state. Moreover, the thirty-year statute of limitations neatly lined up

quod exactum est, a retentatoribus thesauris inferatur et a provincialibus vel a possessoribus quod solutum non fuerit non quaeratur.'

46 CTh Nov. Val. 33's key clause reads: 'Si quis sane barbaris venditionem prohibitam fecerit vel emptum ingenuum ad transmarina transtulerit.' And this is changed in the *interpretatio* to: 'Nam si huiusmodi personas aliqui aut ad extraneas gentes aut transmarina loca transferre aut venundare praesumpserit.' Noted in Matthews 2001; on the term *barbarus*: Wood 2011. On questions of identity, Conant 2015, Pohl and Heydemann 2013, and Pohl, Ganter, Grifoni, and Pollheimer-Mohaupt 2018.

47 CTh Nov. Mar. 3 language shift is: 'iuris quam etiam agonotheticas possessiones, ex consulatu Ausonii et Olybrii dempto civili canone acceperunt, inpositum praediis canonem iuxta fidem publicorum monumentorum civitati, ad quam praedia pertinuerunt.' In the *interpretatio* this becomes: 'Si quid de fiscalibus agris vel aedificiis donatione principis vel venditione vel qualibet ratione ad privatos fortasse pervenerit, id lex ista constituit ut soluto canone a possessoribus in perpetuum teneatur et, inpletis fiscalibus debitis, illi qui possident, heredibus suis relinquendi aut quibus voluerint donandi habeant potestatem.'

48 CTh Nov. Val. 35 with the key interpretation: 'Quae vero actiones perpetuae fuerunt et ad tricennium revocatae sunt placuit adnecti, id est, hereditatis petitio, si tamen ab auctore, cui competebat, fuerit inchoata finalis actio, homicidii, furti, tutelae gestae, de fugitivis, de curialibus vel de collegiatis revocandis, empti venditi, locati et conducti, negotiorum gestorum, mandati, pro socio.'

with the expansion of the Visigothic state in the early 470s, which marked the first formal break with the now Italian-based state under Odoacer and Theodoric.[49] An analysis of these few key laws reveals that these tax provisions demonstrate a formation of a distinct monetary, fiscal, and tax policy at the turn of the sixth century.

Taken together, the second half of the fifth century and the first few decades of the sixth witnessed incremental modifications to monetary and tax laws, which used a mid-fifth-century framework reformed to reflect a new reality. The two titles (9.21 and 9.22) that directly addressed the question of minting recognized this situation, since they adopted a broader set of categories that could be expanded or contracted as needed in a new setting. While these changes were based upon mid-fifth-century realities, Alaric's monetary reforms were local experimentations designed to delineate his state's reach. Yet legal reforms did not occur in isolation but were part of broader structural changes to ideas about money more broadly, which included changes to physical coins. Both were bound up in how people sought to make sense of their economic place in a newly emerging Visigothic state.

Conclusion

This chapter has argued that Visigothic monetary reforms should be contextualized in relation to mid-fifth-century ideas about state governance that began to shift through experimental, incremental changes. It has also suggested that numismatic changes should be brought into broader conversation with these monetary reforms to explain the beginnings of the first 'medieval' states. Rather than examining coins as following a simple post-Roman linear path in which the breakdown of Roman political power naturally equated with the end of economic sophistication and the failure to adopt more advanced eastern Roman ideas, this chapter has focused on the immediate contexts and effects of these monetary and coinage reforms.[50] A model of decline depends on modern ideas of economic growth and an economy that existed as a separate sphere, while assuming the basis for monetary decisions remained solely within the purview of state action. However, focusing on the role of political ('secular') states in changing ideas about the economy and the structures to implement it—both monetary

49 For a discussion of the thirty-year time frame, Esders 2019; and Levy 1951, 187–88. The break in the early 470s is seen as decisive across political histories. See Heather 2005, esp. 406–21.
50 For a similar approach see the articles in Esders, Hen, Sarti, and Fox 2019.

laws and physical coinage—overlooks the expanding role of churches in economic life at the turn of the sixth century. As churches became more central to the daily life of inhabitants of western Europe, governance changes in what constituted economic life should account for churches' expanded role moving forward.[51]

This chapter has outlined a methodology for examining legal monetary reforms alongside the coinage to argue for a broader governance programme that aimed, above all, to shift how the Visigothic state conceptualized its existence against neighbouring states and the eastern Roman empire. Alaric II's governance reforms were part of how new Romes emerged in the post-Roman West that sought to localize Roman ways of living in particular regions. In the case of Visigothic monetary reforms, these small shifts in how laws should be read and applied would not have seemed to be a decisive break with existing ways in which people thought about and used money. Yet these new interpretations of the *Theodosian Code* were not copied everywhere across the Mediterranean world but would become peculiar ways to govern in what would become one corner of the post-Roman world. A divergence with the eastern Roman system had begun, even if it was hardly groundbreaking or did not lead to an immediate revolution.[52] Modifications to different states' modes of government should be contextualized and compared to establish the full contents of the toolbox of governance possibilities, rather than measured against an early sixth-century ideal type. Alaric and Sigismund both, for example, used similar legal monetary powers to structure the economic life of their region, but focused upon different acceptable coinages that could be used in their realm. The *Breviary* provided wide latitude for what was an acceptable currency, while the Burgundian law code narrowed down the potential currencies. Moreover, some coinage changes, such as those under Gundobad who issued new coins, seem to have caused little consternation to their neighbours, while others, such as those under Alaric II, perhaps led to a significant conflict with Clovis and ultimately to Alaric's death. These first post-Roman changes in economic life focused on how to adapt existing laws and coinages to a smaller region of the Mediterranean world, which would be used to govern newly created Romes until the emergence of new national coins in the second half of the sixth century.

51 For the transformation of ideas of wealth, Brown 2012 and Wood 2021. For an example of this work in Italy, Eisenberg and Tedesco 2021.

52 For a comparative example of money as social relation where a revolution did happen, see Edwards (forthcoming).

Bibliography

Arnold, Jonathan J., 'The Battle of Vouillé and the Restoration of the Roman Empire', in *The Battle of Vouillé, 507 CE: Where France Began*, ed. Ralph W. Mathisen and Danuta Shanzer (Boston, MA: De Gruyter, 2012), pp. 111–36

Arnold, Jonathan J., *Theoderic and the Roman Imperial Restoration* (New York, NY: Cambridge University Press, 2014)

Barral i Altet, Xavier, *La circulation des monnaies suèves et visigotiques: contribution à l'histoire économique du royaume visigot* (Munich: Artemis, 1976)

Berndt, Guido M., and Roland Steinacher, 'Minting in Vandal North Africa: Coins of the Vandal Period in the Coin Cabinet of Vienna's Kunsthistorisches Museum', in *Early Medieval Europe*, 16.3 (2008), 252–98

Brown, Peter, *Through the Eye of a Needle: Wealth, the Fall of Rome, and the Making of Christianity in the West, 350–550 AD* (Princeton, NJ: Princeton University Press, 2012)

Carson, R. A. G., J. P. C. Kent, and A. M. Burnett (eds), *The Roman Imperial Coinage*, vol. 10, *The Divided Empire and the Fall of the Western Parts, AD 395–491* (London: Spink and Son, 1994)

Collins, Roger, *Die Fredegar-Chroniken* (Hannover: Hahnsche Buchhandlung, 2007)

Conant, Jonathan, 'Private Documentation and Literacy in Vandal North Africa: The Case of the Albertini Tablets', in *Vandals, Romans and Berbers: New Perspectives on Late Antique North Africa*, ed. by Andrew Merrills (London: Routledge, 2004), pp. 199–224

Conant, Jonathan, *Staying Roman: Conquest and Identity in Africa and the Mediterranean, 439–700* (Cambridge: Cambridge University Press, 2012)

Conant, Jonathan, 'Romanness in the Age of Attila', in *The Cambridge Companion to the Age of Attila*, ed. by Michael Maas (Cambridge: Cambridge University Press, 2015), pp. 156–72

Courtois, Christian, Louis Leschim, Charles Perrat, and Charles Saumagne (eds), *Tablettes Albertini: actes privés de l'époque vandale, fin du V. siècle* (Paris: Arts et métiers graphiques, 1952)

Crusafont, Miquel de, Jaume Benages, and Jaume Noguera, 'Silver Visigothic Coinage', in *The Numismatic Chronicle*, 176 (2016), 241–60

Delaplace, Christine, *La fin de l'Empire romain d'Occident: Rome et les Wisigoths: de 382 à 531* (Rennes: Presses Universitaires de Rennes, 2015)

Depeyrot, Georges, 'Les Monnaies des Lois Barbares', in *Acta Numismática*, 21 (1991), 315–28

Di Cintio, Lucia, *L'interpretatio visigothorum' al 'Codex Theodosianus' il libro IX* (Milan: LED, 2013)

Edwards, Andrew, *The Monied Republic: Capitalism and the American Revolution* (Princeton, NJ: Princeton University Press, forthcoming)

Eisenberg, Merle, 'A New Name for a New State: The Construction of the Burgundian *Regio*', in *The Fifth Century: Age of Transformation*, ed. by Jan Willem Drijvers and Noel Emmanuel Lenski (Bari: Edipuglia, 2019), pp. 157–67

Eisenberg, Merle, and Paolo Tedesco, 'Seeing the Churches Like the State: Taxes and Wealth Redistribution in Late Antique Italy', in *Early Medieval Europe*, 29.4 (2021), 505–34

Esders, Stefan, 'Procopius of Caesarea, the *lex tricennalis*, and the "Time of the Vandals": Historiography, Law, and Political Debate in Mid-Sixth-Century Constantinople', in *Early Medieval Europe*, 27.2 (2019), 197–206

Esders, Stefan, Yitzhak Hen, Laury Sarti, and Yaniv Fox (eds), *East and West in the Early Middle Ages: The Merovingian Kingdoms in Mediterranean Perspective* (New York, NY: Cambridge University Press, 2019)

Evans Grubbs, Judith, *Law and Family in Late Antiquity: The Emperor Constantine's Marriage Legislation* (Oxford: Oxford University Press, 1995)

'FLAME – Framing the Late Antique and Early Medieval Economy', http://coinage.princeton.edu/ [date of access: 3 June 2022]

Garipzanov, Ildar H., 'Coins as Symbols of Early Medieval "Staatlichkeit"', in *Der frühmittelalterliche Staat: europäische Perspektiven*, ed. by Walter Pohl and Veronika Wieser (Vienna: Verlag der österreichischen Akademie der Wissenschaften, 2009), pp. 411–22

Garipzanov, Ildar H., 'Monograms as Graphic Signs of Authority on Early Medieval Coins (from the Mid-Fifth to Seventh Centuries)', in *Graphic Signs of Identity, Faith, and Power in Late Antiquity and the Early Middle Ages*, ed. by Ildar H. Garipzanov, Caroline Goodson, and Henry Maguire (Turnhout: Brepols, 2017), pp. 334–43

Garipzanov, Ildar H., *Graphic Signs of Authority in Late Antiquity and the Early Middle Ages, 300–900* (Oxford: Oxford University Press, 2018)

Gómez Aragonés, Daniel, *Vouillé 507: el nacimiento del Regnum Gothorum de España* (Zaragoza: HRM Ediciones, 2016)

Grierson, Philip, 'Visigothic Metrology', in *The Numismatic Chronicle and Journal of the Royal Numismatic Society*, 13.43 (1953), 74–87

Grierson, Philip, and Mark Blackburn, *Medieval European Coinage: With a Catalogue of the Coins in the Fitzwilliam Museum, Cambridge*, vol. 1, *The Early Middle Ages (5th–10th Centuries)* (Cambridge: Cambridge University Press, 1986)

Halsall, Guy, *Barbarian Migrations and the Roman West, 376–568* (Cambridge: Cambridge University Press, 2007)

Heather, Peter J., *The Goths* (Cambridge, MA: Blackwell, 1996)

Heather, Peter J., *The Fall of the Roman Empire* (London: Macmillan, 2005)

Hendy, Michael F., 'From Public to Private: The Western Barbarian Coinages as a Mirror of the Disintegration of Late Roman State Structures', in *Viator*, 19 (1988), 29–78

Humfress, Caroline, *Orthodoxy and the Courts in Late Antiquity* (New York, NY: Oxford University Press, 2007)

Kent, John, *The Roman Imperial Coinage*, vol. 8, *The Family of Constantine I, A.D. 337–364* (London: Spink, 1981)

Kurt, Andrew, *Minting, State and Economy in the Visigothic Kingdom* (Amsterdam: Amsterdam University Press, 2020)

Lambertini, Renzo, *La codificazione di Alarico II*, 2nd ed. (Torino: Giappichelli, 1991)

Levy, Ernst, *West Roman Vulgar Law: The Law of Property* (Philadelphia, PA: American Philosophical Society, 1951)

Liebs, Detlef, *Römische Jurisprudenz in Gallien (2. bis 8. Jahrhundert)* (Berlin: Duncker & Humblot, 2002)

Liebs, Detlef, 'Zur Überlieferung und Entstehung des Breviarium Alaricianum', in *Atti Dell'Accademia Romanistica Costantiniana: XIV Convegno Internazionale in Memoria Di Guglielmo Nocera* (Perugia: Università degli studi di Perugia, Facoltà di giurisprudenza, 2003), pp. 653–71

Liebs, Detlef, 'Die Kodifizierung des römischen Strafrechts im Breviar Alarichs II', in *Mélanges de l'École française de Rome – Antiquité*, 125.2 (2013), 357–70

Mathisen, Ralph W., '*Peregrini, Barbari*, and *Cives Romani*: Concepts of Citizenship and the Legal Identity of Barbarians in the Later Roman Empire', in *The American Historical Review*, 111.4 (2006), 1011–40

Mathisen, Ralph W., 'D'Aire-sur-l'Adour à Agde: les relations entre la loi séculière et la loi canonique à la fin du royaume de Toulouse', in *Le Bréviaire d'Alaric: aux origines du code civil*, ed. by Michel Rouche and Bruno Dumézil (Paris: PUPS, 2008), pp. 41–52

Matthews, John, 'Interpreting the *Interpretationes* of the *Breviarium*', in *Law, Society, and Authority in Late Antiquity*, ed. by Ralph W. Mathisen (New York, NY: Oxford University Press, 2001), pp. 11–32

McEvoy, Meaghan, *Child Emperor Rule in the Late Roman West, AD 367–455* (Oxford: Oxford University Press, 2013)

McEvoy, Meaghan, 'Becoming Roman?: The Not-So-Curious Case of Aspar and the Ardaburii', in *Journal of Late Antiquity*, 9.2 (2017), 483–511

Metcalf, D. M., J. M. P. Cabral, and L. C. Alves, 'Sixth-Century Visigothic Metrology, Some Evidence from Portugal', in *American Journal of Numismatics (1989–)*, 3.4 (1992), 65–90

Miles, George, *The Coinage of the Visigoths of Spain: Leovigild to Achila II* (New York, NY: American Numismatic Society, 1952)

Mitchell, Timothy, 'Economentality: How the Future Entered Government', in *Critical Inquiry*, 40.4 (2014), 479–507

Mordechai, Lee, and Alan M. Stahl, 'Late Antique and Early Medieval Imitations and the FLAME Database', in *Nordisk Numismatisk Årsskrift*, new series, 2 (*Nordic Numismatic Journal*) (2021), 103–32

Naismith, Rory, *Money and Power in Anglo-Saxon England: The Southern English Kingdoms, 757–865* (Cambridge: Cambridge University Press, 2012)

Nemo-Pekelman, Capucine, 'How Did the Authors of the *Breviarium Alaricanum* Work? The Example of the Laws on Jews', in *Historical Research*, 86.233 (2013), 408–15

Pliego Vázquez, Ruth, *La moneda visigoda* (Seville: Secretariado de Publicaciones, Universidad de Sevilla, 2009)

Pohl, Walter, 'Introduction: Early Medieval Romanness—A Multiple Identity', in *Transformations of Romanness: Early Medieval Regions and Identities*, ed. by Walter Pohl, Clemens Gantner, Cinzia Grifoni, and Marianne Pollheimer-Mohaupt (Berlin: De Gruyter, 2018), pp. 1–37

Pohl, Walter, Clemens Ganter, Cinzia Grifoni, and Marianne Pollheimer-Mohaupt (eds), *Transformations of Romanness: Early Medieval Regions and Identities* (Boston, MA: De Gruyter, 2018)

Pohl, Walter, and Gerda Heydemann (eds), *Strategies of Identification: Ethnicity and Religion in Early Medieval Europe* (Turnhout: Brepols, 2013)

Reinhart, Wilhelm, 'Die Münzen des tolosanischen Reiches der Westgoten', in *Deutsches Jahrbuch für Numismatik*, 1 (1938), 107–35

Reinhart, Wilhelm, *Die Münzen des Westgotischen Reiches von Toledo* (Munich: Kress & Hornung, 1942)

Reinhart, Wilhelm, 'Nuevas aportaciones a la numismática visigoda', in *Archivo Español de Arqueología; Madrid*, 18.60 (1945), 212–43

Roux, Marie, 'Administrative Transitions in Gaul During the Second Half of the Fifth Century: The Example of the Visigothic Kingdom through the Breviary of Alaric', in *The Fifth Century: Age of Transformation*, ed. by Jan Willem Drijvers and Noel Emmanuel Lenski (Bari: Edipuglia, 2019), pp. 221–31

Saint-Sorny, Bruno, 'La fin du roi Alaric II: possibilite d'une nouvelle datation du Breviaire', in *Studi di Storia del Diritto*, vol. 3 (Milan: A. Giuffrè, 2001), pp. 27–90

Shanzer, Danuta, 'Vouillé 507: Historiographical, Hagiographical, and Diplomatic Reconsiderations and Fortuna', in *The Battle of Vouillé, 507 CE: Where France Began*, ed. by Ralph W. Mathisen and Danuta Shanzer (Boston, MA: De Gruyter, 2012), pp. 63–78

Shanzer, Danuta, and Ian Wood, *Letters and Selected Prose of Avitus of Vienne* (Liverpool: Liverpool University Press, 2002)

Stahl, Alan, 'The Transformation of the West', in *The Oxford Handbook of Greek and Roman Coinage*, ed. by William E. Metcalf (New York, NY: Oxford University Press, 2012), pp. 633–54

Steinbach, Sebastian, *Imitation, Innovation und Imperialisierung: Geldwesen und Münzprägung als wirtschaftshistorische Quellen zur ethnischen Identiät und*

Herrschaftsorganisation des spanischen Westgotenreiches (*c.* *572–714*) (Berlin: Lit, 2017)

Tedesco, Paolo, '"The Missing Factor": Economy and Labor in Late Roman North Africa (400–600 CE)', in *Journal of Late Antiquity*, 11.2 (2018), 396–431

Tedesco, Paolo, *State, Taxation, and Power in the Late Roman West* (Oxford: Oxford University Press, forthcoming)

Tomasini, Wallace J., *The Barbaric Tremissis in Spain and Southern France: Anastasius to Leovigild* (New York, NY: American Numismatic Society, 1964)

Vitiello, Massimiliano, *Amalasuintha: The Transformation of Queenship in the Post-Roman World* (Philadelphia, PA: University of Pennsylvania Press, 2017)

Wolfram, Herwig, *History of the Goths*, 2nd ed., trans. by Thomas Dunlap (Berkeley, CA: University of California Press, 1988)

Wood, Ian, *The Merovingian Kingdoms, 450–751* (New York, NY: Longman, 1994)

Wood, Ian, 'Le Bréviaire chez les Burgondes', in *Le Bréviaire d'Alaric: aux origines du code civil*, ed. by Michel Rouche and Bruno Dumézil (Paris: PUPS, 2008), pp. 151–60

Wood, Ian, 'The Term "Barbarous" in Fifth-, Sixth-, and Seventh-Century Gaul', in *Zeitschrift für Literaturwissenschaft und Linguistik*, 41.4 (2011), 39–50

Wood, Ian, 'Entrusting Western Europe to the Church, 400–750', in *Transactions of the Royal Historical Society*, 23 (2013), 37–73

Wood, Ian, 'The Political Structure of the Burgundian Kingdom', in *Chlodwigs Welt: Organisation von Herrschaft um 500*, ed. by Mischa Meier and Steffen Patzold (Stuttgart: Steiner, 2014), pp. 383–96

Wood, Ian, 'The Legislation of *Magistri Militum*: The Laws of Gundobad and Sigismund', *Clio@Themis, Revue Électronique d'histoire Du Droit*, 10 (2016), 1–16

Wood, Ian, 'Creating a Temple Society in the Early Medieval West', in *Early Medieval Europe*, 29.4 (2021), 462–86

About the Author

Merle Eisenberg is an assistant professor of history at Oklahoma State University and a faculty member of the Oklahoma Pandemic Center. He is a late antique and early medieval historian and has published in *The American Historical Review*, *Past & Present*, the *Journal of Late Antiquity*, and *Early Medieval Europe*, among others.

4 A Comparison of Roman and Visigothic Approaches to Exile

Margarita Vallejo Girvés[1]

Abstract

In the Classical and late Roman world, exile was mentioned often in legislation, indicating that it was of particular interest to rulers. Abundant references in literary sources enable us to analyse how legislation was applied in practice, often in response to individual circumstances. There are likewise numerous references to exiles and fugitives in Visigothic legislation, Hispano-Visigothic church canons, and contemporary literary texts. We know concrete details of several particular episodes from narrative sources. However, collectively, these sources suggest that the legal treatment of exiles in the Visigothic kingdom cannot be considered a simple transposition of Roman practices. This chapter aims to determine the relationship between individual cases and Visigothic legislation in order to outline deviations from Roman practice and to understand their potential causes.

Keywords: exile; Late Roman legislation; Visigothic legislation; comparison; case studies

Introduction

For those who were sentenced to exile in the late Roman empire, the punishment entailed removal from their society, their families, and their polities. The penalty of exile was employed to demonstrate to the population as a whole that the behaviour for which the convicted were exiled was absolutely reprehensible. Exile entailed physical exclusion, social shame, and, therefore, a stigma that separated the person from the rest of society. It was not a physical

1 This paper is part of Research Project PGC2018-093729-B-100, Universidad de Alcalá.

Fernández, D., Lester, M. & Wood, J. (eds.), *Rome and Byzantium in the Visigothic Kingdom: Beyond* Imitatio Imperii. Taylor & Francis Group 2023
DOI: 10.5117/9789463726412_CH04

brand but a social one. When the exiled person also had their property and assets partially or totally confiscated or forcibly transferred, they were demoted to a lower level in society, in both their places of origin and exile.

Exile as a judicial punishment, either as *relegatio* or banishment or as deportation to islands as specific destinations, was a very common practice in the late Roman empire.[2] The barbarian kingdoms of the West also employed exile as a punishment for individuals who were found guilty of various crimes and offences. As in the case of the Roman empire, literary and legal sources constitute our main supply of information on this subject, which make possible numerous studies on exile in these societies.[3]

Several important studies have focused on the extent of Roman influence on Visigothic legislation. However, fewer publications have analysed whether Visigothic kings from the reign of Euric (d. 484) until the end of the kingdom in 711 adopted or modified judicial exile as it existed in the late Roman and early Byzantine empires.[4] As we will see in the following sections, the application of exile in the Visigothic laws was less prevalent than in the Code of Justinian (*Codex Iustinianus*, henceforth CJ) and even the Theodosian Code (*Codex Theodosianus*, henceforth CTh). References to *deportatio* or *relegatio ad insulam* disappeared almost completely from the compilation of rules and dispositions known as *Liber Iudiciorum* (henceforth LI). Indeed, the LI is practically devoid of any reference to *deportatio* or *relegatio*. In this chapter, through the examination of a number of particular case studies of judicial exile, I will analyse the extent to which Visigothic engagement with imperial legislation was part of broader processes of ideological and political *imitatio imperii* or not.

Exile in the Late Roman and Early Byzantine World

It is well known that the different variants of *exilium* that I have just mentioned were regularly deployed as punishment for treason and political

2 On the particularities of and differences between these modalities, see Delmaire 2008, 115–32; Washburn 2013, 18–23, 119–21; Vallejo Girvés 1991, 153–58.

3 In addition to the above, the studies by Hillner (2013, 385–434, and 2016) are essential, as she examines not only a multitude of examples, but also provides an in-depth analysis of the previous literature, whose amplitude prevents us from including it here. In addition, the studies found in Hillner, Ulrich, and Engberg (2016), and in Rohmann, Ulrich, and Vallejo Girvés (2018), illustrate the variety of studies related to exile during the different eras and territories of Late Antiquity.

4 Prego de Lis (2006) and Martin (2011, 45–56) pursue this same line of inquiry, although emphasizing specific aspects.

corruption during the last centuries of the Roman Republic and throughout the early empire. They were applied even more frequently from the reign of Emperor Constantine (d. 337) at least until Justinian (d. 565). Evidence of the prevalence of exile abounds in the literary sources, and sources such as the CTh, the *Novellae Theodosii*, the laws of various emperors up until Justinian, and in this emperor's CJ and *Novellae* (henceforth, Nov.) indicate that emperors utilized exile as a sentence for many different crimes.[5] Thus, we find exile as a punishment for economic crimes and corruption, such as negligence in the protection of a minor's fortune, the misuse of irrigation water, the use of public money for private purposes, and fraud in the rendering of wheat tributes.[6] It was also imposed as a penalty against counterfeiting, especially the use of false coins,[7] and served as a punishment for religious offences, particularly in legislation against pagans, heretics, and misconduct of the clergy.[8] Likewise, it was used to punish certain forms of miscarriage of justice and judicial corruption, including unfair sentences, negligence on the part of a judge's staff, delays in the holding of trials,[9] administrative irregularities,[10] hiding or facilitating desertions by soldiers, *coloni*, or slaves,[11] for practices of magic,[12] and, above all, for behaviours contrary to morality, where the punishment was especially used for the correction of familial relationships.[13]

Many of the sentences of exile explicitly specified relegation or banishment *to an island*, especially in the CTh.[14] Specific cases of exile to an island were abundant and are well documented up until and even after Justinian.

5 The confiscation of property was frequently associated with the imposition of exile in its different modalities (cf. *infra*). Likewise, in the CTh it is perfectly clear that exile was imposed on individuals of higher social status, while those of lower status received capital punishment or were condemned to labour in mines for the same crimes. We must also take into account the *Pauli Sententiae* (cf. *infra*).

6 CTh 4.22.2, 8.5.4 and 35, 9.10.3, 9.19.1, 9.23.1, 9.26.1 and 2, 9.32.1, 10.11.1, 10.24.2, 11.14.3, 14.15.6; Nov. Just. 7.1, 116.1, 128.12, 130.6 and 7.

7 CTh 9.19.2, 9.21.1 and 2 (4).

8 CTh 16, fundamentally. Nov. Just. 6.9, 7.1, 120.8, 123.8, 123.31, 123.44.

9 CTh 1.5.3, 2.6 and 9, 2.2.9, 6.30.16 and 17, 9.36.2, 9.39.3, 11.34.1; Nov. Just. 8.8.1, 112.2, 123.27, 124.2, 128.21, 144, 145.

10 CTh 14.3.21; Nov. Just. 134.1, 134.3–5, 134.9 and 11, 134.13.

11 CTh 7.12.1, 7.18.8.

12 CTh 9.16.1–3. It was also defined in CTh 5.7.3, 9.17.1, 11.14.1, 14.16.2, 15.2.3 for various crimes and offences that cannot be included in any of the above.

13 CTh 3.5.5, 3.10.1, 3.16.1 and 2, 9.8.1, 9.9.1, 9.24.1 and 3, 9.25.3, 9.39.2, 12.1.6; Nov. Just. 12, 139, 141, 142.

14 Specifying the modality of exile on islands, CTh 1.5.3 and 5, 3.16.1, 8.5.4, 9.10.3, 9.16.1, 9.21.2 (4), 10.11.1, 9.32.1 (Oasis), 11.34.1, 12.1.6.

Obviously, exile to an island sought, in most cases, the total isolation of the convict from the place or area where they had committed the crime for which they had been punished. However, there were a large number of different types of islands within the Roman and Byzantine empires with very different characteristics, which meant that the actual conditions of exile could vary considerably for the offender. We know that many convicts, both lay and clergy, were exiled to islands, some of which were regular sites for the banishment of people who had received sentences of exile.[15]

Exile in the Visigothic Kingdom of Toulouse

As Roman authority faded across much of western Europe in the fifth century, barbarian leaders such as the Visigoth Euric, who partially dominated areas of Gaul and Hispania, began to take on roles previously reserved for the emperors and their officials, including punishing misconduct and crimes by their subjects.[16] Literary sources document Euric's imposition of exile on individuals found guilty of betrayal or disloyalty—that is, for reasons similar to those that had spurred Roman emperors to sentence a person to exile. For example, Sidonius Apollinaris narrated his own travails in exile, as well as the exiles suffered by the Gallic bishops Crocus and Simplicius.[17] Euric also exiled the bishops Faustus of Riez, Verus of Tours, and Marcellus of Die.[18]

There is no reference, however, to exile as a punishment in either the *Codex Euricianus* (henceforth CE) or in the laws that have been attributed to this king amongst those comprising the LI. Although only a small part of the CE is preserved, the absence of references to exile may be significant. In this regard, it is worthwhile to keep in mind that Carlos Petit, the great expert in the Visigothic criminal system, actually gave up on reconstructing the punitive system of Eurician law.[19]

Alvaro D'Ors attributed the disappearance of the sentence of exile, in any of its forms, to ongoing uncertainty of the boundaries of the territories Euric held. D'Ors suggested that the fluctuating territorial extent of Euric's kingdom must have led the monarch's counsellors, who were in charge of

15 For the fourth century, see Vallejo Girvés 1991, 159–67.

16 Although it is a debated issue, we will not address the territoriality of Visigothic law during this period; for this, see the excellent synthesis by Alvarado 2011, par. 10.

17 Sid. Apol. Ep. 8.3, 9, 13, and 9.3; for Crocus and Simplicius, 7.6, 9. See also Stüber 2019, 41–58.

18 Faustus, *Epistulae* 1.5.16 (ed. Lütjohann 1887); Greg. Tur. Decem libri 10.31 (Verus); *Vita Marcelli* 4 (ed. Dolbeau 1983–1984).

19 Petit 1998, 217.

composing the *Code*, to dispense with exile as a punishment. In his view, during Euric's reign exile and its variants were superseded by other types of sentences, fundamentally pecuniary, which, as we shall see, would be very common in the Visigothic kingdom of Toledo.[20]

It is quite possible that the scarcity of references to exile in the LI skewed D'Ors's analysis, since, as we have seen in cases such as that of Sidonius Apollinaris, exile as a punishment is attested in the Visigothic kingdom of Euric in cases of betrayal and disloyalty. Regarding this issue, Prego de Lis has noted that the extant sections of the CE mainly address issues of private law, which could explain the absence of references to exile therein.[21] Prego de Lis's suggestion may be further corroborated through comparison of Euric's approach to exile with the evidence for exile in the *Breviary of Alaric* (or *Lex Romana Visigothorum*, henceforth LRV), which was compiled by jurists in the Visigothic kingdom of Toulouse during the reign of Alaric II (d. 507). We should also note that Alaric II used exile as a punishment for crimes similar to those attested during Euric's reign, such as the exile of the bishops Volusianus of Tours and Caesarius of Arles.[22]

The Interpretations (*interpretationes*) to the Theodosian Code and to the *Pauli Sententiae* (the Sentences of Paul, henceforth PS) in the LRV listed exile as a punishment for the same crimes as the CTh and the PS.[23] Yet the *interpretationes* to the PS and the provisions of the CTh featured a curious difference related to *deportatio* and *relegatio ad insulam*. The authors of the *interpretationes* to the PS barely modified what the original text defined as *relegatio* or *deportatio ad insulam* and kept this punishment.[24] However, in the *interpretationes* to the CTh, the jurists replaced deportation *ad insulam* with a generic allusion to exile.[25]

Several studies on the authorship of the *interpretationes* included in the LRV have concluded that these commentaries were not entirely the work of jurists from the court or period of Alaric II, but rather of various provincial jurists in the West, especially Gallic, from the last quarter of the

20 D'Ors 2014, 7, 60, 71, 99, 154–55.

21 Prego de Lis 2006, 517 and n. 3.

22 Greg. Tur. Decem libri 2.26 and 10.31; *Vita Caesarii Arelatensis* I, 21 (ed. Krusch 1888).

23 We find some exceptions, as CTh 3.5.5 defined exile to an island while the corresponding *interpretatio* (LRV CTh 3.5.4) did not mention punishment. In CTh 9.10.3, as in the *interpretatio* (= LRV CTh 9.7.2), this was not done either. See di Cintio 2013.

24 Although there are some peculiarities. For example, *interpretationes* to LRV PS 4.7.2 and 5.28.2 added deportation to an island.

25 Thus, CTh 1.5.3 (= LRV CTh 1.5.1), 3.16.1 (= LRV CTh 3.16.1). And CTh 3.5.5 (= LRV CTh 3.5.4) and 9.10.3 (= LRV CTh 9.7.2) omitted any references to deportation or relegation to an island without replacing it with exile.

fifth century.[26] The presence of *relegatio* and *deportatio ad insulam* in the *interpretationes* to the PS and their absence from the *interpretationes* to the CTh suggests that the *ad insulam* punishment was already considered anomalous by some jurists in late fifth-century Gaul, including those who were responsible for interpreting the provisions derived from the CTh.

We also find the replacement of *relegatio* and *deportatio ad insulam* with *exilium* in the *Edictum Theoderici* (the Edict of Theodoric).[27] In his study of this work, Lafferty analysed the innovations that the *Edictum*'s compilers made on the basis of Roman legislation, noting that ancient forms of punishment such as infamy, *damnatio ad bestias*, *deportatio*, and *relegatio ad insulam* were eliminated. In the specific case of *relegatio ad insulam*, he compared the PS with the *Edictum Theoderici*. He observed that, in many cases in which *in insulam deportatur / relegatur* appeared in the PS, the compilers of the *Edictum* substituted *capite puniatur*, *poena*, *exilium dirigantur*, and *perpetui exilii relegatione*.[28] It is curious that the *interpretationes* to the PS in the LRV kept *deportatio* and *relegation ad insulam*, while the *Edictum Theoderici* replaced them with *exilium*, which further supports the contention that this specific punishment became uncommon in the lands of the former western Roman empire during the second half of the fifth century. Obviously, this does not mean that it was not applied on specific occasions, since both the Visigothic and Ostrogothic monarchs had sea and river islands in their territories to which they could banish convicts if they chose to do so. The Ostrogoth Theodoric considered the commutation of the death penalty in favour of *deportatio ad insulam* for those individuals who were able to secure sanctuary in a church, and Queen Amalasuintha was banished to the island on Lake Bolsena by order of Theodahad.[29] These seem to be isolated cases, however, and we have no information suggesting that the Visigoth Alaric II deported anyone to an island, although his kingdom had river and coastal islands to which exiles could have been banished.

The Visigothic monarchs of the kingdom of Toulouse, therefore, seem to have used exile as a punishment in a fashion similar to the late Roman emperors, with the notable exception of exile to islands.[30] As we will see, the imposition of exile was not carried out in the same way in the Visigothic

26 See Gaudemet 1965, Matthews 2011, 18–20, and, especially, di Cintio 2013, with all the previous bibliography and scholastic trends.

27 Shoemaker (2001, 59 *et seq.*, nn. 11–17 (p. 198)) covers their authorship and chronology.

28 Lafferty 2010, 77–78 with n. 24, and 249–50.

29 Cassiodorus, *Variae* 3.47 (ed. Mommsen 1894); see Vallejo Girvés 2018, 134, n. 66.

30 Di Cintio (2013) does not address this issue.

kingdom of Toledo, where all references to *relegatio* and *deportatio ad insulam* disappeared. *Exilium* as a punishment was far less prominent than in the codes compiled under Theodosius II and Justinian.

Exile in the Visigothic Kingdom of Toledo

Before comparing the application of exile by the Visigothic monarchs of Toledo with the directives in the CTh and the CJ, it is necessary to consider a text by Isidore of Seville in which he explained the differences between *relegatio* and *deportatio ad insulam*. In Book I of Isidore's *Differentiarum libri duo*, a didactic work dedicated to explaining the differences between various Latin terms whose meanings were, quite possibly, no longer evident by the early seventh century, we read that:

> [T]here is a big difference between he who is relegated to an island and he who is deported: first, the relegated person takes his property, unless it has been stripped from him by the terms of a sentence; the deportee, on the other hand, cannot take it, unless this is expressly granted. Thus, the relegated person benefits if no reference is made to his property in the sentence, while the deportee is harmed. They are also distinguished by the quality of the destination, as the relegated are afforded certain human considerations, while deportees are usually assigned islands that are desolate and virtually tantamount to a death sentence.[31]

This extract suggests that the Roman concepts of *deportatio* and *relegatio ad insulam* were not common in the Iberian, Visigothic world of the sixth and early seventh centuries. Moreover, it is very interesting that Isidore deemed it necessary to explain that *deportatio ad insulam* was comparable to *summum supplicium*, which meant that the latter concept was still comprehensible in late sixth- and early seventh-century Hispania.[32] Isidore did not include

31 Isidore of Seville, *Differentiae* I, *lemma* 434: 'Inter eum qui in insulam relegatur et eum qui deportatur magna est differentia: primo quod relegatum bona sequuntur nisi fuerint sententia adempta, deportatum non sequuntur, nisi palam ei fuerint concessa. Ita fit ut relegate mentionem bonorum in sentential non haberi prosit, deportato noceat. Item distant et in loci qualitate. Quod cum relegate quidem humanius trasigitur, deportatis uero hae solent insulae adsignari quae sunt asperrimae quaeque sunt paulo minus summon supplicio comparandae' (ed. Codoñer 1992). Agnati (2012, 141–42), refuted the attribution of this text to the jurist Modestinus; Frighetto 2015, 118–19.

32 Isidore of Seville, *Differentiae* I, *lemma* 434: 'quaeque sunt paulo minus summon supplicio comparandae' (ed. Codoñer 1992, 278). In a similar vein, Valastro Canale 2004, 13; Agnati 2012,

any reference to relegation or deportation to islands in the passage that he dedicated to exile in the *Etymologies*, in which he dealt with the other types of exile: 'exile (*exilium*) is so called as if it were "outside the country" (*extra solum*), for someone who is outside the country is called an exile (*exul*). A *relegatus* is one whose possessions accompany him; a *deportatus* is not so accompanied.'[33] The definition offered minimal explanation of what exile constituted, presumably because its meaning was known in Visigothic Hispania. However, Isidore did explain the nature of *relegatus* and *deportatus*. In the provisions of the LI there are hardly any references to either of these two sentences, which, as we have seen, were commonly imposed by late Roman and Byzantine emperors, further explaining Isidore's need to clarify their meaning.[34]

As seventh-century authors likely knew, Justinian ordered a team of jurists to update and compile the provisions of Roman emperors since Hadrian, thereby forming the *Corpus Iuris Civilis*, which also included provisions by the emperor himself issued before 534.[35] Justinian's provisions after this date make up the volume known as the *Novellae Iustiniani*. The same emperor, inspired by an ideology of *renovatio imperii*, conquered part of the Iberian peninsula in the 550s. The Iberian territories dominated by Justinian and his successors until *c.* 625 were subject to Byzantine imperial law, as evidenced in the rulings issued by Pope Gregory the Great in response to the grievances of Bishops Ianuarius of Malaga and Stephanus, who complained of having been unfairly treated by Comentiolus, the Byzantine governor of Hispania.[36] This episode has led some scholars to suggest that 'Justinianic law' was not only known in the Visigothic kingdom of Toledo, but also had a considerable influence on Visigothic legislation.[37] However, the Byzantine occupation of

142–44. On the other hand, in the Merovingian kingdoms, exile to an island was applied in the last quarter of the sixth century. This can be clearly seen in Greg. Tur. Decem libri 5.18, related to the exile of Praetextatus of Rouen to an island. Nevertheless, this author did not use the expressions *relegatus* or *deportatus in insulam*.

33 Isid. Etym. 5.28–29. In addition, in 5.30: 'Proscription (*proscriptio*) is a condemnation of exile a distance', which indicates that Isidore was well aware of imperial legislation in which proscription entailed deportation. See di Cintio 2013, 212. Also 5.31: 'A mine (*metallum*) is where exiles are transported to dig out a vein of ore and hew out marble in slabs.' (trans. Barney et. al. 2006, 125).

34 It is only found in LI 9.2.9 (Erwig), 12.3.8 (Erwig), and 12.3.28 (Erwig).

35 Of special note is Ladner 1975, 191–200.

36 Greg. Mag. Reg. 13.49. Authors such as Presedo (2003, 120–22), Osaba (2003b, 58), and Alvarado (2011, par. 4) thought that Justinianic law should have been known in the Visigothic kingdom, arguing that it was applied in the case of Ianuarius and Stephanus. This argument, however, does not suffice, as we will try to make clear.

37 Osaba 2003b, 58; Dubreucq 2005, 34–35; Alvarado 2011, par. 4; Jiménez Garnica 1985, 745 and n. 39, though only referring to the prohibition of marriages between Goths and Romans.

parts of the southern Iberian peninsula is not proof of Byzantine influence on Visigothic law, since significant hostility between the Visigoths and Byzantines existed until, at least, the second half of the seventh century. In addition, Justinian was considered a heretic by the Church in Hispania due to his leadership in the 'Three Chapters' controversy and his lukewarm defence of the Council of Chalcedon, facts that were well known since *c.* 536. The clearest example of this hostility is the poor opinion of the emperor expressed by the influential Isidore of Seville.[38] We must not forget Isidore's poetic description of his library that revealed the contents of its 'legislative' shelves: 'Theodosius. Paulus. Gaius. Collected here is a most ample series of the laws of justice. These rule the Latin forum with their true speaking.'[39] Here Isidore referred to the provisions of the CTh, as well as to the works of jurisprudence by Gaius and Paulus, but not to the CJ, which, at the time Isidore probably composed these verses, had been in force for more than fifty years.[40]

Exile, perpetual or temporary, is defined in the LI in slightly less than twenty laws unrelated to religion and covering a wide range of offences, serious or slight. Thus, it is the punishment for treason we find in LI 2.1.8 (Erwig). In a similar category, LI 9.2.8 (Wamba), from an earlier date, also punished priests who failed to contribute to the defence of the territory with exile if they could not offset the damage with their property. In LI 9.2.9 (Erwig), we find exile provisions for those of high social position who had disobeyed the king's call to join the army, as this refusal was considered a defiance of a royal order.[41] Exile was also applied to the culprit in LI 6.5.12 and 13 (Chindaswinth and Recceswinth) for the death or mutilation of a slave by a master without the former having received a trial.[42] For those convicted of homosexual practices, Chindaswinth called for penance (in addition to castration), possibly in a monastery (LI 3.5.4), and Egica later cited a canon from the Sixteenth Council of Toledo condemning clerics sentenced for sodomy to perpetual exile (LI 3.5.7).

38 Isid. De viris 18. Cf. Fusco (2012, 87), for whom: '[l]a Spagna rimane in questo periodo sutanzialmente ostile alla recente influenza costantinopolitiana, diversamente da quanto era avvenuto invece nel V secolo, allorché si era assistito ad una recezione attiva (pensó qui al Codice di Eurico, intorno al 470) del romanesimo giuridico.'

39 Isidore of Seville, *Versus* XV: 'Theodosius. Paulus Gaius. Conditur hic iuris series amplissima legum / Veridico Latium quae regit ore forum' (ed. Sánchez Martín 2000, 225).

40 Also, Isid. Etym. 5.1.7, where he did not mention Justinian's either; see Agnati 2012, 141–42 and n. 52; Fusco 2012, 87. Cf. Presedo 2003, 128.

41 Lear (1951, 8–9) is of the same opinion.

42 In LI 6.5.13 (Egica), exile joined penance under the control of the territory's bishop, which could be understood as confinement in a monastery, although this argument cannot be forced.

Slaves guilty of consulting fortune tellers about the life or death of any man would be physically punished and subsequently—according to LI 6.2.1 (Chindaswinth) and 6.2.2 (Erwig)—be transferred to overseas regions to be sold there, a circumstance that, in our view, can be considered a type of exile. Exile or internment in a monastery abounded in family law, especially for punishing incest: LI 3.5.1 and 2 (Recceswinth), 3.5.5 (Recceswinth), 3.6.2 (Recceswinth), and 6.5.18 (*Antiqua*).[43] Exile also appeared as a common punishment for religious infractions, as we observe in LI 12.2.2 (Recceswinth), 12.3.2 (Erwig), LI 12.2.14 (Sisebut), 12.3.1–5, 8–9, 11, and 13 (Erwig), 12.3.19 and 21 (Erwig).[44]

If we exclude the 'religious' stipulations, as they bear some resemblance to Roman imperial legislation, the fifteen provisions on crimes and offences punished with exile in the Visigothic kingdom of Toledo fall into just six categories. However, there are at least sixty cases in which the compilers of the CTh prescribed different types of exile and deportation, as indicated above. In the CJ there was a similar use of exile, in terms of the number and types of cases in which it applied. In his *Novellae*, Justinian punished more than thirty possible crimes with exile.[45] As can be seen, exile was notably more prevalent in the provisions of late Roman and Byzantine emperors—except for issues related to treason and disloyalty to the king and to Catholic doctrine.

Exile as a punishment for treason was a strikingly common and uncontroversial occurrence in the Visigothic legal world. In the late Roman world, traitors were often punished with torture and execution, but the emperor could commute their sentence to exile as a gesture of magnanimity. In the Visigothic kingdom, however, treason was punished with exile in most cases. Confinement to a monastery was also a possible sentence,[46] although often accompanied by amputation (generally of a hand), *decalvatio*, branding with infamy (*infamia*), and the confiscation of property.[47] There were numerous

43 LI 6.5.18 (*Antiqua*) was subsequently modified, eliminating exile. To these we can add LI 4.4.1 (*Antiqua*), which we will analyse *infra*.

44 King 1972, 153. Specifically, the Jewish laws in González Salinero (2014, 204–5). To this we must add 10.2.7 (Recceswinth), because although exile was not indicated as a penalty, the right to recover property for those individuals who had been exiled for more than thirty years was preserved.

45 References to the three in the notes to the section above in 'Exile in Late Roman and Early-Byzantine World'.

46 Lear 1951, 5–6. On the 'disappearance' of the death penalty in the Visigothic kingdom, Deswarte 2008, 156–63, referring especially to Recceswinth's decision.

47 On *decalvatio*, Lear 1951, 15–16; Petit 2001, 105–6; Crouch 2010; Dumézil 2011; Arce 2011, 154–55; Díaz 2012, 98–99.

individuals sentenced for treason who were exiled or confined to monasteries in addition to suffering some of the punishments just mentioned.[48] Among others, we find Leovigild exiling Bishop Masona of Mérida, John of Biclarum, the Suevi Eboricus and Audeca, and possibly Hermenegild;[49] Reccared exiling bishops Sunna of Mérida,[50] Uldila, Sega, and Vagrila;[51] Witteric exiling Count Bulgar;[52] Sisenand exiling Geila, brother of Swinthila; numerous nobles exiled during the reign of Chindaswinth;[53] the aristocratic family of Ricimerus, who protected Valerius of Bierzo (exiled possibly under King Wamba);[54] and the many exiles under King Egica.[55]

Many actions that were considered crimes and offences in the late Roman and Byzantine worlds were viewed in the same way in the Visigothic kingdom of Toledo.[56] However, as a general rule, the Visigothic monarchs replaced exile with other types of physical, social, and financial punishment, especially the confiscation of property.[57] For example, crimes related to corruption, forgery, or mismanagement, which were mostly punishable by exile in late Roman law, received a pecuniary penalty and, on many occasions, flogging and, especially, *decalvatio*, regardless of the social status of the defendant. CTh 9.19.2 punished the falsification of documents with execution, depending on the scale of the deception, whereas LI 7.5.1 (*Antiqua*) on falsifications of royal documents imposed a pecuniary penalty on noblemen and hand amputation on *inferiores*. Those who had been involved in some way in the adulteration or falsification of a will were punished with the loss of assets and deportation to an island according to CTh 9.11.2, while LI 7.5.2

48 In general, Arce 2011, 147–62; Vallejo Girvés 2003, 36–47; Frighetto 2015.

49 Masona was confined to a monastery (VSPE 5.6.66–89 and 110) and, possibly, John of Biclarum as well (Isid. De viris 31). In addition, this might have occurred to other Catholic bishops who resisted the Arianism of Leovigild (Greg. Tur. Decem libri 5.38; Isid. Hist. Goth. 51). Eboricus was confined to a monastery (Ioh. Bicl. 67) and Audeca was tortured, tonsured, ordained a presbyter, and exiled (Ioh. Bicl. 75). See Greg Tur. Decem libri 5.38 for Hermenegild. Cf. also, Isid. Hist. Goth. 51, regarding nobles exiled by Leovigild. See Petit 2001, 107–8.

50 The case of Sunna is peculiar, as it was an expulsion (VSPE 5.11.70–81; Ioh. Bicl. 87). On this issue, from different perspectives, Martin 2011; Vallejo Girvés 2013.

51 Sega's hand was also amputated (Ioh. Bicl. 87); Vagrila's exile was commuted to becoming a slave of the church of Saint Eulalia, after he managed to find sanctuary in it (VSPE 5.11.17–29, 86–103; cf. *infra*). Regarding Uldila, see Ioh. Bicl. 89.

52 *Epistulae Wisigothicae* 12 (13), 14 (ed. Gil 1991).

53 Fredegar 4.82.

54 Val. Ord. quer. 7.

55 Chron. Muz. 37. On exile and the last Visigothic monarchs, see Díaz 2012, 100–103.

56 As we will see, there were also many cases in which the punishment to be applied differed according to the social status of the guilty.

57 For further discussion of financial penalties, see the conclusion to this chapter.

(Chindaswinth) imparted a pecuniary penalty or even enslavement for nobles and flogging for *inferiores* who committed the same crime.

A comparison of the laws against the adulteration or counterfeiting of currencies in the CTh and the LI is very instructive, since the punishments were totally different, although in both cases punishments were established for three social levels (*curiales*, *humiliores*, and slaves). CTh 9.21.1 stated that a *decurion* was to be exiled and his property confiscated; an *humillior* was to receive a perpetual punishment (which was not specified) and lose his property; a slave (*servi*) faced capital punishment.[58] In LI 7.6.2 (Recceswinth), a free man would suffer the loss of his property, the *inferior* would become a slave, and a slave was to have his right hand amputated.[59] Thus, the Visigoths seem to have refrained from systematically employing exile as a punishment for free individuals.

Although they were not fully comparable, laws on the theft or misuse of irrigation waters also present notable differences. A constitution included in CTh 9.32.1, 2 punished a person who illegally drew water from the Nile or exceeded the amount to which he was entitled with death at the stake. Accomplices were to be deported to the oasis (a situation analogous to deportation to an island) and would lose their citizenship, rank, and property. In contrast, LI 8.4.31 (Recceswinth) prescribed a pecuniary penalty for the theft of irrigation water to which others held rights if the defendants were the owners of the land, while they were punished by flogging if they were slaves. Here exile was again absent in the Visigoths' legislation.

Negligence and corruption of judges and magistrates were punished both in CTh 2.1.6 and in LI 6.1.2 (Chindaswinth) with financial penalties, to be paid to the fisc or to those harmed by the conduct. While the CTh also ordered deportation for the corrupt staff of judges, replaced by exile in the *interpretatio* of the LRV, the LI did not stipulate any punishment for the staff. In addition, while negligent behaviour by a judge was punished with exile, confiscation, capital punishment, or torture in Nov. 8.8.1, the judge was only subject to the payment of a pecuniary penalty in LI 2.1.20 (Chindawinth). In this regard, it is interesting to note that, while Justinian punished all unlawful behaviours of judges with exile and the confiscation of property, the Visigothic kings opted for the imposition of monetary

58 Grodzynski 1984, 387.

59 Lear 1951, 11–12; Santiago Vázquez 2011, 63; Pliego Vázquez 2010, 82–86. With regard to amputation with this corrective purpose, López (1912–1913, 118–50) sees the Visigothic monarchs as having been influenced by the provisions of Heraclius, but we must not forget that amputation of the hand as punishment was already imposed by the Romans for treason. As a punishment not related to betrayal, it appeared in Nov. Just. 134.13.

penalties, the confiscation of property, and, in some cases, flagellation. They did not impose exile in any case.[60]

The consultation of fortune tellers, soothsayers, sorcerers, or seers about the life or death of the ruler, or, indeed, of any individual, was punishable in late Roman and Visigothic societies. The penalty was applied both to those who sought the information and to those who dispensed it. However, these more or less comparable situations differed in their punishments, whose severity lessened in the case of the Visigoths.[61] For example, according to CTh 9.16.1 and 2, fortune tellers were to be burned alive, while those who sought their guidance would only be exiled to an island and their property confiscated. But, in LI 6.2.2 (Erwig) and 6.2.5 (Chindaswinth), those who consulted diviners of any sort would be flogged, reduced to servitude (if they were free), and have their property confiscated. If they were slaves, they were tortured and sold overseas—which, of course, was still a type of exile. Fortune tellers and sorcerers were burned alive in the late Roman empire, while in the Visigothic kingdom they were flogged and had their heads shaved.[62]

It is surprising to find exile as a punishment in the provisions of LI 6.5.12 (Chindaswinth) and 13 (Recceswinth), which called for a period of three years of exile under penance for masters who killed or maimed slaves or servants without a judge's authorization, since this provision is not found in late Roman or Byzantine legislation.[63] This is another clear illustration of how the Romans and Visigoths employed exile in varying ways in response to offences not related to treason or disloyalty against the king.

Exile was also set down in LI 4.4.1 (*Antiqua*) concerning the rights of parents who laid claim to adult children they had previously abandoned as infants. Specifically, the law addressed the case of those who, after recovering their child, did not compensate the person who had raised them with money or a slave.[64] The imperial constitutions in CTh 5.9.1 (= LRV CTh 5.7.1), 5.10.1 (= LRV CTh 5.10.1), and CJ 5.4.16 addressed the rights of parents to recover abandoned children and the compensation to be paid to those who raised the children. They also addressed the question of these children's free or unfree status, a decision reserved to those who had found the child.

60 Bianchi 2012, 181–202.

61 Jiménez Sánchez 2005, 69–70.

62 On this difference, Ramis 2017, 21.

63 Petit 2001, 91–92 and n. 4, on Chindaswinth's opposition to slaveowners' infliction of capital punishment on their slaves without a trial.

64 Fossati Vanzeti 1983; Evans Grubbs 2010, 307–9; Evans Grubbs 2013, 97–99; Monnickendam 2019, 5–7.

Therefore, although the Roman provisions did not include exile, they do coincide with Visigothic legislation in requiring compensation for those who had taken care of abandoned children. Justinian determined that all exposed children were free, which never became a norm in Visigothic legislation.[65] This constitutes yet another divergence between Visigothic legislation and the Byzantine law that preceded it.[66] This specific issue is also important because it further corroborates the argument that the influence of Justinianic law in Hispania was not considerable, at least regarding the application of the penalty of exile.

Crimes Against the Family and Sexual Morality[67]

The crimes and offences against sexual morality and the institution of the family in late Roman, Byzantine, and Visigothic legislation shared many similar characteristics, but they were by no means identical. For example, different Visigothic kings punished sexual immorality and actions that undermined the institution of the family. The principles the kings expressed were virtually identical to those present in various imperial constitutions, but the consequences were not. Analysis of these provisions will demonstrate that the Visigoths dispensed with exile as a punishment in many of the cases in which the Romans maintained it.

The laws CTh 9.9.1 and LI 3.2.2 (*Antiqua*) prescribed punishments for an adulterous relationship between a free woman and her slave or freedman. In the CTh, the types of punishment varied depending on whether the union had occurred before or after the law's proclamation. In the former case, the woman would lose her assets and status in public life, while it was implied that the man would be exiled.[68] In the latter case, in which there was conduct involving conscious violation of the law, the mistress would be subject to the death penalty and the partner would be burned at the stake.[69] The *interpretatio* to this provision (LRV CTh 9.6.1) only transmitted the punishments

65 CJ 8.52.3; Evans Grubbs 2013, 97–99.

66 Along the same perspective, Boswell 1980, 205–7.

67 In general, Arjava 2011, 36–37, and Joye 2011. Although I agree with Osaba (2003a), regarding the sway that Constantine's legislative work had on the Visigoths' approach to the family as an institution, I believe that Visigothic law departed from Constantine in terms of how to correct conduct detrimental to the family.

68 CTh 9.9.1, 1.

69 Evans Grubbs 1993, 125–53. In this provision Constantine also dealt with the social category of children born from such a union, as well as their inheritance rights; see also CTh Nov. Anthem. 1.

accorded for couples who joined after the proclamation of the original law. In contrast, LI 3.2.2 (*Antiqua*) prescribed burning at the stake after a public flogging for both parties, with no distinction between the woman and her slave.[70] Therefore, the Visigothic legislation differed from both Constantine's original constitution (CTh 9.9.1) and its later *interpretatio*. In any case, exile was not included at any time in the Visigothic version of this law.[71]

Both late Roman and Visigothic legislation also addressed the abduction of women. Roman punishments for this crime were diverse, in some cases prescribing deportation and exile, and even burning at the stake for those convicted of this crime (CTh 9.8.1 = LRV CTh 9.9.5, 1; CTh 9.24.1 = LRV CTh 9.19.1). Punishments also varied amongst the Visigoths, although in no case was exile prescribed for this crime. Rather, the law ordered pecuniary penalties (including on the promised dowry), enslavement, and flogging for the abductor and his accomplices (LI 3.3.3 (Recceswinth); 3.3.4 (*Antiqua*); 3.3.7 (*Antiqua*)).[72]

Romans and Visigoths also punished unions between relatives, although there were differences according to the degree of their consanguinity,[73] as

70 See Dubreucq 2005, 30–31; Osaba 2013, 120; and Petit 2001, 194–95, on the judge's right to act *ex officio*. With regards to this prohibition on unions between masters and slaves, the Visigothic provision recognized a scenario not previously addressed by late Roman legislation: the appropriate punishment in the event that the couple, aware that they had violated the law, managed to secure sanctuary in a church. Although nothing was said about what was to be done with the male partner, in the Visigothic sphere the woman could be forgiven and spared from the stake to become a slave of whomever the king designated. See Arjava 2011, 36; Álvarez Cora 1997, 15; Osaba 2003b, 56; Osaba 2005, 457–58.

71 A variant addressed a potential union between a free woman and a slave, freedman, or slave of another person, or of the emperor or king. This behaviour had been punished since ancient times; it was the subject of the *Senatus Consultum Claudianum* (SCC), which remained in the provisions of the Christian emperors (for example, CTh 4.12.3), according to which women were reduced to slavery or servitude. It is also found in LI 3.2.3 (*Antiqua*), according to which the couple was to be whipped and the woman handed over to her relatives for them to do what they deemed fit, except put her to death. This Visigothic directive coincided, in a certain sense, with the SCC, as in both directives the couple could be warned up to three times. Justinian abolished the SCC: according to CJ 1.7.24, 1, a woman guilty of this offence could not be reduced to slavery, since this was socially damaging to her family. See Agnati 2017, 257–74, with an extensive analysis and bibliography; Melluso 2000, 47–52.

72 Colman 1983, 66–67; Joye 2011, 37–48, on the differences between these punishments; Osaba 2013, 116–17 and 133–34. Cf. Osaba 2003a, on the influence of Constantine's legislation on the consideration of abduction as a crime. She does not, however, address differences with regards to its punishment. See also Alvarado 2011, par. 9, on the influence of the German right to revenge in such cases.

73 On the pursuit of these types of unions, Evans Grubbs 1993, 132 and, above all, Puliati 2001 on the Roman sphere. In the late Roman world, according to, for example, CTh 3.10.1, followed in LRV CTh 3.10.1, consanguinity reached the fourth degree; in the sphere of Iberian Visigoths

observed in CTh 3.10.1, 1 (= LRV CTh 3.10.1), Nov. 12.1, as well as in LI 3.5.1 (Chindaswinth), 3.5.2 (Reccared), and 3.5.5 (Recceswinth).[74] Contrary to what we have seen in the previous cases, the sentences of Roman, Byzantine, and Visigothic legislators were quite homogeneous in their approach: on all occasions, the property of those guilty was confiscated and the couples were separated and exiled, with the only difference in the Visigothic case being confinement to a monastery to perform penance (LI 3.5.1 (Chindaswinth)). This last penalty was widely applied after Chindaswinth's reign by subsequent Visigothic kings, suggesting that these monarchs held some sort of prerogative concerning monastic institutions.

Roman and Visigothic punishments were also quite similar for those who falsely accused their spouse of having committed an offence or crime in order to obtain a divorce (CTh 3.16.1 and 2 = LRV CTh 3.16.1–2; LI 3.6.2 (Chindaswinth)). In every case the exonerated spouse retained the dowry, while the spouse guilty of false accusations was exiled.[75] Despite this similarity, however, we find some peculiarities in the Visigothic norms. In addition to exile, the law added public flogging and *decalvatio*.[76]

The grounds on which a wife could divorce her husband included homosexuality, a crime in the late Roman and Visigothic worlds that held significantly similar punishments.[77] According to CTh 9.7.3, male homosexual intercourse received the harshest punishments,[78] while male homosexual prostitution was punished with burning at the stake, according to CTh 9.7.6.[79] We do not find any more relevant references until Justinian, who punished passive male homosexuality with death in Nov. 77. To be sure, there was a noticeable change during the reign of this emperor with respect to homosexuality. According to Procopius, under Justinian, those condemned for paedophilia were castrated and paraded in public and, according to Malalas, some bishops found guilty of homosexual practices

it rose to the sixth (LI 3.5.1 (Chindaswinth)). On the reasons for the legal impediments, see Petit 2001, 196–97. On the influence of Isidore of Seville on the increase in the degree of consanguinity, Dubreucq 2005, 31–32.

74 Petit 2001, 194–95, on the judge's right to act *ex officio*.

75 King 1972, 263; Dubreucq 2005, 45–46.

76 Álvarez Cora 1997, 43–44. Arjava (2011, 35) sees many similarities between the handling of divorce in the constitution of the CTh, the *Edictum Theoderici*, and the *Lex Romana Burgundionum*.

77 Dubreucq 2005, 46–47.

78 Callu 1984, 340–41, n. 114; Grodzynski 1984, 378, n. 50.

79 Although not related to exile, on the persecution and punishment of male and female prostitution and the differences between late Roman, Justinianic, and Visigothic laws, see Osaba 2014, 663.

were publicly judged, castrated, and exiled.[80] Both authors make reference to the castration of those found guilty of this crime. Nov. 141 condemned homosexuality and prescribed a series of penalties for it. However, at no time were castration or exile mentioned. Rather, the law stated that the guilty were to be prosecuted, being worthy of the harshest punishment.[81] Nov. 142, meanwhile, prohibited castrating men to render them eunuchs, an action that was punished with exile and property confiscation. Apparently, these practices were considered typical of barbarians and, as such, not permissible in the *res publica*.[82] It can be deduced from these examples that Justinian applied castration infrequently, considering it a barbaric practice antithetical to *romanitas*.[83]

Punishment for sodomy in the Visigothic kingdom was always harsh, although, as in the Justinianic period, we notice an evolution in both the LI and the conciliar legislation. Thus, in LI 3.5.4, Chindaswinth ordered the emasculation of those who were found guilty. In addition, the sexual partners were to be separated from each other and subjected to harsh penance by the bishop of the diocese. Canon 3 of the Sixteenth Council of Toledo, held in the third year of Egica (693), did not mention castration, but rather perpetual exile, while bishops, presbyters, and deacons were to be stripped of their offices if found guilty. Both punishments were specified for those persons from the laity and the minor orders, who were additionally punished with flagellation and *decalvatio*. Shortly afterwards, Egica toughened these punishments in an edict (LI 3.5.7 (Egica)), making the penalty of castration a general punishment for homosexuality regardless of social rank of the persons.[84]

Homosexuality was clearly criminalized during the era of the Christian Roman empire, but Justinian's norms and those of the Visigothic monarchs differed from each other. The penalty prescribed by Chindaswinth's law was, of course, very similar to that which, according to Malalas, Justinian imparted upon homosexual bishops. This may lead us to conclude that this

80 Procopius, *Anecdota* 11.34 (ed. Dewing 1935); Malalas, *Chronographia* 436 (ed. Thurn 2000); Theophanes, *Chronographia a. m.* 6021 (ed. De Boor 1883).

81 Kuster and Cornier 1984, 587–610; Espejo 1991, 73–78 and 154.

82 Boswell 1980, 171–74, and Melluso 2000, 109, on the reasons that prompted Justinian to ban this type of castration.

83 Melluso 2000, 109, n. 387, on the apparent contradiction between the provisions of the Nov. Just. 141 and 142, respectively, with an extensive study of the literature in this regard.

84 Petit 1998, 222. The fundamental study on the proscription of homosexuality in the Visigothic kingdom is that by García López 1996, 309–30, although it is also analysed by Espejo 1991, and Álvarez Cora 1997, 49–51. Cf. Boswell 1980, 175–76.

was a case of Visigothic *imitatio* of Justinian's legislation. However, the penalty for homosexuality stipulated by Nov. 141 did not coincide with the stories in Procopius and Malalas. Thus, we cannot consider Chindaswinth an imitator of Justinian on this matter. We concur with Yolanda García, who convincingly argued that Justinian and Chindaswinth legislated against homosexuality for similar reasons, but that this similarity does not necessarily imply Visigothic *imitatio*. The rationale expressed by both the emperor and the king belonged to a broader Christian ideology that was embraced by leaders during the sixth and seventh centuries, when the punishment of all immoral behaviour was considered essential to bringing about peace and tranquillity among their subjects and achieving the salvation promised by God.[85]

We also find changing legal approaches to those seeking sanctuary in churches. In the late Roman world, ecclesiastical asylum was so respected that those guilty of a serious crime, even one punishable by death, could not be violently removed from churches if they managed to find sanctuary therein. They had to be convinced to depart voluntarily and were therefore often promised that they would not be executed, but rather sent into exile. In this area, however, Justinianic legislation differed from the late Roman period, especially with regard to homicides. While in the fourth and fifth centuries those guilty of homicide who found ecclesiastical asylum were able to avoid execution by going into exile, Justinian expressly excluded them from this prerogative and never allowed the commutation of the death penalty into exile.

The Visigoths do not seem to have followed Justinianic precedents in this regard. According to Visigothic legislation, the right to ecclesiastical sanctuary was to be rigorously respected. Therefore, any individual accused of an offence for which he or she was to receive the death penalty, and who managed to secure ecclesiastical sanctuary, was not to be executed. Rather, their punishment was to become a slave of the king or the family he or she had wronged (LI 3.2.2 (*Antiqua*); 3.3.2 (*Antiqua*); 6.5.16 (Chindaswinth) and 18 (*Antiqua*)). In fact, we can find a practical application of this principle in the case of Sunna's conspiracy against Reccared in Mérida in the late 580s. One of the culprits sentenced to exile, Vagrila, managed to find refuge in the basilica of Saint Eulalia. Respecting the principle of ecclesiastical

85 In addition, García López (1996, 311, n. 6), believes that Visigothic legislation against homosexuality was related to a social prejudice with Germanic roots. Based on Foucault, she states that it was a crime for which the entire community felt damaged collectively. Cf. Salvian of Marseilles, *De Gubernatione Dei* 7.76 *et seq.* (ed. Pauly 1883), on excessive practices by the Goths with regards to the punishment of homosexuality.

asylum, the king decided that he would not be exiled, but rather made a slave of that church.[86]

It should be observed that in Visigothic legislation we find a notable particularity. LI 6.5.18 (*Antiqua*) recognized the possibility that a person guilty of parricide, uxoricide, or fratricide who found sanctuary in a sacred space could be spared from capital punishment. He was, however, to be exiled. It might seem that, in this instance, the Visigothic legislation mimicked the Roman precept of punishing with exile those condemned to death who had secured sanctuary. We believe, however, that there is an important nuance separating these examples. In the Roman legislation, the commutation of the death penalty in favour of exile was, it seems, *obligatory*. In the Visigothic legislation, on the other hand, it was a prerogative that legislators granted to judges, who could choose to exercise it or not. Visigothic legislators, therefore, altered the relationship between the death penalty, ecclesiastical asylum, and exile.

Thus, the Visigoths respected, like the Romans, ecclesiastical asylum, even in extreme cases of homicide. However, penalty commutation did not happen in the same way. The Romans of the fourth and fifth centuries used exile as an alternative punishment. The Visigoths preferred enslavement. Significantly, the Visigoths did not imitate on this matter the decisions of Justinian, who greatly curtailed the right to ecclesiastical sanctuary.

Conclusion

Treason was usually punished with exile throughout Visigothic history, as literary sources and both secular and canon law confirm.[87] This might be considered, at first glance, an imitation of a Roman practice. It is also very possible that exile was more prevalent in Visigothic legislation prior to the LI, based on the fact that three of the references to exile appear in *Antiquae* on family law. This feature finds a significant correlation in the presence of exile in Recceswinth's legislation on family.

In our opinion, however, there is little doubt that the Visigothic monarchs of the second half of the seventh century rarely followed the late Roman

86 Petit 2001, 107; Vallejo Girvés 2018, 121–22.

87 Treason was also punished by confinement in a monastery. On monasteries as a place of exile for the Visigoths, Prego de Lis 2006, 518–28; García López 1996, 316–17, n. 28. As a prison, Díaz 2003, 201–5. In general, on confinement to a monastery in Late Antiquity, Hillner 2016. We intentionally excluded from our analysis exile in canon law, clearly linked to penance in monasteries.

emperors, and in no cases Justinian, when it came to the use of exile in legislation.[88] In addition, they were not as consistent in imposing exile in any of the different varieties which we have surveyed. Nevertheless, as we have noted, there was an exception regarding cases of treason, disloyalty, or failure to aid the king or to defend the territory. For this type of behaviour, the usual sentence was, indeed, exile.

The Visigoths preferred to punish crimes and misconduct through pecuniary penalties and the confiscation of property, which bolstered the public treasury. Exile, in contrast, actually entailed expenses from the perspective of the state, since the authority had to guard or monitor those who were to be removed from their territory.[89] In addition, on numerous occasions they opted for physical punishments other than execution, such as *decalvatio* and flogging, for convicts of all social strata, since these penalties had a greater exemplary effectiveness than exile. It should be noted that these physical punishments were not frequent in the Roman and Byzantine world.[90] It is important, however, to recognize that both head shaving/flogging and exile meant a social stigma for those who received these punishments, although the effects of the former were more visible and immediate for their fellow subjects.

It is also interesting to note that the penalty the Romans used to *complement* exile—the confiscation of property—was precisely what the Visigoths used as *the main form* of punishment in similar crimes and offences,[91] while maintaining a gradation of penalties depending on the defendant's legal and social status. It must also be pointed out that, in some exceptional cases, the Visigoths resorted to exile to punish certain crimes that were not even covered by late Roman legislation.

Bibliography

Agnati, Ulrico, 'Un frammento delle *Differentiae* di Modestino nelle *Differentiae* di Isidoro', in *Ravena Capitale. Uno sguardo ad Occidente: Romani e Goti, Isidoro di Siviglia*, ed. by Gisella Bassanelli Sommariva and Simona Tarozi (Santarcangelo di Romagna: Maggioli Editore, 2012), pp. 129–45

88 See Deswarte 2008, 181–82. Against this perspective, Arce 2011, 168.

89 Petit 1998, 228. In addition, Justinian sought to prevent the imposition of these types of pecuniary penalties; see López 1942–1943, 455–56.

90 Martino 2015, 134; King 1972, 110.

91 To which it is necessary to add the payment of the fines imposed. In general, Díaz 2003, 206; Díaz 2012, 98–99, on the confiscation of assets as a punitive measure.

Agnati, Ulrico, 'L'unione paramatrimoniale di CTh. 4.12.3', in *Index. Quaderni camerti di studi romanistici. International Survey of Roman Law*, 41 (2017), 257–74

Alvarado, Javier, 'A modo de conclusiones: el *Liber Iudicum* y la aplicación del Derecho en los siglos VI a XI', in *Mélanges de la Casa de Velázquez. El derecho hispánico latino de los siglos VI al XII. Le droit hispanique latin du Vie. au XIIe. Siécles*, 41.2 (2011), 109–27

Álvarez Cora, Enrique, 'Derecho sexual visigótico', in *Historia. Instituciones. Documentos*, 24 (1997), 1–52

Arce, Javier, *Esperando a los árabes. Los visigodos en Hispania (507–711)* (Madrid: Marcial Pons, 2011)

Arjava, Antti, 'The Survival of Roman Family Law after the Barbarian Settlement', in *Law, Society, and Authority in Late Antiquity*, ed. by Ralph W. Mathisen (Oxford: Oxford University Press, 2011), pp. 33–51

Barney, Stephen A., W. J. Lewis, J. A. Beach, and Oliver Berghof, *The Etymologies of Isidore of Seville* (Cambridge: Cambridge University Press, 2006)

Bianchi, Paola, 'Il principio di imparzialità del giudice: dal Codice Teodosiano all'opera di Isidoro di Siviglia', in *Ravena Capitale. Uno sguardo ad Occidente: Romani e Goti, Isidoro di Siviglia*, ed. by Gisella Bassanelli Sommariva and Simona Tarozi (Santarcangelo di Romagna: Maggioli Editore, 2012), pp. 181–215

Boswell, John, *Christianity, Social Tolerance and Homosexuality: Gay People in Western Europe from the Beginning of the Christian Era to the Fourteenth Century* (Chicago, IL: University of Chicago Press, 1980)

Callu, Jean-Pierre, 'Le jardín des supplices au Bas-Empire', in *Du Châtiment dans la cité. Supplices corporels et peine de mort dans le monde Antique* (Rome: École Française de Rome, 1984), pp. 313–59

Cassiodorus, *Variae*, ed. by Theodor Mommsen, *Cassiodori Senatoris Variae*, MGH Auctores Antiquissimi, XII (Berlin: Weidmann, 1894)

Cintio, Lucia di, *L'Interpretatio Visigothorum al Codex Theodosianus. Il Libro IX* (Milan: Edizione Universitarie di Lettere, Economia, Diritto, 2013)

Colman, Rebecca V., 'The Abduction of Women in Barbarian Law', in *Florilegium: Carleton University Annual Papers on Classical Antiquity and the Middle Ages*, 5 (1983), 62–75

Crouch, Jace, 'The Judicial Punishment of *Decalvatio* in Visigothic Spain: A Proposed Solution Based on Isidore of Seville and the *Lex Visigothorum*', in *The Mediterranean Review*, 3.1 (2010), 59–81

D'Ors, Álvaro, *El Código de Eurico. Edición, Palingenesía, Indices* (Madrid: Ediciones del BOE, 2014)

Delmaire, Roland, 'Exile, relégation, déportation dans la législation du Bas-Empire', in *Exile et relégation. Les tribulations du sage et du saint durant l'Antiquite*

Romaine et Chrétienne (Ier–Vie. s. ap. J. C.), ed. by Philip Blaudeau (Paris: De Boccard, 2008), pp. 115–32

Deswarte, Thomas, 'Le concile de Tolede VIII (653) et le code de Réceswinthe (654): limitation du pouvoir monarchique et suppression de la peine de mort dans l'Espagne Wisigothique', in *Compilations et codifications juridiques*, vol. 1, *De l'Antiquité à la période moderne*, ed. by David Derousin and Florence Garnier (Paris: Le Manuscrit, 2008), pp. 153–84

Díaz, Pablo, 'Las cárceles en la Hispania Visigoda', in *Castigo y Reclusión en el Mundo Antiguo*, ed. by Sofía Torallas and Inmaculada Pérez Martín (Madrid: Consejo Superior de Investigaciones Científicas, 2003), pp. 193–207

Díaz, Pablo, 'Confiscations in the Visigothic Reign of Toledo: A Political Instrument', in *Expropriations et confiscation dans les royaumes barbares. Une approche régionale*, ed. by Pierfranceso Porena and Yann Rivière (Rome: École Française de Rome, 2012), pp. 93–112

Dubreucq, Alain, 'Le marriage dans la loi des wisigoths', in *Famille, violence et christianisation au Moyen Âge. Mélanges offerts à Michel Rouche*, ed. by Martin Aurell and Thomas Deswarte (Paris: Presses de l'Université de Paris-Sorbonne, 2005), pp. 29–56

Dumézil, Bruno, 'La peine de décalvation dans l'Espagne wisigothique', in *Anthropologie, mythologies et historie de la chevelure et de la pilosité. Le Sens du Poil*, ed. by Bertrand Lançon and Marie Hélène Delavaud-Roux (Paris: L'Harmattan, 2011), pp. 135–47

Edictum Theodereci regis, ed. by Friedrich Bluhme, MGH Leges, V (Hannover: Hahn, 1889), pp. 149–70

Epistulae Wisigothicae, ed. by Luis Gil, *Miscellanea Wisigothica* (Seville: Servicio de Publicaciones de la Universidad de Sevilla, 1991), pp. 1–49

Espejo, Carlos, *El deseo negado. Aspectos de la problemática homosexual en la vida monástica (s. III–VI d. C.)* (Granada: Servicio de Publicaciones de la Universidad de Granada, 1991)

Evans Grubbs, Judith, 'Marriage More Shameful than Adultery: Slave-Mistress Relationships, "Mixed Marriages" and Late Roman Law', in *Phoenix*, 47.2 (1993), 125–54

Evans Grubbs, Judith, 'Hidden in Plain Sight: Exposition in the Community', in *Children, Memory, and Family Identity in Roman Culture*, ed. by Véronique Dasen and Thomas Späth (Oxford: Oxford University Press, 2010), pp. 293–310

Evans Grubbs, Judith, 'Infant Exposure and Infanticide', in *The Oxford Handbook of Childhood and Education in the Classical World* (Oxford: Oxford University Press, 2013), pp. 83–107

Faustus of Riez, *Epistulae*, ed. by Christian Lütjohann, *Sidonius Apollinaris, Epistulae et Carmina. Fauti aliorumque epistulae. Ruricium aliosque Ruricii epistulae*, MGH Auctores Antiquissimi, VIII (Berlin: Weidemann, 1887), pp. 266–98

Fossati Vanzetti, Maria B., 'Vendita ed esposizione degli infanti da Costantino a Giustiniano', in *Studia et Documenta Historiae et Iuris*, 49 (1983), 179–224

Frighetto, Renan, 'El exilio, el destierro y sus concepciones políticas en la Hispania visigoda: los ejemplos de Juan de Bíclaro e Isidoro de Sevilla (siglos VI–VII)', in *Movilidad forzada entre la Antigüedad Clásica y Tardía*, ed. by Margarita Vallejo Girvés, Juan Antonio Bueno Delgado, and Carlos Sánchez-Moreno Ellart (Alcalá de Henares: Servicio de Publicaciones de la Universidad de Alcalá, 2015), pp. 111–34

Fusco, Sandro A., 'L'evolversi della categoría dal "credere" nell'Occidente visigoto: dal Codice Euriciano ad Isidoro di Siviglia', in *Ravena Capitale. Uno sguardo ad Occidente: Romani e Goti, Isidoro di Siviglia*, ed. by Gisella Bassanelli Sommariva and Simona Tarozi (Santarcangelo di Romagna: Maggioli Editore, 2012), pp. 81–100

García López, Yolanda, *Estudios críticos y literarios de la Lex Wisigothorum* (Alcalá de Henares: Servicio de Publicaciones de la Universidad de Alcalá, 1996)

Gaudemet, Jean, 'Le Bréviaire d'Alaric et les *Epitome*', in *Ius Romanum Medii Aevi*, I.2b (1965), 3–57

González Salinero, Raúl, 'The Legal Eradication of the Jewish Literary Legacy in Visigothic Spain', in *Jews in Early Christian Law: Byzantium and the Latin West, 6th–11th Centuries*, ed. by John N. Tolan, Nicholas de Lange, Laurence Foschia, and Capucine Nemo-Pekelman (Turnhout: Brepols, 2014), pp. 195–208

Grodzynski, Dennis, 'Tortures mortelles et categories sociales. Les *Summa Supplicia* dans le droit romain aux IIIe. et Ive. Siècles', in *Du Châtiment dans la cité. Supplices corporels et peine de mort dans le monde Antique* (Rome: École Française de Rome, 1984), pp. 361–403

Hillner, Julia, 'Confined Exiles: An Aspect of the Late Antique Prison System', in *Millennium. Jahrbuch zur Geschichte und Kultur der ersten Jahrtausend*, 10 (2013), 385–434

Hillner, Julia, *Prison, Punishment and Penance in Late Antiquity* (Cambridge: Cambridge University Press, 2016)

Hillner, Julia, Jörg Ulrich, and Jakob Engberg (eds), *Clerical Exile in Late Antiquity* (Frankfurt: Peter Lang, 2016)

Isidore of Seville, *Differentiae*, ed. by Carmen Codoñer, *Isidoro de Sevilla. Diferencias. Libro I. Introducción, edición crítica, traducción y notas* (Paris: Les Belles Lettres, 1992)

Isidore of Seville, *Versus*, ed. by José María Sánchez Martín, *Isidori Hispalensis Versus*, CCSL CXIIIA (Turnhout: Brepols, 2000)

Jiménez Garnica, Ana M., 'El origen de la legislación civil visigoda sobre la prohibición de matrimonios mixtos entre romanos y godos: un problema de fundamento religioso', in *Anuario de Historia del Derecho Español*, 55 (1985), 735–47

Jiménez Sánchez, Juan Antonio, 'La legislación civil y eclesiástica concerniente a las *superstitiones* y a las pervivencias idolátricas en la Hispania de los siglos VI–VII', in *Hispania Sacra*, 57 (2005), 48–78

Joye, Sylvie, 'La transcription du droit de la famille et de la proprieté du droit romain à la loi wisigothique', in *Mélanges de la Casa de Velázquez. El derecho hispánico latino de los siglos VI al XII. Le droit hispanique latin du Vie. au XIIe. Siècles*, 41.2 (2011), 35–53

King, P. D., *Law and Society in the Visigothic Kingdom* (Cambridge: Cambridge University Press, 1972)

Kuster, Harry J., and Raymond J. Cornier, 'Old Views and News Trends: Observations on the Problem of Homosexuality in the Middle Ages', in *Studi Medievali*, 25.2 (1984), 587–610

Ladner, Gerhart B., 'Justinian's Theory of Law and the Renewal Ideology of the *Leges Barbarorum*', in *Proceedings of the American Philosophical Society*, 119.3 (1975), 191–200

Lafferty, Sean D. W., *The Edictum Theoderici: A Study of a Roman Legal Document from Ostrogothic Italy* (PhD Dissertation, University of Toronto, 2010)

Lear, Floyd S., 'The Public Law of the Visigothic Code', in *Speculum*, 26.1 (1951), 1–23

López, Roberto S., 'Byzantine Law in the Seventh Century and its Reception by the Germans and the Arabs', in *Byzantium*, 16 (1942–1943), 445–61

Malalas, *Chronographia*, ed. by Ioannes Thurn, *Ioannis Malalae Chronographia* (Berlin: De Gruyter, 2000)

Martin, Céline, 'L'évêque dans un petit navire. Bannissement et relegation dans les Vies des Saints Pères de Mérida', in *Échanges, Communications et Reseaux dans le Haut Moyen Âge. Études et textes offerts à Stéphanie Lebecq*, ed. by Alban Gautier and Céline Martin (Turnhout: Brepols, 2011), pp. 45–56

Martino, Tomasso, 'Recensione a eds. B. Sère and Jörg Wettlaufer, *Shame Between Punishment and Penance: The Social Usages of Shame in the Middle Ages and Early Modern Times, Firenze 2013*', in *I Castelli di Yale*, 3.1 (2015), 129–34

Matthews, John F., 'Interpreting the *Interpretationes* of the *Breviarium*', in *Law, Society, and Authority in Late Antiquity*, ed. by Ralph W. Mathisen (Oxford: Oxford University Press, 2011), pp. 11–32

Melluso, Marco, *La schiavitú nell'etá giustinianea: disciplina giuridica e rilevanza sociale* (Paris: Presses Universitaires Franc-Comtoises, 2000)

Monnickendam, Yifat, 'The Exposed Child: Transplanting Roman Law into Late Antiquity Jewish and Christian Legal Discourse', in *American Journal of Legal History*, 59.1 (2019), 1–30

Osaba, Esperanza, 'Influenza della leggi costantiniana nella Lex Wisigothorum', in *Diritto @ Storia*, 2 (2003a), http://www.dirittoestoria.it/memorie2/Testi%20

delle%20Comunicazioni/Osaba-LexVisigothorum.htm [date of access: 3 June 2022]

Osaba, Esperanza, 'Reflexiones en torno a las leyes visigodas', in *Monteagudo. Revista de Literatura española, hispanoamericana y teoría de la literatura. Monográfico Retórica y Discurso*, 3 (2003b), 51–72

Osaba, Esperanza, 'Pena capital y derecho de asilo en época visigoda', in *Del derecho penal de Roma al derecho actual*, ed. by Fermín Camacho and Aránzazu Calzada (Madrid: Edisofer, 2005), pp. 453–62

Osaba, Esperanza, 'Las mujeres en la sociedad visigoda de los siglos VI y VII', in *Mulier. Algunas historias e instituciones de derecho romano*, ed. by Rosalía Rodríguez and M. José Bosch (Madrid: Dykinson, 2013), pp. 109–34

Osaba, Esperanza, 'Imagen y represión de la prostitución en época visigoda', in *Fundamina*, 20.2 (2014), 658–66

Petit, Carlos, 'Crimen y castigo en el Reino Visigodo de Toledo', in *Los visigodos y su mundo* (Madrid: Comunidad Autónoma, 1998), pp. 215–37

Petit, Carlos, *Iustitia Gothica. Historia social y teología del proceso en la Lex Visigothorum* (Huelva: Universidad de Huelva, 2001)

Pliego Vázquez, Ruth, 'La falsificación y manipulación de la moneda visigoda', in *Falsificació i manipulació de la moneda. XIV Curs d'historia monètaria d'Hispania*, ed. by Marta Campo (Barcelona: Museu Nacional d'Art de Catalunya, 2010), pp. 81–102

Prego de Lis, Augusto, 'La pena de exilio en la legislación hispanogoda', in *Antigüedad y Cristianismo*, 23 (2006), 515–29

Presedo, Francisco, *La España Bizantina* (Seville: Servicio de Publicaciones de la Universidad de Sevilla, 2003)

Procopius, *Anecdota*, ed. by Henry Bronson Dewing, *Procopius: The Anecdota or Secret History* (Cambridge, MA and London: Harvard University Press, 1935)

Puliati, Salvatore, *Incesta crimina. Regime giuridico da Augusto a Giustiniano* (Milan: Giuffré, 2001)

Ramis Barceló, Rafael, 'Estudio preliminar', in *El Libro de los Juicios* (*Liber Iudiciorum*) (Madrid: Ediciones del BOE, 2017), pp. 11–30

Rohmann, Dirk, Jörg Ulrich, and Margarita Vallejo Girvés (eds), *Mobility and Exile at the End of Antiquity* (Frankfurt: Peter Lang, 2018)

Salvian of Marseilles, *De Gubernatione Dei*, ed. by Frank Pauly, *Salvianus. De Gubernatione Dei. Epistulae. Ad Ecclesiam*, Corpus Scriptorum Ecclesiasticorum Latinarum 8 (Vienna: Verlag der Österreichischen Akademie der Wissenschaften, 1883)

Santiago Vázquez, Javier de, 'Legislación y moneda en la Hispania visigoda', in *Mélanges de la Casa de Velázquez* (*Le droit hispanique latin du VIe. au XIIe. Siècle*), 41.2 (2011), 55–75

Shoemaker, Karl, *Sanctuary and Crime in the Middle Ages (400–1500)* (New York, NY: Fordham University Press, 2001)

Stüber, Till, *Der Inkriminierte Bischof. Könige im Konflikt mit Kirchenleitern im westgotischen und fränkischen Gallien (466–614)* (Berlin and Boston, MA: De Gruyter, 2019)

Theophanes, *Chronographia*, ed. by Carl De Boor, *Theophanis. Chronographia* (Leipzig: Teubner, 1883)

Valastro Canale, Angelo, 'Introduzione', in *Isidoro di Seviglia. Etimologie o origini*, vol. 1 (Torino: Utet, 2004)

Vallejo Girvés, Margarita, '*In Insulam Deportatio* en el siglo IV d. C. Aproximación a su comprensión a través de causas, personas y lugares', in *POLIS. Revista de ideas y formas políticas de la Antigüedad Clásica*, 3 (1991), 153–67

Vallejo Girvés, Margarita, 'Los exilios de católicos y arrianos bajo Leovigildo y Recaredo', in *Hispania Sacra*, 111 (2003), 36–47

Vallejo Girvés, Margarita, 'El éxito de un desterrado arriano. La evangelización de Sunna en Mauritania', in *Marginados sociales y religiosos en la Hispania tardoantigua y visigoda*, ed. by Raúl González Salinero (Madrid and Salamanca: Signifer, 2013), pp. 171–91

Vallejo Girvés, Margarita, 'Case Studies of Church Asylum and Exile in Late Antiquity', in *Mobility and Exile at the End of Antiquity*, ed. by Dirk Rohmann, Jörg Ulrich, and Margarita Vallejo Girvés (Frankfurt: Peter Lang, 2018), pp. 113–37

Vita Caesarii Arelatensis, ed. by Bruno Krusch, *Passiones Vitaeque Sanctorum Aevi Merovingici et Antiquiorum Aliquot*, MGH Scriptores Rerum Merovingicarum, III (Hannover: Hahn, 1888), pp. 433–501

Vita Marcelli, ed. by François Dolbeau, 'La Vie en prose de Saint Marcel, évêque de Die. Histoire du texte et édition critique', in *Francia. Forschungen zur westeuropäischen Geschichte*, 11 (1983–1984), 97–130

Washburn, David A., *Banishment in the Later Roman Empire, 284–476 C.E.* (London: Routledge, 2013)

About the Author

Margarita Vallejo Girvés is Professor of Ancient History at the University of Alcalá, specializing in the History of Late Antiquity. Her research interests include relations between the eastern Roman empire and Visigothic Hispania, exile and the right of asylum in late Roman and Visigothic legislation, and the dynasty of Emperor Leo I (r. 457–474).

5 The Roman Jewel in the Visigothic Crown

A Reassessment of the Royal Votive Crowns of the Guarrazar Treasure

Cecily Hilsdale[1]

Abstract

Since its discovery in the mid-nineteenth century, the celebrated Guarrazar treasure has served as a touchstone for questions about the cultural orientation and prestige policy of the Visigothic kingdom of Toledo. Traditionally, the sumptuous votive crowns and crosses of the treasure have been understood to exhibit the 'influence' of Byzantium. But by looking closely at select elements from the treasure that we describe as 'Roman' or 'Byzantine', this chapter pressures straightforward assumptions of Byzantine influence. In disentangling the Roman from the Byzantine, the chapter argues that the presence of a Roman cross on the votive crown of a Visigothic king complicates narratives of *translatio imperii* in compelling ways, suggesting instead a more nuanced material sense of supersession.

Keywords: Guarrazar treasure; crowns; crosses; Byzantine influence; supersession

In August of 1858, a remarkable cache of early medieval gold crowns and crosses was discovered in Huertas de Guarrazar near Toledo. The fragments were immediately reassembled, found their way into private hands, and within just a few months most were sold to the French government.

1 Many thanks to Molly Lester, Damián Fernández, Jamie Wood, the external reviewers, and all the participants of the 2019 workshop for their helpful feedback. Much of my thinking about the Guarrazar treasure took shape at the Institute for Advanced Study in Princeton and has been supported by the Social Sciences and Humanities Research Council of Canada.

Fernández, D., Lester, M. & Wood, J. (eds.), *Rome and Byzantium in the Visigothic Kingdom: Beyond* Imitatio Imperii. Taylor & Francis Group 2023
DOI: 10.5117/9789463726412_CH05

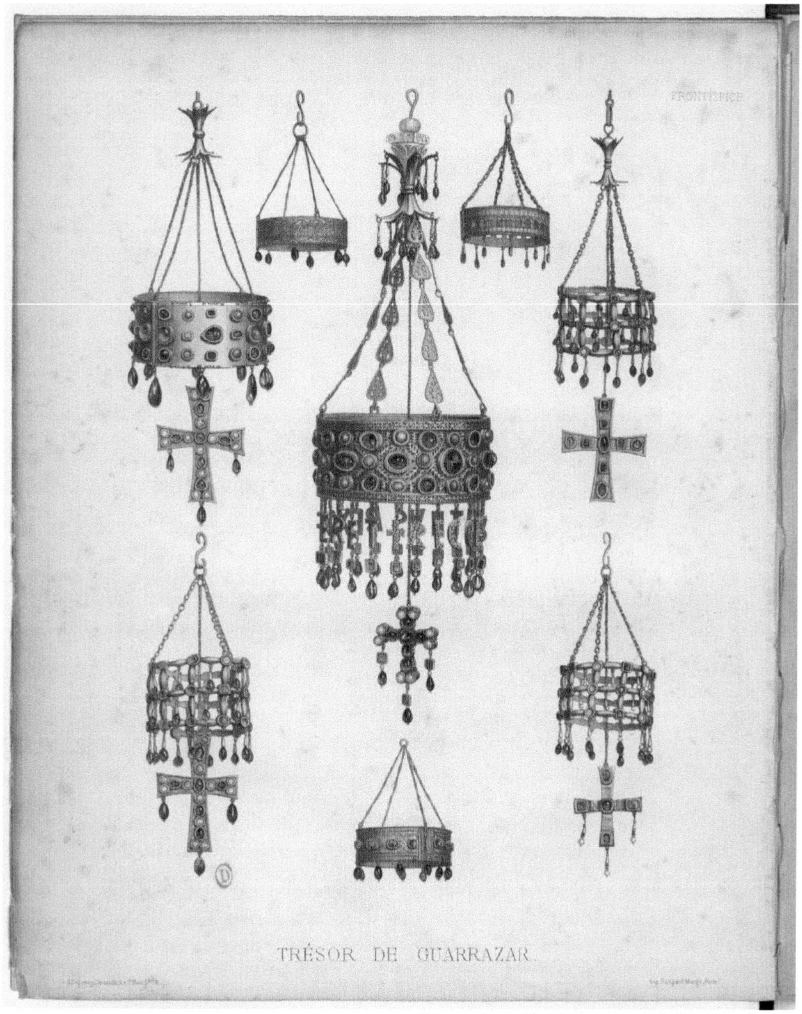

Source gallica.bnf.fr / Bibliothèque de l'INHA / coll. J. Doucet

Figure 5.1: Frontispiece of Ferdinand de Lasteyrie, *Description du Trésor de Guarrazar, accompagnée de recherches sur toutes les questions archéologiques qui s'y rattachent* (Paris: Gide, 1860). Image in the Public Domain, gallica.bnf.fr / Bibliothèque de l'INHA / coll. J. Doucet.

The acquisition was announced in *Le Monde illustré* on 12 February 1859 along with a brief description and illustration, and published more fully by Ferdinand de Lasteyrie in 1860 with a series of detailed colour engravings.[2] The frontispiece of the publication featured this sumptuous ensemble and centred on the largest and most ornate of the crowns, that of the seventh-century Visigothic king Recceswinth (r. 653–672), whose name is spelled out in Latin letters dangling from its lower edge. (See Figure 5.1.)

2 Sommerard 1859; Lasteyrie 1860.

Meanwhile in Spain, diplomatic efforts were underway to repatriate the works. Since the initial announcement of the French acquisition, the Spanish government made valiant efforts to nullify the sale and have the pieces returned. In addition, excavations were carried out at the original site of the discovery.[3] Led by José Amador de los Ríos, four further crowns were unearthed, including one naming another Visigothic king, Swinthila (r. 621–631), which was later stolen and has never been recovered. (See Figure 5.4.) In 1940 leaders of Spain and France 'agreed to an exchange of national treasures'.[4] Along with a Murillo painting of the *Inmaculada* (1678), the ancient Iberian sculpture known as *La Dama de Elche*, and archives from Salamanca, most, but not all, of the pieces of the Visigothic treasure were returned to Spain. As a result, the extant corpus, consisting of ten crowns and eight crosses (as well as a number of loose gems and other fragments), is divided among three collections: the largest portion is in the National Archaeological Museum in Madrid (see Figure 5.2), with other pieces in the National Palace in Madrid and the Cluny in Paris.[5]

I open with an anatomy of this treasure in order to suggest the prominent role of nationalism in the modern movement of these medieval objects. The primacy of national patrimony, the historiography of which has been exceptionally well contextualized by Francisco J. Moreno Martín, also bears relevance for scholarly interpretations of the items, specifically interpretations of their origins.[6] When Lasteyrie first published the pieces, he understood them to be of northern manufacture, akin to fibulas and buckles found in Frankish tombs. By situating them in relationship to Merovingian and Carolingian metalwork, he aligned them within the French cultural orbit. His position was not universally accepted but given that it was the first in-depth study it carried a great deal of weight and set the tone for subsequent scholarship. Written directly in response to Lasteyrie's study, José Amador de los Ríos argued emphatically for the corpus's indigeneity, partaking in no northern traditions.[7] For him, the pieces embodied the

3 The discovery and dispersal of the find is best contextualized by Balmesda 2001, 63–117. On the archaeology of the site itself, see López Quiroga, Morin de Pablos, and Martínez Tejera 2010, 563, and Rojas Rodríguez-Malo, Eger, Catalán, and García 2017, 563–95. Perea 2001 is the main catalogue for the treasure and includes thorough historiographic, epigraphic, scientific, and thematic essays.

4 As phrased by Gisela Ripoll López in Metropolitan Museum of Art 1993, 53; a full account is provided by Gruat and Martínez 2011.

5 García-Vuelta and Perea 2014, 248–49, fig. 1a–1b groups the pieces by location.

6 Moreno Martín 2017. I would like to thank the author for sharing this important essay with me in advance of its publication.

7 De los Ríos 1861 approached the more expanded corpus of objects—i.e., the pieces in Paris as well as those subsequently discovered in Madrid—as the basis for an apologia for the arts of Visigothic Spain more broadly.

Figure 5.2: The Guarrazar Treasure (Museo Arqueológico Nacional, Madrid). Museo Arqueológico Nacional, Inv. RP-2013-10-18. Photo: Doctor Sombra.

'latin-byzantin' style that was native to Visigothic Spain. But how we should understand that style precisely remains somewhat unclear. Debates about origins persisted throughout the twentieth century, with the treasure understood to exhibit a tension between the local and the 'influence' of Byzantium. 'Through all this decadent, Easternized gorgeousness', Pedro de Palol wrote, 'the Visigothic "manner" did not really get lost.'[8]

Drawing on select elements of the Guarrazar treasure, what follows is an attempt to navigate the murky terrain of 'influence' by raising key questions about what makes something Byzantine, how we describe works of this cultural tradition as either Roman or Byzantine, and, further, what that idiom might have meant in early medieval Toledo. Looking closely at one 'Byzantine' piece from the hoard, the cross suspended from Recceswinth's crown, this essay considers its mobilization in the votive ensemble whose conception ultimately was distinctly Visigothic.

The Jewelled Cross as Roman *Ornamenta*

The 9.5-centimetre-tall cross now attached to the crown of Recceswinth is exceptional with respect to the rest of the sumptuous items in the treasure,[9]

8 Palol 1968, 214.

9 On this point there is scholarly consensus. As for technique and metalwork traditions, as early as Lasteyrie the cross was understood as an outlier. Unlike what he perceived to be the

Figure 5.3: Sapphire and Pearl Cross, Guarrazar Treasure (Museo Arqueológico Nacional, Madrid). Museo Arqueológico Nacional. Inv. 71203. Photo: Fundación ITMA, Santiago Relanzón.

and, indeed, with respect to the entire extant corpus of early medieval gemmed crosses, East and West. (See Figure 5.3.) Before assessing the artistic traditions that best characterize the cross in question, it is worth considering

Germanic roots of the rest of the pieces, Lasteyrie (1860, 36) located this cross firmly within antique southern Roman traditions.

in detail what makes the piece so distinctive. The massing of sapphires and pearls of this cross represents a formal logic entirely different from the flat plate work of other gemmed crosses where precious stones are fitted tightly to a flat base.[10] Fundamentally more three-dimensional and architectonic, the gold setting serves as a mere skeletal support for its gems and pearls. Viewed from the front, one sees primarily the reflective surfaces of the sapphires and pearls, each framed by a thin halo of its gold mount. Capitalizing on the visual potential of its individual inset components, the sapphire core presents luminous flashes of light whereas the opaque surfaces of the pearls offer smooth reflective screens. The ultimate effect is a cruciform mass of translucent and reflective surfaces that enhance its overall lustrousness and brilliance.

Viewed from an angle, the architectonic nature of this massing comes into clear focus as the setting becomes legible.[11] The sapphires are mounted on delicate à jour pedestals of foliate forms that bloom into leafy claws to hold the stones in place. This intricate setting mechanism eases the weight of the piece and allows for alternate light sources to enhance the luminosity of the sapphires. In turn, these open settings are framed by tall solid gold capsules that support the eight threaded pearls at the terminal ends of the cross. As the tallest and most massive elements of the cross, these pearl-topped towers offer fortification for the tracery-like interior of the cruciform massing of gemstones. The contrast between the solidity of the pearl towers and the delicacy of the gemstones is evident when viewed from the back as well. Unlike the solid concave bases of the capsules, the base plates for the à jour settings of the sapphires comprise openwork rosettes, diminishing any potential impression of heaviness. The combination of slightly curved and pierced surfaces offers stabilization for the whole piece while also remaining light and variegated.

The back of the cross also preserves the mechanism for a clasp at the far ends of the lateral arms: a hinge on the right and pocket hook on the left (the pin itself is missing). This is clear evidence that the cross previously had served as an object of adornment. Since the earliest studies of the treasure, scholars have noted this unusual feature of this cross—it is the only piece from the treasure to bear traces of a previous life. Most have presumed

10 This point is made unmistakably clear by a quick perusal of Jülich 1986–1987 and Hübener 1975.

11 High-definition zoomable images of the cross, including the reverse, can be seen on the museum's website.

an original function as a fibula or brooch,[12] which sounds right; however, there are no comparable pieces within the entire corpus of extant fibulae or brooches (Roman, Byzantine, or Gothic).[13] Even the most deluxe examples do not compare with this clasped sapphire cross. It is an exquisite and delicate agglomeration of gems and pearls, displaying a degree of complexity and luxury that distinguishes it from all extant brooches of the era.

Although the cross is typologically unique in our extant archive, it is aligned with a tradition that is well attested textually. The ritual fastening of a cloak was part of the formal elevation of late antique imperial figures—the *chlamys* (*paludamentum*) was fastened with a precious brooch on one shoulder. On occasion, gold fibulae were presented to soldiers and high officials. Emperors also gave brooches to neighbouring elites. Procopius mentions a golden brooch explicitly among the symbols of authority that the 'barbarians' hoped to receive from the emperor of the Romans.[14]

Momentarily setting aside issues of previous function, the larger visual idiom represented by this piece requires elaboration. It is best situated within our archive of late antique and early Byzantine jewellery that is characterized by an attention to surface variation with an alternation of heights and thicknesses or permeability of surfaces made possible by openwork boxes, foliate arches and claw mounts, and cylindrical capsules. Although a full contextualization of the cross is beyond the scope of this study, all of its individual elements are attested in the extant archive of jewellery from the fourth to the seventh century.[15] These chronological parameters are broad because so few of the surviving pieces are securely datable and thus unable to anchor the broader corpus with any degree of confidence or precision. Our terminology for this corpus is also ambiguous. What modern scholarship conventionally calls early Byzantine or late antique would have been understood in its own time as simply Roman. In thinking about what is 'Byzantine' or 'Roman' about the cross, one needs to consider what Byzantium meant at that time, and in the context of the

12 In its first publication the original function was described as a fibula: 'le revers porte encore la fibule qui servait à l'attacher au manteau royal' (Sommerard 1859, 106).

13 Recent surveys include Riemer 2010, 283–335, and Baldini Lippolis 1999, 153–66. Note that the cross does not resemble the so-called *Kaiserfibeln*, on which see Schmauder 1998.

14 Proc. Bell. 25.6–7. See MacMullen 1962, 159–66; Janes 1996, 127–53; Deppert-Lippitz 2000, 39–70; Baldini Lippolis 1999, 153–54; Nechaeva 2014, 215–17 and 229–30.

15 Zahn (1913, 107) first described the cross as Byzantine, followed by Schlunk (1945, 203), reiterated in Schlunk 1947, 317, Hauschild and Schlunk 1978, and Ross in Weitzmann 1979, 172. For more recent positions on the cross's origin, see Cortés 2001, 374; Ager, 2010, 89; and García-Vuelta and Perea 2014, 269. The present chapter is part of a larger study that attends to the origins and significance of the cross in greater detail.

present discussion, it is more fruitful to think of Byzantium simply as Rome—not the city but the idea and the imperial pretence with which it was associated.[16] The cross in question may be understood as 'Byzantine' according to modern art historical taxonomies in that it was made according to traditions well-established in and characteristic of production practices of the period. But for the purpose of this essay it is far more appropriate to describe it as 'Roman' because it would have read as such in Visigothic Spain.

The very fact that the cross is composed of six large and brilliant blue sapphires, framed by pearls, and adorned even further by pendants of green glass paste and sapphire beads underscores this point. Crucial in this regard are the sumptuary laws aimed at restricting sapphires, pearls, and emeralds to the imperial context. In what Antje Bosselmann-Ruickbie has rightly characterized as 'probably the most often quoted passage on precious stones in the eastern Roman empire',[17] the sixth-century *Codex Justinianus* preserves the following mid-fifth-century decree: 'No one at all shall be allowed henceforth to fasten or insert pearls, emeralds, and sapphires on their bridles, saddles, and belts.'[18] The specified penalties for preparing 'ornaments decorated with gems and gold, which have been reserved for royal uses' range from excessive fines to capital punishment.[19] The decree aims to define the production of items with these precious materials as a court enterprise: 'royal ornaments ought to be made within My court by palace artisans, and not be prepared everywhere in private houses or offices'; with the goal of protecting 'what is sacred and worthy of adoption in Our dress and ornamentation'.[20]

A few further passages help to clarify the contours of Roman imperial ornament with respect to these precious stones. Claudian describes the

16 Pohl, Gantner, Grifoni, and Pollheimer-Mohaupt 2018; Pohl and Heydemann 2013; Bolgia, McKitterick, and Osborne 2011. See also Drauschke 2007, 53–73 and Drauschke 2008, 367–423.

17 Bosselmann-Ruickbie 2017, 295–96.

18 CJ 11.12.1 (trans. Frier 2016, 2681). Other gems are permitted, but not those; and further, 'no private individual shall be allowed to make anything from gold and gems that belongs to imperial dress and decoration'. Exceptions are made 'for matronly decorations and the wearing of both women's and men's rings'. Stolz (2010, 34–35) provides a succinct summary of the relevant sources on these gemstones. The correlation of ancient gem terminology with modern gem analysis is far from straightforward. This issue is discussed best by Thoresen 2017 and Beghelli 2017, as well as Drauschke 2010, 50–51. Following these authors and others, we should understand *hyakinthoi* as pale blue stones, modern sapphire, or blue corundum, as opposed to lapis lazuli, which is designated by *sappheiros/sappirus*. Kornbluth (2008, 299) points out that as one of the hardest of gemstones, it is rated at nine on the Mohs scale just behind diamond ('talc is one, rock crystal and amethyst seven, and diamond ten').

19 CJ 11.12.1 (trans. Frier 2016, 2681).

20 CJ 11.12.1 (trans. Frier 2016, 2681).

garments of Emperor Honorius as adorned with emeralds, amethysts, and blue hyacinths: 'Indian stones bead the robe and the costly fine-spun stuff is green with emeralds; amethysts are worked in and the brightness of Spanish gold tempers the blue of the hyacinth with its hidden fires.'[21] The association of these stones, especially sapphire, with the emperor increased their potential value for mobilization in the diplomatic arena. The decree's specification of royal use could refer to the emperor's prerogative to disseminate items made with those stones.[22] Procopius included among the symbols of authority Justinian gave to the satraps of Armenia three pale blue stones as the pendants of a fibula: 'The cloak was fastened by a golden brooch in the middle of which was a precious stone from which hung three sapphires (*iakinthoi*) by loose golden chains.'[23] Without mentioning the specific gemstones, Corippus exploits the political potential of gemstones by tracing the political import of the provenance of those affixed to the golden brooch that fastened Justin's cloak at his elevation: 'from the ends of chains hung jewels which the fortunate victory in the Gothic war produced and which Ravenna, loyal to our rulers, brought back, and which Belisarius carried from the Vandal court.'[24] Corippus thus crafts an image of imperial triumph through the spoliated jewels of the emperor's fibula.

The significance of such sumptuous gemstones was also heavily steeped in religious symbolism. Signifying both purity and the adamantine power of the kingdom of God, the sapphire was one of the twelve gemstones of the breastplate of Aaron and was the second foundation stone of the walls of heavenly Jerusalem.[25] As early as the fourth century, we encounter Christian exegesis on these biblical texts.[26] Perhaps not surprisingly, the combination

21 Claudian, *Panegyricus de quarto consulatu Honorii Augusti* 585–88 (trans. Barr 1981, 63).

22 According to the decree, no private individual should prepare anything from the category of imperial dress 'that he wishes to offer some type of gift (*munus*) as it were to the Emperor's Clemency: My Piety does not seek such gifts nor does it ask that royal haberdashery be offered by private people', CJ 11.12.1 (trans. Frier 2016, 2681).

23 Procopius, *Buildings* 3.1.21 (trans. Dewing 1940, VII, 184–85). As noted earlier, Procopius mentions golden brooches as gifts but without noting the added gemstones.

24 Corippus, *In laudem Justini* II, 122 (ed. Cameron 1976, 96, commentary on 159). Justinian's triumphs are then immediately linked to Justin's accession ('The indications of your triumphs, pious Justinian, will remain while Justin is safe and rules the world. The name of both will be sung for all the ages'). As Cameron (1976, 159) notes, these jewels allow Corippus to link the two imperial figures, and 'to invest [Justin] with all the prestige of his predecessor'.

25 Exod. 28:10–13, 17–20 and 19:10–13.

26 Namely, Epiphanios of Salamis in the fourth century and Andrew of Caesarea, Archbishop of Cappadocia in the late sixth to early seventh century. See Avgoloupi 2013, 158; Drauschke 2010, 50; Bosselmann-Ruickbie 2017, 295. See also Zwickel 2002, 50–70; Friess 1980; and Meier 1977.

of emeralds and hyacinths with pearls is the most common combination of altar offerings outlined in the *Liber Pontificalis*, as Michelle Beghelli has pointed out, further supporting the exclusive associations of these stones made plain by the *Codex Justinianus*.[27] The abundance of translucent sapphires on the cross in Madrid, the origin of which has been traced to Sri Lanka, thus suggests the most elite level of patronage and, I would argue, an imperial context replete with Old Testament symbolism and associations of sumptuary restrictions and social exclusivity. Of course, not every extant piece of adornment with sapphire should be understood as imperial in a literal sense,[28] but this unparalleled wearable cross composed of six exceptionally large and clear sapphires with pearls and pendants, without a doubt, signifies the highest order of exclusivity.

The elite, and even authoritative, associations of sapphire are amply attested in early medieval Europe. Flavius Ricimer was presented with a sapphire engraved with his portrait on the occasion of his consulship in 459.[29] While it no longer survives, a sapphire seal of Alaric II is preserved in the Kunsthistorisches Museum in Vienna. Genevra Kornbluth argued that the choice of sapphire for this seal made an implicit claim to the highest status, and, furthermore, that the Ostrogothic ruler Theodoric may have commissioned the piece for Alaric as a gift in an attempt to mediate Frankish-Visigothic tensions.[30] Pope Gregory the Great too capitalized on the prestige value of sapphire. In 603, he sent a letter and three rings as a gift to the daughter of the Lombard queen Theodelinda. While the rings have not survived, we are told that two were adorned with sapphires.[31]

In thinking about the presence in Visigothic Toledo of such a sumptuous sapphire cross that read as both Roman and Christian, it seems impossible that something of this technical virtuosity and prestigious exclusivity would have reached the Visigothic court along with anonymous gold payments as ransom or tribute, or as part of low-level frontier diplomacy or commerce. Such contexts cannot explain the transfer of such a supra-sumptuous prestige

27 Beghelli 2017, 237.

28 Bosselmann-Ruickbie (2017, 302, n. 41) has astutely pointed out that not all gems of the class prohibited in the *Codex Justinianus* should necessarily be understood as imperial, a key observation since rings and women's jewellery were exempt—see note 18 above. Janes (1996, 137–38) argues that during the fourth century the emperor's brooch became more elaborate and jewelled as a means of distinguishing his status from others. On dress and the imperial hierarchy, see Parani 2007, and Stout 1994.

29 On this no longer extant engraved gem, see Spier 2007, 27.

30 Kornbluth 2008.

31 Kornbluth 2008, 329, with bibliography at note 150.

item with imperial associations. If we acknowledge the exceptional nature of the cross in question, with an extravagance that is unparalleled—the size and quality of the sapphires and the technical virtuosity of the settings and the fact that it is a wearable cross—then we should consider an exceptional occasion for its transfer. While intermittent instances of diplomatic exchange between the Visigothic kingdom and Byzantium and the papacy afforded the movement of some symbolically significant prestige items,[32] one potential scenario stands out for the sapphire cross in question: the capture at the siege of Rome in 410 of Galla Placidia and her subsequent marriage to the king of the Visigoths. Although there is no definitive proof of a connection between her and the cross, it is worth exploring this context because of her unique position as heir to the imperial line with the potential for political legitimation.

As the daughter of Theodosius I and granddaughter of Valentinian I, Galla Placidia was doubly imperial by birth.[33] At the siege of Rome, when the temple treasures were supposedly carried off by Alaric, so too was Galla Placidia along with immeasurable treasure, 'incalculable wealth' according to Olympiodorus.[34] Because of her imperial lineage—at that moment she was the sister of the reigning emperor of the West and the aunt of the emperor ruling the East—her value far surpassed the Roman gold and silver. In 414, Galla Placidia and Athaulf were married in Narbonne and then settled in Barcelona. Accounts of their wedding stress its Romanness: in the mansion of one of Narbonne's first citizens, which was 'decorated in the Roman fashion' for the occasion, Galla Placidia 'wore imperial robes', and Athaulf was 'dressed in a military cloak and the rest of the Roman costume', by which we assume he wore and fastened by the shoulder the *chlamys* (*paludamentum*), a sartorial choice linking him to Roman generals and emperors.[35] Although short-lived, their union represented a viable and potentially legitimate imperial regime to rival the imperial administration in Ravenna—indeed it was an affront to Honorius's administration. Tellingly,

32 For example, Gregory the Great is said to have sent relics to commemorate Reccared's conversion, including a cross that contained fragments of the True Cross and the hair of John the Baptist (Greg. Mag. Reg. 9.229b; trans. Martyn 2004, II, 703). Perea (2001, 199–200) has proposed that the two arms of the large processional cross in the Guarrazar treasure may be the remains of that papal relic-cross. See Eger 2004b, 307.

33 The literature on Galla Placidia is vast, with a series of biographical monographs ranging from Oost's classic biography (1968) to Sivan's somewhat speculative study (2011).

34 Olympiodorus, fr. 6 (ed. Blockley 1983, II, 158–59).

35 Olympiodorus, fr. 24 (ed. Blockley 1983, II, 186–89). See Sivan 2011, 9–36, on contemporary Roman wedding rituals.

their child was not given a Gothic name but that of her imperial father.[36] After the death of her husband and child, both within a year, Galla Placidia returned to Honorius's court in Italy, and her story certainly did not end there. In the peripatetic narrative of Galla Placidia we see the movement of wealth beyond measure as well as the embodiment of the legitimate imperial line in her very person from Constantinople to Rome to the Visigothic court. Like precious treasure whose transfer provides authentication to its new possessor, she mediated Old Rome, New Rome, and Visigothic aspirations for authority.[37]

Could the cross now in Madrid be part of this story of plundered treasure and the potential for imperial legitimacy? Could it have once belonged to her as an imperial family heirloom or even have been part of the Roman treasure that was seized along with her? Olympiodorus relates that Galla Placidia was given some of the plunder from Rome as a wedding present. His description of Athaulf's gifts includes 'fifty handsome young men dressed in silk cloths, each bearing aloft two very large dishes, one full of gold, the other full of precious—or rather priceless—stones, which had been carried off by the Goths at the sack of Rome'.[38] The sapphire cross in the Guarrazar treasure could be one of those priceless stones that once belonged to Galla Placidia, coming to the Visigothic court when she did but not returning with her to the imperial court. As an heirloom, it could have been passed through an array of unknown hands over time before ultimately finding itself installed as a central feature of the Visigothic royal votive ensemble.[39] Of course, this

36 The choice of the name Theodosius seems particularly charged in light of the fact that Honorius did not have children. See Díaz 1999, 328–29 and Dunn 2015, 380.

37 Anthropologist Annette Weiner offers a compelling model of 'cosmological authentication' for theorizing this phenomenon. See Weiner 1992 and note 55 below. In stressing the significance of Galla Placidia for legitimating authority, I do not mean to suggest her complicity in such an agenda of legitimation. Leonard (2019) argues that Galla Placidia was a war captive forcibly married to her captor as a 'spear-won bride' and outlines the ethical stakes of describing her otherwise. At the other end of the scholarly spectrum, Dunn (2015) has stressed her agency over victimhood, proposing that she took advantage of her position in Gothic captivity to rival the authority of Honorius and shape the negotiations between the Goths and the empire in the future.

38 Olympiodorus, fr. 24 (ed. Blockley 1983, II, 186–89). Leonard (2019) reads a more sinister message of triumphant hegemony in this passage that draws into alignment Galla Placidia and the nameless men as 'human gold' alongside priceless material riches.

39 It is impossible to account for the location of the cross before it was added to the votive crown of Recceswinth in the mid-seventh century. It may have been kept separate from the official treasure of the Visigoths, portions of which were moved, captured, and lost over the years. Alternatively, it may have been part of the treasure but was safeguarded at moments of instability when the treasure was under threat. Tensions over particular treasury items and their

cannot be proven. Regardless, I would like to propose a similar semantic value for both the person of Galla Placidia, as the physical embodiment and potential of imperial legitimacy, and the cross itself, as the material manifestation of the prestige and pretence of Roman imperium. Both Galla Placidia and the sapphire cross were physical symbols of Rome—they read as imperial. Further, in the Visigothic kingdom, their marriages—short-lived to Athaulf or long-lived to Recceswinth's crown—suggest the possibility of a kind of *translatio imperii*, the starting of a new empire by connecting it in generational and material terms to the older one. In seventh-century Toledo, however, the cross was not worn as adornment but was attached to a crown that was dedicated to a sanctuary. This repurposing complicates the sense of *translatio* in compelling ways, calling into question traditional narratives about Byzantine influence.

The Votive Crown and the Question of Byzantine Influence

Treasure hoards in Iberia constitute an exceptional material archive that complements our textual evidence for the Visigothic practice of offering votive crowns and crosses to churches.[40] Most scholars understand this Visigothic practice as an adoption of Byzantine custom that signalled an embrace of eastern prestige. Diaz and Valverde, among others, have traced this 'prestige policy' back to Leovigild (r. 568–586) who, as Isidore of Seville famously claimed, first distinguished himself as a king in visual terms,

potential loss are made plain by the story of the *missorium* of Aetius as described by Fredegar. In his reading of the narrative, Wood (2000, 312–13) argues that the precious tray, which had been acquired in the mid-fifth century, had become so central to a sense of Visigothic memory that by the mid-seventh century it could not be alienated from the treasury. In other words, the treasure was a malleable collection that involved some degree of divisibility and alienation in addition to augmentation. On the conception of treasure, see the conclusion below and Hardt 1998 and 2009.

40 In addition to Julian of Toledo's *History of Wamba* (cited below), the Visigothic *Liber Ordinum* includes blessings for the dedications of crowns (ed. Férotin 1904, cols. 165–66). The textual record, which is surveyed comprehensively by Bronisch (1999) and Arce (2001a and 2001b), is complemented by the crowns found in both Guarrazar and Torredonjimeno. On the latter see Perea 2009. Unlike official and wearable insignia, the crowns from both these hoards were votive in nature, offerings to a church, although which church, or churches, remains unclear. It is assumed that the crowns and the crosses were deaccessioned from their sanctuary (or sanctuaries) in advance of the early eighth-century Arab conquests. This point, however, remains conjectural. It should be noted that the better state of preservation of the Guarrazar pieces suggests that they were buried carefully, as opposed to the items in the Torredonjimeno treasure. For a comparison of the two, see García-Vuelta and Perea 2014.

meeting his people enthroned and in regal dress.[41] He also first minted coins in his own name and made concerted efforts towards religious unification, which was ultimately secured by Reccared (r. 586–601), under whom we see the firm establishment of Visigothic rule in Hispania and the distinct sacralization of royalty. After his conversion to Nicene Christianity, Reccared dedicated a gold crown in the name of Felix of Girona.[42] Like Reccared's crown dedication, the royal votives of the Guarrazar treasure are generally seen as part of the prestige programme in so far as they convey with sumptuous visual clarity the cultivation of the kind of sacrosanct imperial ritual we associate with Byzantium.

The symbolic cultivation of the Visigoths as heirs to Rome, notably, is set against a political backdrop of tensions with New Rome. It was under King Swinthila, whose crown was stolen from the Royal Armoury, that the Byzantines were expelled fully from the peninsula (625).[43] His votive crown that draws on the visual splendour of Byzantium, therefore, came at the precise moment of Visigothic victory over Byzantium. This prompts us to recognize that the emulation of ritual practices often associated with the eastern empire is not indicative of subservience but rather lends itself to a model of succession or even supersession. In other words, we might think more productively about the 'Byzantinizing' of Visigothic royalty in sequential terms: in laying claim to the mantle of what went before the Visigoths styled themselves as new Romans. Notably, John of Biclarum characterized Reccared as a New Constantine, and the stakes of this invocation have been elucidated particularly well by Santiago Castellanos.[44]

In thinking about the development of a prestige policy at the Visigothic court, however, the particular configuration of the votive crowns of the Guarrazar treasure demands a closer look. While the practice of displaying royal crowns in sacred spaces certainly suggests the adoption

41 Isid. Hist. Goth. 51 in particular and the question of the imperialization of the Visigothic court more generally have generated considerable scholarship. See, for example, Diaz and Valverde 2000, Valverde Castro 2000, Arce 2001a, 2001b, and 2004, and Eger 2009, who surveys the archaeological and art historical evidence.

42 Hist. Wamb. reg. 26. In narrating how the usurper Paul took the crown that had been offered by Reccared Julian stresses that a votive crown should be left in the sacred site of its dedication. As vivid shorthand for condemning a particular rule, votive crown violations are a trope in Byzantine sources as well. The demise of Leo IV after taking for himself the crown dedicated to Hagia Sophia, for example, is narrated in multiple sources.

43 Barbero and Loring (2005, 350–53) characterize the 'most significant accomplishment' of the early seventh-century Visigothic kings as 'the destruction of Byzantine power in the peninsula'. See Vallejo Girvés 2013.

44 Castellanos 2012.

Figure 5.4: Crown of King Suinthila, Guarrazar Treasure (now lost). Photo: Biblioteca del Ateneo de Madrid.

of a pan-Mediterranean prestige practice, for which Constantinople was considered the epicentre and model that was emulated far and wide, sometimes scholars have overlooked the truly inventive nature of the Visigothic golden offerings themselves. In other words, the votive practice embodied by these sumptuous ensembles is a far cry from simple imitation, let alone passive influence. If the ritual practice of votive royal offerings brings the Visigoths into the more longstanding traditions of sacralized

Figure 5.5: Crown of King Recceswinth with Cross, Guarrazar Treasure (Museo Arqueológico Nacional, Madrid). Museo Arqueológico Nacional, Inv. C663. Photo: Fundación ITMA, Santiago Relanzón.

rule represented by Byzantium, it also, and even more so I would argue, represents something startlingly new. The manner in which the crowns invoke their royal donors is indicative of this daring departure. The now lost crown of King Swinthila and that of Recceswinth audaciously spell out royal names, titles, and actions in inset cloisonné letters dangling from their lower edges. (See Figures 5.4 and 5.5.) The glimmering garnet letters enunciate their status as royal offerings in the same way: they each specify their donor's name and rank as king (*rex*) as well as the action of giving.[45] The crowns thus testify to their donors' elevated status as kings and also to their humble piety by expressing their acts of generosity. By strategically combining superiority and humility simultaneously in this way the letters evoke the essence of the gift as theorized by anthropologists since Marcel Mauss.[46] In spelling out the donors' acts of prestation, they make the dedications legible in a performative manner. By this, I mean that the letters at once enact and memorialize their status as sacred donations, in what could easily serve as an illustration of J. L. Austin's conception of a linguistic 'speech act'—where words that when uttered bind, like 'I do' in a wedding ceremony.[47]

Turning from modern linguistics to medieval sources, Isidore of Seville theorizes in more specific terms the conceptual logic of donation. In book six of the *Etymologies*, Isidore discusses sacred and earthly economies of prestation. He describes the dedication of a gift 'made of gold or silver or any other valuable' as follows: 'That which is dedicated (*dedicare*) is "given with speaking" (*dare*, "give" and *dicere*, "speak"), whence it is so called.'[48] The notion of a dedication speaking explains the Visigothic votive crowns perfectly, elaborating the enunciative potential of these sacred gifts. In the act of giving the crowns to the sanctuaries, they speak, ideally in perpetuity.

The format of these locutionary acts is also significant. The names and actions of the Visigothic kings assume the position of the Byzantine emperor's *prependoulia* (or *pendilia*)—the long pearl strands that hung from either side of the imperial crown.[49] In Byzantium, legends surrounded the emperor's

45 +SV[IN]T[H]IL[A]NVS REX OFFE[RE]T and +RECCESVINTHUS REX OFFERET. See Perea 2009, 61, and Eger 2004a on the former, and Perea 2009, 35 on the latter. On the R still in Paris, see Metropolitan Museum of Art 1993, 53–55, and Caillet 1985, 218–27. Unlike the rest of our evidence for medieval votive crowns, those from Visigothic Spain are distinguished by their inclusion of letters that spell out the donations in this way. This unprecedented format is represented both by the Guarrazar treasure and the Torredonjimeno hoard, which includes some letter fragments that must have once been attached to votive crowns in a similar manner (see note 40 above). The Torredonjimeno material is fragmentary and less sumptuous in quality, but it broadens our context for this innovative way of articulating donation.

46 On the relevance of the anthropology of gift-giving for medieval Art History, see Hilsdale 2012.

47 Austin 1975.

48 Isid. Etym. 6.19.24–32 (trans. Barney, Lewis, Beach, and Berghof 2006, 148).

49 De los Ríos (1861) focused on the *pendilia* as a distinctively 'byzantinizing' aspect of the crowns.

prependoulia; their length was associated with the longevity and strength of his rule. For example, in the *Oneirocriticon*, the tenth-century handbook of dream interpretation, the dream of an imperial crown's cut pearl strands is explained as a portend of an untimely demise:

> If anyone whatever dreams that he was wearing a royal crown that had been elegantly placed on his head and embroidered with gems and pearls, he will have dominion and glory analogous to the crown; and if the gems and pearls were hanging down like earrings, his dominion will be in accordance with their length and beauty. If the king dreams that the pendants of his crown were cut off, his reign will be chaotic [*atachia*] and short lived.[50]

Here the dangling strands of pearls stand in metonymically for dominion, their length proportional to one's reign. The royal crowns of the Guarrazar treasure translate the conception of pearl *prependoulia* as a metonym for rule into garnet speech acts.

Latin letters dangle like *prependoulia* from chains attached to the base of each royal crown. However, they encircle the entire circumference thereby precluding the possibility of wearing the crown, marking it definitively as an object of display to adorn a sacred site rather than a royal body. In other words, typologically the crowns imply wearing but their format precludes the possibility of being worn. Further, these *pendilia*-like letter strings add a sonic dimension—or at least the potential for sound tied to movement, like tintinnabula. Even without a faint breeze to set the golden strings into motion, which would create sound, anyone literate and nearby straining to make sense of the garnet letter combinations would, presumably, give voice to them at the same time. In this way, the crowns invite their viewers to inspect, investigate, circumambulate, and even to speak audibly of their regal and generous donors. They thus prompt interpretation and commemoration, making the momentary audible presence of their named donors a permanent possibility in the present and for the future.

The royal votive crowns' innovative format for this invocation transforms what could be seen as an emulation of Byzantine models into a charged reformulation that lays claim to the ritual practice by associating it indelibly with specific Visigothic rulers and, in this way, establishing it firmly as a Visigothic phenomenon. This proposal gains further traction when we consider the longer history of the cross that is now suspended at the

50 *Achmetis Oneirocriticon* (ed. Drexl 1925, 202; trans. Oberhelman 1991, 219). For the context, authorship, and sources, see Mavroudi 2002.

centre of the Recceswinth crown, which brings the discussion from the more abstract idea of Byzantine 'influence' to the concrete consideration of precious treasure and its ability to signal transitions of authority.

Conclusions: Treasure and Supersession

Fully mobilized for dowries and diplomacy, as tribute, inheritance, and splendour, treasure was, as one scholar put it, the king's 'credit rating and his means of maintaining suitable splendour'.[51] The plundering, hoarding, and parsing of treasure became a *topos* in narratives of legitimation for the Visigoths as an essential element of collective identity, co-terminus with royal authority itself: the court was where the treasure was, and the king ideally preserved and augmented it. In describing Theodoric II's daily routine, Sidonius Apollinaris claimed that he inspected his treasure and stable on a daily basis.[52] Conversely the absence of treasure meant instability and ruin, as when it was taken to Ravenna following the Gothic defeat at Vouillé (507) or when Agila (r. 549–554) after his defeat at Córdoba lost his son, much of his army, and 'the whole treasure with its renowned riches'.[53]

Rhetorically speaking, treasure may be the perfect metonym for conveying the idea of supersession. Heirlooms, *ornamenta*,[54] and *ars sacra* are prestige items cherished by their owners and viewers over time. Whether worn on the body, held near, or viewed at a distance as objects of cathected devotion or wonder, treasure was protected and hoarded, kept out of circulation.[55] So too was treasure inherited, given, or taken at key moments of transition. It is no wonder that the genealogy of jewels figures so prominently in the sources. Recall that Corippus describes the jewels of the emperor's fibula as plunder and tribute from the Gothic wars. In fastening his *chlamys* with a brooch

51 Clarke 2012, 90.

52 Sid. Apol. Ep. 2.3–4.

53 Díaz 1999, 335; Isid. Hist. Goth. 45. See also note 39 above.

54 Hardt 1998, 268, offers an expansive definition of *ornamenta* to encompass 'the whole spectrum of decorative objects known from the particularly richly furnished graves and hoard finds of the period'. See also Hardt 2009, 79–80, and note 39 above. Treasure was also donated to churches of course, and while the topic of church treasuries is beyond the scope of this chapter, the medieval Iberian treasury project, on which see Martin 2020, merits special mention.

55 This understanding of treasure encapsulates perfectly what Weiner (1992) would call an inalienable possession, whose value lies beyond its exchangeability. For Weiner, inalienable possessions serve as markers of hierarchy and rank rather than equivalence, and they 'cosmologically authenticate' their owners over time. Pick (2018) has developed these ideas most fruitfully within the context of medieval Spain.

adorned with these historic jewels at his elevation, Justin was invested with the precious relics of his father's military successes. Jewels in this panegyric index the accrual and transmission of imperial power—power that was consolidated by battle across the Mediterranean and then transmitted to the next emperor. Ancient jewels connect Theodosian and Augustan Rome in Claudian's *epithalamion* for the marriage of Honorius and Maria: the groom selected as his gifts for his bride 'the jewels once worn by noble Livia of old and all the proud women of the imperial house'.[56] The late fourth-century imperial groom possessed the ancient Roman treasure—his patrimony—to adorn his bride, who would wear the Augustan *ornamenta* on her body, palpably marking her as a new Augusta. Olympiodorus too, again, drew on the power of old 'precious' and 'priceless' stones for new unions in his description of Athaulf's gifts for Galla Placidia.[57] Here the heirlooms stress not only the Gothic merging with the Roman-Theodosian line but also a claim to that imperial line: the Gothic king was situated structurally in the position of the emperor in that he now possessed the ancient imperial ornament to adorn his Roman bride.

Like treasure, ritual and ceremonial culture more broadly could provide a visual language for making historical claims of supersession. In adopting royal votive practice, the Visigoths partook in the pan-Mediterranean embrace of sacrosanct prestige associated with Constantinople. But, as this essay has demonstrated, the unprecedented format of the royal crowns of the Guarrazar treasure suggests something much more radical. Rather than simply following Roman (Byzantine) precedent, the votive crowns of Visigothic kings outdo those hallowed models. In drawing on the ritual language of royal sacred offerings, they make a bold statement about Visigothic authority by literally and performatively linking their donor's names, rank, and pious generosity. Moreover, the addition to Recceswinth's crown of the cross that I have suggested would have read legibly as Roman makes a further temporal claim: as inheritor of Rome he dedicated his authority to the church.

This reading, to be clear, does not depend on the cross having been associated with Galla Placidia; however, it does ask that we understand the sapphire cross clasp as representing an older Roman tradition and legible as such in seventh-century Toledo. I am convinced that this was the case. In our contemporary moment, audiences accustomed to loudly proclaimed and transparent symbols of luxury may be less conditioned to appreciate

56 *Claudian* I (ed. and trans. Platnauer 1922 [1998], 242–43).

57 See note 38 above.

subtle differences of technique or to recognize fine-tuned thresholds for luxury and hierarchy. But to early medieval eyes the sapphire cross, with its surfeit of luminous stones, must have looked like an imperial heirloom—an ancient but still Christian treasure. And the marrying of such an older Roman sapphire cross to the crown of the new Visigothic king encapsulates the idea of supersession with gem-like clarity: as it was suspended from the centre of the royal Visigothic crown, the cross was converted from an object of adornment—one that bore distinct associations of Roman exclusivity—to the centrepiece of a royal votive ensemble. Dissociated from a Roman elite body, the cross came to stand in for the body of the Visigothic king, and it assumed the place where the king's face would be if it were worn. But, again, the crown could not be worn because the *prependoulia*-like letters—also a translation of the idea of 'Rome'—have precluded that possibility, leaving the viewer to ruminate instead on the name, status, and piety of that physically absent king.

Bibliography

Achmet, *Oneirocriticon*, ed. by F. Drexl, *Achmetis Oneirocriticon* (Leipzig, 1925)

Ager, Barry, 'Byzantine Influences on Visigothic Jewellery', in *Intelligible Beauty: Recent Research on Byzantine Jewellery*, ed. by Chris Entwistle and Noel Adams (London: British Museum, 2010), pp. 72–82

Arce, Javier, 'El conjunto votivo de Guarrazar: función y significado', in *El tesoro visigodo de Guarrazar*, ed. by Alicia Perea (Madrid: Consejo Superior de Investigaciones Científicas, 2001a), pp. 347–54

Arce, Javier, '*Leovigildus rex* y el ceremonial de la corte visigótica', in *Visigoti e Langobardi. Atti del Seminario* (*Roma 28–29 aprile 1997*), ed. by Javier Arce and Pablo Delogu (Florence: All'Insegna del Giglio, 2001b), pp. 79–92

Arce, Javier, 'Ceremonial visigodo/ceremonial "bizantino": un tópico historigráfico', in *Bizancio y la península ibérica: De la antigüedad tardía a la edad moderna*, ed. by Inmaculada Pérez Martín and Pedro Bádenas de la Peña (Madrid: Consejo Superior de Investigaciones Científicas, 2004), pp. 101–15

Austin, J. L., *How to Do Things with Words*, 2nd ed. (Cambridge, MA: Harvard University Press, 1975)

Avgoloupi, Eleutheria, *Simbologia delle gemme imperiali bizantine nella tradizione simbolica mediterranea delle pietre preziose* (*secoli I–XV d.C.*) (Spoleto: Fondazione Centro italiano di studi sull'alto Medioevo, 2013)

Baldini Lippolis, Isabella, *L'oreficeria nell'impero di Costantinopoli: tra IV e VII secolo* (Bari: Edipuglia, 1999)

Balmesda, Luis, 'De la Historia del Hallazgo y la Arqueología de Guarrazar', in *El tesoro visigodo de Guarrazar*, ed. by Alicia Perea (Madrid: Consejo Superior de Investigaciones Científicas, 2001), pp. 63–117

Barbero, A., and M. I. Loring, 'The Catholic Visigothic Kingdom', in *The New Cambridge Medieval History*, vol. 1, *c. 500–c. 700*, ed. by Paul Fouracre (Cambridge: Cambridge University Press, 2005), pp. 346–70

Barney, Stephen A., W. J. Lewis, J. A. Beach, and Oliver Berghof, *The Etymologies of Isidore of Seville* (Cambridge: Cambridge University Press, 2006)

Beghelli, Michelle, 'From the Bible to the *Liber Pontificalis*: Gems and Precious Stones in the Early Medieval Churches: Combinations, Colours and Contexts', in *Gemstones in the First Millennium AD: Mines, Trade, Workshops and Symbolism*, ed. by Alexandra Hilgner, Susanne Greiff, and Dieter Quast (Mainz: Verlag des Römisch-Germanischen Zentralmuseums, 2017), pp. 233–75

Bolgia, Claudia, Rosamond McKitterick, and John Osborne (eds), *Rome Across Time and Space: Cultural Transmission and the Exchange of Ideas, c. 500–1400* (Cambridge: Cambridge University Press, 2011)

Bosselmann-Ruickbie, Antje, 'The Symbolism of Byzantine Gemstones: Written Sources, Objects and Sympathetic Magic in Byzantium', in *Gemstones in the First Millennium AD: Mines, Trade, Workshops and Symbolism*, ed. by Alexandra Hilgner, Susanne Greiff, and Dieter Quast (Mainz: Römisch-Germanisches Zentralmuseum, 2017), pp. 293–306

Bronisch, Alexander Pierre, 'Krönungsritus und Kronenbrauch im Westgotenreich von Toledo', in *Zeitschrift der Savigny-Stiftung für Rechtsgeschichte, Germanistische Abteilung*, 116 (1999), 37–86

Caillet, Jean-Pierre (ed.), *L'Antiquité classique, le haut Moyen âge et Byzance au Musée de Cluny* (Paris: Éd. De la Réunion des musées nationaux, 1985)

Castellanos, Santiago, 'Creating New Constantines at the End of the Sixth Century', in *Historical Research*, 85.230 (November 2012), 556–75

Clarke, Nicola, *The Muslim Conquest of Iberia: Medieval Arabic Narratives* (New York, NY: Routledge, 2012)

Claudian, *Epithalamium de nuptiis Honorii Augusti*, ed. by Maurice Platnauer, *Claudian*, 2 vols (Cambridge, MA: Harvard University Press, 1922 [1998])

Claudian, *Panegyricus de quarto consulatu Honorii Augusti*, ed. by William Barr, *Claudian's Panegyric on the Fourth Consulate of Honorius. Introduction, Text, Translation and Commentary* (Liverpool: Francis Cairns, 1981)

Corippus, *In laudem Iustini Augusti minoris*, ed. by Averil Cameron, *Corippus. In laudem Iustini Augusti minoris* (London: Athlone Press, 1976)

Cortés, Miguel, 'Influencias bizantinas', in *El tesoro visigodo de Guarrazar*, ed. by Alicia Perea (Madrid: Consejo Superior de Investigaciones Científicas, 2001), pp. 367–75

Deppert-Lippitz, Barbara, 'A Late Antique Crossbow Fibula in The Metropolitan Museum of Art', in *Metropolitan Museum of Art Journal*, 35 (2000), 39–70

Dewing, H. B. and Glanville Downey (trans.), *Procopius, On Buildings* (Cambridge, MA: Harvard University Press, 1940)

Díaz, Pablo C., 'Visigothic Political Institutions', in *The Visigoths from the Migration Period to the Seventh Century: An Ethnographic Perspective*, ed. by Peter Heather (Woodbridge: Boydell, 1999), pp. 321–56

Díaz, Pablo C., and M. R. Valverde, 'The Theoretical Strength and Practical Weakness of the Visigothic Monarchy of Toledo', in *Rituals of Power from Late Antiquity to the Early Middle Ages*, ed. by Frans Theuws and Janet L. Nelson (Leiden: Brill, 2000), pp. 59–93

Drauschke, Jörg, '"Byzantine" and "Oriental" Imports in the Merovingian Empire from the Second Half of the Fifth to the Beginning of the Eighth Century', in *Incipient Globalization?: Long Distance Contacts in the Sixth Century*, ed. by Anthea Harris (Oxford: Archaeopress, 2007), pp. 53–73

Drauschke, Jörg, 'Zur Herkunft und Vermittlung "byzantinischer Importe" der Merowingerzeit in Nordwesteuropa', in *Zwischen Spätantike und Frühmittelalter. Archäologie des 4. bis 7. Jahrhunderts im Westen*, ed. by Sebasstian Brather (Berlin and New York, NY: Walter De Gruyter, 2008), pp. 367–423

Drauschke, Jörg, 'Byzantine Jewellery?: Amethyst Beads in East and West during the Early Byzantine Period', in *Intelligible Beauty: Recent Research on Byzantine Jewellery*, ed. by Chris Entwistle and Noel Adams (London: British Museum, 2010), pp. 50–60

Dunn, Geoffrey D., 'Flavius Constantius, Galla Placidia, and the Aquitanian Settlement of the Goths', in *Phoenix*, 69 (2015), 376–93

Eger, Christoph, 'Krone und Kreuz König Svinthilas. Westgotische Hofkunst und "Plate-Inlaying" im 6. Und 7. Jahrhundert', in *Madrider Mitteilungen*, 45 (2004a), 449–506

Eger, Christoph, 'Review of Perea, ed., *El tesoro visigodo de Guarrazar*', in *Germania*, 82 (2004b), 305–10

Eger, Christoph, 'Zur Imperialisierung des westgotischen Königtums aus archäologischer Sicht', in *Spolien im Umkreis der Macht. Akten der Tagung in Toledo 2006*, ed. by Thomas G. Schattner and Fernando Valdés Fernández (Mainz: P. von Zabern, 2009), pp. 151–69

Frier, Bruce W. (ed.), *The Codex of Justinian: A New Annotated Translation, with Parallel Latin and Greek Text Based on a Translation by Justice Fred H. Blume*, 3 vols (Cambridge: Cambridge University Press, 2016)

Friess, Gerda, *Edelsteine im Mittelalter: Wandel und Kontinuität durch zwölf Jahrhunderte* (Hildesheim: Gerstenberg, 1980)

García-Vuelta, Óscar, and Alicia Perea, 'Guarrazar: El taller orfebre visigodo', in *Anales de Historia del Arte*, 24 (2014), 245–71

Gruat, Cédric, and Lucía Martínez, *L'échange: Les dessous d'une négociation artistique entre la France et l'Espagne, 1940–1941* (Paris: Armand Colin, 2011)

Hardt, Matthias, 'Royal Treasures and Representation in the Early Middle Ages', in *Strategies of Distinction: The Construction of Ethnic Communities, 300–800*, ed. by Walter Pohl and Helmut Reimitz (Leiden and Boston, MA: Brill, 1998), pp. 255–80

Hardt, Matthias, *Gold und Herrschaft: Die Schätze europäischer Könige und Fürsten im ersten Jahrtausend* (Berlin: Akademie Verlag, 2009)

Hauschild, Theodor, and Helmut Schlunk, *Die Denkmäler der frühchristlichen und westgotischen Zeit* (Mainz: P. v. Zabern, 1978)

Hilsdale, Cecily J., 'Gift', in *Studies in Iconography*, 33 (2012), 171–82

Hübener, Wolfgang, *Die Goldblattkreuze des frühen Mittelalters*, Veröffentlichung des Alemannischen Instituts 37 (Bühl and Baden: Verlag Konkordia, 1975)

Janes, Dominic, 'The Golden Clasp of the Late Roman State', in *Early Medieval Europe*, 5.2 (1996), 127–53

Jülich, Theo, 'Gemmenkreuze. Die Farbigkeit ihres Edelsteinbesatzes bis zum 12. Jahrhundert', in *Aachener Kunstblätter*, 54.55 (1986–1987), 99–258

Kornbluth, Genevra, 'The Seal of Alaric, *Rex Gothorum*', in *Early Medieval Europe*, 16.3 (2008), 299–332

Lasteyrie, Ferdinand de, *Description du Trésor de Guarrazar, accompagnée de recherches sur toutes les questions archéologiques qui s'y rattachent* (Paris: Gide, 1860)

Leonard, Victoria, 'Galla Placidia as "Human Gold": Consent and Autonomy in the Sack of Rome, CE 410', in *Gender & History*, 31.2 (2019), 334–52

Liber Ordinum, ed. by M. Férotin, *Le Liber ordinum en usage dans l'eglise Wisigothique et Mozarabe d'Espagne du cinquième au onzèeme siècle* (Paris: Firmin-Didot, 1904)

López Quiroga, Jorge, Jorge Morín de Pablos, and Artemio Martínez Tejera (eds), *El tiempo de los bárbaros: pervivencia y transformación en Galia e Hispania (s.s. v–vi d.C.)*, Zona arqueológica 11 (Alcalá de Henares: Museo Arqueológico Regional, 2010)

MacMullen, Ramsay, 'The Emperor's Largesse', in *Latomus*, 21 (1962), 159–66

Martin, Therese (ed.), *The Medieval Iberian Treasury in the Context of Cultural Interchange (Expanded Edition)* (Leiden and Boston, MA: Brill, 2020)

Martyn, John R. C. (trans.), *The Letters of Gregory the Great*, 3 vols (Toronto: Pontifical Institute of Mediaeval Studies, 2004)

Mavroudi, Maria, *A Byzantine Book on Dream Interpretation: The 'Oneirocriticon' of Achmet and its Arabic Sources* (Leiden and Boston, MA: Brill, 2002)

Meier, Christel, *Gemma spiritalis. Methode und Gebrauch der Edelsteinallegorese vom frühen Christentum bis ins 18. Jahrhundert* (Munich: W. Fink, 1977)

Metropolitan Museum of Art, *The Art of Medieval Spain, A.D. 500–1200* (New York, NY: The Metropolitan Museum of Art, 1993)

Moreno Martín, Francisco J., 'Visigoths, Crowns, Crosses and the Construction of Spain', in *Memoirs of the American Academy in Rome*, 62 (2017), 41–64

Nechaeva, Ekaterina, *Embassies, Negotiations, Gifts: Systems of East Roman Diplomacy in Late Antiquity* (Stuttgart: Franz Steiner Verlag, 2014)

Oberhelman, Steven M., *The Oneirocriticon of Achmet: A Medieval Greek and Arabic Treatise on the Interpretation of Dreams* (Lubbock, TX: Texas Tech University Press, 1991)

Olympiodorus, *Fragmenta*, ed. and trans. by R. C. Blockley, *The Fragmentary Classicising Historians of the Later Roman Empire: Eunapius, Olympiodorus, Priscus and Malchus*, 2 vols (Liverpool: Francis Cairns, 1981–1983)

Oost, Stewart Irvin, *Galla Placidia Augusta: A Biographical Essay* (Chicago, IL: University of Chicago Press, 1968)

Palol, Pedro de, *Hispanic Art of the Visigothic Period* (New York, NY: Tudor, 1968)

Parani, Maria G., 'Defining Personal Space: Dress and Accessories in Late Antiquity', in *Objects in Context, Objects in Use*, ed. by Luke Lavan, Ellen Swift, and Toon Putzeys (Leiden and Boston, MA: Brill, 2007), pp. 497–529

Perea, Alicia (ed.), *El tesoro visigodo de Guarrazar* (Madrid: Consejo Superior de Investigaciones Científicas, 2001)

Perea, Alicia (ed.), *El tesoro visigodo de Torredonjimeno* (Madrid: Consejo Superior de Investigaciones Científicas, 2009)

Pick, Lucy K., *Her Father's Daughter: Gender, Power, and Religion in the Early Spanish Kingdoms* (Ithaca, NY: Cornell University Press, 2018)

Pohl, Walter, Clemens Gantner, Cinzia Grifoni, and Marianne Pollheimer-Mohaupt, *Transformations of Romanness in the Early Middle Ages: Regions and Identities* (Berlin: De Gruyter, 2018)

Pohl, Walter, and Gerda Heydemann, *Post-Roman Transitions: Christian and Barbarian Identities in the Early Medieval West* (Turnhout: Brepols, 2013)

Riemer, Ellen, 'Byzantinische und romanisch-mediterrane Fibeln in der Forschung', in *Byzanz – das Römerreich im Mittelalter I: Wedt der Ideen, Welt der Ding* (Mainz: Verlag des Römisch-Germanischen Zentralmuseums, 2010), pp. 283–335

Ríos, José Amador de los, *El arte latino-bizantino en España y las coronas visigodas de Guarrazar: ensayo histórico-crítico* (Madrid: Imprenta nacional, 1861)

Rojas Rodríguez-Malo, Juan Manuel, Christoph Eger, Raúl Catalán, and L. García, 'Wo einst goldene Kronen und Kreuze verborgen wurden – Neue Ausgrabungen in Guarrazar (Vorbericht zu den Kampagnen 2013 und 2014)', in *Oppidum-civitas-urbs: Städteforschung auf der iberischen Halbinsel zwischen Rom und al-Andalus*, ed. by Sabine Panzram (Münster: Lit-Verlag, 2017), pp. 563–95

Schlunk, Helmut, 'Relaciones Entre La Península Ibérica y Bizancio Durante La Época Visigoda', in *Archivo Español de Arqueología*, 18.60 (1945), 177–204

Schlunk, Helmut, *Ars Hispaniae: historia universal del arte hispánico* (Madrid: Editorial Plus-Ultra, 1947)

Schmauder, Michael, 'Imperial Representation or Barbaric Imitation?: The Imperial Brooches (Kaiserfibeln)', in *Strategies of Distinction: The Construction of Ethnic Communities 300–800*, ed. by Walter Pohl and Helmut Reimitz (Leiden and Boston, MA: Brill, 1998), pp. 281–96

Sivan, Hagith, *Galla Placidia: The Last Roman Empress* (Oxford: Oxford University Press, 2011)

Sommerard, M. Edmond du, 'Les couronnes d'or du roi goth Receswinthus trouvées a Guarrazar', in *Le Monde illustré* (February 1859), 106–7, 112

Spier, Jeffrey, *Late Antique and Early Christian Gems* (Wiesbaden: Reichert, 2007)

Stolz, Yvonne, 'The Evidence for Jewellery Production in Constantinople in the Early Byzantine Period', in *Intelligible Beauty: Recent Research on Byzantine Jewellery*, ed. by Chris Entwistle and Noël Adams (London: The Trustees of the British Museum, 2010), pp. 33–39

Stout, Ann M., 'Jewelry as a Symbol of Status in the Roman Empire', in *The World of Roman Costume*, ed. by Judith Lynn Sebesta and Larissa Bonfante (Madison, WI: University of Wisconsin Press, 1994), pp. 77–100

Thoresen, Lisbet, 'Archaeogemmology and Ancient Literary Sources on Gems and their Origins', in *Gemstones in the First Millennium AD: Mines, Trade, Workshops and Symbolism*, ed. by Alexandra Hilgner, Susanne Greiff, and Dieter Quast (Mainz: Verlag des Römisch-Germanischen Zentralmuseums, 2017), pp. 155–217

Vallejo Girvés, Margarita, *Hispania y Bizancio: Una relación desconocida* (Madrid: Akal, 2013)

Valverde Castro, María Rosario, *Ideología, simbolismo y ejercicio del poder real en la monarquía visigoda. Un proceso de cambio* (Salamanca: Ediciones Universidad de Salamanca, 2000)

Weiner, Annette B., *Inalienable Possessions: The Paradox of Keeping-While-Giving* (Berkeley, CA: University of California Press, 1992)

Weitzmann, Kurt (ed.), *Age of Spirituality: Late Antique and Early Christian Art, Third to Seventh Century* (New York, NY: Metropolitan Museum of Art, 1979)

Wood, Ian N., 'The Exchange of Gifts Among the Late Antique Aristocracy', in *El disco de Teodosio*, ed. by Martín Almagro-Gorbea, José Maria Álvarez Martínez, José Maria Blázquez Martínez, and Salvador Rovira (Madrid: Publicaciones del Gabinete de Antigüedades, 2000), pp. 301–14

Zahn, Robert, 'Die Sammlung Friedrich Ludwig von Gans Im Antiquarium', in *Amtliche Berichte Aus Den Königlichen Kunstsammlungen*, 35.3 (1913), 66–160

Zwickel, Wolfgang, 'Die Edelsteine im Brustschild des Hohepriesters und beim himmlischen Jerusalem', in *Edelsteine in der Bibel*, ed. by Wolfgang Zwickel (Mainz: P. von Zabern, 2002), pp. 50–70

About the Author

Cecily J. Hilsdale is Associate Professor of Medieval Art and Architecture at McGill University, and author of *Byzantine Art and Diplomacy in an Age of Decline* (Cambridge, 2014). She specializes in the arts of Byzantium and the Mediterranean, including Byzantine luxury items as diplomatic gifts and the dissemination of eastern styles, techniques, iconographies, and ideologies of imperium.

6 Capitalhood in the Visigothic Kingdom

Damián Fernández[1]

Abstract

Visigothic scholarship has traditionally seen in the choice of Toledo as 'capital' of the kingdom a feature of *imitatio imperii*. Such imitation of Rome or Constantinople would have coincided with changing ideas of capitalhood among Visigothic elites, who progressively abandoned the idea of a 'head city' as the seat of a king (*sedes regia*) and embraced the notion of a royal city (*urbs regia*)—that is, a city with its own intrinsic central status. This chapter challenges this interpretation in two ways. First, the idea of Toledo as *urbs regia* grew within Toledan church circles to affirm the city's primacy within the ecclesiastical province. Thus, strategic use rather than imitation provides a better framework of understanding. Second, it is very likely that this concept of Toledo was not universally accepted; in royal circles and other important cities, the *sedes regia* view probably prevailed.

Keywords: Toledo; capitals; metropolitan sees; Julian of Toledo; Constantinople

Introduction

'The city of Toledo was the first one founded in Hispania and all the Spanish cities were subject to it.'[2] Thus begins the short story of Octavianus,

1 A version of this chapter was first presented at the seminar *Constantinople dans l'Antiquité Tardive* (Université de Lille 3, France, 4 April 2017). I want to thank Javier Arce and Dominic Moreau for their invitation and the ensuing fruitful discussion. I also want to thank the participants of the original workshop held in Princeton in 2019 as well as Samuel Barber, Rosario Valverde Castro, and John Weisweiler, who provided insightful comments and suggestions that significantly improved this work.

2 Civitas Tuletus in Spania primum fundata est ibidem universas deserviunt civitates Spanienses.

Fernández, D., Lester, M. & Wood, J. (eds.), *Rome and Byzantium in the Visigothic Kingdom: Beyond* Imitatio Imperii. Taylor & Francis Group 2023
DOI: 10.5117/9789463726412_CH06

King of Hispania who ruled from Toledo, and his enemy Septemsiderus, preserved in the tenth-century codex of Roda.[3] Octavianus, the story continues, summoned Septemsiderus who, for an unexplained reason, refused to obey the king's order. Preparations for war ensued. The two characters marshalled their armies to face each other in battle, but, as the clash neared, Septemsiderus halted his troops, raised his prayers to God, and Octavianus's forces were miraculously destroyed. The victor settled in Lugo, and his seven children founded eponymous cities in Galicia, León, and northern Portugal, a geographical focus that probably betrays the origin of the anonymous author.[4]

This story, as Ann Christys has pointed out, must be set against the background of the ambiguous status of Toledo among Christian thinkers in the centuries following the Arab conquest.[5] Although later Latin chronicles and histories would emphasize the connection between the Visigothic kingdom of Toledo and the early medieval Christian kingdoms, this association was far from established before the tenth century, when the story of Octavianus and Septemsiderus was probably written.[6] Indeed, the text lies next to references to Babylon and Nineveh in the manuscript, a comparison which is hardly flattering, seeing as these cities fell to the wrath of God for their sins and were eventually destroyed by their enemies.[7] Yet the figure of Octavian (or Augustus) crafted a past modelled after Roman memories, transmitted with more or less accuracy. The twelfth-century *Chronica Pseudo-Isidoriana* also claimed that Octavian founded Toledo (*Toletum fabricavit*)—this time, unambiguously mentioned as the Roman emperor Augustus.[8] It is impossible to tell the extent to which the author of the story in the codex of Roda was aware of the tale of Rome's foundation by a mythical distant relative of Augustus or that Rome eventually subjected all the cities in the Mediterranean to its power.[9] Constantine founded a city that still claimed to be the capital of the Roman polity in the tenth century, and since contacts with Byzantium persisted in the early Middle Ages, many

3 Códice de Roda 197v–98r (Real Academia de la Historia Cod. 78). Gil Fernández 1971, 165–70. I am grateful to Graham Barrett who directed my attention to this story.

4 Linehan 1993, 99–101.

5 Christys 2001, 18–20.

6 For an introduction to the ample bibliography on this question, see Hillgarth 2009, esp. 57–81. For the date, see Díaz y Díaz 1972–1974, 261–62.

7 See the discussion in Díaz y Díaz 1972–1974.

8 *Chronica Gothorum Pseudo-Isidoriana* 5.18 (ed. González Muñoz 2000, 128).

9 Based on the intellectual environment and text production in Navarre, where the codex was compiled, it is highly possible (see Díaz y Díaz 1991). Unfortunately, the story's place of composition remains unknown.

probably knew of this legacy in the peninsular Christian kingdoms.[10] In any event, the narrative of Octavianus and Septemsiderus associates Toledo with an imperial past and a subtle Roman identity, even as it places it against a clearly recognizable early medieval background.

The association between Toledo, Rome, and capitalhood has proven to be quite enduring, and the idea of a Roman or Byzantine Toledo has captured the imagination of current Visigothic scholarship. Although the notion of 'seat' or 'head of a polity' inherited from the Roman past remains underexamined in Visigothic scholarship, comparisons between seventh-century capitals have become analytical templates for different phenomena. For instance, scholars have sought to find parallels between Toledo's monumental buildings and those of Constantinople.[11] Likewise, historians have often highlighted the striking similarities between Byzantine and Visigothic victory parades, accession ceremonies, and liturgical celebrations.[12] Such arguments have even led to the occasional characterization of Toledo as a new or local version of Rome or Constantinople.[13] But contemporary scholarship has sometimes imposed this template upon late antique sources to indicate what late antique writers thought of their capital cities. In other words, Visigothic intellectual, political, and religious elites *must* have thought of Toledo in terms of Roman/Constantinopolitan models. Certain documents would corroborate this interpretation by using the epithet *urbs regia* to describe Toledo—the same expression that late antique authors used to designate Rome or Constantinople. The adoption in Visigothic sources of this terminology is crucial to the modern reassessment of Toledo as an imitation of the head cities in the Roman polity.

Although specialized scholarship often refers to Toledo and other royal residences as capitals, it is still not clear what the concept meant in post-imperial Hispania. The late Roman empire offered at least two models of *caput* cities. On the one hand, Rome (as it were) moved with the emperors during the period of the peripatetic court in the fourth century.[14] On the other hand, as Clifford Ando has recently reminded us, the possibility of decentralizing imperial capitalhood is taken as a given because of the historical outcome—that is, the eventual foundation and capitalhood of

10 Ciggaar 1996, 301–2.

11 García Moreno 1977–1978, 320; Valverde Castro 2000, 184–85; Chavarría Arnau 2018, 62.

12 McCormick 1986, 297–327; Valverde Castro 2000, 181–95. But see the cautionary remarks in Koch 2008. More recently, Javier Arce has pointed out the limits of the imitation paradigm in ceremonies in the case of royal funerary practices (Arce 2020; see also Alonso Álvarez 2008).

13 Hillgarth 1966, 500; Díaz 1999, 336; Valverde Castro 2000, 189; Arce 2011, 75.

14 Mayer 2002. See also Kaldellis 2020.

Constantinople.[15] Yet even during the fourth-century peripatetic period, Rome never lost its position as the symbolic seat of the empire and the centre of the emperor's display of power, which only increased in the early fifth century.[16] Emperors made themselves manifest in the city in ways that did not require their physical presence.[17] The historical memory associated with the city of Rome was unique within the empire. Moreover, we must be cautious in assessing Justinian's characterization of Constantinople as the 'head of the whole world' (*caput orbis terrarum*) and *civitas regia* in the sixth century, and we should not assume that this had gone unchallenged since the early fourth century.[18] This title resulted from a hard-fought battle throughout the fourth and early fifth centuries, as demonstrated in the essays collected by Lucy Grig and Gavin Kelly on the 'two Romes'.[19] Thus, although the emperor's presence could enhance the symbolic and political status of a city, the notion of head city remained at the same time firmly attached to Rome, regardless of the imperial presence, and, eventually, Constantinople.

Visigothic sources show awareness of the special status of Rome and Constantinople, at least until the mid-seventh century. John of Biclarum, in the late sixth century, referred to Constantinople as *urbs regia*, possibly following the terminology of the chronicle of Victor of Tunnuna, which John's explicitly continued.[20] A generation or so later, Isidore described both Rome and Constantinople as the seats of the empire and the capitals or heads of West and East.[21] David Addison also reminds us in this volume that the *passio* of the Innumerable of Zaragoza portrays Rome as *caput gentium*.[22] But did a similar idea of capitalhood permeate the language of the Visigothic kingdom's 'head city'? Were Visigothic 'head cities', and Toledo in particular,

15 Ando 2017, 399.

16 Ando 2017; McEvoy 2010.

17 Weisweiler 2012. See also McEvoy and Moser 2017 (an introduction to several articles in the same issue of *Antiquité Tardive* dealing with specific topics on imperial presence and absence in the city of Rome).

18 'Leges [...] quae vel iudiciorum frequentissimus ordo exercuit vel longa consuetudo huius almae urbis comprobavit, secundum Salvii Iuliani scripturam, quae indicat debere omnes civitates consuetudinem Romae sequi, quae caput est orbis terrarum, non ipsam alias civitates. Romam autem intellegendum est non solum veterem, sed etiam regiam nostram, quae Deo propitio cum melioribus condita est auguries' (*Corpus iuris civilis*, De Conceptione Digestorum 10, ed. Krueger and Mommsen 1887).

19 Grig and Kelly 2012.

20 Ioh. Bicl. 26 and 45.

21 Isid. Etym. 15.1.42.

22 See pp. 232.

special centres, the heads of a polity with a distinct status on their own merits regardless of the presence of the king or the central administration? In other words, did Visigothic kings rule from capital cities in the Roman (or Byzantine) sense? Or did Toledo's status depend on the presence of the king, very much in line with the seats of the fourth-century peripatetic emperors and the fifth-century seats of warlords, emperors, and *magistri militum*?[23]

In his now classic and foundational work on post-imperial capitals, Eugen Ewig sought to debunk the idea of 'nomadic' kings and loosely organized states in the aftermath of Rome.[24] Although Ewig admitted that there were multiple motives for choosing a city as a royal residence, including political reasons, military purposes, or even the city's Roman pedigree, it was the court and its (in his view) rudimentary administration that made a city a capital. Carlrichard Brühl built on Ewig's conclusions and did not doubt Toledo's status as a capital based on its administrative and ecclesiastical role, which he compared to that of Constantinople.[25] Ewig's model to explain the transition from royal seat to Roman-like capital, from *sedes regia* to *urbs regia*, has cast a long shadow over subsequent studies on post-imperial Hispania.[26] In line with contemporary scholarship, Ewig approached the development of Visigothic capitals, Toledo in particular, within the framework of an imitation of or borrowing from Constantinopolitan models.[27]

As this chapter will show, Visigothic sources would eventually adopt the same epithet previously reserved for Rome and Constantinople to refer to Toledo. It is worth wondering, however, whether these sources simply imitated Byzantine ideas or whether they used this concept to address specific concerns in Hispania. Indeed, the adoption of Byzantine idioms of power did not extend to the terminology and conceptualization of Toledo until the mid-seventh century. Only from the 640s onwards did sources begin consistently to attribute a special status to Toledo—a status based on the physical presence of the king, the history of Toledo as the formal seat of kingship, the city's largely invented Christian past, and its contemporary ecclesiastical significance within the kingdom. I will therefore argue that, though part of the impetus for this conceptualization may have come from the monarchy itself, the push for the capitalhood of Toledo in Roman or Constantinopolitan-like terms was fundamentally an enterprise of the city's

23 See Ian Wood's remarks on fifth-century Visigothic courts in this volume.
24 Ewig 1963.
25 Brühl 1967, 201–3.
26 Velázquez and Ripoll 2000 remains the fundamental work from this perspective.
27 Ewig 1963, 31–36. For the academic tradition of 'Byzantinization', see Martin in this volume.

ecclesiastical establishment in a quest for supremacy within the Christian landscape of the kingdom. Yet it is far from certain that other political and ecclesiastical actors uniformly shared this enthusiasm for reframing Toledo's status in the polity of the Visigoths. Rather than a transition from a *caput* city based on the presence of the king to one based on the intrinsic (Christian) value of Toledo, Visigothic sources reveal different notions about the status of Toledo—notions that could perfectly coexist, but that could also raise discordant ideas that could be activated depending on the political circumstances.

The Rise of Toledo

Visigothic kings are attested in different cities after the fall of the kingdom of Toulouse in 507, including Barcelona, Narbonne, Seville, and Mérida. However, for the period before Leovigild's reign, the evidence is fragmentary and frequently limited to short passages in chronicles, which were written sometimes decades or even more than a century after the events.[28] While scholars tend to take royal presence in these cities as a sign of capitals or proto-capitals, the silence of sixth-century sources does not allow us to reconstruct whether royal presence imbued these cities with a special status within the kingdom.

When Leovigild became king in 568 or 569, there was some precedent for Toledo as a royal residence. Both Theudis and Athanagild spent at least some time in the city, although it is difficult to assert the extent to which Toledo

28 In Gaul, Narbonne remained an occasional royal residence. Gesalic was proclaimed king in this city (Isid. Hist. Goth. 37) and Liuva probably also ruled from that city during his short reign (Ioh. Bicl. 24). See also the tax exemption given to Bishop Aquilinus in Tomás-Faci and Martín-Iglesias (2017, 279), which suggests that Leovigild was at Narbonne in 572 as a result of his brother's death. In general, for Narbonne, see Riess 2013, 131–59. Barcelona also hosted kings and their retinues. Gesalic took it as his residence after his defeat of the Burgundians (*Chronica Gallica a. 511*, 87, ed. Burgess 2001, 99; Isid. Hist. Goth. 37) and the *Consularia Caesaraugustana* mentions that Gesalic killed a certain Goiaric at the king's palace (*in palatio*), an event that took place in 511 (Cons. Caes. 91a). Amalaric was assassinated in Barcelona after he was defeated by the Frankish king Childebert in 531 (Cons. Caes. 115a; cf. Greg. Tur. Decem libri 3.10 and Isid. Hist. Goth. 40). Kings also resided in Seville, where Theudigisel was killed in a banquet in 549 (Isid. Hist. Goth. 44), Athanagild rebelled against Agila (Isid. Hist. Goth. 46) and Hermenegild rose against his father (Ioh. Bicl. 54). Despite its late Roman pedigree as capital of the diocese of the *Hispaniae*, Mérida did not feature prominently as a Visigothic royal residence. In the mid-fifth century, Suevic kings are occasionally attested in the city (Hyd. 111 and 129). However, it is only in the second half of the sixth century that a Visigothic king, Agila, resided (and died) in Mérida (Isid. Hist. Goth. 46).

operated as a more or less permanent administrative and political centre.[29] The reason for choosing Toledo has been much debated and the arguments include the supposed (though difficult to prove) presence of Visigothic settlements on the Castilian plateau, the defensive qualities of the city, the late Roman urban infrastructure, and Toledo's location at a crossroads of land routes.[30] While there is evidence of ceremonial life and administrative court infrastructure, these elements were not associated with a specific city and they could be reproduced elsewhere. The admittedly limited sources from this period do not refer to any of these cities in the same way that late antique authors referred to Rome or Constantinople. As Gisela Ripoll has pointed out, the head cities of the fifth and early sixth centuries were royal residences more than kingly cities—*sedes regiae* rather than *urbes regiae*.[31] Gregory of Tours echoed this notion (perhaps also influenced by the Frankish context) when he affirmed that 'Leovigild gave [Hermenegild and Ingund] one of the cities in which, taking residence, they could rule'.[32]

As Toledo enjoyed a more regular royal presence after the mid-sixth century, its centrality within the kingdom increased. It is not clear, however, whether the imagined representation of the city varied during the reigns of Leovigild and Reccared. As mentioned earlier, scholars have repeatedly pointed out topographic similarities in the ceremonial centres of Toledo and Constantinople. For instance, Reccared very likely consecrated a (formerly Arian?) church to the Virgin Mary.[33] This event, and the importance of the cult of Mary, would have paralleled Constantinople's focus on the *theotokos*.[34] To be sure, this cult played an important part in Visigothic liturgy. Yet Marian devotion in the peninsula had diverse origins, including Byzantium, the Latin

29 Because a 'national' council took place in Toledo in 526, it has been suggested that Toledo was a royal residence during Amalaric's reign, yet there is no direct indication of the king's residence in the city. Theudis signed the law on judicial costs in Toledo (*Leges Visigothorum*, 467–69) and may have allowed another council to take place in that city (Isid. Hist. Goth. 41), although it is also possible that Isidore mistook the name of the king who allowed the council to meet. Athanagild probably ruled from Toledo later in his reign, where he died in 568 (Isid. Hist. Goth. 47). Riess (2013, 145–47) is even more sceptical about the pre-Leovigild status of Toledo.

30 Ripoll 2003, 145–48; Velázquez and Ripoll 2000, 531–38; Martin 2003, 214–15; Barroso Cabrera, Carrobles Santos, Morín de Pablos, and Sánchez Ramos 2015, 339–40.

31 Ripoll 2003, 125.

32 'Leuvichildus autem dedit eis unam de civitatibus, in qua resedentes regnarent' (Greg. Tur. Decem libri 5.38).

33 ICERV suppl. 302. The authenticity of this inscription is subject to debate, although most scholars currently accept it as probably genuine. See Velázquez Soriano 2007, 97–98. For the church of St Mary, see Barroso Cabrera and Morín de Pablos 2007, 104–8.

34 Cameron 1978; Mango 2000; Cameron 2004; Pentcheva 2006, 11–35.

West (especially Rome), and autochthonous developments.[35] The Toledan ecclesiastical establishment, however, may have shown a keen interest in the Marian cult, to the extent that Bishop Ildefonsus of Toledo produced a tractate on the virginity of Mary in the early 650s.[36] Yet we must be cautious about placing too much emphasis on *De virginitate*. Ildefonsus was not necessarily interested in developing the figure of Mary as protector of *the* City within the polity. Rather, as Kati Ihnat has pointed out, the efforts to promote the cult of Mary took place against the background of anti-Jewish legislation on forcibly converted Jews (which was not universally embraced among the bishops) and the efforts of the episcopate to avoid apostasy.[37] Indeed, the role accorded to the Virgin in polemical literature of this kind has stronger parallels in the eastern empire. Anti-Jewish legislation gained momentum after Justinian, and eventually included forced baptism of the Jews in the early seventh century, which is reflected in Christian literature at the time and its concern with Judaizing Christians. The defence of Mary's virginity and her ancestry, among other topics, were part of anti-Jewish literature in the East.[38] Thus, there is little evidence of Marian liturgy and literature as a development to enhance Toledo's Christian status as the figure of Mary had in Constantinople, especially after the Avar siege of 626.[39] Instead, as in the Byzantine empire, the Visigothic cult of the Virgin must be read against the background of devotional practices and anti-Jewish polemics that were common to both polities in the seventh century.

Furthermore, written sources of the sixth century (admittedly scanty) did not enthusiastically support a new conceptualization of Toledo. The acts of the Third Council of Toledo do indicate that the gathering took place 'in the royal city of Toledo' (*in civitatem regiam Toletanam*), using the same terminology reserved for Rome and Constantinople.[40] At the same time, this occurrence contrasts with the formula 'in the city of Toledo' otherwise used in the acts.[41] In any event, if the enthusiasm of the Gothic conversion

35 Ihnat 2019.

36 Ildefonsus of Toledo, *De virginitate Sanctae Mariae* (ed. Yarza Urquiola and Codoñer Merino 2007, 145–264).

37 Ihnat 2017. On the legal consequences of the forcible conversion of the Jews, and the specifically royal perspective on the question, see González Salinero 2000 and Martin and Nemo-Pekelman 2008.

38 Shoemaker 1999. See also Cameron 1996, 266. For the early cult of Mary, see Shoemaker 2016.

39 Pentcheva 2006, 37–59.

40 III Toledo, praef. (Coll. Hisp. V, 50).

41 III Toledo, incipit (Coll. Hisp. V, 103), edictum (Coll. Hisp. V, 133), and subscr. (Coll. Hisp. V, 140).

led Christian intellectuals to think of Toledo as a potential new Rome, this fervour was to be rapidly abandoned. Conciliar literature does not repeat the formula of Third Toledo until the mid-seventh century. To be sure, there is a hiatus in national councils of over four decades after 589. But even when councils met with regularity in Toledo during the 630s, the epithet of *civitas* or *urbs regia* disappeared.[42] In this sense, it is symptomatic that John of Biclarum's *Chronicle*, composed in the early 600s, refers to Toledo as *urbs Toletana* while he reserves *civitas regia* for Constantinople.[43] In John's work, Toledo remains the king's seat: he synecdochally described Leovigild's return to the city after his campaigns in 569 by stating that 'King Leovigild returned victorious to his throne/seat' (*solium*).[44]

Thus, although the late sixth and early seventh centuries may have witnessed the adoption of Byzantine ceremonial, Toledo simply remained the city of royal residence and sources rarely conceptualized the city in Constantinopolitan terms.[45] Perhaps it is worth reminding ourselves that the Visigothic monarchy's new rituals were not compulsorily tied to Toledo, but could, and indeed were, reproduced in other cities, as Michael McCormick has pointed out.[46] The recently published charters of San Martín de Asán also remind us that royal Christian patronage extended throughout the kingdom and was not limited to Toledo.[47] Toledo was not seen as a city with intrinsic merits giving it a claim to capitalhood, beyond the presence of the king who chose the city as his residence at the time of the supposed Byzantinization of the Visigothic monarchy.

Towards an *Urbs Regia*

This attitude changed in the mid-seventh century. The first clear evidence comes from the Seventh Council of Toledo in 646, during which the writers of the acts adopted the Roman/Constantinopolitan epithet of

42 *Urbs Toletana* and *ecclesia Toletana* remain the standard formulas in IV Toledo praef. and subscr. (Coll. Hisp. V, 178 and 261), V Toledo, praef., subscr., and Chintila's letter to the council (Coll. Hisp. V, 276 and 287, and Conc. 231–32), and VI Toledo, praef. (*in praetorio Toletano*) and subscr. (Coll. Hisp. 296 and 330).

43 Toledo: Ioh. Bicl. 57, 91, and 93. For Constantinople, see above, note 20.

44 Leovegildus rex […] victor solio reddit (Ioh. Bicl. 12).

45 Cf. Ripoll 2003, 138.

46 McCormick 1986, 304–5. See also Olmo Enciso 2007, 100–106 and Dey 2015, 140–60.

47 Tomás-Faci and Martín-Iglesias 2017. Also, Martín and Larrea 2021, 237–43. See below, note 69.

'royal city' (*urbs regia*). Canon 6 expands on the reasons behind Toledo's pre-eminence: nearby bishops must reside for one month a year in Toledo to give advice to the metropolitan bishop as well as out of respect for the *princeps* and the dignity of the royal seat.[48] Although we should be cautious of drawing too many conclusions from such a brief notice, the separation between the presence of the king and the prestige of the royal seat allowed Toledo to acquire its own regal merits whether the king resided there or not. This multi-layered formulation of Toledo happened at the very moment when bishops, palatine officers, lay magnates, and the king tried to develop formulas that distinguished between the king as a ruler and the institution of the monarchy.[49] In any event, while the canon draws the distinction between the dignity of the king and that of the city, the few words of the canon still associate the special status of the city with the king's presence.

Less than a decade later, Bishop Eugenius (II) signed the acts of the Eighth Council of Toledo in 653 as bishop of the *urbs regia*.[50] The expression 'bishop of the royal city' would remain the standard epithet of the Toledan episcopate through the end of the seventh century in most council signatures, though not in every one of them.[51] In part, this appellation mirrors the formulaic epithet of Constantinople in eastern conciliar documents.[52] However, it is during this period that a new conception of Toledo as capital also emerged. We see this clearly in the work of Eugenius's successor, Ildefonsus. In his *De viris illustribus*, dated to his episcopate between 659 and 667, Ildefonsus qualified Toledo as a 'glorious' or 'renowned' city (*gloriosa urbs*), explaining in the Preface the reason for granting Toledo that epithet:

> I [...] the successor of Eugenius II of blessed memory in that glorious see of the city of Toledo, (which I call glorious not so much from its immense throng of people since it is the presence of our glorious princes that gives

48 'De convicinis episcopis in urbe regia commorandis. Id etiam placuit, ut pro reverentia principis ac regiae sedis honore vel metropolitani civitatis ipsius consolatione convicini Toletanae sedis episcopi, iuxta quod eiusdem pontificis admonitionem acceperint [...] singulis per annum mensibus in eadem urbe debeant commorari' (VII Toledo 6 (Coll. Hisp. V, 356)).

49 This was expressed primarily in the arguments over the proprietary rights to the king's personal possessions and those of the Crown. See VII Toledo 10 and *Decretum*; LI 2.1.6. See also Esders 2019.

50 See also VIII Toledo 10 (Coll. Hisp. V, 428), according to which the election of the new king had to be decided by a council of bishops and senior palace officers 'either in the royal city or in the place where the king had died' ('aut in urbe regia aut in loco ubi princeps decesserit').

51 *Episcopus urbis regiae* in IX, XI, XII, XIV, XV, and XVI Toledo.

52 For mid-Byzantine use of the term, see Alexander 1962, 342–43.

> it glory, but for this reason: that among those who fear God it is considered both a terrible place for the unjust and a place worthy of all veneration by the just) have tried [...] to add to their glorious memory lest I should be condemned for my silence and for covering the gleaming light of the memory of so glorious a See and such glorious men in murky darkness of silence.[53]

Ildefonsus accepts that the presence of the king grants the city renown. In this sense, he still operates within a traditional framework in which royal charisma emanates from the city of royal residence. Or, more likely, he gives a gentle nod to what may still have been the prevalent position among elite circles at court and for the kings themselves. At the same time, he suggests an alternative source of prestige that can compete against or add to the traditional conception of capitalhood in post-Roman Hispania, a status that echoes Constantinopolitan notions of a God-protected city.[54] It is thus not surprising that Ildefonsus defends the growing cult of Mary as protector of the city, which, as Céline Martin has argued, might rely on eastern Roman models.[55]

Ildefonsus mentions at least four miraculous events that allegedly took place in Toledo.[56] More importantly, as Carmen Codoñer Merino has pointed out, the genre of the book breaks with the works it purports to continue (Jerome's *De viris illustribus* and Isidore's continuation of Jerome's work) in one important respect. Ildefonsus's biographies stress less the intellectual merits, in the 'Jeromian' sense, and more the personal virtue of the individuals they describe. There is a subtle but undeniable hagiographical tone to what is purportedly a collection of intellectual biographies following Jerome's model.[57] The emphasis on ascetic virtues was part of Ildefonsus's much broader religious agenda, which advanced a corresponding model of episcopacy.[58] Yet this only reinforced the idea of a special role of Toledo

53 'Ego [...] successor sanctae memoriae alterius Eugenii factus in sede illa gloriosa Toletanae urbis—quam non ex hominum immenso conventu gloriosam dico, cum hanc etiam gloriosum inlustret praesentia principum, sed ex hoc quod coram timentibus Deum iniquis atque iustis habetur locus terribilis omnique veneratione sublimis—conatus sum [...] illorum admiscere memoriae gloriosae, ne incurrerem ex silentio damnum, si tam gloriosae sedi tamque gloriosorum virorum clarescentem memoriae lucem tenebrosi nube silentii contexissem' (Ildef. De viris, praef. (trans. Fear 1997, modified)).

54 Martin 2003, 247.

55 Martin 2003, 227.

56 Ildef. De viris, praef.; cf. 1–2.

57 Codoñer Merino 1972, 32–37; Wood 2012, 635–36.

58 Castro 2016, 54–59; Castro 2019.

within the kingdom, a role granted by the holiness of bishops who embodied Ildefonsus's notions of episcopal office.[59]

To what extent Ildefonsus succeeded is difficult to determine, but his ideas were not accepted unanimously. A few years after Ildefonsus's death, Julian of Toledo advertised the special Christian role of Toledo in the *Historia Wambae regis*, but in terms rather different from Ildefonsus's.[60] Julian's narrative begins with the death of King Recceswinth in the territory of Salamanca and the election of Wamba to succeed him. According to Julian,

> [A]lthough, chosen by divine inspiration and later by the anxious acclaim and the veneration of the people, [Wamba] had already been surrounded by the great pomp of royal ceremony, he would not suffer himself to be anointed by a priest's hand before he had come to the seat of the royal city and had sought the throne of paternal ancestry, at which time only it would be fitting for him to receive the sign of the holy unction.[61]

The subtlety with which Julian combines different and potentially divergent ideas cannot go unnoticed. On the one hand, he reverts to the old idea of Toledo as the seat of the king, the throne (*solium*), which John of Biclarum had already advanced more than half a century earlier.[62] By now, Julian could insist on a well-established continuity of kings who presumably ruled from Toledo. This would imply that residence in Toledo was not a simply personal choice, but a practice rooted in the history of the kingdom, whose origins were immemorial. This is why kings ought to be consecrated in Toledo.[63] The king would not let himself be consecrated by any *sacerdos*

59 Martin 2003, 226–27.

60 The date of composition of the work remains unknown. While most scholars follow Levison's thesis that Julian wrote the *Historia Wambae* before he acceded the episcopate in 680 (Levison 1905, 490–91), Yolanda García López situates Julian's piece in the early years of Erwig's reign (García López 1993, esp. 136). Gregorio García Herrero has posited a later date, towards the end of Julian's episcopacy (García Herrero 1998, 190–203; see also Drews 2021, 323).

61 'Nam eudem virum quamquam divinitus abinceps et per hanelantia plevium vota et per eorum obsequentia regali cultu iam circumdederant magna officia, ungi se tamen per sacerdotis manus ante non passus est, quam sedem adiret regiae urbis atque solium peteret paternae antiquitatis, in qua sibi oportunum esset et sacrae unctionis vexilla suscipere' (Hist. Wamb. reg. 2, trans. Martínez Pizarro 2005, modified).

62 See above, note 44.

63 On this question, the remarks in Collins 1977, 43–49 remain particularly pertinent. See also García López 1993, 130–32. The origins of the ceremony of anointment are not certain. The passage in the *Historia Wambae Regis* is the first unequivocal reference, and it is therefore possible that Julian was insisting on the legitimacy of a ceremony that was relatively recent. However, an ambiguous passage in the acts of the Fourth Council of Toledo might indicate that

other than the bishop of the *urbs regia*. Although there are no indications of a specific Christian value of Toledo in Ildefonsus's terms, the kingly city was the seat of the throne and the place where the Christian sanction of the king would take place.

At the same time, this passage exudes anxiety for Toledo's weakness. Julian emphasizes the incompleteness of Wamba's accession without his anointment in Toledo. And yet it is quite clear from the passage that Wamba could perfectly well have chosen to do otherwise. He had already been proclaimed by the Gothic people (or a metonymy of it) and assumed the royal pomp.[64] No matter how illegitimately Julian presents the 'usurper' Paul in his narrative, it is hardly unlikely that his followers would have considered him a less legitimate king for his consecration in Narbonne.[65] In his letter to Wamba, Paul himself indicates that he is the 'anointed king of the East'.[66] The idea that the special status of Toledo ultimately depended on the king's presence lurks in the background of the grandiose claims about Toledo's unique status and the uninterrupted transmission of royal authority in the city. Julian made his best efforts to remind his readers that the position of Toledo was far from transient. The need for such efforts, however, should warn us against taking Ildefonsus's and Julian's claims as universally accepted.

In sum, a few prominent intellectuals from Toledo argued for the unique position of Toledo within the kingdom by the middle of the seventh century. In their view, the status of the city was due to the presence of the king, the traditional criteria in use until that point in the Visigothic kingdom. In addition, Toledo was a kingly seat in and of itself due to the dignity it had accrued as the seat of government. Finally, mid- and late-seventh-century sources insist that Toledo's role as a centre of Christian veneration granted it a special place within the polity. Nonetheless, we should not assume that these ideas were universally accepted. We should resist the temptation to interpret Julian and Ildefonsus's arguments as representative of a united Visigothic 'Church'. Toledo may have faced challenges to intellectual hegemony from other

the practice dates back at least to the reign of Sisenand (Coll. Hisp. V, 249–50, in reference to Ps 104.15 and 1 Sam 26.9). For a brief discussion, see Barbero de Aguilera 1970, 314–19 and King 1972, 48, n. 5. Cf. the more sceptical view in Drews 2021.

64 For Visigothic ceremonial and its relationship with Byzantium, see Arce 2004. See also LI 1.2.6, for the use of the diadem as a symbol of the kingdom.

65 For the construction of Paul as a tyrant, see Velázquez Soriano 1989, Martínez Pizarro 2005, 78–171, and Castillo Lozano 2019, 81–95. For Narbonne and the brief 'kingdom' in Septimania, see Riess 2013, 188–219.

66 *Unctus rex orientalis* (Hist. Wamb. reg., Ep. Paul).

sees, and the Toledan bishops' arguments were directed inside as well as outside the ecclesiastical community.[67] Since the sources are predominantly ecclesiastical and Toledan, it is hard to reconstruct alternative views. Yet what the documents betray is a conscious effort to undermine alternative, deep-rooted notions of a 'head city'.

Ecclesiastical Politics and the Status of Toledo

It is worth asking, therefore, why Toledo would have developed such a special status in the previously discussed documents. Although Constantinopolitan models may have played a role, I think we need to look into the specifically Iberian context to understand Toledo's seventh-century transformation. The first reason may simply have been its persistence as a royal abode over time. Unlike other royal residences, Toledo retained its status despite the vicissitudes of the Visigothic monarchy, which could have initiated a path-dependent cycle of increasing urban charisma.[68] Toledo became the main focus of royal patronage through the foundation of Christian buildings and enterprises, although it was certainly not the only city where the king performed pious patronage.[69] It is perhaps not

67 See, for instance, Michael Kelly's arguments on the relationship between Seville and Toledo/Agali (Kelly 2021).

68 For the ceremonial growth, see McCormick 1986, 298–302.

69 The literary evidence of royal foundations and benefactions is scattered, but consistent. According to the *Lives of the Fathers of Mérida*, Leovigild donated a fiscal property near Mérida to the monk Nanctus (VSPE 3). He also issued a tax exemption on the Tarraconensis properties of Bishop Aquilinus of Narbonne, though in reward for the latter's *fides* rather than as a pious act. According to another charter of San Martín de Asán, Reccared transferred a privilege from the royal fisc to the monastery, which had previously been granted to a bishop (Tomás-Faci and Martín-Iglesias 2017, 279–81). John of Biclarum's *Chronicle* mentions that Reccared founded and expanded churches and monasteries, but without any indications as to where the king's patronage took place (Ioh. Bicl. 86). Also, during the reigns of Leovigild and Reccared, fiscal slaves founded churches, which were ultimately attributed to the king, at least from the purely legal and canonical perspective (III Toledo 15 (Coll. Hisp. V, 121)). A church in Reccopolis was likely a royal foundation. Although perhaps founded by Leovigild, the chronology is not completely clear, and constructions could have been carried over into the early seventh century (Olmo Enciso 2008). On an ecclesiastical foundation by Recceswinth in or near San Juan de Baños, Palencia, see ICERV 314. Cf. Velázquez and Hernando 2000, on the relationship between this inscription and the church of San Juan de Hornija, perhaps a Chindaswinthian foundation; but note the cautious remarks in Alonso Álvarez 2008 and in Schlimbach 2009. See also the templates of royal donations to churches and monasteries in FW 9–10. It is impossible, however, to determine the location of the original foundations (Córcoles Olaitz 2010, 12–17; Collins 2021, 59–61).

by chance that the first evidence of Toledo as an *urbs regia*, stressing the dignity of the royal seat, dates from 646 during the reign of Chindaswinth, a king who took significant steps towards political and administrative centralization.[70] Also, as Isabel Velázquez has pointed out, this is the period when the notions of *gens* and *regnum* began to transform, and a closer association between king and polity may have facilitated the realignment of Toledo's political symbolism.[71] Toledo could take, in the eyes of the king, a synecdochic aura. Public ceremonies in the city represented the relationship between king and people.[72] The 'agreement' of baptized Jews and the king could take a kingdom-wide force.[73] Moreover, the development of a palatine office may have encouraged an administrative ethos within a silent, sub-elite class that served the needs of the legal, military, and tributary administration.[74] The centripetal force of a stable court may have created a shared experience of capitalhood in an administrative sense, regardless of the physical presence of the king.[75] All in all, the bishops at the council may have picked up on political notions that emanated from the court.

Nonetheless, the sources that either assume or at least aim to construe Toledo's special status beyond the presence of the king were unsurprisingly Toledan and ecclesiastical in nature. The scanty royal documents, such as laws and charters, refer to the city simply as 'Toledo', though this may well derive from Roman diplomatic practice.[76] The inscription of Wamba that celebrated his restoration of Toledo's walls only referred to the *urbs* and *plebs* of Toledo without any special qualification, if we are to believe the testimony of the so-called Mozarabic *Chronicle of 754*.[77] Even documents that were presumably hostile towards a king or Toledo display a language that kings could have embraced perfectly well. The author of the *Lives of the Fathers of Mérida* narrates that, when Leovigild recalled Bishop Masona in to his presence, the king sent envoys who, 'coming to the city of Mérida

70 From different perspectives and interpretations: Thompson 1969, 210–17; Claude 1971, 115–22; García Moreno 1974, 149–55; King 1980; Martin 2011. Cf. Diesner 1979.

71 Velázquez 2003. See now Buchberger 2017, 67ff.

72 Dey 2015, 149.

73 LI 12.2.17. On this *placitum*, see Esders 2016, 57–61.

74 For palace administration, see Martin 2003, 239–54; Isla Frez 2002. For the notarial culture of the kingdom, see Collins 1990, 114–18.

75 For the administrative role of Toledo, see Martin 2003, 239–61.

76 LI 12.1.17 (Recceswinth): *Toletane civitatis*; *Toleto*. LI 4.5.6 and 7 (Wamba): *In Toleto*. Cf. Theudis's law of 546 inserted in the *Breviary*: *Toleto* (*Leges Visigothorum*, 469); LI 9.1.21 (Egica): *Cordoba*; and XIII Toledo, Lex edita: *Toleto*. For royal chancellery, see Canellas López 1979, 37–38.

77 Chron. Muz. 29.

(*urbs Emeretensem*), forced the holy man to speed up in all haste to the city of Toledo (*urbs Toletana*), where the king was'.[78] Behind this phrase, one can sense the affirmation of Mérida's equal standing as well as the almost nonchalant reference to the king being in Toledo as a simple contingency. This is clearly a Méridan perspective of the events, but consistent with royal documents.[79] Similarly, in his rejection of the public life of Toledo (perhaps a council or a business at court), the ascetic Valerius of Bierzo refers to the city in similar terms.[80]

In contrast, the special status of the city of Toledo cannot be dissociated from the push to affirm Toledo's primacy within its own ecclesiastical province and, eventually, the kingdom. By the early sixth century, Toledo headed the newly created ecclesiastical province of Carpetania-Celtiberia, a break-out circumscription from the province of Carthaginensis and perhaps Gallaecia.[81] The reasons for the creation of a new ecclesiastical province remain obscure, but it is clear from two letters by Bishop Montanus attached to the canons of the Second Council of Toledo (521) that the bishop of Toledo believed that he had the authority to intervene in ecclesiastical affairs of other dioceses in the province.[82] These letters may reveal the efforts of an aspiring metropolitan bishop to assert his role rather than the actual influence that metropolitans held before the end of the sixth century.[83] Eventually, Toledo's province would include the rest of Carthaginensis, though when that happened is not certain. According to the *Decree of Gundemar*, included in the acts of the Twelfth Council of Toledo (681), King Gundemar had abolished the ecclesiastical province of Carpetania-Celtiberia in 610, giving Toledo the metropolitan position over Cartagena.[84]

The authenticity of the decree has been questioned, although recent assessments accept the document as genuine. Antonio González Blanco

78 '[Ministri criminis eius] ad Emeretensem urbem venientes virum beatum sub omni celeritate ad urbem Toletanam, in qua rex erat, properare conpellunt' (VSPE 5.6).

79 For a background of the rivalry between Mérida and Toledo, see Collins 1980.

80 'Ad publicum Toletane urbis' (Val. Ord. quer. 7.6).

81 II Toledo (Carpetania-Celtiberia) and III Toledo (Carpetania). Cf. Greg. Tur. Decem libri 6.33 and 44 and Ioh. Bicl. 50. On this episode, see Díaz 2019, 88–92.

82 Coll. Hisp. IV, 356–66. See also Ildef. De viris 2. For a discussion of this episode, see Martin 1998 and 2006. Cf. Isla Frez 2000.

83 Norton 2011, 154–56. For a discussion on the impact of ecclesiastical disputes in the formation of metropolitan authority, see Panzram 2018.

84 XII Toledo, Decretum Gundemari regis (Coll. Hisp. VI, 209–11). In fact, the decree affirms that the province of Carpetania had never existed and, therefore, Toledo had been the metropolitan see of Carthaginensis since the times of Montanus (Orlandis 1980).

has argued that the decree was written ex-post-facto to justify the primacy of Toledo, whose claims were still dubious in the late seventh century even as it was claiming national ascendancy, as we shall see.[85] However, other scholars have pushed back and defended the authenticity of the text.[86] Be that as it may, by the second half of the seventh century, Toledo exercised its primacy over a wide ecclesiastical province. There was also a push to consider Toledo something like the primatial see of the kingdom after 681, when the bishop of the *urbs regia* acquired the right to ordain other bishops appointed by the king from any ecclesiastical province.[87] This move has been interpreted as a borrowing from the idea of Constantinople's patriarchate.[88] Yet the actual impact of this conciliar ruling is uncertain, and later councils never mention a national primatial see explicitly.[89] The 681 decision may have been intended to reverse Wamba's policies.[90] It is likely, however, that the influence of Toledo's bishop on episcopal elections increased in the seventh century less as a result of the status of his see than as a consequence of his proximity to the king and courtly circles.[91]

The construction of Toledo as a prestigious Christian see was a slow process, which probably began in the second half of the sixth century with Leovigild's attempt to bring the relics of St Eulalia to Toledo.[92] Unlike Mérida, Tarragona, or Valencia, Toledo had an unimpressive Christian past.[93] A new Christian history had to be constructed—for instance, via the promotion of Leocadia from a virgin with a *memoria* in Toledo's

85 González Blanco 1986. More recently, Wood 2012, 632.

86 Barbero de Aguilera 1992, 193–95; Velázquez and Ripoll 2000, 544–46; Martin 2003, 244–45; Díaz 2019, 91.

87 XII Toledo, 6. This primacy entailed that the bishop of Toledo would ordain the bishop appointed by the king before sending him to his metropolitan bishop. The bishop of Toledo could also suggest names for the king to appoint as bishop.

88 Ewig 1963, 35; Claude 1971, 170–71.

89 In the late seventh century, Felix of Toledo still referred to the city simply as the metropolitan see of Carthaginensis in *Vita Iuliani* 1; Julian calls it '*Toletana sedes*' in the *Elogium Ildefonsi* (ed. Martín-Iglesias and Yarza Urquiola 2014, 9 and 3). Strikingly, the acts of XIII Toledo, held two years later, do not refer to the city as *urbs regia*, but *Toletana urbs* and so does the law in confirmation of the council.

90 For Wamba's ecclesiastical policy, see Claude 1971, 162–64. For the political context of XII Toledo, see Collins 2004, 96–99; Fernández 2020, 509–11.

91 For the role of social and political networks in episcopal appointments and elections in the Visigothic kingdom, see Wood 2019.

92 VSPE 5.6.

93 For Tarragona, see Pérez Martínez 2012; for Mérida, Mateos Cruz 1999; for Valencia, Ribera i Lacomba 2000.

suburbs in the early sixth century to a confessor in the seventh century.[94] Others later supported this attempt, including Ildefonsus, as Jamie Wood has argued.[95] Yet the reference in Ildefonsus's work to the city's glory depending mostly on its Christian merits rather than the presence of the king should make us suspect that the latter was precisely the alternative idea of Toledo's special status in Visigothic Hispania, and perhaps the dominant one. Particularly during the second half of the seventh century, when centralization and court ceremonial probably achieved their peak of sophistication, we are inclined to suspect a controversy around the respective roles of the king and the bishop of Toledo in the political life of the kingdom.[96]

I do not wish to suggest that Visigothic monarchs did not want to enhance the spiritual prestige of Toledo. Christianity was an integral part of the Visigothic monarchy, and rulers were probably interested in enhancing the Christian power of the city they took as their *sedes*.[97] They may well have wanted to increase the sacred power of Toledo within Hispania, something that interested Leovigild himself. The *Decree of Gundemar*, regardless of its date of composition, affirmed that the city of Toledo was gifted with the antiquity of its title and the veneration of the king's power.[98] The construction of religious buildings appears to have intensified in mid-seventh-century Toledo and it is unlikely that kings were not involved in this process.[99] Rather, I argue that intellectual definitions of Toledo's status and role were interwoven with royal and ecclesiastical agendas that could collude but also collide.[100] Moreover, probably not all church leaders and intellectuals shared the perspective of the ecclesiastical establishment in Toledo. We therefore should be wary of accepting at face value the unanimity that council acts advertised. The mid-seventh-century idea of Toledo as *urbs regia* must not be understood as a uniform and unequivocal development, but as a contested concept within and outside church circles.

94 Velázquez and Ripoll 2000, 554–56.

95 Wood 2012.

96 A summary of the events in Collins 2004, 81–102.

97 For the religious dimensions of Visigothic kingship, see Valverde Castro 2000, 195–215 and Martin 2018.

98 'Haec ipsa sedes sicut praedicta est antiqua nominis sui ac nostri cultu imperii' (XII Toledo, Decretum Gundemari regis (Coll. Hisp. VI, 206)).

99 Velázquez and Ripoll 2000; Barroso Cabrera and Morín de Pablos 2007.

100 A pattern that characterized the relationship between kings and councils. See, for instance, Stocking 2000.

Conclusion

The story of Octavianus and Septemsiderus, with which I started this chapter, was reminiscent of a Toledo associated with Roman emperorship. Admittedly, this may not have been the intention of the anonymous writer, who had no sympathies for the kings that ruled from the city before the Islamic conquest. Other early medieval sources, such as the *Chronicle of 754*, would elevate the status of Visigothic Toledo to an *urbs regia* in less ambiguous terms, although without any Roman connotation.[101] The Arab conquest and the subsequent rise of the Astur-Leonese monarchy forced the discussion over the pre-conquest period that entailed a characterization of Toledo as head of a past and (in the imagination of some) present polity. This characterization was not deprived of Roman sound bites in the description of the city. Roman ideas of Toledo, therefore, proved to be resilient to the Arab conquest, although they also adapted to the early medieval intellectual landscape.

Debates over the status of Toledo and its relationship with Roman traditions did not end with the Middle Ages. Especially over the past century, scholars have pointed out that after the late sixth century, Toledo became not only a capital, but a capital modelled after Rome or Constantinople. The Visigothic monarchy's adoption of apparently Byzantine ceremonials did transform the ritual life of Toledo. While topographical changes are difficult to assess, it is even possible that Constantinople may have inspired some of Toledo's ceremonial infrastructure, or more likely, this infrastructure could be interpreted as being of Constantinopolitan inspiration invoked in specific contexts. As indicated here and in other chapters in this volume, however, it would be at least equally accurate to look into situational contingencies behind the adoption of practices that would otherwise appear to be 'imported'.[102]

The same can be said of notions of Visigothic capitalhood. The idea that Toledo was the head of the polity due to its intrinsic merits rather than because of the king's presence was not at all self-evident in the seventh century, unlike the principle that late antique Romans (and even certain Visigothic authors) applied to Rome and Constantinople. The isolated reference to the city as *civitas regia* in Third Toledo contrasts with the striking silence in other contemporary sources as well as documents from the 620s and

101 Chron. Muz. 11, 21, 34, 37, 39, and 44, although in these cases in association with the episcopal see.

102 For instance, Merle Eisenberg's and Ian Wood's chapters in this volume.

630s. Only in the late 640s does the term re-emerge in conciliar literature. Church authors were aware of Chindaswinth's and Recceswinth's political programmes, which could have translated into new ways of conceiving of Toledo. But the mid-seventh century was also marked by conflicts between the bishops of Toledo and the monarchy. Above all, this was a period during which the see of Toledo fought for ascendancy within the kingdom's sacred and ecclesiastical landscape. These conflicts, I believe, constitute the background against which Toledan ecclesiastical sources sought to transform earlier notions of capitalhood as the seat of the king into the idea of a providentially ordained *urbs regia*.

Ewig's analytical framework for 'head cities' in the successor kingdoms significantly undermined the ideas of barbarian nomadism and 'primitive' statecraft. His model of transition from *sedes regiae* to Roman-like *urbes regiae* advanced the study of Visigothic political culture in multiple ways. Yet, as I hope to have shown in this chapter, his model probably neglects the strategic decisions underlying the adoption of Roman ideas and the ideological tensions among political elites—and beyond. Although we rely primarily on ecclesiastical sources, these documents betray other concurrent ideas of capitalhood, namely that the head of the kingdom was where the king resided, the *sedes regia*. And one may even suspect that the latter dominated over the former, despite the tenacious efforts of Toledo's ecclesiastical establishment to promote the Christian uniqueness of their city.

Bibliography

Alexander, Paul J., 'The Strength of Empire and Capital as Seen through Byzantine Eyes', in *Speculum*, 27.3 (1962), 339–57

Alonso Álvarez, Raquel, 'Hornija, Bamba, Pampliega: Las elecciones funerarias de los reyes hispanovisigodos', in *Territorio, Sociedad y Poder*, 3 (2008), 13–27

Ando, Clifford, 'Triumph in a Decentralized Empire', in *Der römische Triumph in Prinzipat und Spätantike*, ed. by Johannes Wienand and Fabian Goldbeck (Berlin: De Gruyter, 2017), pp. 397–417

Arce, Javier, 'Ceremonial visigodo/ceremonial "bizantino": un tópico historiográfico', in *Bizancio y la península ibérica: de la antigüedad tardía a la edad moderna*, ed. by Inmaculada Pérez Martín and Pedro Bádenas de la Peña (Madrid: Consejo Superior de Investigaciones Científicas, 2004), pp. 101–15

Arce, Javier, *Esperando a los árabes: los visigodos en Hispania, 507–711* (Madrid: Marcial Pons, 2011)

Arce, Javier, 'Las tumbas de los reyes visigodos: un problema histórico', in *Pyrenae*, 51.1 (2020), 131–40

Barbero de Aguilera, Abilio, 'El pensamiento político visigodo y las primeras unciones regias en la Europa medieval', in *Hispania. Revista Española de Historia*, 115 (1970), 245–326

Barbero de Aguilera, Abilio, *La sociedad visigoda y su entorno histórico* (Madrid: Siglo XII, 1992)

Barroso Cabrera, Rafael, and Jorge Morín de Pablos, 'La ciuitas regia toletana en el contexto de la Hispania de la séptima centuria', in *Regia Sedes Toletana. La topografía de la ciudad de Toledo en la tardía antigüedad y alta edad media*, ed. by Jesús Carrobles Santos, Rafael Barroso Cabrera, and Jorge Morín de Pablos (Toledo: Diputación de Toledo, 2007), pp. 97–161

Barroso Cabrera, Rafael, Jesús Carrobles Santos, Jorge Morín de Pablos, and Isabel Sánchez Ramos, 'El paisaje urbano de Toledo en la antigüedad tardía', in *Antiquité Tardive*, 23 (2015), 329–52

Brühl, Carlrichard, 'Remarques sur les notions de "capitale" et de "résidence" pendant le haut Moyen Âge', in *Journal des Savants*, 4 (1967), 193–215

Buchberger, Erica, *Shifting Ethnic Identities in Spain and Gaul, 500–700: From Romans to Goths and Franks* (Amsterdam: Amsterdam University Press, 2017)

Cameron, Averil, 'The Theotokos in Sixth-Century Constantinople: A City Finds its Symbol', in *Journal of Theological Studies*, 29 (1978), 79–108

Cameron, Averil, 'Byzantine and Jews: Some Recent Work on Early Byzantium', in *Byzantine and Modern Greek Studies*, 20 (1996), 249–74

Cameron, Averil, 'The Cult of the Virgin in Late Antiquity: Religious Development and Myth-Making', in *Studies of Church History*, 39 (2004), 1–21

Canellas López, Ángel, *Diplomática Hispano-Visigoda* (Zaragoza: Institución 'Fernando el Católico', 1979)

Castillo Lozano, José Ángel, *Categorías de poder en el reino visigodo de Toledo: los tiranos en las obras de Juan de Bíclaro, Isidoro de Sevilla y Julián de Toledo* (Murcia: Universidad de Murcia, 2019)

Castro, Dolores, 'Toledo, *locus terribilis*. Iglesia y milagro en el *De viris illustribus* de Ildefonso de Toledo', in *En la España medieval*, 39 (2016), 49–72

Castro, Dolores, 'El desierto de Ildefonso de Toledo. Notas sobre la construcción de la autoridad episcopal en el reino visigodo', in *Gerión*, 37.1 (2019), 177–99

Chavarría Arnau, Alexandra, *A la sombra de un imperio. Iglesias, obispos y reyes en la Hispania tardoantigua (siglos V–VII)* (Bari: Edipuglia, 2018)

Christys, Ann, *Christians in Al-Andalus (711–1000)* (Richmond: Curzon, 2001)

Chronica Gallica a. 511, ed. by Richard Burgess, 'The Gallic Chronicle of 511: A New Critical Edition with a Brief Introduction', in *Society and Culture in Late Antique*

Gaul: Revisiting the Sources, ed. by Ralph W. Mathisen and Danuta Shanzer (Aldershot: Ashgate, 2001), pp. 86–100

Chronica Gothorum Pseudo-Isidoriana, ed. and trans. by Fernando González Muñoz, *La chronica gothorum pseudo-isidoriana (ms. Paris BN 6113). Edición crítica, traducción y estudio* (A Coruña: Toxosoutos, 2000)

Ciggaar, Krijnie N., *Western Travelers to Constantinople: The West and Byzantium, 692–1204: Cultural and Political Relations* (Leiden: Brill, 1996)

Claude, Dietrich, *Adel, Kirche und Königtum im Westgotenreich* (Sigmaringen: J. Thorbecke, 1971)

Codoñer Merino, Carmen, *El 'De viris illvstribvs' de Ildefonso de Toledo. Estudio y edición crítica* (Salamanca: Universidad de Salamanca, 1972)

Collins, Roger, 'Julian of Toledo and the Royal Succession in Late Seventh-Century Spain', in *Early Medieval Kingship*, ed. by P. H. Sawyer and I. N. Wood (Leeds: University of Leeds, 1977), pp. 30–49

Collins, Roger, 'Mérida and Toledo: 550–585', in *Visigothic Spain: New Approaches*, ed. by Edward James (Oxford: Clarendon Press, 1980), pp. 189–219

Collins, Roger, 'Literacy and the Laity in Early Medieval Spain', in *The Uses of Literacy in Early Medieval Europe*, ed. by Rosamond McKitterick (Cambridge: Cambridge University Press, 1990), pp. 109–33

Collins, Roger, *Visigothic Spain, 409–711* (Malden, MA: Blackwell, 2004)

Collins, Roger, 'Ambrosio de Morales and the *Codex Vetustissimus Ovetensis*', in *Italy and the East Roman World in the Medieval Mediterranean: Empire, Cities and Elites 476–1204. Papers in Honour of Thomas S. Brown*, ed. by Thomas J. MacMaster and Nicholas S. M. Mantheou (New York, NY: Routledge, 2021), pp. 49–69

Córcoles Olaitz, Edorta, *Las* Formulae Wisigothicae*: aproximación a la práctica jurídica visigoda* (Lecce: Edizione Grifo, 2010)

Corpus iuris civilis. Volumen primum. Institutiones. Digesta, ed. by Paul Krueger and Theodor Mommsen (Berlin: Weidmann, 1887)

Dey, Hendrik W., *The Afterlife of the Roman City: Architecture and Ceremony in Late Antiquity and the Early Middle Ages* (Cambridge: Cambridge University Press, 2015)

Díaz, Pablo C., 'Visigothic Political Institutions', in *The Visigoths: From the Migration Period to the Seventh Century – An Ethnographic Perspective*, ed. by Peter Heather (Woodbridge: Boydell Press, 1999), pp. 321–56

Díaz, Pablo C., 'El esquema provincial en el contexto administrativo de la monarquía visigoda de Toledo', in *Mélanges de la Casa de Velázquez. Nouvelle Série*, 49.2 (2019), 77–108

Díaz y Díaz, Manuel, 'Tres ciudades en el Códice de Roda: Babilonia, Nínive y Toledo', in *Archivo Español de Arqueología*, 45 (1972–1974), 251–66

Díaz y Díaz, Manuel, *Libros y librerías en La Rioja medieval* (Logroño: Instituto de Estudios Riojanos, 1991)

Diesner, Hans-Joachim, 'Politik und Ideologie im Westgotenreich von Toledo: Chindasvind', in *Sitzungsberichte der sächsischen Akademie der Wissenschaften zu Leipzig. Philologish-Historische Klasse*, 121.1 (1979), 1–35

Drews, Wolfram, 'The Image of the Christian Ruler in the Catholic Monarchy of Visigothic Spain: Julian of Toledo's *Historia Wambae*', in *The Good Christian Ruler in the First Millennium: Views from the Wider Mediterranean World in Conversation*, ed. by Philip Michael Forness, Alexandra Hasse-Ungeheuer, and Harmut Leppin (Berlin: De Gruyter, 2021), pp. 311–25

Esders, Stefan, '"Getaufte Juden" im westgotischen Spanien. Die antijüdische Politik König Chintilas zum Jahreswechsel 637/638 und ihre Hintergründe', in *Jüdische Lebenswelten. Von der Antike bis zur Gegenwart*, ed. by Ernst Baltrusch and Uwe Puschner (Frankfurt am Main: Peter Lang, 2016), pp. 53–96

Esders, Stefan, '*Regem iura faciunt, non persona*. Der westgotische Treueid im Kräftefeld personaler und transpersonaler Konzepte der Legitimität politischer Herrschaft', in *Die Macht des Herrschers. Personale und transpersonale Aspekte*, ed. by Mechthild Albert, Elke Brüggen, and Konrad Klaus (Göttingen: Vandenhoeck & Ruprecht, 2019), pp. 70–152

Ewig, Eugen, 'Résidence et capitale pendant le haut Moyen Age', in *Revue Historique*, 230.1 (1963), 25–72

Fear, Andrew, *Lives of the Visigothic Fathers* (Liverpool: Liverpool University Press, 1997)

Felix of Toledo, *Elogium Idelfonsi*, ed. by José Carlos Martín-Iglesias and Valeriano Yarza Urquiola, *Iulianus Toletanus, Felix Toletanus, Iulianus Toletanus (Ps.). Opera II: Elogium Ildefonsi, Vita Iuliani (auctore Felice Toletano), Antikeimena, Fragmenta, Ordo annorum mundi*, CCSL 115B (Turnhout: Brepols, 2014)

Felix of Toledo, *Vita Iuliani*, ed. by José Carlos Martín-Iglesias and Valeriano Yarza Urquiola, *Iulianus Toletanus, Felix Toletanus, Iulianus Toletanus (Ps.). Opera II: Elogium Ildefonsi, Vita Iuliani (auctore Felice Toletano), Antikeimena, Fragmenta, Ordo annorum mundi*, CCSL 115B (Turnhout: Brepols, 2014)

Fernández, Damián, 'Trial Witnesses, Social Hierarchies, and State Building in the Visigothic Kingdom of Toledo', in *Early Medieval Europe*, 28.4 (2020), 509–31

García Herrero, Gregorio, 'Sobre la autoría de la *Insultatio* y la fecha de composición de la *Historia Wambae* de Julián de Toledo', in *Arqueología, paleontología y etnografía*, 4 (1998), 185–214

García López, Yolanda, 'La cronología de la "Historia Wambae"', in *Anuario de Estudios Medievales*, 23.1 (1993), 121–39

García Moreno, Luis A, 'Estudios sobre la organización administrativa del reino visigodo de Toledo', in *Anuario de Historia del Derecho Español*, 44 (1974), 5–155

García Moreno, Luis, 'La cristianización de la topografía de las ciudades de la península ibérica en la antigüedad tardía', in *Archivo Español de Arqueología*, 50.51 (1977–1988), 311–21

Gil Fernández, Juan, 'Textos olvidados del Códice de Roda', in *Habis*, 2 (1971), 165–78

González Blanco, Antonio, 'El Decreto de Gundemaro y la historia del siglo VII', in *Antigüedad y Cristianismo*, 3 (1986), 159–69

González Salinero, Raúl, *Las conversiones forzosas de los judíos en el reino visigodo* (Madrid: Consejo Superior de Investigaciones Científicas, 2000)

Grig, Lucy, and Gavin Kelly, *Two Romes* (Oxford: Oxford University Press: 2012)

Hillgarth, Jocelyn, 'Coins and Chronicles: Propaganda in Sixth-Century Spain and the Byzantine Background', in *Historia: Zeitschrift für Alte Geschichte*, 15.4 (1966), 483–508

Hillgarth, Jocelyn, *The Visigoths in History and Legend* (Toronto: Pontifical Institute of Mediaeval Studies, 2009)

Ihnat, Kati, 'Liturgy Against Apostasy: Marian Commemoration and the Jews in Visigothic Iberia', in *Early Medieval Europe*, 25.4 (2017), 443–65

Ihnat, Kati, 'Orígenes y desarrollo de la fiesta litúrgica de la Virgen María en Iberia', in *Anuario de estudios medievales*, 49.2 (2019), 619–43

Ildefonsus of Toledo, *De virginitate Sanctae Mariae*, ed. by Valeriano Yarza Urquiola and Carmen Codoñer Merino, *Ildefonsi Toletani episcopi De virginitate Sanctae Mariae, De cognitione baptismi, De itinere deserti*, CCSL 114A (Turnhout: Brepols, 2007)

Isla Frez, Amancio, 'Desde el reino visigodo y la ortodoxia toledana: la correspondencia de Montano', in *Studia Storica. Historia Medieval*, 18 (2000), 41–52

Isla Frez, Amancio, 'El *officium palatinum* visigodo. Entorno regio y poder aristocrático', in *Hispania*, 62.212 (2002), 823–47

Kaldellis, Anthony, 'How Was a "New Rome" Even Thinkable? Premonitions of Constantinople and the Portability of Rome', in *Leadership and Community in Late Antiquity: Essays in Honour of Raymond Van Dam*, ed. by Young Richard Kim and A. E. T. McLaughlin (Turnhout: Brepols, 2020), pp. 221–47

Kelly, Michael J., *Isidore of Seville and the* Liber Iudiciorum*: The Struggle for the Past in the Visigothic Kingdom* (Leiden: Brill, 2021)

King, P. D., *Law and Society in the Visigothic Kingdom* (Cambridge: Cambridge University Press, 1972)

King, P. D., 'King Chindasvind and the First Territorial Law-Code of the Visigothic Kingdom', in *Visigothic Spain: New Approaches*, ed. by Edward James (Oxford: Clarendon Press, 1980), pp. 131–57

Koch, Manuel, 'La imperialización del Reino visigodo bajo Leovigildo. ¿Es la *imitatio imperii* de Leovigildo la manifestación de un momento de cambio en la pretensión de poder y la ideología visigodas?', in *Pyrenae*, 39.2 (2008), 101–17

Leges Visigothorum, ed. Karl Zeumer, MGH Leges nationum Germanicarum, I (Hannover: Hahn, 1902)

Levison, Wilhelm, *Historia Wambae regis auctore Iuliano episcopo Toletano*, in *Passiones vitaeque sanctorum aevi Meronvingici*, ed. by Bruno Krusch and Wilhelm

Levison, MGH Scriptores rerum Merovingicarum, V (Hannover and Leipzig: Hahn, 1905), pp. 486–535

Linehan, Peter, *History and the Historians of Medieval Spain* (Oxford: Clarendon Press, 1993)

Mango, Cyril, 'Constantinople as Theotokoupolis', in *Mother of God: Representations of the Virgin in Byzantine Art*, ed. by Maria Vassilaki (Milan: Skira, 2000), pp. 17–25

Martin, Céline, 'Las cartas de Montano y la autonomía episcopal de la Hispania septentrional en el siglo VI', in *Hispania Antigua*, 22 (1998), 403–26

Martin, Céline, *La géographie du pouvoir dans l'Espagne visigothique* (Lille: Presses Universitaires du Septentrion, 2003)

Martin, Céline, 'Montanus et les schismatiques: la reprise en main d'une périphérie hispanique au début du VIe siècle', in *Médiévales*, 51 (2006), 9–20

Martin, Céline, 'Le *Liber Iudiciorum* et ses différentes versions', in *Mélanges de la Casa de Velázquez. Nouvelle série*, 41.2 (2011), 17–34

Martin, Céline, 'Un prince épiscope. Le ministère royal visigothique', in *Le prince chétien de Constantin aux royautés barbares (IVe–VIIIe siècle)*, ed. by Sylvain Destephen, Bruno Dumézil, and Hervé Inglebert (Paris: Association des Amis du Centre d'Histoire et Civilisation de Byzance, 2018), pp. 247–65

Martin, Céline, and Capucine Nemo-Pekelman, 'Les juifs et la cité. Pour une clarification du statut personnel des juifs de l'antiquité tardive à la fin du royaume de Tolède (IVe–VIIe siècles)', in *Antiquité Tardive*, 16 (2008), 223–46

Martin, Céline, and Juan José Larrea (eds), *Nouvelles chartes visigothiques du monastère pyrénéen d'Asán* (Bordeaux: Ausonius, 2021)

Martínez Pizarro, Joaquín, *The Story of Wamba: Julian of Toledo's* Historia Wambae regis (Washington, DC: The Catholic University of America Press, 2005)

Mateos Cruz, Pedro, *La Basílica de Santa Eulalia de Mérida. Arqueología y urbanismo* (Madrid: Consejo Superior de Investigaciones Científicas, 1999)

Mayer, Emanuel, *Rom ist dort, wo der Kaiser ist. Untersuchungen zu den Staatsdenkmälern des dezentralisierten Reiches von Diocletian bis zu Theodosius II* (Mainz: Römisch-Germanischen Zentralmuseum, 2002)

McCormick, Michael, *Eternal Victory: Triumphal Rulership in Late Antiquity, Byzantium and the Early Medieval West* (Cambridge: Cambridge University Press, 1986)

McEvoy, Meaghan, 'Rome and the Transformation of the Imperial Office in the Late Fourth-Mid-Fifth Centuries AD', in *Papers of the British School at Rome*, 78 (2010), 151–92

McEvoy, Meaghan, and Muriel Moser, 'Introducing Imperial Presence in Late Antique Rome (2nd-7th Centuries AD)', in *Antiquité Tardive*, 25 (2017), 15–21

Norton, Peter, *Episcopal Elections, 250–600: Hierarchy and Popular Will in Late Antiquity* (Oxford: Oxford University Press, 2011)

Olmo Enciso, Lauro, 'Nuevos paisajes urbanos y consolidación del estado en época visigoda', in *Hispania Gothorum. San Ildefonso y el reino visigodo de Toledo* (Toledo: Empresa Pública 'Don Quijote de la Mancha 2005', 2007), pp. 161–80

Olmo Enciso, Lauro, 'Recópolis: una ciudad en época de transformaciones', in *Zona Arqueológica*, 9 (2008), 40–63

Orlandis Rovira, José, 'La ambigua jurisdicción de la metrópoli toledana', in *Cuadernos de historia de España*, 63 (1980), 7–11

Panzram, Sabine, 'La formación del orden metropolitano en la Península Ibérica (siglos IV a VI)', in *Pyrennae*, 49.1 (2018), 125–54

Pentcheva, Bissera, *Icons and Power: The Mother of God in Byzantium* (Philadelphia, PA: University of Pennsylvania Press, 2006)

Pérez Martínez, Meritxell, *Tarraco en la Antigüedad tardía: cristianización y organización eclesiástica (III a VIII siglos)* (Tarragona: Arola Ed., 2012)

Ribera i Lacomba, Albert, *Los orígenes del cristianismo en Valencia y su entorno* (Valencia: Ajuntament de València, 2000)

Riess, Frank, *Narbonne and Its Territory in Late Antiquity: From the Visigoths to the Arabs* (Burlington, VT: Ashgate, 2013)

Ripoll, Gisela, 'Changes in the Topography of Power: From *Civitates* to *Vrbes Regiae* in *Hispania*', in *The Construction of Communities in the Early Middle Ages*, ed. by Richard Corradini, Max Diesenberger, and Helmut Reimitz (Leiden: Brill, 2003), pp. 123–48

Schlimbach, Fedor, '*San Román de Hornija*, Chindasvinth und Reciberga. Zur westgotischen Gründung des Klosters in der *Tierra de Campos*', in *Anales de Arqueología Cordobesa*, 20 (2009), 349–78

Shoemaker, Stephen, '"Let Us Go and Burn Her Body": The Image of the Jews in the Early Dormition Traditions', in *Church History*, 68.4 (1999), 775–823

Shoemaker, Stephen J., *Mary in Early Christian Faith and Devotion* (New Haven, CT: Yale University Press, 2016)

Stocking, Rachel, *Bishops, Councils, and Consensus in the Visigothic Kingdom, 589–633* (Ann Arbor, MI: University of Michigan Press, 2000)

Thompson, E. A., *The Goths in Spain* (Oxford: Clarendon Press, 1969)

Tomás-Faci, Guillermo, and Juan Carlos Martín-Iglesias, 'Cuatro documentos inéditos del monasterio visigodo de San Martín de Asán (522–586)', in *Mittellateinisches Jahrbuch*, 52.2 (2017), 261–86

Valverde Castro, María del Rosario, *Ideología, simbolismo y ejercicio del poder real en la monarquía visigoda: Un proceso de cambio* (Salamanca: Universidad de Salamanca, 2000)

Velázquez Soriano, Isabel, 'Wamba y Paulo. dos personalidades enfrentadas y una rebelión', in *Espacio, Tiempo y Forma. Serie II. Historia Antigua*, 2 (1989), 213–22

Velázquez, Isabel, '*Pro patriae gentique Gothorum statu* (4th Council of Toledo, Canon 75, A. 633)', in *Regna and Gentes: The Relationship Between Late Antique and Early Medieval Peoples and Kingdoms in the Transformation of the Roman World*, ed. by Hans-Werner Goetz, Jörg Jarnut, and Walter Pohl (Leiden: Brill, 2003), pp. 161–217

Velázquez Soriano, Isabel, 'El acto epigráfico en la Hispania visigoda (del rey abajo, todos)', in *Hispania Gothorum. San Ildefonso y el reino visigodo de Toledo* (Toledo: Empresa Pública 'Don Quijote de la Mancha 2005', 2007), pp. 87–105

Velázquez, Isabel, and Rosario Hernando, 'Una noticia desconcertante sobre la inscripción de San Juan de Baños ofrecida por Álvar Gómez de Castro', in *Archivo Español de Arqueología*, 73 (2000), 295–307

Velázquez, Isabel, and Gisela Ripoll, '*Toletvm*, La construcción de una *vrbs regia*', in *Sedes regiae (ann. 400–800)*, ed. by Gisela Ripoll, Josep Gurt, and Alexandra Chavarría (Barcelona: Reial Acadèmia de Bones Lletres, 2000), pp. 521–78

Weisweiler, John, 'From Equality to Asymmetry: Honorific Statues, Imperial Power, and Senatorial Identity in Late-Antique Rome', in *Journal of Roman Archaeology*, 25 (2012), 319–50

Wood, Jamie, 'Playing the Fame Game: Bibliography, Celebrity, and Primacy in Late Antique Spain', in *Journal of Early Christian Studies*, 20.4 (2012), 613–40

Wood, Jamie, 'Building and Breaking Episcopal Networks in Late Antique *Hispania*', in *Episcopal Networks in Late Antiquity*, ed. by Carmen Angela Cvetković and Peter Gemeinhardt (Berlin: De Gruyter, 2019), pp. 227–47

About the Author

Damián Fernández is Associate Professor of History at Northern Illinois University. He has published on the social, institutional, and economic history of the Iberian peninsula in Late Antiquity, including a monograph titled *Aristocrats and Statehood in Western Iberia, 300–600 CE*. He is currently co-authoring a translation and commentary of the *Liber Iudiciorum*.

7 Making Rite Choices

Roman and Eastern Liturgies in Early Medieval Iberia

Molly Lester[1]

Abstract

In the sixth and seventh centuries, the liturgy was an important medium through which Iberian kingdoms sought to claim Christian orthodoxy. While some Iberian liturgical practices had ancient origins, others were the product of more recent exchanges across the Mediterranean, and a few were deliberately borrowed from contemporary Rome or the East. This chapter argues that attending to the liturgical dimensions of *imitatio imperii* sheds light on how the mobilization of Roman liturgical traditions variously activated or stripped away their ancient, Roman, or eastern origins. Through invocation or elision of eastern and Roman origins of rites, Visigothic and Suevic elites negotiated their place in the Christian church, defined their relationship to Roman or eastern Christianities, and offered malleable definitions of what was Roman or eastern.

Keywords: liturgy; Old Hispanic liturgy; eastern liturgy; Roman liturgy; creeds; Martin of Braga

In the sixth and seventh centuries, the Mediterranean world witnessed a contest of Christian orthodoxy. Following the fifth-century collapse of western imperial administration, multiple kingdoms claimed to be the rightful heirs of imperial Christianity. The Suevic and Visigothic kingdoms of the 500s and 600s were among these contenders, and Visigothic rulers and intellectuals in particular promoted themselves as the true standard-bearers

1 I am grateful to my co-editors, the anonymous reviewers, Kati Ihnat, Rebecca Maloy, and Christopher Florio for their thoughtful comments and suggestions.

Fernández, D., Lester, M. & Wood, J. (eds.), *Rome and Byzantium in the Visigothic Kingdom: Beyond* Imitatio Imperii. Taylor & Francis Group 2023
DOI: 10.5117/9789463726412_CH07

of Christian orthodoxy in the post-Roman world.[2] Their claim, however, was not without challenge. Those who wished to portray themselves as the heirs of Roman tradition had to grapple not only with other 'barbarian' kingdoms with similar pretensions, but also with other states and churches who still proudly called themselves Romans. The continued existence of the eastern Roman empire forced Visigothic authors to articulate why their kingdom was religiously superior and why eastern Christianity might be considered heretical.[3] The popes of Rome also presented a challenge, and alternately conciliatory and testy exchanges reveal a complicated relationship between the Iberian kingdoms and the papacy.[4]

In this ideological battle, the liturgy (broadly defined as the rites and worship of Christian churches) was an important medium through which Iberian kingdoms sought to claim Christian orthodoxy.[5] Correct ritual and worship were a means to create orthodox churches, to integrate kingdoms, and to construct ecclesiology,[6] and as they pursued these goals, Visigothic and Suevic elites continuously and self-consciously evaluated their own liturgical traditions. In doing so, they were forced to confront the relationship between their own rites and those of other Christian traditions. While some Iberian liturgical practices could be traced back to ancient sources, others were the product of more recent exchanges across the Mediterranean, and a few were deliberately borrowed from contemporary Rome or from the East. Deciding when to highlight and when to obscure the 'Roman' or 'eastern' aspects of a liturgical rite, or what these terms even meant in a liturgical context, was a continuous exercise in relating to, reinventing, or reassessing the presence of Roman Christianity in the Iberian peninsula.

Despite the presence of Roman and eastern traditions in Visigothic and Suevic liturgical discourse, attention to the liturgy has been minimal in discussions of the kingdoms' relationship with the Roman past and other post-Roman polities.[7] Instead, scholarship has largely focused on the Visigothic inheritance of Roman political, legal, and material culture, and (more recently) on Visigothic exchanges with and 'imitations' of the

2 Herrin 1987, 220–49; Stocking 2000.

3 Wood 2005; Montero Herrero 1998.

4 Deswarte 2010; Ferreiro 2020.

5 For early medieval liturgy, see Palazzo 2008. For Old Hispanic liturgy, see Álvarez Martínez 2013; Pinell 1998; Rivera Recio 1965; and Zapke 2007. For a summary of the liturgy of the mass, see Fernández Alonso 1955, 313–23. For the chants of the mass, see Hornby and Maloy 2013, 49–50.

6 For liturgy and Iberian ecclesiology, see Lester 2018.

7 Exceptions are Bravo García 2002; Fernández Jiménez 2004; and Castillo Maldonado 2005.

Byzantine empire.[8] Attending to the liturgical dimensions of *imitatio imperii* sheds light on how Visigothic and Suevic elites negotiated their place in the Christian church, how they defined their relationship to Roman or eastern Christianities, and how their definitions of Roman or eastern were contextually malleable. In some instances, recognizing the original Roman or eastern context of a practice could infuse a rite or alteration with authority, allay fears of heterodoxy, and link a community with the wider Christian world. In other cases, Roman churches were not a model to imitate, but rather a reference point to inform Iberian liturgical discussions and to lend weight to one party's position. Finally, some Iberian elites actually adopted contemporary eastern or Roman liturgical customs, but as in histories or literature,[9] the conscious adoption of other regional rites could involve an explicit identification or a surgically precise excision of the original source. In other words, Iberian Christians could mobilize Roman liturgical traditions even as they activated or stripped away layers of meaning. By examining the variety of Iberian approaches to Roman liturgies, I seek to demonstrate that *imitatio imperii* not only involved appealing to another authority or tradition: it could also manifest as a form of erasure.

In what follows, I will examine how Iberian actors emphasized or elided their relationship with and/or adoption of Roman liturgical customs, defined variously as those from the late Roman empire, the contemporary Byzantine empire, and the city of Rome. After surveying the movement of liturgical knowledge and customs in the early medieval world, I will begin in the sixth-century Suevic kingdom, where bishops actively aligned themselves with the churches of Rome and Constantinople by practising these churches' rites and highlighting liturgical similarities. I will then examine the Visigothic insertion of the Constantinopolitan creed into Eucharistic rites at the Third Council of Toledo in 589. In contrast to the Suevic emphasis on 'Roman' origins or parallels, Visigothic elites at Toledo III navigated their adoption of this custom by simultaneously acknowledging and suppressing its contemporary and eastern origins. Finally, over the course of the seventh century, bishops such as Isidore of Seville and Braulio of Zaragoza increasingly placed the eastern origins of certain liturgical customs within an abstract Christian past rather than linking them to contemporary churches. In the case of the city of Rome, seventh-century authors acknowledged both past and present Roman liturgies as authoritative, yet regarded papal rites as useful parallels to confirm Iberian customs rather than as models to imitate.

8 See the introduction and Martin in this volume.

9 Wood 2012a, 2012b.

Liturgical Drift in the Mediterranean World

Liturgical rituals, prayers, and songs undoubtedly circulated throughout the late antique and early medieval world,[10] yet identifying liturgical exchanges between different regions is methodologically fraught. Written descriptions of late antique liturgies are difficult to generalize into regional traditions, and the earliest extant western liturgical manuscripts date to the late seventh century.[11] We can never be certain whether descriptions of masses, prayers, and chants in ninth- and tenth-century manuscripts accurately depict liturgies of the sixth and seventh centuries.[12] Moreover, capturing what counts as liturgical imitation or adoption produces a fresh set of questions. Demarcating a regional rite risks producing a static rendition that fails to acknowledge fluidity and variation, and broad similarities between all Christian liturgies necessitate a fine-grained approach to identifying transfers between rites.[13] If there was a similarity between geographically distinct rites, how does one determine which rite influenced the other, whether they developed independently, or whether similarities stemmed from one source?

Notwithstanding these questions, it is evident that even as communal horizons contracted in the fifth and sixth centuries, the travellers, traders, pilgrims, refugees, and soldiers who still traversed the Mediterranean world brought with them descriptions of other Christian liturgies or even transplanted rites from one region to another.[14] For example, communities of foreign merchants and craftsmen were common in important urban centres, and enclaves such as the Greek community of Mérida likely included priests who performed eastern rites.[15] Religious migrants and pilgrims similarly

10 Crehan 1976.

11 Vogel 1986, 34–46.

12 Eloquently expressed by Dyer (1982, 24), referring to Roman chant.

13 Liturgists and liturgical historians have long reflected on these challenges, particularly within ongoing debates over the utility of comparative liturgy (as articulated by Anton Baumstark). Both proponents and critics of comparative liturgiology recognize that liturgy is constantly evolving, and while some argue that using extant texts to represent a rite ossifies said rite, others maintain that since texts are what remain of historical liturgies, scholars must use them (see Taft 2001 for an excellent overview). All, however, recognize the dangers of defining and demarcating a 'liturgical family or tradition' (Taft 2001, 197). Geographical proximity and similarities in structures and formulas seem to be the most consistent factors in demarcating a rite. For recent evaluations of methodology, see Gittos 2016 and Berger and Spinks 2016.

14 For late antique and early medieval travel, see Ellis and Kidner 2004 and Claude 2000.

15 For Greek communities in Iberian cities, see Barrett and J. Wood's contributions in this volume.

brought knowledge of other rites or carried their customs with them into new lands. Orosius's Mediterranean-wide journeys, Egeria's fourth-century pilgrimage from Gallaecia to the Holy Land, Hydatius's geographically similar pilgrimage in the early fifth century, Martin of Braga's move from Pannonia to Gallaecia in the 550s, John of Biclarum and Leander of Seville's residence in Constantinople, and the North African monk Donatus's flight to Iberia in the late sixth century all exposed Iberian Christians to different liturgical traditions. Diplomacy and conquest generated even more liturgical exchange. Emperor Justinian's western conquests brought Greek and Syrian bishops to southern Iberia, while Visigothic ambassadors to Gaul and Frankish ambassadors to Iberia attended and observed the liturgies of other kingdoms.[16] Royal marriages often saw a princess of one kingdom bringing her native rites to her new home. While the most famous example is the Roman missionary Augustine of Canterbury's discovery that the Frankish princess Bertha practised Frankish rites in England in 596–597,[17] one wonders whether the Frankish, Visigothic, and Ostrogothic princesses that circulated between the western Mediterranean kingdoms did the same.

Along with travellers came texts and relics. Greek, African, and Gallic canons had long circulated within Iberia, and universal canon collections such as the *Collectio Hispana* embraced canons that reflected temporally and geographically disparate rites. Pastoral and patristic texts also offered descriptions of other regional rites, and esteemed works such as the *Statuta ecclesiae antiqua* and Augustine of Hippo's letters to Januarius lent Gallic and African norms an authoritative lustre.[18] Despite the potential heretical dangers of eastern Christianity, Iberians enthusiastically embraced eastern saints and martyrs, and the feasts of many eastern saints became permanent features of the Old Hispanic sanctoral calendar.[19]

Early medieval Christians also consistently exchanged writings and instructions about liturgies. In 538, for example, Pope Vigilius sent descriptions of Roman sacraments and copies of Roman prayers to the Gallaecian

16 For east Roman bishops, see II Seville 12 (Conc. 171), Vallejo Girvés 2000–2001 and 2008, and Velázquez Soriano 2000. For Visigothic and Frankish ambassadors, see Greg. Tur. Decem libri 5.39.43 and 6.18.33 and 38.

17 For Augustine's liturgical dilemma in Britain, see Meyvaert 1963.

18 Isidore of Seville cited Augustine's letters as authorities in *De ecclesiasticis officiis*, indicating knowledge of the texts in the peninsula by the early seventh century. Iberian bishops probably cited the *Statuta ecclesiae antiqua* in councils under the incorrect title of 'Fourth Council of Carthage' (see Coll. Hisp. IV, 350 and 360, and V, 111). For textual exchange between Iberia and North Africa, see Graham 2011, 158–61.

19 Castillo Maldonado 2005, especially 15–18.

bishop Profuturus of Braga who had earlier written to the pope for advice. Liturgical books crisscrossed the Mediterranean and Atlantic as well. One of the earliest western liturgical manuscripts, the *Verona Orational*, was composed in Iberia (perhaps in north-eastern regions) in the late seventh or the early eighth century and had moved to northern Italy by the mid-eighth century, possibly in the aftermath of Arab and Berber conquests.[20]

In certain cases, scholars have identified specific prayers, chants, and/or rituals that were present in multiple regional rites. Descriptions of Greek responses and chants in western rites, for example, attest to similarities between eastern and western liturgies, even if the mechanics of this exchange are unclear.[21] Extant liturgical manuscripts provide more solid ground for discussion, and examining Iberian manuscripts of the ninth, tenth, and eleventh centuries, scholars have advanced arguments for parallels between the Old Hispanic liturgy and other early medieval rites from Gaul, Rome, and Milan. José Janini has made a convincing case for similarities between the seventh-century Veronese collection of Roman formularies and later Old Hispanic texts such as the eleventh-century *Liber Ordinum*, and Michel Huglo has argued that certain Old Hispanic chants drew on Gallican precedents.[22] Kenneth Levy has explored not only textual similarities, but also melodic correspondences between later Gregorian, Milanese, and Old Hispanic chants;[23] building on Levy's work, Rebecca Maloy and others have identified textual and musical transmissions between Old Hispanic and Franco-Roman responsories.[24] Finally, Dom Louis Brou, Sebastià Janeras, and others have used later manuscripts to explore similarities and differences between Old Hispanic liturgies and various eastern rites.[25]

Yet even with the identification of similarities, the direction and process of liturgical exchanges are difficult to pin down. If these similarities were

20 The dating and origin of this manuscript are uncertain. Some date the manuscript *c.* 800 based on palaeographical grounds, while others argue for an earlier date based on content, marginal additions, and codicology. For a good summary and assessment, see Díaz y Díaz 1997. See Vogel 1986 for the development and genres of liturgical texts.

21 Quasten 1943.

22 Janini 1965; Huglo 1955. However, I find Janini's assertion that a codex identical to the Roman formularies passed over the Pyrenees at an early date and served as a model for the liturgical Latin of Toledo (p. 37) exceedingly optimistic.

23 Levy 1984, 55–61. Gregorian chant was the successor to older Roman liturgies, and eventually replaced Old Hispanic chant in Iberia in the eleventh century. Levy posited that rather than a direct exchange between Gregorian and Old Hispanic traditions, both drew on a (potentially Gallic) branch of Offertory chants that circulated independently (pp. 66, 72, 77).

24 Maloy et al. (forthcoming).

25 Brou 1948; Janeras 1995.

indeed transferences, it is largely impossible to determine when they entered the Iberian repertoire, how they were introduced, or whether they became more widespread beyond our manuscript witnesses.[26] Moreover, as stated earlier, the degree to which later manuscripts represent earlier liturgies is very uncertain. Although seventh-century Iberia witnessed extensive liturgical reform, composition, and standardization, assuming that the manuscripts exactly reproduce practices three centuries earlier is a dangerous leap.[27] For the most part, the mechanics of liturgical exchange in Late Antiquity and the early Middle Ages are invisible to modern eyes.

Roman *Auctoritas* in the Suevic Kingdom

Given that so much about liturgical exchange is opaque, the moments when early medieval authors openly discussed their adoption of another custom, or recognized the extra-regional origins of a practice, are valuable opportunities to investigate the logic and mechanics behind these links. In Iberia, the most dramatic case of explicitly adopting both eastern and Roman liturgical customs occurred in the sixth-century Suevic kingdom in Gallaecia, where anxiety about religious orthodoxy and liturgical practice drove Christian leaders to seek authoritative guides and models. The Suevic royal conversion to Nicene Christianity around 560 presumably accelerated this process as it sharpened the political implications of liturgical decisions.[28] In their letters and councils, Gallaecian bishops eagerly appealed to the city of Rome, to the 'east', and to Constantinople as liturgical authorities and peers, and they both adopted Roman and eastern practices and drew comparisons to their own Gallaecian rite. In doing so, the bishops and (likely) Suevic kings sought to position themselves within the Mediterranean religious and political landscape.[29]

The first evidence for Gallaecian adoption of 'Roman' liturgies stems from the 530s, when Bishop Profuturus of Braga wrote to Pope Vigilius

26 Maloy et al. (forthcoming) offer thoughtful analysis on the possible origins, directions, and mechanisms of exchange between Old Hispanic and Franco-Roman chants.

27 While some assume that the Old Hispanic chant repertoire cohered very early in the seventh century (Randel 2019), Rebecca Maloy and Emma Hornby have recently demonstrated that Old Hispanic chants displayed regional variability well into the eighth and ninth centuries (Maloy 2014; Maloy and Hornby 2016).

28 For the Suevic conversion, see Díaz 2011; Thompson 1980.

29 Deswarte (2010, 134–40) emphasizes local Suevic initiative rather than systematic Roman imposition.

expressing worry over 'ambiguous observations' (*observantiam ambiguam*) within the Gallaecian church. Profuturus's missive is lost, but according to Vigilius's response in 538, the bishop of Braga related that Gallaecian clerics recited different baptismal formulas, celebrated Easter on different days, and practised all sorts of varied customs. The bishop of Rome was only too happy to resolve Gallaecian disagreement by advising Profuturus to perform the liturgy as it was done in Rome, in particular prescribing triple rather than single immersion baptism. Remarkably, Vigilius also sent specific Roman liturgical prayers: 'Wherefore we also directed the text of the same canonical prayer [to be] added below, which (with God favourably inclined) we received from apostolic tradition [...] we likewise added the prayers of Easter day.'[30] The correspondence between Profuturus and Vigilius set an important precedent for the intense liturgical reforms of the 560s. According to the records of the First Council of Braga (561), when the eight bishops in attendance began to address disordered religious customs throughout their sees, they read aloud the letter that Pope Vigilius had sent just over twenty years earlier. They declared their intention to take instruction from apostolic authority, and in canon 4, they mandated that all clerics should celebrate the *ordo* of the mass which Profuturus had received from the authority of the Apostolic See.[31] They echoed this sentiment in the next canon, stating that no one should omit the baptismal *ordo* which Profuturus had earlier received from the see of the Apostle Peter.[32]

The Roman see was not the only liturgical authority available to the reformers at Braga I. When it suited them, the bishops actively combined Roman rites with eastern customs. Prior to embracing Vigilius's Roman liturgies in canons 4 and 5, the bishops had declared in canon 3 that both bishops and priests should address their congregations with '*Dominus vobiscum*' and the people should respond '*Et cum spiritu tuo*', 'as the entire East preserves from apostolic tradition itself and not as the Priscillian depravity altered'.[33] The bishops made it clear that the 'new' custom was in

30 'Quapropter et ipsius canonicae precis textum direximus subter adjectum, quem (Deo propitio) ex apostolica traditione suscepimus. Et ut charitas tua cognoscat, quibus locis aliqua festivitatibus apta connectes, paschalis diei preces similiter [simul] adjecimus' (Vigilius, *Epistula* to Profuturus of Braga, V (PL 69:18)). See also Ferreiro 2020, 279–81, 284–86.

31 I Braga 4 (Conc. 72).

32 'Item placuit, ut nullus eum baptizandi ordinem praetermittat quem et antes tenuit metropolitana Bracarensis ecclesia et pro amputanda aliquorum dubietate praedictus Profuturus ab episcopis scribtum sibi et directum a sede beatissimi apostoli Petri suscepit' (I Braga 5 (Conc. 72)).

33 'Sicut et ab ipsis apostolis traditum omnis retinet Oriens et non sicut Priscilliana pravitas permutavit' (I Braga 3 (Conc. 71–72)).

fact rooted in apostolic tradition, and justified their decision by claiming that Priscillians had distorted the original custom. But in addition to these already powerful explanations, the bishops saw fit to add that the entire East kept this custom as well, deliberately placing themselves within a liturgical tradition kept in eastern churches. The vagueness of the 'East' also avoided direct reference to the eastern Roman empire. It suggested an ahistorical context for the bishops' appeal that evoked the Christian past and perhaps even implied the timelessness and antiquity of the adopted customs. Rather than slavishly adopting Roman liturgies alone, these Gallaecian bishops crafted their own apostolic tradition that embraced Rome and the East, past and present.

The liturgies of Rome and the East also served as a resource to explain or validate pre-existing Iberian customs. Martin of Braga, a Pannonian who had travelled westward and sponsored translations of eastern canons and hagiographies into Latin, frequently appealed to Roman and eastern rites to validate Gallaecian Christianity. In the 560s, Bishop Boniface of an unknown see voiced his suspicions to Martin about the orthodoxy of priests who performed triple immersion baptisms. In his reply (*De trina mersione*), Martin told Boniface that an earlier metropolitan of Braga had asked for the most authoritative formula of baptism from the see of the most blessed Peter. Upon reading the exemplar (whether a copy or an original is unclear), Martin found triple immersion to be the practice the pope had prescribed.[34] He later stated that he based his defence of triple immersion baptism on the written authority of the bishop of Rome, and supported it with ancient sources such as the acts of Sylvester and the writings of Paul.[35]

Alongside older texts and Vigilius's guidance, Martin also justified triple immersion baptism with the extraordinary observation that this was also the custom of the eastern Roman empire. More specifically, this tradition was held by 'the bishop of Constantinople, [who] was observed on the Easter feast by present envoys of this kingdom who had been sent to the empire'.[36] This statement is unique in the Iberian corpus as the only explicit reference

34 'Sed nam et ego manifestius hic cognovit quod de institutione baptismatis metropolitanus huius provinciae ante hos aliquos annos ab ipsa beatissimi Petri cathedra certissimae auctoritatis formulam postulavit. Cuius etiam exemplar curiosius legens, ita reperii scriptum, ut in uno Trinitatis nomine is qui baptizandus es taut tertio perfundatur aut mergatur' (Mart. De trina 2). See Ferreiro 2020, 292–304 for a holistic analysis of the letter.

35 Mart. De trina 3.

36 'Quam ex Romani antistitis auctoritate sacerdotes huius provinciae retinent scriptam, et a Constantinopolitanae urbis praesule, praesentibus huius regni legatis qui ad Imperium fuerant destinati, in ipsa Paschali festivitate pervisa est' (Mart. De trina 3).

to the contemporary Byzantine empire in connection with a liturgical rite practised in the peninsula. In this letter, Martin cut through the vagueness of earlier conciliar references to the 'East' and justified a custom because it was also practised in Byzantium. The religious parallel also might have bolstered ongoing diplomatic efforts to align Byzantine and Suevic interests in the face of an increasingly aggressive Visigothic kingdom.[37] By emphasizing religious solidarity against a common Arian enemy, the parallel between Gallaecian and Constantinopolitan baptism reinforced the orthodoxy of Gallaecian rites and potentially facilitated a working relationship between Suevic and Byzantine leaders and/or their agents.

Overall, Martin combined the ancient past and the Christian present when he defended triple immersion baptism as a custom 'not only handed down through the authority of the See of Rome, but also [which] the ancient custom of the eastern provinces shows, and [which] is written in the explanations of ancient fathers and moreover in [documentary] models of official sacraments'.[38] The Roman see was key to Martin's explanation, and the implication of his letter was that Gallaecian bishops were following Roman precepts. But Martin did not tell Boniface that his practice was an *adoption* of contemporary Byzantine traditions, instead noting eastern parallels to confirm his own. Even for someone as openly enthusiastic about Greek texts and traditions as Martin, he sidestepped characterizing Gallaecian rites as imitations of Byzantine rites.

Although questions always remain about whether canons and letters reflect prescriptive desires or actual practice, Martin's letter provides a potential clue that Roman liturgical rites were indeed practised in parts of Gallaecia. In *De trina mersione*, Martin reassured Boniface that Nicene Christians should not alter their rites simply because heretics imitated them. Arians might draw upon the same scriptures for their liturgical chants (the Psalms) and their readings (the Apostle and the Gospels), but only Nicene Christians understood them correctly.[39] Noticeably absent from Martin's list of readings is (excepting the Psalms) the books of the Old Testament. While many early medieval rites included readings from the Old Testament, the Epistles, and the Gospels, the early medieval Roman rite only contained

37 Vallejo Girvés 1994.

38 'Quod si hoc [i.e., conciliar condemnation of triple immersion] nequeunt demonstrare, teneant a nobis fiducialiter quod et per auctoritatem Romanae sedis est traditum, et Orientalium provinciarum institutio prisca demonstrat, et antiquorum patrum expositionibus, quin etiam officialium sacramentorum documentis scribitur' (Mart. De trina 5).

39 Mart. De trina 4.

two scriptural readings, usually from the Epistles and the Gospels.[40] The letter is suggestive that, at least in the metropolitan see of Braga, bishops might have followed some elements of the Roman liturgy.

Overall, Gallaecian bishops enthusiastically embraced the Roman liturgies that Vigilius had sent to Profuturus, but generally did not explicitly credit the contemporary Byzantine empire as the inspiration behind their adoption of eastern practices. This nuanced navigation of the relationship between Gallaecian, Roman, and eastern liturgies presented a very precise religious and political statement to the early medieval Christian world. Adopting the Roman liturgy as opposed to Visigothic, Frankish, or even local Gallaecian liturgies would have been a powerful statement as to how the Suevic kingdom positioned itself within Christendom.[41] By associating themselves with the Roman church and acknowledging papal authority, Gallaecian bishops could place themselves under papal supervision while avoiding religious 'subservience' to other kingdoms. And by adopting 'eastern' customs defined broadly and ahistorically, Gallaecian authors could associate themselves with the traditions of the ancient Christian East without implying contemporary eastern superiority.

Creeds in the Visigothic Kingdom

Three decades after the First Council of Braga, bishops at the Third Council of Toledo in 589 made an even more delicate decision to transplant an eastern custom into local rites. As in the Suevic kingdom of the 560s, the Visigothic decision to adopt a contemporary 'Roman' liturgical practice occurred within the context of a royal conversion to Nicene Christianity. After the death of the pro-Arian King Leovigild in 586, his son Reccared personally converted to Nicene Christianity in 587 and subsequently called all bishops in the Visigothic kingdom to a council in Toledo in 589 to oversee the conversion of the Gothic people. The records of the council display Reccared's vision of himself as a most orthodox ruler and present a working relationship between ecclesiastics and royal administrators to reform Iberian churches and to ensure justice and religious orthodoxy throughout the kingdom.[42]

40 Romano 2014, 48–49.

41 Deswarte (2010, 138) links the Suevic adoption of Roman customs to their desire to develop a Christian identity unique from the Visigoths.

42 For the Visigothic conversion and Reccared's self-presentation, see Díaz y Díaz 1991; Godoy and Vilella 1986; Herrin 1987, 227–32; Mellado Rodriguez 2011; Saitta 1991; Stocking 2000, 59–88;

Part of this religious reform was the politicization of the Christian liturgy. The council's canons indicate a keen interest in using the liturgy to cultivate and perpetuate Nicene orthodoxy, and their decisions about the kingdom's rites held weighty ecclesiological and political implications.

In this context, Toledo III decreed a striking adoption of an eastern liturgical practice: the insertion of a declaratory Christian creed into the liturgy of the Eucharist.[43] Creeds had long been critically important in baptismal liturgies,[44] but the insertion into the mass was more recent. According to conciliar records, the change was first proposed by Reccared himself: as the assembled bishops turned their attention to ecclesiastical affairs (*disciplinae ecclesiasticae mores*), Reccared declared that to reinforce the conversion, Christians within his realm should recite a creed directly before communion 'like the custom of eastern regions'.[45] It is impossible to determine whether Reccared was the sole author of this proposal or whether he had episcopal assistance, but the king's involvement bolstered the council's effort to employ both state and ecclesiastical officials to enforce Christian norms. The change was noteworthy enough to require extensive explanation and justification, and the council's second canon attributed the change to the Visigothic conversion from Arianism:

> On behalf of reverence for the most holy faith and in order to strengthen the weak minds of men, with the most pious and most glorious lord king Reccared having been consulted, the holy synod resolves that throughout all the churches of Hispania, Gallia, and Gallaecia, the creed of the council of Constantinople, that is the one of 150 bishops, should be recited according to the form (*formam*) of eastern churches, so that before the Lord's prayer is said, the creed should be proclaimed by the people in a clear voice. By this the true faith may have clear testimony, and the hearts of people purified by faith may approach the offered body and blood of Christ.[46]

and Thompson 1960. For interactions and influences between the Visigothic and Byzantine worlds in the context of Toledo III, see Hillgarth 1991.

43 Kinzig (2017, 1: 2, 8–9) links the production of 'declaratory' creeds to moments of doctrinal crisis.

44 Kelly 1950, 30–61; Kinzig 2017, 1:145–64 and 4:1–82.

45 'Ut propter roborandam gentis nostrae nouellam conuersionem omnes Spaniarum et Galliae ecclesiae hanc regulam seruent, ut omni sacrificii tempore ante communicationem corporis Christi uel sanguinis iuxta Orientalium partium morem unanimiter clara uoce sacratissimum fidei recenseant symbolum' (III Toledo, pref. to canons (Coll. Hisp. V, 101)).

46 'Pro reuerentia sanctissimae fidei et propter corroborandas hominum inualidas mentes consultu piissimi et gloriosissimi domni Reccaredi regis sancta constituit synodus ut per omnes

Incorporating a creed into weekly Eucharistic liturgies was a shrewd means of producing orthodoxy. The bishops were aware that conversion was a process, not a singular moment, and by mandating that Christians hear and recite the basics of their faith every time they attended mass, the clerics sought to solidify converts' new theology and to educate the populace.

Incorporating such a dramatic change to the liturgy, much less one identified as originating in the East, risked implying deficiency within Iberian liturgies or the superiority of eastern Christianity. The move could have been even more fraught because the recitation of creeds in the mass was not an ancient custom, but rather a contemporary and theologically charged innovation in the fifth and sixth centuries. According to J. N. D. Kelly and Wolfram Kinzig, the recitation of creeds in the mass likely originated in the sixth-century eastern empire in the context of the Chalcedonian controversy.[47] Although its specific origins are unclear, anti-Chalcedonians in Antioch and Constantinople might have recited the Constantinopolitan creed during the mass, and Chalcedonian clerics seem to have adopted the practice as well. The acts of the Council of Constantinople in 536 referred to the recitation of the creed during mass as customary, and John of Biclarum related that Emperor Justin II mandated in 568 that the creed should be sung before the Lord's Prayer in every church.[48] Although it is impossible to confirm direct knowledge of the tangled history of this practice in the eastern empire, given the number of contacts between the Byzantine and Iberian worlds, it is probable that many Iberian ecclesiastics were aware of the history of this custom.[49]

The Visigothic canon is the first evidence for the incorporation of a creed into a western Eucharistic rite. But the Visigothic practice was not a carbon copy of eastern rites. In the East, the creed was usually recited after the

ecclesias Spaniae, Galliae uel Galliciae secundum formam Orientalium ecclesiarum concilii Constantinopolitani, hoc est centum quinquaginta episcoporum, symbolum fidei recitetur, ut priusquam Dominica dicatur oratio, uoce clara a populo praedicetur, quo et fides uera manifestum testimonium habeat et ad Christi corpus et sanguinem praelibandum pectora populorum fide purificata accedant' (III Toledo 2 (Coll. Hisp. V, 110)). For an excellent analysis of the rhetoric and sequence of this canon, see Pinell 1991, 339–40. See also Fernández Jiménez 2004, 172–73; and Janeras 1995, 104–6.

47 Kelly 1950, 348–51; Kinzig 2017, 1:10.

48 Kelly 1950, 350. See Ioh. Bicl. 2.

49 Kelly (1950, 351–52) proposed a connection between the Visigothic decision and the incorporation of the Constantinopolitan creed into Roman baptismal liturgies earlier in the sixth century, arguing that the Roman decision was in part a condemnation of Ostrogothic Arianism. However, correlation between Roman and Visigothic condemnations of Arianism does not equal causation.

Offertory and before the celebration of the Eucharist.[50] In the Visigothic canon, the creed was placed right before the Lord's Prayer in the midst of the liturgy of the Eucharist. This meant that, while eastern rites usually used the creed to pivot between the first half of the mass (focused on scripture) and the second (focused on sacramental ritual), Iberian rites intended the creed as a ringing proclamation of faith right before baptized Christians received communion. By changing the liturgical sequence and placing the creed at the most sacred moment of the mass, the bishops forged new connections and associations between orthodox doctrine and communion with God, purifying and instructing the Christian faithful before they received the bread and wine. Subsequent evidence suggests that the mandate of the Third Council of Toledo was idealized in Iberian texts in the seventh century. For example, in Isidore of Seville's early seventh-century description of the Eucharistic rite in *De Ecclesiasticis Officiis*, he placed a recitation of the Constantinopolitan creed in the Eucharistic liturgy directly before the laity received communion.[51]

In addition to their unique placement within the sequence of the mass, it is also possible that Iberian credal formulas might have differed from those recited in the East. The Third Council of Toledo had identified the Constantinopolitan creed as the authoritative credal statement, and subsequent authors such as Isidore and Ildefonsus of Toledo reinforced this decision. Yet there were a large number of other creeds circulating in the early medieval West. Most late antique and early medieval western creeds (such as the Apostles' Creed) descended from an older Roman formula, and Roman derivations remained popular in baptismal rites.[52] Another western

50 There appears to be disagreement on the placement of the creed in Byzantine Greek liturgies of the sixth century. Kelly (1950, 350) stated that in eastern Eucharistic liturgies, the creed was recited after the Offertory and before the Pax. Pinell (1991, 333–34) claimed that the creed was recited after the sign of peace and before the preface of the Eucharistic rite. Kinzig (2017, 4:114–18) contrasts fourth-century placements of the creed around the kiss of peace with later placements at the beginning of the Eucharistic rite after unbaptized congregants had exited the church (Liturgies of St Basil and St John Chrysostom). Janeras (1995, 105–6) addresses an apparent mismatch between John of Biclarum's assertion that eastern churches recited creeds before the Lord's Prayer (*oratio dominicana*) and Maximos the Confessor's seventh-century testimony that Constantinopolitan Christians recited creeds before the anaphora (also Kinzig 2017, 4:113). While Janeras suggests that by *oratio dominicana* John actually meant anaphora, it is also possible that the custom had changed between the late sixth century and the mid-seventh century, or that John deliberately described the Constantinopolitan rite as identical to the new Visigothic practice. For a broad comparison of the placement of creeds in masses of early medieval rites, see Pinell 1991, 333–35.

51 Isid. De eccl. 16 (18).

52 Kinzig 2017, 1:11–15.

formula was the *Quincunque vult*, also known as the Athanasian creed. This popular (likely Gallican) creed influenced doctrinal statements of Visigothic councils, which were then preserved in conciliar records and distributed among attendees.[53] In weekly masses across the Visigothic kingdom, priests could have recited any number of credal variations.

Nevertheless, one remarkable piece of evidence suggests that clerics did indeed learn the Constantinopolitan creed in church schools. In the town of Mogarraz, just to the south of Salamanca, a seventh-century slate with a creed scratched on it likely represents a pedagogical exercise from a school.[54] As analysed by José Manuel Ruiz Asencio, the inscription includes two repeated phrases of the Constantinopolitan creed.[55] Given that the lines were likely written in the context of a cathedral or monastic school, it is logical to assume that this creed was the version recited in weekly masses. Still, if the student's spelling, grammar, and word order is any indication, the accuracy of weekly recitation (or at least this student's memory) is up for debate.[56]

Overall, following the eastern example of inserting a creed into the mass was not a straightforward decision. Choosing both formula and placement required a delicate negotiation of the relationship between eastern and western liturgies. Even more so than the earlier canons of Braga, identifying credal recitations in the mass as an 'eastern form' hovered somewhere between acknowledging their contemporary origins in the Byzantine empire and ignoring their origins altogether. Bringing up eastern origins could have raised uncomfortable questions about Byzantine religious pre-eminence during a reformulation of Visigothic religious ideology, yet the bishops' appeal to eastern liturgies placed them in line with eastern practice while eliding any reference to the Byzantine empire. The abstraction of the East could represent an effort to place the Visigothic polity within an orthodox imperial tradition while maintaining its distinctiveness, or it could imply that the

53 For the *Quicunque vult*, see Kelly 1964. Brennecke (2019) has proposed the Visigothic conversion as a possible context for the composition of this creed, but his conclusions are self-admittedly speculative. For theological professions of Visigothic councils, see Madoz 1938 and 1944; Rico Páves 2005. The incorporation of *filioque* into Visigothic creeds is beyond the scope of this article. For the theology of the *filioque* clause in dialogue with eastern theology, see Bravo García 2002 and Gemeinhardt 2002. For theology at Toledo III in general, see González Blanco 1995.

54 For epigraphic and historical analysis of Visigothic slates, see Velázquez Soriano 2004. I exclude analysis of the famous credal inscription found near the basilica of Saint Leocadia, Toledo, because it is currently considered a baptismal creed. For the Toledan inscription, see Jorge Aragonenses 1957.

55 Ruiz Asencio 2004, 1318 for provenance, 1322 for transcription.

56 Ruiz Asencio (2004, 1322–24) proposed that the creed on the slate differed from liturgical creeds, but his assessment relies on the eleventh-century *Liber Ordinum*.

Toledan placement of the creed was not innovative, but rather established. Regardless, Reccared and the bishops gathered at the council employed both explicitness and ambiguity to activate the desirable connotations of their reform while downplaying its more troublesome implications.

Ancient Origins and Present Parallels

After the Third Council of Toledo's insertion of a creed into Eucharistic liturgies, Visigothic engagement with eastern and Roman rites took on a noticeably different tone. In the seventh century, explicit acknowledgements of an eastern origin for an Iberian practice were rare. When they did occur, the 'East' was increasingly conceptualized historically, more frequently appearing as an ancient community rather than a contemporary society. Papal Rome could also serve as an older, authoritative guide, but in some cases, Iberian bishops gestured towards contemporary Roman practice or papal opinions to inform local disagreements about the liturgy. As in the sixth-century Suevic kingdom, seventh-century Visigothic intellectuals were more willing to rely on contemporary Rome than the Byzantine empire as a liturgical authority. Yet seventh-century bishops did not claim to *adopt* Roman practices, but rather cited Roman liturgy as a useful comparison to support or justify a current Iberian practice.[57]

As noted above, sixth-century Iberian bishops had willingly cited ancient eastern Christian communities as liturgical models and authorities. Emerging Iberian collections of canons also reinforced the simultaneous validity and antiquity of eastern liturgical customs. As the production of universal canon collections increased in the sixth and seventh centuries, many collections included and highlighted canons that described liturgical rituals from the late antique East.[58] The *Capitula Martini*, for example, was a collection of canons produced between 569 and 580 in Gallaecia under the supervision of the aforementioned bishop Martin of Braga. The majority of the collection's content stemmed from eastern councils of the fourth century, including Ancyra, Neocaesarea, Gangres, Antioch, and Laodicaea.[59]

57 Unacknowledged and implicit influence and exchange, however, was highly likely. See Ihnat 2019, who places Iberian Marian cult in a Mediterranean context.

58 Although overstated, Sieben (1990, 43–45) asserts that Iberian bishops relied on eastern and African models for their conciliar tradition. For an example of the circulation of canons in the early medieval West, see Mathisen 1999.

59 Martínez Díez 1967 and Gaudemet 1989. Martínez Díez, however, notes that not all of the canons were from eastern councils, and that compilers drew on Toledo I as well.

In particular, a number of canons from Laodicaea, Nicaea, and Neocaesarea described rites of baptism, prayer, martyr festivals, and fasting. Martin and his colleagues did not specify the conciliar sources of the canons and described the content as canons 'established in eastern regions by ancient fathers' or canons 'from the synods of the ancient eastern fathers'.[60] The compilers further accentuated the temporal distance between themselves and the ancient synods by claiming that translation and scribal errors over time had obscured the canons' original meaning, and that they intended to restore the original text. It is difficult to discern whether the compilers intended the liturgical canons in this collection as a blueprint for imitation, as a guide for consultation, or as legitimation for an existing rite. Regardless, when Iberian clerics looked to this collection for liturgical guidance, they turned to the historical rather than the contemporary Christian East.

The emphasis on ancient eastern origins continued in Isidore of Seville's *De Ecclesiasticis Officiis*, a pastoral treatise composed roughly between 600 and 615 for his brother, Bishop Fulgentius of Écija. In this text, Isidore explained the origins of Christian liturgy and explored its contemporary practice in Iberia.[61] While Isidore attributed many rituals and customs to Jewish antiquity or to the time of the apostles, he dated a few to the post-apostolic age. He claimed that 'the Greeks first composed antiphons' and that 'among the Latins', Ambrose of Milan 'was the first to have instituted antiphons, imitating (*imitatus*) the example of the Greeks. From that time on, their usage increased in the western regions.'[62] Isidore also credited 'the first Greeks' with the composition of certain prayers used throughout the church.[63] In these passages, Isidore defined the Greek East linguistically, geographically, and culturally, contrasting it to Latin western regions among which he placed his own 'Hispanic' tradition.[64] Temporally, he relegated the Greeks that invented antiphons and composed prayers to the distant past, locating them within the ancient Christian church rather than the contemporary Byzantine empire and filtering some of their innovations

60 'Sancti canones qui in partibus orientis ab antiquis patribus constituti sunt [...] Canones ex orientalium antiquorum partum synodis' (II Braga, *Capitula Martini* (Conc. 86)).

61 The original title of the work was *De originis officiis*. See Isid. De eccl. 14–15 and 119–20.

62 'Antiphonas Greci primi conpusuerunt [...] Apud Latinos autem primus idem beatissimus Ambrosius antiphonas instituit, Grecorum exemplum imitates; exhinc in cunctis occidius regionibus earum usus increbuit' (Isid. De eccl. 1.7.1).

63 'Quasque primi Greci coeperunt conponere quibus domino supplicaretur' (Isid. De eccl. 1.9.1).

64 Isid. De eccl. 1.13.3. Isidore used 'Latins' and 'the western regions' as rough equivalents, and he further subdivided this community into geographical regions. See Lester 2018.

through western gatekeepers such as Ambrose. Evoking an ancient and eastern origin for contemporary practices traced Isidore's liturgy back to some of the oldest Christian communities while establishing critical distance.

While underscoring the supposedly ancient origins of antiphons and prayers, Isidore did not fail to acknowledge their tangible movement across the Mediterranean. The practices may have been old, but they were not ahistorical: they possessed a distinct transmission history. He characterized Ambrose's adoption of antiphons in Milan as mirroring the *exemplum* of the Greeks, historicizing liturgical transmission and clarifying the link between the ancient East and western antiphons. By imitating or adopting an ancient exemplar, Ambrose and his successors had transposed the past into the present, obscuring any modifications to antiphonal practice that might have occurred in western regions. According to Isidore, western *imitatus* of the East had already occurred before the foundation of the Visigothic kingdom.

Seventh-century Iberian ecclesiastics had a more complicated relationship with the liturgy of Rome. As in the case of the 'East', when the Apostolic See appeared in seventh-century texts as a liturgical authority, it often served as a historical resource that could inform contemporary debates. Papal decretals were authoritative documents safely produced in the past by long-dead popes,[65] and at the Fourth Council of Toledo in 633, Iberian bishops confirmed the legitimacy of reading the Apocalypse in services by citing 'the authority of many councils and the synodal decretals of holy Roman prelates'.[66]

Yet in contrast to their treatment of the East, seventh-century bishops also referred to contemporary Rome as a liturgical authority. In a letter written in the late 630s to Abbot Frunimian, Braulio of Zaragoza addressed the abbot's inquiry on responses to lessons on Good Friday. Frunimian had asked whether *Amen* should be recited or, 'in the customary fashion (*consueto modo*)', a *Gloria* should be chanted. Braulio responded that 'this [a response in general?] was not done amongst us', stating that he had never seen it performed by Isidore nor in the churches of Toledo or Girona. After these Iberian examples, Braulio turned to Rome: 'In Rome, as they say, no

65 Deswarte 2010, 51–65.

66 'Apocalipsin librum multorum conciliorum auctoritas et synodica sanctorum praesulum Romanorum decreta Iohannis euangelistae esse praescribunt et inter diuinos libros recipiendum constituerunt' (IV Toledo 17 (Coll. Hisp. V, 205)). According to this edition, the bishops possibly had in mind the Third Council of Carthage, canon 47, and letters from Popes Innocent I and Hormisdas.

office is celebrated on that day.'[67] Given Braulio's prior references to Isidore, Toledo, and Girona, it is likely that the Zaragozan bishop intended to invoke seventh-century Rome rather than ancient Rome. Braulio did not state, however, that Toledo, Girona, and Isidore derived their practice from the Apostolic See. Instead, Rome served to bolster and validate existing Iberian customs rather than spark innovation.

The same dynamic is visible in canon 6 of the Fourth Council of Toledo, held in 633 only a few years before Braulio's letter. The lengthy canon addressed the orthodoxy of triple versus single immersion baptism, a question that had bothered Iberian bishops since the sixth century. The issue was apparently so fraught that the bishops at Toledo IV turned to an extra-Iberian authority to mediate. The canon included a lengthy citation from Pope Gregory the Great's correspondence with Leander of Seville about proper baptismal practice. In the 590s, Leander had asked Gregory for his opinion on triple versus single immersion baptism, and Gregory had responded that while both submersion practices were inherently legitimate, he recommended single immersion given the Arian connotations of triple immersion baptism. Therefore, to prevent 'the scandal of schism and the employment of heretical dogma', the Iberian bishops embraced Gregory's opinion and ruled against triple immersion baptism.[68] The Iberian bishops' use of Gregory certainly recognized the authority of both Gregory and Leander, and like the Gallaecian use of Vigilius's letter, placed great value on direct papal evaluations of Iberian customs. Yet unlike Pope Vigilius, Gregory had not sent Leander Roman baptismal rites to use in Iberia. Instead, he had provided a theological explanation for prioritizing one existing Iberian practice over another. Forty years later, the bishops at the Fourth Council of Toledo followed Gregory's lead when they framed his letter to confirm an existing custom rather than suggesting a new one. All in all, seventh-century Visigothic Christians were careful to indicate that although the city of Rome was a liturgical authority, they were not borrowing or adopting practices from its rites.

Although scholars should always be wary of neat narratives, the evidence gives the impression of an increasing tendency amongst Iberian ecclesiastics to distance their own liturgies from contemporary eastern or Roman rites.

67 'Per lectiones singulas 'Amen' respondi debeat uel consueto modo decantari 'Gloria', quod neque apud nos fit, neque ubicumque fieri vidimus, nec apud praestantissimae memoriae domnum meum Isidorum, denique nec Toleto quidem uel Gerunda. Romae autem, ut aiunt, nullum eo die celebratur officium' (Braul. Ep. 3).

68 'Propter uitandum autem schismatis scandalum uel haeretici dogmatis usum' (IV Toledo 6 (Coll. Hisp. V, 192)). For the reception of Gregory's work in Iberia, see Wood 2016.

While Suevic sources and Toledo III engaged with and even acknowledged adopted features of eastern liturgies, seventh-century sources increasingly suggested that liturgical transfers from East to West had occurred centuries earlier. For the city of Rome, these sources were more willing to embrace the present as well as the past, and bishops could invoke current popes and practices to inform debates within Iberia. Yet even here, Visigothic authors employed a rhetorical sleight of hand. They were not adopting or imitating a Christianity with Roman overtones, but rather using papal norms to explain the validity of certain Iberian customs.

Conclusion

To return to the theme of this volume, attending to Visigothic and Suevic engagements with eastern and Roman liturgies can nuance our understanding of how Iberians conceptualized their *imitatio* of other rites and complicate our notions of what they 'imitated'. The active selection and implementation of practices, as well as how this process was articulated, display ongoing dialogue between original sources and their Iberian iterations. From clear Gallaecian invocations that forged domestic and international alignments, to the simultaneous claim and erasure of Toledo III, to the seventh-century transformation of eastern and Roman rites into safely distant authorities, Iberian actors seem to have had an awareness that their choices and explanations held implications for local orthodoxy and global ecclesiology. To describe their creative engagements with eastern and Roman customs as imitative is too simplistic, and despite repeated attempts to supersede papal or eastern Roman religious authority, ongoing reliance on and respect for these traditions complicated a straightforward narrative of supersession.

Liturgical discourse in post-imperial Hispania also alerts us to the potentially fluid nature of what was considered 'Roman'. From the liturgies of the ancient 'East' and late antique popes to those of the Byzantine empire and the contemporary city of Rome, elites in the Suevic and Visigothic kingdoms could describe their models and authorities as precisely or as expansively as they wished. Bishops and kings sifted through multiple available rites, combining and excising them to create their own versions of apostolic, papal, or eastern traditions. As we (re)consider *imitatio imperii*, we must keep in mind that Iberian Christians were not only actively selecting and redefining their liturgical 'imitations', but they were also creating and controlling the 'Rome' that they imitated.

Bibliography

Álvarez Martínez, Rosario, Ismael Fernández de la Cuesta, and Ana Llorens Martín, *El canto mozárabe y su etorno: Estudios sobre la música de la liturgia viejo hispánica* (Madrid: Sociedad Española de la Musicologí, 2013)

Berger, Teresa, and Bryan D. Spinks (eds), *Liturgy's Imagined Past/s: Methodologies and Materials in the Writing of Liturgical History Today* (Collegeville, MN: Liturgical Press, 2016)

Bravo García, Antonio Pedro, 'La España visigoda y el mundo bizantino: aspectos culturales y teológicos', in *Toledo y Bizancio*, ed. by Miguel Cortés Arrese (Cuenca: Ediciones de la Universidad de Castilla-La Mancha, 2002), pp. 123–65

Brennecke, H. C., 'Das Athanasianum – ein Text aus dem Westgotenreich? Überlegungen zur Herkunft des *Symbolum quicumque*', in *Das Christentum im frühen Europa. Diskurse – Tendenzen – Entscheidungen*, ed. by U. Heil (Berlin: De Gruyter, 2019), pp. 317–38

Brou, Dom L., 'Les chants en langue grecque dans les liturgies latines', in *Sacris erudiri*, 1 (1948), 165–80

Castillo Maldonado, Pedro, 'Una aproximación a la presencia de Oriente en Occidente: rechazo y atracción hacia el mundo cristiano oriental en las iglesias hispanas de la Antigüedad Tardía', in *'Ilu Revista de Ciencias de las Religiones*, 10 (2005), 5–19

Claude, Dietrich, 'Spätantike und frühmittelalterliche Orientfahrten: Routen und Reisende', in *Voyages et voyageurs à Byzance et en Occident du VI au XIe siècle*, ed. by Alain Dierkens and Jean Marie Sansterre (Geneva: Droz, 2000), pp. 235–53

Crehan, J. H., 'The Liturgical Trade Route: East to West', in *Studies*, 65 (1976), 87–99

Deswarte, Thomas, *Une Chrétienté romaine sans pape. L'Espagne et Rome (586–1085)* (Paris: Classiques Garnier, 2010)

Díaz, Pablo C., *El Reino Suevo (411–585)* (Tres Cantos: Akal, 2011)

Díaz y Díaz, M. C., 'Los discursos del rey Reccared: el "tomus"', in *Concilio III de Toledo: XIV Centenario 589–1989* (Madrid-Toledo, 1991), pp. 223–36

Díaz y Díaz, M. C., 'Consideraciones sobre el oracional visigótico de Verona', in *Petrarca, Verona e l'Europa. Atti del Convegno di studi (Verona 19–23 settembre 1991)* (Padova: Antenore, 1997), pp. 13–29

Dyer, Joseph, 'The Offertory Chant of the Roman Liturgy and its Musical Form', in *Studi musicali*, 11 (1982), 3–30

Ellis, Linda, and Frank L. Kidner (eds), *Essays of Travel, Communication and Geography in Late Antiquity: Sacred and Profane* (Aldershot: Ashgate, 2004)

Fernández Alonso, Justo, *La cura pastoral en la España romanovisigoda* (Rome: Iglesia Nacional Española, 1955)

Fernández Jiménez, Francisco María, 'Influencias y contactos entre la liturgia hispana y las liturgias orientales bizantina, alejandrina y antioquena', in *Bizancio y la Península Ibérica: de la antigüedad tardía a la edad moderna*, ed. by Inmaculada Pérez Martín and Pedro Bádenas de la Peña (Madrid: Consejo Superior de Investigaciones Científicas, 2004), pp. 165–76

Ferreiro, Alberto, *Epistolae Plenae: The Correspondence of the Bishops of Hispania with the Bishops of Rome, Third through Seventh Centuries* (Leiden: Brill, 2020)

Gaudemet, Jean, '"Traduttore, traditore" – Les Capitula Martini', in *Droit de l'Eglise et vie sociale au Moyen Age* (Northampton: Variorum Reprints, 1989), VI

Gemeinhardt, Peter, *Die Filioque-Kontroverse zwischen Ost- und Westkirche im Frühmittelalter* (Berlin: De Gruyter, 2002)

Gittos, Helen, 'Researching the History of Rites', in *Understanding Medieval Liturgy: Essays in Interpretation*, ed. by Helen Gittos and Sarah Hamilton (Farnham: Routledge, 2016), pp. 13–37

Godoy, C., and J. Vilella, 'De la "Fides gothica" a la ortodoxia nicena: inicio de la teología política visigótica', in *Antigüedad y Cristianismo III: Los Visigodos: Historia y Civilización* (Murcia: Universidad de Murcia, 1986), pp. 117–44

González Blanco, Antonio, 'Lenguaje y teología en el tercer concilio de Toledo', in *Antigüedad y Cristianismo XII: Homenaje al Prof. Dr. D. Antonio Yelo Templado al cumplir 65 años* (Murcia: Universidad de Murcia, 1995), pp. 375–84

Graham, Stacey, 'The Transmission of North African Texts to Europe in Late Antiquity', in *Medieval Manuscripts, Their Makers and Users: A Special Issue of Viator in Honor of Richard and Mary Rouse*, ed. by Henry Ansgar Kelly and Christopher Baswell (Turnhout: Brepols, 2011), pp. 151–67

Herrin, Judith, *The Formation of Christendom* (Princeton, NJ: Princeton University Press, 1987)

Hillgarth, Jocelyn N., 'El Concilio III de Toledo y Bizancio', in *Concilio III de Toledo: XIV Centenario 589–1989* (Madrid-Toledo, 1991), pp. 297–306

Hornby, Emma, and Rebecca Maloy, *Music and Meaning in Old Hispanic Lenten Chants: Psalmi, Threni and Easter Vigil Canticles* (Woodbridge: The Boydell Press, 2013)

Huglo, Michel, 'Les "Preces" des Graduels aquitains empruntées a la liturgie hispanique', in *Hispania sacra*, 8.16 (1955), 361–83

Ihnat, Kati, 'Orígenes y desarrollo de la fiesta litúrgica de la Virgen María en Iberia', in *Anuario de Estudios Medievales*, 49.2 (2019), 619–43, https://doi.org/10.3989/aem.2019.49.2.09

Janeras, Sebastià, 'Elements orientals en la litúrgia visigótica', in *Miscellània litúrgica catalana*, 6 (1995), 93–127

Janini, José, 'Roma y Toledo: nueva problemática de la liturgia visigótica', in *Estudios sobre la liturgia mozárabe*, ed. by Juan Francisco Rivera Recio (Toledo: Disputación Provincial, 1965), pp. 33–53

Jorge Aragonenses, Manuel, 'El primer credo epigráfico visigodo y otros restos coetáneos, descubiertos en Toledo', in *Archivo Español de Arte*, 30 (1957), 295–323

Kelly, J. N. D., *Early Christian Creeds* (London: Longmans, Green, 1950)

Kelly, J. N. D., *The Athanasian Creed* (London: Adam and Charles Black, 1964)

Kinzig, Wolfram, *Faith in Formulae: A Collection of Early Christian Creeds and Creed-Related Texts*, 4 vols (Oxford: Oxford University Press, 2017)

Lester, Molly, 'Mapping Liturgical Identity in Early Medieval Iberia and Beyond', in *Visigothic Symposium*, vol. 2 (n.p.: Punctum Books, 2018), pp. 114–30

Levy, Kenneth, 'Toledo, Rome, and the Legacy of Gaul', in *Early Music History*, 4 (1984), 49–99

Madoz, José, 'Le symbole du IVe Concile de Tolède', in *Revue d'histoire ecclésiastique, Louvain*, 34 (1938), 5–20

Madoz, José, 'La teología de la Trinidad en los símbolos toledanos', in *Revista Española de Teología*, 4 (1944), 457–77

Maloy, Rebecca, 'Old Hispanic Chant and the Early History of Plainsong', in *Journal of the American Musicological Society*, 67.1 (2014), 1–76

Maloy, Rebecca, Mason Brown, Ben Cefkin, Ruth Opara, Megan Quilliam, and Melanie Shaffer, 'Revisiting "Toledo, Rome, and the Legacy of Gaul": New Evidence from the Divine Office', in *Plainsong in Medieval Music* (forthcoming)

Maloy, Rebecca, and Emma Hornby, 'Fixity, Flexibility, and Compositional Process in Old Hispanic Chant', in *Music and Letters*, 97 (2016), 547–74

Martínez Díez, Gonzalo, 'La colección canónica de la iglesia sueva, los capitula martini', in *Bracara Augusta*, 21 (1967), 224–43

Mathisen, Ralph, 'Between Arles, Rome and Toledo: Gallic Collections of Canon Law in Late Antiquity', in *Fronteras religiosas entre Roma, Bizancio, Damasco y Toledo: El nacimiento de Europa y del Islam (siglos V–VIII)*, ed. by S. Montero (Madrid: Universidad Complutense, 1999), pp. 33–46

Mellado Rodríguez, Joaquín, 'Luces y sombras en las actas del III Concilio de Toledo', in *Pro tantis redditur: homenaje a Juan Gil en Sevilla*, ed. by Rocío Carande and Daniel López-Cañete Quiles (Seville: Universidad de Sevilla, 2011), pp. 281–92

Meyvaert, Paul, 'Diversity within Unity: A Gregorian Theme', in *Heythrop Journal*, 4.2 (1963), 141–62

Montero Herrero, Santiago, 'L'idee ecumeniche di Isidoro di Sivigla', in *L'ecumenismo politico nella coscienza dell'occidente*, ed. by Luciana Aigner Foresti et al. (Rome: L'Erma di Bretschneider, 1998), pp. 397–404

Palazzo, Éric, 'Performing the Liturgy', in *The Cambridge History of Christianity*, vol. 3, *Early Medieval Christianities c.600–1100*, ed. by Thomas F. X. Noble and Julia M. H. Smith (Cambridge: Cambridge University Press, 2008), pp. 472–88

Pinell, Jordi, 'Credo y comunión en la estructura de la misa hispánica según disposición del III Concilio de Toledo', in *Concilio III de Toledo: XIV Centenario 589–1989* (Madrid-Toledo, 1991), pp. 333–42

Pinell, Jordi, *Liturgia hispánica* (Barcelona: Centre de Pastoral Litúrgica, 1998)

Quasten, J., 'Oriental Influences in the Gallican Liturgy', in *Traditio*, 1 (1943), 55–78

Randel, Don Michael, 'Leander, Isidore, and Gregory', in *Journal of Musicology*, 36 (2019), 498–522

Rico Páves, José, '*Totius fons et origo divinitatis.* La persona del Padre en los símbolos de fe de los concilios de Toledo (ss. V–VII)', in *Revista Española de Teología*, 65 (2005), 173–95

Rivera Recio, Juan Francisco (ed.), *Estudios sobre la liturgia mozárabe* (Toledo: Disputación Provincial, 1965)

Romano, John F., *Liturgy and Society in Early Medieval Rome* (Burlington, VT: Ashgate, 2014)

Ruiz Asencio, José Manuel, 'Pizarra visigoda con Credo', in *Escritos dedicados a José María Fernández Catón*, vol. 2, ed. by Manuel Cecilio Díaz y Díaz, Mercedes Díaz de Bustamante, and Manuela Domínguez García (León: Centro de Estudios e Investigación San Isidoro, 2004), pp. 1317–28

Saitta, Biagio, 'La conversione di Reccaredo: necessita politica o convinzione personale', in *Concilio III de Toledo: XIV Centenario 589–1989* (Madrid-Toledo, 1991), pp. 375–86

Sieben, Hermann Josef, *Die Partikularsynode: Studien zur Geschichte der Konzilsidee* (Frankfurt am Main: J. Knecht, 1990)

Stocking, Rachel, *Bishops, Councils, and Consensus in the Visigothic Kingdom, 589–633* (Ann Arbor, MI: University of Michigan Press, 2000)

Taft, Robert F., 'Anton Baumstark's Comparative Liturgy Revisited', in *Comparative Liturgy Fifty Years after Anton Baumstark (1872–1948): Acts of the International Congress, Rome, 25–29 September 1998*, ed. by Robert F. Taft and Gabriele Winkler (Rome: Pontificio Istituto Orientale, 2001), pp. 191–232

Thompson, E. A., 'The Conversion of the Visigoths to Catholicism', in *Nottingham Medieval Studies*, 4 (1960), 4–35

Thompson, E. A., 'The Conversion of the Spanish Suevi to Catholicism', in *Visigothic Spain: New Approaches*, ed. by Edward James (Oxford: Oxford University Press, 1980), pp. 77–92

Vallejo Girvés, Margarita, 'La embajada sueva en Constantinopla o la búsqueda de un aliado contra la amenaza visigoda (S. VI)', in *Estudios humanísticos. Geografía, historia y arte*, 16 (1994), 61–70

Vallejo Girvés, Margarita, 'Las sedes eclesiásticas hispanobizantinas en su incorporación al reino visigodo de Toledo', in *Cassiodorus. Rivista di Studi sulla Tarda Antichità*, 6–7 (2000–2001), 13–35

Vallejo Girvés, Margarita, 'La iglesia hispana en el contexto teológico mediterráneo: ¿integración, ausencia o exclusion?', in *De Roma a los bárbaros. Poder central y horizontes locales en la Cuenca del Duero*, ed. by S. Castellanos and I. Martín Viso (León: Universidad de León, 2008), pp. 205–26

Velázquez Soriano, Isabel, 'Zonas y problemas eclesiásticos durante la época de la presencia bizantina en Hispania (una reflexion sobre los textos)', in *V Reunió d'Arqueologia Cristiana Hispànica: Cartagena, 16–19 d'abril de 1998*, ed. by Tena Núria and Josep M. Gurt (Barcelona: Institut d'Estudis Catalans, 2000), pp. 585–600

Velázquez Soriano, Isabel, *Las pizarras visigodas: Entre el latín y su disgregación. La lengua hablada en Hispania siglos vi–viii* (Valladolid: Real Academia Española, 2004)

Vogel, Cyrille, *Medieval Liturgy: An Introduction to the Sources*, rev. and trans. by William G. Storey and Niels Krogh Rasmussen (Washington, DC: Pastoral Press, 1986)

Wood, Jamie, 'Heretical Catholics and Catholic Heretics: Isidore of Seville and the Religious History of the Goths', in *From Orosius to the Historia Silense: Four Essays on Late Antique and Early Medieval Historiography of the Iberian Peninsula*, ed. by David Hook (Bristol: University of Bristol, 2005), pp. 17–50

Wood, Jamie, *The Politics of Identity in Visigothic Spain: Religion and Power in the Histories of Isidore of Seville* (Leiden: Brill, 2012a)

Wood, Jamie, 'Playing the Fame Game: Bibliography, Celebrity, and Primacy in Late Antique Spain', in *Journal of Early Christian Studies*, 20.4 (2012b), 613–40

Wood, Jamie, 'A Family Affair: Leander, Isidore, and the Legacy of Gregory the Great in Spain', in *Isidore of Seville and his Reception in the Early Middle Ages*, ed. by Andrew Fear and Jamie Wood (Amsterdam: Amsterdam University Press, 2016), pp. 31–56

Zapke, Susana (ed.), *Hispania Vetus: Musical-Liturgical Manuscripts from Visigothic Origins to the Franco-Roman Transition (9th–12th Centuries)* (Bilbao: Fundación BBVA, 2007)

About the Author

Molly Lester is Assistant Professor of History at the United States Naval Academy. She is a historian of late antique and early medieval Christianity and has published on orthodoxy and heresy, liturgy, and canon law in Visigothic Iberia. Her current book project is *The Word as Lived: Orthodoxy and Liturgy in Early Medieval Iberia*.

8 Ethnicity and *Imitatio* in Isidore of Seville

Erica Buchberger[1]

Abstract

This paper examines the ways Isidore of Seville appropriated Roman ethnic terms, origin stories, and models of triumphant victory and strategically altered them to better reflect the Hispania he experienced and wanted to build: one ruled by Catholic Goths destined to unite the peoples under their rule in faith. It begins by demonstrating the normalization of *gens* as a descriptor for a people united politically or religiously, not just by purported kinship. It then shows how he refashioned existing origin stories to give the Goths greater antiquity—and thus legitimacy and status—while neutralizing any negative connotations previous authors had envisioned. It finishes with examples of Isidore's broader tale of the Goths' progression from barbaric outsiders to worthy insiders destined for Hispania.

Keywords: Isidore of Seville; ethnicity; *populus*; *gens*; origins

Analyses of *imitatio imperii* commonly focus on the ceremonial and symbolic aspects of the Roman empire—victory celebrations, creation of a capital, ceremonial dress and language, imagery on coins, and legal pronouncements—not ethnicity. Perhaps one reason is that in modern English, 'imitation' carries derogatory connotations of uninspired copying that remove the agency and creativity of the imitator. Imitated items and practices are seen as poor copies of originals, the latter of which are much more worthy of attention.[2] Under this definition, one would expect an imitator of Rome

1 Thanks to Fred Astren, Riccardo Pizzinato, the anonymous reviewers, and the attendees of the workshop that preceded this volume for comments and suggestions.

2 Ziolkowski 2001, 295–96.

Fernández, D., Lester, M. & Wood, J. (eds.), *Rome and Byzantium in the Visigothic Kingdom: Beyond* Imitatio Imperii. Taylor & Francis Group 2023
DOI: 10.5117/9789463726412_CH08

to claim to be Roman, resembling Athaulf's claim that Goths were unable to submit to law and so should join and revive Rome, not replace *Romania* with *Gothia*.[3] Following this logic, the Visigoths may be considered imperfect imitators of Roman ethnic concepts since the identity they claimed was not 'Roman' but 'Gothic', a poor copy of the original.

However, this is not how the classical rhetorical tradition understood *imitatio*. Students learned Latin grammar and rhetoric by replicating styles and forms, but this required careful selection of appropriate material to emulate as they wrote on new topics in new ways to rival rather than parrot the original. *Aemulatio* was such a central part of *imitatio* that texts regularly paired the terms.[4] Using this definition, Visigothic authors did not *just* imitate; they borrowed Roman ethnic concepts, adapted their stories of Gothic origins, and asserted their legitimacy within Hispania in order to supersede the empire, not to become it. They were active participants in negotiating their identities in dialogue with Roman norms from a common cultural landscape.[5] This *imitatio* is not only far from uninspired 'imitation', but it also more accurately reflects how early medieval ethnicity is now commonly understood. Ethnic identity is no longer seen as a fixed or innate trait, but as a dynamic process involving actors making strategic choices within specific historical contexts using the repertoires of identification available to them.[6] Similarly, historians are increasingly understanding *imitatio imperii* as not merely copying a static model, but as emulating useful models from a repertoire and adapting them for particular purposes wholly one's own.[7]

In what follows, I examine such adaptations of Roman ethnic terms and concepts in Visigothic Hispania. Given space constraints, I focus on Isidore of Seville since his writings had a profound influence within the Visigothic kingdom and beyond and his *Etymologies* provide definitions to which historians regularly refer. To prevent confusion, I will avoid the term 'imitation', instead selecting language that will highlight the distinction between the different ways of understanding *imitatio imperii* discussed above: rote copying on the one hand and emulation, appropriation, and rhetorical *imitatio* on the other.

3 Oros. Hist. 7.43.

4 Ziolkowski 2001; Mayernik 2016, 3–6.

5 On cultural commonalities across the Mediterranean and former Roman provinces, see especially the recent volumes Esders, Fox, Hen, and Sarti 2019; Esders, Hen, Lucas, and Rotman 2019; and Cvetković and Gemeinhardt 2019. That such commonalities could trigger parallel developments, see McCormick 1986, 395–96; Ziolkowski 2001, 303.

6 Reimitz 2015; Pohl, Gartner, and Payne 2012; Pohl and Heydemann 2013.

7 Chrysos 2003; Majnarić 2017; Frighetto 2016.

Isidore was bishop of Seville from the early seventh century until his death in 636. Of his highly influential, prolific writings on a wide variety of topics, the most relevant on ethnicity are his *Etymologies* and *History of the Goths*. The *Etymologies* (or *Origins*) is a wide-ranging collection of knowledge emphasizing ancient authority and understanding concepts through word origins.[8] Because of their antiquarian bent, we should not assume his definitions here reflect contemporary meanings (though they may). Isidore crafted his oeuvre deliberately to influence his present, but here he also aimed to summarize eternal truths from ancient times.[9] Two versions of Isidore's *History* survive: an initial, shorter redaction ending with the death of King Sisebut in 621, and a second, more developed redaction updated through Swinthila's victories over the Byzantine or east Roman empire in 625. This includes the rhetorical bookends known in modern times as the *Prologue* or *Laus Spaniae* and the *Recapitulation* or *Laus Gothorum* which situate Gothic history in geographical context in Hispania and assert the Goths' manifest destiny in the province.[10]

It is now well known that Isidore sought as a cultural broker to encourage unity in the kingdom under Gothic rule and Catholic faith.[11] Among his strategies, as I have argued elsewhere, he emphasized a common religious identity as Catholics and a common political identity as subjects of a Gothic king. Over the course of the seventh century, these commonalities came to override distinctions between Goths and Romans by descent until ethnically all Christian subjects could claim to be Goths. This process was aided by the inherently multi-layered nature of ethnicity, with multiple modes of identification (religious, political, descent, cultural) operating simultaneously and the most salient ones potentially influencing the others.[12] Isidore crafted his historical writings to promote and legitimize Gothic dominance by reformulating models of ethnicity and of history writing, depicting God's favour shifting from the Romans to the Goths in Hispania, and presenting a narrative of Gothic manifest destiny.[13]

The obvious place to begin is with the terms for peoples, *populus* and *gens*. The only explicit ancient definition of *populus* is Cicero's: 'an assembly of a multitude united in agreement on law and in partnership for the common

8 Barney, Lewis, Beach, and Berhof 2006, 3–28.

9 Barney, Lewis, Beach, and Berhof 2006, 10–17.

10 Wood 2012, 4–6, 68–73; Merrills 2005, 185.

11 Castellanos 2020, 29; Reimitz 2014, 48–49; Wood 2013, 126; Fontaine 1959 and 2000; Merrills 2006, 38.

12 Buchberger 2017, esp. 22–24, 33–100; Abrams 2012, 21; Pohl 2018b, 4–9; Halsall 2018, 41–42.

13 Buchberger 2017, 68. Compare John of Biclarum: Ioh. Bicl. 85–92; Humphries 2019, 101, 109.

good.'[14] It included all citizens, divided into elite patricians and common *plebs*.[15] According to Livy, the Latins and the Romans were each a *populus* born from multiple peoples, called *gentes* before union and *populi* after agreeing to common law.[16] The only ancient definitions of *gens* pertain to its technical meaning in republican law (particularly the Twelve Tables), obsolete by the early empire.[17] However, in both technical and broader senses, authors regularly used *gens* to indicate purported shared origins, applying to groups ranging from ancient families to large nations.[18] In Late Antiquity, Christian authors adapted these terms to describe the Christian people. Augustine's *populus Dei* was similar to the Roman *populus*, being constituted by adherence to a covenant with God. It could comprise many ethnic *gentes*, but unlike those who became part of the ancient Roman *populus*, they often retained a separate ethnic identity, in part because this sometimes coincided with a political identity associated with a post-Roman kingdom. *Gentes* could also be a religious other contrasted with either Old Testament Israel or the Christian *populus*.[19]

At first glance, it seems that Isidore adopted the ancient meaning of *populus* and *gens* nearly wholesale. His definition of *populus* in *Etymologies* copies Cicero's almost verbatim: 'a human multitude united in agreement on justice and in partnership for community harmony.'[20] Isidore continues, borrowing from Gaius's *Institutes*, that it is 'distinct from the *plebs*, because a populace consists of all the citizens, including the elders of the city'.[21] In fact, because he does not include its application to the Christian people, his definition of *populus* looks not just classicizing but antiquated from a seventh-century perspective.[22] With *gens*, Isidore was more flexible, defining

14 'Populus autem non omnis hominum coetus quoquo modo congregatus, sed coetus multitudinis, juris consensu et utilitatis communione sociatus' (Cicero, *De re publica* 1.39 [25]; trans. adapted from Keyes 1928, 64–65).

15 Gai Inst. 1.3.

16 Livy, *Ab urbe condita* 1.2, 8–9 (ed. Foster 1919); Geary 2002, 49–50.

17 Smith 2006, 13–17.

18 See the listings in Lewis and Short 1933, s.v. *populus* and *gens*.

19 Aug. De civ. Dei 19.24; Adams 1991, 113–14; Heydemann 2016, 29–31, 38; Pohl 2018a, 11–12, 21, 23–24; Geary 2002, 54–55. On ethnicity as part of Christian models of peoplehood, see Buell 2005, esp. 138–66.

20 'Populus est humanae multitudinis, iuris consensu et concordi communione sociatus' (Isid. Etym. 9.4.5; trans. adapted from Barney, Lewis, Beach, and Berhof 2006, 203 [Isidore] and Dyson 1998, 78, 950 [Augustine]). Isidore accessed Cicero's definition via Augustine (Aug. De civ. Dei 2.21, 19.21). See also Furtado 2008, 410, n. 5; Adams 1991, 109–11, 120.

21 Isid. Etym. 9.4.5 (trans. Barney, Lewis, Beach, and Berhof 2006, 203). Cf. Gai Inst. 1.3. See Elfassi 2011, 29.

22 Furtado 2008, 410, n. 5.

it as 'a number of people sharing a single origin, or distinguished from another nation (*natio*) in accordance with its own grouping'.[23] This modifies the common ancient association with descent to acknowledge the possibility of other self-selected criteria.[24]

In many cases, Isidore uses *populus* and *gens* in line with his definitions and with ancient and Christian practice. The legal aspect of *populus* appears in his definitions of law as 'the ordinance of the *populus*' and of civil law as 'law which each *populus* or city' establishes for itself, in numerous examples of ancient Roman legal practice (such as the *populus* creating *decemviri* to write laws), and in describing leaders as selected by or serving their people (such as the Greek *basileus* being the pedestal supporting the *populus*).[25] Most of these references concern biblical Israel, Greeks, and Romans. Isidore also uses *populus* for a multitude or crowd, often in the context of public speeches necessary for functional rule of law, but also for audiences at spectacles and plays.[26] Despite omitting religious meanings from his definitions, Isidore does refer to both biblical Israel and Christians as a *populus* or *populus Dei*. Like the Romans, they participated in their rule by selecting leaders and heard speeches and sermons about God's law as a *populus*.[27]

Similarly, Isidore adopts the late antique Christian distinction between a Christian *populus* and pagan *gentes* or *gentiles*. The Apostles spread the Christian faith among the *gentes*, and *gentiles* wrote hymns to Apollo.[28] Even the Romans, who were a *populus* or three connected *populi* when Romulus divided them into three legal assemblies, become a *gens* when listed among other pagans who named the months.[29] Law continues to play a role, as *gentiles* are those 'without the law' who 'have not yet believed'; like Livy's Romans, they should cease to be called *gentes* or *gentiles* once they convert and therefore agree to follow the (Christian) law.[30] *Gentes* also appear, as in classical texts, as nations born of a common ancestor or as multiple peoples in the world. Abraham was the father of many *gentes*, Jesus came to save all *gentes*, and there were once as many languages as *gentes* in the world.[31]

23 Isid. Etym. 9.2.1 (trans. Barney, Lewis, Beach, and Berhof 2006, 192).

24 Pohl and Dörler 2015, 137.

25 Isid. Etym. 2.10.1, 5.10, 5.5; 5.1.3; 9.3.18 (trans. adapted from Barney, Lewis, Beach, and Berhof 2006, 73, 118).

26 For example, Isid. Etym. 6.8.2, 18.16.1, 18.45.

27 Isid. Etym. 7.6.63, 8.5.67; 7.12.24, 7.6.65, 15.4.15.

28 Isid. Etym. 6.2.48, 1.39.17.

29 Isid. Etym. 9.3.7, 5.33.5.

30 Isid. Etym. 8.10.2–4 (trans. Barney, Lewis, Beach, and Berhof 2006, 183).

31 Isid. Etym. 7.7.2; 7.2.7, 7.8.7; 9.1.1.

When referring to named peoples in *Etymologies*, however, Isidore diverges strikingly from this tidy pattern adopted from older Roman usage. One would expect him to label a people *gens* if referring to shared origins, and *populus* when referring to legal constitution, yet there are some peoples he calls both *gens* and *populus* without differentiation. The Albani are both among the Scythian *gentes* and inhabitants of a region 'named for the colour of its *populus*'.[32] The Bessians are a *populus* sharing Thrace with other *nationes* and *gentes*, and the Garamantes a *populus* of Africa near Ethiopian *gentes*.[33] Yet Ethiopia's name derives from the colour of its *populi*, not *gentes*.[34] The Galicians are a *gens* named by Teucer and whiter than other *populi* of Hispania.[35] Italus gave his name to the province of Italy, which then did likewise for the *gens*, yet elsewhere Isidore calls the Italians a *populus*.[36] Romulus named both *gens* (Romans) and *civitas* (Rome), yet more often Isidore writes of the Roman *populus*.[37] There are no clear contextual distinctions to explain Isidore's varied terminology in these cases. Sometimes *populus* suggests a region's population and appears in Book 14 on world regions, and *gens* refers to peoplehood itself and features in Book 9 on languages and peoples, but not always.[38] Nor is there an identifiable ancient precedent Isidore might be following.

His terminological usage in the *History of the Goths* is even more ambiguous, with the Goths alternately labelled as *populus*, *populi*, and *gens*. His clearest innovation is in the realm of law and leadership, which should take *populus* according to both his definitions and ancient precedent. Yet Isidore relates that Athanaric accepted governance of the Gothic *gens* and that Leovigild and Reccared each improved the *gens*, one territorially and the other in faith.[39] Following his own advice that once adhering to Catholic Christian law a people should no longer be a *gens*, Isidore changes to *populus* when describing the Catholic King Reccared's merciful reduction of tribute his *populus* owed and Swinthila as virtuous ruler of the *populi*.[40] This also serves to legitimize the Goths as rightful heirs to Rome on the peninsula, replacing one *populus* governed by law with another. Yet even here there

32 Isid. Etym. 9.2.65, 14.3.34 (trans. adapted from Barney, Lewis, Beach, and Berhof 2006, 288).
33 Isid. Etym. 14.4.6, 9.2.125.
34 Isid. Etym. 14.5.14, 14.5.9.
35 Isid. Etym. 9.2.110–11.
36 Isid. Etym. 14.5.18, 9.2.85.
37 Isid. Etym. 9.2.84.
38 Examples of exceptions: Isid. Etym. 9.2.55, 9.2.94, 14.3.40, 14.6.5.
39 Isid. Hist. Goth. 6, 52; Adams 1969, 772–73; Adams 1997, 4.
40 Isid. Hist. Goth. 55, 64.

are exceptions. For example, he relates the great strength of the Gothic *gens* to its right to rule in the *Recapitulation*, after their conversion.[41] He refers to the Arian heresy the *Gothorum populus* held previously, as if they were still a *populus* as Arians, despite describing them before this point as a *gens* poisoned with heresy by Valens and persecuting those Catholic Christians among their number.[42] The Goths also appear as a *gens* ruling multiple other *gentes*, or sometimes multiple *populi*. Reccared's conversion recalled the *populi* of the Gothic *gens* to the faith, mountain *populi* were terrified by Swinthila's army, and Rome sees the Goths served by many *gentes* and even Hispania itself.[43] It is not clear who these various peoples are, but there is precedent in classical texts and his *Etymologies* that suggests the population of individual cities or the general multitude.[44] Most of the time when referring to other peoples, Isidore adheres to ancient norms by using *gens*, but in one passage Rome appears as both 'mistress of all *gentes*' and 'victor over all *populi*', seemingly meaning the same thing.[45]

These divergences in the *History* from the classical norms he followed in other writings suggest that a transformation of ethnic terminology was taking place—whether by Isidore's design, more generally across the post-Roman West, or probably both. Gerda Heydemann has shown *gens* becoming more 'elastic' in Cassiodorus's writings in sixth-century Italy as he worked to balance old definitions with the new reality of ruling Christian *gentes*.[46] Helmut Reimitz has demonstrated also that the seventh-century chronicler known as Fredegar reworked older texts for a world of *gentes*.[47] Similarly, Benjamin Cornford has highlighted Paul the Deacon's broadening of the term *populus* in eighth-century Italy.[48] Even within Visigothic Iberia, the Third (589) and Fourth (633) Councils of Toledo employ language similar to Isidore's, mixing classical usages with contemporary adaptations. As records of bishops' decisions in assembly, the councils describe the Christians as a *populus* (or *populus Dei*) far more than Isidore in his *History* and *Etymologies*.[49] Otherwise, though, they align closely with Isidore's usages, presenting Visigothic kings as rulers of *gentes* or *populi* fairly interchangeably

41 Isid. Hist. Goth. 69.
42 Isid. Hist. Goth. 7, 6.
43 Isid. Hist. Goth. 52, 63, 70.
44 Isid. Etym. 9.4.3, 9.2.85, 9.2.98; Livy, *Ab urbe condita* 22.7.6 (ed. Foster 1919).
45 Isid. Hist. Goth. 67 (trans. adapted from Wolf 1999, 108).
46 Heydemann 2016, 44–46, 51–52.
47 Reimitz 2015, 222–31.
48 Cornford 2006, 57–58.
49 For example, III Toledo, prologue (Coll. Hisp. V, 100); IV Toledo 6, 18 (Coll. Hisp. V, 193, 209).

and the *gens* as an assembly of political actors consenting to be ruled and protected by the king alongside the stability of the country.[50] Some of Toledo IV's similarities to Isidore's writings may relate to his presiding over that council, but this was not the case for Toledo III.[51] Together, all of these examples reveal that Isidore and his contemporaries engaged in creative adaptation of ancient Roman terms for peoples. *Gens* was being normalized as a descriptor for a people united politically or religiously, not just by purported kinship. The rhetorical *imitatio* Isidore and others engaged in borrowed a classical framework for ethnicity but modified it to describe a changed political and social reality where barbarian *gentes*, not Rome, ruled in the West.

Another way Isidore drew on and reworked Roman ethnic models is his creation of an origin story for the Goths. Here again, he did not adopt ancient and late Roman tales from biblical genealogy (Gog and Magog) and classical ethnography (Scythians and Getae) wholesale and uncritically. Instead, Isidore refashioned them in order to give the Goths greater antiquity—and thus legitimacy and status—while neutralizing any negative connotations previous authors had envisioned.[52] He particularly aimed to portray them as older than the Romans, to endow them with strong and victorious characteristics, and to establish their development from barbarians to worthy successors of Rome in Hispania. They were to supersede the Romans, not simply copy them.

As a churchman living in a society that valued both classical heritage and biblical authority, Isidore drew from both of these sources for the Goths' past. From ancient Greek and Roman ethnography, he linked them to the Getae described by Herodotus and Pliny. From biblical genealogy, he traced them to Noah via Magog and the related Gog that Ezekiel prophesied would lay waste to Israel in punishment for its sins. In doing so, he followed in the footsteps and adapted the interpretations of Ambrose of Milan, Jerome, Augustine of Hippo, and Orosius.[53] These late antique Christian authors had all speculated about the Goths and other barbarians' connection to Gog or the Getae, but for them the Goths were outsiders, heretics, or rhetorical foils in the story of Christianity's triumph; for Isidore, they were the rightful, Catholic rulers of his kingdom whose dominance he strove to support. His

50 For example, III Toledo, prologue (Coll. Hisp. V, 54); IV Toledo 75 (Coll. Hisp. V, 251, 256). For further discussion of the conciliar language, see also Velázquez 2003; Martin 2008.

51 Stocking 2000; Castellanos 2020, 36–37.

52 I explore Isidore's Gothic origin legend in more detail in Buchberger 2022.

53 Coumert 2007, 103–214.

selective reuse and refashioning of his predecessors' accounts reflects this different perspective.[54]

The Goths' origin story appears twice in Isidore's *History of the Goths*. Chapters one and two state:

> The people (*gens*) of the Goths is a very ancient one. Some suspect that they originated from Magog, son of Japheth, on the basis of the similarity of the last syllable, or they conclude the same from the prophet Ezekiel. But in the past, learned men were in the habit of calling them 'Getae' rather than 'Gog' or 'Magog'. However, the meaning of their name in our language is *tectum*, by which is meant strength, and rightly so, for there was never a people (*gens*) on earth that succeeded in exhausting the Roman empire to such an extent. These were the ones that Alexander himself declared should be avoided, the ones that Pyrrhus feared, the ones that made Caesar shudder.[55]

The *Recapitulation* begins in much the same manner: 'The Goths originated from Magog, the son of Japheth, and have been proved to have a common origin with the Scythians. That is why they are not much different in name: with one letter changed and one removed, "Getae" becomes "Scythae".'[56] The *Etymologies* similarly tell, under the section 'On the Names of Peoples (*De gentium vocabulis*)':

> The Goths are thought to have been named after Magog, the son of Japheth, because of the similarity of the last syllable. The ancients called them Getae rather than Goths. They are a brave and most powerful people (*gens*), tall and massive in body, terrifying for the kind of arms they use. Concerning them, Lucan [*Civil War* 2.54]: 'Let here a Dacian press forward, there a Getan rush at the Iberians.'[57]

To depict the Goths and Getae as one and the same, Isidore appealed to ancient authorities, asserting that 'learned men' or the 'ancients' called the Goths 'Getae'. This statement at the beginning of his *History* copies nearly word for word Jerome's *On Genesis*, a subtle appeal to more recent authority.[58]

54 Humphries 2010; Clark 2011; Merrills 2005, 62–64; Wood 2013, 153–55.
55 Isid. Hist. Goth. 1–2 (trans. Wolf 1999, 80–81).
56 Isid. Hist. Goth. 66 (trans. Wolf 1999, 107).
57 Isid. Etym. 9.2.89 (trans. Barney, Lewis, Beach, and Berhof 2006, 197).
58 Jerome, *On Genesis* 10.2 (PL 23:935–1009, at col. 951).

He also uses etymological links, such as the similarity of 'Scythae' to 'Getae' and of 'Gog' to 'Goth', and demonstrates a belief that a people's character is reflected in the meaning of its name, borrowing Jerome's assertion that 'Gog' means 'roof (*tectum*)'.[59] Yet he also innovated by claiming that *tectum* meant 'strength', co-opting the definition for 'Gaza' preceding Gog in Jerome's *Book of Hebrew Names* in order to suggest that the Goths were strong by their very nature.[60] This is an important adaptation, because many contemporaries, including Ambrose, Augustine, and Jerome, emphasized Gog and Magog's apocalyptic role as enemies of Christendom.[61] Isidore needed to claim their antiquity without these connotations. He does so by focusing on more neutral geographical and genealogical overlaps than on character: people think both Scythians and Goths descended from Magog, and their countries were named after him.[62] No apocalypse is needed.[63]

Furthermore, Isidore implied Gothic kinship with other peoples so that the Goths could appropriate their strengths and victories. Orosius's *Histories* asserted that the Goths were savage Getae whom Alexander, Pyrrhus, and Caesar feared, bolstering the claim by including them among Scythian tribes.[64] Isidore borrowed this, mostly in Orosius's words, and invented an episode where the Goths supported Pompey against Caesar with great valour.[65] He thus makes the Goths champions of republican liberty against tyranny. Changing Pliny's and Orosius's descriptions of Parthians and Bactrians from neighbours to fellow Scythian peoples, Isidore associates the Goths with their powerful empires, implying the Goths are naturally capable of ruling. From both Amazons and Scythians they attain the ferocity of warriors.[66] They also harness the Dacians' strength against Rome through Isidore's creative etymology: 'people think they were called Dacians (*Dacus*) as if the word were *Dagus*, because they were begotten "from the stock of the Goths" (*de Gothorum stirpe*).'[67] Occasionally Isidore mentions a negative trait, like savageness, but he mostly highlights positive characteristics:

59 Jerome, *On Ezekiel* 11.38 (PL 25:25–490D, at col. 356); Jerome, *Hebrew Names* (PL 23:771–858, at cols. 831 and 837).

60 Coumert 2007, 113–14; Wolfram 1988, 29.

61 Ambrose, *De fide* 2.16.137–38 (PL 16:523–698); Aug. De civ. Dei. 20.11; Jerome, *On Genesis* 10.2 (PL 23:935–1009, at cols. 950–51); Jerome, *On Ezekiel* 11.38 (PL 25:25–490D, at cols. 356–57).

62 Isid. Etym. 9.2.27, 14.3.31; Wood 2012, 163.

63 Palmer 2014, 39; Gautier Dalché 1985, 279–80; Bøe 2001, 184–86.

64 Oros. Hist. 1.16.2–3, 7.24.5; Merrills 2005, 62; van Nuffelen 2012, 109–11.

65 Isid. Hist. Goth. 3; Merrills 2005, 213.

66 Isid. Etym. 9.2.62, 9.2.43–44; Wood 2013, 154–58.

67 Isid. Etym. 9.2.90 (trans. Barney, Lewis, Beach, and Berhof 2006, 197). See also Pohl and Dörler 2015, 137; Carbó García 2004, 182–85, 188, 190–91.

strength, bravery, victory, antiquity, and northern hardiness. In a society where classical and biblical heritage each had value, he took advantage of the rhetorical promise of both to depict the Goths as a superior people.

Isidore's Gothic origin story supports his broader tale of the Goths' progression from barbaric outsiders to worthy insiders destined for Hispania. He borrowed heavily from his fellow Iberian Orosius, whose interpretation of contemporary conflicts as advancing God's plan to spread Christianity via the Roman empire had made the Goths key players in the Christian story.[68] Isidore's *Recapitulation* describes the Goths' journey from 'icy peaks' across the Danube into Roman territory, recalling classical descriptions of Scythia and biblical accounts of the land of Magog.[69] But the Goths also make a journey of character, highlighted through the characteristics presented in his origin story which ultimately bolstered the Goths in Isidore's present. Once enemies of Rome who were defeated only with 'enormous struggle', they are now victorious people to be feared.[70] They soon became Christian, but of the heretical Arian sort. Isidore blames the Arian Roman emperor Valens for their heresy as well as for their rebellion, as the Goths were only 'forced to rebel' at Adrianople in 378 when Rome oppressed them 'against the tradition of their own liberty'.[71] Because Isidore had earlier claimed that the Goths supported liberty against Caesar's tyranny, the reader is primed to accept such a tradition.

Like Augustine and Orosius, Isidore contrasts the threat that Gothic kings Radagaisus and Alaric posed to Christian society, though without his predecessors' emphasis on God's plan for humanity.[72] While the former authors express relief that God chose Alaric instead of the more vicious Radagaisus to punish Rome, Isidore leaves these two threats disconnected. He describes Radagaisus as 'of Scythian stock (*genus*), dedicated to the cult of idolatry, and wild with fierce barbaric savagery', much as Orosius does, but Alaric as 'a Christian in name' and fighting with restraint.[73] He borrows Orosius's account of the Gothic soldiers during Alaric's 410 sack of Rome who escorted a nun and the relics she guarded to safety, to show their piety and respect.[74] For Isidore, the difference between the two men shows the development of the Goths toward an earthly destiny:

68 Merrills 2005, 39–43; van Nuffelen 2012, 164; Wood 2012, 154.

69 Isid. Hist. Goth. 66 (trans. Wolf 1999, 107–8).

70 Isid. Hist. Goth. 5 (trans. Wolf 1999, 82).

71 Isid. Hist. Goth. 7–9 (trans. Wolf 1999, 85).

72 Aug. De civ. Dei 1.1, 1.7, 5.23; Oros. Hist. 7.37.5–9; Clark 2011, 33–36; Brown 2000, 311.

73 Isid. Hist. Goth. 14–15 (trans. Wolf 1999, 86).

74 Isid. Hist. Goth. 16–17.

unlike Radagaisus, Alaric's Goths transcended their Scythian ancestors by becoming Christian and civilized, and their future is not violent destruction but Christian mercy.

In 589, Reccared completed the Goths' spiritual journey by converting to Catholicism and banning Arianism, 'recalling all the *populi* of the entire Gothic *gens* to the observance of the correct faith and removing the ingrained stain of their error'.[75] He soon defeated the Franks 'with the help of his newly received faith', showing conversion improving the Goths' already impressive military prowess.[76] Swinthila then defeated the Romans (Byzantines) for good in the early 620s, conquering their remaining fortresses and uniting the peninsula under Gothic, Catholic rule. Isidore's *Recapitulation* celebrates this among other examples of the Goths' mastery of peoples in Hispania: the Vandals put to flight, the Alans extinguished, the Sueves threatened with extermination, and 'Rome itself, victor over all peoples' submitting to 'the Getic triumphs'. These peoples, and even Hispania itself, now rightly served the Goths.[77]

These final lines recall the *Prologue* with which the *History* began: a panegyric praising Hispania and foreshadowing its eventual perfect union with the Goths. Following the classical genre of *encomium*, with clear parallels to Pliny's *Natural History* and Pacatus Drepanius's panegyric for Theodosius, Isidore stresses the region's exceptional fertility bestowed by its creator and personifies Hispania as both a supportive mother and the Goths' cherished bride.[78] The province is the 'sacred and always fortunate mother of princes and *gentes*' where 'the Getic *gens* is gloriously prolific'. It is thus a place worthy of such an ancient people (hence 'Getic', referring to the ancient Getae) and also of 'golden Rome, the head of all peoples' that 'rightly' desired Hispania long ago and 'betrothed' her to itself. However, Isidore writes, 'now it is the most flourishing *gens* of the Goths, who in their turn, after many victories all over the world, have eagerly seized and loved you'.[79] Isidore's rhetoric and the *topoi* he employs are borrowed directly from his ancient and late antique predecessors, but his goal is different from theirs. He did not aim to support or revive Rome, or to make the Goths into Romans; he wanted the Goths to replace the Romans in Hispania. In alluding to Rome's fading glory, Isidore transfers its superiority to the Goths as its

75 Isid. Hist. Goth. 52 (trans. Wolf 1999, 102).

76 Isid. Hist. Goth. 54 (trans. Wolf 1999, 103).

77 Isid. Hist. Goth. 67 (trans. mine).

78 Pliny, *Natural History* 37.77 (201) (ed. Eichholz 1962); Pacatus, *Panegyric* 4.2–5 (ed. Nixon and Rodgers 1994); Rodríguez Alonso 1965, 113–19; Merrills 2005, 185–96, 227.

79 Isid. Hist. Goth., prologue (trans. Wolf 1999, 79–80).

destined Iberian heirs.[80] It is now the Gothic *gens* in charge, superseding the Roman *populus*, and Rome's own cultural and literary motifs emulated and refashioned helped it happen.[81]

As I hope this chapter has demonstrated, Isidore of Seville appropriated Roman ethnic terms, origin stories, and models of triumphant victory and strategically altered them to better reflect the Hispania he experienced and wanted to build: one ruled by Catholic Goths destined to unite the peoples under their rule in faith. He was not alone in seeking to capitalize on Roman prestige through *imitatio*, nor was ethnicity the only avenue through which to do so, as the other chapters of this volume make clear. From literature and language to law, from religious practice to art and architecture, residents of the Visigothic kingdom reinterpreted the Roman legacy to create something new. Too often such adaptations have been described as merely derivative, seeking and failing to become truly Roman.[82] But this ignores the conscious choices authors made in dynamic dialogue with their neighbours, past and present, removing the authors' agency in the process. It also ignores the fact that Isidore was not trying to make the Goths 'Roman' but to manipulate the borders of Gothic identity such that all under Gothic rule, including those of Roman descent, could find a home among the Gothic *gens* divinely destined to rule Hispania. That he explicitly promotes 'Goths' rather than 'Romans' illuminates the true nature of his *imitatio*, and hopefully this look through an ethnic lens can help us see beyond assumptions of 'mere imitation' in other areas, too.

Bibliography

Abrams, Lesley, 'Diaspora and Identity in the Viking Age', in *Early Medieval Europe*, 20.1 (2012), 17–38

Adams, Jeremy duQuesnay, 'The Political Grammar of Isidore of Seville', in *Arts Libéraux et philosophie au Moyen Âge: IVe Congrès international de philosophie médiévale* (Paris: Vrin, 1969), pp. 763–75

Adams, Jeremy duQuesnay, *The 'Populus' of Augustine and Jerome: A Study in the Patristic Sense of Community* (Ann Arbor, MI: University of Michigan Press, 1991)

Adams, Jeremy duQuesnay, 'The Political Grammar of Early Hispano-Gothic Historians', in *Medieval Iberia: Essays on the History and Literature of Early*

80 Merrills 2005, 193, 198–99, 227.

81 Wood 2012, 147–55; Wood 2013, 126–33, focusing on Isidore's *Chronicle*; McCormick 1986, 326–27.

82 E.g., Goffart 2008, 863–64.

Medieval Spain, ed. by D. J. Kagay and J. T. Snow (New York, NY: Peter Lang, 1997), pp. 1–25

Barney, Stephen A., W. J. Lewis, J. A. Beach, and Oliver Berhof, *The Etymologies of Isidore of Seville* (Cambridge: Cambridge University Press, 2006)

Bøe, Sverre, *Gog and Magog: Ezekiel 38–39 as Pre-Text for Revelation 19,17–21 and 20,7–10* (Tübingen: Mohr Siebeck, 2001)

Brown, Peter, *Augustine of Hippo: A Biography* (Berkeley, CA: University of California Press, 2000)

Buchberger, Erica, *Shifting Ethnic Identities in Spain and Gaul, 500–700: From Romans to Goths and Franks* (Amsterdam: Amsterdam University Press, 2017)

Buchberger, Erica, 'Origin Legends of Visigothic Spain in Isidore of Seville's Writings', in *Origin Legends in Early Medieval Western Europe*, ed. by Lindy Brady and Patrick Wadden (Leiden: Brill, 2022), pp. 25–45

Buell, Denise Kimber, *Why This New Race: Ethnic Reasoning in Early Christianity* (New York, NY: Columbia University Press, 2005)

Carbó García, Juan Ramón, 'Godos y getas en la historiografía de la Tardoantigüedad y del Medievo: un problema de identidad y de legitimación sociopolítica', in *Studia Historica. Historia Antigua*, 22 (2004), 179–205

Castellanos, Santiago, 'Isidore of Seville: Historical Contexts', in *A Companion to Isidore of Seville*, ed. by Andrew Fear and Jamie Wood (Leiden: Brill, 2020), pp. 21–41

Chrysos, Evangelos, 'The Empire, the *Gentes*, and the *Regna*', in *Regna and Gentes: The Relationship Between Late Antique and Early Medieval Peoples and Kingdoms in the Transformation of the Roman World*, ed. by Hans-Werner Goetz, Jörg Jarnut, and Walter Pohl (Leiden: Brill, 2003), pp. 13–19

Cicero, *De re publica*, ed. by Clinton W. Keyes, *Cicero, On the Republic. On the Laws* (Cambridge, MA: Harvard University Press, 1928)

Clark, Gillian, 'Augustine and the Merciful Barbarians', in *Romans, Barbarians, and the Transformation of the Roman World: Cultural Interactions and the Creation of Identity in Late Antiquity*, ed. by Ralph Mathisen and Danuta Shanzer (Burlington, VT: Routledge, 2011), pp. 33–42

Cornford, Benjamin, 'Paul the Deacon's Understanding of Identity, his Attitude to Barbarians, and his "Strategies of Distinction" in the *Historia Romana*', in *Texts and Identities in the Early Middle Ages*, ed. by Richard Corradini, Rob Meens, Christina Pössel, and Philip Shaw (Vienna: Verlag der Österreichischen Akademie der Wissenschaften, 2006), pp. 47–60

Coumert, Magali, *Origines des peuples: Les récits du haut moyen âge occidental (550–850)* (Paris: Institut d'études augustiniennes, 2007)

Cvetković, Carmen Angela, and Peter Gemeinhardt (eds), *Episcopal Networks in Late Antiquity: Connection and Communication Across Boundaries* (Berlin: De Gruyter, 2019)

Dyson, R. W., *The City of God Against the Pagans* (Cambridge: Cambridge University Press, 1998)

Elfassi, Jacques, 'Quelques sources non repérées du premier livre des Différences et des Étymologies d'Isidore de Séville, ou comment deux œuvres s'éclairent mutuellement', in *Voces*, 22 (2011), 25–38

Esders, Stefan, Yaniv Fox, Yitzhak Hen, and Laury Sarti (eds), *East and West in the Early Middle Ages: The Merovingian Kingdoms in Mediterranean Perspective* (Cambridge: Cambridge University Press, 2019)

Esders, Stefan, Yitzhak Hen, Pia Lucas, and Tamar Rotman (eds), *The Merovingian Kingdoms and the Mediterranean World: Revisiting the Sources* (London: Bloomsbury, 2019)

Fontaine, Jacques, *Isidore de Séville et la culture classique dans l'Espagne wisigothique* (Paris: Institut d'études augustiniennes, 1959)

Fontaine, Jacques, *Isidore de Séville: genèse et originalité de la culture hispanique au temps des Wisigoths* (Turnhout: Brepols, 2000)

Frighetto, Renan, 'Do *imperium* ao *regnum* na antiguidade tardia: o exemplo do reino hispano-visigodo de Toledo (séculos VI–VII)', in *História*, 35 (2016), e91, https://doi.org/10.1590/1980-436920160000000091 [date of access: 3 June 2022]

Furtado, Rodrigo, 'From *gens* to *imperium*: A Study of Isidore's Political Lexicon', in *Latin vulgaire--latin tardif VIII: actes du VIIIe colloque international sur le latin vulgaire et tardif, Oxford, 6–9 septembre 2006*, ed. by Roger Wright (Hildesheim: Olms-Weidmann, 2008), pp. 408–14

Gautier Dalché, Patrick, 'Isidorus Hispalensis, *De gentium uocabulis* (Etym. IX,2): quelques sources non repérées', in *Revue d'Etudes Augustiniennes et Patristiques*, 31.3–4 (1985), 278–86

Geary, Patrick J., *The Myth of Nations: The Medieval Origins of Europe* (Princeton, NJ: Princeton University Press, 2002)

Goffart, Walter, 'Rome's Final Conquest: The Barbarians', in *History Compass*, 6.3 (2008), 855–83

Halsall, Guy, 'Transformations of Romanness: The Northern Gallic Case', in *Transformations of Romanness: Early Medieval Regions and Identities*, ed. by Walter Pohl, Clemens Gantner, Cinzia Grifoni, and Marianne Pollheimer-Mohaupt (Berlin: De Gruyter, 2018), pp. 41–57

Heydemann, Gerda, 'People(s) of God?: Biblical Exegesis and the Language of Community in Late Antique and Early Medieval Europe', in *Meanings of Community*

Across Medieval Eurasia, ed. by Eirik Hovden, Christina Lutter, and Walter Pohl (Leiden: Brill, 2016), pp. 25–60

Humphries, Mark, '"Gog is the Goth": Biblical Barbarians in Ambrose of Milan's *De fide*', in *Unclassical Traditions: Alternatives to the Classical Past in Late Antiquity*, ed. by Richard Flower, Christopher Kelly, and Michael Williams (Cambridge: Cambridge University Press, 2010), pp. 44–57

Humphries, Mark, 'Narrative and Space in Christian Chronography: John of Biclaro on East, West, and Orthodoxy', in *Historiography and Space in Late Antiquity*, ed. by Peter Van Nuffelen (Cambridge: Cambridge University Press, 2019), pp. 86–112

Lewis, Charlton T., and Charles Short, *A Latin Dictionary* (Oxford: Clarendon Press, 1933)

Livy, *Ab urbe condita*, ed. by B. O. Foster, *Livy, History of Rome, vol. 1, Books 1–2* (Cambridge, MA: Harvard University Press, 1919)

Majnarić, Ivan, '*Aemulatio Imperii* and the South-Eastern Frontier of the Carolingian World', in *Imperial Spheres and the Adriatic: Byzantium, the Carolingians and the Treaty of Aachen (812)*, ed. by Mladen Ančić, Jonathan Shepard, and Trpimir Vedriš (Abingdon: Routledge, 2017), pp. 43–56

Martin, Céline, 'La notion de *gens* dans la péninsule ibérique des VIe–VIIe siècles: quelques interprétations', in *Identité et ethnicité: concepts, débats historiographiques, exemples (IIIe–XIIe siècle)*, ed. by Véronique Gazeau, Pierre Bauduin, and Yves Modéran (Caen: Publications du CRAHM, 2008), pp. 75–89

Mayernik, David, *The Challenge of Emulation in Art and Architecture: Between Imitation and Invention* (Abingdon: Routledge, 2016)

McCormick, Michael, *Eternal Victory: Triumphal Rulership in Late Antiquity, Byzantium and the Early Medieval West* (Cambridge: Cambridge University Press, 1986)

Merrills, Andrew, *History and Geography in Late Antiquity* (Cambridge: Cambridge University Press, 2005)

Merrills, Andrew, 'Comparative Histories: The Vandals, the Sueves, and Isidore of Seville', in *Texts and Identities in the Early Middle Ages*, ed. by Richard Corradini, Christina Pössel, and Philip Shaw (Vienna: Verlag der Österreichischen Akademie der Wissenschaften, 2006), pp. 35–46

Pacatus, *Panegyric*, ed. by C. E. V. Nixon and Barbara Saylor Rodgers, *In Praise of Later Roman Emperors: The Panegyrici Latini*, with Latin text of R. A. B. Mynors (Berkeley, CA: University of California Press, 1994)

Palmer, James, *The Apocalypse in the Early Middle Ages* (Cambridge: Cambridge University Press, 2014)

Pliny the Elder, *Natural History*, ed. by D. E. Eichholz, *Pliny the Elder: Natural History, vol. 10, Books 36–37* (Cambridge, MA: Harvard University Press, 1962)

Pohl, Walter, 'Disputed Identifications: Jews and the Use of Biblical Models in the Barbarian Kingdoms', in *Barbarians and Jews: Jews and Judaism in the Early Medieval West*, ed. by Yitzhak Hen and Thomas F. X. Noble (Turnhout: Brepols, 2018a), pp. 11–28

Pohl, Walter, 'Introduction: Early Medieval Romanness – A Multiple Identity', in *Transformations of Romanness: Early Medieval Regions and Identities*, ed. by Walter Pohl, Clemens Gantner, Cinzia Grifoni, and Marianne Pollheimer-Mohaupt (Berlin: De Gruyter, 2018b), pp. 3–39

Pohl, Walter, and Philipp Dörler, 'Isidore and the *gens Gothorum*', in *Antiquité Tardive*, 23 (2015), 133–41

Pohl, Walter, Clemens Gantner, and Richard Payne (eds), *Visions of Community in the Post-Roman World: The West, Byzantium, and the Islamic World, 300–1100* (Farnham: Ashgate, 2012)

Pohl, Walter, and Gerda Heydemann (eds), *Strategies of Identification: Ethnicity and Religion in Early Medieval Europe* (Turnhout: Brepols, 2013)

Reimitz, Helmut, 'The Historian as Cultural Broker in Late Antiquity', in *Western Perspectives on the Mediterranean: Cultural Transfer in Late Antiquity and the Early Middle Ages, 400–800 AD*, ed. by Andreas Fischer and Ian Wood (London: Bloomsbury, 2014), pp. 41–54

Reimitz, Helmut, *History, Frankish Identity and the Framing of Western Ethnicity, 550–850* (Cambridge: Cambridge University Press, 2015)

Rodríguez Alonso, Cristóbal, *Las historias de los godos, vándalos y suevos de Isidoro de Sevilla. Estudio, edición crítica y traducción* (León: Centro de Estudios e Investigaciones 'San Isidoro', 1965)

Smith, C. J., *The Roman Clan: The Gens from Ancient Ideology to Modern Anthropology* (Cambridge: Cambridge University Press, 2006)

Stocking, Rachel L., *Bishops, Councils, and Consensus in the Visigothic Kingdom, 589–633* (Ann Arbor, MI: University of Michigan Press, 2000)

Van Nuffelen, Peter, *Orosius and the Rhetoric of History* (Oxford: Oxford University Press, 2012)

Velázquez, Isabel, '*Pro patriae gentisque Gothorum statu*', in *Regna and Gentes: The Relationship Between Late Antique and Early Medieval Peoples and Kingdoms in the Transformation of the Roman World*, ed. by Hans-Werner Goetz, Jörg Jarnut, and Walter Pohl (Leiden: Brill, 2003), pp. 161–217

Wolf, Kenneth Baxter, *Conquerors and Chroniclers of Early Medieval Spain*, 2nd print ed. (Liverpool: Liverpool University Press, 1999)

Wolfram, Herwig, *History of the Goths* (Berkeley, CA: University of California Press, 1988)

Wood, Jamie, *The Politics of Identity in Visigothic Spain: Religion and Power in the Histories of Isidore of Seville* (Leiden: Brill, 2012)

Wood, Jamie, '*Religiones* and *gentes* in Isidore of Seville's *Chronica maiora*', in *Post-Roman Transitions: Christian and Barbarian Identities in the Early Medieval West*, ed. by Walter Pohl and Gerda Heydemann (Turnhout: Brepols, 2013), pp. 125–68

Ziolkowski, Jan, 'The Highest Form of Compliment: *Imitatio* in Medieval Latin Culture', in *Poetry and Philosophy in the Middle Ages: A Festschrift for Peter Dronke*, ed. by John Marenbon (Leiden: Brill, 2001), pp. 293–307

About the Author

Erica Buchberger is Associate Professor of History at the University of Texas Rio Grande Valley. Her research focuses on ethnic and religious identity in early medieval Gaul and Iberia. She is the author of *Shifting Ethnic Identities in Spain and Gaul, 500–700: From Romans to Goths and Franks*, and co-editor of *Inclusion and Exclusion in Mediterranean Christianities, 400–800* with Yaniv Fox.

9 Re-imagining Roman Persecution in the Visigothic Passions

David Addison[1]

Abstract

Despite the intervening centuries, the Iberian martyr passions show how important the later Roman world—especially its sites of judicial torture and spectacular punishment—was to the Visigothic Christian imaginary. For most Christians, the dominant notion of sanctity remained the urban martyr, who, more than the bloodless 'confessor', was commemorated in the liturgy, who attracted large-scale civic devotion, and whose cult sites underlay the spiritual topography of the kingdom's cities. I argue that the passions attempted to reinterpret the Roman city—to make its ancient physical vestiges legible within a Christian framework which served ideals of civic Christianity in the present. The Visigothic civic imaginary, therefore, was intimately tied into the memory of the Roman city.

Keywords: martyrdom; sanctity; urban history; memory; liturgy; popular religion; material religion; passions; Prudentius

Introduction: Martyrs and Confessors[2]

No texts from the Visigothic period were more consistently engaged with the memory of the Roman past than the martyr passions. Though redacted

1 Drafts of this chapter have been read by Julia Smith, Lisa Lodwick, and Kati Ihnat, each of whom provided insightful and stimulating comments. I am grateful also to the editors of this volume and to the anonymous peer reviewers, both of whose comments have greatly improved the text. Finally, I owe a debt to the organizers and participants of the 2019 Princeton University workshop where I first presented a version of this chapter. All errors, of course, remain my own.

2 For general accounts of the cult of saints in Visigothic Hispania: García Rodríguez 1966; Castillo Maldonado 2005. Brown 1981 remains fundamental for wider paradigms.

Fernández, D., Lester, M. & Wood, J. (eds.), *Rome and Byzantium in the Visigothic Kingdom: Beyond* Imitatio Imperii. Taylor & Francis Group 2023
DOI: 10.5117/9789463726412_CH09

mainly in the sixth and seventh centuries, the Iberian passions vividly evoked the world of the Roman persecutions over two centuries earlier. Modern historians put little faith in their historical veracity—only the *Passio Fructuosi, Augurii et Eulogii*, known to Augustine of Hippo, appears in corpora of 'genuine' ancient passions—but what they do reveal is the cultivation of a useful Roman past by post-Roman Christians.[3] This past was presented to a wide audience through liturgical reading.[4] In Robert Markus's words, 'on a large number of the year's days, a Christian who attended a church service would be liturgically thrust back into the age of the martyrs'.[5] Historians, however, have been more inclined to think about the other side of the equation—how the martyrs, in relics or legendary retellings, were brought into a new medieval world. Markus's insight has not been sufficiently appreciated.

It is frequently suggested that the figure of the bloody martyr was superseded by new modes of sanctity, particularly that of the ascetic 'confessor' saint. This assertion rests on a strand of argument advanced by late antique Christian authorities themselves. The idea of martyrdom and the genre of the martyr passion were deeply embedded in the violence of the Roman persecutions and the distinctive Roman cultural world of judicial tortures and spectacular entertainments.[6] Nonetheless, a more universal vision of 'martyrdom', wrested from this specific context, emerged in the thought of figures like Augustine of Hippo and Gregory the Great.[7] The latter's doctrine of the 'two martyrdoms' was particularly influential. The first was that of the bloody martyr whose inner virtue was made manifest in violent passion; the other was that of the ascetic, whose historical context did not provide opportunity for outer, manifest struggle. Alike in their inner struggle against vice, the two were distinguished only by historical serendipity.[8]

With martyrdom generalized into an inner conflict against vice, sanctity could be drawn away from the increasingly distant figures of the Roman martyrs and brought into the world of the holy bishop or abbot, the eremitic miracle-worker, or the lone ascetic. A vast corpus of hagiography from Gaul and elsewhere concerns such people, and the works of exceptionally vocal figures like Gregory of Tours have been allowed to cast a heavy shadow over

3 On 'authentic passions', see Rebillard 2017, 1–27 with the *Passio Fructuosi* at 258–62 (with English trans.).

4 De Gaiffier 1954a.

5 Markus 1990, 99.

6 On passions' 'Romanness': Bowersock 1995; Shaw 2003; Grig 2004.

7 On Augustine: Ployd 2018.

8 Greg. Mag. Dial. 3.26, with Straw 1999 and Leyser 2000.

historians' understandings of post-Roman sanctity.[9] Only recently has it become clear that those who promoted such visions of saints' cult, including Gregory the Great, were arguing positions which aroused significant controversy in their time.[10] Such ideas did indeed reach Visigothic Hispania, as did some appetite for confessor *vitae*, but the Visigothic evidence suggests that this ideal of sanctity was far less widespread outside of ascetic circles than that of the bloody martyr.[11]

In the liturgical cult of the church, the Roman-era martyrs, rooted strongly in time and place, remained central. If the evidence of the eleventh- and twelfth-century manuscripts of the *Liber missarum* is any guide, the only Iberian confessor saint to receive liturgical cult in the Visigothic period was Aemilian, a sixth-century hermit whose *vita* was written by Braulio of Zaragoza. Given such patronage, he was the exception not the rule.[12] Though liturgical texts (and passions) did occasionally use the word 'confessor' for figures like Leocadia of Toledo, here the word was understood in the manner closer to that in which Cyprian of Carthage had originally used it—that is, to refer to someone who suffered persecution but died in prison rather than by direct execution.[13] The historic Roman context of violence—not the ascetic struggle of inner virtue or the miraculous deeds of holy people—predominated in the liturgical side of Visigothic saints' cult. The passions have a claim to being more representative of the regular lay encounter with the saints than confessor hagiography, which had an ambiguous relation to popular piety.[14]

Martyr texts tell us most of all about urban cult and civic Christianity. Staging their action in the civic and judicial landscape of the persecution-era Roman city, they became a key means of articulating and asserting a

9 On Gregory of Tours: Van Dam 1993; on Merovingian *vitae*: Van Uytfanghe 1987; Kreiner 2014.

10 See esp. Dal Santo 2012 on Gregory the Great's *Dialogi*. For earlier scepticism: Hunter 1999. Isidore of Seville was sceptical about contemporary miracles: Isid. Sent. 1.24.1–4b, with commentary in Cazier 1994, 129–32.

11 For Gregory's 'two martyrdoms' in Hispania: Isid. Etym. 7.11.4 and Valerius, *De uana seculi sapientia* 9 (ed. Díaz y Díaz 2006, 180), with commentary in de Vogüé 1989. For the influence of Gregory's *Dialogi*: VSPE, *praefatio*. On Visigothic confessor hagiography more generally: Castellanos 2004; Velázquez 2005, 150–245.

12 See *Liber missarum* II (ed. Janini 1982–1983, xvii–xxxix, for provenance). The texts for Aemilian are in *Liber missarum* I, 149.1327–35, 494–99; but note that he does not appear in Verona Orational. On Braulio and Aemilian: Castellanos 2011.

13 E.g., Cyprian, *Epistula* 12 (ed. Hartel 1868–1871, 502–4). Pacian of Barcelona attests Cyprian's categories in fourth-century Iberia, e.g., in *Epistula* 2.7.8 (ed. Anglada Anfruns 2012, 91).

14 Castellanos 2004 presents hagiography as a largely elite genre. Cf. Kreiner 2014.

particular vision of civic community, developed in explicit dialogue with images of Roman civic life and the urban crowd. In many ways this Roman past was an imagined past—a legitimating forebearer for the contemporary community—but in other ways it demonstrated that there was sufficient continuity in the urban fabric of post-Roman cities to render the passions' social and cultural world legible to contemporary audiences. The passions need to be set against the actual history of Visigothic urbanism and, particularly, of Christianity's changing place within it. These texts imagined a history, but at the same time they were, as a genre, some of the most distinctive products of that real later Roman world. As well as their re-imaginings and anachronisms, we need to explore the passions' more direct relationship to the physical and cultural vestiges of Roman urbanism. They speak of a complex dialogue between past and present, not the simple overwriting of the former by the latter.

The Passions and the *Pasionario*

Perhaps the largest obstacle in the study of the Iberian passions has been the difficulty in placing them in time and space. None can be securely attributed to a named author, and some cannot even be pinned down to a single century. As composite texts, re-using and elaborating on older material from both written and oral traditions, they render the notion of a single author ill-fitting.[15] In the *Passio Felicis*, it is true, the hagiographer states that he was a deacon and that, along with people from his region, he translated Felix's body out of Girona, but his autobiographical candour has no parallel elsewhere in the corpus.[16] Furthermore, the corpus cannot usually be analysed in terms of factions or interest groups as the material from Rome can be—the evidence is simply not fine-grained enough.[17] Even the city of composition is sometimes unknown, and as the case of Felix shows, not every text was composed in the main cult centre.

15 See the wider scholarship on hagiographical *réécriture*: esp. Goullet and Heinzelmann 2003; Goullet 2005. Given our slight knowledge of the earliest texts of the Iberian tradition, however, it is often unclear if we are dealing with texts which have undergone conscious, focussed *réécriture* or texts which have experienced more general, cumulative alterations through the vicissitudes of transmission.

16 *Passio Felicis* 21 (PH). The translation was likely to a basilica in Narbonne attested in Greg. Tur. In gloria mart. 91, with discussion in Reiss 2013, 80–92, 117–23. Ildef. De viris. 9 complicates matters by referring to a *sepulchrum sancti Felicis martyris* in Girona in the seventh century.

17 Cooper 1999; Leyser 2000. Various Roman passions are translated in Lapidge 2018.

The Iberian passions are almost always read within the context of a collection known as the *Pasionario Hispánico*. This collection, preserved in tenth- and eleventh-century manuscripts from the northern Spanish monasteries of San Pedro de Cardeña and Santo Domingo de Silos, contains all of the passions relevant to this study, alongside a host of post-Visigothic passions and a large corpus of texts pertaining to saints from other regions. In the middle of the twentieth century the passionary was edited in full by Ángel Fábrega Grau, chiefly on the basis of the earliest manuscript (the tenth-century Cardeña manuscript now in the British Library).[18] Pilar Riesco Chueca subsequently re-edited only the passions pertaining to Iberian martyrs, using a wider range of *Pasionario* manuscripts.[19] Valeriano Yarza Urquiola has recently published a critical edition of the entire *Pasionario*, distinguishing and separately editing the tenth- and eleventh-century redactions.[20] It is crucial to understand, however, that these are editions of the *Pasionario* as a collection, not of each individual passion according to its earliest manuscripts. While we have evidence for Iberian collections preceding the extant *Pasionario* manuscripts (including mentions of now-lost ninth-century collections), it cannot be presumed that these were examples of the *Pasionario Hispánico* in the form attested in later manuscripts.[21] Indeed, it is worth pushing back against the common assumption that all such Iberian manuscripts represent versions of a singular liturgical collection with general Iberian scope: as Fernand Peloux has recently argued, this idea owes much to the twentieth-century nationalist imagination.[22]

It is clear, nonetheless, that the *Pasionario* manuscripts preserve numerous texts which circulated in the Visigothic period. Crucially, this is not to say that the collection itself dates back to this era. The earliest evidence we have for such a collection comes at the opening of the ninth century: Guy Philippart has identified a core corpus of forty-eight passions in the oldest (tenth-century) manuscript which, he argues following Henri Quentin, was known to a Frankish writer who augmented Bede's martyrology around 806 (albeit perhaps not in a version identical to the extant *Pasionario* manuscripts).[23] Individual passions can, however, be securely dated to

18 London, BL, add. ms. 25600. See Fábrega Grau 1950–1953, with the MSS. discussed at I, 25–57.

19 Riesco Chueca 1995, with MSS. at xv–xix.

20 Yarza Urquiola 2020, with MSS. at I, 11–13, 291–332. This edition appeared too late to be taken into detailed consideration.

21 Martín 2009.

22 Peloux 2018.

23 Philippart 2014, 42–48, drawing on Quentin 1908, 139–221. Cf. Peloux 2018, 130–33. The oldest *Pasionario* manuscript is London, BL, add. ms. 25600.

the Visigothic period or even earlier. These need to be taken on their own terms. The contributions of various scholars in the wake of Fábrega's edition have established a more-or-less agreed-upon corpus of passions circulating in the Visigothic period.[24] There is not the space to detail all the textual considerations upon which these judgements are grounded, but I will lay out one particularly important line of argument.

Many of the passions involve the legendary persecuting governor Datian, and these are often considered as a group. Datian is first attested in Augustine's and Prudentius's discussion of the Iberian martyr Vincent, indicating that the governor was already present in Vincent's now-lost fourth-century passion.[25] The passions frequently borrowed characters and episodes from each other, in Hispania as elsewhere.[26] From Vincent's text, Datian came to be implicated in more and more martyrdoms—including those already attributed to other governors—until he appeared in the near-identical historical prefaces to the *Passio Leocadie* and *Passio Vincenti, Sabine et Christete*.[27] Here he was written up as the author of a spree of violence, slaughtering the martyrs Félix of Girona, Cucuphas of Barcelona, Eulalia of Barcelona, the Innumerable of Zaragoza, Justus and Pastor of Complutum, Leocadia of Toledo, Vincent, Sabine, and Christeta of Ávila, and Eulalia of Mérida. In Baudouin de Gaiffier's view, these long prefaces marked the furthest elaboration of Datian's legend.[28] Manuel Díaz y Díaz gave them

24 The main contributions are: Fábrega Grau 1950–1953, I; Díaz y Díaz 1957 and 1964; García Rodríguez 1966; Castillo Maldonado 1999, 21–70.

25 On the passion known to Augustine and Prudentius, see Saxer 2002, 67–97.

26 E.g., the recurring character of the *matrona* Lucina in the Roman corpus, discussed in Cooper 1999.

27 *Passio Leocadie*, 2–3 (PH); *Passio Vincenti, Sabine et Christete* 2–3 (PH). Fábrega Grau (1950–1953, I, 72) provided a *terminus post quem* via their dependency on a fifth-century Gallic passion from Toulouse, the *Passio Saturnini* (for a recent critical edition see Cabau 2001). The Visigothic prefaces' curious claim that the martyred bodies of the child martyrs Justus and Pastor emitted milk rather than blood (at 3: *pro cruore lac* [...] *fundens*) indicates another intertext, hitherto unexplored. It seems to derive from apocryphal traditions concerning the apostle Paul's beheading, the closest parallel being pseudo-Abdias, *Passio sancti Pauli* 8 (ed. Eastman 2015, 184: *pro sanguine lac cucurrit*). This text has traditionally been connected to sixth-century Gaul, though on shaky grounds: see Rose 2013a and 2013b. Apocryphal traditions around Paul's beheading were, however, already circulating in the Latin West by the fifth century, albeit without precise verbal parallels: see Maximus of Turin, *Sermo* 9.2 (ed. Mutzenbecher 1962, 32: *dicitur fluxisse lactis magis unda quam sanguinis*). A separate possibility is that the Visigothic prefaces draw on Prud. Peri. 10.700, where it is said of an infant undergoing judicial torture that *plus unde lactis quam cruoris defluat*. Prudentius's image has been seen to play on a Juvenalian intertext rather than apocrypha on Paul: Tsartsidis 2017, 81.

28 De Gaiffier 1954b. This was a reaction against Fábrega Grau 1950–1953, I, 68–75, which posited a now-lost common liturgical text, a '*Passio de communi*', which served as the base for

a *terminus ante quem* in the last years of the seventh century owing to dependencies found in Valerius of Bierzo.[29] If we accept these arguments we have good reason to place the passions of the martyrs listed above before the end of the Visigothic period.[30] In addition, we can add, on separate grounds, the passions of Fructuosus, Augurius, and Eulogius of Tarragona, Vincent of Zaragoza, Justa and Rufina of Seville, and Mantius (said to have been martyred by Jews in the post-Roman period).[31] Aside from the early outliers of the *Passio Fructuosi, Augurii et Eulogii* and the 'version brève' of Vincent's *passio*, these are all dated no earlier than the sixth and seventh centuries.

In a few cases, there are critical editions of individual passions based on the full range of manuscripts, including those outside the *Pasionario* tradition.[32] This is true for our earliest text, the *Passio Fructuosi, Augurii et Eulogii*, which survives in a mid-eighth-century Frankish passion collection held in Munich.[33] It is also true for the *Passio Vincentii*, which has been edited in three substantially different redactions by Victor Saxer. These include a fifth-century 'version brève' and a sixth-century 'version commune' (of which the *Pasionario* text is an example), as well as a Carolingian redaction (*c.* 870) from Saint-Germain-des-Prés.[34] The earlier testimonies of passions give us confidence in the reliability of the *Pasionario* as a channel of transmission. The eighth-century Munich collection gives texts of the *Passio Fructuosi* and *Passio Vincentii* ('version commune') differing little from the *Pasionario* texts. A different eighth-century Carolingian passion collection preserved in a Turin manuscript gives a text of the *Passio Eulalie Emeritensis* closely mirroring the *Pasionario* manuscripts.[35]

Some cases are more complicated. The *Passio Innumerabilium Cesaraugustanorum*, for example, is first known in a ninth-century manuscript from

the whole 'cycle of Datian'. See García Rodríguez 1966, 251–53, and Guerreiro 1992b, 18, n. 10, for positive discussion of de Gaiffier's argument. Yarza Urquiola 2020, I, 19–21, returns to Fábrega's view.

29 Díaz y Díaz 1957, 456.

30 Eulalia of Barcelona's cult continues to arouse controversy, and I omit it from further discussion. See García Rodríguez 1966, 289–303.

31 On Justa and Rufina: García Rodríguez 1966, 231–34. On Mantius: Díaz y Díaz 1982; Gil 1984, 189–93; Fernández Catón 1983; González Salinero 2018. I discuss Fructuosus et al. and Vincent below.

32 For the Gallic diffusion of Iberian passions: Guerreiro 1992a.

33 Franchi de'Cavalieri 1935, 183–94, with the MSS. discussed at 168–81. The Munich MS. is BSB, Clm 3514, 145–48, described in Bierbrauer 1990, 16. MS. viewable online at: http://daten.digitale-sammlungen.de/0001/bsb00017241/images/index.html [last accessed 16 July 2021].

34 Saxer's various studies and editions are collected in Saxer 2002.

35 Turin, BNU, MS. D.V.3, ff. 104v–111r. The text is edited by Caterina Mordeglia in Goullet 2014, 446–57. I am grateful to Jamie Kreiner for notifying me of this edition.

Saint-Germain-des-Prés in a redaction significantly divergent from the *Pasionario* text.[36] While both versions were printed in the *Acta Sanctorum*, no subsequent edition of the variant Carolingian text has been made.[37] Rosa Guerreiro's suggestion that it represents a local Aragonese redaction does not seem to be the most plausible explanation.[38] Instead, the Carolingian version was likely edited in the ninth century by the monks of Saint-Germain-des-Prés in much the same manner as the *Passio Vincentii*. Both re-written texts appear for the first time in a Saint-Germain manuscript which collected texts pertaining to the monk Usuard's journey to Hispania.[39] The Saint-Germain version of the *Passio Innumerabilium* plays down any local specificities and displays a much more muted tendency for *laus urbis* in comparison to the Iberian redaction. The Iberian text, by contrast, has the marks of a text written to be preached in Zaragoza, with exhortations to an audience and abundant references to the glory of the city and its festivals.[40] All this suggests that the Saint-Germain text was a result of *réécriture* in a monastic context, distancing it from the oral, civic sensibilities of the original text preserved in the Iberian manuscripts. The *Pasionario* tradition is therefore a more secure line of transmission than that which ran through Saint-Germain. Due caution is essential and more philological work on the passions is needed, but it remains the case that Visigothicists have more secure passions at their disposal than do many early medievalists: we can have confidence in the Visigothic provenance of many texts in the *Pasionario*.

Oblivion and Eternity

While the passions transmitted in later monastic manuscripts were used perhaps for private reading or in monastic liturgy, here I want to re-situate them in their Visigothic context, where they were highly public and wide-reaching texts, chiefly delivered orally.[41] Re-placing them in the context of

36 Paris, BN, lat. 13760, ff. 83r–89v. MS. viewable online at: https://gallica.bnf.fr/ark:/12148/btv1b90767846 [last accessed 6 August 2022].

37 Smedt, Van Hoof, and de Backer 1887, 643–49, with the Carolingian text edited from a tenth-century Saint-Amand MS. (Paris, BN, lat. 5568), derivative of Paris, BN, lat. 13760. On these MSS.: Smith 1996, esp. 161–62.

38 Guerreiro 1992a, 152.

39 On the MS.: Decker 1990 and Saxer 2002, 293–94. On Usuard: Nelson 1993 and Christys 1998.

40 *Passio Innumerabilium Cesaragustanorum* 13–14 (PH). For discussion of its original context: Tovar Paz 1994, 226–30.

41 *Pace* the more monastic interpretations of Díaz y Díaz 1992 and Gil 2000.

urban cult, as texts preached about the Christian past of the various cities of Hispania, we see them in dialogue not only with the Roman past but also with Roman modes of memorializing. I want to think, in particular, about how passions engaged with the physical environment of the Roman and post-Roman city. Doing so requires an examination of how the passions related to anterior memorial culture. Christian memorialization claimed to transcend the empty material memorialization of Roman society, but at the same time it developed new ways of understanding the physical world—particularly Roman urban and suburban sites—as sanctified by connection with a martyr and their deeds.[42] The underlying logic of this 'materialization' of the holy can be elaborated in some detail.

The passion most consciously attentive to the relationship between classical and Christian ways of remembering was the *Passio Innumerabilium Cesaragustanorum*.[43] Opening with a discourse on the nature of mortality and memory, it positions itself against the literary memorialization of 'the deeds of worldly ancient men' in history and literature. It describes these men as violent people, pouring out 'the blood of innocents' and seeking glory only in fighting and defending their homes and property. Their memorialization—occurring 'in the schools of the Greek philosophers', 'the studies of the Latin peoples', and 'the remembrances of the historians and equally the books of the poets'—is a frantic attempt to stave off the oblivion of mortality.[44] People might try to create a more lasting memory through inscribing words in marble or bronze, but all is bound to fail. Christian memorialization, in contrast, is aimed at those who had already attained eternal life—those already resident in the 'eternal dwelling-places'.[45]

The contrast between ancient heroes and martyrs was well known in other passions—it was used similarly, for example, in the opening of the *passio* for the second-century martyrs of Lyon, preserved in Eusebius's *Historia ecclesiastica*.[46] In the bluntest sense, passions cast Roman culture as a foil against which Christian eternity can stand out, and identify it accordingly

42 On sanctity and place: Sotinel 2005.

43 I cite from the PH.

44 *Passio Innumerabilium Cesaragustanorum* 2–3 (PH), quotes at 2: 'Priscorum mundialium gesta uirorum, quorum obstinatio extitit inrumpere acies bellatorum cruoremque effundere innoxium seruantium iura terrarum tectaque uel claustra domorum, non solum Grecorum gimnasia concrepant filosoforum, sed etiam ethnicorum studia personant latinorum. Celebritatem quippe nominis eorum tam monumenta storicorum quam etiam libri concinunt poetarum.'

45 *Passio Innumerabilium Cesaragustanorum* 3 (PH): 'in mansionibus eternis'.

46 Its influence, via Rufinus's translation, is possible, though there are no clear verbal borrowings. For Eusebius's and Rufinus's texts: *Historia ecclesiastica* 5.1.3–4 (ed. Schwartz and Mommsen 1903–1908, 400–403).

with empty glories and fleeting pleasures. Various Iberian martyrs are depicted dramatically abandoning elements of classical culture. Thus, Justus and Pastor, infant martyrs, reject schooling from 'the teacher or doctor of this world (*istius seculi*)' and rush off to seek martyrdom instead.[47] Félix of Girona rejects the liberal education he was receiving in his native North Africa, saying: 'What is the philosophy of this world to me?'[48]

The stark dichotomy set up between Roman and Christian culture was a trope that co-existed with a very substantial borrowing of elements of the Roman cultural imagination. Military metaphors for martyrdom are well known: martyrs could be 'soldiers of Christ', and Christ could be 'our emperor who arms his martyrs with the triumphal standard'.[49] More interesting for our purposes is the binding of martyr cult into the civic world of Roman cities. Rome itself could be understood in a new Christian way—as 'that *caput gentium*, most noble of cities, golden Rome' with 'two consuls of Christ, the great holy apostles Peter and Paul', in the words of the *Passio Innumerabilium Cesaragustanorum*.[50] The curious phrase *caput gentium* ('head of the peoples' or 'gentiles')—a play on the classical *caput mundi*—appears also in Isidore's *De laude Spaniae*, where the Visigoths are described as coveting *aurea Roma caput gentium*.[51] This has no martyrial context, however, and it is more plausible to connect the *Passio Innumerabilum*'s imagery to a sermon of Augustine's on Peter and Paul, which describes the martyred apostles as 'two lights of the *gentes*' held by *Roma, caput gentium*.[52] This is uncertain but, either way, it remains true that there were strong precedents for re-using ancient civic imagery in martyr cult. Indeed, martyrs were key tools in the Christian reinterpretation of traditional urban culture. They were, more broadly, sites in which the Roman cultural past was confronted and re-interpreted.

47 *Passio Iusti et Pastori* 2 (PH): 'iam non ad studium magistri iustius seculi uel doctoris ire ceperunt.'

48 *Passio Felicis Gerundensis* 3 (PH): 'Quid mici est filosophia huius mundo?'

49 *Passio Innumerabilium Cesaragustanorum* 3 (PH): 'militum Christi [...] imperatoris nostri, qui triumfali uexillo [...] suos martyres perarmauit?'

50 *Passio Innumerabilium Cesaragustanorum* 13 (PH): 'ipsa caput gentium, nobilissima urbium, aurea Roma, qui cum duobus consulibus Christi, magnis scilicet sanctis apostolis Petro et Paulo, gestat innumerabilium martirum suaue olentia incrementa rosarum.' For the Christianization of the classical imagery of Rome cf. Prud. Peri. 2, on the martyr Laurence.

51 Isid. Hist. Goth., *De laude Spaniae*, lines 26–27. Deswarte 2010, 96, notes the parallel, though without reference to the sermon below.

52 Augustine of Hippo, *Sermo* 381, line 49 (ed. Partoens and Van Der Wiel 2020, 212): 'Habet ergo Roma, caput gentium, duo luminaria gentium.' For the cult of Peter and Paul in Hispania: García Rodríguez 1966, 146–53; Deswarte 2010, 92–97.

The main architect of the Christian understanding of late Roman civic culture in Hispania was Prudentius of Calahorra. Deeply imbued with the classical poetic canon, he had served in high—though somewhat unclear—office in the western imperial administration.[53] He came to exert a major influence over later Iberian passions and liturgical compositions. The question of how Christianity should relate to the anterior classical literary heritage and its role in memorialization was especially vital in poetry. Prudentius's Iberian predecessor, the Constantinian-era versifier of scripture Juvencus, had stated that ancient poetry served only to 'bind together lies about the deeds of ancient men', all the while utilizing its aesthetic achievements in the service of scripture.[54] Horace and Ovid had both famously suggested that their literary work could attain a transcendence and longevity denied to physical monuments doomed to crumble.[55] Juvencus considered ancient poetry as equally awaiting oblivion—equally part of the mutable world that God will bring to an end when he wishes. Prudentius shared this conception of poetry, yet as Cillian O'Hogan has eloquently shown, he also had a vision of martyr cult which borrowed heavily from the Roman civic imaginary.[56] Thus, while the martyrs belonged to universal Christian history, their deaths could also be imagined as sacrifices purifying particular cities and citizenries as bounded, localized entities.[57] Martyr commemoration was about things eternal, but it was tied tightly to physical spaces, monuments, and objects on earth. To understand this seeming paradox, we need to think more broadly about Christian 'materiality'.

It has long been established that martyrs and other saints allowed the holy to be manifested in particular objects. Patricia Cox Miller has suggested that there was a 'material turn' in late antique Christian culture, involving relics, new thinking on the body, aesthetic trends, and so on.[58] While some ecclesiastical figures, notably Vigilantius of Calagurris, vigorously opposed the notion of the divine's substantial interpenetration of the material world, historians tend, nonetheless, to identify relics as indicative of a new religious mentality and praxis.[59] As the 'moveable wealth' of holiness, they

53 His career is known from the remarks in his *Praefatio* (ed. Cunningham 1966, 1–2).

54 Juvencus, *Euangeliorum libri IIII, Praefatio* 16 (ed. Huemer 1891, 2): 'quae veterum gestis hominum mendacia nectunt'. See Green 2006.

55 On Horace and Ovid: O'Hogan 2016, 21–23. On similar sentiments in Eusebius of Caesarea: Castelli 2004, 104–5.

56 O'Hogan 2016. On Prudentius and martyr cult: Palmer 1989; Roberts 1993; Hershkowitz 2017.

57 Petruccione 1995.

58 Miller 2009.

59 Hunter 1999.

were capable of transcending their origins: they could be brought into new centres like monasteries, or be bought and sold, stolen and divided up.[60] The Iberian passions do discuss relics, but in relatively muted terms, tending to emphasize the importance of the bodily integrity of the martyr's corpse rather than its capacity to be split or traded.[61] A notable exception is the *Passio Felicis*, in which the author, a presbyter, recounts how he produced portable blood relics from the martyr's body.[62] The passions, with their civic sensibilities, were usually, however, more concerned with the way in which sites were rendered special by connection with a martyr's life. It is this 'immovable wealth' that will elucidate the rootedness of martyr cult in the topography, as well as the imaginary, of the late Roman city.

Topographies of Martyrdom

Martyr cults were typically conservative as regards late Roman topography. When the near-identical historical prefaces to two later-seventh-century texts—the *Passio Leocadie* and *Passio Vincenti, Sabine et Christete*—built up a unified historical narrative of the Diocletianic persecution in Hispania, grouping together different pre-existing cults by the legendary activity of the governor Datian, they gave a catalogue of cities not dissimilar to that given in a poem of Prudentius's on the Innumerable of Zaragoza. Prudentius opened by evoking the end times. Each city walks in a line, like an imperial procession, to the seat of judgement, bearing the martyrs with which it is blessed.[63] While the Visigothic prefaces do not follow Prudentius's imperial imagery, they do retain his fundamentally urban focus, with one key difference: while Prudentius included some North African, Gallic, and Italian cities, the Visigothic prefaces describe only Iberian examples. They mark the contours of Visigothic political topography, constructing a usable past better adapted for the shape of the new polity, and thus narrower than Prudentius's more expansive late Roman vision. They did so, however, without allowing the centrality of cities to recede.

The civic basis of martyr cult comes across most sharply in instances where a martyr's patronage was contested. While martyrs were, in theory,

60 On relics: Smith 2012, 2015; Wiśniewski 2019; on thefts: Geary 1990.

61 E.g. *Passio Fructuosi, Augurii et Eulogii* 6 (ed. Franchi de'Cavalieri 1935, 192–93); Prud. Peri. 6.130–41.

62 *Passio Felicis* 22 (PH).

63 Prud. Peri. 4.1–76.

all equally deserving of worship by everyone, most martyrs were bound up with local civic identity, and their special patronage was subject to more or less exclusive claims. Vincent's cult was contested between Zaragoza—where he had served as deacon—and Valencia—his place of martyrdom and burial. The sermon known as *Gloriosissimi*, probably preached in Valencia, shows how exclusive a local sense of connection to a martyr could be:

> Although this special friend of Christ should be worshipped by all Christians, with the relics of the martyrs, for his holy confession, he is nevertheless our holy servant joined by the piety of our people, for which reason he is ours in stock (*genere*), ours from faith, ours in vestment (*stola*), ours in duty, ours in burial, ours in patronage.[64]

Similar rhetoric, awash with first-person plurals and metaphors of kinship, is known in parallel Gallic cases. Drawing on sermons preached in Lyon, Lisa Bailey has connected similar language to civic competition and anxiety over urban status.[65] The author of this particular Iberian sermon is uncertain, but the competition between Valencia and Zaragoza over Vincent's patronage is certainly the correct context in which to place it. It has been argued that it was written to be preached by Justinian of Valencia, the mid-sixth-century bishop of the city, though it is unclear whether he composed it himself or whether—as some manuscripts say—it was written by his brother Justus of Urgell.[66] Either way, its attachment to the martyr is strikingly exclusive.

A city's claim to special connection with the martyr was not solely about the possession of relics. The locations of suffering and martyrdom attained a special connection to the martyrs in their own right; and did so in ways that more closely bound memory to physical monuments. In the near-identical prefaces to the later-seventh-century *Passio Leocadie* and *Passio Vincenti, Sabine et Christete*, the various martyrdoms of Zaragoza were described as follows:

> If the human tongue would pass over in silence how many insults and blows were in that place—of how many tortures and how many effusions

64 *Gloriosissimi* 1 (ed. Martín-Iglesias and Abellán 2012, 243): 'Qui licet precipuus Christi amicus ab omnibus christianis cum reliquis martiribus pro sancta sit confessione colendus, est tamen nobis uernula quadam et gentili pietate coniunctus, eo quod sit noster ex genere, noster ex fide, noster in stola, noster in gloria, noster in officio, noster in tumulo, noster in patrocinio.'

65 Bailey 2010, 41–45.

66 Its recent editors, Martín-Iglesias and Abellán, argue the traditional case for Justus's authorship; Linage Conde 1972 argued influentially for Justinian's. Meyer is sceptical of any attribution (2012, 141–42). On Justus and Justinian: Isid. De viris, 20–21.

> of blood had been carried out—the land itself, polluted with the blood of Christians, would speak, for there would be no excepted place which would not hold the revivified and most flourishing ashes of the martyrs in the site of cremation.[67]

Zaragoza did certainly hold ashes of martyrs, but the prior image—that of the land, wet with blood, attesting their martyrdoms—reflects a different logic. Martyrs could be thought of as literally writing their deeds on the earth in blood. Prudentius opens his poem for the local martyrs of Calahorra, Emeterius and Chelidonius, with the following words: 'Two martyrs' names are enrolled in heaven; there Christ registered them in golden letters, but on earth he recorded the names in figures of blood.'[68] Michael Roberts has called this bloody writing 'the indelible stain of blood that constitutes the minimal Passion text'.[69] According to Prudentius's imagery, the written passion composed by humans is secondary to the indelible passion written on the ground, itself corresponding to the eternal and immutable passion written in heaven.[70] Martyrs' bloody writing roots the passion in a location, and renders a spot holy by anointing it or consecrating it with blood.

Numerous Visigothic sources attest the importance of sites made holy by bloodshed. Eugenius II of Toledo, former deacon of Zaragoza, wrote a verse inscription for a basilica in Zaragoza dedicated to Vincent, stating that Vincent had shed blood from his nose on the spot on which the church was built.[71] A more striking example is provided by the church built in the amphitheatre at Tarragona. While epigraphic evidence is mute on the point, it seems overwhelmingly likely that this Visigothic-era church was placed in the old Roman amphitheatre where the city's martyrs Fructuosus, Augurius, and Eulogius were believed to have been martyred.[72] Their passion places their deaths in the amphitheatre and, as Jordina Sales Carbonell has

67 I translate from *Passio Leocadie* 3 (PH): 'Quanta in ibidem ludibria quantaque berbera, quot cruces, quotque effusiones sanguinum in ea operatus fuerit, si humana lingua taceat, ipsa que polluta est christianorum sanguinibus terra, loqueretur, eo quod nullus exceptus fuerit qui bustuali situ non teneat rediuibos ac florentissimos cineres martyrum locus.' See also *Passio Vincenti, Sabine et Christete* 3 (PH).

68 Prud. Peri. 1.1–3: 'Scripta sunt caelo duorum martyrum uocabula,/ aureis quae Christus illic adnotauit litteris,/ sanguinis notis eadem scripta terris tradidit' (trans. Roberts 1993, 11).

69 Roberts 1993, 13.

70 Cf. Prud. Peri. 10.1111–35, where perishable imperial documents telling of martyrdom are contrasted to the imperishable account taken by an angel.

71 Eugenius of Toledo, *Carmina* 10.7–8 (ed. Alberto 2006, 222).

72 Godoy Fernández 1995.

shown, parallel cases are known from elsewhere in the Mediterranean.[73] The presence of different cult sites in the same city, some based on body relics and others on sites of bloodshed, is a phenomenon known elsewhere in the Mediterranean, too (as, for example, in Arles).[74] Michael Kulikowski has emphasized that Iberian cult sites tended to develop outside of cities, typically on the site of a Roman necropolis, thereby decentring communal focal points away from the prior symbolic heart of the Roman city.[75] This was true in Tarragona, for example, as well as for Mérida and Toledo where the major cult sites lay outside the walls.[76] Yet in all these cases there is also evidence of intramural building—which is more difficult to identify archaeologically—from around the sixth century. This was a hinge-point in Visigothic urbanism, with Christianity engaging more directly with the fabric of monumental Roman urbanism and claiming spaces once at the symbolic heart of the ancient city. The sanctification of intramural sites became newly important.

Valencia is a well-documented case.[77] Preceded by some precocious fifth-century burials, most of the buildings of the Valencian 'episcopal complex' are datable to the sixth century. These include the cathedral, a cruciform mausoleum, a baptistry, and other edifices.[78] A large number of burials are present in the area, some of which indicate high prestige and others whose simultaneous multiple inhumations have been connected to waves of the Justinianic plague.[79] Especially interesting is a building indicated by a seventh-century apse built over the ruins of a third-century peristyle house. Later tradition and modern archaeological work have sought to identify this as the location of the prison in which Vincent was incarcerated. That the Roman house was used in this way seems unlikely—especially since it seems to have had a subsequent phase of use in food-production before its destruction—but its later monumentalization suggests that Visigothic-era Christians may, nonetheless, have already made this connection.[80] Christianity's growth in the civic spaces of cities involved new logics of cult, sometimes based on

73 Sales Carbonell 2014 and 2016.

74 Bailey 2010, 44–45, with background in Loseby 1996.

75 Kulikowski 2004, 215–55, 287–310.

76 Mar et al. 1996; Chavarría Arnau 2018, 81–84; Mateos Cruz 1999, esp. 179–95; Gurt i Esparraguera and Diarte Blasco 2012.

77 Summarized in Diarte Blasco 2012, 234–44 and Löx 2017.

78 Soriano Sánchez 1994; Alapont Martín and Ribera i Lacomba 2006 and 2009.

79 Gruber 2018. Keller et al. 2019 demonstrate the presence of the pathogen *Y. pestis* in one grave from the episcopal site at l'Almoina.

80 Alapont Martín and Ribera i Lacomba 2009 affirm the traditional thesis; Löx 2017 gives a sceptical take.

relics but sometimes based instead on the physical sites of past suffering. Since most of the Iberian passions were composed in the sixth and seventh centuries, while this change in Visigothic urbanism was in motion, they ought to be read as part of a new Christian engagement with the Roman urban past.

The Roman Crowd and the Christian Congregation

Thinking of the passions' relationship to the physical vestiges of Roman urbanism, the material they contain about public space and crowds acquires new significance. 'Public' is a word with a wide semantic range, both in its Latin root, *publicus*, and in its modern scholarly uses. In its narrowest sense it could just denote 'the state' as opposed to 'private' citizens, as when Chindaswinth ruled that masters could not kill their slaves *extra publicum iudicium* (that is, without going through the systems of royal justice).[81] Isidore glossed the term *publicus* minimally, citing the Roman jurist Ulpian's definition of *ius publicum*.[82] More relevant here, however, is the broader notion of 'publicness' as representativeness and openness—as things occurring before the eyes of a given community. In this sense we can refer to 'public spaces' that were not controlled by the state. We can also describe bishops addressing themselves to a Christian 'public' inasmuch as they were seen as the representative of a given community and exercised their authority before its scrutiny. A vision of a Christian 'public', worked out in dialogue with Roman civic ideas, was particularly apparent in the passions.[83]

Passions' main action occurred in public trials before the spectating eyes of the crowd. Eulalia of Mérida's passion described the young girl entering the city's forum like an *adventus*, claiming that 'there assembled an innumerable crowd, vast beyond measure, such that there was no-one left in their house'.[84] The crowd was an important background character in a passion, rarely discussed but essential to its logic. While martyrs were themselves witnesses to Christ's truth, they also needed their confession to be witnessed by others.[85] Interestingly, the Iberian passions do not depict the crowd as 'pagan' or inherently hostile. Instead, they were ready and able to witness

81 LI 6.5.12.

82 Isid. Etym. 5.8.

83 On ecclesiastical 'publicness' in a somewhat different, rural context: Addison 2020.

84 *Passio Eulalie Emeritensis* 7 (PH): 'Facta est turba innumerabilis, ingens nimis, ita ut in domo sua nemo remaneret.' On late Roman and Visigothic ceremonial: McCormick 1986, 297–327.

85 On Christian subversions of judicial confession: Grig 2004, 67–77. In the Iberian corpus, see esp. *Passio Vincentii* [version brève] 2 (ed. Saxer 2002, 138).

the truth set forth in the person of the martyr. This is a remarkable feature of the Iberian texts, not present in all other traditions.[86] Governors thus had to avoid the public gaze. In the *Passio Iusti et Pastoris*, the governor Datian:

> [O]rdered that they be arrested without being heard, and ruled that they be sent away, fearing that if they were led to his presence for interrogation they would ready the souls of those standing around them for the confession of Christ's name, or that if he did not prevail over them it would be seen publicly (*publice*) that his malice was overcome by little infants.[87]

The spectating crowd is an oppressive burden to the governor, ready to witness the martyr's triumph.

Prospective martyrs, then, did not witness their faith exclusively in these open environments, but cycled between periods of imprisonment and periods of 'public' confession. This heightened the symbolic importance of the publicity of martyrdom. Vincent and his bishop Valerian were incarcerated after their first encounter with Datian. The sixth-century passion expressed this in a language of publicness: they are 'secluded for so long from the common light of public intercourse (*publicae conuersationis*)'.[88] When Vincent is later returned to prison—'isolated from all public light (*publica luce*) and damned to perpetual night'—he miraculously produces a startlingly bright light, a synecdoche of the entire coming-to-publicness that passions dramatized.[89] A derivative story appeared in the *Passio Felicis* in which the light converts the jailers.[90] The martyr thus finds a receptive audience even in prison. Later in Vincent's passion, Datian tries to destroy the remains of the martyr's body to avoid attracting a cult, exclaiming: 'Let him be submerged in the sea, that we might not blush daily under the eyes of all! The seas will conceal his victory.'[91] It is notable that the sixth-century

86 I am grateful to Peter Brown for drawing my attention to this theme.

87 *Passio Iusti et Pastoris* 3 (PH): 'Inauditos eos iussit conpreendi et cedi precepit, timens ne, dum eos ad interrogandum ad eius presentiam perduceret, aliorum circumstantium ad confessionem Christi nominis animos preparassent aut ne, dum in eis non preualuisset, suam publice prospiceret malitiam ab infantulis superari.'

88 *Passio Vincentii* [version commune] 3 (ed. Saxer 2002, line 27): 'a communi tamdiu publicae conuersationis luce seclusos'.

89 *Passio Vincentii* [version commune] 17–19 (ed. Saxer 2002, lines 148–83, quote at 17, line 151–52): 'ab omni publica luce sepositum et perpetua nocte damnatum'.

90 *Passio Felicis* 17 (PH). The dependency is probably to the 'version brève'.

91 *Passio Vincentii* [version commune] 23 (ed. Saxer 2002, lines 221–22): 'Inmergatur pelago, ne erubescamus cotidie sub oculis omnium. Victoria eius uel maria celabunt.' This episode was echoed in *Passio Felicis* 18 (PH).

'version commune' brings out the language of publicness far more than the fifth-century 'version brève'.

The figure of the crowd ought to be understood within the concrete pastoral context of the passions.[92] They were to be read liturgically on feast days. They were a literature that was repetitive and stereotyped, easier than most ecclesiastical genres to be appreciated by audiences who were not necessarily all literate.[93] The manner in which martyrs provided spectacles thus had a double significance. The martyr was a spectacle before the Roman crowd—Eulalia of Mérida furnished 'such a pleasing spectacle to the citizens'; Justa and Rufina were *spectacula Dei*, contesting in the 'stadium of spiritual contest'—but the passion text was *itself* also a spectacle set before the early medieval Christian congregation.[94] The audience was encouraged to see themselves mirroring the crowd who watched expectantly as the martyr contested with the governor.[95] It is this role into which congregants were 'thrust back', as Markus would have it—that of the 'public' before whom the martyr could symbolically enact Christianity's conquest of the Roman civic sphere.

The sense of unanimity and harmony anachronistically placed onto the Roman crowd articulated an idealized Christian community to the medieval audience and gave a history to the Christian community in the city.[96] I do not want to presume a functionalist model in which an authentic sense of consensus was forged by these means: coercion, exclusion, and the flattening out of real inequalities are always by-products of such nominally consensual visions of community.[97] The passions, with their homogenous crowds, show this amply. Jews do appear in some passions, but always as people miraculously converted. They are there as extreme cases showing the power of the martyr to manifest Christ's power even to those who were, as anti-Jewish rhetoric went, typically insensate to spiritual truths.[98] Visions of community are prone to exclude as well as include, but the point here is that the particular integrative picture of civic community presented by the passions was one construed with reference to an imagined—and somewhat anachronistic—Roman civic past.[99]

92 For the broader historiography of early medieval crowds: Bobrycki 2018, esp. 3–17.

93 On audience comprehension: Van Uytfanghe 2001.

94 *Passio Eulalie Emeritensis* 17 (PH): 'tam gratissimum exspectaculum ciuibus'; *Passio Iuste et Rufine* 3 (PH): 'spiritalis agonis stadium'.

95 Grig 2004, 42–47. On spectacle and martyrdom, see also Castelli 2004, 104–33.

96 For similar images in Gallic sermons: Bailey 2010, 51.

97 Ginzburg 2012.

98 *Passio Eulalie Emeritensis* 6 (PH); *Passio Vincenti, Sabine et Christete* 11–12 (PH); *Passio Mantii* (PH). See Castillo Maldonado 2006, and Guerreiro 1993, and, more broadly, Drews 2006.

99 See Buc 2001, 123–57.

There are some reasons to question whether audiences would have seen these notions as having any *specifically* Roman content, as opposed to reflecting phenomena still present in society. The strongest argument supporting this objection lies in the fact that spectacular punishments and public trials were not confined to the Roman period.[100] Visigothic penal law insisted on 'publicness' both in terms of 'public' agents of justice and in terms of openness before a notional community: 'The judge, whenever the guilty one is to be killed, should exercise discipline not in secret or hidden places, but publicly, in an assembly.'[101] The same was true for floggings and whippings: they were to be held *publice, in conventu publice*, or *in conspectu omnium*.[102] Even the means of governmental violence depicted in the passions would not, for the most part, have been alien to Visigothic practice. One could be burned alive, like Eulalia of Mérida or the martyrs of Tarragona, under Visigothic penal law.[103] Torture was certainly permitted as part of serious criminal inquiries.[104] The only specifically Roman punishment mentioned in regard to the persecutions was damnation to the mines or quarries—though this occurs not in a passion but in Justus of Urgell's commentary on the Song of Songs.[105] While it is a fascinating piece of evidence for memory of the persecutions, it does not connect to the passion corpus in any direct way.

We can see more evidence of rupture, however, when considering the broader changes in cities' urban fabric. In Zaragoza we have remarkable but exceptional evidence of games being held, presumably in the theatre, as late as 504.[106] Despite this, some infrastructure in the same city, like the sewers under the forum, had already ceased functioning by the end of the fourth century, and a number of large buildings were abandoned during the fifth.[107] Pilar Diarte Blasco's systematic survey of the archaeology of 'public spaces' in Hispania suggests that the growth of the ecclesiastical presence

100 Petit 1991 gives an excellent overview of Visigothic penal law and catalogues relevant citations. In what follows, I draw heavily on this resource.

101 LI 7.4.7 (*antiqua*): 'Iudex, quotiens occisurus est reum, non in secretis aut in absconsis locis, sed in conventu publice exerceat disciplinam.'

102 LI 3.4.7 (*antiqua*); 6.4.2 (Chindaswinth); 7.2.6 (*antiqua*); 9.2.2 (*antiqua*); 9.2.4 (*antiqua*); 12.2.4 (Sisebut).

103 LI 3.2.2 (*antiqua*); 11.2.1 (*antiqua*); 12.2.11 (Recceswinth).

104 LI 6.1.2. The same term *quaestio* appears in both Visigothic legislation and passions.

105 Justus of Urgell, *Explanatio in Cantica Canticorum* 5.115 (ed. Guglielmetti 2011, 90–92). On penal condemnation to mines: Gustafson 1994. I am grateful to Henry Gruber for his comments on penal servitude.

106 The games are attested in Cons. Caes., anno 504, line 444. See Jiménez Sánchez 2006 and Beltrán Lloris 1993.

107 Diarte Blasco 2012, 84–91.

followed a brief hiatus in which certain public buildings and spaces fell into abeyance.[108] As Damián Fernández has noted, this abeyance did not constitute a straightforward decline in occupation, but rather a process of transformation and re-use, with ancient monumental spaces coming to be used for private dwellings or productive functions.[109] There was a hiatus in their 'publicness'—if not in occupation—and this implies a greater sense of historical break than is suggested by the continuity of punishments' 'publicness'. Christian authorities certainly relied on a certain degree of urban continuity to make their images legible and immediate, but they were not merely stewarding a continuously existing 'public' sphere. Through their spoliation of the Roman civic imaginary, they rearticulated the urban community and its history in new ways.

Conclusion

The passions shed light on a world of civic religiosity which is not well represented in other, more well-thumbed Visigothic sources. They suggest a different sense of Christian community and, indeed, a different relationship to the Roman past than that found in confessor piety or in the grand historical works of writers like Isidore. Though the local civic imaginary of martyr passions was partly an inheritance from the late Roman world, continuity was not inevitable. The civic imaginary long evoked in martyr passions acquired a particular urgency and relevance in the period in which Christianity came to take hold over the monumental hearts of cities—that is, the sixth and seventh centuries. Here the passions, preached at festivities and in the liturgy, were key instruments in the development of a vision of the Roman civic which appropriated and re-interpreted aspects of the physical and the imagined city for newly Christian times.

Theirs was a vision of 'public' Christianity, providing a dramatic and legitimizing account of the emergence of Christianity as a major force in the civic world of the Roman city. They did this in such a way as to suggest a genealogical relation between, on the one hand, the martyr before their 'public' and, on the other, the later preacher before their congregation. In dialogue with the still present vestiges of Roman civic life, passions repeatedly re-interpreted and re-enacted a Roman past as a myth of origins for both the urban Christian *populus* and the 'publicness' of the church as

108 Diarte Blasco 2012, 311–13.
109 Fernández 2017, 126–39.

the institution claiming to represent this community. The passions speak, therefore, of the continued importance of an idea of the Roman past in the Visigothic present, and one which was not only imaginary but also rooted in a creative engagement with the real vestiges of the Roman world.

Bibliography

Addison, David, 'Property and Publicness: Bishops and Lay-Founded Churches in Post-Roman Hispania', in *Early Medieval Europe*, 28.2 (2020), 175–96

Alapont Martín, Llorenç, and Albert V. Ribera i Lacomba, 'Cementerios tardoantiguas de Valencia: arqueología y antropología', in *Anales de Arqueología Cordobesa*, 17.2 (2006), 161–94

Alapont Martín, Lorenç, and Albert V. Ribera i Lacomba, 'Topografía y jerarquía funeraria en la Valencia tardoantigua', in *Morir en el Mediterráneo Medieval*, BAR International Series, S2001, ed. by Jorge López Quiroga and Artemio Manuel Martínez Tejera (Oxford: John and Erica Hedges, 2009), pp. 59–88

Augustine of Hippo, *Sermo* 381, ed. by Gert Partoens and Laurens Van Der Wiel, 'Augustine's s. 381 for the *natalis* of Peter and Paul: Manuscript Transmission and New Critical Edition', in *Nos sumus tempora. Studies on Augustine and his Reception Offered to Mathijs Lamberigts*, Bibliotheca Ephameridum Theologicarum Lovaniensium 316, ed. by Anthony Dupont, Wim François, and Johan Leemans (Leuven: Peeters, 2020), pp. 189–212

Bailey, Lisa K., *Christianity's Quiet Success: The Eusebius Gallicanus Sermon Collection and the Power of the Church in Late Antique Gaul* (Notre Dame, IN: University of Notre Dame Press, 2010)

Beltrán Lloris, Miguel, 'El teatro de *Caesaraugusta*. Estado actual de conocimiento', in *Teatros romanos de Hispania*, ed. by Sebastián F. Ramallo Ascensio (Murcia: Universidad de Murcia, 1993), pp. 93–118

Bierbrauer, Katharina, *Die Vorkarolingischen und karolingischen Hss der Bayerischen Staatsbibliothek*, Katalog der illuminierten Handschriften der Bayerischen Staatsbibliothek in München 1 (Wiesbaden: Reichert, 1990)

Bobrycki, Shane, 'The Flailing Women of Dijon: Crowds in Ninth-Century Europe', in *Past & Present*, 240.1 (2018), 3–46

Bowersock, Glen W., *Martyrdom and Rome* (Cambridge: Cambridge University Press, 1995)

Brown, Peter R. L., *The Cult of the Saints: Its Rise and Function in Latin Christianity* (London: SCM Press, 1981)

Buc, Philippe, *The Dangers of Ritual: Between Early Medieval Texts and Social Scientific Theory* (Princeton, NJ and Oxford: Princeton University Press, 2001)

Castellanos, Santiago, *La hagiografía visigoda. Dominio social y proyección cultural* (Logroño: Fundación San Millán de la Cogolla, 2004)

Castellanos, Santiago, *Poder social, aristocracias y* hombre santo *en la Hispania Visigoda: La* Vita Aemeliani *de Braulio de Zaragoza*, Biblioteca de Investigación 20 (Logroño: Universidad de La Rioja, 2011)

Castelli, Elizabeth A., *Martyrdom and Memory: Early Christian Culture Making* (New York, NY: Columbia University Press, 2004)

Castillo Maldonado, Pedro, *Los Mártires Hispanorromanos y su Culto en la Hispania de la Antigüedad Tardía* (Granada: Universidad de Granada, 1999)

Castillo Maldonado, Pedro, '*Angelorum participes*: The Cult of the Saints in Late Antique Spain', in *Hispania in Late Antiquity: Current Perspectives*, ed. by Kim Bowes and Michael Kulikowski (Leiden: Brill, 2005), pp. 151–88

Castillo Maldonado, Pedro, 'Judíos, conversos y relapsos en la hagiografía narrativa tardoantigua Hispana', in *Studia Histórica—Historia Antigua*, 24 (2006), 185–203

Cazier, Pierre, *Isidore de Séville et la naissance de l'Espagne catholique*, Théologie historique 96 (Paris: Beauchesne Éditeur, 1994)

Chavarría Arnau, Alexandra, *A la sombra de un imperio. Iglesias, obispos y reyes en la Hispania tardoantigua (siglos V–VII)*, Munera 43 (Bari: Edipuglia, 2018)

Christys, Ann, 'St-Germain-des-Prés, St Vincent and the Martyrs of Cordoba', in *Early Medieval Europe*, 7.2 (1998), 199–216

Cooper, Kate, 'The Martyr, the *Matrona* and the Bishop: The Matron Lucina and the Politics of Martyr Cult in Fifth- and Sixth-Century Rome', in *Early Medieval Europe*, 8.3 (1999), 297–317

Cyprian, *Epistulae*, ed. by Wilhelm Hartel, *S. Thasci Caecili Cypriani opera omnia*, 3 vols, Corpus Scriptorum Ecclesiasticorum Latinorum 3 (Vienna: Gerold, 1868–1871)

Dal Santo, Matthew, *Debating the Saints' Cult in the Age of Gregory the Great*, Oxford Studies in Byzantium (Oxford: Oxford University Press, 2012)

Decker, Andrea, 'Die *membra disiecta* eines Aimoin-Codex: ein Beitrag zum Skriptorium von Saint-Germain-des-Prés', in *Scriptorium*, 44.2 (1990), 193–206

Deswarte, Thomas, *Une Chrétienté romaine sans pape. L'Espagne et Rome (586–1095)*, Bibliothèque d'histoire médiévale 1 (Paris: Classiques Garnier, 2010)

Diarte Blasco, Pilar, *La configuración urbana de la* Hispania *tardoantigua. Transformaciones y pervivencias de los espacios públicos romanos (s. III–VI d.C.)*, BAR International Series 2429 (Oxford: Archaeopress, 2012)

Díaz y Díaz, Manuel Cecilio, 'Correcciones y conjeturas al Pasionario Hispánico', in *Revista de Archivos, Bibliotecas y Museos*, 63 (1957), 453–65

Díaz y Díaz, Manuel Cecilio, 'Anotaciones para una cronología del Pasionario hispánico', in *Hispania Sacra*, 17.33 (1964), 515–28

Díaz y Díaz, Manuel Cecilio, 'La *Passio Mantii* (*BHL* 5219)', in *Analecta Bollandiana*, 100 (1982), 327–339

Díaz y Díaz, Manuel Cecilio, 'The Christian Origins of the Peninsula as Seen in Some Seventh Century Texts', in *Vie chrétienne et culture dans l'Espagne du VIIe au Xe siècles* (Ashgate: Variorum, 1992), pp. 87–94

Drews, Wolfram, *The Unknown Neighbour: The Jew in the Thought of Isidore of Seville* (Leiden: Brill, 2006)

Eugenius of Toledo, *Carmina*, ed. by Paulo Farmhouse Alberto, *Eugenius Toletanus, Opera omnia*, CCSL 114 (Turnhout: Brepols, 2006)

Eusebius, *Historia Ecclesiastica*, ed. by Eduard Schwartz and Theodor Mommsen, *Eusebius Werke, 2: Die Kirchengeschichte*, Die griechischen christlichen Schriftsteller der ersten drei Jahrhunderte, 2 vols (Leipzig: J.C. Hinrichs'sche Buchhandlung, 1903–1908)

Fábrega Grau, Ángel, *Pasionario Hispánico (siglos VII–XI)*, Monumenta Hispaniae sacra. Serie litúrgica 6, 2 vols (Madrid and Barcelona: Consejo Superior de Investigaciones Científicas, 1950–1953)

Fernández, Damián, *Aristocrats and Statehood in Western Iberia, 300–600 C.E.* (Philadelphia, PA: University of Pennsylvania Press, 2017)

Fernández Catón, José María, *San Mancio: culto, leyenda y reliquias. Ensayo de crítica hagiográfica*, Fuentes y estudios de historia leonesa 30 (León: Centro de Estudios e Investigación 'San Isidoro', 1983)

Franchi de'Cavalieri, Pio, 'Gli atti di S. Fruttuoso di Tarragona', in *Note agiografiche, fascicolo 8*, Studi e testi 65 (Vatican City: Biblioteca Apostolica Vaticana, 1935), pp. 183–94

Gaiffier, Baudouin de, 'Le lecture des Actes de martyrs dans la prière liturgique en Occident. À propos du Passionnaire hispanique', in *Analecta Bollandiana*, 72 (1954a), 134–66

Gaiffier, Boudouin de, '*Sub Daciano praeside*: étude de quelques passions espagnoles', in *Analecta Bollandiana*, 72 (1954b), 378–96

García Rodríguez, Carmen, *El culto de los santos en la España romana y visigoda* (Madrid: Consejo Superior de Investigaciones Científicas, 1966)

Geary, Patrick J., *Furta Sacra: Thefts of Relics in the Central Middle Ages*, rev. ed. (Princeton, NJ: Princeton University Press, 1990)

Gil, Juan, 'Interpretaciones latinas', in *Habis*, 15 (1984), 185–200

Gil, Juan, 'La pasión de Santa Eulalia', in *Habis*, 31 (2000), 403–16

Ginzburg, Carlo, 'The conversion of the Jews of Minorca (A.D. 417–18)', in *Threads and Traces: True, False, Fictive*, trans. Anne C. Tedeschi and John Tedeschi (Berkeley, CA: University of California Press, 2012), pp. 25–33

Gloriosissimi, ed. by Jose Carlos Martín-Iglesias and Salvador Iranzo Abellán, 'Justo de Urgel, *Sermo de S. Vincentio* (*CPL* 1092): estudio de su tradición manuscrita, edición crítica y traducción', in *Anuario de Estudios Medievales*, 42.1 (2012), 229–51

Godoy Fernández, Cristina, 'La *memoria* de Fructueux, Augure et Euloge dans l'arène de l'amphithéâtre de Tarragone: nouvelle hypothèse sur son implantation', in *Antiquité Tardive*, 3 (1995), 251–62

González Salinero, Raúl, 'Perfiles de un debate sobre la *Passio Mantii*', in *Hispania Sacra*, 70.141 (2018), 185–210

Goullet, Monique, *Écriture et réécriture hagiographiques. Essai sur les rééctritures de Vies de saints dans l'Occident latin medieval* (*VIIIe–XIIIe s.*), Hagiologia 4 (Turnhout: Brepols, 2005)

Goullet, Monique, *Le Légendier de Turin. MS. D.V.3 de la Bibliothèque Nationale Universitaire*, Millennio Medievale 103 (Florence: SISMEL-Edizioni del Galluzzo, 2014)

Goullet, Monique, and Martin Heinzelmann (eds), *La réécriture hagiographique dans l'Occident médiéval: transformations formelles et idéologiques*, Beihefte der Francia 58 (Ostfildern: Jan Thorbecke Verlag, 2003)

Green, Roger P. H., *Latin Epics of the New Testament: Juvencus, Sedulius, Arator* (Oxford: Oxford University Press, 2006)

Grig, Lucy, *Making Martyrs in Late Antiquity* (London: Duckworth, 2004)

Gruber, Henry, 'Indirect Evidence for the Social Impact of the Justinianic Pandemic: Episcopal Burial and Conciliar Legislation in Visigothic Hispania', in *Journal of Late Antiquity*, 11.1 (2018), 193–215

Guerreiro, Rosa, 'Le rayonnement de l'hagiographie hispanique en Gaule pendant le haut Moyen Âge: circulation et diffusion des *Passions* hispaniques', in *L'Europe héritière de l'Espagne wisigothique*, Collection de la Casa de Velázquez 35, ed. by Jacques Fontaine and Christine Pellistrandi (Madrid: Casa de Velázquez, 1992a), pp. 137–57

Guerreiro, Rosa, 'Un archétype ou des archetypes du Paisionnaire hispanique? Prudence et le métier d'hagiographie', in *De Tertullien aux Mozarabes, I: Antiquité tardive et Christianisme ancient* (*IIIe–VIe siècles*). *Mélanges offerts à Jacques Fontaine*, Collection des Études augustiniennes. Série Antiquité 132, ed. by Louis Holtz and Jean-Claude Fredouille (Paris: Institut d'Études Augustiniennes, 1992b), pp. 15–27

Guerreiro, Rosa, 'La imagen del judío en los textos hagiográficos y patrísticos, Siglos V al VIII', in *Espacio, Tiempo y Forma: Serie II: Historia Antigua*, 6 (1993), 437–50

Gurt i Esparraguera, Josep M., and Pilar Diarte Blasco, 'La basílica de Santa Leocadia y el final de uso del circo romano de Toledo: una nueva interpretación', in *Zephyrus*, 69 (2012), 149–63

Gustafson, Mark, 'Condemnation to the Mines in the Later Roman Empire', in *The Harvard Theological Review*, 87.4 (1994), 421–33

Hershkowitz, Paula, *Prudentius, Spain, and Late Antique Christianity: Poetry, Visual Culture, and the Cult of Martyrs* (Cambridge: Cambridge University Press, 2017)

Hunter, David G., 'Vigilantius of Calagurris and Victricius of Rouen: Ascetics, Relics, and Clerics in Late Roman Gaul', in *Journal of Early Christian Studies*, 7.3 (1999), 401–30

Jiménez Sánchez, Juan Antonio, 'Los últimos *ludi circenses* realizados en *Hispania* en época visigoda', in *Faventia*, 28.1–2 (2006), 99–113

Justus of Urgell, *Explanatio in Cantica Canticorum*, ed. by Rossana E. Guglielmetti, *Giusto d'Urgell, Explanatio in Cantica Canticorum. Un vescovo esegeta nel regno visigoto*, Per verba. Testi mediolatini con traduzione 27 (Florence: SISMEL-Edizioni del Galluzzo, 2011)

Juvencus, *Euangeliorum libri IIII*, ed. by Johann Huemer, *Gai Vettii Aquilini Juvenci Evangeliorum libri quattuor*, Corpus Scriptorum Ecclesiasticorum Latinorum 24 (Vienna: Tempsky, 1891)

Keller, Marcel, Maria A. Spyrou, Christiana L. Scheib, Gunnar U. Neumann, Andreas Kröpelin, Brigitte Haas-Gebhard, Bernd Päffgen, Jochen Haberstroh, Albert Ribera i Lacomba, Claude Raynaud, Craig Cessford, Raphaël Durand, Peter Stadler, Kathrin Nägele, Jessica S. Bates, Bernd Trautmann, Sarah A. Inskip, Joris Peters, John E. Robb, Toomas Kivisild, Dominique Castex, Michael McCormick, Kirsten I. Bos, Michaela Harbeck, Alexander Herbig, and Johannes Krause, 'Ancient *Yersinia pestis* Genomes from Across Western Europe Reveal Early Diversification During the First Pandemic (541–750)', in *PNAS*, 116.25 (2019), 12363–72

Kreiner, Jamie, *The Social Life of Hagiography in the Merovingian Kingdom*, Cambridge Studies in Medieval Life and Thought: Fourth Series (Cambridge: Cambridge University Press, 2014)

Kulikowski, Michael, *Late Roman Spain and its Cities* (Baltimore, MD: Johns Hopkins University Press, 2004)

Lapidge, Michael, *The Roman Martyrs: Introduction, Translations, and Commentary*, Oxford Early Christian Studies (Oxford: Oxford University Press, 2018)

Leyser, Conrad, 'The Temptations of Cult: Roman Martyr Piety in the Age of Gregory the Great', in *Early Medieval Europe*, 9.3 (2000), 289–307

Liber missarum, ed. by José Janini, *Liber missarum de Toledo y libros místicos*, 2 vols, Serie litúrgica, Fuentes 3 and 4–8 (Toledo: Instituto de Estudios Visigótico-Mozárabes, 1982–1983)

Linage Conde, Antonio, 'Tras las huellas de Justiniano de Valencia', in *Hispania Antiqua*, 2 (1972), 203–16

Loseby, Simon T., 'Arles in Late Antiquity: *Gallula Roma Arelas* and *Urbs Genesii*', in *Towns in Transition: Urban Evolution in Late Antiquity and the Early Middle Ages*, ed. by Neil J. Christie and Simon T. Loseby (Aldershot: Scolar Press, 1996), pp. 45–70

Löx, Markus, 'The Urban Centre of Valencia in Late Roman and Visigothic Times', in *Journal of Late Antiquity*, 10.1 (2017), 131–65

Mar, Ricardo, Jordi López, O. Tobías, I. Peña, and L. Palahí, 'El conjunto paleocristiano del Francolí en Tarragona. Nuevas aportaciones', in *Antiquité Tardive*, 4 (1996), 320–24

Markus, Robert A., *The End of Ancient Christianity* (Cambridge: Cambridge University Press, 1990)

Martín, José Carlos, 'Códices hagiográficos latinos de origen hispánico de los siglos IX–XIV. Con un apéndice sobre el siglo XV. Ensayo de inventatio', in *Analecta Bollandiana*, 127.2 (2009), 313–63

Martín-Iglesias, Jose Carlos, and Salvador Iranzo Abellán, 'Justo de Urgel, *Sermo de S. Vincentio* (*CPL* 1092): estudio de su tradición manuscrita, edición crítica y traducción', in *Anuario de Estudios Medievales*, 42.1 (2012), 229–51

Mateos Cruz, Pedro, *La basílica de Santa Eulalia de Mérida. Arqueología y urbanismo*, Enejos de 'Archivo Español de Arqueología' 19 (Madrid: Consejo Superior de Investigaciones Científicas, 1999)

Maximus of Turin, *Sermones*, ed. by Almut Mutzenbecher, *Maximi episcopi Taurinensis Collectionem sermonum antiquam nonnullis sermonibus extravagantibus adiectis*, Corpus Scriptorum Ecclesiasticorum Latinorum 23 (Turnhout: Brepols, 1962)

McCormick, Michael, *Eternal Victory: Triumphal Rulership in Late Antiquity, Byzantium and the Early Medieval West* (Cambridge: Cambridge University Press, 1986)

Meyer, Sofia, *Der heilige Vinzenz von Zaragoza: Studien zur Präsenz eines Märtyrers zwischen Spätantike und Hochmittelalter* (Stuttgart: Franz Steiner Verlag, 2012)

Miller, Patricia Cox, *The Corporeal Imagination: Signifying the Holy in Late Ancient Christianity* (Philadelphia, PA: University of Pennsylvania Press, 2009)

Nelson, Janet, 'The Franks, the Martyrology of Usuard, and the Martyrs of Cordoba', in *Martyrs and Martyrologies*, Studies in Church History 30, ed. by Diana Wood (Oxford: Blackwell, 1993), pp. 67–80

O'Hogan, Cillian, *Prudentius and the Landscapes of Late Antiquity* (Oxford: Oxford University Press, 2016)

Pacian of Barcelona, *Epistulae*, ed. by Ángel Anglada Anfruns, *Pacianus Barcinonensis, Opera quae extant*, CCSL 69B (Turnhout: Brepols, 2012), pp. 53–153

Palmer, Anne-Marie, *Prudentius on the Martyrs*, Oxford Classical Monographs (Oxford: Clarendon Press, 1989)

Passio Innumerabilium Cesaragustanorum [Saint-Germain-des-Prés redaction], ed. by Charles de Smedt, Guillaume Van Hoof, and Joseph de Backer, in *Acta sanctorum, Novembris, Tomus primus* (Paris: Victor Palme, 1887), pp. 643–49

Passio sancti Pauli, ed. by David L. Eastman, *The Ancient Martyrdom Accounts of Peter and Paul* (Atlanta, GA: SBL Press, 2015)

Passio Saturnini, ed. by Patrice Cabau, '*Opusculum de passione ac translatione sancti Saturnini, episcopi Tolosanae civitatis et martyris*. Édition et traduction provisoires', in *Mémoires de la Société Archéologique du Midi de la France*, 61 (2001), 59–77

Passio Vincentii, ed. by Victor Saxer, *Saint Vincent, diacre et martyr: culte et légendes avant l'An Mil*, Subsidia hagiographica 83 (Brussels: Société des Bollandistes, 2002)

Peloux, Fernand, 'Le légendier de Moissac et le Passionnaire hispanique. Enquête ouverte sur la circulation d'une collection wisigothique dans le haut Moyen Âge', in *Le légendier de Moissac et la culture hagiographique méridionale autour de l'an mil*, Hagiologia 15 (Turnhout: Brepols, 2018), pp. 129–52

Petit, Carlos, 'Crimen y castigo en el reino visigodo de Toledo', in *La Peine: deuxième partie*, Recueils de la Société Jean Bodin pour l'histoire comparative des institutions 56 (Brussels: De Boeck Université, 1991), pp. 9–71

Petruccione, John, 'The Martyr Death as Sacrifice: Prudentius, *Peristephanon* 4.9–72', in *Vigiliae Christianae*, 49.3 (1995), 245–57

Philippart, Guy, 'Les légendiers, des origins au début du IXe siècle', in *Le Légendier de Turin. MS. D.V.3 de la Bibliothèque Nationale Universitaire*, Millenio Medievale 103, ed. by Monique Goullet (Florence: SISMEL-Edizioni del Galluzzo, 2014), pp. 7–74

Ployd, Adam, '*Non poena sed causa*: Augustine's Anti-Donatist Rhetoric of Martyrdom', in *Augustinian Studies*, 49.1 (2018), 25–44

Prudentius, *Praefatio*, ed. by Maurice P. Cunningham, *Aurelii Prudentii Clementis Carmina*, CCSL 126 (Turnhout: Brepols, 1966)

Quentin, Henri, *Les martyrologes historiques du Moyen Âge. Étude sur la formation du martyrologe romain*, Études d'histoire des dogmes et d'ancienne littérature ecclésiastique (Paris: Gabalda, 1908)

Rebillard, Éric, *Greek and Latin Narratives about the Ancient Martyrs*, Oxford Early Christian Texts (Oxford: Oxford University Press, 2017)

Reiss, Frank, *Narbonne and its Territory in Late Antiquity: From the Visigoths to the Arabs* (Farnham: Ashgate, 2013)

Riesco Chueca, Pilar, *Pasionario Hispánico: introducción, edición crítica y traducción* (Seville: Universidad de Sevilla, Secretaría de Publicaciones, 1995)

Roberts, Michael, *Poetry and the Cult of the Martyrs: The 'Liber Peristephanon' of Prudentius*, Recentiores: Latin Texts and Contexts (Ann Arbor, MI: University of Michigan Press, 1993)

Rose, Els, '*Abdias scriptor vitarum sanctorum apostolorum*? The "Collection of Pseudo-Abdias" Reconsidered', in *Revue d'histoire des textes*, 8 (2013a), 227–68

Rose, Els, '*Virtutes apostolorum*: Origin, Aim, and Use', in *Traditio*, 68 (2013b), 57–96

Rufinus, *Historia Ecclesiastica*, ed. by Eduard Schwartz and Theodor Mommsen, *Eusebius Werke*, vol. 2, *Die Kirchengeschichte*, Die griechischen christlichen Schriftsteller der ersten drei Jahrhunderte, 2 vols (Leipzig: J.C. Hinrichs'sche Buchhandlung, 1903–1908)

Sales Carbonell, Jordina, 'Implantación de iglesias en edificios de espectáculos romanos: orígenes de un proceso de medievalización de la ciudad antigua', in *Studi Romani*, 62.1–4 (2014), 71–102

Sales Carbonell, Jordina, 'Arqueología e identidad religiosa: edilicia cristiana y arquitectura lúdica en Hispania', in *La religión como factor de identidad*, ed. by Juana Torres and Silvia Acerbi (Madrid: Escolar y Mayo, 2016), pp. 47–59

Shaw, Brent D., 'Judicial Nightmares and Christian Memory', in *Journal of Early Christian Studies*, 11.4 (2003), 533–63

Smith, Julia M. H., 'A Hagiographer at Work: Hucbald and the Library at Saint-Amand', in *Revue Bénédictine*, 106.1–2 (1996), 151–71

Smith, Julia M. H., 'Portable Christianity: Relics in the Medieval West (*c.* 700–1200)', in *Proceedings of the British Academy*, 181 (2012), 143–67

Smith, Julia M. H., 'Relics: An Evolving Tradition in Latin Christianity', in *Saints and Sacred Matter: The Cult of Relics in Byzantium and Beyond*, Dumbarton Oaks Symposia and Colloquia, ed. by Cynthia Hahn and Holger A. Klein (Washington, DC: Dumbarton Oaks Press, 2015), pp. 41–60

Soriano Sánchez, Rafaela, 'Las excavaciones arqueológicas de la Cárcel de San Vicente (Valencia)', in *Saguntum*, 27 (1994), 173–86

Sotinel, Claire, 'Les lieux des culte chrétiens et le sacré dans l'Antiquité tardive', in *Revue de l'histoire des religions*, 4 (2005), 411–34

Straw, Carole, 'Martyrdom and Christian Identity: Gregory the Great, Augustine, and Tradition', in *The Limits of Ancient Christianity: Essays on Late Antique Thought and Culture in Honor of R.A. Markus*, ed. by William E. Klingshirn and Mark Vessey (Ann Arbor, MI: University of Michigan Press, 1999), pp. 250–66

Tovar Paz, Francisco Javier, *Tractatus, sermones atque homiliae. El cultivo del género literario del discurso homilético en la Hispania tardoantigua y visigoda* (Cáceres: Universidad de Extremadura, 1994)

Tsartsidis, Thomas, *Commentary on Prudentius' 'Hymn to Romanus' 1–650* (*Peristephanon 10*) (PhD thesis, University of Edinburgh, 2017)

Valerius of Bierzo, *De uana seculi sapientia*, ed. by Manuel Cecilio Díaz y Díaz, *Valerio del Bierzo. Su persona. Su obra*, Fuentes y estudios de historia leonesa 111 (León: Centro de Estudios e Investigación 'San Isidoro', 2006)

Van Dam, Raymond, *Saints and their Miracles in Late Antique Gaul* (Princeton, NJ: Princeton University Press, 1993)

Van Uytfanghe, Marc, *Stylisation biblique et condition humaine dans l'hagiographie mérovingienne (600–750)*, Verhandelingen van de Koninklijke Academie voor Wetenschappen, Letteren en Schone Kunsten van België, Klasse der Letteren 120 (Brussels: AWLSK, 1987)

Van Uytfanghe, Marc, 'L'hagiographie antique tardive: une littérature populaire?', in *Antiquité Tardive*, 9 (2001), 201–18

Velázquez, Isabel, *Hagiografía y culto a los santos en la Hispania visigoda: aproximación a sus manifestaciones literarias*, Cuadernos Emeritenses 32 (Mérida: Museo Nacional de Arte Romano, 2005)

Vogüé, Adalbert de, '*Martyrium in occulto*: le martyre du temps de paix chez Grégoire le Grand, Isidore de Séville et Valerius du Bierzo', in *Fructus centesimus: Mélanges offerts à Gerard J.M. Bartelink à l'occasion de son soixante-cinquième anniversaire*, Instrumenta patristica 19, ed. by Antoon A. R. Bastiaensen, Anthony Hilhorst, and Corneille H. J. M. Kneepkens (Dordrecht: Kluwer Academic Publishers, 1989), pp. 125–40

Wiśniewski, Robert, *The Beginnings of the Cult of Relics* (Oxford: Oxford University Press, 2019)

Yarza Urquiola, Valeriano, *Passionarium Hispanicum, Saeculum X–XI*, 2 vols, CCSL 171–171a (Turnhout: Brepols, 2020)

About the Author

David Addison is an Examination Fellow at All Souls College, Oxford. In 2021 he completed his DPhil thesis, *Layperson, Ascetic, and Cleric in Iberian Christianity, c. 500–711*. His next project is a comparative study of Christian monastic and ascetic culture in the late antique Atlantic regions of continental Europe and the British Isles.

10 Romanness in Visigothic Hagiography

Santiago Castellanos[1]

Abstract

This chapter evaluates the use (or not) of Roman identities and institutions in Visigothic hagiography. Visigothic hagiographical materials display a telling absence of 'Romanness', understood as a collective or individual consciousness of belonging to a Roman cultural tradition. This absence is tied to the erosion of ethnic binaries during the political construction of the Gothic kingdom, a process in which both the Roman aristocracy and the Catholic episcopate participated. I argue that in the seventh century, invocations of Roman heritage did not represent a continuation of ethnic conflict; rather, the hagiographers in their treatment of Rome's legacy were less interested in articulating the Roman identities of contemporary individuals than in placing their subjects within a world with recognizably Roman features.

Keywords: Romanness; Visigothic kingdom; hagiography; Christianism; Late Roman aristocracy; ethnicity

In the first third of the seventh century, a cleric from the ecclesiastical and monastic complex of St Eulalia, in *Emerita* (Mérida), in southwestern Hispania, felt it appropriate to note the Roman origin of one of the figures in the text that he was writing, the *Lives of the Fathers of Mérida*, a series of accounts of the lives of ecclesiastics from sixth-century Mérida.[2] This

1 This chapter is part of the research project HAR2016-76094-C4-1-R. I am grateful to the editors for their patient review of the text and their comments for improving it, and to the anonymous reports; of course, any error is my sole responsibility.

2 Elsewhere in the volume, Graham Barrett offers an alternative interpretation for the dating and composition of the first version of the work. See Maya Sánchez 1992 for the edition of the *Vitas sanctorum patrum Emeretensium* (VSPE), which should be consulted for details of authorship and dating, alongside Velázquez 2008a). On the social, ideological, and political context of the VSPE, see Collins 1980; Chaparro 1992; Velázquez 1994; Arce 1999; Castellanos 2003; Díaz 2010.

Fernández, D., Lester, M. & Wood, J. (eds.), *Rome and Byzantium in the Visigothic Kingdom: Beyond* Imitatio Imperii. Taylor & Francis Group 2023
DOI: 10.5117/9789463726412_CH10

anonymous hagiographer made explicit reference to the Roman origins of the *dux* Claudius, a military leader and governor in the service of the Gothic king Reccared (r. 586–601) in the province of Lusitania, stating that he was of noble lineage and had been born to Roman parents: 'Idem vero Claudius nobili genere hortus Romanis fuit parentibus progenitus.'[3]

The Méridan hagiographer's invocation of the Lusitanian *dux*'s 'Roman' parentage is strikingly unique within the text, and his evident desire to underscore a figure's Roman heritage is more suggestive than it may seem. Given that the Iberian peninsula was (depending on the region) subject to Roman rule for more than half a millennium, we might expect to find a strong sense of Romanness among its inhabitants well into the post-Roman period. I will refer to 'Romanness' as a collective or individual consciousness of belonging to a Roman cultural tradition. Such tradition(s) could have been received through numerous ways, such as the persistence of Roman law, the memory of aristocratic families of Roman origins, and the cult of late Roman saints, among others. Yet by the time the hagiographer composed his work, more than a century separated the end of Roman rule in Hispania and the composition of the VSPE, and we might assume that the sense of belonging to a Roman world had faded as well. Attachment to Roman identity likely varied across the peninsula, as Roman rule had ceased to function in the western, central, and even southern provinces long before it did so in Tarraconensis. Given the potential for Roman identity to have variously endured and declined depending on location, the hagiographer's highly selective invocation of 'being Roman' deserves further consideration.

While recent analyses have focused on Romanness in other areas in Europe from the end of the western Roman empire onwards,[4] this chapter evaluates the uses and non-uses of Roman identities and institutions in Visigothic hagiography. I will argue that in the seventh century, invocations of Roman heritage did not represent a continuation of ethnic conflict between Romans and Goths. In the extant sources, we find a few references to *Romani* (the VSPE being one of the principal instances) with different meanings.[5] Yet ethnicity was not an absolute and unchanging concept in the Visigothic kingdom.[6] Allusions to *Gothi* and *Romani* in Visigothic-era texts gradually changed over the course of the sixth century, to the point that there was a certain tendency by the end of the seventh century to

3 VSPE 5.10.32–36.
4 Pohl 2014.
5 Arce 2018.
6 Buchberger 2017. The conceptual and general arguments by Walter Pohl are essential (Pohl 1998).

identify all the subjects of the *regnum Gothorum* as *Gothi*.[7] Nevertheless, it was a requirement to be a *Gothus* in order to become *rex Gothorum*, which suggests that the binary ethnic distinction between Goth and Roman was crucial in some very specific instances, but not in others.[8]

Roman and Gothic identity do not seem to have featured in Visigothic hagiography as prominently as in other sources. Apart from the allusion to Claudius's Roman identity in the VSPE, there are no other references of a similar nature in the Visigothic-era hagiographies analysed in this chapter: the Life of Saint Aemilian or *Vita Sancti Aemiliani* (henceforth, VA), the Life of Fructuosus or *Vita Fructuosi* (henceforth, VF), the 'auto-hagiographic' writings of Valerius of Bierzo, and the rest of the VSPE (the *Vita Desiderii* by Sisebut will not be considered here as its setting is primarily Merovingian). In general, barring the exceptions examined below, the hagiographers were not at all interested in marking historic or contemporary identities as 'Roman'.[9]

Instead, I suggest that the hagiographers had other aims, such as creating a fixed written memory based on oral traditions. In particular, hagiographers invoked Roman identities and sketched a Roman social background to pursue their own agendas and to create a world their readers would recognize. Within this agenda, neither the explicit identification with the Roman past nor the expressions of Roman identity were of particular importance. Rather than speaking to ethnic categorization, the hagiographers' treatment of Rome's legacy was only one part of an overall attempt to fix the memory of a relatively recent, yet no longer extant world. They were less interested in articulating the Roman identities of contemporary individuals than in placing their subjects within a world with recognizably Roman features. The Roman past lived on in descriptions of historical landscapes and topographies and discussions of institutions, socio-economic classes, and religious structures.

Historical Contexts of Holy Men and Hagiographers

To examine how these hagiographies selectively activated Roman legacies, we must understand the historical contexts of both the hagiographers and the holy men they depicted. Although all the texts under consideration

7 Buchberger 2017.

8 V Toledo 3; VI Toledo 17.

9 This matter was naturally different in the case of the *Passiones*, which referred to the Roman background of the martyrs and were mostly set in Roman contexts. With regard to the *Passiones*, see the chapter by David Addison in this volume.

were written in the seventh century, two (the VSPE and the VA) were set in the context of the sixth-century consolidation of the Visigothic kingdom of Hispania. The origins of the shift in the focus of Visigothic activity to Hispania can be traced to the conquests in eastern Tarraconensis at the end of the fifth century. The process of consolidating Visigothic rule in the peninsula intensified after the battle of Vouillé (507) and the victory of Clovis's Franks over the Goths of Alaric II. This military event undoubtedly marked the end of any Visigothic ambitions to establish their hegemony in Gaul, and from then on Hispania took on a growing importance for the Visigothic monarchy. Even then, however, the end of the Visigothic kingdom in Gaul and the beginnings of the Visigothic kingdom in Hispania did not constitute a single episode, but rather a process. As late as the year 531, upon King Amalaric's death, Goths were still migrating from Gaul to Hispania,[10] and Gothic interest in the southern areas of the peninsula seems to have expanded only under Theudis (r. 531–548). In the middle of the sixth century, the growth of Gothic influence in Hispania occurred even in the context of civil war and the establishment of competing courts of Agila and Athanagild (in Córdoba, Seville, and Mérida). When Leovigild acceded to the throne with his brother Liuva in 568/9, the Visigothic monarchy and its aristocracy were present in a good portion of Hispania, but they were far from controlling the entire peninsula.[11]

The reigns of Leovigild (*c.* 568/9–586) and Reccared (586–601) provide the political background for the events of the VSPE and, to some degree, of the VA. Leovigild consolidated the administrative, tax, and military structures of the *regnum Gothorum*, and extended the territorial boundaries of the kingdom through a series of conquests. The Visigothic monarchy was still Arian, and Nicene sources, which dominate the surviving record, present Leovigild as a king who was hostile to Christian orthodoxy, and even as a persecutor. Meanwhile, the same sources present Reccared, his son and successor, as a champion of orthodoxy. After converting from Arianism to Catholicism in 587, Reccared convened the Third Council of Toledo in 589, bringing about the conversion of the entire *gens* and the *regnum* of the *Gothi*, in addition to the kingdom of the Sueves, which had been conquered by his father in 585. Iberian sources, essentially those of John of Biclarum and Isidore of Seville, and those written outside of the peninsula, namely those of Gregory of Tours and Gregory the Great, produced the particular images of Leovigild and Reccared mentioned above for ideological reasons.

10 Proc. Bell. 5.13.13. See Arce 2018.
11 A quick overview in Castellanos 2020.

It is not absolutely certain, however, that Leovigild's religious policy was consistently hostile towards Nicenes, and sources from Iberia are silent about the conversion of Hermenegild, son of Leovigild and brother of Reccared, to Nicene Christianity in the course of his rebellion against his father between around 579 and 585. Yet external sources do mention this important detail.[12]

Although both the VSPE and the VA are set in the sixth century, they were written at different points in the seventh century: the former is dated approximately toward the end of the first third of the seventh century and the latter to the first half of the seventh century. The seventh-century worlds of Braulio, the author of the VA, and the Méridan hagiographer were quite different from that of Leovigild and Reccared. For one thing, the Visigothic monarchy had expanded its territorial control across the peninsula. After 589, the Catholic kingdom headed by Reccared, the nobility, and the bishops was able to defend the frontiers that had been expanded by Leovigild's conquests. Reccared and his successors also held on to Septimania, in southern Gaul. Offensives against imperial troops in the south-east concluded with their expulsion by King Swinthila around 625.

The bishops, including Isidore of Seville, also developed a new religious and political ideology that fused Visigothic monarchy and Catholic religion and reached its zenith at the Fourth Council of Toledo, held in 633.[13] This cooperative approach put the administrative organization of the church at the disposal of the state, and it allowed kings to make use of the church's powerful ability to produce influential discourses. Religious discourses served to justify the *Gothi's* presence in Hispania and the hegemony of the *regnum*. Clerical preaching throughout the realm sought to discourage any tendency towards localism or rebellion.

This was the general political and ideological context within which both Braulio's VA and the VSPE were written. Of course, each text had its own ideological agendas that shaped their presentation of the late sixth century. Braulio wished to promote Aemilian's oratory and the cult of his relics, particularly since he had family interests in it. Braulio's 630s narrative of the political events and conquests of the 570s and 580s related these episodes to Aemilian's holy power. Leovigild appeared as an avenging sword against incredulous local rulers as a result of Aemilian's prophecies. Leovigild's conquest of Cantabria in 574 is presented in the context of a different, divine plan: the victory of a Catholic holy man over challenges to his thaumaturgical and prophetic capacity.[14]

12 Greg. Tur. Decem libri 5.38; Greg. Mag. Dial. 3.31.

13 Stocking 2000; Velázquez 2003.

14 VA 33.

The VSPE also reflects the connection between the local and the central. Leovigild and Reccared appeared with treacherous and benevolent tints respectively and served as vehicles to advance the author's efforts to narrate internal conflicts within the city. As in the case of Braulio's VA, the local loyalties of the VSPE's author in the seventh century profoundly shaped the presentation of the characters and the interpretation of events from the sixth century. The author was aligned with one of the parties to the sixth-century disputes, the monastic complex of St Eulalia, and sought to justify the Nicene bishops' control over the city's premier cult site. Moreover, the VSPE does not refer once to Hermenegild, omitting the detail that the city was a war theatre during his rebellion against his father (as alluded to in Gregory of Tours). It is clear, therefore, that there is a complex relationship between the VSPE, a hagiographical account by a clergyman from Mérida, and the political events of the preceding decades, which resulted in particular emphases, silences, and manipulations in the hagiographical text.[15]

The VF and the autobiographical works of Valerius of Bierzo were written in the second half of the seventh century.[16] Fructuosus of Braga (d. 665/667) was active in the mid-seventh century and Valerius of Bierzo probably wrote his texts in the 690s. All too often, the period from the mid-seventh century onward has been viewed retrospectively, as bound inevitably for a particular end, namely the collapse of the Visigothic kingdom and the defeat of King Roderic by the conquering Arab-Berber armies in 711. In recent years, scholars have rejected the idea of a weakened kingdom in the late Visigothic period.[17]

In contrast to the VA and the VSPE, the author of the VF and Valerius made very few references to the broader political context in which their main characters operated.[18] For example, the VF intentionally omits Fructuosus's important role as a bishop in favour of his earlier life as a monk, a decision

15 Fouracre 1990. On the Merovingian material, see also Kreiner 2014. A recent essay about the narratives in that period, in Ghosh 2016. With regard to Leovigild, see García Moreno 2008. On Reccared and the use of his kingdom in the sources, Castellanos 2007. The passage from Gregory of Tours featuring Leovigild as a persecutor, leading a *magna persecutio*, is Greg. Tur. Decem libri 5.38; and Leovigild is shown as a persecutor in Isid. Hist. Goth. 50.

16 For the origins of the VF, see Díaz y Díaz 1953; Maya Sánchez 1978; Codoñer 1987; for an overview, see Andrés Sanz 2010. The edition of the texts by Valerius used is Díaz y Díaz 2006. On Valerius and his writings, there are, among other publications, Collins 1986; Martín Iglesias 2009 and 2010; Díaz 2013.

17 A summary in Díaz and Poveda 2016.

18 Overviews of these periods are given in Díaz 2007; González Salinero 2017; Castellanos 2018. In respect of the historical context of the end of the kingdom and the immediately preceding period, see Díaz and Poveda 2016, which also gives extensive bibliographic references.

that Codoñer has pointed out was likely due to the monastic origin of the text.[19] The choice is striking because Fructuosus was bishop of Braga, one of the most important sees of the realm, and corresponded with other powerful bishops, such as Braulio of Zaragoza. The VF, however, only offers glimpses of Fructuosus as a member of the socio-political elite through a brief mention of his father's high status and a reference to royal intervention to limit Fructuosus's efforts to travel to the Holy Land. Valerius also sought to downplay his own elite connections. He presents himself as an outsider, a non-conformist character, a presentation that was more related to his radical religious agenda than to his own actions. Valerius's activities took place in a world of landowners, with whom he was not uncomfortable, and he shows awareness of episcopal power, regardless of his apparent disagreements with his bishop's decisions.

Despite the hagiographers' own social practices, the VF and Valerius's writings present overall a tense relationship between the holy men and the socio-political elite. Kingdom-level political events and characters are not as visible as the local worlds of these holy men. Yet the indirect testimony of these texts reveals a great deal about local elite society—the great landowners and bishops—that formed the political base of the Visigothic *regnum*.

The Direct Use of Romanness

Given the different historical contexts of the VSPE's composition (the mid-seventh century) and the events it narrated (late sixth century), the direct evocations of the 'Roman' identities, political alliances, and enmities of some of its central figures are striking. The VSPE is a hagiographic text that is composed of five books or *opuscula*.[20] The first book is about Augustus, a young servant of the St Eulalia complex. The second is about a gluttonous and drunken monk from the monastery of Cauliana, a few miles from the city. The third is about Nanctus, an abbot who arrived in *Emerita* from Africa and to whom the Arian King Leovigild gave a fiscal property (*locus fisci*) for him to lead an ascetic life. The fourth book focuses on the bishops Paul and Fidel, whose episcopates probably coincide with the beginning of the second half of the sixth century although the exact dates are uncertain. The fifth and main piece is dedicated to Masona, who was bishop of Mérida

19 Codoñer 1987, 190.

20 On the VSPE, see the chapter by Graham Barrett in this book. Besides, see the introduction to the edition by Maya Sánchez 1992, and the introduction to the translation by Velázquez 2008a.

from at least 572/573 (the date cited by John of Biclarum) and who died *c.* 605/606. Masona's successors, Innocentius and Renovatus, are also very briefly mentioned in this book.

In the story of Masona, the Méridan hagiographer's choice to identify *dux* Claudius's Roman origins (as outlined in this chapter's opening paragraphs) may reveal something about the possible valences of Roman identity in sixth- and seventh-century Mérida. Studies of hagiography have shown that these texts are valuable sources for exploring the local worlds they describe despite the many distorting *topoi* typical of the genre. Hagiographies frequently offer vivid day-to-day details and place individuals in specific local contexts, regardless of their ideological underpinnings or specific narrative structures.[21]

The author of the VSPE occasionally invokes the 'Roman' backgrounds of the figures with whom Méridan bishops interacted. The hagiographer's desire to note that Claudius was of Roman origin was presumably not baseless: in the 630s, local tradition likely remembered this important historical figure, and there was no reason not to record Claudius's ancestry. Claudius had been an important figure as Reccared's political and military right-hand man in Mérida. Claudius faced the task of thwarting plots at a time when multiple conspiracies arose in Mérida, Toledo, and Narbonne, several decades before the first version of the VSPE was written.[22] Nor is Claudius the only figure in the VSPE who had 'Roman' origins. In the story of Bishop Paul, the bishop aids a married couple of senatorial background when the wife has a health crisis. They subsequently donate their estate to him.[23] The same invocation of the heritage (*genus*) of both the senatorial couple and *dux* Claudius links them, explicitly or implicitly, with a Roman past.

In addition to 'Roman' heritage, the VSPE invokes connections with the popes of Rome. The hagiographers in Mérida appeal to a different idea of Rome when they describe Gregory the Great (r. 590–604) in the work's preface as the holiest and most conspicuous bishop of the City of Rome, making a word play on his name Gregory and the adjective *egregious*. By invoking the name of Gregory and stating that the work was written in the manner of his *Dialogues*, the preface associates the VSPE with one of the most prestigious contemporary Latin hagiographies. The connections with

21 On the hagiography of the Iberian Visigothic kingdom as a whole, see Castellanos 2004; Velázquez 2007. John of Biclarum's mention of Masona is in his chronicle, Ioh. Bicl. 30.

22 On the revolts, see Castellanos 2007.

23 VSPE 4.2.3–5: 'Contigit cuiusdam primarii ciuitatis ex genere senatorum nobilissimi viri ergotrasse matrona, que et ipsa inlustri stigmate progenita nobilem traebat prosapiem.'

papal Rome go beyond textual emulation. Through his friend Leander of Seville, Gregory had been kept well-informed about events in Hispania, including the conversion of Reccared, and he had corresponded with the aforementioned Claudius himself.[24]

The purposes of these 'Roman' identifications are varied. Clarifying the fact that Claudius was of Roman origin sheds light on the allegiances and activities of local elites, as prominent sectors of the Hispano-Roman aristocracy decided to collaborate with the Gothic kingdom. The identification presumably offered a contrast to aristocrats of Gothic origin, which by the 580s were well established in Mérida and other major cities.[25] Given Paul's collaborative relationship with the married senatorial couple, the couple's 'Roman' origins might have served to highlight the prestigious stature of the bishop's lay allies. Or perhaps these clerics had familial or social links to members of the local aristocracy who had a Roman background and wished to promote it. The VSPE presents Roman ancestry in a positive light, as in the case of Masona, without a doubt the principal 'holy man' in the work, who is identified as a Goth.[26]

Despite these strategic invocations of Roman and Gothic identity, constructing ethnic identities was not a priority for the hagiographers of the VSPE.[27] Ethnicity, in the sense of a Gothic-Roman binary in both political and religious terms, was likely not the sense in which the Méridan hagiographers used the term 'Roman' in referring to Claudius's origins, nor 'Goth' in alluding to those of Masona. Rather, these hagiographers aimed to fix an oral memory in written form that would enhance emotional responses to the monastic and ecclesiastic complex of St Eulalia. The references to the respective Roman and Gothic origins of Claudius and Masona did not intend to illustrate the identities of two ethnic groups in conflict. According to the hagiographer's narrative, both Romans and Goths worked together to achieve a greater good: the triumph of orthodoxy and, importantly for the ecclesiastical parties in Mérida, the central role of the complex of St Eulalia in the process.[28]

24 VSPE, praef. 2–4: 'qua sanctissimus egregiusque uates, Romane presul urbis'. About the connections, Díaz 2008; Wood 2016.

25 The best-known case comes from Mérida itself, especially those listed in VSPE 5 on Gothic *nobiles* and Masona. The conversion of the Arian bishops at the Third Council of Toledo is another example of the wider Gothic presence in the cities of Hispania in the late 580s (Castellanos 2007, 243–67).

26 VSPE 5.2.1–3.

27 Ethnicity was likewise of no interest to Braulio of Zaragoza when writing his *Vita Aemiliani*, or to the anonymous compilers of the *Vita Fructuosi*. Castellanos 2004.

28 In VSPE 5.5.8–9, Leovigild appoints Sunna as an Arian bishop. The text does not present this as a conflict between Goths and Romans, but as a conflict between Arians and orthodox Christians, especially over the control of the complex of St Eulalia (VSPE 5.5.32–35). Within the

Other Romanness: Roman Topographies

Apart from the examples in the VSPE noted above, there are no direct references to 'ethnic' Romanness in other Visigothic-era hagiographies. However, this does not translate into the complete absence of Roman ideas and institutions from the saints' lives. Indeed, the geo-historical contexts for the events recounted in the *vitae* and the texts' composition were deeply shaped by the empire's legacy. Although there was no simple continuity between late Roman socio-political configurations and those of the *regnum Gothorum*,[29] the political, administrative, economic, and cultural structures of the Visigothic kingdom had their roots in the Roman period. In a basic sense, the Visigothic landscape of the sixth and seventh centuries was the result of urban, provincial, and rural precedents stretching back deep into the imperial past.[30]

The Roman imprint is evident in multiple *vitae*. Mérida, for example, was one of the greatest cities in Hispania, founded in the time of Augustus and more than likely the administrative capital of Hispania from the end of the third through the fifth century.[31] The city's continued importance is reflected in Fructuosus's travels to southwest Iberia, including his stop to worship St Eulalia at Mérida and to the zone around *Gades* (Cádiz), a journey doubtlessly taken along the Roman road that had linked Astorga (in León) to Mérida for centuries.[32] As we shall presently see, hagiographers depicted the activities of their 'holy men' within a geo-historical environment with undeniably Roman features.

In many *vitae*, large rural properties provide a background for the actions of the holy men. Holy men performed sacred powers and engaged in religious conflicts within large rural properties that operated according to long-established Roman socio-economic practices. As we have already seen, in Mérida, the protagonists are clearly connected with local notables and the local church. In the VA, the local Roman background is made clear

ideological framework of the text, the reaction against this event was massive, comprising the *populus* (VSPE 5.5.36–41). During the revolt of Gothic nobles against Masona, and ultimately against Reccared, the text stresses that Claudius, who was 'Roman' as indicated earlier, intervened in favour of Masona, who had been identified as a Goth (VSPE 5.10.1–8).

29 On administrative structures, see Martin 2003; with regard to the way the kingdom was rooted in Roman social and economic structures, see Castellanos 2020.

30 Kulikowski 2004.

31 On late Roman Mérida, Sastre de Diego 2015, with the archaeological and historical keys, and the main bibliography.

32 VF 11–15.

through the association of holy men with pre-eminent individuals who possess enslaved individuals (described as *servi* or *ancillae* in the text). For example, Honorius, a prominent figure in the enclave of *Parpalines*, is shown to possess an extensive estate with its own private church. Somewhat similar is Ebronanto, an estate on which Valerius of Bierzo lived and which also had its private church.[33]

Even though the rural and rather mountainous upper reaches of the Ebro in northern Hispania were a world apart from Mérida, they also still contained recognizably Roman features. The rustic Bierzo of Fructuosus was a territory that had been organized under Roman rule into *castella* and large estates. Fructuosus's life also revolved around many older cities and provinces originally founded in the early Roman empire. It has already been remarked that Fructuosus was initially active not only in the Bierzo district (the *Bergidum* of both Roman and Visigothic sources), but also in Mérida and the zone around Cádiz. And although the role of Fructuosus as a bishop is given a passing mention in the VF, the city of Braga, the capital of Gallaecia since late Roman times, was a major setting for his later life.

Late antique topography also shaped the experiences and writings of Valerius of Bierzo. A few decades after Fructuosus, the Bierzo of Valerius (a self-styled 'holy man') continued to reflect the hierarchical territorial organization of the Roman period. The chief city of the district, Astorga, lay outside the Bierzo proper, although it appears in Valerius's texts as the diocesan see held by Isidore, a bishop with whom Valerius came into conflict.[34] At the time of Valerius's activities, there were several recently established monastic enclaves, such as the monasteries founded by Fructuosus, while others had roots going much further back, as was the case for *Castrum Petrense* (perhaps Castro Pedroso in Oencia or Pedrero de Somoza in Maragarería).[35]

A deeply Roman landscape also provides the setting for the VA, written by Braulio of Zaragoza (bishop 631–651) for Frunimian, who was likely his brother and the abbot of the community of monks living in caves in the mountains around the former *oratorium* of the saint.[36] Before his death

33 VA 18; 20; 21; 24; 29; Val. Ord. quer. 13–16.

34 Val. Ord. quer. 21.

35 On the historical backdrop of the works of Valerius, see Díaz 2012; Martin 2017–2018. The different proposals about Castro Petrense, in Díaz 2012, 386.

36 There has been scholarly discussion on whether Frunimianus was truly the brother of Braulio, but Vitalino Valcárcel and José Carlos Martín Iglesias have persuasively argued that the two men were indeed brothers. On various aspects of the VA, Castellanos 1998. About Frunimian as Braulio's brother, Valcárcel 1990–1991; Martín Iglesias 2010. Contra, Kelly 2016.

in 574/575, Aemilian had spent most of his time in the mountainous land surrounding his *oratorium*, which lay in the upper reaches of the Ebro valley within the Roman province of Tarraconensis, in what is the modern region of La Rioja. The bishop of Tarazona, another Roman city and situated farther down the Ebro valley, temporarily placed him in charge of the parish of *Vergegio* (Berceo, La Rioja). Although this geography has often been interpreted as hinting at a hierarchy of lands in a zone with large late Roman estates,[37] the question of the geo-historical context in which Aemilian operated within Cantabria is more complicated. While some have suggested that the Cantabria mentioned by Braulio indicates a city, it is most likely that in Late Antiquity, and more specifically the Visigothic period, this referred to a territory comprising today's region of Cantabria, the northern parts of the current provinces of Burgos and Palencia, and the upper reaches of the Ebro.[38] Therefore, Braulio evokes a typically Roman city-territory landscape but one that is rapidly changing in the course of Late Antiquity.

Aemilian's oratory lay in the Distercian or Dercetian mountains, today's Sierra de la Demanda. Other landmarks in the region included *Castellum Bilibium*, near modern Haro in the Rioja region, and *Amaia*, perhaps the strongest point in the territorial structure of Cantabria in Late Antiquity. The latter was a hill-fort of considerable size in the area of what is now Peña Amaya in the modern province of Burgos,[39] a region with roots in the transformational period of the fifth century. In the north of the province of Tarraconensis, where Aemilian lived, new village communities sprung up along with numerous *castella*, a phenomenon that archaeology has uncovered across the peninsula. Braulio's biography of Aemilian, therefore, takes place in a small world that resulted from territorial changes after the fifth century.[40]

In contrast to the rural focus of the VA, the VSPE offers a detailed depiction of an urban context of Mérida. From the reforms of Diocletian (r. 284–305) onwards, epigraphic evidence indicates that Mérida became the *de facto* capital of late Roman Hispania, as the see of the *vicarius Hispaniarum*. The evolution of the city's layout in Late Antiquity is well known, and in

37 VA 10.25–26 and 12.9 (*Vergegio*). Castellanos 1998.

38 Regarding this problem of Cantabria, see Castellanos 1998; Martin 2003, 76–77. A different interpretation seeing Cantabria as a city is in García Moreno 2008, 64–70.

39 VA 9.14–15 (*castellum Bilibium*), 11.4 (*Dircetii montis secreta*); 16 (*Amaia*).

40 Quirós Castillo 2013a, with particular attention to the case of Peña Amaya. On the state of knowledge of *castella* in northern Hispania, see the range of contributions in Quirós Castillo and Tejado Sebastián 2012. See also Tejerizo and Canosa 2018.

the time of the Visigothic kingdom, Mérida retained the greater part of its Roman urban structure in spite of some significant changes. Striking new developments included the privatization of larger public spaces and the narrowing of streets as residential buildings spilled out into them. The construction of churches and oratories, also found in the city's *suburbia*, gave the town the Christian topography that forms the backdrop for the VSPE's narrative.[41]

It is important to note that the majority of these topographical and urbanistic changes occurred in the late Roman period rather than the Visigothic era. For example, the city walls were Roman but underwent considerable restructuring in the fifth century. This is hinted at by the controversial inscription mentioning cooperation between the Gothic *dux* Salla and Bishop Zeno, dating from the times of King Euric (r. 466–484) and confirmed by archaeological findings.[42] Furthermore, several of the most important locations mentioned in the VSPE, such as the mausoleum and the first church of St Eulalia in the *suburbium*, date from this time, as does the first cathedral, in all probability. In addition to the Roman roots of the urban landscape, the VSPE bore witness to ongoing repairs and updates, such as renovation work undertaken by Bishop Fidel and the construction of a new *xenodochium* by Masona in the Visigothic period.[43]

Overall, the backdrop for the seventh-century hagiographies situated within the Visigothic kingdom of Toledo is essentially Roman. Readers of these hagiographies would recognize places that still bore a Roman imprint, including cities such as Mérida, Astorga, Tarazona, Toledo, and Cádiz, as well as other settlements that largely stemmed from the Roman territorial organization. This does not in itself imply that the hagiographers had any ideological intent to highlight and foreground the 'Roman' identity of locations or individuals. Rather, references to such places were inevitable because the historical landscape in which the 'holy men' had lived and where the authors set their narratives were 'Roman'. Yet the hagiographies did not need to make the 'Roman connection' explicit: their audiences would have

41 On the archaeological panorama of Mérida in Late Antiquity and Visigothic times, see Mateos 2000; Alba Calzado and Mateos Cruz 2008; Mateos and Alba 2011; Mateos and Caballero 2011; Alba Calzado 2011; Sastre de Diego 2011 and 2015.

42 On this inscription, see Arce 2008; Koch 2008; Velázquez 2008b. See also the recent comments by Damián Fernández (Fernández 2017, 165–68). On the city walls and archaeological confirmation of fifth-century rebuilding, the author would like to express his gratitude for the information provided on the site of excavations by Isaac Sastre, Javier Martínez, and Santiago Feijoo. See Feijoo Martínez and Alba Calzado 2014, 94.

43 VSPE 4.6.32; 5.3.13.

immediately recognized a territorial hierarchy and a topography that still shaped the worlds of those who read these texts.

Becoming Non-Roman from a Roman Starting-Point: The Use of Social Structures

Just as the geographical and topographical backdrop of the lives of the 'holy men' was rooted in the Roman past, the same was true of the socio-economic structures that framed the narratives, miracles, and other components of these texts. The vocabulary of status, titles, and privileges of the hagiographers' actors derived from the late Roman world—from kingship to slavery, reaching every social stratum.

To be sure, some of these social structures were 'new', and the most striking non-Roman element in the *vitae* is the Gothic monarchy. In some *vitae*, Gothic kings seem to represent a negative force affecting the 'holy man'. This emerges in the VF, for example, where a king (perhaps Recceswinth, although the *vita* is unclear) prevented Fructuosus from making a journey to the east.[44] In the VSPE, Book 3 mentions Leovigild's donation to the Nicene holy man Nanctus. However, in Book 5, Leovigild is depicted as a formidable opponent of Bishop Masona, and the Méridan hagiographer stresses that the king is a persecuting Arian opposed to the Nicene bishop. After trying to bolster the position of Sunna, the Arian bishop of the city, against Masona, the king openly confronts the latter by successively exiling him and supporting an alternative Nicene bishop, Nepopis.

In contrast, in the VSPE Reccared is praised for his role in rendering the kingdom orthodox. Interestingly, the authors emphasize the bishop's autonomy in relation to Reccared. This is especially clear in the account of the 587 rebellion of Sunna and many nobles against Reccared, which is concluded in favour of the king through the armed intervention of *dux* Claudius. One of the nobles, Vagrila, seeks asylum in the basilica of St Eulalia. The king sentences him to perpetual service to the saint's complex, but Bishop Masona acts independently and frees Vagrila. Through this act of clemency, Masona's reputation is burnished in comparison to that of Reccared as the saint acted on his own initiative in interpreting and applying the sentence.[45]

The author also highlights the close relationship between the bishopric and the monastic complex of St Eulalia, rather than the profile of any

44 VF 2; 17. Vallejo Girvés (2012, 414) suggests that this was probably Recceswinth.

45 VSPE 5.11.86–114.

individual bishop or ruler. It was this civic-religious identity, not 'Romanness' or 'Gothicness', let alone loyalty to the monarchy, that seems to have been the main concern of those associated with the complex of St Eulalia who produced the first version of the VSPE during the first third of the seventh century.[46] References to Gothic monarchs enabled the hagiographers to stress the virtues of the Catholic bishops; they were not mentioned in order to bolster the Gothic monarchy.[47]

Something rather similar occurred in Braulio's depiction of Leovigild in the VA. As noted above, Leovigild appears on the occasion of his conquest of Cantabria around the year 574. This was not just an incidental detail—Leovigild is presented as the avenging arm of God, even though he was an Arian. This characterization is the result of Braulio's desire to highlight the prophetic abilities of Aemilian, who reportedly foresaw the conquest of Cantabria. Some local notables ignored the 'holy man', seeing his prophecy as a symptom of senile dementia. Braulio stresses how Leovigild did indeed conquer Cantabria and killed the nobleman, Abundantius, who had been most opposed to Aemilian. The monarchy here appears as a complement, a narrative resource deployed for maximum effect on the audience to justify the holy man's role as prophet.[48] In brief, the authors used kings to play up one feature or another of the 'holy men' whose cults they aimed to enhance. Yet nowhere did the hagiographies refer to kingship as a non-Roman institution, another example of their indifference towards discussing or even emphasizing ethnic identities.

While Gothic kings and their agents might have replaced Roman emperors and governors as hagiographical protagonists, the hagiographies mention members of other social groups whose status and privileges stemmed from Roman traditions. By the time that the hagiographies were written, decades had passed since the Goths had settled in Hispania, a process that by necessity took account of social arrangements dating back to the Roman period.[49]

The presentation of the peasants and the nobles in the hagiographies deserves some attention. Peasants do not often appear as a clearly defined social group—the peasantry—in Visigothic sources, and hagiographies are no exception. In legal texts, the meaning of the term *servi* is unclear; it

46 Key aspects about the transformation of Roman civic identities in Late Antiquity in Hispania were exposed by San Bernardino 1996.

47 Several specific passages show the atrocious picture the hagiographers draw of Leovigild and his confrontation with Masona: VSPE 5.4.9–12; 5.5.1, 8–19; 5.6.37-48, 110-111. With regard to Vagrila: VSPE 5.11.86–114.

48 VA 33.

49 Buchberger 2017.

often includes agricultural workers who were dependent upon the *domini*. Elsewhere, the word may also denote slaves who worked in the fields, and in cities.[50] In general, however, peasants dependent upon a magnate were sometimes included in the generic term *servi*. It is even more difficult to identify references to free, independent peasants. Some archaeologists have recently made the suggestion that the new peasant communities which archaeology has been uncovering in the Iberian peninsula might correspond to such an independent peasantry, but there are serious doubts as to whether this is the case.[51]

The peasantry, like all other social groupings mentioned in the *vitae*, entered the saints' 'sphere of activity' in accordance with the hagiographers' narrative purpose. For example, in the VF, the author relates an anecdote of a *rusticus*, or peasant, who attacks Fructuosus because of the very poor appearance of the saint's clothing. In this passage, the author stresses the poorness of the saint's clothes in order to highlight his ascetic dedication over his episcopal status.[52] This episode is not recounted to make a point about social class, but rather to demonstrate the virtues of Fructuosus. The vocabulary the author of the VA uses to describe local powers and relationships of social dominance, such as *servus* and *ancilla*, were fully rooted within the late Roman tradition. The same is true of the slaves manumitted by Masona in Mérida, a tale that was less about recording the Méridan church's privileged place in the social hierarchy (which of course it had), but rather to stress the generosity of the 'holy man' who led it.[53]

In the treatment of the aristocracy there are more references to social classes and offices with Roman antecedents. It has already been seen that the most direct allusion to Roman titles is found in the VSPE's references to Gregory the Great and to the Roman origins of the *dux* Claudius. This particular office is also mentioned in the VF, where the author states that Fructuosus's father was a *dux*, a title that implied either a military command or a status as provincial governor within the Visigothic kingdom. Moreover,

50 With regard to the peasantry, see García Moreno 2001; Díaz 2007, 463–99. On the possibility that these were mostly communities of independent peasants, as put forward recently by several archaeologists, the relevant bibliography can be found in Tejerizo 2017 and Quirós Castillo 2013b. As for doubts about this supposed independent status, at least with regard to peasant villages in general, see Castellanos 2020.

51 Vigil-Escalera 2015; Tejerizo 2017.

52 VF 11.

53 VA 18; 24; 29; 33. On the lexis of social dominance in the VA, Escalona Monge and Rodríguez Cerezo 1988; Castellanos 1998. The *comites* and Sunna in VSPE 5.10.1–8. The manumissions by Masona are described in VSPE 5.13.1–21.

senatorial status is invoked to describe the married couple helped by Paul in the VSPE. The term *senator* is not used to revive Roman positions but to demonstrate that the couple were among the longest-standing aristocratic lineages in Mérida. The hagiographer employs an anachronistic term that carried great prestige in Roman times to stress the couple's position at the summit of the local social hierarchy. The couple's status legitimates the fortune they give Paul, which he later uses in negotiations to ensure that his nephew Fidel will succeed him as bishop.

The invocation of *senator* also appears in the VA. Writing in the seventh century, Braulio utilizes this word to describe several personages with whom Aemilian has relationships. Once again, the aim is to underscore the very high rank held by these figures, such as Sicorius, Abundantius, and Honorius, in the mosaic of local powers on the upper reaches of the Ebro in the sixth century. The same interpretation must be put on the mention of a *senatus* of Cantabria. In this case, the term probably refers merely to some gathering of local potentates who managed to build up a regional powerbase that was sufficiently effective for Leovigild to undertake a military campaign against them.[54]

While the hagiographers clearly use Roman terminology at points, they also speak of new Gothic political institutions when it suits their purpose. In addition to the already-discussed case of kingship, there were also references to the monarchy's delegates at local level, the *comites*, such as those who joined Sunna in the revolt against Reccared.[55]

From this brief review of references to social statuses of Roman origin, certain features emerge. Terms such as *senatores*, *senatus*, *ancillae*, *servi*, and the like appear in the VSPE and the VA. These relationships of dependence had taken shape within the 'Roman' rural estates analysed in the previous section. But the hagiographers were not interested in painting an 'accurate' picture of social relations in the Visigothic kingdom. Rather, they related each figure (notables, peasants, slaves, dependents, and so forth) to the *miracula* and activities of the holy men about whom they were writing.[56] As in the case of landscape, social categories of Roman origin help situate the miraculous deeds of the holy men within a conceptual map familiar to their readers.

54 I have studied the references to local and regional powers in post-Roman Spain in Castellanos 2013.

55 VSPE 5.10.1–25; 5.11.38.

56 Concerning property in the context of the VSPE, see Díaz 1992–1993. In respect to the archaeological site suggested as Parpalines, see Espinosa 2003. Ebronanto is mentioned in Val. Ord. quer. 10.17. On estates and the social relationships of Valerius, Díaz 1986; Martin 2015.

Conclusion: Romanness Is Not the Question

Hagiographers writing during the seventh century in the Visigothic kingdom of Toledo had no particular interest in stressing Romanness as a personal identity, nor in highlighting the continuity of Roman topographical traditions. It was only very sporadically that they mentioned Romanness, such as the Roman familial origin of Claudius, the Roman provincial structure, or the 'senatorial' status of Iberian elites. Even in these cases, the echoes of the empire were of no great interest in and of themselves. Instead, they were deployed to highlight one feature or another of the exemplary holy men. These features allowed the hagiographers to frame their narratives and ensured that the messages that they articulated were recognized by their audiences.

Romanness thus was of scant interest in a world where the *gens Gothorum* had gradually come to become a dominant identity. Aside from its presence in preserved ancient laws, Romanness as a personal identity had little impact in the seventh-century *leges*, a situation that is also reflected in the hagiographic genre.[57] The eastern Roman empire and the distant past were considered Roman. Hagiographies constantly evoke a world of Roman-era landscapes, Roman urban topography, and Roman social relations. Yet they remain stubbornly silent about relating these features to any Roman identity. Rome, whatever the term meant in the minds of the readers, was not deemed necessary to celebrate the saints' powers. We must therefore see hagiographies as another discursive practice that resignified the Roman past (and present) in the imagination of the individuals and communities in the Visigothic kingdom.

Bibliography

Alba Calzado, Miguel, 'Los espacios domésticos en la ciudad visigoda de Emerita (ss. V–VIII)', in *Actas Congreso Internacional 1910–2010: el yacimiento emeritense* (Mérida: Ayuntamiento de Mérida, 2011), pp. 521–46

Alba Calzado, Miguel, and Pedro Mateos Cruz, 'El paisaje urbano de Emerita en época visigoda', in *Zona Arqueológica*, 9 (2008), 261–73

Andrés Sanz, María Adelaida, 'Vita Fructuosi (CPL 1293)', in *La Hispania visigótica y mozárabe. Dos épocas en su literatura* (Salamanca: Universidad de Salamanca, 2010), pp. 221–24

57 Castellanos 2020, 18–19.

Arce, Javier, 'The City of Mérida (Emerita) in the Vitas Patrum Emeretensium (VIth century A.D.)', in *East and West: Modes of Communication*, ed. by Evangelos Chrysos and Ian Wood (Leiden: Brill, 1999), pp. 1–14

Arce, Javier, 'La inscripción del puente de Mérida de época del rey Eurico (483 d.C.)', in *Pyrenae*, 39.2 (2008), 121–26

Arce, Javier, 'Goths and Romans in Visigothic Hispania', in *Transformations of Romanness*, ed. by Walter Pohl, Clemens Gantner, Cinzia Grifoni, and Marianne Pollheimer-Mohaupt (Berlin and Boston, MA: De Gruyter, 2018), pp. 371–78

Buchberger, Erica, *Shifting Ethnic Identities in Spain and Gaul, 500–700: From Romans to Goths and Franks* (Amsterdam: Amsterdam University Press, 2017)

Castellanos, Santiago, *Poder social, aristocracias y 'hombre santo' en la Hispania visigoda: la 'Vita Aemiliani' de Braulio de Zaragoza* (Logroño: Universidad de La Rioja, 1998)

Castellanos, Santiago, 'The Significance of Social Unanimity in a Visigothic Hagiography: Keys to an Ideological Screen', in *Journal of Early Christian Studies*, 11.3 (2003), 387–419

Castellanos, Santiago, *La hagiografía visigoda. Dominio social y proyección cultural* (Logroño: Fundación San Millán de la Cogolla, 2004)

Castellanos, Santiago, *Los godos y la cruz. Recaredo y la unidad de Spania* (Madrid: Alianza Editorial, 2007)

Castellanos, Santiago, 'Redefiniendo el poder local en la "Hispania" tardoantigua. Hacia el "*loci senior*"', in *Magistrados locales de 'Hispania': aspectos históricos, jurídicos, lingüísticos*, ed. by Estíbaliz Ortiz de Urbina (Vitoria-Gasteiz: Universidad del País Vasco, 2013), pp. 333–48

Castellanos, Santiago, *Los visigodos* (Madrid: Síntesis, 2018)

Castellanos, Santiago, *The Visigothic Kingdom in Iberia: Construction and Invention* (Philadelphia, PA: University of Pennsylvania Press, 2020)

Chaparro, César, 'Significado de las Vitas sanctorum patrum Emeretensium: lectura desde sus fuentes', in *Humanitas. In honorem Antonio Fontán* (Madrid: Gredos, 1992), pp. 339–49

Codoñer, Carmen, 'Sobre la Vita Fructuosi', in *Athlon: Satura Grammatica in honorem Francisci R. Adrados*, vol. 2 (Madrid: Gredos, 1987), pp. 183–90

Collins, Roger, 'Merida and Toledo: 550–585', in *Visigothic Spain: New Approaches*, ed. by Edward James (Oxford: Clarendon, 1980), pp. 189–219

Collins, Roger, 'The "Autobiographical" Works of Valerius of Bierzo: Their Structure and Purpose', in *Antigüedad y Cristianismo*, 3 (1986), 425–42

Díaz, Pablo C., 'Iglesia propia y gran propiedad en la autobiografía de Valerio del Bierzo', in *Actas I Congreso Internacional Astorga romana* (Astorga, 1986), pp. 297–303

Díaz, Pablo C., 'Propiedad y explotación de la tierra en la Lusitania tardoantigua', in *Studia Historica. Historia Antigua*, 10–11 (1992–1993), 297–310

Díaz, Pablo C., 'La Hispania visigoda', in *Hispania tardoantigua y visigoda*, ed. by Pablo C. Díaz, Francisco J. Sanz Huesma, and Clelia Martínez Maza (Madrid: Istmo, 2007), pp. 257–611

Díaz, Pablo C., 'Gregorio Magno y el reino visigodo. Un conflicto de poderes', in *Gregorio Magno, l'Impero e i 'Regna'*, ed. by Claudio Azzara (Florence: SISMEL, Edizioni del Galluzzo, 2008), pp. 59–80

Díaz, Pablo C., 'Mérida tardoantica: l'apoteosi di una città cristiana', in *Reti Medievali Rivista*, 11.2 (2010), 67–79

Díaz, Pablo C., 'Percepción del espacio y la naturaleza en Valerio del Bierzo', in *Estudios de Historia Antigua en homenaje al prof. Manuel Abilio Rabanal*, ed. by Juan Manuel Abascal, Antonio Caballos Rufino, Santiago Castellanos García, and Juan Santos Yanguas (León: Universities of Leon and Seville, 2012), pp. 383–98

Díaz, Pablo C., 'Valerio del Bierzo: la equívoca marginalidad de un asceta tardoantiguo', in *Marginados sociales y religiosos en la Hispania tardorromana y visigoda*, ed. by Raúl González Salinero (Madrid: Signifer, 2013), pp. 293–315

Díaz, Pablo C., and Pablo Poveda, '*Qui patrie excidium intulerunt.* Hispania 711: explicaciones desesperadas para un colapso inesperado', in *Reti Medievali*, 17.2 (2016), 1–28

Díaz y Díaz, Manuel C., 'A propósito de la Vita Fructuosi', in *Cuadernos de Estudios Gallegos*, 8 (1953), 155–78

Díaz y Díaz, Manuel C., *Valerio del Bierzo. Su persona. Su obra* (León: Centro de Estudios e Investigación San Isidoro, 2006)

Escalona Monge, Julio, and Tomás M. Rodríguez Cerezo, 'El léxico sobre relaciones de dependencia en un texto de época visigoda. Un ensayo metodológico', in *Studia Historica. Historia Antigua*, 6 (1988), 201–10

Espinosa, Urbano, 'El enclave "Parpalines" de la "Vita Sancti Aemiliani": espacio rural y aristocracia en época visigoda', in *Iberia*, 6 (2003), 79–110

Feijoo Martínez, Santiago, and Miguel Alba Calzado, 'La decadencia de Mérida en el siglo IX', in *Bataliús III. Estudios sobre el reino aftasí*, ed. by Juan Zozaya Stabel-Hansen and Guillermo Kurtz Schaefer (Badajoz: Comunidad Autónoma de Extremadura, 2014), pp. 93–110

Fernández, Damián, *Aristocrats and Statehood in Western Iberia, 300–600 CE* (Philadelphia, PA: University of Pennsylvania Press, 2017)

Fouracre, Paul, 'Merovingian History and Merovingian Hagiography', in *Past & Present*, 127 (1990), 3–38

García Moreno, Luis A., 'From *coloni* to *servi*: A History of the Peasantry in Visigothic Spain', in *Klio*, 83 (2001), 198–212

García Moreno, Luis A., *Leovigildo. Unidad y diversidad de un reinado* (Madrid: Real Academia de la Historia, 2008)

Ghosh, Shami, *Writing the Barbarian Past: Studies in Early Medieval Historical Narrative* (Leiden: Brill, 2016)
González Salinero, Raúl, *Introducción a la Hispania visigoda* (Madrid: UNED, 2017)
Kelly, Michael J., 'The Politics of History-Writing: Problematizing the Historiographical Origins of Isidore of Seville in Early Medieval Hispania', in *Isidore of Seville and his Reception in the Early Middle Ages: Transmitting and Transforming Knowledge*, ed. by Andrew Fear and Jamie Wood (Amsterdam: Amsterdam University Press, 2016), pp. 93–110
Koch, Manuel, '*Nunc tempore potentis Getarum Eurici regis*. El impacto visigodo en Hispania a través de la inscripción del puente de Mérida (483 d.C.)', in *Pyrenae*, 39.2 (2008), 137–42
Kreiner, Jamie, *The Social Life of Hagiography in the Merovingian Kingdom* (Cambridge: Cambridge University Press, 2014)
Kulikowski, Michael, *Late Roman Spain and its Cities* (Baltimore, MD: Johns Hopkins University Press, 2004)
Martin, Céline, *La géographie du pouvoir dans l'Espagne visigothique* (Lille: Presses Universitaires du Septentrion, 2003)
Martin, Céline, 'Valérius et l'ennemi. Grands propriétaires, clercs, cénobites et ermites face au contrôle du sacré dans le Bierzo du VIIe siècle', in *Compétition et sacré au Haut Moyen Âge: entre médiation et exclusion*, ed. by Philippe Depreaux, François Bougard, and Régine Le Jan (Turnhout: Brepols, 2015), pp. 67–84
Martin, Céline, 'The Asturia of Valerius: Bierzo at the End of the Seventh Century', in *Visigothic Symposium*, 2 (2017–2018), 60–78
Martín Iglesias, José Carlos, 'La biografía dentro de la autobiografía: el caso de Valerio del Bierzo (siglo VII)', in *Las biografías griegas y latinas como género literario: De la Antigüedad al Renacimiento, Algunas calas*, ed. by Vitalino Valcárcel Martínez (Vittoria: UPV [University of the Basque Country], 2009), pp. 319–342
Martín Iglesias, José Carlos, 'Braulio de Zaragoza'; 'Valerio del Bierzo', in *La Hispania visigótica y mozárabe. Dos épocas en su literatura* (Salamanca: University of Salamanca, 2010), pp. 95–100; 202–21
Mateos, Pedro, 'Augusta Emerita, de capital de la Diocesis Hispaniarum a sede temporal visigoda', in *Sedes Regiae (ann. 400–800)*, ed. by Gisella Ripoll and Josep María Gurt (Barcelona: Reial Acadèmia de Bones Lletres, 2000), pp. 491–520
Mateos, Pedro, and Miguel Alba, 'El paisaje urbano de Mérida en torno al año 711', in *Zona Arqueológica*, 15 (2011), 27–35
Mateos, Pedro, and Luis Caballero, 'El paisaje urbano de Augusta Emerita en época tardoantigua (siglos IV–VII)', in *Actas Congreso Internacional 1910–2010. El yacimiento emeritense* (Mérida: Ayuntamiento de Mérida, 2011), pp. 505–19
Maya Sánchez, Antonio, 'La versión primitiva de la Vita Fructuosi', in *Habis*, 9 (1978), 169–96

Maya Sánchez, Antonio, *Vitas Sanctorum Patrum Emeretensium*, CCSL 116 (Turnhout: Brepols, 1992)

Pohl, Walter, 'Telling the Difference: Signs of Ethnic Identity', in *Strategies of Distinction: The Construction of Ethnic Communities, 300–800*, ed. by Walter Pohl and Helmut Reimitz (Leiden: Brill, 1998), pp. 17–69

Pohl, Walter, 'Romanness: A Multiple Identity and its Changes', in *Early Medieval Europe*, 22.4 (2014), 406–18

Quirós Castillo, Juan Antonio, 'Defensive Sites of the Early Middle Ages in North-West Spain', in *Landscapes of Defence in Early Medieval Europe*, ed. by John Baker, Stuart Brookes, and Andrew Reynolds (Turnhout: Brepols, 2013a), pp. 305–39

Quirós Castillo, Juan Antonio (ed.), *El poblamiento rural de época visigoda en Hispania. Arqueología del campesinado en el interior peninsula*r (Bilbao: Universidad del País Vasco, 2013b)

Quirós Castillo, Juan Antonio, and José María Tejado Sebastián (eds), *Los castillos altomedievales en el noroeste de la Península Ibérica* (Bilbao: Universidad del País Vasco, 2012)

San Bernardino, Jesús, *El santo y la ciudad. Una aproximación al patrocinio cívico de los santos en época teodosiana (386–410 d.C.)* (Écija: Graf. Sol, 1996)

Sastre de Diego, Isaac, 'El cristianismo en la Mérida romana y visigoda. Evidencias arqueológicas y fuentes escritas', in *Actas Congreso Internacional 1910–2010: el yacimiento emeritense* (Mérida: Ayuntamiento de Mérida, 2011), pp. 563–85

Sastre de Diego, Isaac, *Mérida capital cristiana. De Roma a Al-Andalus* (Mérida: Museo Nacional de Arte Romano, 2015)

Stocking, Rachel, *Bishops, Councils, and Consensus in the Visigothic Kingdom, 589–633* (Ann Arbor, MI: University of Michigan Press, 2000)

Tejerizo, Carlos, *Arqueología de las sociedades campesinas en la Cuenca del Duero durante la primera Alta Edad Media* (Bilbao: Universidad del País Vasco, 2017)

Tejerizo, Carlos, and Jorge Canosa, 'Power, Control and Social Agency in Post-Roman Northern Iberia: An Archaeological Analysis of Hillfort Occupations', in *Journal of Medieval Iberian Studies*, 10.3 (2018), 295–323

Valcárcel, Vitalino, '¿Uno o dos Frunimianos en Vita Emiliani y cartas de Braulio de Zaragoza?', in *Faventia*, 12–13 (1990–1991), 367–71

Vallejo Girvés, Margarita, *Hispania y Bizancio. Una relación desconocida* (Madrid: Akal, 2012)

Velázquez, Isabel, '¿Hagiografía versus prosopografía? En torno a las Vitas Sanctorum Patrum Emeretensium', in *Latinitas Biblica et Christiana. Studia philologica varia in honorem Olegario García de la Fuente* (Madrid: UEM, 1994), pp. 497–506

Velázquez, Isabel, '*Pro patriae gentisque Gothorum statu* (4th Council of Toledo, Canon 75, A. 633)', in *Regna and Gentes: The Relationship Between Late Antique and Early Medieval Peoples and Kingdoms in the Transformation of the Roman*

World, ed. by Hans-Werner Goetz, Jörg Jarnut, and Walter Pohl (Leiden: Brill, 2003), pp. 161–217

Velázquez, Isabel, *La literatura hagiográfica. Presupuestos básicos y aproximación a sus manifestaciones en la Hispania visigoda* (Burgos: Junta de Castilla y León, 2007)

Velázquez, Isabel, *Vidas de los Santos Padres de Mérida* (Madrid: Trotta, 2008a)

Velázquez, Isabel, 'El puente de Mérida: algo más que un problema de traducción', in *Pyrenae*, 39.2 (2008b), 127–35

Vigil-Escalera Guirado, Alfonso, *Los primeros paisajes altomedievales en el interior de Hispania. Registros campesinos del siglo quinto d.C.* (Bilbao: Universidad del País Vasco, 2015)

Wood, Jamie, 'A Family Affair: Leander, Isidore and the Legacy of Gregory the Great in Spain', in *Isidore of Seville and His Reception in the Early Middle Ages: Transmitting and Transforming Knowledge*, ed. by Andrew Fear and Jamie Wood (Amsterdam: Amsterdam University Press, 2016), pp. 31–56

About the Author

Santiago Castellanos is Permanent Associate Professor of History at University of León, Spain. He works on late Roman empire and the Visigothic kingdom in Hispania. His latest book is *The Visigothic Kingdom in Iberia: Construction and Invention* (University of Pennsylvania Press, 2020).

11 Empire and the Politics of Faction

Mérida and Toledo Revisited

Graham Barrett[1]

Abstract

When Reccared presided over the conversion of the Visigoths in 589, John of Biclarum wrote that he embodied Constantine at Nicaea and Marcian at Chalcedon. It is tempting to see late antique state formation through the lens of such *imitatio imperii*, but what did that mean in practice? Our understanding of the 'baptism of Spain' is coloured by the polemical *Lives of the Fathers of Mérida*, but this beguiling seventh-century text can also reveal elements of Visigothic 'imperial' governance, enabling us to diagnose the available resources and dynamics of rulership. From its partisan sketches of civic politics and factions, we can reconstruct something of royal interactions with local élites and how Visigothic kings had to work with or around local actors, in doing so recapitulating a defining feature of Roman *imperium*.

Keywords: Visigothic kingship; local politics; hagiography; epigraphy; Mérida; Toledo

Now the aforementioned King Reccared, as we have said, took part in the holy council, recalling for our times how the *princeps* of old, Constantine the Great, enlightened the holy synod of Nicaea by his presence, as well as

1 I should like to express my gratitude here to the editors for their labours; to Roger Collins, Helmut Reimitz, Isaac Sastre de Diego, Chris Wickham, and Ian Wood; and to Francisco del Águila Gómez, the Indiana Jones of Cádiz. For primary sources, I give section and where appropriate line numbers: all translations are my own. For Church councils, Coll. Hisp. is the edition of reference for Elvira, Tarragona, Girona, I Zaragoza, Lérida, Valencia, and I–XV Toledo; see Conc. for all others.

Fernández, D., Lester, M. & Wood, J. (eds.), *Rome and Byzantium in the Visigothic Kingdom: Beyond* Imitatio Imperii. Taylor & Francis Group 2023
DOI: 10.5117/9789463726412_CH11

Marcian, the most Christian *imperator*, at whose instigation the decisions of the synod of Chalcedon were confirmed.[2]

Introduction

What distinguishes a kingdom from an empire? For a passing moment in the early fifth century Athaulf may have mused on converting Rome into a Gothic *imperium*, yet the realm ruled by his descendants from the late sixth to the early eighth called itself variously the 'homeland' or 'kingdom of the Goths' or the 'kingdom of Hispania', never an empire.[3] Much about it was imperial, of course, in that capacious Roman sense: the provinces which its kings administered, the cities they founded, the laws they enacted as 'prince' and 'Flavius', their codes and coins, legations and letters, their votive crowns.[4] As in the *Donation of Constantine*, where the emperor places a tiara upon the head of the pope to wear henceforth in all papal processions 'in imitation of our imperial power', Rome casts so long a shadow that too often what we mean by *imitatio imperii* is any such emulation of its symbols of authority.[5] But can we go beyond—*is* there a beyond—symbolism? While our source materials often seem limited to a sterile sequence of kings and bishops, laws and canons, rendering so much of Visigothic history top-down and normative tedium, one remarkable offset is the *Vitas sanctorum patrum Emeretensium* (VSPE: 'Lives of the Holy Fathers of Mérida'), which can take us deep into contemporary structures of power and enable us to say something more concrete about their 'imperial' nature.[6]

Emerita Augusta, 'the Rome of Spain', was founded by the emperor Augustus in 25 BCE to settle retired (*emeriti*) veterans of the Cantabrian Wars: it was the capital of the province of Lusitania and, from the fourth century, the diocese of Hispaniae.[7] As conjured by Roger Collins in a classic essay, the VSPE brings to life through local eyes the world of this major urban centre and subtly sketches its passage in the later sixth century from something like an autonomous city-state to a component of the kingdom of Toledo.[8]

2 Ioh. Bicl. 91.

3 Oros. Hist. 7.43.5–6; Velázquez Soriano 2003; Barrett 2020, 54–64.

4 See Koch 2008.

5 Valla 2007, app., 'The Donation of Constantine', 17; Scholl 2017.

6 Maya Sánchez 1992; trans. Fear 1997, 45–105; Velázquez Soriano 2008, 45–125; cf. Stocking 2007.

7 Ford 1855, 2: 472; see Mateos Cruz 2000; Arce 2002; Sastre de Diego 2015; Alba Calzado 2018.

8 Collins 1980; Kulikowski 2004, 274–76, 290–93; Panzram 2010; cf. Wickham 2005, 221–22.

The hagiography is characterized by a magical realism more beguiling than the typical dutiful effort, seeming and at times being treated as 'one of the most truthful pages of the history of Spain', but serving nonetheless to screen a pointed polemic.[9] In the foreground is an epic struggle waged by Bishop Masona and the virgin martyr Eulalia, patroness of the city, against the imposition of heterodoxy from without; in the background is the consolidation of the state by Leovigild (568–586) and the conversion of the Visigoths from Arian to Nicene Christianity under his son Reccared (586–601). Taking advantage of this rich narrative, what I mean to explore here is a specifically structural rather than symbolic *imitatio imperii*. What this text can contribute is not so much hard data about elements of imperial Roman governance in Visigothic Iberia as a diagnosis of the available resources of rulership and the dynamics which resulted from them.[10] Through its polemical sketches of civic politics and factions we can reconstruct something of royal interactions with local élites which recalls the relationship between cities and emperors in the Roman world. To make their influence felt on the ground in Mérida, successive Visigothic kings had to work with or around local actors claiming to represent the city, to respond to local parties aiming to rule the city, and in doing so they recapitulated a central and defining feature of *imperium*.

Authors and Agendas

The VSPE presents itself as the work of an anonymous deacon of Mérida, and its composition is traditionally dated to the bishopric of Stephen I (*c.* 633–635), successor to Renovatus, the last holder of the office cited in it.[11] The text is divided into five *opuscula* or booklets. The first three consist of miracles attending the deaths of a boy named Augustus and a reformed alcoholic monk, and the murder of Abbot Nanctus, an immigrant from Africa, by misguided rustics. The last two describe at considerably greater length the eventful episcopal careers of Paul and Fidel, uncle and nephew somewhat mysteriously arrived from the East, and of Masona, stout yeoman of orthodox faith, with brief final notices of Innocent and

9 Cossío 1914, 23; Collins 1980, 192–94; Velázquez Soriano 1994; Castellanos 2003; Velázquez Soriano 2008, 28–32; see e.g., García Iglesias 1974; Orlandis 1991, 171–86; Teixeira and Carneiro 2020.

10 See Fouracre 1990.

11 García Moreno 1974, 439, 'Stephanus', 171; 438, 'Renovatus', 171; Ramírez Sádaba 2003, 274–76.

Renovatus. But the composition of the text turns out to be more complicated. From the manuscript transmission one can see that in subsequent decades the VSPE underwent some light editing, before being fully revised into a new edition featuring a different title, an index, the interpolation of a hagiographic corpus celebrating Fructuosus of Braga, the addition of sundry other passages, and general linguistic emendation. Four appendices (now lost), including a confession in the name of 'Paul' addressed to Bishop Festus (*c.* 672–680), provide a date for the new edition, and in the past the whole work has been ascribed to a non-existent 'Paul the deacon' by erroneously combining the two authorial personas.[12] We are dealing with an open text, which has changed form and content over time. The fact that the earliest manuscripts are from the tenth century should further caution against assuming that the first version as reconstructed is the text as originally written: one copy includes only books four and five, raising the possibility that what we have today might encompass multiple originally independent components.[13] Before we draw on the VSPE as an eyewitness to Visigothic Mérida, we need to give these questions proper consideration. And on closer inspection the text turns out to have not one but two authors, with distinct agendas, which must inform how we use it to frame the constraints and opportunities applying to the Visigothic kings as they founded their kingdom.

The first part of the VSPE comprises books one to three. In the preface, its author is clear about his agenda: to bolster the faith of his readers and listeners, after the example of Gregory the Great's *Dialogues*, by relating current and local miracles, 'events which have taken place in the present day in the city of Mérida'.[14] The *Dialogues* were written in 593/94, which gives us a secure *terminus post quem* for the text, and indeed this seems to be the earliest citation of Gregory's work.[15] From the context of his stories, the Méridan hagiographer likely had some role in monastic education, since he mentions in his account of 'innocent, simple, and illiterate' Augustus that the author often visited the 'house of the distinguished virgin Eulalia' where the child lived, while schoolboys busily learning their letters set the scene for the marvellous reform of the inebriated monk.[16] The author of the text

12 Garvin 1946, 1–6; Maya Sánchez 1978; Maya Sánchez 1992, xxxi–xliii, lv–lviii; García Moreno 1974, 442, 'Festus', 172; cf. Smedt 1884, 8–15.

13 London, British Library, Additional MS 17357 (early 13th c.): Maya Sánchez 1992, xx–xxi; Gaiffier 1976–1977; see also Reeve 1983, 244, n. 42; Henriet 2004, 159; and now esp. Collins 2021.

14 VSPE pr. 15–16; Chaparro Gómez 1992.

15 See Greg. Mag. Reg. 3.50; Zimmerman 1959, vii–viii; Moreira 2000, 139, n. 10; Varela Rodríguez 2019, 137–38, 145.

16 VSPE 1.2–4; 2.61–63; Suárez Fernández 2016, 269–72; Menéndez Bueyes 2019, 31–32.

calls himself a 'deacon of Christ' under the authority of an abbot, and the second miracle plays out at the monastery of 'Cauliana' (Cubillana), 'nearly eight miles outside' of Mérida to the northeast, which was perhaps the home of this deacon.[17] He also displays two attitudes which mark him out from the second author. One is a critical stance on wealth: he describes Cauliana with diffident qualification as 'the very rich monastery (so they say)', while in book three he has the evil peasants despise the shabby appearance of Nanctus, a sign of saintly humility.[18] More unexpectedly, he is discreetly tolerant of Leovigild, villainous king of the later books, who 'though he was Arian' makes a donation to the abbot of Cauliana from the royal estate, and 'though he was not of the proper faith' sentences the murderers of Nanctus appropriately for their crime.[19] While not Arian himself, this author brings to mind Leovigild as presented to us by Gregory of Tours, demanding of one such bishop why he did not perform miracles like true believers were doing.[20] The first part of the VSPE cracks open the door for virtuous Arians, if not quite so far as performing miracles, then at least to be in communion with the holy.

The second part, consisting of books four and five, is flagged as separate by several indicators before we even contemplate its author. Book three ends with a unique responsory 'Thanks be to God', as if serving as the *explicit* for an originally stand-alone text.[21] The next two books are then headed by a collective title, 'Here begins the death and miracles of the holy bishops of Mérida', and introduced by a preface declaring a new agenda: to narrate local miracles not from the present but the past, 'the deeds of the holy fathers of old' handed down by tradition.[22] Taken together this recalls the multiple different internal prefaces and complex composition of the ten books of *Histories* by Gregory of Tours.[23] And if we look for the two distinctive attitudes of our first author, we find a total contrast. The second author is positive about money, lingering lovingly on the scale of the patrimony bequeathed to Bishop Paul by the wealthiest senatorial family of Lusitania, and portraying Masona as a patron rich beyond measure, processing in pomp with his entourage showing him all due subservience 'as if before a

17 VSPE 1.96–100; 2.4–5.

18 VSPE 2.38–40; 3.44–48; Chavarría Arnau 2004; Fernández 2016b, 527.

19 VSPE 3.37–40; 3.54–56; cf. Velázquez Soriano 2008, 22–23; Dumézil and Joye 2012, 20–22.

20 Greg. Tur. In gloria confess. 13.

21 VSPE 3.61.

22 VSPE 4 tit.; 4 pr. 8–10.

23 Greg. Tur. Decem libri, pr.; 1 pr.; 3 pr.; 5 pr.; Murray 2008.

king'.[24] In another contrast to the first, this author is damning of Leovigild, seen as a brutal Arian tyrant whose 'diabolical' scheming against the heroic Masona, a new Elijah come to confront Baal, earns him a wondrous slave beating from Eulalia.[25] That feigner of piety 'wrecked rather than ruled Hispania' and fully deserved his divine judgement of death and hell.[26] The model is royal persecutor and episcopal martyr, and the language draws heavily on the *Passion* of Desiderius of Vienne by the Visigothic king Sisebut (612–621): composed in approximately 615, it provides a rough *terminus post quem* for this second part (the bishopric of Renovatus is of unknown date, and has been deduced solely from his appearance in the narrative).[27] But such casting also represents a minority view of Leovigild; because of his role as effective founder of the Visigothic kingdom, other contemporary writers such as John of 'Biclarum' (probably Vallclara, near Tarragona; possibly Béjar, near Salamanca) and Isidore of Seville are more neutral about him, balancing his culpable Arianism against the achievements of his reign.[28]

One last point crucial to the perspective of our second author is the unusual status of the archdeacon Eleutherius. The VSPE presents him as a cautionary tale of excessive ambition: when he sees the elderly Masona nearing the end of his life, Eleutherius excitedly takes to travelling about with an entourage of his own, but the bishop miraculously regains sufficient vim and vigour to pray successfully for the death of his would-be successor.[29] In doing so, Masona ignores the appeals made by the mother of the impatient archdeacon, rebuffing her with terse words recalling Pontius Pilate and, remarkably, making her one of those who denied that Jesus of Nazareth was King of the Jews.[30] Yet in the basilica of Santa Eulalia de Mérida, there is the following tripartite inscription on the stairs leading down to the late Roman crypt:

> Gregory, distinguished man and servant of God, lived for 56 years, 5 months. He rested in peace on 16 October in era 530 [492 CE].
>
> Perpetua, handmaiden of God, lived 16 years. She rested in peace during 27 June in era 620 [582 CE].

24 VSPE 4.2.61–76; 5.3.52–57; Fernández 2016b, 534.

25 VSPE 5.4.4–12; 5.8.14–25; cf. Díaz Duckwen 2018; Lorenzo-Rodríguez 2020, 213.

26 VSPE 5.9.1–9.

27 Maya Sánchez 1994; Fear 2001; Martín 2000, 144–45.

28 Ioh. Bicl. 79 (cf. 57); Isid. Hist. Goth. 49, Castellanos 2018, Barroso Cabrera, Morín de Pablos, and Sánchez Ramos 2020, 172–201.

29 VSPE 5.13.11–16; 5.13.45–66.

30 VSPE 5.13.69–74; John 19:22; Fear 1997, 102, n. 230.

> A † Ω. Eleutherius, archdeacon and servant of God in the church of Mérida, lived 33 years. He rested in peace on 29 December in era 643 [605 CE].[31]

How can we account for this honorific treatment, and the placement *ad sanctam*, of a cursed antagonist of mighty Masona?[32] The epigraphic notice of Eleutherius is clearly an addition to the earlier two, and could be unrelated, but one possible reading is that these three persons were all from the same family. We do have other collective inscriptions, not least the 'family epitaph' of Isidore of Seville (d. 636); if this was the case, the archdeacon was a member of an aristocratic lineage stretching back over a century.[33] Might Eleutherius have been the real insider, and Masona the outsider—along with his hagiographer? Masona, indeed, is last attested in 597, whereas Eleutherius lived on for nearly another decade: we might even ask whether our hagiographer reversed the order of their deaths to maximize the force of his polemic.[34]

This possibility takes us deep into the politics of faction at the most local level, within the church of Mérida itself, and it changes how we understand the position and so the agenda of our author.[35] Churches were often riven by internal division: Ildefonsus of Toledo, for example, recalls in the preface to his *On Distinguished Men* how one Gerontius the priest, flush with royal favour, felt able to treat Bishop Justus of Toledo with contempt and marvellously lost his wits in appropriate punishment.[36] John of Biclarum too records the renown not only of Masona but also of a priest named John, contemporary and colleague in Mérida, of whom the VSPE says nothing at all.[37] Another score settled, only this time by silence? We are not being told the whole story, and the simplest explanation for the text as it stands is that the second author, promoting his party, at some point took up the work of the first into a seemingly comprehensive but subtly partisan history of the holy in Mérida, perhaps carrying over the original epilogue or composing it himself. Some mild revision may have smoothed over any more obvious stylistic differences between the two

31 Ramírez Sádaba and Mateos Cruz 2000, 37; CILAE 1287 (https://cil2digital.web.uah.es/inscripciones/ficha/696/1287).

32 Mateos Cruz 1999, 160–63; Castellanos 2003, 406–16; Castellanos 2020, 105–7; cf. Godoy Fernández 1995, 278–81.

33 Ramírez Sánchez 2008, 165–72; Martín 2010.

34 Toledo (597); cf. García Moreno 1974, 435, 'Massona', 169.

35 Castillo Maldonado 2007, 266–69.

36 Ildef. De viris, pr. 44–50; Castro 2016, 64–65.

37 Ioh. Bicl. 30, 51.

parts, but the disjuncture of objectives and attitudes is clear to see (see Table 1).[38] Both constituent texts remain products of and witnesses to the politics of faction, and as we shall see the politics in turn constrained and conditioned the intersection of royal with urban, giving the Visigothic kingdom its imperial character.

Part One		
First Preface		Written post-593/94
1	The Death of the Young Boy Named Augustus	Set *c.* later 6th c.?
2	The Death of a Certain Monk of Cauliana	Set *c.* later 6th c.?
3	The Death of a Certain Abbot Nanctus	Set in 568–586 (see VSPE, 3.3–5)
Explicit		
Part Two		
Second Preface		Written post-615
4	The Death and Miracles of the Holy Bishops of Mérida (Paul and Fidel)	Set *c.* 530s–560s
5	The Life and Mighty Works of the Holy Bishop Masona (followed by Innocent and Renovatus)	Set *c.* 570s–620s
Epilogue		

Table 1: The internal structure and chronology of the *Vitas sanctorum patrum Emeretensium*. Sources: Kampers 1979, 95, 'Paulus', 32–33; 96, 'Fidelis', 33; 195, 'Nanctus', 57–58; 361, 'Augustus', 93; García Moreno 1974, 435, 'Massona', 166–69; 437, 'Innocentius', 170; 438, 'Renovatus', 171; Jorge 2002, 76.

Greeks and Gifts

Book four of the VSPE begins part two of the text, but it also inaugurates a new era in the episcopal and civic history of Mérida. Many a narrative from late antique Iberia involves an arrival from North Africa, which retained economic and cultural links to the peninsula; here, however, a Greek doctor named Paul comes from the East and after a time becomes bishop, putting an end to unspecified troubles under his predecessor.[39] Later some traders from his home in Greece make an appearance seeking an audience, improbably bringing with them his nephew Fidel, whom Paul recognizes. The bishop subsequently browbeats the merchants with threats and bribes into leaving

38 See Stover and Kestemont 2016, esp. 154.

39 VSPE 4.1; Osland 2012; Graham 2005, 118–33, 174–86.

Fidel behind 'for comfort in my captivity'.[40] There is no reason to doubt the plausibility of these episodes as such: the fourth-century Aphrodisias portable sundial, a marine navigation aid, includes Mérida as the main port of call in Hispaniae even though the river route from the sea was not directly navigable.[41] The city, furthermore, remained a major administrative and economic hub well beyond the end of Roman rule, with Greek epigraphy only dying out in the seventh century, similar to the city of Mértola to the southwest down the Guadiana River.[42] What calls for more comment is the suspect vagueness of the text as to the background and context of both Paul and Fidel, which, when read alongside the evocation of 'captivity', suggests intrigue, political (or criminal) exile, or possibly (like Gundovald in Gaul) some kind of mission on behalf of the eastern empire.[43]

And indeed, the career of Paul as bishop quickly takes a strange turn when the wife of a local senatorial aristocrat loses her unborn child in the womb and calls upon his medical expertise to avert her own death: after praying for forgiveness, he performs surgery to extract the dead foetus.[44] The operation, much discussed, is neither an abortion nor a caesarean but an embryotomy, a risky procedure described by the seventh-century Greek physician Paul of Aegina, another possible point of contact with the East. Medicine and merchants seem to have been linked in the minds of contemporaries: in an interesting collocation, Visigothic law treats doctors (required to draw up contracts with their patients in case they should kill them) and foreign traders in the same book, albeit separated by legislation on grave robbery.[45] It was not until the high Middle Ages, however, that consistent canon law against the clergy practising medicine was formulated, so why does Paul ask forgiveness, and why did the author choose to relate the story?[46] After all, in the early tenth-century *Life* of Patriarch Ignatius, for example, when doctors proposed to perform an embryotomy on a woman suffering a breech birth, appeal to the saint was sufficient to turn the baby

40 VSPE 4.3.38–40.

41 Talbert 2017, 8; Álvarez Martínez 1983, 65–70, 83–84; cf. Arce 1999, 11–14; Retamero 1999, 271–77.

42 García Moreno 1972; Hoz García-Bellido 2007; Vizcaíno Sánchez 2007, 289–322; Alves-Dias, Gaspar, and Lopes 2013; Hoz 2014, 437–57; Reynolds 2015.

43 Greg. Tur. Decem libri 6.24.

44 VSPE 4.2; Sanabria Escudero 1964, 75–80; Curado 2004.

45 VSPE 4.2.43–50; Paul of Aegina, *Epitome of Medicine* 6.74 (ed. Heiberg 1921–1924); LI 11.1.3–4; 11.3; Pérez Martín 1987; cf. Mistry 2015, 93–125; Tsoucalas, Laios, Karamanou, and Sgantzos 2015; Martínez and González 2017, 47–49.

46 Amundsen 1978.

around inside her, making surgical intervention unnecessary.[47] The point of our second author must be to counter a failure of holiness on the part of Paul, for a properly 'holy father of Mérida' should have been able to resolve the situation via prayer.[48] An echo of this case seems to sound a generation later, when the monk Tarra wrote to Reccared denying accusations of moral turpitude and complaining that he had been evicted from the monastery of Cauliana as if 'aborted from the womb'; his invocation of one Fidel (or a *fidelis*) as his character witness may be mere coincidence, or a barbed reminder of what others had been allowed to get away with in the past.[49] There was something unsavoury about these people, and part two of the VSPE has a consistent tone of apologetic.

The operation is the making of Paul, who receives half of the property of the grateful couple at once and the other half after their deaths, leaving him the wealthiest man in Mérida, lord of a great estate.[50] Looking to found a dynasty, he holds the local clergy hostage to his money, ordaining his nephew Fidel as his successor and requiring acceptance by the terms of his will if they wish to inherit his patrimony thereafter.[51] Even so, in order to secure the office against clerical opposition, Fidel is compelled to repeat the threat to take away all those properties 'by Church law'.[52] Once he has bought the bishopric, he embarks upon a restoration and building campaign at both the intramural cathedral church of Santa María and the extramural basilica of Santa Eulalia, efforts which, though undeniably impressive, do put one very much in mind of money laundering.[53] But since the author himself invokes canon law—correctly, if defensively—on the right of the bishop to dispose of his personal possessions, we may pause for a moment to consider the legality of the episcopal actions described here.[54] Bishops were explicitly barred from designating their own successors and, since Simon Magus, from purchasing office.[55] At the end of his life, Fidel also makes a point of sweeping benefactions, remitting all debts owed by the crowds who

47 Nicetas David, *Life of Patriarch Ignatius* 86 (ed. Smithies and Duffy 2013).

48 See McClanan 2002, 44–45; Dal Santo 2012, 159–83, 221–32.

49 Velázquez Soriano 1996, 294: 32–33, 45–46; Stocking 2000, 104–5; Mistry 2015, 93–94; Mistry 2018, 166–70.

50 VSPE 4.2; Díaz 1992–1993.

51 VSPE 4.4; García Iglesias 1989; Norton 2007, 207; Fuentes Hinojo 2012.

52 VSPE 4.5.4–9.

53 VSPE 4.6.24–32; Velázquez Soriano 2007, 261–68.

54 II Braga (572) cap. 15; cf. Lérida (546) 16; Valencia (549) 2; IX Toledo (655) 4, 6–7; Martínez Díez 1959, 171–73; Juan 1998; Castillo Maldonado 2012, 17–25; Roca 2015, 10–11.

55 II Braga (572) cap. 8; IV Toledo (633) 19; XI Toledo (675) 9; Acts 8:9–24; Martínez Díez 1959, 34–38.

surround him like a Roman patron receiving morning *salutatio* from his clients: given that ecclesiastical property was inalienable, however, was this permitted?[56] Indeed, one of the acts of his successor Masona which most enrages the archdeacon Eleutherius is the manumission of Church slaves with gifts of money and other goods. Canon law on the issue endeavoured to walk a fine line between a Christian spirit of charity and preserving the institutional endowment, but it remained very much a source of argument, debate, and in the main opposition.[57] To what degree will such tensions with canon law have been felt? While the applicability of individual Church councils can be unclear, and general dissemination of all their precepts likely came only with the first conciliar compilation by Isidore of Seville (perhaps supporting a later date of composition for the second sector of the VSPE), for the most part the canonical sensitivity perceptible in the text concerns the infringement of commonly accepted principles.[58]

Money was in short both the strength and the weakness of these bishops, and the author engages in much special pleading on their behalf. Furthermore, if we take the insider status of Eleutherius, whom he damns, and combine it with the serial violations of canon law by Paul, Fidel, and Masona, whom he exonerates, the possibility begins to emerge that our writer represents a controversial faction in Mérida which had slipped from its position of power by the time of writing. Beyond its vulnerability to legalistic criticism, can we say anything more about this group? It was not obviously an east Roman faction, since the author makes no mention of the revolt of Athanagild (which received imperial assistance from the emperor Justinian) late in the bishopric of Paul, even though his rival Agila was killed in Mérida itself.[59] Neither was it necessarily confessional, for the author is silent too about the rising of Hermenegild against his father Leovigild with imperial aid from Tiberius II, even though the city supported the Nicene prince, providing a perfect opportunity to criticize the Arian king for retaking it by force.[60] In fact, Hermenegild has been excised from the narrative altogether: whereas Gregory the Great credited the conversion of Reccared to 'the example of his martyr brother', our author, despite drawing

56 VSPE 4.10; II Braga (572) cap. 14–15; III Toledo (589) 3; VI Toledo (638) 15; IX Toledo (655) 3; I. Wood 1999, 195–98, 203–6; I. Wood 2013, 58–62; S. Wood 2006, 9–11, 16–25.

57 VSPE 5.13.17–38; I Seville (590) 1–2; II Seville (619) 8; IV Toledo (633) 67–74; IX Toledo (655) 11–16; X Toledo (656) decr. 2; Mérida (666) 20–21; III Zaragoza (691) 4; XVI Toledo (693) 5; Martínez Díez 1959, 125–46; Castellanos 1998; Buenacasa Pérez 2004; Río 2017, 92.

58 Coll. Hisp. 1, esp. 257–325.

59 Isid. Hist. Goth. 46–47.

60 Greg. Tur. Decem libri 6.18; Drews 2019.

directly on this passage of the *Dialogues*, quietly alters the text to 'Christ the Lord'.[61] Nor was it a Greek faction, any more than it was of another ethnic group; Masona, we read, was wholly dedicated to God in spite of being a 'Goth', a label which seems to have borne some of the narrative burden of Arianism.[62] What we are left with is a faction of individuals, competing with other individuals for power and authority over the local scene.

Martyrs and Miracles

According to the VSPE, the primary spiritual resource at hand for civic actors looking to make their mark was the virgin martyr Eulalia, and her body in its basilica is in a sense the protagonist of the text.[63] Writing in the late fourth or early fifth century, Prudentius hymned her torture and execution at the hands of the Roman governor Datian in 303/4, specifying that she had been buried in a church just outside the walls of Mérida, and had there become the object of cult for her robust defence of the Christian faith.[64] The development of her shrine seems to have been almost immediate; the curious early medieval chronicle of Pseudo-Isidore even puts the construction of it—called *Delicata* ('Luxurious') presumably in error for *Dedicata* ('Consecrated', to Eulalia)—during the reign of Diocletian (284–305), in effect within a year or two of her death.[65] Already celebrated by Augustine in a sermon from the 410s, as patroness of Mérida she quickly became a force to be feared: so Heremigarius, a Suevic leader, found in 429 when he was hurled head-first into the Guadiana River for his bad attitude.[66] With power came recognition, and by 450 she was the dedicatee of a church founded in the Narbonnese countryside, while a striking fifth- or sixth-century sculptural depiction of her Prudentian martyrdom found near Lebrija in Andalucía is further testimony to the early spread of her cult (though the subject has

61 Greg. Mag. Dial. 3.31; VSPE 5.9.10–17; Hillgarth 1966, 499; Marcotegui Barber 2003; Barroso Cabrera, Morín de Pablos, and Sánchez Ramos 2020, 15–135.

62 VSPE 5.2.1–11; Koch 2012, 273–309; Koch 2014 and 2020; Stadermann 2017, esp. 225–53, 258–72, 282–94; Buchberger 2017, 53–61; Whelan 2019, 184–89; Wood (forthcoming); cf. Liebeschuetz 2015, 94–95.

63 See Guiance 2005; Panzram 2007.

64 Prud. Peri. 3.186–215; García Rodríguez 1966, 284–303; San Bernardino Coronil 1996; Mentxaka 2020.

65 Pseudo-Isidore, *Chronicle* 7 (cf. 12) (ed. González Muñoz 2000); Mateos Cruz 1999, 197–201; and see now Gil 2020, 2: 1233, 1239 (cf. 1255).

66 Augustine, *Sermons* 313G, 3 (ed. Morin 1930); Hyd. 80; Claude 1978, 33, 'Heremigarius', 659.

also been identified as an unknown male martyr, or Saint Thecla).[67] When Abbot Nanctus made his journey from Africa during the reign of Leovigild, it was at least partly on pilgrimage to her relics.[68]

The narrative of the VSPE can be read as a struggle to define and control the space of urban Mérida and its hinterland, and to this end its bishops had, or sought to have, a special relationship with Eulalia as the exclusive mediators of her power.[69] In the text, she appears before the hard-pressed Masona to offer comfort, presented in classic patron-client terms as a 'most tender mistress (*domina*)' to her 'most faithful and humble servant (*servulus*)', while all holders of the episcopal office were apparently buried close by her altar for the prestige and authority which that association brought to their successors.[70] Strictly speaking this is another illicit activity, in that canon law was set against interment 'within the basilicas of the saints' and only permitted burial outside their walls if absolutely necessary, but it was common enough, and was practised too by the bishops of Toledo at the tomb of Leocadia.[71] As Gregory of Tours found with Saint Martin, however, maintaining control over and getting benefit out of a suburban shrine from an urban cathedral could throw up unexpected challenges, as other parties with equal or greater access to the site pursued divergent agendas.[72] In this context, one can read the *xenodochium* or hostel-hospital which Masona, following in the medical footsteps of Paul, built adjacent to the extramural basilica of Santa Eulalia as an effort to bind the latter more tightly to him. One might also regard his grant of 2,000 *solidi* from the episcopal patrimony to Redemptus, the deacon in charge of the extant *xenodochium*, for distribution to the needy as a hard-currency scheme to gain a reliable man on the spot, even as Masona promoted his intramural palace as the point for townsmen and countryfolk alike to apply for the dole.[73]

67 Chalon 2010; Gnilka 2011; Recio Veganzones 1979; cf. Schlunk and Hauschild 1978, 60–61; Vidal Álvarez 2002, 229–32, 237.

68 VSPE 3.3–8; Recio Veganzones 1995.

69 See Teja 2019; Castro 2020.

70 VSPE 5.8.1–5; 5.15.1–3; Chaparro Gómez 1986; Brown 2015, 50–68.

71 See I Braga (561) 18; Ildef. De viris 13; Julian of Toledo, *Codicil on Ildefonsus* 41–45 (ed. Martín-Iglesias and Yarza Urquiola 2014); Felix of Toledo, *Life of Julian* 12 (ed. Martín-Iglesias and Yarza Urquiola 2014); Fear 1997, 104, n. 237; Scholz 1998; Díaz 2000, 158–59; López Quiroga and Martínez Tejera 2009.

72 See e.g., Greg. Tur. Decem libri 9.33, 10.12; Wood 2001.

73 VSPE 5.3.13–41; Pachá 2014, 262–68; Utrero Agudo and Moreno Martín 2015, 106–14; Underwood 2018, 382–84; Kurt 2020, 266–67; cf. Mateos Cruz 1995; 2022; Martínez Jiménez, Sastre de Diego, and Tejerizo García 2018, 168–69; Watson 2020, 4–12, 24–25.

The same process of 'topographic binding' is clearly perceptible in the anonymous *Passion* of Eulalia, written no later than the mid-seventh century.[74] Prudentius had given her whereabouts at the outbreak of persecution as her family home, 'secluded in the countryside far from the city', but this later treatment situates her elsewhere. More precisely, it places her in the *villa* of 'Promtiano' (from *promptuarium*, 'storeroom', in North African usage designating a monastery), located at milestone 38 from Mérida in the vicinity of Puebla de Sancho Pérez: there the *vehiculum publicum* or prefect's carriage arrives to bring her back to the city, and she spurs on its driver to make the long journey within an impossible hour.[75] The space separating suburban and urban is miraculously compressed, before the civic setting of her interrogation is conjured through evocation of the forum and tribunal, neighbouring districts whence the crowds have gathered, and of the gates of the *praetorium* or headquarters around which the governor paces in a fury.[76] The text then ends where it begins, beyond the city walls, at the site of her execution. The extramural location also provides the setting for the recovery and burial of her body, and the coming of pilgrims to be healed or to follow in her footsteps.[77]

If we revisit the VSPE with this spatial technique in mind, we can recognize how the second author creates his own sacred topography through visionary processions linking the bishops and power bases of Mérida. On one occasion, Bishop Fidel dispatches a boy on business outside the city, who sees on his return a fiery globe followed by a company of the saints together with the bishop, passing from the church of San Fausto to that of Santa Lucrecia—possibly the hermitage of Loreto—and back over the bridge to the southwest gate.[78] Another man witnesses Fidel setting out from Santa Eulalia and 'going amongst the basilicas of the martyrs', while a third beholds a holy host moving in pageant from the cathedral to the adjacent baptistery of San Juan, where the saints send demonic agents to the episcopal palace to deal the same bishop a death-blow; from there the bishop is taken out to Santa Eulalia for burial with the saint (see Figure 11.1).[79] By these serial narratives,

74 Gil 2000; and see now Yarza Urquiola 2020, 1, 21–23, 434–44.

75 Prud. Peri. 3.37–38; *Passio Eulalie Emeritensis* (PH), 4, 4–5; Mateos Martín de Rodrigo 2009, 223; Mateos Martín de Rodrigo 2018 and 2019; cf. Symmachus, Ep. 6.37 (ed. Seeck 1883, 163); Hudson 2021, 208–47.

76 *Passio Eulalie Emeritensis*, 7, 15; cf. Cordero Ruiz 2010; Cordero Ruiz and Franco Moreno 2012.

77 *Passio Eulalie Emeritensis*, 16, 19.

78 VSPE 4.7.

79 VSPE 4.8; 4.9; 4.10.1–3.

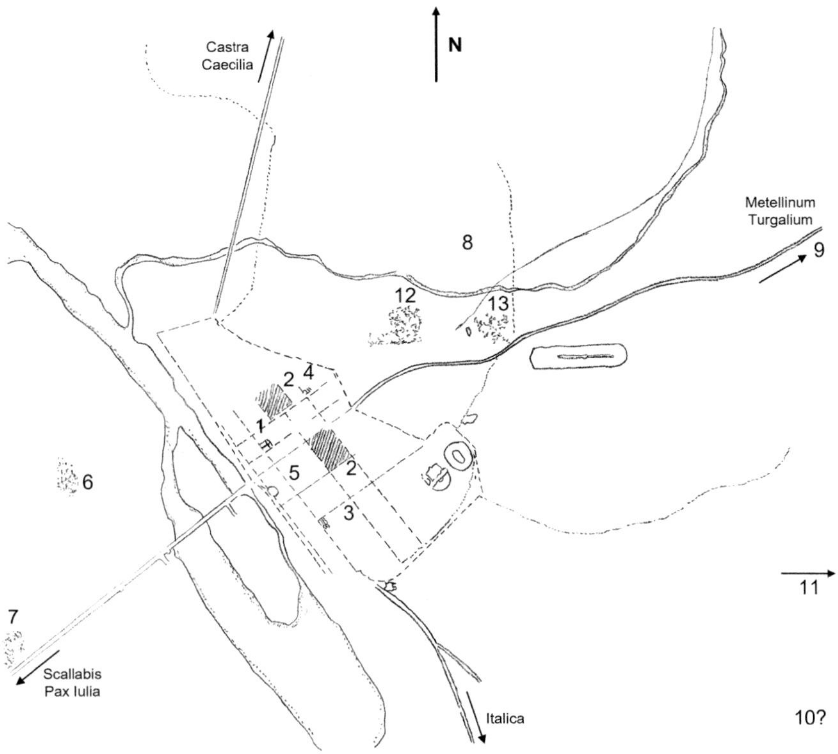

Figure 11.1: The City of Mérida in Late Antiquity

<u>Legend:</u>

1. Episcopal complex
2. Roman forum
3. Church of San Andrés
4. Church of Santiago
5. Alcazaba (fortress)
6. Hermitage of Loreto
7. Church of San Fausto
8. Church of Santa Lucía
9. Monastery of 'Cauliana' (Cubillana)
10. Church of San Cipriano (unknown)
11. Church of Santa María de Quintilina
12. Basilica of Santa Eulalia
13. *Xenodochium* (hostel-hospital)

Shaded extramural areas = Christian cemeteries
Dotted lines = aqueduct channels

Adapted from Mateos Cruz 1999, 191, fig. 74, with permission.

the churches of Mérida, intramural and extramural, are bound together under the divine authority of its bishop. Collectively they describe both the act of processing around the walls of the city with the saints, common practice to ensure its protection, and an *adventus* or ceremonial entry into the city, the most potent symbolic means of expressing dominance over it.[80]

Relics and Rulers

When we come to the climax of the VSPE, the career of Masona and his stand against Leovigild in the contest between Mérida and Toledo for mastery, patroness and topography have key roles to play. By his prayers and through the agency of Eulalia, the province of Lusitania remains free of plague and hunger. Even before his ordination, Masona has dwelt devotedly in her basilica, and with her favour he in turn becomes the patron of Mérida, leading the citizenry as one 'around the basilicas of the martyrs' to pray for rain during a drought.[81] At length, the conflict with the 'king of the Arians' for confessional supremacy comes to centre on possession of one of her relics. When Leovigild has the bishop brought before him in Toledo, he demands with threats the tunic of Eulalia in order to display it there in the Arian basilica; roundly rebuffed, he orders a search of both the cathedral and the church of Santa Eulalia back in Mérida, yet to no avail, since Masona is himself wearing the garment underneath his own clothes.[82] Canon law was uncomfortable with bishops making a spectacle of carting relics about, even within their own churches, and this clever ruse may have seemed to contemporaries as unscrupulous as the actions of the king, though it is not unlike the citizens of Zaragoza, under Frankish siege, circling the walls with the tunic of Vincent as their totem.[83] What we might miss, however, is the significance of the antagonists converging on the same saints and relics. Amongst the four recently discovered sixth-century documents from San Martín de Asán in Huesca (Aragón) are a diploma of 572 from Leovigild to the bishop of Narbonne (who in turn made a donation to this monastery a few years later) and a diploma of 586 from Reccared, new or imminent convert, to the same foundation.[84] Networks or affinities of kings, bishops, and monasteries which we might otherwise have processed respectively as dogmatically Arian and Nicene, in implacable opposition, instead meet

80 Dietz 2005, 172–73; Fuentes Hinojo 2008; Feijóo 2015, 315–18; Brubaker and Wickham 2021, 121–23; cf. Díaz 2010.

81 VSPE 5.2.12–20; 5.3.4–7; 5.14.7–12; Chaparro Gómez 1979; Pérez Sánchez 1992–1993 and 2002.

82 VSPE 5.6; Teja 2018.

83 III Braga (675) 5; Greg. Tur. Decem libri 3.29; Castellanos 1996, 11–15; cf. Guiance 2009, 119–20.

84 Tomás-Faci and Martín-Iglesias 2017, docs 2 (279), 4 (280–81).

in pious acts at a single institution.[85] On one level this is obvious, since the saints, if they were not allies, could make for powerful enemies. During the struggle against Hermenegild, Leovigild had occasion to order the return of loot taken by his troops from a monastery of Saint Martin lest vengeance be exacted, and soon after coming to the throne Reccared made a general restoration of seized property.[86] But this also demonstrates a broader point about contemporary power relations: pragmatic considerations of politics come before maintenance of theological purity, and the VSPE, to say nothing of our sources more broadly, may be applying religious labels to what are better analysed as personal and plastic relations of party and faction.

Leovigild convened a synod at Toledo in 579 to proclaim that Nicene believers who wished to join his faith need not be re-baptized, but simply receive a laying-on of hands, take communion, and hear the Arian Christology: thus seduced, records John of Biclarum, all too many changed sides 'for ambition rather than by force'.[87] Like the first author of the VSPE, the king was willing to meet non-Arians somewhere in the middle, and insofar as he himself identified as Arian, factional 'Arianism' (as opposed to dogmatic Arianism) was a potential route to power for his subjects. For the king, correspondingly, it could be a way into local politics, and we can see how this worked in the person of Sunna, the Arian bishop whom Leovigild appointed as rival to Masona in Mérida.[88] This troublemaker 'usurped certain basilicas with all their privileges at royal command' before setting his eyes on Santa Eulalia, appealing to the king for a decree transferring it into his control. Instead, a debate is held before judges at the episcopal palace, and after visiting the basilica to pray Masona proves the victor, finally leading his followers back there in another celebratory act of topographic binding.[89] Sunna had clearly sought to establish his power base outside the walls at Santa Eulalia and to confine his Nicene counterpart to the intramural cathedral, but having failed he convinces Leovigild to haul our hero off to Toledo, where the episode of the tunic plays out, and the king ultimately exiles Masona 'for three years and then some'.[90] In his place Nepopis is installed, carefully using the passive voice (*subrogatur* [...] *substituitur*): impious, devilish, Satanic, 'harbinger of Antichrist', and 'bishop of someone

85 Davies 2007, 113–38.
86 Greg. Tur. In gloria confess. 12; Ioh. Bicl. 86.
87 Ioh. Bicl. 57.217–19; Mülke 2009; Lester 2020.
88 See Wood 2019, 235–40.
89 VSPE 5.5; Fernández 2020, 524–25.
90 VSPE 5.6; 5.7.1–4.

else's city', a grave crime indeed in the eyes of canon law.[91] The second author says nothing at all of the course of his episcopate, but fast forwards to the miraculous appearance of Eulalia before Leovigild to beat him into restoring the exiled Masona, and to the failed attempt by Nepopis to liberate the riches of the churches and dispatch them 'to his own city'.[92]

From the perspective of the king, the overall strategy is laid bare by a case discussed at the Twelfth Council of Toledo in 681. Stephen II of Mérida testified that he had been forced by Wamba (672–680) to ordain a new bishop at a monastery in the village of 'Aquis' (probably Alange, to the southeast of the city). This was not an episcopal seat but the site of 'the venerable body of the most holy confessor Pimenius', apparently the dearly departed prelate of Medina Sidonia. The whistle-blower testimony led to a realization that the king had been making other uncanonical appointments in the suburbs of the royal capital and beyond; though the new bishop was removed from office, a proper diocese was sought for him since he had been ordained 'not out of ambition but by force', reversing the critical language used of converts at the Arian synod of 579.[93] Similarly, in the VSPE, when Reccared is at last enjoined to take action against Sunna, still on the scene in Mérida throughout the reign of Nepopis and the restoration of Masona, an offer of ordination 'in whatever other city' is held out to him, even if he obstinately refuses the required conversion and penance and so is exiled to Mauretania.[94] Again, there is no outright deposition. For kings, bishops could be a lever of access to civic politics and to the power of saintly bodies, but they were also powerful local actors in their own right, to be co-opted as agents wherever possible and confronted only with extreme care.[95] For bishops, kings could likewise be a useful tool, a lever of access to appointment or promotion. They might signal such a partnership through factional 'Arianism', or have the label attributed to them by others on the outside looking in, but this was not in the first place about religion. One can read right past the fact that our second author says nothing about Nepopis and his doctrinal allegiance: the simplest interpretation of the situation is that he replaces Masona as the 'Nicene' bishop while Sunna stays on as 'Arian'

91 VSPE 5.6.135–40; II Braga (572) cap. 7; cf. II Braga (572) cap. 6, 9, 12; XI Toledo (675) 4.

92 VSPE 5.8; Fuentes Hinojo 2011, 320–33.

93 XII Toledo (681) 4; García Moreno 1974, 187, 'Pimenius', 97; Carmona Barrero and Calero Carretero 2016; Pachá 2019.

94 VSPE 5.11.53–81; Martin 2011; Vallejo Girvés 2013.

95 See e.g., XVI Toledo (693) 9; Orlandis and Ramos-Lissón 1986, 491–93; Martin 2003, 113–22, 198–203; Osland 2011.

bishop, both owing their position in some measure to the king regardless of his and their beliefs.[96]

The tribulations of our hero do not reach an end with his return to Mérida, the death of Leovigild, and the succession and conversion of Reccared: he soon faces an attempt on his life by Sunna and elements of the Gothic aristocracy, in which residential topography plays an important role. On false pretences, Sunna invites Masona to his house, but Masona counters this by inviting Sunna to his own house, the palace. Picking up *en route* the future king Witteric (603–610) to administer the fatal blow, the conspirators arrive only to be told to wait while Masona fetches his next-door neighbour Claudius, *dux* or military commander of the city of Mérida, evidently positioned strategically to exercise immediate influence over the episcopal complex. Once they have entered and been seated, Witteric finds himself mystically prevented from striking down either Masona or Claudius, both of whom we now learn were the intended targets; the plotters leave in a huff, while Witteric remains behind at the palace to offer his confession and himself as hostage. There he reveals a fall-back scheme to murder the bishop during the Easter procession from the 'senior church' or cathedral to the basilica of Santa Eulalia, when the villains would fall on him and his fellow celebrants at the same city gates earlier sanctified by the vision of Fidel.[97] On the appointed day, Claudius slaughters some of the would-be revolutionaries, detains the others, and arrests Sunna at home together with his cronies, binding them over to Reccared for sentencing to exile by law.[98]

This is the world of medieval Rome, fighting on the streets amongst fortified homes and religious processions.[99] It provides context for a noted late antique metrical inscription from Mérida, dating perhaps to the 580s and dedicating an unidentified *domus* to Eulalia. The text could be a claim staked to that space, or perhaps a sign of the factional affiliation of the occupants, whoever the cited 'enemy' might be:

> † Kindly disposed, hold this house in your ownership, Eulalia the martyr, so that the enemy [or Enemy], recognizing it, may withdraw in disorder, and so that this house, together with its inhabitants, may prosper in your favour. Amen.[100]

96 Alonso Campos 1986; Martín Viso 2008, 234–39; García Moreno 1974, 436, 'Nepopis', 170.

97 VSPE 5.10; 5.11.1–28; see Zerjadtke 2019, 76–80, 107–17.

98 VSPE 5.11.38–61; LI 2.1.8; Petit 2009, 39–42.

99 Wickham 2014, 181–258.

100 HE 13 (2007), 173, 62–64; CILAE 1407 (https://cil2digital.web.uah.es/inscripciones/ficha/942/1407); cf. Trillmich 2004; Gil 2009; Kurt 2016, 32.

By the late fifth century, the cityscape had been transformed from one dominated by imperial monuments, public spaces, and large decorated peristyle houses to one animated by reused fabric and smaller utilitarian subdivision apartments. Nevertheless, the power players of our drama still moved amongst the grandest churches and semi-private residences which set the stage for the performance of élite status.[101] After Masona has finally regained his lost basilicas by royal writ, one Vagrila seeks sanctuary at the extramural site, and is handed a penance of enslavement to the Church for his participation in the plot, obliged to march on foot before the horse of his priest 'without the support of any carriage (*vehiculum*)'.[102] Recreating both the language of transit and the route taken by Eulalia in her passion, the bishop summons him back 'to the *atrium* which is situated within the walls of the city', the reception hall of the episcopal palace, to be pardoned along with all his family and estates, a performative procession once more linking these two foremost homes in the cityscape.[103]

The conspiracy suppressed, the last major event to be narrated before the death of Masona is the Frankish invasion of Gallia Narbonensis in support of certain Arian (or 'Arian') rebels. The author signals that he is treating it in brief, but the absence of Claudius, the erstwhile ally of Masona who according to John of Biclarum had commanded the successful defence for Reccared like Gideon against the Midianites, stands out regardless.[104] Instead we read only of victory, heralded by Masona and his congregation with Psalms, a procession to the basilica of Santa Eulalia, and Easter mass in celebration of peace.[105] A century earlier, when the great bridge over the Guadiana had been repaired in 483, a famous commemorative inscription cemented and celebrated the nexus of patronage between King Euric (466–484), the *dux* Salla, and Bishop Zeno which had made it happen.[106] Why then in the telling of this moment of final victory should the partnership of Reccared and Claudius be fractured from Masona? Perhaps it had for the time being superseded the need for the king to work with and through the bishop of Mérida to wield authority at the local level. Perhaps this was the moment when some other faction within the city (say, that of Eleutherius) took the opportunity to side-line the lineage of Paul, Fidel, and Masona with all

101 Osland 2016 and 2017; Mateos Cruz and Sánchez Ramos 2020; and see e.g., Alba Calzado 1996, 1997, 2004, and 2011.

102 VSPE 5.11.86–103.

103 VSPE 5.11.86–114; Godoy Fernández and Tuset Bertrán 1994.

104 VSPE 5.12.1–24; Ioh. Bicl. 90; Judges 7.

105 VSPE 5.12.25–37.

106 Fernández 2016a; Fernández 2017, 166–68; Osland 2019.

their many liabilities, along with their champion the second author of the VSPE.[107] Certainly the last two bishops profiled, Innocent and Renovatus, are scarcely more than virtuous types, and the writer passes swiftly on to his closing remarks evoking the tombs of the bishops and of Eulalia, through whom all signs and wonders are possible.[108]

Conclusion

> In what case do the names of cities belong [to express location]? When they are first or third declension, *e.g. Emerita, Emeritae, Carthago, Carthaginis*, they belong in the dative case: if someone asks, 'Where are you?', answer in the dative case, 'I am at Mérida', 'I am at Cartagena'. But when they are second declension, *e.g. Toletum, Toleti*, they belong in the genitive case: answer in the genitive case, 'I am at Toledo'.[109]

When Reccared presided over the Third Council of Toledo and the conversion of the Visigoths in 589, he embodied Constantine at Nicaea and Marcian at Chalcedon—no, he surpassed them, for those prior assemblies had only condemned the heresies of Arius and his ilk, whereas the 'baptism of Spain' obliterated Arianism once and for all.[110] It is tempting to see the formation of the Visigothic state through the lens of *imitatio imperii* interposed by such sources, the orthodox prince imposing his will upon the confessional factions of his realm, forging unity from diversity by his *fiat*.[111] Yet the outward Arians and Nicenes mixed up together in gift and patronage at San Martín de Asán compel us to rethink the relationship between royal politics and religious identities. The VSPE grants us unique access to the local horizon of civic concord and conflict, and what at first seems to be the message of this complex and compelling text is the confrontation of an Arian faction sponsored from Toledo with a Nicene resistance on the ground in Mérida championed by its bishop Masona, a triumphant victory of the heavenly over the earthly city, the 'Peninsular Rome' over the 'Constantinople of the West'.[112] But the shadowy second narrator of the drama is no simple partisan for the victorious side: witness his suppression from the historical record of

107 See Dey 2018, 179–80.

108 VSPE 5.14; 5.15.

109 Julian of Toledo, *Art of Grammar* 1.4.75–76 (ed. Maestre Yenes 1973).

110 Ioh. Bicl. 91; Linehan 1993, 22–31; Stocking 2000, 59–88.

111 Castellanos 2012.

112 Escudero Manzano 2016, 728–29; Castillo Maldonado 1999, 36–38.

Hermenegild, christened martyr by Gregory the Great (and recognized as such by Valerius of Bierzo), and his absence of interest in the aftermath of 589.[113] With the coming to light of the funerary slab of the archdeacon Eleutherius, prominently placed in the necropolis beneath the basilica of Santa Eulalia, we can appreciate that this source is only secondarily about either royal politics or religious identities: it is firstly an account of civic factions competing amongst themselves for advantage, a struggle in which confession was foremost a flag of allegiance.[114] At the same time, it is a settling of scores, not by the winners but by a spokesman for the losers, an answering of charges, a setting of the record straight by those in outright defeat or incipient decline.

Much of part two of the VSPE is concerned with property and its intersection with ecclesiastical politics: the career of Bishop Paul, the terms of his testament and their execution, the power struggle surrounding his nephew Fidel and his irregular claim to episcopal succession. Rather than simply pass over them in silence, the author is all too ready to engage in special pleading for their dubious arrangements; sides had been taken, and they still mattered generations later, however uncanonical murmuring about bishops *post mortem* might be.[115] What emerges is a city with a bipolar topography, the cathedral within the walls where Masona was based, the basilica of Santa Eulalia without the walls where his rival Sunna sought to preside. The author tries to bind these together for good through narrative, but his miraculous midnight processions dramatize the challenge of controlling both at once. We can discern at least two factions in Mérida: one tracing its origin back to Paul, looking for legitimacy through custodianship of Eulalia herself and running up the 'Nicene' banner in so doing, the other vilified as 'Arian' but for much of the story simply better at mobilizing royal favour, its members including Sunna, Nepopis (seemingly Arian and Nicene bishop respectively), and maybe even the first author, responsible for part one of the VSPE. By the end of the action, the latter party, allied with Leovigild, has lost and the former, those sympathetic to Reccared, are in the ascendant. We may even glimpse a third faction emerging, pro-Reccared too and counting Claudius and perhaps Eleutherius in its number, ultimately to leave our second author on the margins. Emblematic of the prevailing fluidity of affinity is the important bit player Witteric, sometime 'Arian' rebel, a chancer whom we find before long sitting on the throne of a Nicene realm.[116]

113 Valerius of Bierzo, *On the Empty Wisdom of the World* 6 (ed. Díaz y Díaz 2006).

114 Castillo Lozano 2020.

115 Mérida (666) 17.

116 Castillo Lozano 2016–2017, 171–75.

But was this the triumph of orthodoxy, of 'all become one kingdom in harmony' as Leander of Seville proclaimed in celebration of official conversion?[117] Just over a decade later, two deposed and exiled bishops in the east Roman enclave around Cartagena side-stepped the exarch (governor) and appealed to Gregory the Great in Rome, who briskly set aside the merits of the case and intervened through an envoy to arrange reinstatement: both bishops and pope stood to gain from each other by exchanging reciprocal recognition to the exclusion of rival players in the game of power.[118] In spite of its charged rhetoric of theology and theocracy, not everyone in the world of Late Antiquity prioritized doctrinal commitment above everything else.[119] In Hispania, *something* had to be done about those Arians, whether of commitment or convenience, after 589; *some* flexibility and accommodation were required to reconcile them to the new dispensation, even extending to their churches and relics.[120] Key to this process is the politics of faction, which at the most local level centred on confession no more than on property, on private belief no more than on personal profit: religious identities could be discursive, deployed by the various parties to secure and signal their affinities, within and beyond the city. Leovigild had aimed to found a kingdom on such a confessional label, but at least one faction, in Mérida, used its opposite to pull away and apart; for Reccared at Toledo, whatever he believed, there were to be no more 'Arians', only the new badge of loyalty to his own regime.[121]

Where then does this place us on the passage from Roman emperorship to Visigothic kingship? Looking back to the beginning, it was the collision of Rome with the Hellenistic world at the moment of its return to rule by a king in all but name which gave the Roman empire its distinctive mode of operation, as the Greek city-states presumed from the habit of ages to present their petitions for advantage directly to Augustus and expect a personal response.[122] However much the state expanded in size and scope over the centuries which followed, the language of imperial government retained a critical register of dialogue between the emperor and the cities (and their factions), on their terms as much as on his, as a means of realizing

117 Leander of Seville, *Homily*, III Toledo; Godoy Fernández and Vilella Masana 1986.

118 Greg. Mag. Reg. 13.47–50 (ed. Norberg 1982); Salvador Ventura 2013, 255–57; Ferreiro 2020, 173–76; Wood 2020.

119 Markus 1988, 72–104; Cameron 2011, 14–32; Whelan 2018, esp. 139–217.

120 III Toledo (589) 9; II Zaragoza (592) 1–3; Collins 1991; cf. Mikat 1984; Chavarría Arnau 2017; Chase 2020.

121 See Valverde 1999.

122 Millar 1992, 611–20.

rule on the ground.[123] And this remained true even after Rome in what had been Augusta Emerita, where the contours of local society offered both a challenge and an opportunity for the imposition of authority.[124] As Julian of Toledo reminds us in his treatise on grammar, the Visigothic kingdom was a realm of cities: it understood itself as such, and had to be conquered and governed as such. The lesson of the *Lives of the Fathers* is that Toledo, without Mérida, would have been inconceivable as we know it.[125] In ruling through engagement with their subjects as dynamic civic societies the Visigothic kings were imitating their imperial forebears, and the politics of faction practised to this end is the respect in which their kingdom most closely resembled an empire.

Bibliography

Alba Calzado, Miguel A., 'Consideraciones arqueológicas en torno al siglo V en Mérida', in *Mérida: Excavaciones Arqueológicas*, 2 (1996), 361–86

Alba Calzado, Miguel A., 'Sobre el ámbito doméstico de época visigoda en Mérida', in *Mérida: Excavaciones Arqueológicas*, 3 (1997), 387–418

Alba Calzado, Miguel A., 'Sobre las casas de atrio o/y peristilo: intervención arqueológica realizada en el nº 19 de la calle Suárez Somonte (Mérida)', in *Mérida: Excavaciones Arqueológicas*, 10 (2004), 257–76

Alba Calzado, Miguel A., 'Los espacios domésticos en la ciudad visigoda de Emerita (ss. V–VIII)', in *Actas del Congreso Internacional 1910–2010. El yacimiento emeritense*, ed. by J. M. Álvarez Martínez and P. Mateos Cruz (Mérida: Museo Nacional de Arte Romano, 2011), pp. 521–46

Alba Calzado, Miguel A., 'Secuencias en la transformación de *Augusta Emerita* (siglos I–IX): tres concepciones distintas de ser ciudad', in *Entre civitas y madīna. El mundo de las ciudades en la Península Ibérica y en el norte de África* (*siglos IV–IX*), ed. by S. Panzram and L. Callegarin (Madrid: Casa de Velázquez, 2018), pp. 51–74

Alonso Campos, José Ignacio, 'Sunna, Masona y Nepopis: las luchas religiosas durante la dinastía de Leovigildo', in *Antigüedad y Cristianismo*, 3 (1986), 151–58

Álvarez Martínez, José María, *El puente romano de Mérida* (Badajoz: Museo Nacional de Arte Romano, 1983)

123 Lenski 2016, 1–23, 167–206.

124 Castellanos 2020, 59–82; cf. Ripoll 2000; Velázquez and Ripoll 2000, 541–43.

125 See Brown 1974, 27, 32–33.

Alves-Dias, Maria Manuela, Catarina Gaspar, and Virgilio Lopes, 'Mértola en la Antigüedad tardía: nuevos datos arqueológicos y epigráficos', in *Habis*, 44 (2013), 247–67

Amundsen, Darrel W., 'Medieval Canon Law on Medical and Surgical Practice by the Clergy', in *Bulletin of the History of Medicine*, 52.1 (1978), 22–44

Arce, Javier, 'The City of Mérida (*Emerita*) in the *Vitas patrum Emeritensium* (VIth Century AD)', in *East and West: Modes of Communication*, ed. by E. Chrysos and I. Wood (Leiden: Brill, 1999), pp. 1–14

Arce, Javier, *Mérida tardorromana: 300–580 d.C.* (Mérida: Museo Nacional de Arte Romano, 2002)

Augustine of Hippo, *Sermons*, ed. by G. Morin, *Sancti Augustini Sermones post Maurinos reperti* (Rome: Tipografia Poliglotta Vaticana, 1930)

Barrett, Graham, 'Hispania at Home and Abroad', in *Beyond the Reconquista: New Directions in the History of Medieval Iberia (711–1085)*, ed. by S. Barton and R. Portass (Leiden: Brill, 2020), pp. 52–119

Barroso Cabrera, Rafael, Jorge Morín de Pablos, and Isabel M. Sánchez Ramos, *Hermenegildus rex. Príncipe, usurpador y mártir* (Madrid: Audema, 2020)

Brown, Peter, '*Mohammed and Charlemagne* by Henri Pirenne', in *Daedalus*, 103.1 (1974), 25–33

Brown, Peter, *The Cult of the Saints: Its Rise and Function in Latin Christianity*, new ed. (Chicago, IL: University of Chicago Press, 2015)

Brubaker, Leslie, and Chris Wickham, 'Processions, Power, and Community Identity: East and West', in *Empires and Communities in the Post-Roman and Islamic World, c. 400–1000 CE*, ed. by W. Pohl and R. Kramer (Oxford: Oxford University Press, 2021), pp. 121–87

Buchberger, Erica, *Shifting Ethnic Identities in Spain and Gaul, 500–700: From Romans to Goths and Franks* (Amsterdam: Amsterdam University Press, 2017)

Buenacasa Pérez, Carles, 'Espiritualidad vs racionalidad económica: los dependientes eclesiásticos y el perjuicio económico a la iglesia de Dumio en el testamento de Ricimiro (656)', in *Polis*, 16 (2004), 7–32

Cameron, Alan, *The Last Pagans of Rome* (Oxford: Oxford University Press, 2011)

Carmona Barrero, Juan Diego, and José Ángel Calero Carretero, 'La diócesis de Aquis en tiempos de Wamba (667–681). Propuestas para su identificación con Alange', in *La enseñanza en Tierro de Barros. Actas de las VII Jornadas de Historia de Almendralejo y Tierra de Barros* (Almendralejo: Asociación Histórica de Almendralejo, 2016), pp. 181–204

Castellanos, Santiago, 'Las reliquias de santos y su papel social: cohesión comunitaria y control episcopal en Hispania (ss. V–VII)', in *Polis*, 8 (1996), 5–21

Castellanos, Santiago, 'El testamento de Ricimiro de Dumio en el contexto de la consolidación episcopal en la Hispania tardoantigua', in *Hispania Antiqua*, 22 (1998), 427–38

Castellanos, Santiago, 'The Significance of Social Unanimity in a Visigothic Hagiography: Keys to an Ideological Screen', in *Journal of Early Christian Studies*, 11.3 (2003), 387–419

Castellanos, Santiago, 'Creating New Constantines at the End of the Sixth Century', in *Historical Research*, 85.230 (2012), 556–75

Castellanos, Santiago, 'Política y registro hagiográfico en la Hispania visigoda: Leovigildo en las *Vitae*', in *Studia historica in honorem Prof. Urbano Espinosa Ruiz*, ed. by M. J. Castillo Pascual and P. Iguácel de la Cruz (Logroño: Universidad de La Rioja, 2018), pp. 485–99

Castellanos, Santiago, *The Visigothic Kingdom in Iberia: Construction and Invention* (Philadelphia, PA: University of Pennsylvania Press, 2020)

Castillo Lozano, José Ángel, *Categorías de poder en el reino visigodo de Toledo: los tiranos en las obras de Juan de Bíclaro, Isidoro de Sevilla y Julian de Toledo. Antigüedad y Cristianismo* 33–34 (2016–2017)

Castillo Lozano, José Ángel, 'Luchas de poder en la Mérida visigoda', in *Intus-Legere Historia*, 14.2 (2020), 104–23

Castillo Maldonado, Pedro, '¿Rivalidades ciudadanas en textos hagiográficos hispanos?', in *Florentia Iliberritana*, 10 (1999), 29–40

Castillo Maldonado, Pedro, '*In ecclesia contra ecclesiam*: algunos ejemplos de disputas, violencias y facciones clericales en las iglesias tardoantiguas hispanas', in *Antiquité Tardive*, 15 (2007), 263–76

Castillo Maldonado, Pedro, '*In hora mortis*: deceso, duelo, rapiña y legado en la muerte del obispo visigótico', in *Hispania Sacra*, 64.129 (2012), 7–28

Castro, Dolores, 'Toledo, *locus terribilis*. Iglesia y milagro en el *De viris illustribus* de Ildefonso de Toledo', in *En la España Medieval*, 39 (2016), 49–72

Castro, Dolores, 'El obispo en movimiento. El itinerario de Masona entre Mérida, Toledo y el exilio', in *Obispos y monasterios en la Edad Media. Trayectorias personales, organización eclesiástica y dinámicas materiales*, ed. by A. Vanina Neyra and M. Pérez (Buenos Aires: Sociedad Argentina de Estudios Medievales, 2020), pp. 23–53

Chalon, Michel, 'L'inscription d'une église rurale du territoire narbonnais au Ve siècle', in *Pallas*, 84 (2010), 145–75

Chaparro Gómez, César, 'Notas de lexicología: el campo léxico de la colectividad en *Vitas sanctorum patrum Emeretensium*', in *Estudios dedicados a Carlos Callejo Serrano* (Cáceres: Diputación Provincial de Cáceres, 1979), pp. 223–44

Chaparro Gómez, César, '*Famulus, servus* y otros términos referidos al servicio en *Vitas sanctorum patrum Emeretensium*', in *Actas de las Primeras Jornadas sobre manifestaciones religiosas de la Lusitania* (Cáceres: Universidad de Extremadura, 1986), pp. 51–59

Chaparro Gómez, César, 'Significado de las *Vitas sanctorum patrum Emeretensium*: lectura desde sus fuentes', in *Humanitas in honorem Antonio Fontán* (Madrid: Gredos, 1992), pp. 339–49

Chase, Nathan P., 'From Arianism to Orthodoxy: The Role of the Rites of Initiation in Uniting the Visigothic Kingdom', in *Hispania Sacra*, 72.146 (2020), 427–38

Chavarría Arnau, Alexandra, 'Monasterios, campesinos y *villae* en la Hispania visigoda: la trágica historia del abad Nancto', in *Mélanges d'Antiquité tardive. Studiola in honorem Noël Duval*, ed. by C. Balmelle, P. Chevalier, and G. Ripoll (Turnhout: Brepols, 2004), pp. 113–25

Chavarría Arnau, Alexandra, 'Finding Invisible Arians: An Archaeological Perspective on Churches, Baptism, and Religious Competition in 6th-Century Spain', in *Hortus Artium Medievalium*, 23.2 (2017), 674–85

Claude, Dietrich, 'Prosopographie des spanischen Suebenreiches', in *Francia*, 6 (1978), 647–76

Collins, Roger, 'Mérida and Toledo, 550–585', in *Visigothic Spain: New Approaches*, ed. by E. James (Oxford: Clarendon Press, 1980), pp. 189–219; repr. in R. Collins, *Law, Culture, and Regionalism in Early Medieval Spain* (London: Variorum Collected Studies, 1992), § I

Collins, Roger, '¿Dónde estaban los arrianos en el año 589?', in *Concilio III de Toledo: XIV Centenario, 589–1989* (Toledo: Arzobispado de Toledo, 1991), pp. 211–22

Collins, Roger, 'An Unreliable Witness? *Vitas sanctorum patrum Emeretensium* and Religious Conflict in Visigothic Spain', in *Revista Diálogos Mediterrânicos*, 21 (2021), 36–58

Cordero Ruiz, Tomás, 'Una nueva propuesta sobre los límites del *Ager emeritensis* durante el imperio romano y la Antigüedad tardía', in *Zephyrus*, 65 (2010), 149–65

Cordero Ruiz, Tomás, and Bruno Franco Moreno, 'El territorio emeritense durante la Antigüedad tardía y la Alta Edad Media', in *Visigodos y omeyas: el territorio*, ed. by L. Caballero Zoreda, P. Mateos Cruz, and T. Cordero Ruiz (Madrid: Consejo Superior de Investigaciones Científicas, 2012), pp. 147–69

Cossío, Manuel B., *El entierro del Conde de Orgaz* (Madrid: V. Suárez, 1914)

Curado, Blas, *La medicina en Mérida según la Vida de los padres emeritenses* (Mérida: Museo Nacional de Arte Romano, 2004)

Dal Santo, Matthew, *Debating the Saints' Cult in the Age of Gregory the Great* (Oxford: Oxford University Press, 2012)

Davies, Wendy, *Acts of Giving: Individual, Community, and Church in Tenth-Century Christian Spain* (Oxford: Oxford University Press, 2007)

Dey, Hendrik, 'Privileged Cities: Provincial, Regional, and Imperial Capitals', in *Antiquité Tardive*, 26 (2018), 163–95

Díaz, Pablo C., 'Propiedad y explotación de la tierra en la Lusitania tardoantigua', in *Studia Historica. Historia Antigua*, 10–11 (1992–1993), 297–309

Díaz, Pablo C., 'El peregrino en la ciudad: expresionismo religioso en la *Hispania* tardoantigua', in *Iberia*, 3 (2000), 151–66

Díaz, Pablo C., 'Mérida tardoantica: l'apoteosi di una città cristiana', in *Reti Medievali*, 11.2 (2010), 67–79

Díaz Duckwen, María Luján, 'La Biblia dentro de la hagiografía tardoantigua. Un ejemplo hispano: *Vitas sanctorum patrum Emeritensium*', in *Bibliotheca Augustiniana*, 9.1 (2018), 90–105

Díaz y Díaz, Manuel C., *Valerio del Bierzo. Su persona. Su obra* (León: Caja España de Inversiones-Archivo Histórico Diocesano de León, 2006)

Dietz, Maribel, *Wandering Monks, Virgins, and Pilgrims: Ascetic Travel in the Mediterranean World, A.D. 300–800* (University Park, PA: Pennsylvania State University Press, 2005)

Drews, Wolfram, 'Hermenegild's Rebellion and Conversion: Merovingian and Byzantine Connections', in *East and West in the Early Middle Ages: The Merovingian Kingdoms in Mediterranean Perspective*, ed. by S. Esders, Y. Fox, Y. Hen, and L. Sarty (Cambridge: Cambridge University Press, 2019), pp. 74–86

Dumézil, Bruno, and Sylvie Joye, 'Les *Dialogues* de Grégoire le Grand et leur postérité: une certaine idée de la réforme?', in *Médiévales: Langues, Textes, Histoire*, 62 (2012), 13–31

Escudero Manzano, Gonzalo J., 'Aproximaciones hermenéuticas sobre el Agustinianismo en la Hispania tardoantigua: Mérida a principios del siglo VII', in *Cauriensia*, 11 (2016), 713–30

Fear, Andrew T., *Lives of the Visigothic Fathers* (Liverpool: Liverpool University Press, 1997)

Fear, Andrew T., 'The Ghost of Saint Desiderius', in *La Corónica*, 29.2 (2001), 79–93

Feijóo, Manuel, 'Espacios urbanos e identidad religiosa en el Occidente europeo durante la Antigüedad tardía', in *Antesteria*, 4 (2015), 311–25

Felix of Toledo, *Life of Julian*, ed. by José Carlos Martín-Iglesias and Valeriano Yarza Urquiola, *Iulianus Toletanus, Felix Toletanus, Iulianus Toletanus* (*Ps.*). *Opera II: Elogium Ildefonsi, Vita Iuliani* (*auctore Felice Toletano*), *Antikeimena, Fragmenta, Ordo annorum mundi*, CCSL 115B (Turnhout: Brepols, 2014)

Fernández, Damián, 'Persuading the Powerful in Post-Roman Iberia: King Euric, Local Powers, and the Formation of a State Paradigm', in *Motions of Late Antiquity: Essays on Religion, Politics, and Society in Honour of Peter Brown*, ed. by J. Kreiner and H. Reimitz (Turnhout: Brepols, 2016a), pp. 107–28

Fernández, Damián, 'Property, Social Status, and Church Building in Visigothic Iberia', in *Journal of Late Antiquity*, 9.2 (2016b), 512–41

Fernández, Damián, *Aristocrats and Statehood in Western Iberia, 300–600 CE* (Philadelphia, PA: University of Pennsylvania Press, 2017)
Fernández, Damián, 'Trial Witnesses, Social Hierarchies, and State Building in the Visigothic Kingdom of Toledo', in *Early Medieval Europe*, 28.4 (2020), 509–31
Ferreiro, Alberto, *Epistolae plenae: The Correspondence of the Bishops of Hispania with the Bishops of Rome* (*Third through Seventh Centuries*) (Leiden: Brill, 2020)
Ford, Richard, *A Handbook for Travellers in Spain*, 3rd ed., 2 vols (London: John Murray, 1855)
Fouracre, Paul, 'Merovingian History and Merovingian Hagiography', in *Past & Present*, 127 (1990), 3–38
Fuentes Hinojo, Pablo, 'Patrocinio eclesiástico, rituales de poder e historia urbana en la Hispania tardoantigua (siglos IV al VI)', in *Studia Historica. Historia Antigua*, 26 (2008), 315–44
Fuentes Hinojo, Pablo, '*Adventus praesulis*: consenso social y rituales de poder en el mundo urbano de la Antigüedad tardía', in *Studia Historica. Historia Antigua*, 29 (2011), 293–339
Fuentes Hinojo, Pablo, 'Sucesión dinástica y legitimidad episcopal en la Mérida visigoda', in *En la España Medieval*, 35 (2012), 11–33
Gaiffier, Baudouin de, 'Le légendier hispanique', in *Homenaje a Fray Justo Pérez de Urbel*, 2 vols (Silos: Abadía de Silos, 1976–1977), vol. 2, pp. 117–23
García Iglesias, Luis, 'Aspectos económico-sociales de la Mérida visigótica', in *Revista de Estudios Extremeños*, 30.2 (1974), 321–62
García Iglesias, Luis, 'Las posesiones de la iglesia emeritense en época visigoda', in *Estudios sobre la Antigüedad en homenaje al profesor Santiago Montero Díaz. Anejos de Gerión* 2 (Madrid: Universidad Complutense de Madrid, 1989), pp. 391–401
García Moreno, Luis A., 'Colonias de comerciantes orientales en la Península Ibérica: s. V–VII', in *Habis*, 3 (1972), 127–54
García Moreno, Luis A., *Prosopografía del reino visigodo de Toledo* (Salamanca: Universidad de Salamanca, 1974)
García Rodríguez, Carmen, *El culto de los santos en la España romana y visigoda* (Madrid: Consejo Superior de Investigaciones Científicas, 1966)
Garvin, Joseph N., *The Vitas sanctorum patrum Emeretensium* (Washington, DC: Catholic University of America Press, 1946)
Gil, Juan, 'La pasión de Santa Eulalia', in *Habis*, 31 (2000), 403–16
Gil, Juan, 'Inimicus (Vives, ICERV 348)', in *Habis*, 40 (2009), 247–50
Gil, Juan, *Scriptores Muzarabici saeculi VIII–XI*. Corpus Christianorum Continuatio Mediaevalis 65A-B, 2 vols (Turnhout: Brepols, 2020)
Gnilka, Christian, 'Die Seelentaube bei Prudentius', in *Philologus*, 155.1 (2011), 167–83

Godoy Fernández, Cristina, *Arqueología y liturgia. Iglesias hispánicas (siglos IV al VIII)* (Barcelona: Universitat de Barcelona, 1995)

Godoy Fernández, Cristina, and Francesc Tuset Bertrán, 'El *atrium* en las *Vitas sanctorum patrum Emeretensium.* ¿Una fórmula de la llamada arquitectura de poder?', in *Archivo Español de Arqueología*, 67.169–70 (1994), 209–21

Godoy Fernández, Cristina, and Josep Vilella Masana, 'De la *Fides gothica* a la Ortodoxia nicena: inicio de la teología política visigótica', in *Antigüedad y Cristianismo*, 3 (1986), 117–44

Graham, Stacey R., *The Dissemination of North African Christian and Intellectual Culture in Late Antiquity* (PhD Dissertation, University of California, Los Angeles, 2005)

Guiance, Ariel, 'Santos, reliquias y milagros en la hagiografía visigoda', in *Pecia*, 8–11 (2005), 245–60

Guiance, Ariel, 'Observations about a Controversial Hagiography: The *Vita vel gesta sancti Ildefonsi*', in *Imago Temporis. Medium Aevum*, 3 (2009), 99–122

Henriet, Patrick, 'La lettre d'Alphonse III, *rex Hispaniae*, aux chanoines de Saint-Martin de Tours (906)', in *Retour aux sources. Textes, études et documents d'histoire médiévale offerts à Michel Parisse*, ed. by S. Gouguenheim et al. (Paris: Picard, 2004), pp. 155–66

Hillgarth, Jocelyn N., 'Coins and Chronicles: Propaganda in Sixth-Century Spain and the Byzantine Background', in *Historia*, 15.4 (1966), 483–508; repr. in Jocelyn N. Hillgarth, *Visigothic Spain, Byzantium, and the Irish* (London: Variorum Collected Studies, 1985), § II

Hoz, María Paz de, *Inscripciones griegas de España y Portugal* (Madrid: Real Academia de la Historia, 2014)

Hoz García-Bellido, María-Paz de, 'Las inscripciones griegas como testimonio de la presencia de orientales en la Mérida visigoda', in *Munus quaesitum meritis. Homenaje a Carmen Codoñer*, ed. by G. Hinojo Andrés and J.C. Fernández Conde (Salamanca: Universidad de Salamanca, 2007), pp. 481–89

Hudson, Jared, *The Rhetoric of Roman Transportation: Vehicles in Latin Literature* (Cambridge: Cambridge University Press, 2021)

Jorge, A. M. C. M., *L'épiscopat de Lusitanie pendant l'Antiquité tardive (IIIe-VIIe siècles)* (Lisbon: Instituto Português de Arqueologia, 2002)

Juan, María Teresa de, 'La gestión de los bienes en la Iglesia hispana tardoantigua: confusión patrimonial y sus consecuencias', in *Polis*, 10 (1998), 167–80

Julian of Toledo, *Art of Grammar*, ed. by M. A. H. Maestre Yenes, *Ars Iuliani Toletani episcopi. Una gramática latina de la España visigoda. Estudio y edición crítica* (Toledo: Diputación de Toledo, 1973)

Julian of Toledo, *Codicil on Ildefonsus*, ed. by José Carlos Martín-Iglesias and Valeriano Yarza Urquiola, *Iulianus Toletanus, Felix Toletanus, Iulianus Toletanus (Ps.).*

Opera II: Elogium Ildefonsi, Vita Iuliani (auctore Felice Toletano), Antikeimena, Fragmenta, Ordo annorum mundi, CCSL 115B (Turnhout: Brepols, 2014)

Kampers, Gerd, *Personengeschichtliche Studien zum Westgotenreich in Spanien* (Münster: Aschendorff, 1979)

Koch, Manuel, 'La imperialización del reino visigodo bajo Leovigildo. ¿Es la *imitatio imperii* de Leovigildo la manifestación de un momento de cambio en la pretensión de poder y la ideología visigodas?', in *Pyrenae*, 39.2 (2008), 101–17

Koch, Manuel, *Ethnische Identität im Entstehungsprozess des spanischen Westgotenreiches* (Berlin: De Gruyter, 2012)

Koch, Manuel, 'Arianism and Ethnic Identity in Sixth-Century Visigothic Spain', in *Arianism: Roman Heresy and Barbarian Creed*, ed. by G. M. Berndt and R. Steinacher (Farnham: Ashgate, 2014), pp. 257–70

Koch, Manuel, 'Who are the Visigoths? Concepts of Ethnicity in the Kingdom of Toledo: A Case Study of the *Vitas sanctorum patrum Emeretensium*', in *The Visigothic Kingdom: The Negotiation of Power in Post-Roman Iberia*, ed. by S. Panzram and P. Pachá (Amsterdam: Amsterdam University Press, 2020), pp. 157–71

Kulikowski, Michael, *Late Roman Spain and its Cities* (Baltimore, MD: Johns Hopkins University Press, 2004)

Kurt, Andrew, 'Lay Piety in Visigothic Iberia: Liturgical and Paraliturgical Forms', in *Journal of Medieval Iberian Studies*, 8.1 (2016), 1–37

Kurt, Andrew, *Minting, State, and Economy in the Visigothic Kingdom: From Settlement in Aquitaine through the First Decade of the Muslim Conquest of Spain* (Amsterdam: Amsterdam University Press, 2020)

Lenski, Noel, *Constantine and the Cities. Imperial Authority and Civic Politics* (Philadelphia, PA: University of Pennsylvania Press, 2016)

Lester, Molly, '*Persecutio*, *Seductio*, and the Limits of Rhetorical Intolerance in Visigothic Iberia', in *Heirs of Roman Persecution: Studies on a Christian and Para-Christian Discourse in Late Antiquity*, ed. by É. Fournier and W. Mayer (London: Routledge, 2020), pp. 213–33

Liebeschuetz, Wolf, *East and West in Late Antiquity: Invasion, Settlement, Ethnogenesis, and Conflicts of Religion* (Leiden: Brill, 2015)

Linehan, Peter, *History and the Historians of Medieval Spain* (Oxford: Oxford University Press, 1993)

López Quiroga, Jorge, and Artemio M. Martínez Tejera, '*De corporibus defunctorum*: lectura e interpretación histórico-arqueológica del canon XVIII del primer concilio de Braga (a. 561) y su repercusión en la arquitectura hispana de la Antigüedad tardía', in *Morir en el mediterráneo medieval. Actas del III Congreso internacional de arqueología, arte e historia de la Antigüedad y Alta Edad Media peninsular*, ed. by J. López Quiroga and A. M. Martínez Tejera (Oxford: Archaeopress, 2009), pp. 153–84

Lorenzo-Rodríguez, Abel, '*More infantie a tergo corporis emendari*: violencia y disciplina en los ámbitos escolares hispanos (siglos IV–XII)', in *En la España Medieval*, 43 (2020), 205–22

Marcotegui Barber, Beatriz, 'El tratamiento historiográfico de San Hermenegildo', in *Anuario de Historia de la Iglesia*, 12 (2003), 289–302

Markus, Robert A., *Saeculum: History and Society in the Theology of St Augustine*, rev. ed. (Cambridge: Cambridge University Press, 1988)

Martin, Céline, *La géographie du pouvoir dans l'Espagne visigothique* (Villeneuve-d'Ascq: Presses Universitaires du Septentrion, 2003)

Martin, Céline, 'L'évêque dans un petit navire. Bannissement et relégation dans les *Vies des saints pères de Mérida*', in *Échanges, communications et réseaux dans le haut Moyen Âge*, ed. by A. Gautier and C. Martin (Turnhout: Brepols, 2011), pp. 45–56

Martín, José Carlos, 'Une nouvelle édition critique de la "Vita Desiderii" de Sisebut', in *Hagiographica*, 7 (2000), 127–80

Martín, José Carlos, 'El *Epitaphium Leandri, Isidori et Florentinae* (*ICERV* 272) o la compleja transmisión manuscrita de un texto epigráfico. Nueva edición y estudio', in *Euphrosyne*, 38 (2010), 139–63

Martín Viso, Iñaki, 'Propriété foncière et articulation socio-politique au Nord-Ouest de la Lusitanie (VIe et VIIe siècles)', in *Le Bréviaire d'Alaric. Aux origines du Code civil*, ed. by M. Rouche and B. Dumézil (Paris: Presses de l'Université Paris-Sorbonne, 2008), pp. 213–39

Martínez, Javier, and Patricia González, 'Knowledge and Specialised Trades in the Late Antique West: Medicine vs Engineering', in *Journal for Late Antique Religion and Culture*, 11 (2017), 38–58

Martínez Díez, Gonzalo, 'El patrimonio eclesiástico en la España visigoda. Estudio histórico-jurídico', in *Miscelánea Comillas*, 32 (1959), 5–200

Martínez Díez, Gonzalo, and Félix Rodríguez, *La colección canónica hispana*, 6 vols (Madrid: Consejo Superior de Investigaciones Científicas, 1966–2002)

Martínez Jiménez, Javier, Isaac Sastre de Diego, and Carlos Tejerizo García, *The Iberian Peninsula between 300 and 850: An Archaeological Perspective* (Amsterdam: Amsterdam University Press, 2018)

Mateos Cruz, Pedro, 'Identificación del Xenodochium fundado por Masona en Mérida', in *IV Reunió d'arqueología cristiana hispànica*, ed. by J. M. Gurt and N. Tena (Barcelona: Institut d'Estudis Catalans, 1995), pp. 309–16

Mateos Cruz, Pedro, *La basílica de Santa Eulalia de Mérida. Arqueología y urbanismo* (Madrid: Consejo Superior de Investigaciones Científicas, 1999)

Mateos Cruz, Pedro, '*Augusta Emerita*, de capital de la *Diocesis Hispaniarum* a sede temporal visigoda', in *Sedes regiae (ann. 400–800)*, ed. by G. Ripoll and J. M. Gurt (Barcelona: Reial Acadèmia de Bones Lletres, 2000), pp. 491–520

Mateos Cruz, Pedro, 'A propósito del edificio identificado como el *xenodochium* de Masona en Mérida. Aspectos cronológicos y funcionales', in *SPAL: Revista de Prehistoria y Arqueología de la Universidad de Sevilla*, 31.1 (2022), 426–42

Mateos Cruz, Pedro, and Isabel Sánchez Ramos, 'Arquitectura residencial urbana en *Lusitania* en la Antigüedad tardía. Topografía, edilicia y dinámicas de transformación', in *Mytra*, 6 (2020), 397–429

Mateos Martín de Rodrigo, Antonio, *Las pasiones de Santa Eulalia de Mérida o África e Hispania* (Mérida: Museo Nacional de Arte Romano, 2009)

Mateos Martín de Rodrigo, Antonio, 'Santa Eulalia de Mérida y la *mansio Perceiana*', in *El Hinojal*, 11 (2018), 8–33; 13 (2019), 8–41

Maya Sánchez, Antonio, 'La versión primitiva de la *Vita Fructuosi*', in *Habis*, 9 (1978), 169–96

Maya Sánchez, Antonio, *Vitas sanctorum patrum Emeretensium*, CCSL 116 (Turnhout: Brepols, 1992)

Maya Sánchez, Antonio, 'De Leovigildo perseguidor y Masona mártir', in *Emerita*, 62.1 (1994), 167–86

McClanan, Anne L., '"Weapons to Probe the Womb": The Material Culture of Abortion and Contraception in the Early Byzantine Period', in *The Material Culture of Sex, Procreation, and Marriage in Premodern Europe*, ed. by A. L. McClanan and K. R. Encarnación (New York, NY: Palgrave, 2002), pp. 33–57

Menéndez Bueyes, Luis R., '*Sine cerere et libero friget Venus*: el alcoholismo como problema de salud en el monacato visigodo', in *Hispania Sacra*, 71.143 (2019), 25–38

Mentxaka, Rosa, 'Reflexiones histórico-jurídicas sobre el martirio de Eulalia de Mérida', in *Seminarios Complutenses de Derecho Romano*, 33 (2020), 141–178

Mikat, Paul, *Doppelbesetzung oder Ehrentitulatur: zur Stellung des westgotisch-arianischen Episkopates nach der Konversion von 587/89* (Opladen: Westdeutscher Verlag, 1984)

Millar, Fergus, *The Emperor in the Roman World (31 BC–AD 337)*, 2nd ed. (London: Duckworth, 1992)

Mistry, Zubin, *Abortion in the Early Middle Ages, c. 500–900* (Woodbridge: York Medieval Press, 2015)

Mistry, Zubin, 'The Womb of the Church: Uterine Expulsion in the Early Middle Ages', in *Cultural Constructions of the Uterus in Pre-Modern Societies, Past and Present*, ed. by M. E. Couto-Ferreira and L. Verderame (Newcastle: Cambridge Scholars Publishing, 2018), 155–74

Moreira, Isabel, *Dreams, Visions, and Spiritual Authority in Merovingian Gaul* (Ithaca, NY: Cornell University Press, 2000)

Mülke, Markus, 'Romana religio oder catholica fides? Die Westgotenkönig Leovigild und das arianische Reichskonzil von 580 n.Chr. in Toledo', in *Frühmittelalterliche Studien*, 43.1 (2009), 53–70

Murray, Alexander Callander, 'Chronology and the Composition of the Histories of Gregory of Tours', in *Journal of Late Antiquity*, 1.1 (2008), 157–96

Nicetas David, *Life of Patriarch Ignatius*, ed. and trans. by Andrew Smithies and John M. Duffy, *Nicetas David: The Life of Patriarch Ignatius* (Washington, DC: Dumbarton Oaks, 2013)

Norton, Peter, *Episcopal Elections, 250–600: Hierarchy and Popular Will in Late Antiquity* (Oxford: Oxford University Press, 2007)

Orlandis, José, and Domingo Ramos-Lissón, *Historia de los concilios de la España romana y visigoda* (Pamplona: Universidad de Navarra, 1986)

Orlandis, José, *La vida en España en tiempo de los godos* (Madrid: Rialp, 1991)

Osland, Daniel, 'Tribute and Coinage in the Visigothic Kingdom: On the Role of the Bishop', in *Anas*, 24 (2011), 71–95

Osland, Daniel, 'Documenting Change in Late Antique Emerita through the Ceramic Evidence', in *Journal of Late Antiquity*, 5.2 (2012), 322–44

Osland, Daniel, 'Abuse or Reuse? Public Space in Late Antique Emerita', in *American Journal of Archaeology*, 120.1 (2016), 67–97

Osland, Daniel, 'Housing in Late Antique Augusta Emerita: The End of the Peristyle House', in *Oxford Journal of Archaeology*, 36.1 (2017), 85–106

Osland, Daniel, 'Text and Context: Patronage in Late Antique Mérida', in *Studies in Late Antiquity*, 3.4 (2019), 595–625

Pachá, Paulo, 'Gift and Conflict: Forms of Social Domination in the Iberian Early Middle Ages', in *Networks and Neighbours*, 2.2 (2014), 251–77

Pachá, Paulo, 'To Name and Control: Space and Power in the Integration Process of the Visigothic Kingdom of Toledo', in *Mélanges de la Casa de Velázquez*, 49.2 (2019), 109–31

Panzram, Sabine, 'Eulalia und die Bischöfe von Merida. Von der "Handlungsmacht" einer Heiligen zur Zeit der Westgoten', in *Formen und Funktionen von Leitbildern*, ed. by J. Hahn and M. Vielberg (Stuttgart: Franz Steiner Verlag, 2007), pp. 177–225

Panzram, Sabine, 'Mérida contra Toledo, Eulalia contra Leocadia: listados "falsificados" de obispos como medio de autorepresentación municipal', in *Espacios urbanos en el Occidente mediterráneo (s. VI–VIII)*, ed. by A. García (Toledo: Toletum Visigodo, 2010), pp. 123–30

Paul of Aegina, *Epitome of Medicine*, ed. by Johann L. Heiberg, *Paulus Aegineta*, 2 vols (Leipzig: Teubner, 1921–1924)

Pérez Martín, Antonio, 'Observaciones a Liber Iudiciorum 11.3', in *Historia, Instituciones, Documentos*, 14 (1987), 141–59

Pérez Sánchez, Dionisio, 'Sociedad y relaciones de dependencia en la Lusitania tardorromana y visigoda', in *Studia Historica. Historia Antigua*, 10–11 (1992–1993), 311–18

Pérez Sánchez, Dionisio, 'Algunas consideraciones sobre el ceremonial y el poder político en la Mérida visigoda', in *Studia Historica. Historia Antigua*, 20 (2002), 245–66

Petit, Carlos, '*Rex iudex*. El momento judicial del rey de Toledo', in *Procesos, inquisiciones, pruebas. Homenaje a Mario Sbriccoli*, ed. by E. Conte and M. Madero (Buenos Aires: Manantial, 2009), pp. 39–75

Pseudo-Isidore, *Chronicle*, ed. by F. González Muñoz, *La chronica gothorum pseudo-isidoriana (ms. Paris BN 6113). Edición crítica, traducción y estudio* (Noia: Toxosoutos, 2000)

Ramírez Sádaba, José Luis, 'Epigrafía monumental cristiana en Extremadura', in *Repertorio de arquitectura cristiana en Extremadura. Época tardoantigua y altomedieval*, ed. by P. Mateos Cruz and L. Caballero Zoreda (Madrid: Consejo Superior de Investigaciones Científicas, 2003), pp. 271–91

Ramírez Sádaba, José Luis, and Pedro Mateos Cruz, *Catálogo de las inscripciones cristianas de Mérida* (Mérida: Museo Nacional de Arte Romano, 2000)

Ramírez Sánchez, Manuel, 'La escritura de las inscripciones cristianas de Mérida. Algunas notas a propósito de varias publicaciones recientes', in *Paleografía I. La escritura en España hasta 1250*, ed. by J. A. Fernández Flórez and S. Serna Serna (Burgos: Universidad de Burgos, 2008), pp. 160–72

Recio Veganzones, Alejandro, 'Probable representación martirial de Santa Eulalia de Mérida en la plástica visigoda', in *Revista de Estudios Extremeños*, 35.3 (1979), 539–62

Recio Veganzones, Alejandro, 'La mártir Eulalia en la devoción popular: Prudencio primer promotor de su culto, peregrinaciones, expansión de sus reliquias e iconografía (ss. IV–VII)', in *IV Reunió d'arqueología cristiana hispànica*, ed. by J. M. Gurt and N. Tena (Barcelona: Institut d'Estudis Catalans, 1995), pp. 317–36

Reeve, Michael D., 'Martial', in *Texts and Transmission: A Survey of the Latin Classics*, ed. by L. D. Reynolds (Oxford: Clarendon Press, 1983), pp. 239–44

Retamero, Félix, 'As Coins Go Home: Towns, Merchants, Bishops, and Kings in Visigothic Hispania', in *The Visigoths from the Migration Period to the Seventh Century: An Ethnographic Perspective*, ed. by P. Heather (Woodbridge: Boydell & Brewer, 1999), pp. 271–305

Reynolds, Paul, 'Material Culture and the Economy in the Age of Saint Isidore of Seville (6th and 7th Centuries)', in *Antiquité Tardive*, 23 (2015), 163–210

Rio, Alice, *Slavery after Rome, 500–1100* (Oxford: Oxford University Press, 2017)

Ripoll, Gisela, '*Sedes regiae* en la *Hispania* de la Antigüedad tardía', in *Memorias de la Real Academia de Buenas Letras de Barcelona*, 25 (2000), 371–401

Roca, María J., 'La distinción entre patrimonio eclesiástico y privado de obispos y clérigos en la España visigoda', in *e-Legal History Review*, 20 (2015), 1–16

Salvador Ventura, Francisco, 'The Bishops and the Byzantine Intervention in Hispania', in *The Role of the Bishop in Late Antiquity: Conflict and Compromise*, ed. by A. Fear, J. Fernández Ubiña, and M. Marcos (London: Bloomsbury, 2013), pp. 245–61

San Bernardino Coronil, Jesús, '*Eulalia Emeritam suam amore colit*: consideraciones en torno a la fiabilidad de un testimonio prudenciano (*PE.* 3.186–215)', in *Habis*, 27 (1996), 205–23

Sanabria Escudero, Manuel, 'La medicina emeritense en las épocas romana y visigoda', in *Revista de Estudios Extremeños*, 20.1 (1964), 53–84

Sastre de Diego, Isaac, *Mérida, capital cristiana. De Roma a al-Andalus* (Mérida: Museo Nacional de Arte Romano, 2015)

Schlunk, Helmut, and Theodor Hauschild, *Hispania Antiqua. Die Denkmäler der frühchristlichen und westgotischen Zeit* (Mainz: Verlag Philipp von Zabern, 1978)

Scholl, Christian, 'Imitatio Imperii? Elements of Imperial Rule in the Barbarian Successor States of the Roman West', in *Transcultural Approaches to the Concept of Imperial Rule in the Middle Ages*, ed. by Christian Scholl, Torben R. Gebhardt, and Jan Clauß (Frankfurt: Peter Lang, 2017), pp. 19–40

Scholz, Sebastian, 'Das Grab in der Kirche: zu seinen theologischen und rechtlichen Hintergründen in Spätantike und Frühmittelalter', in *Zeitschrift der Savigny-Stiftung für Rechtsgeschichte: Kanonistische Abteilung*, 84.1 (1998), 270–306

Smedt, Charles de, *Anonymi libellus de vitis et miraculis patrum Emeritensium Paulo diacono Emeritensi vulgo inscriptus* (Brussels: Polleunis, Ceuterick & Lefébure, 1884)

Stadermann, Christian, *Gothus. Konstruktion und Rezeption von Gotenbildern in narrativen Schriften des merowingischen Gallien* (Stuttgart: Franz Steiner Verlag, 2017)

Stocking, Rachel L., *Bishops, Councils, and Consensus in the Visigothic Kingdom, 589–633* (Ann Arbor, MI: University of Michigan Press, 2000)

Stocking, Rachel L., 'Review Article: Continuity, Culture, and the State in Late Antique and Early Medieval Iberia', in *Early Medieval Europe*, 15.3 (2007), 335–48

Stover, Justin A., and Mike Kestemont, 'The Authorship of the *Historia Augusta*: Two New Computational Studies', in *Bulletin of the Institute of Classical Studies*, 59.2 (2016), 140–57

Suárez Fernández, Ana, 'Un relato de fantasmas hispanovisigodo: el caso del pequeño Augusto en las *VSPE*', in *Estudios Medievales Hispánicos*, 5 (2016), 263–90

Symmachus, *Epistulae*, ed. by Otto Seeck, *Q. Aurelii Symmachi quae supersunt*, MGH Auctores Antiquissimi, VI.1 (Berlin: Weidmann, 1883)

Talbert, R. J. A., *Roman Portable Sundials: The Empire in Your Hand* (Oxford: Oxford University Press, 2017)

Teixeira, Cláudia, and André Carneiro, 'From Invisible to Tangible Power in Late Antique Rural Lusitania: Between Text and Material Evidence', in *Urban Transformations in the Late Antique West: Materials, Agents, and Models*, ed. by A. Carneiro, N. Christie, and P. Diarte-Blasco (Coimbra: Coimbra University Press, 2020), pp. 303–19

Teja, Ramón, 'El simbolismo mágico de la túnica de Santa Eulalia de Mérida en el enfrentamiento entre el obispo Masona y Leovigildo', in *Eulogía. Estudios sobre cristianismo primitivo. Homenaje a Mercedes López Salvá*, ed. by P. de Paz Amérigo and I. Sanz Extremeño (Madrid: Escolar y Mayo, 2018), pp. 265–74

Teja, Ramón, '*Intra muros* y *extra muros*: la "guerra" entre nicenos y arrianos por el control de los espacios públicos y religiosos en la Mérida de Leovigildo y Masona', in *Studi e Materiali di Storia delle Religioni*, 85.1 (2019), 202–14

Tomás-Faci, Guillermo, and José Carlos Martín-Iglesias, 'Cuatro documentos inéditos del monasterio visigodo de San Martín de Asán (522–586)', in *Mittellateinisches Jahrbuch*, 52.2 (2017), 261–86

Trillmich, Walter, 'La inscripción de una *domus* encomendada a la mártir Eulalia: un documento del encuentro final entre católicos y arrianos en *Emerita*', in *Anas*, 17 (2004), 145–60

Tsoucalas, Gregory, K. Laios, M. Karamanou, and M. Sgantzos, 'Bishop Paul of Mérida, and the First Known Caesarean Section on a Living Woman', in *Journal of Obstetrics and Gynaecology*, 35.2 (2015), 203

Underwood, Norman, 'Medicine, Money, and Christian Rhetoric: The Socio-Economic Dimensions of Healthcare in Late Antiquity', in *Studies in Late Antiquity*, 2.3 (2018), 342–84

Utrero Agudo, María Ángeles, and Francisco Moreno Martín, 'Evergetism among the Bishops of Hispania between the Sixth and Seventh Centuries: A Dialogue between Archaeological and Documentary Sources', in *Journal of Early Christian Studies*, 23.1 (2015), 97–131

Valerius of Bierzo, *On the Empty Wisdom of the World*, ed. by Manuel C. Díaz y Díaz, *Valerio del Bierzo. Su persona, su obra* (León: Centro de Estudios e Investigación 'San Isidoro', 2006)

Valla, Lorenzo, *On the Donation of Constantine*, trans. by G. W. Bowersock (Cambridge, MA: Harvard University Press, 2007)

Vallejo Girvés, Margarita, '¿El éxito de un desterrado arriano? La evangelización del obispo Sunna en Mauritania', in *Marginados sociales y religiosos en la Hispania tardorromana y visigoda*, ed. by R. González Salinero (Salamanca: Signifer, 2013), pp. 171–91

Valverde, María R., 'Leovigildo: persecución religiosa y defensa de la unidad del reino', in *Iberia*, 2 (1999), 123–32

Varela Rodríguez, Joel, 'Algunos problemas del uso de Gregorio Magno por Isidoro de Sevilla', in *Revue d'Études Augustiniennes et Patristiques*, 65.1 (2019), 135–64

Velázquez, Isabel, and Gisela Ripoll, '*Toletum*, la construcción de una *urbs regia*', in *Memorias de la Real Academia de Buenas Letras de Barcelona*, 25 (2000), 521–78

Velázquez Soriano, Isabel, '¿Hagiografía *versus* prosopografía? En torno a las *Vitas sanctorum patrum Emeretensium*', in *Latinitas Biblica et Christiana. Studia philologica varia in honorem Olegario García de la Fuente*, ed. by F. Sojo Rodríguez (Madrid: Universidad Europea de Madria, 1994), pp. 497–506

Velázquez Soriano, Isabel, 'El *Suggerendum* de Tarra a Recaredo', in *Antiquité Tardive*, 4 (1996), 291–98

Velázquez Soriano, Isabel, '*Pro patriae gentisque Gothorum statu* (4th Council of Toledo, Canon 75, a. 633)', in *Regna and Gentes: The Relationship between Late Antique and Early Medieval Peoples and Kingdoms in the Transformation of the Roman World*, ed. by H.-W. Goetz, J. Jarnut, and W. Pohl (Leiden: Brill, 2003), pp. 162–217

Velázquez Soriano, Isabel, '*Baselicas multas miro opere construxit* (*VSPE* 5.1.1). El valor de las fuentes literarias y epigráficas sobre la edilicia religiosa en la Hispania visigoda', in *Hortus Artium Medievalium*, 13.2 (2007), 261–68

Velázquez Soriano, Isabel, *Vidas de los santos padres de Mérida* (Madrid: Trotta, 2008)

Vidal Álvarez, Sergio, 'Problemas en torno a la iconografía del Libro de Daniel en la escultura hispánica de los siglos IV–VII', in *Madrider Mitteilungen*, 43 (2002), 220–38

Vizcaíno Sánchez, Jaime, *La presencia bizantina en Hispania (siglos VI–VII): la documentación arqueológica. Antigüedad y Cristianismo*, 24 (2007)

Watson, Sethina, *On Hospitals: Welfare, Law, and Christianity in Western Europe, 400–1320* (Oxford: Oxford University Press, 2020)

Whelan, Robin, *Being Christian in Vandal Africa: The Politics of Orthodoxy in the Post-Imperial West* (Berkeley, CA: University of California Press, 2018)

Whelan, Robin, 'Ethnicity, Christianity, and Groups: Homoian Christians in Ostrogothic Italy and Visigothic Spain', in *Inclusion and Exclusion in Mediterranean Christianities, 400–800*, ed. by Y. Fox and E. Buchberger (Turnhout: Brepols, 2019), pp. 167–98

Wickham, Chris, *Framing the Early Middle Ages: Europe and the Mediterranean, 400–800* (Oxford: Oxford University Press, 2005)

Wickham, Chris, *Medieval Rome: Stability and Crisis of a City, 900–1150* (Oxford: Oxford University Press, 2014)

Wood, Ian, 'Social Relations in the Visigothic Kingdom from the Fifth to the Seventh Century: The Example of Mérida', in *The Visigoths from the Migration Period to the*

Seventh Century: An Ethnographic Perspective, ed. by Peter Heather (Woodbridge: Boydell & Brewer, 1999), pp. 191–223

Wood, Ian, 'Topographies of Holy Power in Sixth-Century Gaul', in *Topographies of Power in the Early Middle Ages*, ed. by M. de Jong, F. Theuws, and C. van Rhijn (Leiden: Brill, 2001), pp. 137–54

Wood, Ian, 'Entrusting Western Europe to the Church, 400–750', in *Transactions of the Royal Historical Society*, 23 (2013), 37–73

Wood, Ian, 'Arianism and Identity among the Early Medieval *Gentes*: Variations in Time and Space' (forthcoming)

Wood, Jamie, 'Building and Breaking Episcopal Networks in Late Antique *Hispania*', in *Episcopal Networks in Late Antiquity: Connection and Communication across Boundaries*, ed. by C. A. Cvetković and P. Gemeinhardt (Berlin: De Gruyter, 2019), pp. 227–47

Wood, Jamie, 'Conflicts over Episcopal Office in Southern Hispania: Comparative Perspectives from Visigothic and Byzantine Territories', in *The Visigothic Kingdom: The Negotiation of Power in Post-Roman Iberia*, ed. by S. Panzram and P. Pachá (Amsterdam: Amsterdam University Press, 2020), pp. 353–72

Wood, Susan, *The Proprietary Church in the Medieval West* (Oxford: Oxford University Press, 2006)

Yarza Urquiola, Valeriano, *Passionarium hispanicum*. CCSL 171–171A, 2 vols (Turnhout: Brepols, 2020)

Zerjadtke, Michael, *Das Amt 'Dux' in Spätantike und frühen Mittelalter. Der 'ducatus' im Spannungsfeld zwischen römischem Einfluss und eigener Entwicklung* (Berlin: De Gruyter, 2019)

Zimmerman, O. J., *Gregory the Great: Dialogues* (Washington, DC: Catholic University of America Press, 1959)

About the Author

Graham Barrett is Senior Lecturer in Late Antiquity at the University of Lincoln. His research focuses on the sociocultural history of Latin in western Europe from the fifth to the eleventh century, and he is the author of *Text and Textuality in Early Medieval Iberia: The Written and the World, 711–1031* (Oxford University Press, 2023).

12 The Agents and Mechanics of Connectivity

The Mediterranean World and the Cities of the Guadiana Valley in the Sixth Century

Jamie Wood

Abstract

This chapter explores connections between the upper Guadiana valley, especially the cities of Mérida and Mértola, and the Byzantine world in the sixth century. By analysing archaeological evidence in conjunction with written sources, it identifies continued linkages to North Africa and the eastern Mediterranean in this period. Although the ceramic assemblages indicate that the scale of such connectivity was considerably reduced compared to previous centuries, hagiography and epigraphy both point towards the presence of well-established 'Greek' ecclesiastical elites at both cities in the middle decades of the sixth century who, alongside other local leaders, played a pivotal role in managing connections to outsiders, including traders who brought goods from beyond Hispania to the Guadiana basin.

Keywords: bishops; ceramics; economic relations; Greeks; Guadiana valley; local elites; Lusitania; material culture; Mérida; Mértola; trade; Lives of the Fathers of Mérida

Introduction

Studies that examine Byzantine influence or presence in Hispania tend to focus on two locations: the nascent Visigothic court at Toledo that developed from the mid-sixth century onwards, and the province that was established under Justinian on the southern coast of Hispania in the mid-sixth century,

Fernández, D., Lester, M. & Wood, J. (eds.), *Rome and Byzantium in the Visigothic Kingdom: Beyond* Imitatio Imperii. Taylor & Francis Group 2023
DOI: 10.5117/9789463726412_CH12

the capital of which lay at Cartagena. Historical and art historical scholarship has tended to focus geographically on the imperial presence in the south-east of the Iberian peninsula, on elite-level religious and political interactions, and on the 'influence' that Byzantine culture and theology exerted on the Visigothic kingdom.[1] Archaeologists, meanwhile, have tended to address economic issues.[2] The roles of what are assumed to be peripheral regions and the people that inhabited them have, in general, been overlooked in favour of examples of imperial-royal interactivity.

This approach to relations between the Byzantine world and post-Roman Hispania is at odds with much recent work on the Iberian peninsula, which has adopted a regional perspective. Many scholars, often drawing more directly on material evidence, have sought to move beyond centralizing sources and the Toledo-focused narratives that they propagated.[3] This chapter focuses on connectivity (evidence for linkages to the eastern Mediterranean and the north of Africa) and interactivity (cases in which we can see active engagement and/or reciprocal exchange with such regions) on a micro-regional level. Drawing on Horden and Purcell's definition of connectivity as 'the various ways in which microregions cohere, both internally and also with one another', it suggests that interactivity occurred geographically far from centres of royal and imperial power and was driven forward by local and regional elites, including ecclesiastical leaders.[4] Furthermore, connections in such small worlds were the result of 'habitual face-to-face interaction'.[5] I seek to refocus attention away from the Toledo-Cartagena-Constantinople axis by offering a case study of sixth-century connections between the Byzantine world and Mérida and Mértola, two cities in the Guadiana river valley in southwestern Iberia. Decentring the analysis reveals that it was not only kings, emperors, and their agents that were responsible for the continued (if, compared to preceding centuries, reduced) integration of large parts of Hispania into the Byzantine-Mediterranean world in the sixth century, but also local

1 The classic historical study remains Vallejo Girvés 1993, now augmented by Vallejo Girvés 2012.

2 The key archaeological overview is provided by Vizcaíno Sánchez 2007.

3 For summaries of this trend in scholarship, see: Wood 2015, esp. 9–10; Wood and Martínez Jiménez 2016. See Bernardes 2009, 326 for a call for more regional studies. See Díaz and Menéndez-Bueyes 2015 for the rise of localism in post-Roman Gallaecia. Conant (2010, 14–21) has demonstrated how the cult of the saints can offer further indications of the complex nature of the entanglement between Africa and the Iberian peninsula in Late Antiquity, which seems to have been driven forward largely at local rather than 'national' levels.

4 Horden and Purcell 2000, 123.

5 Tartaron 2018, 73.

elites and communities of 'eastern' and African migrants and merchants operating on regional and inter-regional levels.[6]

While imperial support for the movement of troops and officials and the collection of taxes had largely broken down in the western Mediterranean by the late fifth century, determined efforts were made in some of the post-Roman kingdoms to maintain taxation and supply systems such as the *annona*.[7] The end of the central Roman government in the West did not, however, result in the end of pan-Mediterranean interactivity, and some scholars of late antique Iberia have argued that there was considerable continuity in 'state' institutions at local and supra-local levels in some regions.[8] Building on this work, I focus on two key issues: the agents of such connectivity and its practical functioning, or mechanics. The evidence from sixth-century Mérida and Mértola reveals a great deal about the resilience (or otherwise) of socio-economic networks and other long-distance connections. Mérida in particular has been well excavated and is the subject of extensive extant written records, which provide valuable opportunities to triangulate between textual and material evidence for long-distance connections. This city offers insights into the mechanics and agents of connectivity, that is, *how* it might have happened and *who* might have been responsible.

In what follows, I argue that the communities of the Guadiana valley maintained connections to the Byzantine world throughout Late Antiquity, despite falling outside of Visigothic and imperial control for much of the period. For most of the sixth century, the Visigoths did not control large swathes of the Iberian peninsula and local elites ruled many cities and regions. Suggestions of a more unitary Visigothic rule represent a fundamental misreading of the evidence for post-Roman Hispania and are the result of uncritical acceptance of the triumphalist narratives of pro-Toledan propagandists writing in the seventh century.[9] In this geo-political context, local initiative—both by elites in the Guadiana valley and by those who were seeking to supply them with goods and information—drove forward connectivity. The socio-economic mechanics of the small worlds of the

6 García Moreno (1972, 153) suggests that colonies of eastern merchants in Hispania played an important role in the Byzantine occupation of important parts of the south-east of the peninsula. While this is an intriguing proposition, direct evidence for concerted cooperation between such merchants and the imperial government is lacking. On Visigothic Iberia and Byzantine Africa see, more recently, García Moreno 2002.

7 Bjornlie 2016; Arnold 2016, 91.

8 Fernández 2017; Curchin 2013–2014 and 2014; Kulikowski 2004.

9 See Castellanos 2020, 3–5, 9, 13–17, 20, 29 for more on this.

region, rather than the political and ideological considerations of the Byzantine and Visigothic governments, thus played a significant role in determining whether connectivity continued or was curtailed.[10] The local and regional elites who drove these connections were diverse. In addition to the civic leaders and local aristocrats on which recent scholarship has focused, as well as representatives of the Visigothic state, we should also include ecclesiastical leaders and communities with Greek or African origins, many of whom worked in cooperation with traders who brought goods from overseas. Local and regional leadership depended, after all, to a considerable extent on a continued ability to control the mechanics of connectivity, such as the transport networks of rivers and roads, the redistribution of imported goods, the display of wealth, and the ability to levy fees on merchants.

My analysis draws on a range of written sources, especially the *Vitas Sanctorum Patrum Emeritensium* (VSPE), a seventh-century hagiography written in several stages that focuses on the sixth-century bishops of Mérida. I also rely on important epigraphic material from Mértola and other elements of material culture such as mosaics. The core of my chapter, however, is an analysis of shifting patterns of pottery importation from the Byzantine world to the upper Guadiana valley. Tracking shifting patterns in the importation and exportation of ceramics is one means of understanding long-distance economic connections.[11] The presence of ceramics from the eastern Mediterranean, such as Late Roman C (Phocaean Ware) and Late Roman D (Cypriot Ware), within pottery assemblages serves as an indicator of connectivity between production zones and Hispania. The presence of African Red Slip ware may point towards continuing contact with North African production and distribution sites. Changes in the frequency with which such ceramics are recovered from excavations can help to demonstrate how interactivity changed over time, and shifting distribution patterns of amphorae, ceramic lamps, metalwork, and other kinds of imported goods can further nuance this picture.

10 For a similar point in relation to the early Roman period in the province of Lusitania, see: Edmondson 1990, 150–51: 'Although Roman and/or Italian soldiers, traders, administrators were important vehicles of cultural change, the main impetus came from the periphery (that is, from the provincial élite) rather than from the imperial capital.' On 'small worlds', see Davies 1988.

11 Wickham 2005, 693: 'I would argue indeed that ceramics are the firmest support for any account of exchange in our period.' Bernardes 2009, 327: 'The absence or presence of imported pottery can tell us, e.g., about the abandonment or continued occupation of sites.'

The Guadiana Valley

Although it may not have been under direct Visigothic or imperial control for much of the sixth century, the Guadiana valley was by no means a backwater.[12] Mérida, former capital of late Roman Hispania (and of the province of Lusitania) and still a significant political, ecclesiastical, and economic centre, lay on the river's middle reaches on the border with the province of Baetica. Downstream, the Guadiana river formed the border between Lusitania and Baetica, where it passes through the territory of the *conventus* capital of Beja and eventually through the city of Mértola, the last safely navigable point on the river in the modern day (68 km from the sea). Some parts of this river valley were intensively settled during the Roman period: for example, the hinterlands of the two Roman colonies in the valley, Mérida and Beja, had the highest concentration of villa sites in Lusitania.[13] Due to its rich archaeological and textual record, Mérida has been the subject of considerable attention in scholarship on post-Roman Iberia, although less notice has been paid to the broader provincial context in which Mérida existed and its elites operated.[14]

There was great variety to the political landscape of post-Roman Hispania, and the long transition from Roman to Visigothic rule involved complex processes of negotiation, conflict, and compromise between a range of local leaders and a sometimes-splintered Visigothic elite. In some places there was considerable continuity in civic government into the sixth century and beyond,[15] and in the western regions of the peninsula, aristocrats maintained traditional lifestyles and ways of thinking about government throughout the period.[16] The VSPE reports how a married Méridan couple of senatorial background donated their estate to the Greek Bishop Paul after he had saved the wife's life, and there are other hints in the text about the continuity of civic institutions such as councils.[17] Paul passed on the bishopric to his nephew, Fidel, creating a Greek 'dynasty'.[18] Ecclesiastical leaders were not, despite the rhetoric of some sources, set apart from the

12 Kulikowski 2004, 272–73 on the 'independence' of southern Iberia in the first half of the sixth century; also, Collins 1980.

13 Edmondson 1990, 150.

14 A notable exception is Cordero Ruiz's (2013) study of the city's hinterland in Late Antiquity.

15 For recent studies, see Curchin 2013–2014 and 2014; Fernández 2017.

16 Fernández 2017.

17 VSPE 4.2. On continuity of civic institutions in late antique Hispania, including in Mérida, see Fernández 2020.

18 VSPE 4.4–5.

immediate social and political context in which they lived and worked; they were often part of or related to local elite families and sought to intervene actively in disputes within their cities and regions.[19] It is not surprising, therefore, that there are other examples of episcopal dynasties from late antique Hispania; the evidence for Mérida simply provides richer insights into their activities.[20]

In contrast to urban centres, we are less well served in evidentiary terms in identifying post-Roman occupation of rural sites. Nonetheless, recent archaeological investigations point towards continuous occupation at the majority of rural sites in the southwest of the Iberian peninsula from the fifth century onwards, irrespective of the type of site (villa, secondary settlements, or smaller sites), while Damián Fernández's recent monograph demonstrated convincingly the continuity of aristocratic life in urban and rural contexts across the region in Late Antiquity.[21] Elites operating at regional and local levels thus retained considerable power even after the upper Guadiana valley fell out of the control of the central Roman state. In the post-Roman period, to this mix of 'local' elites (rural and urban) must be added those individuals and groups with connections to external powers such as the Visigothic monarchy, the Byzantine empire, and the papacy, as well as neighbouring bishops within Hispania who often involved themselves in the affairs of their peers.[22]

Communication networks to a large extent determined the type, scope, and scale of connectivity between the communities of the Guadiana valley and the Mediterranean world. In post-Roman Iberia, 'river valleys favoured the most direct and regular' means of interaction between elites beyond the local level, including via the Roman road system.[23] Rivers were rarely navigable beyond their lower courses, although the middle and upper courses could be navigated with smaller vessels. It is not clear if the Guadiana could be navigated to Mérida in Late Antiquity, although further downstream Mértola was directly accessible to the sea and the mouth of the Guadiana was a point of 'intense Mediterranean-Atlantic

19 Wood 2019.

20 On episcopal dynasties in late antique Hispania, see: Wood 2019; more generally, see Rapp 2005, 195–99.

21 Bernardes 2009, 328–29, 342 (continuity at urban and rural sites); Fernández 2017.

22 It is hardly surprising, as explored by Graham Barrett elsewhere in this volume, that there was considerable factional fighting between competing members of such elites. See Wood 2019 on how such local contexts influenced conflict over episcopal office in Mérida and elsewhere.

23 Fernández 2017, 3–4. See García Moreno 1972, 142 on the importance of the coasts and great navigable rivers of Hispania in Antiquity.

interaction' dating back to the Bronze Age.[24] García Moreno's seminal study of 'oriental' merchant colonies in the Iberian peninsula in Late Antiquity noted the presence of easterners in Mérida and Mértola, arguing that the main function of such communities (in the Guadiana valley and elsewhere in post-Roman Hispania) was commercial.[25] Mérida also provides the most extensive narrative evidence for the presence of individuals from the Byzantine world in Hispania in the sixth century. As we shall see, the VSPE narrates the lives of two Greek bishops of the city, including interactions with traders from their homeland. Several sites along the Guadiana have also been subject to extensive excavation, which has revealed further evidence for connection to the Byzantine-Mediterranean world.

Although from the fifth to the seventh century there was a clear reduction in long-distance trade across Hispania, the rhythm of such shifts differed from region to region (and from micro-region to micro-region).[26] There is evidence in the Guadiana valley for traders who came from (or had linkages to) the Byzantine world, suggesting the maintenance of active commercial contacts across the period.[27] At Mérida and Mértola there were probably established communities (termed 'colonies' in García Moreno's classic article[28]) of easterners, and in both places people identified as Greek or using Greek script held ecclesiastical office, suggesting that they could call on considerable local support.[29] The material record, especially ceramics, provides ample evidence of their impact on the local economy into the late sixth and even the early seventh century. Communities with historic links to the Byzantine-Mediterranean world were therefore part of the complex fabric of post-Roman society in the Guadiana valley, and their leaders presumably played an important role in maintaining connections with the eastern Mediterranean and Africa during the sixth century. Such connections no doubt contributed to the Mediterranean 'influences' that have frequently been identified in southwestern Iberia in the post-Roman period.[30] Connectivity is thus visible across a range of material and textual registers.

24 Fernández 2017, 4–5; 233, n. 8.

25 García Moreno 1972, 142.

26 Bernardes 2009, 344; Fernández 2017, 216–18, 220.

27 García Moreno 1972, 146.

28 García Moreno 1972.

29 Decker 2009, 244–45.

30 Bernardes 2009, 330.

The Provincial Capital: Mérida

Capital of late Roman Hispania after the reforms of Diocletian,[31] Mérida's strategic significance in the fifth century is indicated by the various references that the chronicler Hydatius makes to the city. He mentions the manoeuvres of various barbarian groups around the city, its patronage by Saint Eulalia, and the activities of its bishop.[32] In terms of its monumentality, the city has been described as 'top tier', boasting walls, aristocratic housing, and public buildings during the late Roman period.[33] Its administrative function was partially responsible for its vitality in the post-Roman period, during which Mérida—and cities like it across the south of the peninsula—continued to function as a centre of territorial control, provincial administration, and fiscal activity. It also operated as a hub for an intensively exploited agricultural hinterland and served as a route-focus for roads and waterways.[34] The elites of post-Roman Mérida were therefore well-placed to negotiate power relations with the emerging Visigothic state. New ecclesiastical buildings were erected in the city during this period and are further evidence for the wealth of urban elites, religious and otherwise. As we shall see, continued imports from the Mediterranean also act as an index of sustained connection to broader commercial networks.[35]

There is good evidence for the presence of 'Greeks' in fifth- and sixth-century Mérida. Epigraphy reveals that Greek speakers lived in the city during this period and, combined with other textual references, this suggests that easterners 'formed an important group economically in Mérida and in other towns throughout Spain'.[36] Indeed, as Fernandes and Valério have demonstrated, there is evidence for Greek speakers across the province of

31 See Fernández 2017, 33 for a summary of the establishment of the city as provincial capital.

32 Hyd. 80 (90): the Sueve Heremigarius caused an affront to Eulalia and was defeated, drowning afterwards, near to Emerita; 122 (130): Manichees hiding in Asturica were exposed by reports to Antoninus, bishop of Emerita; 129 (137): Rechila, Suevic king, died in Emerita; 130 (138): Pascentius, a Manichee from Rome, was arrested in Emerita by Bishop Antoninus, who had him tried and expelled from Lusitania; 175 (182): Theodoric, Gothic king, deterred from pillaging Emerita by warnings from the martyr Eulalia; 179 (186): Theodoric left Emerita; 239 (245): Goths pursuing Suevic envoys, made for Emerita.

33 Fernández 2017, 44–45.

34 Osland 2016, 68–69.

35 Martínez Jiménez and Tejerizo García 2015, 90–92; Collins 1980. For a detailed study of the city's relations with its territory, see Cordero 2013.

36 Decker 2009, 244–45; according to García Moreno (1972, 138–39), onomastic evidence suggests that there was a Greek-'oriental' colony engaged in trade with the eastern Mediterranean in the city from the imperial period through to the sixth century.

Lusitania throughout the sixth century.[37] Although 'none of the easterners in southern Lusitania whose occupations are identifiable were traders' and 'all [were] connected with the Church', it seems likely that these Greek-speaking communities included, or at least interacted regularly with, merchants from the Mediterranean world.[38] Church authorities seem to have played a prominent role in overseeing relations with Greek merchants who came to Mérida,[39] a duty that should be understood in the context of their broader leadership in the city and their responsibility for the management of relations with outsiders such as kings, foreign visitors, and neighbouring bishops.[40]

Ecclesiastical mediation is further evidenced by the fact that monastic and episcopal sites across the peninsula often have relatively high levels of imported goods, including from the eastern Mediterranean and Africa. Indeed, in a recent article Paul Reynolds suggested that further attention should be paid to the role of such sites and the ecclesiastical elites that controlled them in mediating trade.[41] It would also be profitable to explore how ecclesiastical leaders interacted with royal, urban, and aristocratic elites. For instance, the mid to late sixth century witnessed the movement of the monastic founders Nanctus and Donatus from Africa, with the support of King Leovigild and a noblewoman called Minicea respectively.[42] Although bishops predominate in the written records for this period, ecclesiastical elites did not operate separately from other social leaders; rather, they were born from the upper echelons of society and their activities were funded by prominent 'secular' figures, as in the cases of Bishop Paul and Abbot Nanctus in Mérida.

Close reading of narrative sources can further deepen our understanding of the contacts that existed between the cities of the Guadiana and the Mediterranean world in Late Antiquity. Indeed, the classic proof text for the continued connection of Hispania to the eastern Mediterranean, the VSPE, devotes some attention to the interactions between Greek merchants and the city's bishop. This hagiography was composed in several stages in the late sixth and seventh centuries,[43] and provides the most textured account of the socio-political life of a city in late antique Hispania. It focuses

37 Fernandes and Valério 2013.

38 Reynolds 2015, 206–7, 209.

39 Reynolds 2015, 206–9.

40 Wood 2019.

41 Reynolds 2015, 205–8.

42 Nanctus: VSPE 3.2; Donatus: Ildef. De viris 3; see also Ioh. Bicl. 18, s. a. 570.

43 On the date, see: Velázquez 2008, 11–15.

on the development of the bishopric of Mérida in the sixth century and is especially concerned with conflicts over the episcopate.[44] The text suggests how connections to the Mediterranean world may have occurred. One of the most significant disputes in Mérida was the establishment of Paul as bishop in the sixth century. The text relates that 'it is often told how a holy man called Paul, a Greek by nationality and a doctor by trade, came from the lands of East to the city of Mérida'.[45] Although some scholars have called into question the reliability of the VSPE as a source (discussed in more detail in Graham Barrett's chapter in this volume),[46] historically, many Greeks had indeed worked as doctors in the Roman world.[47] In addition, in the Visigothic legal code, laws on doctors (LI 11.1.1–8) were placed alongside those dealing with overseas merchants (*transmarini negotiatores*; LI 11.3.1–4), reinforcing the association of the medical profession with foreigners.[48] Paul inherited the wealth of a senatorial couple after he had saved the woman's life by using his medical skills, later using the possibility that he could withdraw this endowment to ensure that his nephew, Fidel, succeeded as bishop.

According to the hagiographer, Fidel arrived in the city in a group of Greek merchants who came to Mérida in ships from the East. Fidel's arrival was apparently a complete shock to Paul, who discovered his identity by accident. The account of the arrival of the Greeks, who came from the same region as Paul, suggests that eastern traders were a common presence in mid-sixth-century Mérida, while a fragmentary inscription in Greek to a deacon suggests that Paul and Fidel were not the only ecclesiastics with connections to the eastern Mediterranean.[49] The VSPE indicates that there was a customary protocol (*ex more*) for the reception of traders:

> One day some Greek traders from the region from which he himself had come, arrived in their ships from the East and put in on the shore of

44 Further explored in Graham Barrett's chapter in the present volume.

45 'Referunt multi sanctum uirum nomine Paulum, natione Grecum, arte medicum, de Orientis partibus in Emeretensem urbem aduenisse' (VSPE 4.1).

46 On the Greek origins of Paul and Fidelis as 'mythological', see Arce 2002, 209–12.

47 Blockley 1980, 89–90, with references.

48 D'Ors 1958; for further discussion, see p. 329 and 337 below. The other title in book 11, LI 11.2, deals with the violators of tombs.

49 ICERV 418, García Moreno 1972, 139. Based on onomastic evidence, García Moreno (1972, 147–48) suggested that the Bishop Nepopis, temporarily imposed by Leovigild on the Nicene population of Mérida in the early 580s, was of Egyptian origin and goes on to argue that Nepopis was able to rally support among the city's colony of easterners.

> Spain. When they came to the city of Mérida, according to custom they presented themselves on arrival to the bishop.[50]

Retamero suggested that the reception took place in the *atrium*, 'a specific place of ceremony where the bishop showed himself and his entourage in solemn events'.[51] Godoy and Tuset surveyed the full range of references to the *atrium* in the VSPE and showed that it functioned as a multi-purpose space for meetings, judicial proceedings, audiences, and the distribution of charity to the poor.[52] Interaction between the bishop and the merchants involved the repeated exchange of gifts, beginning with the presentation of a gift from the merchants to the bishop to thank him for receiving them into the city: 'On the following day they sent him a small gift to thank him.'[53] The gift was carried by Fidel, and 'when he had been presented before Paul and the holy man had joyfully received the gift he had brought as a token of thanks, the bishop began to question him point by point as to what he was called and from what province or town he came'.[54] Once he realized that Fidel was his nephew, Paul determined that he should stay in Mérida rather than return home, warning the merchants as follows: 'He replied "Let it be clear to you that if you do not leave me him, you shall not return to your own country, but accept a goodly sum of money from me and depart in safety, travelling in peace."'[55] After his demands had been met, Paul made two final 'gifts' for Fidel, one to his sister back east and the other to the merchants themselves: 'He sent various gifts to his sister through them and also rewarded the sailors generously so that, enriched by his presents, they returned to their country with great joy.'[56] It is hard to read these 'gifts' as anything other than forced payment, albeit apparently

50 'Accidit die quadam de regione qua ipse oriundus extiterat negotiatores Grecos in nauibus de Orientibus aduenisse atque Spanie litora contigisse. Quumque in Emeretensem ciuitatem peruenissent, ex more episcopo prebuerunt occursum' (VSPE 4.3).

51 Retamero 1999, esp. 273–74.

52 Godoy Fernández and Tuset Bertrán 1994, esp. 214.

53 'sequenti die ad eum munusculum miserunt pro gratiarum actione' (VSPE 4.3).

54 'Quumque eius fuisset presentatus obtutibus et que grato animo directa detulerat gratanter uir sanctus suscepisset, eum cepit singillatim sciscitari quo uocaretur nomen, de qua prouincia uel de qua ciuitate esset' (VSPE 4.3).

55 'E contra ille ayt: 'Conpertum uobis sit quia si istum mici non dimittitis, uos in patriam uestram minime reuertitis. Sed accipite a me pecuniam copiosam et abite securi pergentes cum pace' (VSPE 4.3).

56 'Qui diuersa per eos munera mittens sorori ipsis quoque nautis multa largitus est dona. Ac sic ditati eius muneribus regressi sunt in patriam suam cum gaudio magno' (VSPE 4.3).

they were generous enough that the merchants left satisfied.[57] Overall, the impression is of a carefully scripted exchange, the terms of which were set by the bishop.

In the VSPE, the bishop is responsible for managing interactions with the eastern merchants. His power is emphasized repeatedly: the merchants had to come to him when they arrived; he interrogated Fidel; and he forbade the merchants' departure if they did not leave Fidel in Mérida. Of course, as an episcopal source the VSPE is likely to focus on the power of the bishop and to downplay that of other authority figures within the city, although references to royal officials in Mérida and other cities elsewhere in the text (e.g., VSPE 5.10–12) suggest that the author was not entirely blind to other powers within the city.[58] It is also perhaps likely that eastern (Greek-speaking) visitors would have wanted to meet with a Greek bishop before anyone else. In Mérida, the bishop was responsible for mediating contact with the easterners just as he managed relations with other external powers, including the Visigothic king and the bishops of other cities.[59] We might also consider the bishops' reception of the foreign merchants as a local analogue to their roles as ambassadors.[60] In both cases, they would have been acting as representatives of their cities to outsiders.

It therefore seems likely that in the mid-sixth century any visitors of significance to Mérida would have had to present themselves before the bishop of the city upon arrival. Such a practice was not necessarily automatic because it is highly likely that there were other authorities (civic elites and officials, representatives of the Visigothic king) within the city, with whom traders might have sought contact. Other cities—like Mértola, to be explored in the next section—lacked bishops, and alternative channels for connectivity would have been developed out of necessity. In Mérida, however, the bishop's responsibility for welcoming and caring for visitors may be further underlined by the foundation of a *xenodochium*, or hostel for travellers and the poor (*peregrinorum et egrotantium*), by Fidel's successor, Masona.[61] While elsewhere in the late antique and early medieval Mediterranean *xenodochia* seem to have ministered to the sick as well as to visitors

57 Retamero 1999, 271.

58 On the tripartite relationship between local civic elites, bishops, and royal officials in post-Roman Hispania, see Fernández 2020.

59 See Collins 1980 for what the text reveals about relations between the bishops of Mérida and Visigothic monarchs.

60 On bishops as ambassadors in Late Antiquity, see Gillett 2003, 113–71 and Ian Wood's chapter in this volume.

61 VSPE 5.3; García Moreno 1972, 140.

from afar,[62] Masona's foundation may be yet more evidence for the role of the bishop in providing infrastructural support for incomers, whether they were traders or pilgrims to the shrines of the city's patron, Saint Eulalia.

Ecclesiastical authorities, sometimes with the support of royal authorities and local elites, acted as key mediators of contact with outside traders at Mérida. It is not unlikely that they played a similar role in other cities in the middle decades of the sixth century as the Visigothic kings struggled to establish their authority, especially in the south. As noted above, it has been suggested that ecclesiastical institutions may have managed trade more generally in late antique Iberia, which would align with the fiscal, judicial, and economic functions that bishops fulfilled throughout the Visigothic period.[63]

In addition to these ecclesiastical connections, there is strong material evidence for interaction between Mérida and the Byzantine world.[64] Some items that are likely to have been exchanged remain invisible archaeologically. From where, for example, did the silk liturgical garments that are mentioned in the VSPE come?[65] The *Liber Iudiciorum* includes earlier laws on overseas merchants trading in items such as precious metals, clothing, or other ornaments, and although in some cases we may be able to trace the material remains of such imports, in most cases this is impossible.[66] Coupled with the issue of archaeological invisibility, the posited early medieval 'container revolution' could mean that the ceramic record further under-represents levels of importation.[67]

Although there is no doubt that there were shifts in the scale and focus of both importation and local production during the fifth century and afterwards,[68] it has been suggested that elements of the material culture of sixth- and early seventh-century Mérida had a markedly 'eastern' character that exerted a significant influence on Hispano-Visigothic artistic production more generally. For example, 'Byzantine-style' niches were produced in the city, from which sculptural traditions resembling those of Ravenna and Syria

62 Dey 2008, 403–5.

63 Reynolds 2015, 205–8; Koon and Wood 2009; Fernández 2006.

64 García Moreno 1972, 140–42.

65 E.g., VSPE 4.6.

66 LI 11.3.1. See, for example, Cecily Hilsdale's chapter in this volume.

67 On strategies for addressing the issue of archaeological invisibility, see Zanini 2006.

68 Alba Calzado 2003, 299: there were higher quantities of sigillata at Mérida before the fifth century, while rather than localization or regionalization of the city's ceramic record in the 'Visigothic period', there were a range of shifts in the modes of production towards a more household-based approach (at 303–4, 306, 312, 314).

may have been diffused throughout the rest of the peninsula. It has been argued that such influences may be traced to the mid-sixth-century episcopates of Paul and Fidel.[69] Although the identification of some episcopal complexes and monastic foundations is controversial, pottery and other imported goods have been found at enough attested ecclesiastical sites to suggest that their inhabitants were significant consumers of imported materials.[70]

Imported pottery offers more quantitative evidence for the scale of connection to the Byzantine world in the sixth century. Given the wealth of the archaeological record for Mérida, it is surprising that there have been so few publications relating to the late Roman ceramic finds. Nonetheless, the city's pottery record contrasts with other sites in the south, with substantial imports of TSHT (Terra Sigillata Hispánica Tardía) from elsewhere in Hispania in the fourth and fifth centuries.[71] This is perhaps a reflection of the city's status and its connections with the rest of the peninsula (of which it was capital during the late Roman period). Indeed, the fact that Mérida is located inland raises the possibility that some ceramics—especially those of Baetican origin—may have reached the city overland from the neighbouring province (probably via Seville) rather than via the Guadiana.[72] The cities of the upper Guadiana seem to have functioned as much as hubs for land transport as they did for fluvial communications. Local ceramics were important too, and the city produced local-regional painted wares in the fourth and fifth centuries.[73]

A meta-analysis of the ceramic record from thirty-four sites dated between the fourth and the eighth centuries demonstrated a substantial decline in fineware imports to the city across the course of the fifth century, although there was never a complete loss of ties with the Mediterranean, especially North Africa.[74] Mediterranean forms manufactured in the sixth century made their way to the city, although in reduced numbers compared to the fourth and fifth centuries. At some sites in the city, sixth-century forms predominate.[75] The most common imports in the fifth and sixth centuries

69 Barroso Cabrera and Morín de Pablos 2007, 78.

70 Reynolds 2015, 205–8.

71 Reynolds 2010, 62.

72 Osland 2012, 332–34, 341 (including reference to the importation of Baetican finewares); Fernández (2017, 5) notes how Mérida was a key stopping point on the Via de la Plata, the main road from Baetica to Gallaecia; 112: supply with TSHT probably occurred via the road network.

73 Reynolds 2010, 65.

74 Osland 2012, 322, 328, 333, 343–44; 341: conversely, demand for imported coarsewares was never great in Mérida in the period from the fourth to the sixth century.

75 Osland 2012, 333; Osland 2016, 82–83.

were ARS (African Red Slip) and 'late terra sigillata (and sigillata-derived) wares from southern Gaul, Hispania Tarraconensis, and Baetica', while there were also small numbers of ARS D forms dating later than the third quarter of the fifth century.[76] Production of TSHT, TSHTM (southern TSHT), and Iberian imitations of Gallic Gray Ware trailed off in the late fifth century, yet small-scale imports of late ARS forms dating from the sixth and into the seventh centuries continued.[77] Analysis of lamps suggests that importation from North Africa ceased in the second quarter of the sixth century, following a marked reduction in scale after the middle of the fifth. Interestingly, at the end of the fifth century and in the early sixth, lamps from Byzacena augment the previously dominant Zeugitanian imports.[78] Although lack of publication of pottery assemblages, especially for rural sites, is a limiting factor, there seems to have been limited importation of ceramics to the region around Mérida, suggesting that the city and its immediate territory consumed those imports in the sixth century and later.[79] Overall, in the fifth and sixth centuries there was a decline in the frequency of imported ceramics in relative proportion to all ceramic finds.[80] However, contacts with the Mediterranean world were maintained—albeit on a reduced scale—even after the Visigoths had gradually established their rule over Mérida and other southern cities during the second half of the sixth century.[81]

Continued demand in this late period is highly likely to have been driven by elite elements of the population as costs increased when goods became harder to acquire.[82] Within the context of an overall reduction in connection into Byzantine Mediterranean economic networks, Méridan elites were likely responsible for continued interactions in the second half of the sixth century and the early 600s, just as they were before. Ecclesiastical leaders seem to have played a significant role in managing relations with traders, while competitive display among the elite probably meant that some imported goods continued to be desired for their prestige value. People from the eastern Mediterranean and Africa, including but not restricted to traders and ecclesiastics, were present in Mérida throughout the period and would have played a role in these interactions.

76 Osland 2012, 331–32.
77 Osland 2012, 334.
78 Quaresma, Bustamante-Álvares, and Sabio 2018, 139–47.
79 For an overview of the ceramic evidence for Extremadura, see: Alba Calzado 2003.
80 Osland 2012, 344.
81 Osland 2012, 333. On the Visigothic conquest of Hispania more generally, see Collins 2004, 26–63.
82 Osland 2012, 322, 334, 342–44; Osland 2016, 87.

The Port on the River: Mértola

In Antiquity, Mértola (ancient *Myrtilis*) benefitted from its ability to control movement along the upper Guadiana. The city functioned as the port for the *conventus* capitals of Beja and Mérida, linking 'the Lusitanian countryside and its dense villa network with the Atlantic-Mediterranean routes' and serving as an important *entrepôt* for imported goods and a redistribution hub for agricultural products from what is nowadays known as the Baixo Alentejo.[83] Mining also played an important role in the economy of the region.[84] Mértola was likely the last consistently navigable point on the river and managed movement upriver towards Mérida, the provincial capital.[85] It was also the point at which several important land routes converged, connecting them to the Algarve coast and, further afield, to the Mediterranean.[86]

The city occupies a dominant location over the Guadiana and thus was in a good position to control access upriver (and downriver). Indeed, Hydatius's lone reference to Mértola points towards its strategic importance: 'The *comes* Censurius, who had been sent as an envoy to the Sueves and then been besieged by Rechila in Martylis where he was staying, surrendered under terms.'[87] Its defences were augmented by the construction of a new wall, perhaps in the late third or early fourth century, although a fifth- or sixth-century date has been proposed for some alterations. This may not have been a purely military act, additionally functioning as a statement of the city's prestige.[88]

The construction of a bath complex over part of the forum underscored the wealth of the city's elites in Late Antiquity, while the discovery of mosaic flooring points towards the existence of high-status housing.[89] Further religious and military renewal took place in the mid-fifth century.[90] These can be related to a more general transformation of the classical cityscape across the Iberian peninsula, as what had been public spaces were gradually

83 Fernández 2017, 113–14; Kulikowski 2004, 122; Lopes 2017, 355, 371.

84 Bernardes 2009, 330; Lopes 2017, 356.

85 Fernández 2017, 4–5.

86 Lopes 2017, 349; 355–56.

87 Hyd. 113.

88 Kulikowski 2004, 122; Fernández 2017, 113–14, 234–35, n. 14 (for dates of walls) and 25 (possible doubts about the chronology). Lopes 2017, 351 (the outer wall of the cryptoportico is the only section of the wall that can be safely and securely dated to the late Roman period), 361. On the possible fifth or sixth century ('Byzantine') date, see Macias 2005, 23–40. On city walls in late antique Lusitania, see De Man 2011.

89 Kulikowski 2004, 122 (baths); Fernández 2017, 238, n. 67.

90 Bernardes 2009, 330.

privatized and/or taken over by Christian buildings.[91] Mértola developed along similar lines, and by the fifth and sixth centuries, the space occupied by the old forum had been taken over by a Christian basilica and baptistery.[92] These buildings were supported by the cryptoportico, also constructed at some point in Late Antiquity. In the same period, another baptistery was constructed nearby.[93] Outside the city walls, a three-nave basilica of *c.* 900 m² was built in the mid-fifth century.[94] Extensive investment in ecclesiastical building projects during the fifth and sixth centuries further points towards the wealth of the elite of Mértola. Over one hundred Christian inscriptions dating between the fifth and seventh centuries have been uncovered, underlining the vibrancy of the city's religious culture.[95]

Excavations at the extramural basilica uncovered sixth-century graves and funerary inscriptions that provide indications about the composition of the city's elite, especially its ecclesiastical hierarchy.[96] There are several inscriptions written in Greek and recording individuals with Greek names, which suggests the presence of a permanent community with eastern connections, as in Mérida.[97] A number of these inscriptions are clearly Christian in content or decoration.[98] Particularly interesting is a funerary inscription for a certain Eutyches, a reader, son of Zosimus, who came from Libissa in Bithynia and died in *aera* 583 (= 544 CE).[99] Following the inscription to Eutyches, there are two further notices about Patricius, son of Gerasimus (a presbyter), and a fragmentary funerary inscription to a third person. Torres has argued that these three individuals were members of the same family, that their epitaphs followed chronologically the order of death of the commemorands, and that the references to the positions of reader and presbyter were an indication of the family's elevated social status.[100] Five other Greek inscriptions have been found in the basilica.[101]

91 For an overview of the development of urban spaces in this period, see Avelino Gutiérrez 2015.

92 Kulikowski 2004, 122; Fernández 2017, 130.

93 Lopes 2017, 371.

94 Macias, 1995; Fernández 2017, 132.

95 Bernardes 2009, 330.

96 Fernández 2017, 132.

97 García Moreno 1972, 138: 'concuerda perfectamente con que sean miembros de una colonia de greco-orientales.'

98 CIPTP 50, 59, 61, 98–99 (both 'probably' from Mértola).

99 CIPTP 37 = ICERV 524.

100 Torres 1995, 265. CIPTP 37 notes that there are 'evidentes semelhanças paleográficas' between the first two elements of the inscription.

101 Torres 1995, 264.

'Byzantine' outsiders were not only Greeks or 'easterners', but could come from Africa as well: the epigraphic record also includes inscriptions commemorating individuals who came from Africa or had typically African names.[102] Detailed analysis of funerary inscriptions from Mérida and Mértola has suggested that there were considerable similarities in terms of the cities' international connections, but differences in terms of organizational scale and status.[103] Although Greeks reached more exalted positions in Mérida due to its status as capital of Lusitania and as a bishopric, easterners also occupied positions within the ecclesiastical hierarchy at Mértola.

The city continued to play an important commercial role into the late sixth century and beyond.[104] Ceramic evidence includes fragments of Phocaean and Cypriot sigillata ware dating between the mid-fifth and the mid-sixth century, further pointing towards Mértola's connections to the eastern Mediterranean.[105] Importations of African sigillata occurred between the end of the fourth and the early seventh century, with a peak in the period 480–520.[106] Import activity was accompanied by investment in new buildings. In the forum area, a mosaic pavement was discovered in 2000 that affirmed the city's importance in the fourth to the sixth century and its continued contacts with the Mediterranean.[107] The baptistery has architectural similarities to examples from southern Gaul, northern Italy, and Carthage that have been dated between the fourth and seventh centuries,[108] while the mosaic stylistically parallels examples from elsewhere in Hispania, Tunisia, North Africa, and Ravenna. Building on this evidence, some have suggested broader 'Byzantine' influence dating to the early sixth century.[109] Indications of Mértola's connection to the Byzantine world thus extend beyond the epigraphic record to other elements of the late antique material culture of the city.

Beyond the existence of international connections, the evidence from Mértola reveals how civic elites sought to manage their linkages to the Byzantine East and North Africa by investing in defensive construction and

102 García Moreno 1972, 138, n. 56.
103 Alves Días and Gaspar 2014.
104 Kulikowski 2004, 122.
105 Delgado 1992, 132–33.
106 For a comprehensive survey of the evidence for Mértola and the region to the south, see Fernandes 2012.
107 Lopes 2008, 35–36.
108 Lopes 2008, 37.
109 Lopes 2009; Lopes 2008, 38–39. Bernardes (2009, 330, 343) points towards 'Mediterranean' influence.

other civic and transportation infrastructure. The building of the Torre do Rio in Late Antiquity connected the river to the intramural zone, extending the already formidable city walls. It served to secure the city's water supply in case of siege and to control the port zone; it may also have facilitated the loading and unloading of goods in the port and their movement into the city.[110] Construction of the Torre do Rio was roughly contemporary with that of the cryptoportico (which was sealed and used as a cistern shortly after construction).[111] Similar techniques and materials were used at both sites, suggesting contemporaneity and perhaps coordination.[112] Lopes notes that an important structural element in the defensive system of the port zone in the Roman period was a semi-circular tower associated with another rectangular tower about 100 m from Torre do Rio, although excavations suggest a very broad possible chronology of construction in two phases between the fourth century BCE and the fourth century CE.[113] While investment in urban defences tends to be seen as a sign of insecurity, it can also be read as a prestige statement, emphasizing the confidence of the city's elite. As we have seen, evidence relating to ecclesiastical building suggests that the leaders of Mértola were not lacking in resources in Late Antiquity.[114]

Maintaining and Controlling Communications in the Guadiana Valley

Elsewhere in the Iberian peninsula, defensive construction took place to control river crossings, including the reoccupation and fortification of hilltop settlements.[115] For example, at Córdoba in the late fifth or early sixth century, a fort was developed 'to protect the river port and guarantee access to the head of the bridge'.[116] Active maintenance of river infrastructure at Mértola in Late Antiquity (and before) is matched by work that was done on the Roman bridge over the river at Mérida, where an inscription records that the Gothic *dux* Salla helped Bishop Zeno rebuild the walls and bridge

110 Lopes 2017, 365, 367–70; the reuse of a second-century inscription provides a *terminus post-quem* for the date of construction, though a sixth-century chronology is possible due to the high levels of building elsewhere in the city in that period.

111 Lopes (2017, 364) notes that the construction was paradigmatically late Roman.

112 Santos Silva et al. 2006.

113 Lopes 2017, 353–54.

114 Fernández 2017, 137.

115 Tejerizo-García and Canosa-Betés 2018.

116 Casal García 2018, 120.

of the city in 483.[117] Osland has recently stressed the leading role that Zeno probably took in this project, also noting that Salla was likely an active collaborator.[118] Interestingly, the inscription does not just mention the bridge itself, but the fact that its disrepair had affected the road network: 'The road suspended over the river had lost its use / And the fallen bridge denied a free journey.' Furthermore, Salla's work on the bridge occurred 'after he had renewed the city with remarkable walls', indicating that urban defence and the broader transport infrastructure were tied up with efforts to maintain the river crossing.[119] Attempts were also made to maintain other elements of the city's water-related infrastructure, such as the aqueducts.[120] The river and road network, alongside the defences, thus played a central role in the efforts of the urban elite to advertise their patronage of Mérida, in this case in cooperation with a Gothic commander.[121]

Recent archaeological investigations, alongside references in textual sources, have suggested the existence of a Roman road network running beside the Guadiana in the hinterland of Mértola.[122] The navigability of the Guadiana up to Mértola led Bernardes to suggest that the lower river should be considered as a continuation of the coast and that defensive constructions at coastal sites across southern Lusitania may provide further parallels.[123] It is highly likely that, in the absence of an overarching central authority until the late sixth century, local and regional elites instigated this series of efforts to control access points across the south-west of the peninsula. Some degree of coordination between the leaders of individual communities was, at least in theory, possible, while Zeno's cooperation with Salla also demonstrates that the Visigoths were potentially active agents in such processes.[124] Fernández has further argued that the recently discovered charters of the Pyrenean monastery of San Martín de Asán suggest that in

117 ICERV 363; Fernández 2017, 123–24; Kulikowski 2004, 205–6, 210, 380–81 (n. 41); at 210 Kulikowski notes that there is no archaeological evidence for work on the bridge during the fifth century, but there is much evidence for work on the city's walls during the same period.

118 Osland 2019, esp. 614–23.

119 See Fernández 2017, 166 for translation of the inscription; Osland 2016, 89 discusses the reinforcement of the walls briefly.

120 Martínez Jiménez (2019, 186–203) suggests that there were attempts to maintain the aqueducts in Mérida in the sixth century.

121 See Fernández (2017, 167) for the significance of the advertised cooperation between the Goths and the bishop; further developed in Osland 2019, 614–23.

122 Lopes 2017, 357.

123 Bernardes 2009, 338–40.

124 Fernández 2017, 165.

the second half of the sixth century local communities were expected to finance infrastructure work.[125]

Osland suggests convincingly that Salla's concerns when supporting bridge renovations in Mérida would have been not only strategic, but also based on an acknowledgement of 'the city's apparent dependence on the bridge for its economic well-being'.[126] The management of rivers and interactions with foreign traders at ports were also concerns for Visigothic monarchs, most notably in the laws governing the activities of the *transmarini negotiatores* and their interactions with the population of Hispania.[127] Other laws suggest public interest in maintaining riverine communications in the face of possible 'privatization'. For example, an *antiqua* on the enclosure of *flumina maiora* states that rivers should not be blocked to such an extent that boats (*naves*) could not pass.[128] While the Visigothic monarchs of the seventh century sought to regulate contact with outsiders, the elites of fifth- and sixth-century Mértola and Mérida—perhaps in cooperation with the Visigothic monarchy[129]—funded infrastructure projects associated with the fluvial transport network that opened up opportunities for the movement of individuals, ideas, and goods at the same time as they secured elite control through defensive construction. The ability of these elites to secure their authority over the territory of the city and to exploit its resources depended, after all, on maintaining their cities as functioning transport hubs.

Conclusion

Significantly, trading and ecclesiastical connectivity to the Greek-speaking world pre- and post-dated the definitive establishment of Visigothic control over the Guadiana valley, pointing towards the importance of local and regional elites in driving forward such linkages. The pottery evidence, texts, epigraphy, and other archaeological material demonstrate the

125 Fernández 2021, 110–14.
126 Osland 2019, 622.
127 LI 11.3.1–4, all of which are *antiquae*. See p. 326 above. One of the anti-Jewish laws (LI 12.3.20) lays down procedures for dealing with Jews who arrived in the kingdom from foreign territories or provinces. On foreign merchants, see: D'Ors 1958 and, more recently, Mariezcurrena 1999.
128 LI 8.4.29. Interestingly, the law defines *flumina maiora* as those rivers into which sea fish can enter, García Moreno 1972, 145.
129 These *antiquae* laws could date from either the reign of Euric (d. 484) or Leovigild (d. 586), as discussed in D'Ors 1958, 468 and Mariezcurrena 1999, 148–49, although the consensus is for an earlier date.

continued integration of the south-west of the Iberian peninsula into Mediterranean-wide circuits of exchange in the sixth century, even if on a considerably reduced scale in comparison to the fifth century and earlier. The point at which Visigothic kings asserted their authority over the region in the mid-to-late sixth century coincides with a reduction in material evidence for connection to the Byzantine-Mediterranean world, but not its complete cessation. During the seventh century, as the Visigothic state tightened its control, the cities of the Guadiana valley still maintained connections to the outside world. The authors of the VSPE had access to Pope Gregory I's *Dialogues*, demonstrating that even as the flow of ceramic imports slowed to a trickle, the elites of the upper Guadiana retained a strong interest in the cultural patrimony of the Byzantine Mediterranean.[130]

Analysis of the cities of Mérida and Mértola demonstrates that people with connections to the Byzantine world were not unusual in the upper Guadiana valley and should not necessarily be understood as 'outsiders'. Rather, as under the Roman empire, 'ethnic' colonies, alongside local elites, played an important role in maintaining international connections, especially economically.[131] The individuals and groups in Mérida and Mértola with linkages to the eastern Mediterranean and North Africa should thus be seen as an integral element in the population of the region. Their leaders were as responsible for managing connections to the Byzantine-Mediterranean world as the Hispano-Roman aristocracy or the Visigothic monarchs and their agents.

Local elites, including ecclesiastical authorities, also played a key role in the management of connectivity. They invested in the maintenance of the transport network and associated infrastructure (e.g., the *xenodochium* in Mérida), just as they paid for defensive and religious construction.[132] Investment in control of the river and transport infrastructure supported trade and the movement of religious personnel (and ideas), and secured sites militarily and for political purposes, as suggested by the collaboration between Bishop Zeno and the Gothic noble Salla in the maintenance of the bridge at Mérida in 483. Clearly civil and ecclesiastical officials did not act independently of one another in the provincial capital, and similar infrastructure projects at Mértola presumably also required local-level elite cooperation.

130 VSPE, praef. 1–2.

131 On ethnic communities and trade in the Roman world, see Terpstra 2013.

132 Lopes 2017, 373.

Along the southwest coast of the peninsula and inland, at cities such as Faro (*Ossonoba*), Luz de Tavira (*Balsa*), and Beja (*Pax Iulia*),[133] ceramic, epigraphic, and architectural evidence suggests continued commercial relations with the eastern Mediterranean and/or North Africa until the seventh century despite the aforementioned pattern of an overall gradual reduction in long-distance trade.[134] A broadly similar chronology has been observed for the Guadiana valley. Despite their geographical distance from the coast, perhaps due to the navigability of the Guadiana and investment in infrastructure around it, the cities of Mértola and Mérida remained connected into Mediterranean circuits of economic, intellectual, and ecclesiastical exchange into the seventh century. At Mérida, pottery and other material remains suggest continued connection to Africa and the eastern Mediterranean, as do inscriptions in Greek. Downriver at Mértola, the epigraphic record demonstrates the presence of Greek speakers in the sixth century, some of whom held ecclesiastical office, while Cypriot, Phocaean, and African pottery suggests the importation of goods from across the Byzantine Mediterranean.

Taking a micro-regional approach raises some important questions about the nature of the 'Byzantium' with which the elites of the upper Guadiana valley engaged—what we see is not 'imperialism', nor is it just a projection of Byzantine 'soft-power' or cultural predominance, nor is this simply evidence of 'Byzantine' 'presence' or 'influence'. Much more was going on: shifting interactions between different microregions across the post Roman Mediterranean (cities on the upper Guadiana with some specific locations in the 'Byzantine' East and North Africa) resulted in exchanges of goods and movements of people that were at times affected by religious or political considerations and occasionally refracted by highly partial written sources. I have suggested that it is only by understanding the contexts in which the local elites that controlled cities such as Mérida and Mértola operated that we can begin to unpick not just the existence of exchange between post-Roman Iberia and the Byzantine world, but also *how* and *why* it developed in specific ways and took on specific forms. Exploration of the cities of Mérida and Mértola together demonstrates how 'religious',

133 The city of Beja, more distant from the Guadiana, was dependent on Mértola's port for access to international networks. In the mid-sixth century, the Bishop Apringius of Beja had an extensive library and may even have been of eastern extraction: García Moreno (1972, 147) notes the 'Greco-oriental' origin of his name and suggests that he came from the East; Fernandes and Valério (2013, 97) also propose a Syrian origin for Apringius.

134 Bernardes 2009, 331 (ceramics); 341 (epigraphy); 341 (architecture); 344 (general reduction in long-distance trade from the fifth to the seventh century, with some regional differentiation).

'political', and 'economic' connections should not be considered in isolation but were overlapping and mutually interdependent in the Guadiana valley and beyond.

Bibliography

Alba Calzado, Miguel A., 'Apuntes sobre la cerámica de época tardoantigua (visigoda) y altomedieval (emiral) en Extremadura, a partir del registro arqueológico emeritense', in *Repertorio de arquitectura cristiana en Extremadura: época tardoantigua y altomedieval*, Anejos de Archivo español de arqueología, ed. by Pedro Mateos Cruz and Luis Caballero Zoreda (Mérida: Consejo Superior de Investigaciones Científicas, 2003), pp. 293–332

Alves Dias, M. Manuela, and Catarina Gaspar, 'A população de Mérida e de Mértola nas fontes epigráficas', in *Wisigothica after M. C. Díaz y Díaz*, mediEVI 3, ed. by Carmen Codoñer and Paulo Farmhouse Alberto (Florence: Sismel – Edizione del Galluzzo, 2014), pp. 329–39

Arce, Javier, *Mérida Tardorramana, 300–580 d.C.* (Mérida: Museo Nacional de Arte Romano, 2002)

Arnold, Jonathan J., 'Ostrogothic Provinces', in *A Companion to Ostrogothic Italy*, ed. by Jonathan J. Arnold, M. Shane Bjornlie, and Kristina Sessa (Leiden: Brill, 2016), pp. 73–97

Avelino Gutiérrez, José, 'The Other Iberian Peninsula: The Cities of Early Medieval Spain', in *New Directions in European Medieval Archaeology: Spain and Italy Compared. Essays for Riccardo Francovich*, Collection Haut Moyen Âge 24, ed. by Sauro Gelichi and Richard Hodges (Turnhout: Brepols, 2015), pp. 135–84

Barroso Cabrera, Rafael, and Jorge Morín de Pablos, *Regia Sedes Toletana: El Toledo Visigodo a través de su escultura monumental* (Toledo: Auditores de energia y medio ambiente, 2007)

Bernardes, João Pedro, 'As Transformações no Fim do Mundo Rural Romano no Sudoeste Peninsular: evidências e problemas arqueológicos (sécs. V–VII)', in *Anales de Arquelogía Cordobesa*, 20 (2009), 323–48

Bjornlie, M. Shane, 'Governmental Administration', in *A Companion to Ostrogothic Italy*, ed. by Jonathan J. Arnold, M. Shane Bjornlie, and Kristina Sessa (Leiden: Brill, 2016), pp. 47–72

Blockley, R. C., 'Doctors as Diplomats in the 6th Century', in *Florilegium*, 2 (1980), 89–100

Casal García, María Teresa, 'The *rabad* of Šaqunda in Ummayad Córdoba (750–818 AD)', in *Entre Civitas y Madīna: El Mundo de las Ciudades en la Península Ibérica y en el Norte de África (Siglos IV–IX)*, ed. by Sabine Panzram and Laurent Callegarin (Madrid: Casa de Velázquez, 2018), pp. 119–32

Castellanos, Santiago, *The Visigothic Kingdom in Iberia: Construction and Invention* (Philadelphia, PA: University of Pennsylvania Press, 2020)

Collins, Roger, 'Mérida and Toledo: 550–585', in *Visigothic Spain: New Approaches*, ed. by Edward James (Oxford: Clarendon Press, 1980), pp. 189–219

Collins, Roger, *Visigothic Spain, 409–711* (Oxford: Blackwell, 2004)

Conant, Jonathan P., 'Europe and the African Cult of Saints, Circa 350–900: An Essay in Mediterranean Communications', in *Speculum*, 85 (2010), 1–46

Cordero Ruiz, Tomás, *El territorio emeritense durante la Antigüedad Tardía (siglos IV–VIII): genésis y evolución del mundo rural lusitano*, Anejos de Archivo español de arqueología 66 (Mérida: Consejo Superior de Investigaciones Científicas, 2013)

Curchin, Leonard A., 'Senators or Curials? Some Debatable *nobiles* in Late Antique Hispania', in *Hispania Antiqua*, 37–38 (2013–2014), 129–35

Curchin, Leonard A., 'The Role of Civic Leaders in Late Antique Hispania', in *Studia historica, Historia antigua*, 32 (2014), 281–304

D'Ors, Álvaro, 'Los "transmarini negotiatores" en la legislación visigótica', in *Estudios de Derecho internacional: homenaje al profesor Camilo Barcia Trenes* (Santiago de Compostela: Octavio y Félez, 1958), pp. 467–83

Davies, Wendy, *Small Worlds: The Village Community in Early Medieval Brittany* (London: Duckworth, 1988)

De Man, Adriaan, *Defensas Urbanas Tardias da Lusitânia* (Mérida: Museo Nacional de Arte Romano, 2011)

Decker, Michael, 'Export Wine Trade in West and East', in *Byzantine Trade, 4th–12th Centuries: The Archaeology of Local, Regional and International Exchange. Papers of the Thirty-eighth Spring Symposium of Byzantine Studies, St John's College, University of Oxford, March 2004*, ed. by Marlia Mundell Mango (Farnham: Ashgate, 2009), pp. 239–52

Delgado, Manuela, 'Cerâmicas romanas tardias de Mértola originárias do Médio Oriente', in *Arqueologia Medieval*, 1 (1992), 125–33

Dey, Hendrik W., 'Diaconiae, xenodochia, hospitalia and monasteries: "Social Security" and the Meaning of Monasticism in Early Medieval Rome', in *Early Medieval Europe*, 16.4 (2008), 398–442

Díaz, Pablo C., and Luis R. Menéndez-Bueyes, 'Gallaecia in Late Antiquity: The Suevic Kingdom and the Rise of Local Powers', in *Culture and Society in Medieval Galicia: A Cultural Crossroads at the Edge of Empire*, The Medieval and Early Modern Iberian World 58, ed. by James D'Emilio (Leiden: Brill, 2015), pp. 146–75

Edmondson, Jonathan C., 'Romanization and Urban Development in Lusitania', in *The Early Roman Empire in the West*, ed. by T. F. C. Blagg and Martin Millett (Oxford: Oxbow, 1990), pp. 149–74

Fernandes, Edgar Miguel Cruz Monteiro, *Cerâmicas finas norte-africanas e mediterrânicas orientais no Baixo Guadiana (séculos V a VII)* (MA dissertation, Faculdade de Ciências Sociais e Humanas, Universidade Nova de Lisboa, 2012)

Fernandes, Edgar Miguel Cruz Monteiro, and Miguel Filipe Grandão Valério, 'Comunidades helenógrafas en la Lusitania visigoda (s. vi)', in *Pyrenae*, 44 (2013), 69–108

Fernández, Damián, 'What Is the *De Fisco Barcinonensi* About?', in *Antiquité Tardive*, 14 (2006), 217–24

Fernández, Damián, *Aristocrats and Statehood in Western Iberia, 300–600 CE* (Philadelphia, PA: University of Pennsylvania Press, 2017)

Fernández, Damián, 'Transformaciones institucionales y liderazgo cívico en la Hispania post-imperial', in *Urban Transformations in the Late Antique West: Materials, Agents, and Models*, ed. by A. Carneiro, N. Christie, and P. Diarte-Blasco (Coimbra: Coimbra University Press, 2020), pp. 259–78

Fernández, Damián, 'El sistema tributario visigodo y los documentos de San Martín de Asán', in *Nouvelles chartes visigothiques du monastère pyrénéen d'Asán*, Scripta Mediævalia 42, ed. by C. Martin and J. J. Larrea (Bordeaux: Ausonius, 2021), pp. 105–23

García Moreno, Luis A., 'Colonias de comerciantes orientales en la Península Ibérica. S. V–VII', in *Habis*, 3 (1972), 127–54

García Moreno, Luis A., 'El Africa bizantina y España (siglos VI–VII): intercambios politicos y culturales', in *Quaderni Catanesi di Studi Antichi e Medievali*, 1 (2002), 140–90

Gillett, Andrew, *Envoys and Political Communication in the Late Antique West, 411–533* (Cambridge: Cambridge University Press, 2003)

Godoy Fernández, Cristina, and Fracesc Tuset Bertrán, 'El *atrium* en las *Vitas sanctorum patrum Emeritensium*. ¿Una formula de la llamada arquitectura de poder?', in *Archivo Español de Arqueología*, 67 (1994), 209–21

Horden, Peregrine, and Nicholas Purcell, *The Corrupting Sea: A Study of Mediterranean History* (Malden, MA: Blackwell, 2000)

Koon, Sam, and Jamie Wood, 'Unity from Disunity: Law, Rhetoric and Power in the Visigothic Kingdom', in *European Review of History*, 16 (2009), 793–808

Kulikowski, Michael, *Late Roman Spain and its Cities* (Baltimore, MD: Johns Hopkins University Press, 2004)

Lopes, Virgílio, 'A arquitectura e os mosaicos do complexo baptismal de Mértola', in *Revista de História da Arte*, 6 (2008), 33–41

Lopes, Virgílio, 'Late Antiquity in Portugal: The Mosaics', in *11th International Colloquium on Ancient Mosaics*, ed. by Mustafa Şahin (Istanbul: Zero Books, 2009), pp. 585–95

Lopes, Virgílio, 'A cidade portuária de Mértola no período Romana e na Antiguedade Tardia', in *Puertos atlánticos béticos y lusitanos y su relación comercial con el*

Mediterráneo, Hispania Antigua, Serie Arqueológica 7, ed. by Juan M. Campos Carrasco and Javier Bermejo Meléndez (L'Erma di Rome: Bretschneider, 2017), pp. 348–77

Macias, Santiago, 'A basilica palaeocristá de Mértola', in *IV Reunió d'arqueologia cristiana hispánica* (Barcelona: Institut d'Estudis Catalans, 1995), pp. 277–96

Macias, Santiago, *La kura de Beja et le territoire de Mértola entre l'Antiquité Tardive et la Reconquête*, vol. 1 (Thèse de Doctorat en Histoire, Université Lumière Lyon II, 2005)

Mariezcurrena, Salvador I., 'Puertos y comercio marítimo en la España visigoda', in *Polis: revista de ideas y formas políticas de la Antigüedad*, 11 (1999), 135–60

Martínez Jiménez, Javier, *Aqueducts and Urbanism in Post-Roman Hispania* (Piscataway, NJ: Gorgias, 2019)

Martínez Jiménez, Javier, and Carlos Tejerizo García, 'Central Places in the Post-Roman Mediterranean: Regional Models for the Iberian Peninsula', in *Journal of Mediterranean Archaeology*, 28.1 (2015), 81–103

Osland, Daniel, 'Documenting Change in Late Antique Emerita through the Ceramic Evidence', in *Journal of Late Antiquity*, 5.2 (2012), 322–44

Osland, Daniel, 'Abuse or Reuse? Public Space in Late Antique Emerita', in ***American Journal of Archaeology***, 120.1 (2016), 67–97

Osland, Daniel, 'Text and Context: Patronage in Late Antique Mérida', in ***Studies in Late Antiquity***, 3.4 (2019), 581–625

Quaresma, José Carlos, Macarena Bustamante-Álvares, and Rafael Sabio, 'Les lampes africaines de l'Antiquité Tardive provenant d'Augusta Emerita (Mérida, Espagne)', in *Rei Cretariae Romanae Fautorum Acta*, 45 (2018), 139–47

Rapp, Claudia, *Holy Bishops in Late Antiquity: The Nature of Christian Leadership in an Age of Transition*, The Transformation of the Classical Heritage 37 (Berkeley, CA: University of California Press, 2005)

Retamero, Felix, 'As Coins Go Home: Towns, Merchants, Bishops and Kings in Visigothic Hispania', in *The Visigoths from the Migration Period to the Seventh Century: An Ethnographic Perspective*, Studies in Historical Ethnoarchaeology 4, ed. by P. Heather (Woodbridge: Boydell and Brewer, 1999), pp. 271–320

Reynolds, Paul, *Hispania and the Roman Mediterranean, AD 100–700: Ceramics and Trade* (London: Duckworth, 2010)

Reynolds, Paul, 'Material Culture and the Economy in the Age of Saint Isidore of Seville (6th and 7th Centuries)', in *Antiquité Tardive*, 23 (2015), 163–210

Santos Silva, A., J. M. Ricardo, M. Salta, P. Adriano, J. Mirão, A. Estêvão Candeias, and S. Macias, 'Characterization of Roman Mortars from the Historical Town of Mértola', in *Heritage Weathering Conservation*, 1 (2006), 85–90

Tartaron, Thomas, 'Geography Matters: Defining Small Worlds of the Aegean Bronze Age', in *Maritime Networks in the Ancient Mediterranean World*, ed. by

Justin Leidwanger and Carl Knappett (Cambridge and New York, NY: Cambridge University Press, 2018), pp. 61–92

Tejerizo-García, Carlos, and Jorge Canosa-Betés, 'Power, Control and Social Agency in Post-Roman Northern Iberia: An Archaeological Analysis of Hillfort Occupations', in *Journal of Medieval Iberian Studies*, 10.3, (2018), 295–323

Terpstra, Taco, ***Trading Communities in the Roman World: A Micro-Economic and Institutional Perspective*** (Leiden: Brill, 2013)

Torres, Cláudio, 'A cidade paleocristã de Mirtylis', in *IV Reunió Cristiana Hispànica, Lisboa (1992)* (Barcelona: Institut d'Estudis Catalans; Universitat de Barcelona, 1995), pp. 263–66

Vallejo Girvés, Margarita, ***Bizancio y la España tardoantigua (SS. V–VIII): Un capitulo de historia mediterránea*** (Alcalá de Henares: Universidad de Alcalá de Henares, 1993)

Vallejo Girvés, Margarita, ***Hispania y Bizancio: una relación desconocida*** (Madrid: Akal, 2012)

Velázquez, Isabel, ***Vidas de los santos Padres de Mérida*** (Madrid: Trotta, 2008)

Vizcaíno Sánchez, Jaime, *La presencia bizantina en Hispania (siglos VI–VII): la documentación arqueológica*, Antigüedad y Cristianismo 24 (Murcia: Universidad de Murcia, 2007)

Wickham, Chris, *Framing the Early Middle Ages: Europe and the Mediterranean, 400–800* (Oxford: Oxford University Press, 2005)

Wood, Jamie, 'Borders, Centres and Peripheries in Late Roman and Visigothic Iberia', in *International Journal of Regional and Local History*, 10.1 (2015), 1–17

Wood, Jamie, 'Building and Breaking Episcopal Networks in Late Antique Hispania', in *Episcopal Networks in Late Antiquity*, Arbeiten zur Kirchengeschichte, ed. by P. Gemeinhardt and C. Cvetovic (Berlin: De Gruyter, 2019), pp. 227–47

Wood, Jamie, and Javier Martínez Jiménez, 'New Directions in the Study of Visigothic Spain', in *History Compass*, 14.1 (2016), 29–38

Zanini, Enrico, 'Artisans and Traders in the Early Byzantine City: Exploring the Limits of Archaeological Evidence', in *Late Antique Archaeology*, 3.1 (2006), 371–411

About the Author

Jamie Wood is Professor of History and Education at the University of Lincoln. He has published extensively on Isidore of Seville's historiography, bishops in Visigothic Hispania, and the social functions of violence. His current project explores political, economic, and religious connections between the Iberian peninsula and the Byzantine world in Late Antiquity.

13 Staying Roman after 711?

Ann Christys[1]

Abstract

Historians of the first half century after 711 rely on the so-called Mozarabic Chronicle, written within the east Roman chronographic tradition. Several statements in the chronicle appear to be corroborated by coins and lead seals with Arabic inscriptions found in the peninsula that also have Byzantine antecedents. This chapter looks at the ways that material evidence for imitation, reinvention, or the strategic adoption of the Roman and Byzantine past can inform the debate about rupture and continuity in Iberia after 711.

Keywords: Islamic conquest of Spain; coinage of al-Andalus; Arabic lead seals; *Chronica Muzarabica*/Chronicle of 754; Byzantine North Africa

When the Muslims conquered al-Andalus, they found in the city of *Qurṭuba* [Córdoba] the ruins (*'athār*) of a massive bridge that spanned the river, held on several arches of firm pillars, the work of the people of ancient civilizations now vanished, of which only traces remained (*al-'umam al-māḍīa al-dāthara lam yabqā minhā*).[2]

Mārida [Mérida] was one of the first places that the kings of the *'ajm* [non-Muslims] and the emperors before them chose to settle as [...] a foundation on which to build. It was completed in the time of the Caesar *Uktūbiyān* [Octavian]. The first Caesar began it and the second Caesar completed it. The rulers visited frequently and renewed the monuments, excellently made, the decorations, and the astonishing marble. They were

1 I would like to thank the editors, the anonymous reviewers and in particular Merle Eisenberg for their help with this chapter.

2 *Fatḥ al-Andalus* (ed. Molina 1994, 46); *La conquista de al-Andalus* (trans. Penelas 2002, 37); all translations, unless credited, are the author's.

Fernández, D., Lester, M. & Wood, J. (eds.), *Rome and Byzantium in the Visigothic Kingdom: Beyond* Imitatio Imperii. Taylor & Francis Group 2023
DOI: 10.5117/9789463726412_CH13

> able to bring in water stored in a construction known as *al-barīqa* [from Latin *Aqua Barraeca*] [which] workmen [both] before [...] and after them were incapable of contriving.[3]

When the forces of Ṭāriq ibn Ziyād crossed the Straits of Gibraltar in 711, followed a year later by those of Mūsā ibn Nuṣayr, the governor of North Africa appointed by the caliph in Damascus, they found all around them the material traces of Roman and Visigothic Hispania. In Córdoba, Roman walls, gates, and streets formed the template of the new capital. Visigothic buildings abutting the southern wall of the city served as the palace and administrative centre of the first Umayyad emir, ʿAbd al-Raḥmān I (756–788).[4] The Great Mosque of Córdoba may have replaced a Visigothic basilica on the same site.[5] Roman hydraulic systems were repaired to supply the garden palaces of Rusāfa,[6] al-Rūmanīya,[7] and Madīnat al-Zahrā'[8] outside Córdoba. In Mérida, Visigothic and Roman spolia were reworked into the ninth-century citadel;[9] excavation of a tenth-century domestic building revealed an Islamic phase 'entirely dependent on the Roman-Visigothic past'.[10] Roman statues stood over the gates of Córdoba and Madīnat al-Zahrā', where Roman basins stood in the patios.[11]

The conquerors also brought with them from North Africa residues of the classical past in the form of coinage and lead seals derived from Byzantine minting practices. That the new rulers had so many options to choose from—east Roman and Islamic elements from North Africa meeting Visigothic and west Roman from Iberia—makes for a complicated discussion from which few firm conclusions may be drawn. Following a brief presentation of some of the literary evidence for the conquest period, this chapter focuses on the material evidence, in particular on the coins and lead seals with Arabic inscriptions found in the peninsula, to assess how the evidence for imitation, reinvention, or strategic adoption of the Roman and Byzantine past can inform the debate about rupture and continuity in Iberia after 711.

3 Al-Rushātī, *Kitāb Iqtibās al-Anwā* (ed. Molina López and Bosch Vila 1990, 54); Elices Ocón 2017, 254.
4 Murillo Redondo et al. 2010b.
5 Although this is disputed: Arce Sainz 2015.
6 Murillo Redondo 2013; Murillo Redondo et al. 2010a.
7 Anderson 2013, 50–59.
8 Vallejo Triano 2010, 92–101.
9 Alba Calzado 2018.
10 Mateos Cruz and Alba Calzado 2000, 144.
11 Calvo Capilla 2014.

Several Arabic histories of al-Andalus mention the aqueduct of Mérida, Córdoba's Roman bridge, and the building, or rebuilding (*banā*) of the latter by one of the first governors of the new province, al-Samḥ (718–721).[12] Infrastructure repair was of course a recurring problem, as a late fifth-century inscription on the bridge at Mérida reminds us.[13] Yet on the whole the conquerors' response to the legacy of Roman building in the peninsula seems muted, perhaps because of the time taken to record it. Most of the histories attributed to Andalusi writers of the Umayyad period (756–*c.* 1031) were written in the tenth century and they survive mainly in the form of citations by later compilers. The anonymous *Conquest of al-Andalus*, the source of the description of the bridge cited at the head of this article, is a short digest of the work of one or more historians of the eleventh century.[14] Sections of the source of the second above-cited passage—the *Kitāb Iqtibās al-Anwā*[15] of al-Rushātī (1074–1147) of Almería—may survive in the author's hand.[16] He gave a chain of transmission (*isnads*) of material cited from earlier chroniclers, among them 'the sheikhs of Mérida' and 'a book written by the Christians' which he said had remained untranslated for a long time.[17] Al-Rushātī's main source was probably Aḥmad al-Rāzī (d. 955), who was active at the Umayyad court—although al-Rushātī did not mention al-Rāzī in connection with Mérida. Al-Rāzī was remembered for a description of al-Andalus that has not survived. It percolated through later compilations and translations, most notably a Castilian version of the fifteenth century, the *Crónica del Moro Rasis*,[18] but al-Rāzī's original text cannot be reconstructed.[19] The *Crónica* and late medieval histories of al-Andalus in Arabic should be treated with care, recognizing that the sources on which they were based were manipulated in the process of compilation.

The instability of ethnic labelling adds to this air of uncertainty. Historians and geographers writing in Arabic were not clear what they meant by the term 'Roman'. They employed the label '*Rūm*' ('Roman') principally for the Byzantines, their fleets, and their embassies to Córdoba. But it was

12 Ibn al-Quṭīya, *Ta'rīkh iftitāḥ al-Andalus* (ed. al-Abyārī 1982, 38) (trans. James 2009, 59); *Akhbār Majmū'a* (ed. Lafuente Alcántara 1867, 23–24) (trans. James 2012, 58–59); *Fatḥ al-Andalus* 11 (ed. Molina 1994, 46) (trans. Penelas 2002, 37); *Dhikr bilād al-Andalus* (ed. Molina 1983, 31) (trans. Molina 1983, 37).

13 Fernández 2017, 166 and see Barrett and Wood in this volume.

14 *Fatḥ al-Andalus* (ed. Molina 1994, xxvii–xxviii).

15 The title could be translated as '*florilegium*'.

16 al-Rushātī, *Kitāb Iqtibās al-Anwā* (ed. Molina López and Bosch Vila 1990, 31, 34).

17 al-Rushātī, *Kitāb Iqtibās al-Anwā* (ed. Molina López and Bosch Vila 1990, 54–55).

18 *Crónica del Moro Rasis* (ed. Catalán and de Andrés 1975).

19 Molina 1982–1983.

a portmanteau term that could be used for almost anyone or anything of Christian origin, particularly from outside the world of Islam, including slaves. Ibn Ḥabīb, writing in the ninth century (the unique manuscript of his *History* dates from the thirteenth),[20] mentioned a fleet of the *Rūm* whom the Muslims had defeated during the caliphate of Uthmān (644–656),[21] and he noted that ships of the *Rūm* were operating off the coast of North Africa in 711.[22] Yet he also said that Mūsā encountered brave horsemen of the *Rūm* in Spain during his campaign of 712–713;[23] these men must have been of Visigothic origin. The nearest that Ibn Ḥabīb came to an explanation for the ethnonym *Rūm* is his statement that 'the inhabited world is 44,000 *farasangs* and 12,000 of these are allocated to *al-Sind* (China) and *al-Hind* (India) and 8,000 to Gog and Magog and 3,000 to the *Rūm* and 1,000 to the Arabs'.[24] Al-Rāzī and other historians working in tenth-century Córdoba also used *Rūm* for Christians, but they were more likely to call them *al-Ifranj* (Franks). These historians would have known something of the Roman empire, since they seem to have read Latin histories in translation, among them a version of Orosius's *Seven Histories Against the Pagans*.[25] It is, however, difficult to untangle the evidence for the audience for this and other Latin histories in Arabic, which may have been translated for Christians literate in Arabic.[26] More generally, the pre-Islamic history of Hispania/al-Andalus was treated in the Arabic sources with a fanciful antiquarianism. Historians and others characterized the surviving monuments as the works of 'the ancients',[27] beginning with the eponymous Ispān and the Andalūsh people.[28] Arabic historians preserved varying accounts of the conquest of al-Andalus that included fantastic stories about the House of Bolts in Toledo where the last Visigothic ruler Rodrigo found a picture of the turbaned men who were to overthrow him, the discovery of the Table of Solomon in Toledo, and other wonders.[29] It is difficult to extract from these versions of the past any usable information about what 'the inheritance of Rome' looked like in immediately post-conquest Iberia.

20 Ibn Ḥabīb, *Ta'rīkh* (ed. Aguadé 1991).
21 Ibn Ḥabīb, *Ta'rīkh* 324 (ed. Aguadé 1991, 113).
22 Ibn Ḥabīb, *Ta'rīkh* 394 (ed. Aguadé 1991, 136).
23 Ibn Ḥabīb, *Ta'rīkh* 430 (ed. Aguadé 1991, 148).
24 Ibn Ḥabīb, *Ta'rīkh* 13 (ed. Aguadé 1991, 17).
25 *Kitāb Hurūshiyūsh* (ed. Penelas 2001).
26 Christys 2006.
27 *al-awā'il* ('the ancestors', literally 'the first men').
28 Christys 2018; Elices Ocón 2017.
29 Clarke 2012.

Until recently, few scholars of Visigothic Hispania have ventured into al-Andalus. One exception is Javier Arce, who argued that the classical culture of Visigothic Hispania was preserved into the Islamic period, to be revived in the kingdom of Asturias by Christians coming from the south in the tenth century to found or re-found monasteries.[30] This argument relies on dating the so-called 'Mozarabic' churches of northern Iberia and assessing the relative contribution of Visigothic and Islamic styles to their architecture, a controversy that is still far from being resolved.[31] Another sign that modern compartmentalization of the study of Iberia after 711 is breaking down is that Arabists writing about the first half century after the conquest are increasingly turning to a Latin text, the so-called *Chronica Muzarabica*, also known as the *Chronicle of 754* from the date of its last entry.[32] Written by a Christian who lived through civil war between Berber and Arab factions in al-Andalus during the 740s, the text was copied after the *Chronicle* of John of Biclarum as a link in the chain of chronicles that stretches in its various recensions from Eusebius to the thirteenth, fourteenth, and seventeenth centuries.[33] The author of the *Chronicle of 754* knew John of Biclarum's work and had other sources of information about Byzantium that have yet to be identified.[34] He used this information to write three parallel histories—of the Byzantine empire, the Islamic empire, and the transition from Visigothic Hispania to al-Andalus, which Burgess and Kulikowski described as 'one of the most ambitious chronographic works in Latin of the Early Middle Ages'.[35] In comparison with the Arabic sources, the *Chronicle of 754* is a sober and near-contemporary narration. Furthermore, it appears to be corroborated by material evidence for the conquest that, like the chronicle, also has east Roman antecedents. Reading the *Chronicle* together with this evidence shows us that what looks new after 711 can, from a different starting point, also look familiar.

The Coinage of the Conquest

Historiography of the Islamic conquest and settlement of Hispania has taken a material turn that reflects not only frustration with the literary evidence

30 Arce Martínez 2000.

31 Arce Sainz 2014; Caballero Zoreda and Mateos Cruz 2000; Maser 2014.

32 Ed. Gil 2018.

33 Cardelle de Hartmann 1999.

34 López Pereira 1980, 96–98.

35 Burgess and Kulikowski 2013.

and new archaeological discoveries, but also reasons that have as much to do with modern Spanish politics as with scholarship, as we shall see. After an exhaustive study of the Arabic narratives of the conquest,[36] Eduardo Manzano organized his history of the first centuries of al-Andalus around a study of the Islamic military and how taxation was structured to pay for the conquest and settlement of Iberia. Manzano emphasized how quickly the Muslim governors were able to establish a coinage for a new realm with a new name, faith, and language.[37]

The earliest post-conquest coins minted in the peninsula are gold *dinars* dated to 93–95 AH/711–713 CE. Some ten coins are known for 711–712 and about twenty for 712–713. The mints of the Iberian peninsula also produced silver *dirhams* for almost every year starting in 103/721–722.[38] Unfortunately, although a significant number of coins from al-Andalus have been published, nearly all are without provenance. Basing his discussion of this coinage on an estimation of the number of dies, Trent Jonson has argued that most of the new Islamic coin finds could have come from one or two hoards;[39] he concluded that the number of new coins issued seems to have been small and that it is likely that Visigothic coinage remained in circulation.[40]

Dinars minted in al-Andalus have many features in common with those issued in North Africa after 84/703–704.[41] Based on *solidi* issued by the Byzantine mint at Carthage before its first capture by the Muslims in 695, the first Islamic *dinars* from North Africa are globular in shape, but a variety of inscriptions in Latin replace the emperor busts and cross on steps of the Byzantine model. From 89/708–709 variations on the *shahāda* (the Muslim statement of faith) in Latin appear on the obverse. The reverse carries the name of the mint and dating formulae. Indiction dating, which had been used, although inconsistently, on coins from Byzantine Carthage, was reintroduced. *Dinars* with the *shahāda* in Arabic appeared in 97/715–716 in North Africa and in 98/716–717 in Iberia. In contrast to North Africa, in al-Andalus, the obverse carried a seven, eight, or nine-pointed star (see Figure 13.1), and the *hijri* (AH) dating appeared with the Indiction. Within six years of the conquest the name of the mint appeared in Arabic as 'al-Andalus'.

Since the Muslim governors of al-Andalus did not follow the usual practice of adapting the local coinage, it has been assumed that mints travelled with

36 Manzano Moreno 1999; the relevant passages are collected in Manzano Moreno 2012.
37 Manzano Moreno 2006, 55.
38 Jonson 2014, 1: 231.
39 Jonson 2014, 2: 356.
40 Jonson 2014, 2: 396.
41 Jonson 2014, 1: 34–36.

Figure 13.1: Andalusi *dinar* dated Indiction XI, also dated XCIII = AH 71/711. From http://www.andalustonegawa.50g.com/gov_trans_types.htm; thanks to Ibrahim and Gaspariño.

the armies of Ṭāriq and Mūsā and operated independently from the old Visigothic mints.[42] Jonson, however, noted that the fineness of the Islamic coins is 'similar to [...] the Visigoth coinage minted in the last few decades prior to the Muslim conquest'.[43] It is possible that moneyers brought over from North Africa reminted Visigothic coins, just as mobile mints seem to have been used earlier to rework Byzantine issues into Visigothic issues during campaigns against the Byzantine enclave of *Spania* in the early seventh century.[44] It is also possible that native moneyers may have minted coinage for the new masters, as had been the case after the Muslim conquest of Syria.[45] Visigothic mints were still functioning in the conquest period, with the last issues being thirteen coins of the last known Visigothic ruler, Agila II (710–713), the majority from Narbonne.[46] A small number of *semisses* and *tremisses* were also minted, as had also been the case at the Byzantine mint in Carthage,[47] as well as small copper *fulūs* imitating North African coinage, but with legends written only in Arabic. The *fulūs* have not attracted much attention until recently; only two can be dated to the period of the conquest and the early governors.[48]

Many aspects of these coins remain unexplained. It is not clear why the first Andalusi *dinars* copied North African coins issued in 703–706 rather

42 Crusafont i Sabatier, Balaguer, and Grierson 2013, 57.
43 Jonson 2014, 2: 320, 328; on Visigothic coinage see Eisenberg in this volume.
44 Pliego Vázquez 2009, 1: 193; Kurt 2019.
45 Pottier, Schulze, and Schulze 2008.
46 Pliego Vázquez 2009, 2: 45.
47 Jonson 2014, 1: 37.
48 Gasc 2019.

than more recent issues. Islamic issues from the Carthage mint might have crossed the Straits before 711, but this is only speculation since relations between the Visigothic mainland and North Africa are undocumented for the early years of the eighth century. Byzantine coins may also have been familiar in the peninsula, some of them minted in Byzantine *Spania* in the sixth and early seventh centuries,[49] although there is no clear evidence for Byzantine coinage or for mints in the southeast that predate Swinthila's recapture of *Spania* in 625.[50] The process of transition from Byzantine to Muslim rule in North Africa is obscure,[51] and there may have been a period during which local Byzantine rule in North Africa was tolerated in return for tribute.[52] This may help to explain anomalies in the North African coinage. For example, despite the fact that Carthage continued to mint coins for the Byzantine emperors until the end of the first reign of Justinian II in 695, early Islamic coins in North Africa used the portrait of Heraclius, which was also on the first *solidus* to be copied in the eastern Islamic world, rather than that of Justinian II. This part of the Islamic world was also slow to adopt the coinage reforms introduced in the East under 'Abd al-Malik (r. 685–705), which had gradually transformed the Byzantine *solidus* into the first aniconic *dinar* dated 77/696–697 with the first aniconic *dirham* following a year later. It was not until twenty years later that North African coinage first carried the *shahāda* in Arabic and the Indiction date was replaced with '*ferritus in Africa anno* [...]' and the date according to the Islamic calendar.

The speed of change was even slower in al-Andalus than across the Straits. Manzano attempted to account for the use of Indiction dating in al-Andalus by pointing out that the *Chronicle of 754* mentions three censuses, during the governorships of al-Samḥ (718–720),[53] Uqbah ibn al-Hajjāj (734–740),[54] and Yusuf al-Fihrī (747–756),[55] which could have been undertaken at fifteen-year intervals.[56] Yet the *Chronicle of 754* does not use Indiction dating, which had dropped out of Iberian chronicle practice two generations earlier.[57] Although Almudena Ariza has argued that some

49 Wood 2010.
50 Pliego Vázquez 2009, 1: 115–21.
51 Kaegi 2010.
52 Kaegi 2010, 210.
53 Chron. Muz. 57.
54 Chron. Muz. 67.
55 Chron. Muz. 75.
56 Manzano Moreno 2006, 74–75.
57 Trans. Wolf 1990, 57.

features of the Andalusi *dinars* were imposed from Damascus soon after the conquest,[58] numismatic change is usually slow. Delay in adopting 'Abd al-Malik's aniconic reforms and the retention of obsolete features look like relics of Byzantine minting practice, from which Islamic coinage in the West was only slowly evolving.

Looking back to the Islamic conquest of Syria and Palestine, however, we find that there may have been other reasons for continuing to mint currency that looked Byzantine. In Syria the minting of pseudo-Byzantine coins may have begun soon after the Battle of Yarmuk in 636.[59] Under Persian rule, workers associated with the Byzantine mint at Antioch had produced Byzantine *folles*, supplemented later by unskilled moneyers who made coins of lower quality. The new Arab rulers seem to have done the same, producing coins whose obverses are characteristic of the mints of Neapolis, Emesa, and Cyprus during the period immediately before 636. Iran under the Arabs also continued to mint Sassanian *dirhams* with the images of Khusrau II or Yazdgard III and legends in Pahlavi. Pseudo-Byzantine coinage was accepted both in the East and in the Maghreb and Iberia because it was similar to contemporary imperial coinage still in circulation. When, according to the *Maronite Chronicle* of *c.* 640, the caliph Mu'āwiya 'minted gold and silver [...] it was not accepted because it had no cross on it'.[60]

This may explain why the first attempt to mint *dinars* in al-Andalus was short-lived. Manzano suggested that Mūsā's recall to Damascus in 713 is reflected in the coin finds,[61] since only four coins survive for that year and none for the period during which Mūsā's son succeeded him as governor. Minting of *dinars* in small numbers recommenced under al-Ḥurr (716–717). Mūsā's ties with the Damascus regime were close. He fought for Mu'āwiya, the first Umayyad caliph, and may have gone to Egypt with 'Abd al-Malik b. Marwān as early as 697/8.[62] Yet the delay in adopting 'Abd al-Malik's reformed coinage in al-Andalus suggests that he made no attempt to control the transition from Byzantine to orthodox Islamic minting practice, perhaps because both the conquered peoples and the armies of the conquest coming from North Africa may have been happier with pseudo-Byzantine currency that was closer to what they recognized as real money.

58 Ariza Armada 2016.
59 Pottier, Schulze, and Schulze 2008.
60 Palmer 1993, 29.
61 Manzano Moreno 2006, 55–61.
62 *Khalifa b. Khayyat's History* (trans. Wurzel 2015, 139); Benhima and Guichard 2017.

The Lead Seals

Like the coinage, a number of lead seals with Arabic inscriptions found in the peninsula seem to provide evidence for attempts at administrative reform linked to regime change in the years immediately after 711, which the *Chronicle of 754* appears to corroborate. The seals leaped to prominence at the time of deeply divisive commemorations of the conquest in 2011, when they were heralded as 'new documents on the Umayyad conquest of Spain [...] fundamental to the understanding of the early days of the Muslim presence in the Iberian peninsula'.[63] This hyperbole and the weight that has been placed on these undistinguished artefacts, previously overlooked, is understandable at a time when some Spanish academics are helping to promote the view that their homeland could never have been subject to Muslim domination and therefore the conquest never happened.[64] For some scholars of the opposing camp, the seals are incontrovertible evidence both for the conquest and for a new period in Spanish history that was fundamentally new and Islamic.

More than 150 Islamic lead seals survive from the Iberian peninsula, allocated to almost fifty different types depending on the content of their inscriptions.[65] Half of the seals were chance findings from sites in the southwest of the peninsula, but in 2005 more than seventy seals were discovered through the supervised use of metal detectors in the spoil heaps resulting from repeated excavation of a Roman *municipium* at Ruscino (France)[66] on the *Via Domitia* that passes through Narbonne. Those seals that are legible all bear the same legend: *maghnūm ṭayyib* ('licit booty') on one side and '*qusim*, or *qasm bi-arbūna*' ('distributed in Narbonne') on the other. (See Figure 13.2) Although the Ruscino seals carry neither the name of a ruler, nor the place where they were issued and are undated, they seem to relate to the redistribution by the governor al-Samḥ (718–721) of the booty taken in his campaign against Narbonne, which is recorded in the *Chronicle of 754*:

> In the western regions the Arabs achieved many military victories under their leader al-Samḥ. He undertook a census of Hispania Ulterior and Hispania Citerior. He divided by lot among his allies the booty, arms and

63 Ibrahim 2011, 147.
64 Fancy 2019; García Sanjuán 2013, 2019; Wolf 2019.
65 Ibrahim 2015.
66 Baratta 2015.

Figure 13.2: Seal of Andalusi governor al-Samḥ (718–21). From http://www.andalustonegawa.50g.com/Seals.html; thanks to Ibrahim and Gaspariño.

> whatever else in the way of plunder the Arab people in Spain had not yet divided and added a portion of all the moveable and immoveable goods to the fisc. Afterwards he made Narbonne his own.[67]

Many of the seals found elsewhere in the peninsula also carry legends that appear to refer to the conquest period. The inscriptions are difficult to decipher and where they carry personal names these cannot always be identified. Three governors are named: al-Samḥ, his predecessor al-Ḥurr (717–718), and his successor Anbasa (721–725). One of seals of al-Ḥurr has been over-stamped on an earlier issue, but it is not clear whether the original predates the conquest. The latest datable issue is a single seal apparently naming the first Umayyad emir ʿAbd al-Raḥmān I (756–788).[68]

Lead seals were of course common from Antiquity. Although it is not clear whether they were in use in Visigothic Hispania, more than 80,000 seals are now known for Byzantium. They were mostly discovered in archaeological contexts, especially in Istanbul.[69] They are difficult to date, and their interpretation is challenging. Byzantine seals before *c.* 700 were usually impressed with the name and title of the owner or an invocation to Christ, the Virgin, or a saint, and sometimes images; later issues were more likely to be aniconic. A much smaller number of Byzantine seals have

67 Chron. Muz. 57 (trans. Wolf 1990, 138).

68 Ibrahim 1995.

69 Brubaker and Haldon 2001, 129–37; Brandes 2002, 281.

been found in North Africa;[70] some may be dated by their portraits, as may a few seals with Latin inscriptions from Carthage and the surrounding area, issued from the 670s onwards. Some of these seals witness the activities of *commerciarioi* based in Constantinople who travelled to North Africa, probably in connection with the procurement of grain for the army, and whose activities in North Africa are known from the middle of the seventh century. The seals disappear around the time of Gregory's revolt in 647 and reappear only in 673–674, shortly after Constantinople tried to reimpose fiscal control over the region.[71] In 672/3 the office of the *commerciarioi* was reformed, possibly as a response to the Arab conquests and the threat to Constantinople, and their seals began to carry the Indiction dating.[72] Wolfram Brandes concluded that the Indiction was added to the seals as a part of this reorganization, in parallel with a coinage reform of 688, although the reason for this is not known.[73]

The material and inscriptions of the seals from al-Andalus are quite unlike other Islamic seals of the same period. Few lead seals have been published for eastern Islamic lands or Egypt in the early conquest period, and none for the Maghreb.[74] Later written sources remembered the first Umayyad caliph Mu'āwiya (661–680) as the first to establish a register of seals. They were used on safe-conducts and tax demand notes, which carried the name of the official making the demand.[75] In Egypt, the seals were made of clay and both seals and fragments of the papyri that were attached to them survive. The earliest Islamic seals from Egypt were impressed with living forms, either human or animal; the move to aniconic seals coincided with 'Abd al-Malik's coinage reform. Until the mid-eighth century the governor's name inscribed on the seal might be either in Greek or in Arabic and the attached note in Greek, Greek and Arabic, or Coptic, combining the indigenous languages and formulae with those of the conqueror.[76] In al-Andalus, however, the seals are inscribed in Arabic alone. The Andalusi seals also look anomalous within the Muslim world because their inscriptions, such as those relating to peace pacts, discussed below, do not seem to have any parallel in Egypt, Syria, or Mesopotamia.

Some of the single seal finds from southern Iberia, like those from Ruscino, concern taxation and redistribution of land and goods. A seal with the

70 Morrisson and Seibt 1982; Brandes 2002, 309.
71 Haldon 2016, 241; Prigent 2006.
72 Brandes 2002, 312.
73 Brandes 2002, 322.
74 Sénac and Ibrahim 2017.
75 Sijpesteijn 2012.
76 Heidemann and Sode 1997; Sijpesteijn 2013, 67–71.

legend 'al-Ḥurr orders the division of al-Andalus' seems to match an entry in the *Chronicle of 754* saying that al-Ḥurr 'restored to the Christians the small estates that had originally been confiscated for the sake of peace so as to bring in revenue to the public treasury'.[77] Several seals mention division (*qasm*); others have *fay' Allāh*, which is another term for the portion of the spoils of war due to the state, perhaps referring to immovable goods. A seal with an inscription naming Beja, now in southern Portugal, refers to the allocation of wheat. Most of these seals cannot be dated, although it has been suggested that the use of early Kufic script may rule out a date later than the conquest period.[78] For this reason a seal that appears to read 'the emir Abd Allāh' is attributed to the early governor Abd Allāh b. Malik (al-Samḥ, mentioned above) rather than the emir 'Abd Allāh (888–912) because the epigraphy looks early.[79]

The author of the *Chronicle of 754* had already suggested that Mūsā's greed was the reason for his recall to Damascus, suggesting that norms for the distribution of booty were already in force in the eighth century.[80] Nevertheless, recent discussion of the terminology used on the seals may be vulnerable to the charge of anachronism. Some of the seals are inscribed with the word '*jizya*', the poll-tax levied on non-Muslim subjects. Seals with the legend '*ahl*' ('the people of') the cities of Seville and Beja could also refer to the *jiyza*.[81] A clay seal from Egypt mentioning *jizya* has been linked to the financial reforms of an early eighth-century governor (Qurra ibn Sharīk 709–719).[82] Yet Islamic theory on the allocation of the spoils of conquest and the treatment of the conquered peoples was not formalized until the ninth century.[83] It was at this period that two chroniclers writing in Arabic about the conquest of Spain—Ibn Ḥabīb (d. 853) and Ibn 'Abd al-Ḥakam (803–871)—commented on the illegal retention of booty due to the state by Mūsā b. Nuṣayr and others.[84] Some of the inscriptions name individual cities—Seville, Jaén, Sidonia, Ilbira (Elvira, near Granada), Ocsonaba (Faro), and perhaps Mérida[85]—and seem to relate to their capture. The terms used in the inscriptions—*ṣulḥ* and *maṣālaḥa* ('conciliation' or 'settlement')—are

77 Chron. Muz. 53 (trans. Wolf 1990, 137).
78 Ibrahim 2011.
79 Ibrahim 2015, no. 4.
80 Chron. Muz. 45–46.
81 Ibrahim 2011.
82 Heidemann and Sode 1997.
83 Crone 2004, 304.
84 Christys 2014.
85 Gaspariño and Ibrahim 2019.

those used in later historiographical debates about the legal distinction between conquest by force or pact.[86] They were derived from the teachings of Malik ibn Anas (711–795), which were not introduced into al-Andalus until the middle of the ninth century. Unless the norms of taxation and settlement later attributed to Malik and others were already in force in 711, it is possible that these norms and the seals that represent them post-date the conquest by at least a century. Going further, Janina Safran has recently argued that Maliki jurists from the ninth to the twelfth centuries revised the narrative of the conquest of Spain according to Maliki norms, as part of the history of their own community.[87]

The prominence of the lead seals in the current polemic around the conquest has co-opted information derived not only from the *Chronicle of 754*, but from the later Arabic sources to reinforce the seals' importance. The following will serve as an example. Tawfiq Ibrahim interpreted a seal that appears to read '*muṣālaḥa libīr*(*a*)' (the settlement of Livira) as a reference to a peace treaty between the conquerors and the people of Elvira, near Granada:

> Elvira [...] was reputed in Visigoth[ic] times to have had a substantial Jewish population. So, following the not very exquisite treatment Jews had long received from the Visigoth[s] [...] it would therefore be of little wonder if they [...] entered into a peace pact with the new masters of the terrain as this seal seems to indicate. If so, this would have probably occurred [...] when 'Abd al-Azīz, [the son of Mūsā ibn Nuṣayr] [...] must have necessarily passed through the area on his way to Orihuela where the pact of Tudmīr would be established. The possible pact with Elvira may have been established just before Mūsā's departure in 95/713.[88]

Visigothic anti-Jewish legislation is well documented, but the supposed betrayal of Hispania to the Muslims by the Jews is a trope. Indeed, there is almost no reliable evidence for the Jewish population of al-Andalus between 711 and the tenth century. Furthermore, the Arabic sources give varying accounts of the itineraries of the conquerors, and the pact of Tudmīr is controversial.[89] It is a lot of history for a single undated and difficult-to-read

86 Pliego Vázquez and Ibrahim 2021; Manzano Moreno 2006, 36.

87 Safran 2019.

88 Ibrahim 2011, no. 1.

89 For the pact of Tudmīr, see Franco-Sánchez 2014; Gutiérrez Lloret 2014; Manzano Moreno 2014.

inscription to bear. We must hope that more work on the seals will help to clarify their value as evidence for the conquest period.

One further caveat is our uncertainty about how Islamic the armies of the conquest were.[90] Historians writing in Arabic characterized the invading forces as largely Berber. This begs a number of questions. The ethnonym 'Berber' used for the inhabitants of North Africa was coined by these historians only in the ninth century.[91] It conceals differences across the region that were so profound that it is unlikely that the inhabitants of North Africa considered themselves a single group.[92] By the eighth century few of these 'Berbers' had converted to Islam in North Africa; most may have been either still pagan or Christian. The adoption of Roman status symbols—clothing, regalia, and titles—and political organization is well documented in the period *c.* 535–565, following the Justinianic occupation of North Africa.[93] The North African elite continued to use both Roman and indigenous names, and they took Roman titles and celebrated Roman martyrs.[94] Some of these men may still have been Christians who identified as Roman when they accompanied their Muslim leaders to Spain.[95] Both the *Chronicle of 754*[96] and the slightly earlier *Chronica byzantia-arabica*[97] chronicled the sudden appearance of 'Saracens' and their leader Muḥammad in Syria. But the *Chronicle of 754* does not characterize the 'Saracens' and the 'Moors' who accompanied Ṭāriq and Mūsā as men who imposed a new faith on Hispania. After reporting the initial shock of the conquest, the chronicler presents a series of governors as being either just or unjust in relation to their treatment of the Christian population. He notes that although a few churchmen abandoned their flock, many Christians and their institutions flourished.[98] Acculturation to Arabic language and culture and conversion to Islam were gradual and Christians would continue to play a significant role in Andalusi society until the tenth century.[99]

90 Manzano Moreno 1998.
91 Rouighi 2011.
92 Fenwick and Merrills 2021.
93 Merrills 2021.
94 Conant 2012, 280.
95 Stouraitis 2014.
96 Chron. Muz. 7.
97 *Chronica byzantia-arabica* 13 (ed. Gil 2018, 312).
98 They may have functioned as tax gatherers for the new regime, although there is no clear evidence for this, in contrast to the Islamic conquest of Syria-Palestine: see Walmsley 2010, 27–29.
99 Christys 2002, 184–86.

Conclusion

Just as we have learned to be wary of Arabic historiography of the conquest, so we should not rush to accept the material evidence as proof that everything changed in 711. On the one hand, there is a strong case that the move towards aniconic coins with Arabic inscriptions, the lead seals with Arabic inscriptions relating to the conquest and settlement of cities and the distribution of land and goods, and the passages from the *Chronicle of 754* about the new rulers' tax reforms, add up to a coherent account of a well-managed conquest and the transition to a new system of government. This process was later codified into history by writers who knew little of the Roman or Byzantine past and read the conquest as the implementation of Islamic norms. Yet many questions about the coins, seals, and chronicles remain unresolved. Rachel Stocking's argument that 'a dialogue between text and artifact is the only means of grasping a complex and shifting late antique world' holds equally true for the period after 711.[100] Care must be taken when interpreting both the written and the material evidence, so that assumptions made about the one are not transferred to the other.[101]

We may cautiously conclude that, like the *Chronicle of 754*, the *dinars* and perhaps the lead seals evolved from Roman tradition. They may have already been familiar in Visigothic Hispania from Byzantine rule in the peninsula and the closeness between southern Spain and North Africa. They were recognizably Byzantine even in their new guise in the baggage of the armies of a new regime. It seems that 711 was too early to give up being Roman in Hispania. In the first years after the conquest some, perhaps many, aspects of society may have remained the same under a change of leadership.

Bibliography

Akhbār Majmūʿa, ed. by Emilio Lafuente Alcántara, *Akhbār Majmūʿa, Crónica anónima del siglo XI* (Madrid, 1867)

Alba Calzado, Miguel, 'Secuencias en la transformación de *Augusta Emerita* (siglos I–IX): tres concepciones distintas de ser ciudad', in *Entre civitas y madīna. El mundo de las ciudades en la Península Ibérica y en el norte de África (siglos iv–ix)*,

100 Stocking 2007.

101 Carvajal López 2019.

Collection de la Casa de Velázquez 167, ed. by Sabine Panzram and Laurent Callegarin (Madrid: Casa de Velázquez, 2018), pp. 51–74

Anderson, Glaire D., *The Islamic Villa in Early Medieval Iberia* (Farnham and Burlington, VT: Ashgate, 2013)

Arce Martínez, Javier, '"*Gothorum laus est civilitas custodita*". Los visigodos conservadores de la cultura clásica: el caso de Hispania', in *Visigodos y Omeyas: Un debate entre la Antigüedad Tardía y la Alta Edad Media (Mérida, April, 1999)*, Anejos de Archivo Español de Arqueología 23, ed. by Luis Caballero Zoreda and Pedro Mateos Cruz (Madrid: Consejo Superior de Investigaciones Científicas and Consorcio de la Ciudad Monumental de Mérida, 2000), pp. 11–20

Arce Sainz, Fernando, 'Arquitectura religiosa cristiana en al-Andalus. Propuesta para su comprensión y estudio', in *Von Mozarabern zu Mozarabismen. Zur Vielfalt kultureller Ordnungen auf der mittelalterlichen Iberischen Halbinsel*, ed. by Matthias Maser, Klaus Herbers, Michele C. Ferrari, and Hartmut Bobzin (Münster: Aschendorff, 2014), pp. 235–57

Arce Sainz, Fernando, 'La supuesta basílica de San Vicente en Córdoba: de mito histórico a obstinación historiográfica', in *Al-Qanṭara*, 36.1 (2015), 11–44

Ariza Armada, Almudena, 'Los dinares bilingües de al-Andalus y el Magreb', in *Revista Numismática Hécate*, 3 (2016), 137–58

Baratta, Giulia, 'Excavation in Ruscino (Perpignan – France) / Ruscino (Perpignan), Francia', in *Archeologia ed epigrafia a Macerata. Cinquant'anni di ricerche in Ateneo*, ed. by Sofia Cingolani, Silvia Marengo, and Gianfranco Paci (Macerata: Università di Macerata, 2015), pp. 62–64

Benhima, Yassir, and Pierre Guichard, 'Mūsā ibn Nuṣayr, Retour sur l'histoire et le pouvoir d'un gouverneur omeyyade en Occident musulman', in *Bulletin d'études orientales*, 66 (2017), 97–116

Brandes, Wolfram, *Finanzverwaltung in Krisenzeiten. Untersuchungen zur byzantinischen Administration im 6.–9. Jahrhundert*, Forschungen zur byzantinischen Rechtsgeschichte 25 (Frankfurt am Main: Löwenklau-Gesellschaft, 2002)

Brubaker, Leslie, and John Haldon, *Byzantium in the Iconoclast Era c. 680–850: The Sources. An Annotated Survey*, Birmingham Byzantine and Ottoman Manuscripts 7 (Aldershot, Burlington, VT, Singapore, and Sydney: Ashgate, 2001)

Burgess, R. W., and Michael Kulikowski, *Mosaics of Time: The Latin Chronicle Tradition from the First Century BC to the Sixth Century AD*, vol. 1, *A Historical Introduction to the Chronicle Genre from its Origins to the High Middle Ages* (Turnhout: Brepols, 2013)

Caballero Zoreda, Luis, and Pedro Mateos Cruz (eds), *Visigodos y Omeyas: Un debate entre la Antigüedad Tardía y la Alta Edad Media (Mérida, April, 1999)*, Anejos de Archivo Español de Arqueología 23 (Madrid: Consejo Superior de Investigaciones Científicas and Consorcio de la Ciudad Monumental de Mérida, 2000)

Calvo Capilla, Susana, 'The Re-use of Classical Antiquity in the Palace of Madinat al-Zahrā' and its Role in the Construction of Caliphal Legitimacy', in *Muqarnas*, 31 (2014), 1–34

Cardelle de Hartmann, Carmen, 'The Textual Transmission of the Mozarabic Chronicle of 754', in *Early Medieval Europe*, 8.1 (1999), 13–29

Carvajal López, José C., 'After the Conquest: Ceramics and Migrations', in *Journal of Medieval Iberian Studies*, 11.3 (2019), 323–41

Catalán, Diego, and María Soledad de Andrés, *Crónica del Moro Rasis* (Madrid: Editorial Gredos, 1975)

Christys, Ann, *Christians in al-Andalus (711–1000)* (Richmond: Curzon, 2002)

Christys, Ann, '"How Can I Trust You, Since You are a Christian and I am a Moor?" The Multiple Identities of the *Chronicle of Pseudo-Isidore*', in *Texts and Identities in the Early Middle Ages, Forschungen zur Geschichte des Mittelalters*, ed. by Richard Corradini, Rob Meens, Christina Pössel, and Philip Shaw (Vienna: Verlag der Österreichischen Akademie der Wissenschaften, 2006), pp. 359–72

Christys, Ann, 'From *ǧihād* to *diwān* in Two Providential Histories of Hispania/ al-Andalus', in *'Guerra santa' e conquiste islamiche nel Mediterraneo (VII–XI secolo)*, ed. by Marco Di Branco and Kordula Wolf (Rome: Viella, 2014), pp. 79–94

Christys, Ann, '"Made by the Ancients": Romanness in al-Andalus', in *Transformations of Romanness: Early Medieval Regions and Identities*, Millennium-Studien zu Kultur und Geschichte des erstens Jahrtausends n. Chr./ Millennium Studies in the Culture and History of the First Millennium C.E. 71, ed. by Walter Pohl, Clemens Gantner, Cinzia Grifoni, and Marianne Pollheimer-Mohaupt (Berlin and Boston, MA: Walter de Gruyter, 2018), pp. 379–92

Chronica byzantia-arabica, ed. by Juan Gil, *Chronica Hispana saeculi VIII et IX*, Corpus Christianorum. Continuatio Mediaevalis 45 (Turnhout: Brepols, 2018), pp. 307–23

Clarke, Nicola, *The Muslim Conquest of Iberia: Medieval Arabic Narratives* (Abingdon and New York, NY: Routledge, 2012)

Conant, Jonathan, *Staying Roman: Conquest and Identity in Africa and the Mediterranean, 439–700* (Cambridge: Cambridge University Press, 2012)

Crone, Patricia, *Medieval Islamic Political Thought* (Edinburgh: Edinburgh University Press, 2004)

Crusafont i Sabatier, Miguel, Anna M. Balaguer, and Philip Grierson, *Medieval European Coinage: With a Catalogue of the Coins in the Fitzwilliam Museum, Cambridge*, vol. 6, *The Iberian Peninsula* (Cambridge: Cambridge University Press, 2013)

Dhikr bilād al-Andalus, ed. by Luis Molina, *Dhikr bilād al-Andalus. Una descripción anónima de al-Andalus*, 2 vols (Madrid: Consejo Superior de Investigaciones Científicas, 1983)

Elices Ocón, Jorge, 'El pasado pre-islámico de al-Andalus: fuentes árabes, recepción de la antigüedad y legitimación en época omeya (ss.VIII–X)' (doctoral thesis, Universidad Autónoma de Madrid, 2017), http://hdl.handle.net/10486/679950

Fancy, Hussein, 'The New Convivencia', in *Journal of Medieval Iberian Studies*, 11.3 (2019), 295–305

Fatḥ al-Andalus, ed. by Luis Molina, *Fatḥ al-Andalus* (*La conquista de al-Andalus*) (Madrid: Consejo Superior de Investigaciones Científicas, 1994)

Fenwick, Coriander, and Andy Merrills, 'Authority Beyond Tribe and State in the Early Medieval Maghrib', in *Al-Masāq*, 33.1 (2021), 1–13

Fernández, Damián, *Aristocrats and Statehood in Western Iberia, c. 300–600 C.E.* (Philadelphia, PA: University of Pennsylvania Press, 2017)

Franco-Sánchez, Francisco, 'El tratado de Teodomiro en su contexto histórico y paleográfico', in *eHumanista/IVITRA*, 5 (2014), 312–48

García Sanjuán, Alejandro, *La conquista islámica de la Península Ibérica y la tergiversación del pasado: del catastrofismo al negacionismo* (Madrid: Marcial Pons Historia, 2013)

García Sanjuán, Alejandro, 'Denying the Islamic Conquest of Iberia: A Historiographical Fraud', in *Journal of Medieval Iberian Studies*, 11.3 (2019), 306–22

Gasc, Sebastián, 'Numismatics Data about the Islamic Conquest of the Iberian Peninsula', in *Journal of Medieval Iberian Studies*, 11.3 (2019), 342–58

Gaspariño, Sebastián, and Tawfiq Ibrahim, 'Nuevo "precinto de paz" (musalaha) de lugar desconocido', in *Manquso*, 10 (2019), 5–6

Gutiérrez Lloret, Sonia, 'La materialidad del Pacto de Teodomiro a la luz de la arqueología', in *eHumanista/IVITRA*, 5 (2014), 262–88

Haldon, John, *The Empire That Would Not Die: The Paradox of Eastern Roman Survival 640–740* (Cambridge, MA and London: Harvard University Press, 2016)

Heidemann, Stefan, and Claudia Sode, 'Metallsiegel in der islamischen Welt, ihre Forschungsgeschichte und orientalische Bleisiegel aus einem Siegelfund in Konstantinopel', in *Res Orientales X, Sceaux d'Orient et leur employ*, Groupe pour l'Étude de la Civilisation du Moyen-Orient (Leuven: Peeters, 1997), pp. 41–60

Ibn Ḥabīb ['Abd al-Malik ibn Habib], *Kitab al-Ta'rikh*, ed. by Jorge Aguadé, *Ta'rīkh: 'Abd al-Malik ibn Habib Kitab al-Ta'rikh* (Madrid: Consejo Superior de Investigaciones Científicas, 1991)

Ibn al-Quṭīya [Abū Bakr Muḥammad ibn 'Umar ibn al-Quṭīya], *Ta'rīkh iftitāḥ al-Andalus*, ed. by Ibrāhīm al-Abyārī, *Ta'rīkh iftitāḥ al-andalus'* (Beirut: Dār al-kitāb al-miṣrī, 1982)

Ibrahim, Tawfiq, 'Un precinto en nombre de 'Abd al-Rahman I', in *Al-Qanṭara*, 16 (1995), 143–45

Ibrahim, Tawfiq, 'Nuevos documentos sobre la conquista omeya de Hispania: Los precintos de plomo', in *711. Arqueología e historia entre dos mundos*, vol. 1,

Arqueología 15, ed. by Luis A. García Moreno and Alfonso Vigil-Escalera (Alcalá de Henares: Museo Arqueológico Regional, 2011), pp. 146–61

Ibrahim, Tawfiq, 'Additions to the Lead Seals of the Umayyad Conquest of the Iberian Peninsula', in *Villa 5, Monnaies du haut Moyen Âge: histoire et archéologie (péninsule Ibérique – Maghreb, Viie–Xie siècle)*, Études Médiévales Ibériques, ed. by Philippe Sénac and Sébastien Gasc (Toulouse: Presses universitaires du Midi, 2015), pp. 115–32

Ibrahim, Tawfiq, and Sebastian Gaspariño, *The Coins of Al-Andalus: The Tonegawa Collection*, https://rah-es.academia.edu/TawfiqIbrahimتوفيقابراهيم [date of access: 3 June 2022]

James, David, *Early Islamic Spain: The History of Ibn al-Quṭīya* (Abingdon and New York, NY: Routledge, 2009)

James, David, *A History of Early Al-Andalus. The Ajbār maŷmū'a: A study of the Unique Arabic Manuscript in the Bibliothèque Nationale de France, Paris, with a Translation, Notes and Comments* (London and New York, NY: Routledge, 2012)

Jonson, Trent, 'A Numismatic History of the Early Islamic Precious Metal Coinage of North Africa and the Iberian Peninsula', 2 vols (DPhil thesis, University of Oxford, 2014)

Kaegi, Walter, *Muslim Expansion and Byzantine Collapse in North Africa* (Cambridge: Cambridge University Press, 2010)

Kitāb Hurūshiyūsh, ed. by Marte Penelas, *Kitāb Hurūshiyūsh (Traducción Árabe de las Historiae Adversus Paganos de Orosio)* (Madrid: Centro Superior de Investigaciones Científicas, 2001)

Kurt, Andrew, 'Visigothic Currency in its Making and Movement: A Varying State of Circumstances', in *Visigothic Symposia*, 3 (2019), 165–97

López Pereira, José Eduardo, *Estudio Crítico sobre la crónica mozárabe de 754* (Zaragoza: Anubar, 1980)

Manzano Moreno, Eduardo, 'Árabes, beréberes e indígenas: Al-Andalus en su primer período de formación', in *L'Incastellamento: Actes des Recontres de Gérone (26–27 Novembre 1992) et de Rome (5–7 Mai 1994)*, Collection de l'École Française de Rome 241, ed. by Miquel Barceló and Pierre Toubert, (Rome: École Française de Rome and Escuela Española de Historia y Arqueología en Rome, 1998), pp. 157–78

Manzano Moreno, Eduardo, 'Las fuentes árabes sobre la conquista de al-Andalus: una nueva interpretación', in *Hispania*, 59.2 (1999), 389–432

Manzano Moreno, Eduardo, *Conquistadores, Emires y Califas Los Omeyas y la formación de al-Andalus* (Barcelona: Crítica, 2006)

Manzano Moreno, Eduardo, 'Los relatos de la conquista de al-Andalus en las fuentes árabes: un estudio sobre su procedencia' (Madrid: Consejo Superior de Investigaciones Científicas, 2012), https://digital.csic.es/handle/10261/44814 [date of access: 2 June 2022]

Manzano Moreno, Eduardo, 'La transmisión textual sobre Teodomiro', in *eHumanista/IVITRA*, 5 (2014), 243–61

Maser, Matthias, 'Von Mozarabern zu Mozarabismen? Überlegungen zu einer perspektivischen Neuausrichtung der Forschung', in *Von Mozarabern zu Mozarabismen. Zur Vielfalt kultureller Ordnungen auf der mittelalterlichen Iberischen Halbinsel*, ed. by Matthias Maser, Klaus Herbers, Michele C. Ferrari, and Hartmut Bobzin (Münster: Aschendorff, 2014), pp. 21–40

Mateos Cruz, Pedro, and Miguel Alba Calzado, 'De Emerita Augusta a Marida', in *Visigodos y Omeyas: Un debate entre la Antigüedad Tardía y la Alta Edad Media (Mérida, April, 1999)*, Anejos de Archivo Español de Arqueología 23, ed. by Luis Caballero Zoreda and Pedro Mateos Cruz (Madrid: Consejo Superior de Investigaciones Científicas and Consorcio de la Ciudad Monumental de Mérida, 2000), pp. 143–68

Merrills, Andy, 'The Men Who Would Be King: Moorish Political Hierarchies and Imperial Policy in Byzantine Africa', in *Al-Masāq*, 33.1 (2021), 14–29

Molina, Luis, 'Sobre la procedencia de la historia preislámica inserta en la crónica del moro Rasis', in *Awrāq*, 5–6 (1982–1983), 133–39

Morrisson, Cécile, and Werner Seibt, 'Sceaux des commerciaires byzantins du VIIe siècle trouvés à Carthage', in *Revue Numismatique*, 6th series, 24 (1982), 222–40

Murillo Redondo, Juan Francisco, 'Qurtuba califal. Origen y desarrollo de la capital omeya de al-Andalus', in *Awrāq*, 7 (2013), 81–103

Murillo Redondo, Juan Francisco, Fátima Castillo Pérez de Siles, Elena Castro del Río, María Teresa Casal, and Teresa Dortez Cáceres, 'La almunia y el arrabal de al-Rusafa, en el Yanib al-Garbi de Madinat Qurtuba', in *El Anfiteatro Romano de Córdoba y su entorno urbano. Análisis Arqueológico (ss. I–XIII d.C.)*, Monografías de arqueología cordobesa 19:2, ed. by Desiderio Vaquerizo Gil and Juan Francisco Murillo (Córdoba: Universidad de Córdoba and Gerencia Municipal de Urbanismo del Ayuntamiento, 2010a), pp. 565–614

Murillo Redondo, Juan Francisco, Alberto León Muñoz, Elena Castro del Río, María Teresa Casal García, Raimundo Ortiz Urbano, and Antonio José González Ruíz, 'La transición de la civitas clásica cristianizada a la madina islámica a través de las transformaciones operadas en las áreas suburbiales', in *El Anfiteatro Romana de Córdoba y su entorno urbano. Análisis Arqueológico (ss. I–XIII d.C.)*, Monografías de arqueología cordobesa 19:2, ed. by Desiderio Vázquez Gil and Juan Francisco Murillo (Córdoba: Universidad de Córdoba and Gerencia Municipal de Urbanismo del Ayuntamiento, 2010b), pp. 503–46

Palmer, Andrew, *The Seventh Century in the West-Syrian Chronicles*, Translated Texts for Historians 15 (Liverpool: Liverpool University Press, 1993)

Penelas, Marte, *La conquista de al-Andalus*, Fuentes Arábico-Hispanas 28 (Madrid: Consejo Superior de Investigaciones Científicas, 2002)

Pliego Vázquez, Ruth, *La moneda visigoda*, 2 vols (Seville: Universidad de Sevilla, 2009)

Pliego Vázquez, Ruth, and Tawfiq Ibrahim, 'A Bilingual Lead Seal from the Umayyad Conquest of the Iberian Peninsula', in *Al-Qanṭara*, 42 (2021), 1–8

Pottier, Henri, Ingrid Schulze, and Wolfgang Schulze, 'Pseudo-Byzantine Coinage in Syria Under Arab Rule (638–*c.* 670) Classification and Dating', in *Revue Belge de Numismatique et de Sigillographie*, 154 (2008), 87–155

Prigent, Vivien, 'Le rôle des provinces d'Occident dans l'approvisionnement de Constantinople (618–717). Témoignages numismatique et sigillographique', in *Mélanges de l'École française de Rome. Moyen Âge*, 118 (2006), 269–99

Rouighi, Ramzi, 'The Berbers of the Arabs', in *Studia Islamica*, 1 (2011), 67–101

Al-Rushātī [Abū Muḥammad al-Rushātī], *Kitāb Iqtibās al-Anwā*, ed. by Emilio Molina López and Jacinto Bosch Vila, *Al-Andalus en el Kitāb Iqtibās al-Anwār y en el Ijtiṣār Iqtibās al-Anwār*, Fuentes Arábico-Hispanas 7 (Madrid: Consejo Superior de Investigaciones Científicas, 1990)

Safran, Janina, 'Cultural Memories of the Conquest of al-Andalus Between the Ninth and Twelfth Centuries C.E.', in *Journal of Medieval Iberian Studies*, 11.3 (2019), 359–77

Sénac, Philippe, and Tawfiq Ibrahim, 'Notes sur les Sceaux de la conquête Omeyyade. Première moitié du VIIIe siècle', in *Mélanges Jean-Claude Cheynet*, Travaux et Mémoires 21:1, ed. by Béatrice Caseau, Vivien Prigent, and Alessio Sopracasa (Paris: CNRS and Association des Amis du Centre d'Histoire et Civilisation de Byzance, 2017), pp. 645–56

Sijpesteijn, Petra M., 'Seals and Papyri from Early Islamic Egypt', in *Seals and Sealing Practices in the Near East: Developments in Administration and Magic from Prehistory to the Islamic Period. Proceedings of an International Workshop at the Netherlands-Flemish Institute in Cairo on December 2–3, 2009*, ed. by Ilona Regulski, Kim Duistermaat, and Peter Verkinderen (Louvain: Peeters, 2012), pp. 171–82

Sijpesteijn, Petra M., *Shaping a Muslim State: The World of a Mid-Eighth-Century Egyptian Official* (Oxford: Oxford University Press, 2013)

Stocking, Rachel, 'Review Article: Continuity, Culture and the State in Late Antique and Early Medieval Iberia', in *Early Medieval Europe*, 15.3 (2007), 335–48

Stouraitis, Iohannis, 'Roman Identity in Byzantium: A Critical Approach', in *Byzantinische Zeitschrift*, 107.1 (2014), 175–220

Vallejo Triano, Antonio, *La ciudad califal de Madīnat al-Zahrā'. Arqueología de su excavación* (Córdoba: Almuzara, 2010)

Walmsley, Alan, 'Coinage and the Economy of Syria-Palestine in the Seventh and Eighth Centuries', in *Money, Power and Politics in Early Islamic Syria: A Review of Current Debates*, ed. by John F. Haldon (Aldershot: Ashgate, 2010), pp. 21–44

Wolf, Kenneth B., *Conquerors and Chroniclers of Early Medieval Spain*, Translated Texts for Historians 9 (Liverpool: Liverpool University Press, 1990)
Wolf, Kenneth B., 'Myth, History and the Origins of al-Andalus: A Historiographical Essay', in *Journal of Medieval Iberian Studies*, 11.3 (2019), 378–401
Wood, Jamie, 'Defending Byzantine Spain: Frontiers and Diplomacy', in *Early Medieval Europe*, 18 (2010), 292–319
Wurzel, Carl, *Khalifa ibn Khayyat's History on the Umayyad Dynasty (660–750)*, prepared for publication by Robert Hoyland, Translated Texts for Historians 63 (Liverpool: Liverpool University Press, 2015)

About the Author

Ann Christys is an independent scholar who studies the historiography of Spain between the eighth and eleventh centuries. Her doctoral thesis appeared as *Christians in al-Andalus, 711–1000* (2002) and she has also published a monograph on written evidence for Vikings in the peninsula: *Vikings in the South: Voyages to Iberia and the Mediterranean* (2015).

Index

For Product Safety Concerns and Information please contact our EU representative GPSR@taylorandfrancis.com Taylor & Francis Verlag GmbH, Kaufingerstraße 24, 80331 München, Germany

Batch number: 10341603

Printed by Printforce, the Netherlands